WAS IRELAND A COLONY?

This book is the third in a series sponsored by the Social Sciences Research Centre at the National University of Ireland, Galway (series editor: Ricca Edmondson). The series focuses on re-evaluating issues central to public life in Ireland. Two previous titles are *Health Promotion: Multi-Discipline or New Discipline?* ed. Ricca Edmondson and Cecily Kelleher, 2000, *Issues in Irish Public Policy*, ed. George Taylor, 2002. This publication was grant-aided by the Publications Fund of National University of Ireland, Galway.

WAS IRELAND A COLONY?

Economics, Politics and Culture
in Nineteenth-Century Ireland

Editor
TERRENCE McDONOUGH
National University of Ireland, Galway

IRISH ACADEMIC PRESS
DUBLIN • PORTLAND, OR

First published in 2005 by
IRISH ACADEMIC PRESS
44 Northumberland Road, Dublin 4, Ireland

and in the United States of America by
IRISH ACADEMIC PRESS
c/o ISBS, Suite 300
920 NE 58th Avenue
Portland, Oregon 97213-3786

Website: www.iap.ie

British Library Cataloguing in Publication Data
An entry is available on request

ISBN 0-7165-2798-7 (cloth)
ISBN 0-7165-2806-1 (paper)

Library of Congress Cataloging-in-Publication Data
An entry is available on request

Contents

PART III IDEOLOGY

PART IV CULTURE

Introduction

TERRENCE MCDONOUGH

In 1992 the Cork anthropologist Joseph Ruane[1] published an influential survey on the question of colonialism and Irish historical development. Among many other insights, Ruane contended that the language and themes of colonialism were widely employed by historians in discussing Ireland between the late medieval period and the eighteenth century. Thereafter, he observes, 'reference to colonialism has been unusual'.[2] This observation is the starting point of this volume.

It would not be surprising to see the issue of the Irish colonial experience fading from consideration after independence and the creation of the Free State in the early twentieth century. The reasons for the silence on this question concerning the nineteenth century are more obscure. Ruane notes that 'the language of colonialism simply stopped with the advent of the nineteenth century, without explicit discussion or justification'.[3] Finding that an account of colonial experience was unnecessary to comprehensively understand Irish society could explain this neglect of the influence of colonialism on the Irish nineteenth century. It is the contention of this volume, however, that the colonial experience of Ireland cannot be ignored in the development of a complete understanding of the nineteenth century. Further, an account of colonialism[4] is broadly necessary in the realms of economics, politics, ideology, and culture.

The primary concern of this volume is the positive contribution a colonial perspective can make to the understanding of nineteenth-century Ireland. A comprehensive discussion of the reasons for the widespread failure to make this observation to date is substantially beyond our present scope and intentions. Nevertheless, it appears that the nineteenth century has been constructed as a firebreak to the consideration of twentieth-century Ireland in colonial or post-colonial terms. There are a number of reasons why such a firebreak could be considered necessary. Even a cursory reading of the documents of recent controversies in Irish historiography reveals a pervasive anxiety not to give historical aid and comfort to the Provisional IRA (Irish Republican Army). If nineteenth-century Ireland cannot be seen in colonial terms then neither can Northern Ireland in the later twentieth century. Further, and especially since the Republic of Ireland entered the European Community in 1973, southern elites have looked to Europe for identity and advancement. The metropolitanisation of Irish historical experience does service to this identification. There has been an aversion to seeing Irish historical experience on the contrary as analogous to the remoter parts of the Third World. The extinguishing of the Irish colonial experience as early as the turn of the nine-teenth century would establish modern Irish history as partaking of the European mainstream. Indeed this perspective can regard union with the United Kingdom of Great Britain and Ireland as a kind of bridge to the mainland of European society and culture.

Events at the end of the twentieth century have challenged the utility of the chasm created in the nineteenth century between earlier colonial experi-ence and modern Ireland. The paramilitary cease-fires in Northern Ireland and the replacement of British direct rule with a power-sharing executive with Sinn Féin participation can be expected to slowly drain a substantial fraction of the political anxiety from Irish historical debate. The success of the Irish economy, the so-called Celtic Tiger, has raised Irish living standards to average European levels. The elimination of a certain economic performance anxiety could give Irish elites the confidence to base their participation in European affairs from their unique national experience rather than a constructed cos-mopolitanism. Lastly, the 150th anniversary of the Great Famine has led to a reassessment in some quarters of the less than benign influence of British policy-making in this period.

Indeed, since Ruane's essay appeared, new work on the nineteenth century has been carried out in a range of academic disciplines. This volume brings this new work in the fields of economics, history, and culture together for the first time. New scholarship has cast a provisional rope bridge across the chasm of neglect of colonialism that has characterised Irish nineteenth-century studies. One cable of the bridge consists of approaching both the industrial and agri-cultural economy from critical perspectives drawn from economic develop-ment theory. Another cable examines Irish political institutions and is informed by a close consideration of the making and implementation of British policy during the famine. Perhaps the strongest cable has been the application of post-colonial and Marxist literary theory to understanding Irish culture and ideology in the nineteenth century.

Cultural studies frequently occupy a privileged position within the academy as cultivating the field most remote from the concerns of power. Economics by contrast potentially deals with questions of production, distribution and ex-ploitation, issues at the heart of the contemporary social order. Consequently economics in the academy is more heavily policed than a subject like English. Critical perspectives are harder to maintain and are relegated to the margins of the discipline. Critical positions on the Irish economy had a brief flourishing in the Irish nineteenth century itself,[5] but have largely remained dormant in Ireland since. Nevertheless, this situation has recently begun to change and the first cable steadying our course across the Irish nineteenth century is formed by the application of two versions of Marxian development theory to understanding the trajectory of the Irish economy.

In 1993 the University of Ulster sociologist Ronnie Munck published *The Irish Economy: Results and Prospects*, including a chapter on the nineteenth century.[6] Munck's analysis drew heavily on dependency theory. Rooted in a Marxist analysis of imperialism, dependency theory argues that the development of peripheral regions in the world economic system has been subordinated to the interests of the metropolitan core. This subordination does not necessarily lead to a complete absence of development but assures that peripheral economies remain dependent on the metropolitan economies and hence backward and exploited. Munck identifies the main external factor causing dependency as 'the domination by foreign interests over key sectors of the economy'.[7]

Despite a relatively healthy expansion in the eighteenth century, the Act of Union marked a new era in which Ireland 'assumed the dependent position of classical imperialism whereby it was subordinated as a provider of cheap labour and raw materials to the dominant power'.[8] Munck concludes his discussion of the Irish economy before independence: 'development prospects were always conditioned and more often determined by the political, military, cultural and economic subordination to Britain'.[9] Political, military, cultural and economic subordination to another country might of course be one definition of colonialism.

Denis O'Hearn from Queens University deepened the dependency analysis through a detailed consideration of both the cotton and linen industries. O'Hearn[10] compares the development of the Irish and English cotton industries between 1780 and 1830, arguing that Irish cotton was peripheralised by Britain, while British cotton served as the leading sector of an internationally dominant economy. Consistent with Munck's analysis, O'Hearn contends that this peripheralisation was accomplished within a relationship of colonisation though the strategy pursued in this period was the imposition of a free trade regime rather than the promulgation of direct regulation over the subordinated economy.

The production of linen expanded in Belfast in the wake of cotton's decline. The relative success of the linen industry is often cited as a counter-example to the deindustrialising impact of integration with the larger British economy. O'Hearn[11] argues strongly, however, that the exchange of linen for cotton was not an equal one. The market was smaller and more volatile. Both wages and profits were lower than in comparable areas of cotton manufacture. Higher value added stages of production such as printing and dyeing remained in England. Perhaps most importantly, the linkages which cotton created with other industries in the vicinity of its production were much fewer in the case of linen. As a result, linen was 'limited in its ability to induce the rates of technical, organizational, and material change that we associate with the rise of capitalism elsewhere, and was particularly limited in its ability to act as a "leading sector" by inducing new linkages to other economic activities in the region'.[12] In the opening chapter of this volume, 'Ireland in the Atlantic Economy', O'Hearn brings these arguments forcefully together.

While it is strong on analysing the consequences of external domination on an underdeveloped economy, as a Marxian perspective, dependency theory is surprisingly neglectful in its treatment of internal class relations. In the Irish case, the dependency school is proficient at explaining the absence of particular kinds of industrial development, but relatively silent on the nature of the predominantly agricultural and rural economy that was actually present in Ireland. It would be remarkable if the internal dynamics of Ireland's agricultural economy did not strongly influence the character of Ireland's development and the relationship between the Irish economy and its British counterpart.

In 1994 the Maynooth economic sociologist Eamonn Slater and the present editor[13] published a long article arguing that nineteenth-century Ireland was dominated by essentially feudal class relations. Since a great deal of the history of the nineteenth century is dominated by the conflict between landlords and tenants, it might be thought that such a contention would not be controversial. Indeed, nineteenth-century observers frequently identified aspects of feudal economic relations as responsible for Ireland's failure to produce a modern agricultural economy. Recent historiography has, however, emphasised the modernising aspects of Irish society and has projected this process back into the nineteenth century. This is partly due to the post-war dominance of the modernisation perspective within development theory and is partly a reaction against 'the backward glance' of Irish nationalism, romanticising a Celtic and peasant past. In the second chapter, 'Colonialism, Feudalism and the Mode of Production in Nineteenth-Century Ireland', Slater and McDonough set out to rectify modernisation theory's denial of the importance of pre-capitalist class relations in modern Irish history and situate the development of these class relations in Ireland's colonial situation.

Major publications by Christine Kinealy and Peter Gray have re-evaluated the motivations behind the formulation of British economic policy during the famine and its administration in Ireland. Kinealy's study, *This Great Calamity*, appeared in 1994 and centred on the course of the famine and the administration of famine relief in Ireland. Grey's *Famine, Land and Politics* was published in 1999 and concentrated on the ideology and politics involved in making famine policy in Britain. Both books reached similar conclusions.

Kinealy[14] observes that the government reduced its involvement in food imports and made relief more difficult to obtain in the second year of the famine in the face of more widespread potato blight. The government again changed its relief policy in Black '47 in an attempt to force local resources to support the stricken. Famine relief was henceforth regarded as a local responsibility rather than a national one. It was this failure of policy that transformed the crop failure into a famine. Government inaction found its justification in an economic orthodoxy that advocated non-intervention and fiscal rectitude. Further, Kinealy found that the particular nature of the government response to the famine suggested a more covert agenda and motivation. The government was using the famine to

> facilitate various long-desired changes within Ireland. These included population control and the consolidation of property through a variety of means, including emigration, the elimination of small holdings, and the sale of large but bankrupt estates ... The government measured the success of its relief policies by the changes which were brought about in Ireland rather than by the quality of relief *per se*.[15]

Gray identifies the goal of this policy of benign neglect as the Anglicization of the structures of Irish society. The mass of small holdings were to be swept away, paving the road for capital investment in land. 'The core of anglicization lay in the extension to Ireland of the tripartite division of labour between landlord, capitalist tenant farmer, and landless wage-labourer.'[16]

Gray contends that policy debate drew not only on orthodox political economy, but also 'on more pervasive popular and Christian concepts of economic laws, which were in turn heavily laden with moral, religious, and political presuppositions and concerns'.[17] This Christian position held that the divine will generally operated through the laws of cause and effect. God's economic will could best be divined by allowing the natural laws of the economy to operate without overt interference. This view was mixed with an evangelical providentialism to produce a 'moralist' and non-interventionist response to the famine crisis within the liberal administration by such figures as Charles Trevelyan and Charles Wood. Famine policy was 'the fruit of a powerful social ideology that combined a providentialist theodicy of "natural laws" with a radicalised and 'optimistic' version of liberal political economy'.[18] In her essay 'Was Ireland a Colony? The Evidence of the Great Famine', Christine Kinealy examines the consequences of these insights into British policy-making for Ireland's colonial status.

It is only a short step from studying colonialism's economic aspects to realising that in complicated and often subtle ways colonialism would find expression in material culture. Archaeological research can provide exciting new information about the material dimensions of colonialism. Archaeological artefacts can be understood as the physical expression of the interactions between members of different classes and cultures. Charles Orser's excavations at Ballykilcline in County Roscommon have demonstrated that nineteenth-century Ireland is fertile ground for such an analysis. Orser makes this point forcefully in the closing essay of this volume's consideration of economics, 'The Material Implications of Colonialism in Nineteenth-Century Ireland'.

It is a cliché that the Irish are obsessed with history. To the degree that history is implicated in the creation of the social order in Ireland (or disorder in the case of the six counties) it may find itself sharing scrutiny and surveillance commonly confined to the more policy-oriented fields of economics and political science. It is certainly true that more critical perspectives on the British state in Ireland in the nineteenth century have recently emerged in the work of younger scholars employed in the British rather than the Irish academy. This work has found focus in the glaring light of the Great Famine that bifurcated the century in Ireland. I have already discussed the contributions of Christine Kinealy and Peter Gray in this area. History and politics forms the second cable in our colonial rope bridge, a kind of handhold across the nineteenth century.

Peter Gray's study looks at the colonial character of the Dublin Castle administration through the contested constitutional role of the Lord-Lieutenant. Several attempts were made to abolish the Irish lord lieutenancy and the viceregal court, either replacing the position with a secretary of state for Ireland or transferring all Irish executive powers to the home secretary. Virginia Crossman brings her studies of Irish local government in the nineteenth century to bear on the colonial question. A micro-historical perspective on colonial structures and individual practices is developed by Nicola Drucker. The hunting and shooting activities of the Grehan family range from Clonmeen House to colonial India. India appears again with Ireland on a broader imperial stage in 'The Sinews of Empire: Ireland, India and the Construction of British Colonial Knowledge'. Tony Ballantine examines the role of Ireland both as an apt site for the construction of British colonial knowledge and the source of trained personnel for the subjugation of the empire.

We have also included a section examining the dynamics of ideology and the relationship of colonialism to the history of ideas in the Irish nineteenth century. In 'Defining Colony and Empire in Nineteenth-Century Irish Nationalism', Sean Ryder confronts head on questions raised by the undoubted support of many nineteenth-century nationalists for Irish participation in empire and the reluctance of many contemporary critics of British rule to analyse Ireland in colonial terms. In the process he develops a complex and nuanced understanding of the concepts of colony and empire in the nineteenth century and the years leading up to it.

Amy Martin takes up the construction of Irish racial difference in 'Becoming a Race Apart: Representing Irish Racial Difference and the British Working Class in Victorian Critiques of Capitalism'. This essay looks at this question innovatively in the context of emerging Victorian critiques of English capitalism. Martin demonstrates that both conservative and radical views of the condition of British society were heavily bound up with ideas concerning the impact of growing Irish immigration on a previously unified nation. The English working class was seen to be the vulnerable site of this influence, malign in the view of Carlyle, revolutionary in the view of Engels.

McDonough, Slater, and Boylan look at the consequences of Ireland's anomalous position within the United Kingdom for the development of Irish political economy. Strangely, it was the colonial character of Irish society that made it ripe for the ideological application of the most advanced elements of economic science. The English colonial administration had created a deeply divided society and an impoverished moral economy. A concerted attempt was made to fill this gap with political economy. A changing balance of forces after the famine encouraged an explosion of innovation in Irish economics.

In 'Two Kinds of Colony: "Rebel Ireland" and the "Imperial Province"', Pamela Clayton looks at the different views of Ireland North and South within imperial ideology. Clayton argues that since the seventeenth century plantations, Ireland had been a mixed colony with a strong settler element. Despite this, the Irish, in common with other colonised peoples, were subjected to racist stereotyping, including implications that they were not an 'imperial race' even as they were serving the empire in large numbers. Finally, Clayton examines Protestant claims to imperial loyalty and considers the evidence for and against these claims.

The last section of the volume examines the insights post-colonial and allied Marxist studies have brought to the study of Irish nineteenth-century culture. The opening essay surveys the field and identifies two primary areas of study. Both concern attempts to construct Irish identity. The first involves the attempted recovery of a prelapsarian 'authentic' Celtic past and a definition of what is distinctive in Irish identity as coincident with those points at which it is most different from the metropole. The second involves the failure of the Irish novel to achieve a secure representation of the bourgeois subject in an Irish context. Both of these projects arise as a response to Ireland's colonial condition.

In her essay 'Ireland in 1812: Colony or Part of the Imperial Main?', Valerie Kennedy expands a number of these themes in relation to the imagined community in Maria Edgeworth's *The Absentee*. Kennedy argues that Edgeworth's own situation, the historical context of her Irish works, and the works themselves, are all replete with contradictions which find their origin in Ireland's colonial context. Through an examination of the work of the Banim brothers, Willa Murphy looks at how secrecy defines the world of the colony and the clandestine spaces where colonial subjects invent a world of their own making, screened off from the scrutinising eyes of the law. This is a space in which they might imagine themselves differently. Lionel Pilkington undertakes a sceptical consideration of whether the initial productions of the Irish Literary Theatre in the nineteenth century and Brian Friel's *Translations* in the twentieth century secure a transition from the colonial condition of Irish theatre to a 'national' or post-colonial condition respectively. Catherine Wynne describes how aspects of the Irish landscape itself become colonial topography in nineteenth-century Irish fiction.

Charles Orser discovers that the twentieth-century Irish landscape is literally grounded in a nineteenth century riven by colonialism. In this introduction we have briefly argued that an exclusion of the colonial condition renders many aspects of nineteenth-century Irish society incomprehensible. These aspects are found within the Irish economy, Irish political institutions, Irish ideology and culture. We hope that by an integrated study of economy, politics, ideology, and culture this volume will contribute to establishing the high ground for a more nuanced and less blinkered account of Irish history than the dominant modernisation perspective now allows.

By way of concluding this introduction, we can observe that Charles Orser's archaeological spadework discovers that upturning Irish soil, like Irish history, yields 'social documents deeply engaged on both sides of the colonialist struggle'.

NOTES

1. J. Ruane, 'Colonialism and the Interpretation of Irish Historical Development', in M. Silverman and P.H. Gulliver (eds), *Approaching the Past: Historical Anthropology through Irish Case Studies* (New York: Columbia University Press, 1992).
2. Ibid., p. 296.
3. Ibid., p. 318
4. Colonialism is notoriously difficult to define. Ruane provides a definition partially based on its use within the Irish literature:

   > Colonialism as a process refers to the intrusion into and conquest of an inhabited territory by representatives (formal and informal) of an external power; the displacement of the native inhabitants (elites and/or commoners) from resources and positions of power; the subsequent exercise of economic, political, and cultural control over the territory and native population by the intruders and their descendants, in their own interests and in the name and interests of the external power.

   See Ibid., p. 295. Ruane's emphasis on economic, political, and cultural control vindicates the multidisciplinary approach of this volume.
5. T. A. Boylan and T. McDonough, 'Dependency and Modernization: Perspectives from the Irish Nineteenth Century', in T. D. Foley, and S. Ryder (eds), *Ideology and Ireland in the Nineteenth Century* (Dublin: Four Courts Press, 1998).
6. R. Munck, *The Irish Economy: Results and Prospects* (London: Pluto Press, 1993).
7. Ibid., p. 2.
8. Ibid., p. 13.
9. Ibid., p. 2.
10. D. O'Hearn, 'Innovation and the World-System Hierarchy: British Subjugation of the Irish Cotton Industry, 1780–1830', *American Journal of Sociology*, 100, 3 (1994), pp. 587–621.
11. D. O'Hearn, 'Irish Linen: A Peripheral Industry', in M. Cohen (ed.), *The Warp of Ulster's Past* (New York: St Martin's, 1997 pp.161–90).
12. Ibid., p. 165.
13. E. Slater and T. McDonough, 'Bulwark of Landlordism and Capitalism: The Dynamics of Feudalism in Nineteenth Century Ireland', *Research in Political Economy*, 14 (1994).
14. C. Kinealy, *This Great Calamity: The Irish Famine 1845–52* (Dublin: Gill & Macmillan, 1994).
15. Ibid., p. 353.
16. P. Gray, *Famine, Land and Politics: British Government and Irish Society 1843–50* (Dublin: Irish Academic Press, 1999), p. 9.
17. Ibid., p. 7.
18. Ibid., p. 331.

PART I
ECONOMICS

CHAPTER ONE

Ireland in the Atlantic Economy

DENIS O'HEARN

W as Ireland a colony? In many senses this is a semantic question and the answer depends on how we define colonialism. A narrow definition of colonialism is based on a particular set of formal characteristics, the absence of which means an area is not a colony. These characteristics include territorial conquest as part of a general European expansion; the implantation of settlers to control indigenous populations and organise new economic units; and the exploitation of raw materials and other commodities through the exploitation of cheap or enslaved labour on confiscated lands, see, for example, Bottomore.[1]

Perhaps the most important but often forgotten characteristic of colonialism, however, is its dynamic. Its success is best indicated by the institutionalisation of local political and economic structures so that direct control is eventually superseded by *reliable* local governance – that is, by local political institutions that do not challenge rules of free trade and investment *or* the protection of intellectual property rights that have increasingly characterised world capitalism. Wallerstein[2] argues that the creation of an aiding and abetting authority is one of the four defining characteristics of the incorporation of a region into the world system, while the deepening institutionalisation of that authority defines peripheralisation. Robinson[3] emphasises the importance of collaborators and collaborating institutions in colonialism and later in the more powerful system of 'free trade imperialism'. To complete the circle, Fanon[4] bitterly warns of the dangers inherent in the post-colonial situation where 'bourgeois nationalists' continue the controlling work that was previously done by a colonial authority. Thus, the imperialism of the twentieth century is a far more powerful system of core control over peripheral regions than was the direct colonialism of the sixteenth to nineteenth centuries, yet the one depended on conditions created by the other.

By a formal reckoning, then, Ireland *was* indisputably a colony between the sixteenth and nineteenth centuries, before the focus of this volume begins. Although Canny argues that Ireland was neither entirely kingdom nor colony, he insists that any characteristics of 'kingdom' that emerged came out of first being a colony.[5] Not only were settlers implanted on Irish lands, for the political purpose of imposing order and the economic purpose of procuring commodities such as timber, there were also elements of what Balandier[6] has called a 'colonial situation': the assertion of ethnic or cultural superiority over a supposedly inferior indigenous people; the subjugation of the indigenous economy to the purposes of the metropole; the imposition of force to maintain political order and stability; and the use of ethnic stereotypes to justify metropolitan domination.

Although Ireland was formally incorporated as a region of the 'United Kingdom' after the Act of Union in 1801, and 'ceased' being a colony by the strictest definition, the colonial situation remained, even if, as Hechter[7] reminded us, it was an *internal colonial situation*.

In a sense, then, as I will argue in this chapter, Britain's integration of Ireland into the United Kingdom was analogous to the transition from formal colonialism to free trade imperialism in other parts of the world *rather than* the acceptance of the island as an equal member of a regional 'nation'. Union helped Britain control Ireland politically and subjugate it economically, institutionalising regional unequal development between the regions rather than repairing it. When this solution began to unravel in the twentieth century, the south of Ireland *delinked* and *reintegrated* into a new Atlantic economy that was under the hegemonic control of the US and regulated by its 'open door' policy toward US trade and investments. Meanwhile, having lost its hegemonic position and unable to control the lesser regions of its 'union', Britain again ruled by force and violence in the north of Ireland until the union began to break up going into the twenty-first century.

In this context, the formal meaning of colonialism is not very important. The important questions about the relationship between Ireland and England (and, later, between Ireland and the US and Europe) have to do with the degree to which Irish economic change was continually restricted after the sixteenth century and subsumed under the interests of core states that were developing Atlantic and world economic power. British domination of the Irish economy from the moment that Ireland was effectively incorporated into the British economic empire created a path dependency that cut off certain (mostly industrial) options for Irish economic change, while pushing its economy in more restricted, *peripheral* directions. This is not to say, like the straw person created by some revisionist economic historians, that England always and intentionally impoverished Ireland, making the Irish the 'most oppressed people ever'.[8] But it does mean that English policy integrated Ireland in a subordinate position within its strategy for creating an Atlantic economy, with English power and manufactures at its centre; and this form of integration severely limited subsequent Irish economic change, despite formal changes in British political and economic control of Ireland. After introducing the concept of path dependency, therefore, I will discuss the development of the sixteenth to eighteenth century Irish economy at some length before examining Ireland's failed attempt to achieve upward mobility to the core in the nineteenth century through the introduction of its own cotton industry.

COLONIAL CONTROL AND ECONOMIC PATH DEPENDENCY

Much of recent Irish economic history takes the form of narratives that describe key periods, such as the rise of the linen industry, the effects of the woollen acts, or the effects of the Act of Union. Emphasis is on the distinctive features of each period and debate centres on whether one or another variable 'caused' a given outcome. At their extreme, such analyses explain a given outcome by a discrete proximate market event, such as a sudden move in prices or a war-induced recession (see, for example, Cullen[9]). In so far as these histories recognise that certain kinds of outcomes recurred across time, they tend to explain them by an unfortunate scarcity of certain 'endowments', such as raw materials and a dynamic entrepreneurial class (for an evaluation of such 'causes' of Irish industrial underdevelopment, see O Grada[10]). While careful consideration of causal regularity is scarce, there is practically no recognition of processes that have *cumulative causation*, i.e., where characteristics that are chosen or imposed in one period influence outcomes in subsequent periods.

Analysis of such *path dependency* is more common among social scientists who want to explain historical economic change. Mechanisms, once introduced, can 'lock in' given trajectories of economic change. Often, these mechanisms are set in train by the introduction of something – a technology, policy, or social relation – that is one of several contingencies at a critical historical juncture, or turning point. The initial change may have been imposed, chosen because of short-term considerations, or even introduced through chance, yet it can have significant long-term consequences that are often inefficient or disadvantageous. What is important is that a change, once made, has cumulative causality; changes in one period affect and limit what happens in subsequent periods.

Mainstream economists who discuss path dependency usually focus on a limited set of circumstances where a discrete technological 'choice' at one period has effects on subsequent technologies. Under certain conditions – such as increasing returns to scale due to large set-up costs or learning effects – one technology or even one producer can take over a market even though they are not efficient in the long run. Applied to trade theory, the early history of market shares among regions or countries may determine trade patterns over the long run. Industrial location, for instance, is often the outcome of processes that are subject to 'historical accident', may be sub-optimal, but locked in by decisions taken in the early history of settlement. Regional prosperity and uneven development can thus be self-reinforcing.[11]

Path-dependence in this form is still a neoclassical concept in so far as it is explained within the parameters of equilibrium economics. Special conditions create multiple equilibria, among which sub-optimal paths may be chosen. Exit from a sub-optimal path is not possible by individual actions but takes a 'big push' by a central authority such as a developmental state, which co-ordinates actions by many individuals until they achieve exit into a new, more productive equilibrium path.[12]

But self-reinforcing processes are also common to critical theories of economic change. Dependency and world-system approaches, for example, concentrate on structural relationships that are imposed by core powers and which 'lock in' vast regions to peripheral locations within global divisions of labour. Although their specific forms of production and associated technologies may change over time, these regions remain identifiably peripheral or semi-peripheral. Whether or under what conditions peripheral states may exit to a more advantageous position through policy choice is a key debate within the study of economic change.

Haydu[13] introduces local agency by moving beyond simple path dependency to a method that he calls *reiterative problem solving*. 'Continuities across temporal cases', he claims, 'can be traced in part to enduring problems, while more or less contingent solutions to these problems are seen as reflecting and regenerating the historical individuality of each period'.[14] Rather than focusing on how an initial change determines a cumulative subsequent trajectory, this brings choice back to each critical juncture, where one must explain why one solution is chosen instead of another and how this solution sets a new historical direction and limits future choices. Outcomes at a given switch point are thus products of the past rather than historical 'accidents', the preferred term of path dependency. Solutions embody contradictions, create further crises, and also give tools with which to understand future crises. Solutions at one time may close off future options, but they also shape future switch points and can even create new possible solutions in future periods.

A study that appears to follow such a problem solving approach is Senghaas's analysis of how some small, predominantly agrarian European export economies evolved into mature industrial societies while others were peripheralised. Senghaas recognises that path-dependent mechanisms meant that divisions of labour established at the end of the Middle Ages 'continued to determine the development paths of individual societies and entire continents well into the nineteenth and twentieth centuries'.[15] But he also insists that individual societies go through critical turning points where policy choices determine whether they will achieve autocentric industrial development or revert into peripheralisation.

In Europe, the turning point came when small countries, having been compelled to turn towards the world market, realised the gap that had opened up between them and the industrialised European core after the industrial revolution. They faced a choice between continuing to adapt to an externally-imposed division of labour or trying to develop international competitiveness by protecting domestic infant industries. Those who accepted their narrow role of exporter to an associated core power – Ireland, Portugal, Spain, Romania – were peripheralised further and failed to industrialise. But some small countries broke out of underdevelopment, says Senghaas, by dissociating from their dominant core trading partner, inducing a broad-based agricultural revolution, and spreading the gains from agricultural productivity to raise the average incomes of all sectors. By opening up the domestic market, they created demand for new domestic industrial products, especially the specialised processing of local agricultural produce. From such beginnings, successful countries slowly built up an industrial base, moving to free trade *only* after they had gone a substantial way towards equalising their development levels with the already industrialised countries.

The development of linkages between economic sectors was key to the process. Where productivity gains were sectorally limited, dualistic structures impeded the opening up of the domestic market. Growth remained exogenously determined and dependent. But the Scandinavian countries switched from exports of staples to processing and exporting finished and semi-finished manufactures. As a result, they graduated 'in Britain's footsteps' from suppliers of raw materials to mature capitalist economies.[16] They developed linked economies, not overspecialised and dependent ones, not only improving their productivity but also their terms of trade.

Unlike some critical approaches, Senghaas does not see the decision on a turning point as being primarily imposed from outside or determined by historical structure. Rather, in his successful European cases, 'the decision on autocentric development or peripheralization was taken *within the respective societies themselves*, and ... reflected different *internal* social conditions for the processing of the opportunities and restrictions which the world market offered'. He concludes that 'the causal relationship posited by the world system approach between the *autocentric* industrial development of one group of societies and the *periphery* development of another group, does not exist at all'.[17]

From a critical perspective this is perhaps the most contentious of his findings. It is a rather amazing jump to analyse a limited number of European cases where there was, perhaps, a wide degree of choice in development policy and then to assume that other countries have similar latitude. As Cumings[18] notes with respect to similar attempts by small Asian countries to attain indigenous development by selectively protecting and developing their domestic markets, 'many called, few are chosen'. In most cases, small countries that attempt such a development are sanctioned by powerful core economies. Thus, in order to succeed, countries must make the right policy choices, have the capacity to implement them *and* avoid sanction by the core powers of the world economy. Even Senghaas recognises that in all of his successful cases the 'sovereign power of self-determination' was critical, so that internal policy could respond properly to changing world economic conditions. Both structural constraints (such as colonialism) and time constraints (*when* a country attains self-determination) can undermine a country's attempts to develop.

Once we consider processes of cumulative causation, we reframe the question 'was Ireland a colony?' The new question is, 'did Ireland have the choice and capacity to achieve an alternative development path during the nineteenth century, as was done by some small European economies? If not, why not?' A crucial comparative research question, then, is *when is local choice possible and when is it not*.

IRELAND'S INCORPORATION AND EARLY PATH DEPENDENCY

Most historians of the Elizabethan and Cromwellian periods emphasise the transformation of Irish agrarian society. Few have analysed the transformation of Irish towns. Yet the removal of Catholic merchants and their attempted replacement by Protestants had crucial consequences on subsequent Irish class structure and economic change. Pre-plantation towns were centres of local government, military defence, trade and commerce. Apart from Dublin and Belfast, however, most of them were dominated by Irish and old Anglo-Irish Catholics.[19]

Cromwell transferred economic and political power in these towns to more 'reliable' citizens. He barred Catholics from local government and merchant trades and removed them from Irish towns. Attempts were made to bring Protestant settlers to towns and by 1660, according to a contemporary source, 'the corporate towns [were] mostly inhabited by English and Protestants and governed by them, whereas before the war, it was difficult for a Protestant to get office in any town' (quoted in Barnard).[20] As in the countryside, however, the English found it difficult to attract Protestant merchants and tradesmen. Barnard cites evidence that the modal town settler was a failed English businessman who sought new opportunity in Ireland. A contemporary dismissed Galway's settlers as 'a few mechanick barbers and taylers' and 'mean persons unfit to carry on the trade of soe great a porte'.[21]

The removal of Catholics from Irish towns helped destroy Ireland's independent economic structures, making it more dependent on England's core economy. Before Cromwell, Catholic merchants controlled Ireland's small merchant fleet and dominated a dynamic trade with Europe and the Americas. Galway merchants, for instance, had considerable trade with Spain, Portugal, France and the West Indies. The removal of these contacts increased Ireland's dependence on trade with England, a crucial element in its incorporation into the English Atlantic project. It also obliterated Ireland's equivalent of the English new merchant class. The exclusion of native Irish from merchant and industrial activities was copper-fastened by penal laws which forbade Catholics from owning property or engaging in the professions. Along with the trade and shipping restrictions of the Navigation Acts, the destruction of the indigenous Irish merchant class, a rather invisible episode in Irish colonial history, created a negative path-dependence that severely reduced its long-term development options and capabilities.

The Navigation Acts did not greatly effect Ireland's trade outside of the empire, which was damaged more by the destruction of its traditional commercial classes, with their European trade contacts, than by law. But the Acts did restrict and channel Irish trade with the empire. Acts of 1660, 1663, 1670 and 1671 excluded Ireland from directly importing practically all American plantation commodities.[22] This made Irish export trades less attractive because merchants could not directly import plantation goods in return. Acts of 1696 even excluded non-enumerated colonial goods from direct import into Ireland. Stopping in England before continuing to Ireland added significant transactions costs. These laws were intended to restrict English imports of East Indian silks and calicoes and, as we shall see, to restrain the emerging Irish woollen industry.

The Navigation Acts were primarily intended to restrict foreign (especially Dutch) competition in commerce on the high seas, a key to achieving global hegemony.[23] But Ireland's merchant marine also declined due to the twin damages of core sea domination and the loss of its native merchant class. By 1698, only 18 per cent of recorded Irish trade was carried in Irish ships.[24] Also by this time, the bulk of Irish trade was with England rather than the continent, and was restricted by British limitations on Irish exports.[25] Even Cullen admits that the Navigation Acts were 'a grievance to the Irish merchant'.[26]

English policy caused major long-term damage to Irish developmental prospects precisely through its distortion of Irish class formation. Irish merchants who were restricted in their ability to import lost motivation to export. Without exports, a central motor for developing industry and increasing the productivity of labour is removed, especially from an island economy with a small internal market. The Navigation Acts thus took trade and shipping from the hands of Irish merchants and gave them to English merchants, limiting Ireland's development potentials as it enhanced the class power of English merchants, the driving force of English capitalism.

But the *exceptions* to the Navigation Acts affected Irish economic change as much as their restrictions. Under the Act of 1663 Ireland could ship only servants, horses, and victuals directly to the colonies. Direct shipments of linen were allowed after 1705. Even after the Navigation Laws were mostly removed in 1778, the Irish could not export wool, woollen and cotton manufactures, hats, glass, hops, gunpowder or coal to the colonies.[27] Thus, trade restrictions were designed not only to suppress Irish competition with England but to encourage Irish production of commodities that were crucial to England's Atlantic commercial project. The two most important examples of this process were the transformations of Irish production from live cattle exports to provisions and from wool to linen.

At the start of the seventeenth century the English landed gentry held sufficient political power to protect their interests from external threat. After the Cromwellian resettlement, lean Irish cattle were exported to southern England in large numbers and fattened and sold to the growing English urban populations. It was a familiar way for the new settlers to profit. Southern English graziers, their own kith and kin, provided familiar trading networks for their product. But landlords and breeders from northern and western English counties, a powerful political force, complained that Irish cattle damaged their trade. Their first cattle bill was part of the 1663 Navigation Act. Apart from requiring imports from plantations to land first in England, it placed a prohibitively high duty on Irish cattle exports to England. The bill was extended in

1665 to totally prohibit Irish cattle, sheep and provisions exports to England –
products that made up three-quarters of Irish exports. Live cattle exports
immediately fell, from 37,544 in 1665 to 1,054 in 1669.[28]

Edie argues that the cattle bills were a watershed in English treatment of
Ireland as a colony, indicating that 'in so far as it was within English power to
do so, Irish interests were to be subordinated to the political and economic
needs of England'.[29] Parliamentary debates over the cattle bills clearly support
this argument. Neither side wanted to *impoverish* the Irish but *all* sides wanted to subjugate their economy. They argued about how best to do this and
whether the cattle bills sacrificed English imperial interests to the narrow
interests of northern stockmen. The solution was to merge narrow class interests with the broader interests of empire by encouraging the Irish to substitute the (less profitable) provisions trade for the (more profitable) live cattle
trade. Proponents and opponents of the cattle bills both proposed giving
Ireland provisioning contracts for the English navy.[30] The English Privy
Council, for example, suggested that such a trade with friendly countries
would keep Ireland from reopening its trade with the English plantations in
America.[31]

There is little indication that the transition to provisions would have
occurred without the negative inducement of the cattle bills. In 1664 the
Council of Trade concluded that the Irish were not suited for the provisions
trade. In 1665 only 28 per cent of Irish cattle were exported in barrels; yet 96
per cent were barrelled by 1669.[32] Nearly all of these provisions went to the
Atlantic maritime trade: English merchant ships and continental colonial powers. The French reportedly fed their slaves in Martinique exclusively on Irish
provisions. The Portuguese and Dutch colonies were other major customers.

Irish provisions soon became a conscious and effective instrument of
English hegemony. By supplying cheap Irish provisions to France and Holland
from within the British empire, England gained the power to *strategically withdraw* key commodities from its imperial rivals in times of hegemonic competition. During wars with France and Holland in 1672, Spain in 1739, and the
Austrian War of Succession in 1741, England not only withdrew Irish provisions from its enemies' but simultaneously cheapened them for the English
navy.[33] During the American war of Independence, England stopped exports of
Irish provisions to France and the American colonies, followed by an embargo
on linen exports.

This was also an early form of flexible accumulation, where Irish regions
were forced to depend on *peripheral subcontracting* that was considerably unstable precisely because of recurring hegemonic conflict. When England periodically found a strategic advantage in cutting off provisions to competitors like
Holland or France, Ireland paid the cost. Indeed, embargoes created surpluses
of Irish provisions, so the English profited doubly by buying Irish victuals at
especially cheap prices.

The Cattle Acts, however, had another important effect beyond encouraging Irish provisions. They also encouraged the Irish to hold sheep instead of cattle because they could still export wool to England.[34] Sheep herding, however, depressed Irish incomes and destabilised subsistence, inducing the larger sheep farmers to seek profits by linking forward into wool manufacture. Wool, the leading core industry of the time, was still relatively labour-intensive and could be produced with rudimentary equipment. Ireland's advantage in labour costs made it competitive and an Irish cottage industry in woollens grew rapidly after 1670. By the 1680s, Irish woollen products were competing on English markets.[35]

London merchants reacted by trying to stifle the Irish infant industry. Edie shows that the common political sentiment in England was to crush competitive Irish trades and make Ireland a supplier of raw materials and a consumer of English goods.[36] Protectionist pressures intensified in the 1690s as the Irish industry recovered from the Jacobite War and economic crisis hit the English industry.[37] The 'moderate' English plan, pushed by the Board of Trade and the ruling Whig Junto and widely publicised in popular writings, was to compensate Ireland's loss of wool by encouraging linen production. This was hardly a benevolent sentiment. When the English Board of Trade was set up in 1696 it was instructed to find a way to acquire linen from within the empire to relieve English dependence on Baltic linen.[38] The supply of linen critical for the burgeoning English naval and commercial fleets, as well as for its new Atlantic colonies. Yet Holland's role as broker for flax and linen destabilised English access. Securing a stable supply of linen and, if possible, flax under English control was thus important to the emerging English hegemonic project. But the English state could not induce sufficient domestic production of linen since woollen (and later cotton) manufactures were far more profitable, less labour-intensive, less burdensome to grow and process, and their markets were more stable.

English parliament prohibited Irish exports of woollen manufactures with its Woollen Act of 1699. Although some Irish historians argue that the Act was not motivated by a desire to subjugate Irish industry,[39] English economic historians are less forgiving. Ellison[40] provides extensive quotes from English parliament that demonstrate a clear British intent to replace Irish woollens with linen and provisions. He documents repeated English government suggestions from the 1650s to encourage linen, provisions and fisheries in place of woollens. The transition to linen was finally insured after the Woollen Act[41] as Ireland's woollen industry went into stagnation.

England encouraged Irish linen as it discouraged woollens. It allowed plain Irish linen to enter England duty free after 1696, it funded skilled immigrants to boost linen production, and a Linen Board was established in 1711.[42]

This was not an exchange of equivalents – wool and, later, cotton had characteristics that enabled them to become leading core capitalist sectors. Linen was peripheral in terms of its limited market, low profits, low wages, and lack of innovation. English woollens and cotton textiles began under rural putting-out systems where merchants and landed interests organised the supply of the raw material and put it out to households or small 'factories' for a piece-wage. The bottlenecks encountered in spinning required more and more extensive putting out, which in turn imposed expenses that eventually encouraged the mechanisation of yarn production. In linen, cottage producers cultivated their own raw materials, which they processed and wove into textiles in an integrated domestic production system, until they sold the cloth to merchants in the market-place.43 Merchant capital accumulation concentrated in later links of the commodity chain like bleaching and marketing, while households were remarkably resistant to capitalist incursions into raw material supply, spinning and weaving. Irish linen production thus remained organised in households until well into the nineteenth century while English woollens and cotton came under the control of emergent capitalists. As Dobb[44] argues, although this system left petty producers formally independent, it enabled their exploitation through trade or *unequal exchange*.

From the Irish perspective, the *dependent* nature of linen is crucial. For the next 200 years, Irish linen depended almost entirely on English markets, whether for home consumption or re-export. There it faced severe and largely disadvantageous competition from other textiles, most notably cotton. High value-added stages of production such as printing and dyeing remained in England. And linkages to local sectors such as machine-building and transport – which made woollens and cotton so valuable to the English economies – came late and were substantially fewer in linen. The Irish industry depended on English inputs, technologies, transport, distribution and finance. While linen created some new economic activity in Ireland, it was strictly limited geographically; limited in its ability to induce the rates of technical, organisational and material change that we associate with the rise of capitalism elsewhere; and particularly limited in its ability to act as a 'leading sector' by inducing new linkages to other regional economic activities.

The reason for Ireland's market dependence was neither laziness nor lack of desire to export abroad on the part of Irish merchants. For two centuries after the suppression of the native merchant class in the seventeenth century, Irish merchants still tried to reach American and continental markets in linen, cotton and other manufactures. But more than a century of British maritime policy and Navigation Acts gave British traders competitive advantages that the Irish could not overcome. The underdevelopment of Irish industry as a whole left Irish merchants unable to secure economies of scale and lower transactions costs that were crucial to success in overseas trade. Ireland only exported meat, butter, and corn in any quantity – and these predominantly to England – so Irish shippers could not mix loads to make long-distance trade profitable. Irish poverty and dependence on English imports, and the fact that many of the greatest 'Irish' consumers, its absentee landlords, did their consuming in England, meant that Irish exporters were unable to make up return loads even after the repeal of the Navigation laws allowed them to import directly from the colonies. Irish demand for tobacco, sugar, rum, or even flax seed or raw cotton was too small to sustain a profitable return trade from the Americas. The lack of development of the internal market not only stifled demand for local production, which Senghaas emphasised, but also stifled the development of a commercial class and commercial infrastructure based on long-distance trade. Finally, undeveloped commerce and banking meant that Irish merchants could only give short-term credit –two months as opposed to eight months given by English merchants – leaving them at a distinct disadvantage. Even with its linen 'industry', the dependent and disarticulated Irish economy could not create the many broader linked activities in shipping and distribution that were induced by core English industries.

Viewed in the context of the Navigation Acts and other measures to establish English control of world trade, the cattle acts and subsequent encouragement of Irish provisions and the Woollen Act and transformation of Irish industry into linen were important local manifestations of global hegemonic strategy. But they also locked Ireland tightly into an Atlantic division of labour that was substantially controlled by England in the interests of hegemony and English core industrialisation. The changes that took place from the earliest years of England's effective incorporation of Ireland, such as the decimation of the local merchant class and any effective Irish sea commerce, were intensified by the restrictions of the Navigation Acts and subsequent transformations of Irish industry and agrarian production. This created a path dependency where Irish entrepreneurs, mainly settler landowners and city merchants, could only compete through their advantages in access to cheap labour; they were at significant disadvantage in access to raw materials, markets and, subsequently, left without inducements to innovate through changes in the organisation or technologies of production. Ireland's path as producer of foodstuffs for England and peripheral, non-innovative industrial products with low profitability, was set well before the Act of Union liberalised its economic affairs with England at the beginning of the nineteenth century. Although 'market mechanisms' rather than Atlantic imperial policies determined the fate of Irish economic change in the nineteenth century, the outcome of continued peripheralisation, as we shall see, was precisely the same.

NINETEENTH CENTURY INDUSTRIALISATION: FROM CONTROL BY FORCE TO CONTROL BY COMPETITION

Linen's semiperipheral character and the instability of its markets made it an unreliable staple industry. When war and rising prices disrupted flax supply, farmer-spinners and farmer-weavers moved into subsistence farming.[45] Up to three-quarters of the linen looms in the north of Ireland were reported idle during the depression of 1773.[46] Unlike core English textiles, Irish linen entrepreneurs could not compete by introducing technology or factory organisation. Their advantages lay in cheap domestic labour, cheapened further by supplementing a 'family wage' with subsistence farming. Limitations of raw material supply and final demand gave Irish capital little rationale to innovate.

An Irish cotton industry, on the other hand, was established as Ireland attained some relative autonomy and Britain repealed its more egregious restrictions on Irish trade and industry. As linen stagnated during 1770–80, the newly semi-independent Irish parliament attempted to encourage cotton manufactures with bounties and protection against imports of English calico and muslin. New spinning technology was introduced, including water-driven mills, and cotton began to replace linen in north-eastern Ireland. Monaghan reports that in 1760 there were 400 linen looms and no cotton looms in the Belfast region while an 1810 census reported 860 cotton looms and 6 linen looms. [47] Merchants and landlords attempted with less success to set up cotton manufactures in other parts of Ireland, including traditional woollen regions around Cork and areas where there was little tradition of textile manufacturing.

Cotton was an obvious choice for capital investment. Northern Irish bleachers and drapers who tried to set up linen weaving factories in the vicinities of their works were not very successful. On the other hand, cotton was already becoming a *leading sector* in England and Irish capital attempted to follow this English path as they had tried before in cattle and woollens.

A century of Navigation and Woollen Acts, and more than a century of class transformation, however, left Irish commerce woefully underdeveloped. As a result, a division of labour within cotton developed with the Irish concentrating in areas where cheap labour was an advantage while the English industry held parts of cotton production that were more capital-intensive and more tied into global markets.

Most innovations in the early cotton industry were in spinning: major technical innovations like the water frame, the mule and the jenny; and innovative factory-based production. The stimulus for these changes was the bottleneck spinning created for weaving. Without an adequate pool of sufficiently cheap labour, of the kind that induced the *extensive* growth of Irish flax cultivation and spinning to increase the supply to weavers, English capital required other means to increase the supply of cotton yarn. These included a remarkable series of technical innovations in the late eighteenth century and the centralisation of spinning in factories.

Even with this vast increase in yarn supply, however, weaving did not become a bottleneck on spinning. Rather, factory spinners *encouraged* traditional social relations in weaving for a time by using the export market as a vent for their surplus yarn. The putting-out system continued to dominate weaving until the 1840s.[48] A significant proportion of factory-spun yarn was put out to Ireland, which already had a network of domestic weavers scattered throughout the countryside and a rudimentary commercial network in the form of the brown linen markets that could be adapted to the purpose of putting out. Thus, returning to the analysis of Senghaas on small European states' recognition of 'turning points', Irish elites and policy-makers recognised the developmental gap that had opened up between Ireland and England, and they attempted to break out of the established role as provider of peripheral exports. But because of the structural restraints that had been imposed throughout the sixteenth and seventeenth centuries, the pattern of uneven development was reproduced *within* the 'core' cotton sector.

Elsewhere I use Irish customs data to estimate the growth of subsectors of Irish and English cotton between 1782 and 1822.[49] I find that growth rates in the Irish and British cotton industries were nearly equivalent: the British industry grew by about 6 per cent per year, and the Irish industry by 5 per cent. On the other hand, the Irish industry went through two phases. Cotton output grew rapidly and relatively smoothly until the turn of the century and thereafter became slower and more erratic. From 1782–1801, both the English and Irish industries grew at 7 per cent. But after 1801, the British industry continued to grow rapidly (5.1 per cent annually) while the Irish industry stagnated at about 2½ per cent. Moreover, growth rates of Irish cotton varied considerably after 1801, with periods of severe recession, indicating that it was more unstable than British cotton.[50]

The Irish cotton industry was so successful in its early years that the Lancashire cotton manufacturers rejected outright Prime Minister Pitt's 1785 proposals to normalise trade duties with Ireland (in return for higher Irish contributions to the costs of empire and in hopes of moderating Irish demands for legislative independence). They regarded Ireland as a commercial threat because of its abundant low-wage labour, plentiful water power and state incentives to industry.[51] Robert Peel even threatened to move his cotton manufactures to Ireland if the propositions were enacted.[52] Fifteen years later the English manufacturers pressed Pitt to *withdraw* Irish cotton duties immediately under the Act of Union, so that they could gain free access to Irish markets. The Manchester Chamber of Commerce argued that the removal of duties would 'direct the capital and industry of both countries to prosecuting those various manufactures for which each possessed the greatest natural qualifications'.[53]

In between, the English industry had consolidated its domination of the most profitable parts of the cotton industry (spinning, engineering, transport/distribution) through innovations in productive organisation and technologies, as well as the control of access to the raw material. Cheap Irish labour was no longer a threat and, indeed, was an advantage if English spinners could put out their yarns for cheap weaving, thus increasing their profits on the final product. Irish weaving became a peripheral, subsidiary sector to English spinning.

For a time, Ireland's relative advantages in cheap labour costs and water power enabled it to remain 'competitive' with Britain in the sense that its cotton industry survived. But in the unstable commercial conditions of the early nineteenth century England clearly won out. The distinct trajectories of the British and Irish cotton industries are shown by the growth rates of spinning and weaving output in Ireland and Britain. Irish yarn output (spinning) increased rapidly from 1782–88, but was stagnant thereafter. On the other hand, British yarn exports to Ireland increased rapidly after 1790 and rose steadily until the 1820s. British yarn was woven in Ireland for British dealers who re-imported the fabric for finishing and marketing around the world. Between 1790 and 1822 Irish weaving of British cotton yarn rose by more than 5 per cent annually and the Irish cotton industry became concentrated in weaving. But English yarn supplies fluctuated considerably and periodically glutted the Irish market, especially under free trade after the union. This made the Irish cotton trade very unstable and Irish capital, quite rationally, refused to innovate much. As a result, the Irish industry was vulnerable when technical changes and factory organisation finally swept the British weaving sector.

When the US imposed trade barriers against Britain in 1809, British manufacturers began dumping cloth as well as yarn in Ireland. Irish manufacturers could not respond by exporting their own cloth because they lacked a solid export infrastructure – the by-product of more than a century of British restrictions on its colonies' trade with countries other than England. Irish attempts to export cloth to America ended in disaster, and Irish customs records show only a handful of small cotton textile shipments from Ireland to America after 1805.

The Irish cotton industry finally collapsed after England removed Irish tariffs on yarn in 1816 and cloth in 1824. Between 1825 and 1835 Irish yarn output fell from 3.6 to 2.3 million pounds and cloth output fell from 6.3 to 2.9 million pounds weight.[54] As English weaving was mechanised, the Manchester manufacturers began to export finished cloth to Ireland rather than putting out there. English cloth exports to Ireland averaged less than 80,000 yards before 1815, but reached 850,000 yards in 1822. British cloth exports rose to 5 million yards in 1825 and 14 million in 1835, while yarn exports fell from three million to half a million pounds weight.[55]

Belfast spinners moved into spinning flax when they became unable to compete in cotton. Both the number of cotton spinning mills and imports of cotton wool into Belfast fell dramatically between the early 1820s and 1835.[56] Dublin and Cork found no adaptive response. The recession of 1825–26 caused the greatest run of company failures in Dublin history to that time. The Cork industry entirely collapsed, causing emigration 'on a scale unique by pre-Famine standards'.[57] As Irish labour advantages decreased, Irish weavers failed to remain competitive even in the coarser lines.

The reasons why England dominated, subjugated and eventually caused the destruction of the Irish cotton industry are several, and are closely tied into its domination of the Atlantic economy. Thus, in Mjoset's[58] terminology, English success was the result of cumulative processes that caused a 'virtuous cycle' of development while Ireland was locked into a 'vicious cycle' of under-development and industrial peripheralisation.

English spinners first came to dominate the cotton industry because their diversified market access enabled them to realise economies of scale. But this had to be created with the help of state sponsorship and the advantages of empire, which had been built up over the previous centuries. Throughout the world-system, England established market access through its use of sea-power to dominate international commerce and to regulate its imperial trade laws and practices. The large English spinners increasingly subjugated Irish weaving through their dealers in Ireland, who regularly reduced their Irish yarn prices to undercut local competition.[59] The pressure to sell yarn to Irish weavers increased during the 1790s with the size and throughput of English spinning mills. Eventually, the largest English spinners colluded to share out the Irish market at agreed minimum prices.[60] The introduction of free trade under the union enabled spinners to dump their yarn in Ireland and elsewhere during difficult periods such as the wartime period after 1803, when 'the export effort sometimes resembled a gigantic dumping operation'.[61] Meanwhile, smaller spinners were at a disadvantage on foreign markets because of high transactions costs and unfavourable credit terms.

Market control was equally if not more important at the front end, where better access to the raw material gave a distinct competitive advantage. Since raw cotton cannot be grown in Europe, access was a potential constraint on the growth of the industry, especially on spinning. English trade advantages under the Navigation Acts were supplemented by the efforts of the British Board of Trade to induce cotton cultivation in Asia, Africa and America. Unlike the inelastic supply of flax and wool, American cotton planters were able to increase their supply of cotton even faster than its rapidly expanding demand. After the saw gin made it economical to process upland cotton, the southern US went in a decade from exporting no cotton to become Britain's major source of cotton in 1803.[62] When British producers needed extra supplies, the Board of Trade generated them from India, Brazil, Egypt and elsewhere.[63]

England's advantageous access to this supply, and Ireland's disadvantageous access, was a crucial reason why its capital could capture and localise innovations while peripheralising the Irish industry. In the 1790s, as spinners increased their demands for consistent supplies of raw cotton and the importance of importers being close to spinners increased, cotton supplies centralised in Liverpool.[64] The larger spinners around Liverpool developed special relations with cotton brokers, enabling them to get the best and most consistent quality of cotton. Brokers sent samples to their favoured customers so that they could make purchasing decisions before their competitors.[65] A consistently diverse supply of cotton allowed the large Lancashire spinners to spin a variety of weights of yarn, giving them market flexibility when certain weights were in oversupply. Bigger scale, better technology and skilled machine operatives enabled them to more easily switch production to different weights of yarn. By 1800, there was a hierarchy of supply of raw cotton by the buyer's size and proximity to Liverpool – the most consistent and cheapest supply in Lancashire, higher prices in Glasgow, and the highest prices and most uneven quality in Ireland and beyond.[66] In an earlier article I[67] show that the supply of cotton wool in Ireland, apart from being inferior in quality, was less stable than in Britain and became particularly unstable after 1800.

This cumulative effect of differences in English and Irish trade capabilities, soured the Irish environment for innovation, regardless of considerable efforts to enhance it by the Irish state and its prospective industrial class. Irish weavers worked in homes and small weaving sheds even after power-looms had displaced hand looms in England.[68] The persistence of the hand loom was a rational response to the low price of Irish labour, which induced entrepreneurs to use a different factor mix than in England.[69] But while it was rational to use cheap labour, the substitution of labour for machines was a semiperipheral adaptive response that cumulatively constrained the region's long-term ability to participate in capitalist industrialisation.

The Irish cotton industry became dependent on England for its inputs. Not only was the Irish industry less mechanised than the British, it relied on Britain for what machinery it had,[70] especially second-hand English steam engines and cotton machinery. Everyday supplies such as card brushes, rollers and spindles, full sets of mules, dressing machines and mill gearing were also supplied from Manchester.

Like the control of trade, the control of machinery trade and concentration of engineering in Lancashire was explicit British policy. Cotton merchants and manufacturers, including otherwise vehement Manchester free traders, opposed machinery exports and the emigration of skilled machinists, even to Ireland under the 'union'. The British state complied with comprehensive and rigorously enforced protective legislation.[71] While Ireland had freer access to British machinery after the union, even the most advanced Irish producers remained a step or two behind the English industrial core. Eventually, this was not enough, and short-term 'dependent development' turned into failure and peripheralisation back into the linen industry.

The Irish path to factory linen production was the demise after 1825 of Irish cotton, which was relatively mechanised and centralised around Belfast. The crucial result in Ireland was that the mechanisation of linen caused a domestic industry that had been spread throughout the northern half of Ireland to become concentrated in a few factories around Belfast. From the point of view of the Atlantic economy, linen production became concentrated in north-eastern Ireland as traditional linen-producing in Leeds and Scotland moved into more profitable activities like jute and clothing manufacture.[72] Cheap Irish labour began producing linen yarn for higher value-added making-up industries in England and Scotland. Irish yarn exports rose from 4–4.5 million pounds in the 1820s to 9 million pounds in 1857 and 28 million in 1865.[73] This route to industrialisation was left open to north-eastern Irish capital because linen, already one of the most peripheral textile industries in the eighteenth century, was becoming increasingly peripheral in terms of its development potential *even as it mechanised and centralised in factories*. Linen's peripherality is indicated by its relatively low wages and low profitability,[74] but particularly by its slow rates of technical change, severe market limitations and lack of linkages.

Technical Change in Linen

By the 1790s, some mechanised 'dry-spinning' of linen with steam power was introduced in England and Scotland and spread over the following thirty years, although it could not produce fine yarns because of the tendency of dry flax to break. Steam-powered spinning was only introduced in Ireland forty years after it appeared in England, and then very slowly and only with subsidies from the Linen Board.[75]

The new wet spinning process that enabled factories to spin finer yarns after the 1820s, gave Irish linen a new lease on life as a replacement for the collapsing cotton industry. It also transformed linen into a more concentrated and proletarian industry as cotton mill production was transformed to linen. The economies of wet-spinning were first joined with steam power by a Belfast cotton spinner who transferred his business to linen. By 1838, there were forty spinning mills in Ireland and there were eighty by 1853.

Even as factory spinning finally became routine, mechanisation of linen weaving lagged behind. In Manchester, where the first steam loom was installed in 1806, there were 2,000 power looms by 1818 and 10,000 by 1823. Power-looms were used in Scottish linen weaving as early as 1810, but were barely known in Ireland until after 1850.[76] Some small weaving factories appeared in Ireland in the 1820s as mill spinners desired to work their yarns into cloth, yet domestic hand-weaving prevailed for some time.

As usual, the main explanation of this slow rate of technical change is the availability of cheap labour. Rather than competing intensively by using machines, the Irish industry continued to compete by reducing wages and extending the use of hand labour in factories. Only the massive cuts in Irish labour supply due to starvation and emigration in the 1840s restored an upward push to wages. This, in turn, finally induced the mechanisation of linen weaving. The first power looms in Irish linen were installed in 1847 by an English engineer and their number in Ireland rose from less than 100 in 1850 to more than 12,000 in 1868, 21,000 in 1881 and 32,000 in 1899.[77] Finally, half a century after the rise of steam powered factory production in Lancashire, the Irish industry was a mechanised factory system.

Market Limitations

While cheap labour is the most common explanation for a lack of innovation in Irish linen, demand limitations also reduced any rationale for capital accumulation and innovation. The differences between cotton and linen manufactures in this respect could hardly be more apparent. While English cotton cloth output grew by 3.6 per cent per annum between 1824 and 1890, Irish linen cloth output actually *fell* on average by 0.21 per cent per year.[78] Despite the common perception of Irish factory linen production as the centre of a vibrantly rising industrial sector in the north-east of Ireland, linen was a stagnant industry during the rise of capitalist factory production, hardly capable of leading a broad and rapid economic expansion. During the nineteenth century the existing level of linen output was simply concentrated from the northern half of the island to the Lagan valley. A stagnant level of output was produced in mechanised factories, creating unemployment and underemployment in the countryside along with migration to Belfast and emigration from Ireland altogether. Some rural hand spinners became machine weavers in Belfast, while the overwhelming proportion of urban men worked as general labourers. Those who remained in the countryside were generally consigned to chronic poverty and famine.

Low Linkages

Demand for the final product is not the only impulse to industrial development. Perhaps the most significant developmental characteristic of core activities is that they link in clusters: one activity induces many others so that the original activity is only a part of its associated economy. Irish linen lacked such linkages. The British cotton industry was the centre of a wide cluster of innovations, with technical spin-offs in mechanical engineering, chemicals and steam-power.[79] It was a bulwark of the English export trade, with important linkages to shipping.[80] And it induced the development of shipping, canal and rail technologies, which would be the centre of the 'second industrial revolution', and the improvement of post and communications.[81] Cotton may have consumed half of the increment in steel production and fabrication through its demand for power-looms, printing cylinders, steam-engines and boilers (not to mention the steel-consumption of transport and mining machinery). Other linkages included machine oils, wooden bobbins, chemicals and dyes, and rubber and leather machine belts. Murray estimates that 154 ancillary industries supplied the cotton sector by 1870.[82] To this we may add the consumer demand generated by the industry's workers.

The only significant linkages with Irish linen were in the engineering industry of north-eastern Ireland. Even here the linkages were far weaker than other textiles. The scale and quality of Irish engineering was different from England, where a cumulative process spanning both the wool and cotton economies created demand for highly specialised smithing crafts. Irish smiths, however, never specialised.[83] The specialised industry that emerged in Ireland was very small. By 1800, there were only two foundries in Belfast, rising to eight in the 1830s and twenty in 1870, after which the numbers fell off. There were more foundries in Dublin until they declined under English competition after 1850. Northern Irish iron making never spread beyond textile and marine engineering and steel or aluminium founding never took off.[84]

Even in textile engineering local producers were strictly limited to products that were either too costly to transport from England or which could not be adapted from cotton to linen. The erection and repair of water wheels for linen and flax mills, bleach works, and corn mills was mostly carried out by local firms. But as the vastly superior turbine technology took over in the second half of the nineteenth century, mills imported their turbines from Britain and elsewhere.[85]

Irish founders produced some new steam engines, basic technologies that were extremely expensive to transport, although Geary[86] cites evidence of a tendency to import used British steam machines. Moreover, the tenure of steam in the linen industry lasted only a few years, as water power still dominated well past the 1850s and electric motors and internal combustion engines began to replace steam by 1875. The more specialised British engine makers had clear advantages in these technologies and again imports came to dominate Irish power plant.

The largest engineering sector that was tied to linen was textile machinery. Yet this was also foreign dominated when machines for linen could be adapted from cotton. Some extremely basic flax breaking and scutching machinery was produced in Ireland but even this basic trade declined in the second half of the nineteenth century. Neither carding nor hackling machines were made in Ulster before 1850, the former being imported from Leeds while hackling continued to be done mostly by hand. And nearly all early dry and wet-spinning machines were English.[87] Power looms were introduced fairly rapidly after 1850 but they were readily adapted from cotton machines so Belfast imported them from England. Only the Jacquard loom for weaving damask was produced in Ireland, but this was a relatively minor part of the industry. Finally, finishing machinery before 1850 was crude but English firms began to compete seriously in improved machinery for finishing, bleaching, and dyeing after 1850 and linen finishing became dependent once more on British imports. Machine printing was not introduced into Irish linen until the twentieth century, and relied entirely on British machine makers.[88]

Overall, then, the engineering associated with linen never reached leading-sector proportions in the same way as in the English Midlands. Belfast engineering, in many ways like linen, was outstanding less in terms of its absolute size than in its size relative to the largely non-industrialised rest of Ireland. But the contrasts between linkages in English cotton and Irish linen were greater still, as Murray's estimates of 154 English ancillary sectors indicates. Examination of the purchasing records of Belfast textile manufacturers indicates that everyday supplies like brushes, rollers, spindles, and spare parts were also supplied from Manchester.

CONCLUSIONS

Although this chapter aims to explain the peripheralisation of nineteenth-century Irish industry, it began with a rather extensive review of earlier cycles of economic transformation that were explicitly tied into England's efforts to build an Atlantic economy within which it had a hegemonic role. From the moment of Ireland's incorporation into the English-led regional economy, it was forced through a series of social structural changes that would have cumulative effects on its later development. Most important were transformations of Irish class structure on the land and the limitations on Irish commerce, including the destruction of its local commercial classes and trading structures and the restrictions that were placed on settler economic activities by policies like the Navigation Acts, the Cattle Acts and the Woollen Act. The settlement of English and Scottish landowners encouraged attempts to follow the English model of development, but the destruction of Irish commerce and the continual regulations on Irish industry ensured that these attempts would not be successful. This left prospective Irish entrepreneurs open to transformation into peripheral industries that were non-competitive with respect to English capital and, at the same time, favourable to the broad strategy of building the Atlantic economy.

Irish industry was not destroyed, then, but subjugated and turned towards England's global interests. Irish settler participation in competitive trades like cattle and woollen manufactures was turned to products that were important to the imperial project, like provisions and linen. While 'industry' was traded for 'industry', this was not an exchange of equivalents because potentially leading core activities were exchanged for clearly peripheral ones. Ireland competed in provisions and linen through its advantages in cheap labour, but this hindered any impulse to innovate as was happening in English industry.

Ireland's nineteenth–century transformation, from cotton to linen and from domestic industry to rural agrarian underdevelopment, ultimately took place in the environment of free trade rather than mercantilism. Yet centuries of restrictions had by this time transformed the Irish economy in such a way that it could not compete with England. Without global trading infrastructures, it had access neither to the markets nor to the raw materials that were necessary to compete in cotton. Competing instead by extending the exploitation of cheap labour, Ireland's main competitive advantage, its activities became concentrated in less profitable and less innovative sectors: first, in cotton weaving instead of spinning, finishing and linked trades like engineering; eventually, in linen instead of cotton. Yet linen was a stagnant and peripheral sector, with enough linkages to create a small industrial economy in the north-east, but insufficient outward multipliers to prevent the larger Irish economy from sinking further into underdevelopment, famine and agrarian concentration.

Under circumstances where colonialism had transformed Irish class structure and productive capacities in such a way that it could not compete in core industry, the liberal environment of free trade and union could have only had underdeveloping effects on Ireland. Unlike earlier periods where Ireland's economic peripheralisation was based on active *colonial* restrictions, nineteenth-century imperialism was powerful precisely because uneven development was regulated by the market itself. A modernisationist discourse emerged where the Irish were themselves to blame because they did not respond adequately and efficiently to market signals, *despite* having been conferred the 'advantages' of full membership in the union and 'equal' opportunity to compete within the rules of free trade (with certain exceptions, of course, like England's continuing protection of its intellectual property in the form of machinery).

The story of repeated Irish attempts to industrialise, and repeated peripheralisation, indicates that optimistic, locally-centred models like that of Senghaas need modification. Repeated Irish attempts to break out of underdevelopment by industrialising confirm the concept of 'turning points' in the developmental process or, in Haydu's terms, that local agents repeatedly attempt contingent solutions to enduring problems, the nature and outcomes of which reflect the historical individuality of each period. But processes of cumulative causality limit the abilities of local agents to successfully carry out these solutions, they are modified by more powerful associated core powers and, in the case of peripheral zones like Ireland, the outcome appears to be repeated *re*peripheralisation and the regeneration of regional uneven development. Contrary to Senghaas, therefore, it appears that local agents do *not* always, or perhaps even usually, have sufficient power and resources to break out of 'vicious' cycles of underdevelopment to 'virtuous' ones of development.

The subjugation of regions like Ireland and the semiperipheral character of their few industrial activities is not simply an academic issue. The vulnerability of the Belfast region as a semiperipheral industrial zone (and it was largely Belfast, rather than the whole of Ulster or even northern Ireland that constituted the industrial zone after 1830) left it woefully exposed as its associated British core declined during the twentieth century. Lacking even the option of dependence on ascending core regions such as the United States and Europe after the Second World War, the post-partition north-eastern economy declined rapidly to become one of the most depressed regions of the European periphery. England's gift of linen, although it outlasted the simultaneous gift of provisioning for a long time and went through several distinct phases, was a mixed blessing at best.

NOTES

1. T. Bottomore, *Dictionary of Marxist Thought* (Oxford: Blackwell, 1991).
2. I. Wallerstein, *The Modern World-System III: The Second Era of Great Expansion of the Capitalist World-Economy* (New York: Academic Press, 1988).
3. R. Robinson, 'Non-European Foundations of European Imperialism: Sketch for a Theory of Collaboration', in Roger Owen and Bob Sutcliffe (eds), *Studies in the Theory of Imperialism* (New York: Longman, 1983), pp. 117–40.

4. F. Fanon, *The Wretched of the Earth* (New York: Grove Press, 1968).
5. N. Canny, *Kingdom and Colony: Ireland in the Atlantic World, 1560–1800* (Baltimore: Johns Hopkins University Press, 1988).
6. G. Balandier, *Sociologie Actuelle de l'Afrique Noir* (Paris, Presses Universitaires de France1963).
7. M. Hechter, *Internal Colonialism: The Celtic Fringe in British National Development, 1536–1966* (Berkeley: University of California Press, 1975).
8. L. Kennedy, *Colonialism, Religion and Nationalism in Ireland* (Belfast: Institute of Irish Studies, 1996).
9. L.M. Cullen, *An Economic History of Ireland since 1660* (London: Batsford, 1972).
10. C. O Grada, *New Economic History of Ireland* (Cambridge: Cambridge University Press, 1994).
11. W.B. Arthur, 'Self-reinforcing mechanisms in economics', in P.W. Anderson, K. Arrow and D. Pines (eds), *The Economy as an Evolving Complex System* (Reading, MA: Addison-Wesley, 1988).
12. P.N. Rosenstein-Rodin, 'Problems of industrialization of Eastern and South-Eastern Europe', *Economic Journal*, 55 (1943), pp. 202–11.
13. J. Haydu, 'Making use of the past: time periods as cases to compare and as sequences of problem solving', *American Journal of Sociology*, Vol. 104., no. 2 (1998), pp. 339–69.
14. Ibid., p. 354.
15. D. Senghaas, *The European Experience: A Historical Critique of Development Theory* (Leamington Spa: Berg, 1985), p. 14.
16. Ibid., p. 88.
17. Ibid., p. 155.
18. B. Cumings, 'The origins and development of the Northeast Asian political economy: industrial sectors, product cycles, and political consequences,' in F.C. Deyo (ed.), *The Political Economy of the New Asian Industrialism* (Ithaca, NY: Cornell University Press), pp. 44–83.
19. Despite this catholic dominance, Lord Deputy Arthur Chichester in 1610 claimed that the native Irish were 'indisposed and unapt' to town life. See R.J. Hunter, 'Towns in the Ulster Plantation', *Studia Hibernica*, 11 (1971), pp. 40–79.
20. T.C. Barnard, *Cromwellian Ireland: English Government and Reform in Ireland 1649–60* (Oxford: Oxford University Press, 1979).
21. Ibid., pp. 57, 59, 60.
22. A.E. Murray, *History of the Commercial and Financial Relations between England and Ireland from the Period of the Restoration* (New York: Burt Franklin, 1903), p. 43.
23. G. Modelski and W.R. Thompson, *Sea Power in Global Politics, 1494–1943* (Seattle: University of Washington Press, 1988).
24. L.A. Harper, *The English Navigation Laws: A Seventeenth-Century Experiment in Social Engineering* (New York: Columbia University, 1939), p. 283.
25. Neoclassical economic historians like Cullen argue that British state policies had little effect on Irish shipping and, in any case, could be evaded by smuggling. See Cullen, *An Economic History of Ireland since 1660*. But Harper claims that 'vigorous' enforcement of the Navigation Acts decisively limited Irish trades. See Harper, *The English Navigation Laws*, pp. 117, 119, 123, 128, 152, 155, 261.
26. Cullen, *An Economic History of Ireland since 1660*, p. 38.
27. Harper, *The English Navigation Laws*, pp. 401–2.
28. J. O'Donovan, *The Economic History of Live Stock in Ireland* (Cork: Cork University Press, 1940), p. 53.
29. C.A. Edie, 'The Irish Cattle Bills', *Transactions of the American Philosophical Society*, 60, 2 (1970), p. 5.
30. Ibid., pp. 21–2.
31 Ibid., p. 36; and O'Donovan, *The Economic History of Live Stock in Ireland*, p. 62.
32. O'Donovan, *The Economic History of Live Stock in Ireland*, p. 51.
33. A.E. Murray, *History of the Commercial and Financial Relations between England and Ireland*, p. 71.
34. Ibid., p. 38; and O'Donovan, *The Economic History of Live Stock in Ireland*, p. 79.
35. Cullen, *An Economic History of Ireland since 1660*, p. 23; and Murray, *History of the Commercial and Financial Relations between England and Ireland from the Period of the Restoration*, p. 104.
36. Edie, 'The Irish Cattle Bills', p.51.
37. P. Kelly, 'The Irish Woollen Export Prohibition Act of 1699: Kearney Revisited', *Irish Economic and Social History*, 7 (1980), pp. 22–44.
38. Ibid., pp.22–44.
39. Ibid. and L.M.Cullen (ed.), *Formation of the Irish Economy* (Cork: Mercier, 1969).

40. T. Ellison, *The Cotton Trade of Great Britain* (London: Wilson, 1886).
41. Kearney makes a great deal of the fact that mercantilism was not a fully coherent set of poli-
    cies carried through by unified English governments. This argument, however, ignores the
    reality of class struggle and class-state relations in seventeenth century capitalism generally
    and England in particular. The Irish Woollen Act and accompanying linen measures were no
    less mercantilist just because an ascendant coalition of woollen manufacturers and new mer-
    chants forced them through parliament against the wishes of the monarch. Nor was the cam-
    paign launched at the same time by East Anglian and London silk weavers against the East
    India Company any less mercantilist because it originated among ascendant sections of capi-
    tal against opposition from others. See H.F. Kearney, 'The political background to English
    mercantilism, 1695–1700', *The Economic History Review*, 11 (1959), pp. 484–96.
42. C. Gill, *The Rise of the Irish Linen Industry* (Oxford: Clarendon, 1925); and M. Cohen, 'Peasant
    differentiation and proto-industrialization in the Ulster countryside: Tullylish, 1690–1825',
    The Journal of Peasant Studies, 17, 3 (April 1990), pp.413–32.
43. See P. Kriedte, H. Medick and J. Schlumbohm, *Industrialization before Industrialization*
    (Cambridge: Cambridge University Press, 1981), pp. 98–101. The distinctions between Irish
    and Scottish linen production and their relation to theories of *protoindustrialization*, are dis-
    cussed in detail by Gray. See J. Gray, 'The Irish and Scottish linen industries in the eighteenth
    century: an incorporated comparison', in M. Cohen (ed.), *The Warp of Ulster's Past:
    Interdisciplinary Perspectives on the Irish Linen Industry 1700–1920*, pp. 37–70.
44. M. Dobb, *Studies in the Development of Capitalism* (London: Routledge and Kegan Paul, 1963), p.
    209.
45. W.H. Crawford, *Domestic Industry in Ireland: the Experience of the Linen Industry* (Dublin: Gill &
    Macmillan, 1972); and A. Durie, 'The Scottish linen industry in the eighteenth century: some
    aspects of expansion,' in L.M. Cullen and T.C. Smout (eds), *Comparative Aspects of Scottish and
    Irish Economic and Social History* (Edinburgh: J. Donald, 1976), p. 91.
46. J.J. Monaghan, 'The rise and fall of the Belfast cotton industry', *Irish Historical Studies*, 3, 9
    (March 1942), p. 1.
47. Ibid., p. 3.
48. D. Landes, *The Unbound Prometheus: Technological Change and Industrial Development in Western
    Europe from 1750 to the Present* (Cambridge: Cambridge University Press, 1969), pp. 42–4.
49. Because all of the raw material for the industry was imported, rates of growth of Irish and
    British cotton production can be estimated from their retained imports of cotton wool.
50. D. O'Hearn, 'Innovation and the World-System Hierarchy: British Subjugation of the Irish
    Cotton Industry, 1780–1830', *American Journal of Sociology*, 100, 3 (1994), pp. 587–621.
51. M.M. Edwards, *The Growth of the British Cotton Trade* (Manchester: Manchester University
    Press, 1967), p. 11.
52. Ironically, the English industrialists demanded free trade with France because they desired
    access to its markets and perceived no threat from the local industry. See A. Redford,
    Manchester Merchants and Foreign Trade (Manchester: Manchester University Press, 1934), p.
    127.
53. Ibid., p. 142.
54. Irish Railway Commissioners, *Second Report of the Commissioners Appointed to Consider and
    Recommend a General System of Railways for Ireland* (1837) (original volume in National Library
    of Ireland).
55. The remaining yarn exports came mainly from Scottish spinners who were attempting to com-
    pete in an ever more difficult environment by their own adaptive response of putting out in
    Ireland. See D. Dickson, 'Aspects of the Irish cotton industry', in L.M. Cullen and T.C. Smout
    (eds), *Comparative Aspects of Scottish and Irish Economic and Social History*, p. 111.
56. Dickson, 'Aspects of the Irish cotton industry', p. 110; Irish Customs 1823: Exports and
    Imports of Ireland;
    and Railway Commissioners 1837, p. 73.
57. Dickson, pp.100–15.
58. L. Mjoset, *The Irish Economy in a Comparative Institutional Perspective* (Dublin: National
    Economic and Social Council, 1992).
59. Edwards, *The Growth of the British Cotton Trade*, p. 140.
60. Even around Belfast, where there were some modern mills, the finer yarns continued to be
    imported from England. Ironically, the skilled Ulster weavers were especially dependent on
    the British industry because Ulster's mills could not spin the fine yarns they needed to weave

high-quality cloth. See F. Geary, 'The rise and fall of the Belfast cotton industry: some problems', *Irish Historical Studies*, 8 (1981) pp.38 **[AU?]**. The dependent Ulster weavers were typically controlled by British spinners under the putting out system.

61. Edwards, *The Growth of the British Cotton Trade*, pp. 74, 128–30.
62. E. Baines, *History of the Cotton Manufacture in Great Britain* (London: Fisher, Fisher and Jackson, 1835), p. 302.
63. Ellison, *The Cotton Trade of Great Britain*, p. 87; and Redford, *Manchester Merchants and Foreign Trade*, pp. 217ff.
64. Edwards, *The Growth of the British Cotton Trade*, pp. 107–10.
65. Ellison, *The Cotton Trade of Great Britain*, p. 177.
66. Edwards, *The Growth of the British Cotton Trade*, pp. 107–10.
67. D. O'Hearn, 'Innovation and the World-System Hierarchy', pp. 587–621.
68. E.R.R. Green, *The Lagan Valley* (London: Faber and Faber, 1944); and J. Mokyr, *Why Ireland Starved: a Quantitative and Analytical History of the Irish Economy, 1800–1850* (Boston: Allen & Unwin, 1983), pp.176–7.
69. F. Geary, 'The Belfast cotton industry revisited', *Irish Historical Studies*, 26 (1989), p. 262.
70. The ratio of steam to water horsepower was about 7.5:1 in Lancashire and 2:1 in Belfast. See ibid., p. 262.
71. A.E. Musson, and E. Robinson, *Science and Technology in the Industrial Revolution* (Manchester: Manchester University Press, 1969); and Redford, *Manchester Merchants and Foreign Trade*, pp. 131,133.
72. W.E. Coe, *The Engineering Industry of the North of Ireland* (Belfast: Institute of Irish Studies, 1969).
73. Gill, *The Rise of the Irish Linen Industry*, p. 319.
74. See D. O'Hearn, 'Irish Linen: A Peripheral Industry', in M. Cohen (ed.), *The Warp of Ulster's Past: Interdisciplinary Perspectives on the Irish Linen Industry, 1700–1920*, pp. 161–90.
75. A. Takei, 'The first Irish linen mills, 1800–1824', *Irish Economic and Social History*, 21 (1994), pp.28–38.
76. Gill, *The Rise of the Irish Linen Industry*, p. 268.
77. Ibid., p. 329.
78. E. Boyle, 'The Economic Development of the Irish Linen Industry, 1825–1913', unpublished Ph.D. dissertation (Belfast: Queens University, 1979), pp. 254–81; and Ellison, *The Cotton Trade of Great Britain*, Table B; and M. Blaug, 'The productivity of capital in the Lancashire cotton industry during the nineteenth century', *Economic History Review*, 13, 3 (1961), pp. 358–81.
79. Musson and Robinson, *Science and Technology in the Industrial Revolution*.
80. R. Davis, *Rise of the English Shipping Industry in the Seventeenth and Eighteenth Centuries* (Newton Abbot: David & Charles, 1962).
81. Redford, *Manchester Merchants and Foreign Trade*.
82. J. Murray, *Handbook for Shropshire, Lancashire and Cheshire* (London: Murray, 1870).
83. Coe, *The Engineering Industry of the North of Ireland*, p. 16.
84. Ibid., pp. 24–31.
85. Ibid., p. 37. 88. Ibid., p. 73.
86. Geary, 'The Belfast cotton industry revisited', p. 262.
87. Coe, *The Engineering Industry of the North of Ireland*, p. 63.
88. Ibid., p. 73.

CHAPTER TWO

Colonialism, Feudalism and the Mode of Production in Nineteenth-Century Ireland

EAMONN SLATER and TERRENCE MCDONOUGH

INTRODUCTION

In the previous chapter, Denis O'Hearn analysed the dependent character of Irish industrialisation throughout the nineteenth century. The insertion of the Irish economy in the Atlantic economic system served to undermine autonomous industrial development. The failure of an autonomous industrial growth process left the Irish economy predominantly rural in character. Consequently it is essential to understand the class relations which were dominant in agriculture and which underlie the dynamic of the rural economy in the nineteenth century.

We will argue in this chapter that the Irish economy remained predominantly feudal in character up until the late nineteenth century. We will argue further that the dynamic development of Irish agriculture in the nineteenth century can be understood as developments within the feudal system. These changes were driven by the adoption of alternative landlord strategies in the extraction of rent from the tenantry. Following a distinction drawn by Marx between different ways of expanding profit in a capitalist system, we will argue that the extraction of feudal rent before the Famine was of an absolute character, that is it relied on increasing the amount of labour applied to producing the rent. After the Famine, the extraction was of a relative character. Rather than increasing the amount of labour applied to the land, landlords attempted to increase the productivity of labour through new agricultural techniques and the consolidation of tenant land holdings.

Finding feudalism in the agricultural history of a Western European state is hardly surprising. The observation of feudal social relations in the Irish nineteenth century is remarkable only for feudalism's persistence well into the modern period. This persistence serves to dramatically distinguish the Irish economy from that of the rest of the United Kingdom, which was the leading capitalist economy throughout the nineteenth century. Coupled with the stunted development of industry, such a profound disjunction in the economy calls into question the equal status of Ireland within the Union. While the details of the development of the Irish agricultural economy before the nineteenth century are outside the scope of this volume, it was the establishment of the colonial relationship between Ireland and Britain which conditioned the persistence of feudalism in Ireland beyond its time in the rest of Western Europe.

The Cromwellian conquest and settlement of Ireland introduced a British feudalism in Ireland at precisely the time when the English aristocracy had begun to decisively lose its sway over British society. The motivation for this settlement was more political and military than economic, given the importance to Britain of securing the western island against opposing European influences. Nevertheless the instrument of this security was the establishment of a powerful Protestant landholding class loyal to British interests. The economic and social dominance of this class was to outlast that of their British counterparts, at least partially because strategic necessity forged a strong bond between Irish landed and British imperial interests.

While it undermined the legitimacy that a long tradition might have bestowed, the absence of traditional ties between the Cromwellian settlers and the indigenous peasantry freed the new landlords from a range of customary obligations and left the peasantry without customary protections. The religious disability of the peasantry under the Penal Laws served to shore up this inequity in tenurial relations. While retaining power vis-à-vis a subordinated peasantry, the fitful character of industrialisation under the Union preserved the landlord class from the potential challenges which would have emanated from a dynamic middle class. Thus the colonial character of Irish feudalism advantaged landlords in conflict with both the peasantry and alternative elites. It was these advantages which pushed feudalism in Ireland into the nineteenth century.[1]

THE PERSISTENCE OF FEUDALISM IN IRELAND

The agrarian character of the economy of nineteenth century Ireland is hardly in doubt. In 1870, only 3 per cent of the population owned land.[2] The majority of the dispossessed were not urban proletarians, however, but rural dwellers. In 1841, when statistics begin to become reliable, less than 14 per cent of the population lived in towns of 2,000 or more. Almost three-quarters of the occupied males were engaged in farming.[3] Comparable figures for Britain indicate that under one-quarter of the British labour force were similarly engaged.[4]

Since the plantations of the sixteenth and seventeenth centuries, the land surface of Ireland had been divided into landed estates. For example, in the division of Munster, landed estates of 12,000, 8,000, 6,000 and 4,000 acres were created (although Sir Walter Raleigh received about 40,000 acres). Some estates were as small as 100 acres, but it was the large landed estate that predominated.[5] Twenty years after the 1845 famine, about 2,000 owners of landed estates, each with 2,000 acres or more, owned two-thirds of the country's land surface.[6] Indeed, half of that surface belonged to less than 800 individuals. These landlords enjoyed a gross annual rental in the region of £10 million. This was at a time when the total United Kingdom central expenditure on civil government amounted to 6.6 million.[7]

Rent broadly considered as a payment in return for access to the land as a factor of production is a category that exists in capitalist as well as feudal economies. Without getting into the extensive literature that discusses the theory of rent within a capitalist market framework, we will establish that Irish rent in the nineteenth century cannot be considered to be capitalist rent in this sense. Rent in Ireland was rather the extraction of surplus from the peasantry obtained through extra- (that is, other than) economic coercion.

Within a Marxian framework, the key factor that distinguishes feudal from capitalist modes of production is the specific form through which surplus labour[8] is extracted from the labouring classes. In the feudal case, the surplus is appropriated as rent from the direct producers through the application of extra-economic coercion, that is, through political or ideological coercion or some combination of the two. Extra-economic coercion is most often necessary because the direct producers have access to the means to produce their own subsistence. This definition is similar to the one proposed by Laclau[9] and is consistent with Marx's treatment of this question.[10]

Under capitalist relations of production, rent results from a competitive relationship between agricultural capitals seeking access to the land which is held monopolistically by landlords. It is necessary therefore to look critically at Irish rent as a competitive rent relationship. A close reading of nineteenth-century accounts establishes the non-capitalist nature of this rent. Most theorists of the nineteenth century who discussed the Irish rental relationship were generally at pains to develop the difference between normal economic rent under capitalistic agriculture and the rent paid by Irish tenants.[11] They generally referred to the Irish rental system as the cottier rent system.

John Stuart Mill suggests that competition is also a feature of the cottier system that regulates the level of this money rent, but it is competition of a peculiar sort:

> The produce, on the cottier system, being divided into two portions, rent, and the remuneration of the labourer, the one is evidently determined by the other. The labourer has whatever the landlord does not take; the condition of the labourer depends on the amount of rent. But rent, being regulated by competition, depends upon the demand for land, and the supply of it. The demand for land depends on the number

of competitors, and the competitors are the whole population. The effect, therefore, of this tenure, is to bring the principle of population to act directly on the land, and not as in England on capital. Rent, in this state of things, depends on the proportion between population and land. As the land is a fixed quantity, while population has an unlimited power to increase, unless something checks that increase, the competition for land soon forces up rent to the highest point consistent with keeping the population alive.[12]

The import of Mill's analysis is that in Ireland competition is not carried on by capitalists, but by the whole population seeking its subsistence through entry to the land. We must be mindful here that the existence of this competition by the whole population is initially conditioned by the conquest of Ireland by the British. This conquest began a process of the elimination of the customary access of the indigenous peasantry to the land. While the peasantry remained, the Gaelic tribal chief was replaced by new landlords who had no traditional obligations to the actual occupiers of the soil. The competition for the land referred to by Mill therefore has the political subjugation of the older Gaelic order as its necessary condition of existence.

The importance of this continued political intervention was recognised by Cliffe Leslie.[13] Leslie considered that the Irish legal structure was actually feudal in nature and that the feudal domination over the Irish economy tended to undermine the necessary legal security for industrial and agricultural enterprises. He suggests that the origin of this legal insecurity was in the state's passage of the Penal Laws[14] and that this legal interference was the determining factor in allowing the landlord class to exploit the tenants. In consequence, Leslie argues the Irish rental relationship was different from the capitalist rent relationship:

> Rent under these circumstances became, not what political economists define it, the surplus above average wages and profit, but the surplus above minimum wages, without any profit at all.[15]

It is evident in this passage that by minimum wages Leslie is referring to the minimum subsistence requirement.

Wilmot Horton further highlights the non-capitalist nature of the Irish peasant's demand for land:

> In that country [Ireland], from the deficiency of employment for the labouring population, and from the practice which has prevailed of letting land in minute portions, and sacrificing the permanent improvement of estates to the object of obtaining the greatest amount of present rent; the possession of land is sought, not by capitalists for the purpose of profit, but by mere labourers for the purpose of obtaining the bare means

of subsistence ... He [the tenant] has no capital, he therefore requires no profit: he looks only for the means of subsistence, and his habits render a very small allowance sufficient to provide those means. He knows that many others, in the same condition with himself, are prepared to offer any rent which they have the slightest hope of being enabled to pay, in order to obtain possession of the land. Having but little to lose, the apprehension of his ultimately finding himself unable to fulfil his contract is not so powerful as the fear of being outbidden in the offer of rent, and thereby losing his only present resource. Under these circumstances, he offers a rent which, in many instances, he is utterly unable to pay.[16]

The concluding part of this passage indicates the market distorting consequences of the dispossession and re-entry of the Irish peasantry in relation to the land. The contract entered into between the peasant and the landlord is not one of equals and cannot be expected to be fulfilled as if it were entered into on this basis. Despite the appeal to the principles of supply and demand, it must be recognised that the supply of land is limited and actively monopolised while the demand for land is conditioned by the dispossession of the native population. Longfield develops this perspective arguing that an Irish cottier tenant gains a profit not from production but from fraud:

The general character of the Irish tenant was, that he was willing to offer any rent in order to obtain possession of a farm, but without any intention of regularly paying that rent. On the contrary his object was to derive a profit, not by applying skill and capital to the cultivation of his farm, but, by denying that he had any money, by defrauding his landlord and evading the payment of his rent.[17]

In other words, the level of rent is established in a direct relationship between the tenant and the landlord, only indirectly mediated by market considerations in the letting of land. Vaughan emphasises that 'rent levels, when compared with the official tenement valuation, showed great differences and individual estates often recorded high coefficients of variation'.[18]

The monopoly position which the landlord holds over the tenant is not only achieved by his ownership of the land, but also by the direct producer's inability to acquire an economic existence outside the agricultural sphere of production. The lack of industrial development in Ireland therefore tied the Irish tenant to the land. This economic bondage could only be broken by emigration.

Butt neatly summarises the case for the feudal character of cottier rents in the following:

Land is not an article of which the supply can be proportioned to the demand. The tenant on an estate cannot deal with his landlord on equal terms. It is the power of the tenant to endure exaction, and nothing like the competition of other persons offering him lands, that limits the amount to which it is possible for a landlord to raise his rents ... How often do we hear it said that a proprietor is a harsh and oppressive land-lord, because high rents are exacted on his estate! We frequently hear a landlord praised as kind and generous, because his farms are let at a low valuation. The very language of ordinary life is sufficient to show that the fixing of rent depends upon something very different from the laws of demand. We do not speak of a harsh and oppressive grocer, because he sells his goods at a high price, or speak of a kind and indulgent draper, because he is contented with small profits and quick sales ... But in a country like Ireland, ... rent has not yet entirely lost its character of a feudal impost, regulated by the share which the landlord thinks fit to allot as compensation for the letting of the soil.[19]

The non-capitalist and feudal character of Irish rent is further underlined by the fact that the total amount of rent rose with the creation of subtenan-cies. In this type of subletting, the rent charged to the occupier must cover all the rents to the various intermediate landlords (known as middlemen) as well as the head landlord. There is a tendency for subletting to double the rent. This trend occurs because the middlemen attempt to reproduce the same life-style as that of their head landlord by increasing the level of rent charged. Kevin O'Neill in his study of Co. Cavan backs this assumption by suggesting that the ratio between the rent paid by the subtenant and the head tenant is in a ratio of 2:1.[20] The level of rent paid by the actual occupier is not deter-mined by a competitive market situation and it bears no relationship to the actual productivity of the agricultural operation. In opposition to a competitive rent which would be determined by demand and supply, the middleman's rent is created by their position which allowed them to intervene between the direct producers and the head landlord imposing an extra charge on these pro-ducers.

The persistence of non-monetary feudal dues, perhaps, more dramatically indicates the feudal nature of Irish rent. These were observed by Sigerson:

> Besides the rent aids and reliefs, the tenant had to pay certain 'dues' in kind, and perform certain 'duties'. Contributions of poultry, eggs etc., were required as 'duty fowl', 'duty eggs', and so forth. The 'duty work' to be performed consisted in labour given to plant, reap, and gather the landlord's crops, to thresh his corn, draw home his turf, or like agricul-tural services. A rate of payment was occasionally fixed, but this payment was always less than the market value of the labour.[21]

In addition to these non-monetary exactions, tenants were subjected to a variety of estate rules that went well beyond the usual contractual obligations of lessees. These rules included obtaining permission from the landlord to marry, forbidding the exercise of overnight hospitality, encouraging the atten-dance of children at Protestant schools, fines for setting snares and traps, and maintaining the secrecy of landlord/tenant dealings.[22] This social control over the tenantry was not in essence a mere contractual relationship.

It might be objected that, contrary to the usual feudal practice, Irish leas-es tended to be yearly or at will. While this is superficially similar to capitalist contractual practice, in the context of a fundamentally feudal system yearly leases represent merely the extent of the subjugation of the peasantry to the will of the landlord. This is most obvious in the case of the tenants who held their land without lease at the will of the landlord.

This insecurity had its origins in British domination of the island. The 1641 rebellion and the subsequent Cromwellian conquest of Ireland swept away existing feudal custom and prevented the establishment of a manorial system on the European or British model. Seebohm observes:

> A custom, such as the legal maxim, cannot be created de nova. It must grow, and it must have existed time out of mind. Therefore the tenants of the newly created manors, being 'tenant at will' as the copyhold ten-ants of English manors are nominally must of necessity be really tenants at will in Ireland, seeing that in newly created manors no customs could be pleaded in favour of their fixity of tenure and rents.[23]

The bastardised English feudal system in Ireland failed to introduce any customary rights to the Irish feudal tenantry. In consequence, no tenurial cus-toms were legally recognised. Tenant insecurity was increased by the legal dis-advantage under which the Irish population suffered. This was unlike the legal situation on the mainland in that the British tenantry were protected by Common Law.[24]

The relationship between the subjugation of the tenant to the landlord and the length of the lease is reflected in the history of Irish land tenure. From the seventeenth century onwards, leaseholds evolved from being of long duration to much shorter leases and finally to a point in the nineteenth century where no leases were issued at all. The logical conclusion of this trend was reached where the direct tenant held the land from the landlord 'at will' or from year to year. According to Solow,[25] by the middle of the nineteenth century, 70–75 per cent of all tenants in Ireland were yearly tenants or tenants-at-will. Tenancies-at-will were implied from the payment of rent, without the exis-tence of a written agreement and could be terminated by the landlord at any time. Thus the evolution of the yearly tenancy demonstrates that far from indicating a commercial relationship of equality between landlord and tenant, short leases indicated the radical subjection of the tenant's interests to those of the landlord.

The analysis of nineteenth-century Ireland as a social formation dominated by the extraction of feudal rent must also meet the objection that production in Ireland was highly integrated with the economy of the rest of the United Kingdom, which was in turn highly integrated into a world market. The economy of the UK at this time is uncontroversially capitalist in character. It is also widely accepted that the world market at this time and subsequently can be characterised as a capitalist world market. Due to either or both of these factors, the economy in Ireland has generally been assumed, often without explicit discussion, to be capitalist in nature.[26]

Yet there is no warrant for this kind of assumption. Producers may bring commodities to capitalist markets and exchange them for money without thereby establishing themselves as capitalist producers. Marx sees this possibility in Volume II of *Capital* in the following:

> In every production not directed towards satisfying the producer's own immediate needs, the product must circulate as a commodity i.e. be sold, not so that a profit may be made on it, but simply so that the producer may live.[27]

Marx in Volume I of *Capital* applies this observation specifically to the Irish tenantry:

> The scattered means of production that serve the producers themselves as means of employment and subsistence, without valorizing themselves through the incorporation of the labour of others, are no more capital than a product consumed by its producer is a commodity.[28]

Having established the feudal character of the Irish rental relationship, it is necessary to theoretically examine the general forms of the extraction of feudal rent. This task is similar to the one undertaken by Marx in his analysis of the distinction between absolute and relative surplus value within the capitalist mode of production. Marx himself opens up the possibility of analysing feudal rent in an analogous manner. In his discussion of Richard Jones, Marx suggests that pre-capitalist rent relationships can exist in two specific forms:

> In discussing forced labour and the forms of serfdom [or slavery] which correspond to it more or less, Jones unconsciously emphasises the two forms to which all surplus value [surplus labour] can be reduced. It is characteristic that, in general, real forced labour displays in the most brutal form, most clearly the essential features of wage labour.
>
> Under these conditions [where there is serf labour] rent can only be increased either by the more skilful and effective utilization of the labour of the tenantry [relative surplus labour], this however is hampered by the inability of the proprietors to advance the science of agriculture, or by an increase in the total quantity of the labour exacted...[29]

If surplus labour in pre-capitalist production can be divided up into relative and absolute characteristics, it should be possible to locate this distinction with regard to the concept of rent, which, as we have seen is the essential form in which surplus labour is pumped out of the direct producer in nineteenth-century Ireland.

Marx has suggested that absolute surplus labour is concerned with increasing the total quantity of labour extracted, while relative surplus labour attempts to increase the surplus by more skilful and effective utilisation of labour. It is our contention that the period following the famine is dominated by the extraction of relative rent. Prior to the famine, absolute rental extraction is important, though after 1815, the Irish agricultural economy begins a period of transition to the relative rental regime.

THE ABSOLUTE RENTAL REGIME

Absolute surplus labour can be extracted either by means of increasing the amount of surplus labour extracted from each worker on the land or by increasing the number of workers on the land. The first of these possibilities can be pursued through the simple expedient of raising the rent charged on a particular tenancy. The higher the increase, the more surplus labour is expropriated from the tenant, all other things being equal. The tenant must devote an increasing portion of his time on the land to producing his rent and correspondingly less time to producing his own standard of living. In its more aggressive forms absolute rental value extraction has traditionally been referred to as rackrenting.

The second route through which absolute rental value extraction may be pursued is through increasing the number of peasants on the land. Concretely, this was accomplished through the division of the available land into smaller plots let out to a larger number of tenants. In Ireland, this subdivision was accomplished both by the employment of middlemen through the mechanism of subletting and also through family subdivision.

The following testimony of the Poor Law Inquiry indicates the presence of the tendency towards increasing subdivision of tenancies and the consequent growth in population on the land in early-nineteenth century Ireland:

> In Ireland the peasant population has been suffered to multiply without the imposition of any check; on the contrary, the landlords, both superior and inferior, conceived it to be their interest to encourage the increase; and although in the present day, the superior landlords have begun to perceive the errors of their system, ... Besides the absence of that species of control which has been mentioned as existing in other countries, it will be found that the payment of a money-rent, or the calculation of it in money, by a peasantry who get nothing beyond their subsistence from the

soil, is of itself an influential cause of redundant population ... This procedure has allowed the proprietors to withdraw themselves from the
immediate superintendance of their estates.[30]

The final subdivision of the land under the absolute rental value regime
involved the development of a system of unpaid productive labour, which has
given its name to this entire period of the absolute rental regime – the cottier
system. The Poor Law Inquiry attempts to define cottierism in the following:

> The most prevalent meaning of the term 'cottier' is that of a labourer
> holding a cabin, either with or without land, as it may happen [but com-
> monly from a quarter to three acres are attached], from a farmer or other
> occupier, for whom he is bound to work, either constantly at a certain
> fixed price [usually a very low one], or whenever called upon, or so many
> days in the week at certain busy seasons, according to the custom of the
> neighbourhood.[31]

Accordingly, the relationship between the tenant and the cottier is not a wage
labour relationship but rather a form of developed feudal labour rent, where
the cottier works a number of days in the year on the tenant's plot and the rest
on his own cottier plot.

T.W. Freeman[32] illustrates the tendency towards subdivision with an example from the townland of Fossabeg in Co. Clare. The townland had 300 acres
of arable land and 60 acres of bog. The lease expired in 1847 after 54 years.
The area had originally been farmed by one tenant but by 1847 it had ninety-
six, eighty-one of whom lived in houses within the townland. There were
forty-eight other cabins on the land, occupied by undertenants, and in all
700–800 persons endeavoured to live off little more than half one square mile.

Absolute rent, pursued either through the increase in rental charges or
through subdivision has a tendency to absorb all the normal rewards of commodity production. The ultimate limit of absolute rental value is reached
when the rackrented tenant can only obtain a meagre physical subsistence
from his production. As a result of this tendency, not only did absolute rental
value rob the tenant of any potential profit, but also of the money needed for
capital investment. This trend forced the Irish tenant into using exclusively
products of the natural economy, and their associated production techniques.
The direct producer will substitute the spade for the plough, manure for
guano, and family labour for wage labour etc.

The ability of absolute rental regimes to push the tenant's share of the
total product to absolute subsistence is reflected in the Irish tenantry's
propensity to become exclusively dependent upon the potato in the
Pre-Famine period. Not only did they come to subsist on the potato, but on
the most prolific variety:

Though most of the small occupiers and labourers grow apples and cups, they do not use them themselves, [they sell them] with the few exceptions mentioned, except as holiday fare, and as a little indulgence on particular occasions. They can only afford to consume the lumpers or coursest quality themselves, on account of the much larger produce, and consequent cheapness of that sort. The apples yield ten to fifteen per cent less than the cups, and the cups ten to fifteen per cent less than the lumpers, making a difference of twenty to thirty per cent between the produce of the best and the worst qualities.[33]

By relying on the most prolific potato, the tenant was able to limit the amount of his land given over to subsistence production to minimum size, thereby allowing the rest for the production of rent.

The collapse of the ability of the agricultural system to produce the physical means of subsistence is an inherent tendency of the absolute rental regime. This is determined by rackrenting and the continual subdivision of the land in order to accommodate a growing population. Squeezed between high rents and small plots, the tenants tended to engage in ever more intensive farming. Grain production and the pig were produced as surplus production for the rent, while the potato crop grown on ever smaller plots of land became the staple crop for physical subsistence. Consequently, the failure of or even a contraction in potato production could be disastrous. Tragically, this occurred during the Famine period (1845–49).

THE TRANSITION PERIOD, 1815–1850

The tendency of the absolute rental value regime towards crisis played a large role in the transition to the relative rental regime that dominated the Irish feudal mode of production up to the 1880s. A period of transition existed in the first half of the century. Its boundaries were marked on both sides by crisis. The transition began with the economic crisis that followed the end of the Napoleonic Wars in 1815. The terminus of this transition period is marked by the Great Famine. Both of these events were conditioned by the particular character of the absolute rental value regime. The relationship of the dynamics of absolute rent to the Great Famine is explained briefly above. The fall of agricultural prices that accompanied the 1815 crisis was particularly detrimental to the continuation of the absolute rental value regime.

The subdivision within the absolute rental regime is greatly facilitated by rising prices. It is obvious that the rising number of renters and the increasing level of rent can be more easily accommodated if agricultural prices are rising. Conversely, this process finds it difficult to operate in a situation of falling prices. If the direct producer finds himself unable to pay his rent, each middleman in turn would fail to pay their respective rents and the whole system is then in danger of collapse. Between 1760 and 1815, Ireland experienced rising prices. Louis Cullen has documented the economic crisis and consequent declining prices that befell Ireland in 1815 after the boom years of the Napoleonic Wars:

> The boom was halted with the termination of hostilities in 1815. Prices fell sharply from their inflated level, and the trend was now downward. Despite a 10 per cent rise in the volume of exports between 1815 and 1820, their value fell. The volume of exports rose further in 1821; their value fell still further. A major economic crisis occurred in the spring of 1820, the most severe in two decades. It was in the main a consequence of falling prices, induced by falling markets in England where severe depression was experienced in 1819. Grain prices fell through 1818 and 1820: between 1818 and 1822 they were halved. Prices of beef and pork fell by about a third between 1819 and 1820. The abrupt character of the crisis in 1820 was contributed to by monetary deflation.[34]

The slump in agricultural prices caused many farmers extreme difficulty in keeping up high rental payments.[35] The landlords as a class were determined to do something about the increasing amount of rent arrears. In service of this goal, the landlords attempted to reform estate management. This reform chiefly involved getting rid of their middlemen and directly running the estates. After 1815, landlords in general refused to renew leases of middlemen, especially leases for lives.[36][37] This was of necessity a long drawn out process as the head landlords had to wait until leases for lives expired before they could take over their lands directly. The increasing tendency of Catholic middlemen to support O'Connell in Parliamentary elections hastened their demise.

With the introduction of the Poor Law Act of 1838 and its extension in 1843, the landlords were called upon by law to contribute to the support of the poor. This acted as a further incentive for landlords to prevent subletting and subdivision. Donnelly suggests that landlords began a vigorous reform of the management of their estates in the 1830s and 1840s.[38]

After retaking direct control of their estates, the landlords appointed estate agents, whose job was to personally supervise the estate tenants with regard to their rent payments, tenants' family settlements, etc. Especially important were the agent's efforts to encourage consolidation. In this new type of estate management the landlord and his agents began to take an interest in the economic and social affairs of the direct tenants, especially with regard to the relationship between the numbers of people on the land and their subsequent ability to produce the rent.

THE FAMINE AND ITS AFTERMATH

Marx characterises the years after the famine in the following way:

> The depopulation of Ireland has thrown much of the land out of culti-
> vation, greatly diminished the produce of the soil, and in spite of the
> greater area devoted to cattle breeding, brought about an absolute
> decline in some of its branches, and in others an advance scarcely worth
> mentioning, and constantly interrupted by retrogressions. Nevertheless,
> the rents of the land and the profits of the farmers increased along with
> the fall in the population, though not so steadily as the latter. The rea-
> son for this will easily be understood. On the one hand, with the throw-
> ing together of smallholdings, and the change from arable to pasture
> land, a larger part of the total product was transformed into a surplus
> product. The surplus product increased although there was a decrease in
> the total product of which the surplus product formed a fraction.[39]

This decrease in the total product produced, although the amount of surplus product increased, is an indication of the changeover from absolute rental
production to relative rental production. The institution of the relative rental
regime involved a conscious attempt by the Irish landlords to increase the efficiency of the Irish tenantry as rent producers, thereby increasing the rate of
rental extraction. In 1851, the new agent of the Guinness estates in Wexford
and Wicklow intended 'to negotiate the surrender of farms, put them into condition, drain, and consolidate them with a view to letting them at some future
period in large tracts to solvent and improving tenants'.[40] Crucial to this particular transition period is a necessary decline in population to allow for consolidation and the emergence of relative rental production.

The reorganisation of Irish agriculture and its feudal rental regime was
greatly accelerated by the impact of the potato famine. This was due to the
process of depopulation and the subsequent consolidation of farm holdings.
Between 1845 and 1851, the number of farm holdings under 15 acres
decreased by 25 per cent.[41] In Co. Cork between 1844 and 1851, the percentage decrease of holdings between 1 and 5 acres was 61.8 per cent, between 5
and 15 acres was 53.5 per cent, and over 15 acres, 11 per cent.[42]

Clearances during the famine years were far easier since the ability of the
tenants to resist this kind of coercion was lowered. For example, Donnelly on
Co. Cork's clearances:

> Before the Famine many improving landowners were satisfied with
> something less than wholesale clearances of cottiers when the leases of
> middlemen expired; they rearranged farms and added land to already
> large holdings, they often placed the more industrious smallholders on
> better ground while transferring the less promising ones to poorer plots

or relegating them to the position of a labourer. This restraint, however, was rarely in evidence after the potato failures. Now when old leases to middlemen terminated, head landlords commonly conducted sweeping clearances of cottiers. [43]

Starvation and epidemic diseases had, in any case, completely undermined the cottier's will to resist by the summer of 1847, when the evictions began on a large scale ...[44]

These clearances sometimes involved inducements like sponsored emigration which not only cleared the tenant off the land but cleared him and his family out of the country as well.[45] Nevertheless, forced eviction was the ultimate form of coercion used.

After the Famine, landlords found it easier to introduce on to their landed estates the new management system of the estate agent, and to increase their social control over the tenantry. The evolution of estate rules was crucial in this process. Estate rules provided a number of strictures with which the tenant had to comply, on pain of being either evicted or fined. These rules varied widely from estate to estate and could include limits on the personal behaviour of the tenant. More important from the point of view of extracting rent through increased productivity, these rules often included interventions in the production process of the tenant, specifying such things as proper crop rotations, etc. Especially significant in this process was the landlord's ability to have the ultimate decision over the tenants' marriage partners and their succession to the land. The landlord or his agent generally had to give the tenant permission for his son to get married, because one and only one son inherited the occupancy of land.

The promulgation of these estate rules implied a more active administration of the estate by the landlord or his representatives. The estate agent and various kinds of bailiffs replaced the middlemen previously relied on to enforce the collection of rent under the dominance of the absolute rental value regime. The estate agent was given wide authority to run the day-to-day business of the estate.

The overall consequence of the landlord's attempt to limit the amount of people surviving on the land was the creation of a surplus population of non-inheriting sons and daughters without access to the means of production. This surplus population had no alternative but to seek their livelihood outside the agricultural sphere of production, usually through emigration. Previously, under the absolute rental regime, and its inherent process of family subdivision, the leaseholder had a large pool of labour to call upon, in order to produce his rent charge. But with the coming of the new type of estate management, the direct tenant still had to produce the same level of rent (or an increase) with fewer direct producers. The declining numbers of direct producers had to create more rent per producer if they were to remain on the land.

In consequence of the near demise of the absolute rental regime, spade husbandry and its various forms of direct labour co-operation become spatially restricted and structurally subordinate to the specific labour processes which operated under the relative rental regime.[46] The declining labour force under relative rental value production forced the tenant to attempt to introduce new technical means of production. The following testifies to this trend:

> Thus, there is abundant evidence that, from the late forties to the early sixties, a rapidly decreasing agricultural population sought to maintain, almost undiminished, the area of tillage. Obviously, such a result could only be achieved by having recourse on a large scale to the use of labour-saving agricultural implements and machinery, or by resorting to less intensive methods of manual cultivation.[47]

The most important innovation was adoption of the all-metal Scottish swing plough. Its use had become common throughout Ireland by the middle of the nineteenth century.[48] This new type of plough technology marks a watershed according to Hooper:

> The great abundance of labour and low rate of wages - some of it could not find employment on any terms - coupled with the smallness of the holdings up to late in the forties, and the defective appliances for horse husbandry, led inevitably to spade cultivation. When the consolidation of holdings took place after the famine, and emigration on a large scale set in, the way was paved for the expansion of plough husbandry.[49]

Plough husbandry superseded spade husbandry as the dominant labour process under the Irish feudal mode of production after the Famine period. Crucially, plough husbandry depended upon the tenant's ability to accumulate the necessary capital and to apply that capital on the land in the form of permanent improvements. The ability to accumulate capital depended on the level of rent demanded and the size of the holding that the tenant worked. Carrying out permanent improvements also depended on tenurial security.

Without tenurial security, the landlord was able to either confiscate improvements or to confiscate the value of those improvements through increases in rent. The consequence of this was detrimental to the development of plough husbandry in Ireland. The tendency was for the tenant to invest in fluid capital alone or in fixed capital that could be removed from the farm, for example, farm implements. Therefore, those aspects of plough husbandry used most prominently included purchased seeds, especially artificial grasses and clover, and the use of fertiliser, for example, guano. Those features of plough husbandry that involved fixed capital that could not be carried away were certainly underdeveloped. The lack of permanent improvements in the form of drainage, outhouses and adequate fencing severely stunted the development of plough husbandry.

Crucial in this stunted development of plough husbandry was the subsequent evolution of the pasturage system of cattle production. This is indicated by G.F. Shaw in 1868:

> Our agricultural statistics show, for the last twenty years, a marked tendency towards the production of more cattle and less corn, and this increased number of cattle has been fed not to any extent by an increased quantity of green crops, but by turning land from tillage into permanent pasture (quoted in Monsell).[50]

These new grasslands were the physical manifestation of pasturage – an extensive system of cattle production. Although competing with tillage since the 1820s, cattle production only became dominant after the Famine. Cattle numbers doubled from 2.7 million in 1848 to 5 million in 1914.[51] Not only was cattle production competing with tillage production but it was also competing with plough husbandry as a mixed system of farming. Pringle outlines the characteristics of the pasturage or grazing system:

> The grazing system, as pursued in Ireland with reference to the rearing of live stock, may be described as a system which is based altogether on unassisted nature. Art has nothing whatever to do with it, beyond saving a crop of hay on some piece of old pasture which has been specially reserved for 'meadowing'. There are no houses on such farms for sheltering cattle during winter, ... Not a turnip is to be seen.[52]

This extensive grazing system of cattle and sheep production has given rise to an assumption that it signalled the emergence of agrarian capitalism in Ireland.[53] However, this grazing system fit into the Irish system of short term and insecure tenure rather than that of a dynamic capitalist mode of production. Pasturage was an alternative use for a consolidating field system and competed with the agricultural revolution associated with plough husbandry. David Jones describes the overall characteristics of this type of cattle production in the following:

> In contrast to the fruit-grower and cereal producer, the grazier's initial outlay in working capital and fixed assets is minimal. He has only a fraction of the capital expenditure of the tillage farmer since he has little need to invest in such fixed assets as storage buildings, implements and manures. Thus the individual who has decided to invest in a herd of bullocks needs only to acquire a grass holding for his purpose. Moreover, the physical development of bullocks and sheep on open grazing is relatively rapid. As a result, bullocks and sheep can be profitably sold again within a short space of time. The grazier could therefore realize the full value of maximum net gain on his capital outlay within a much shorter space

of time than the tillage farmer. This meant that he did not need for the efficient operation of his enterprise, the same guarantee of tenurial security as the tillage farmer.[54]

The existence of the Irish rental regime tended to discourage the tenant from investing in permanent improvements on the land. As we have already argued, the consequence of this relationship was that the tenant was far more likely to invest in fluid capital rather than fixed capital. Since the major inputs of grazier production consisted of fluid capital, seed and cattle or sheep, it was a type of production ideally suited for insecure landlord dominated tenurial systems.

THE END OF FEUDALISM

In the opening section of this essay, we argued that the Irish social formation in the nineteenth century can most accurately be described as feudal in character and that the persistence of feudalism could be ascribed to the colonial relationship between Britain and Ireland. Specifically, we have argued that the trajectory of Irish society from the late eighteenth century to 1815 depends on the development of the logic of an absolute rental regime. The first half of the nineteenth century can best be characterised as a period of transition between rental regimes. Finally, the remainder of Ireland's feudal history to the 1880s is dominated by a relative rental regime. Not only was Ireland in the nineteenth century feudal in character but its dynamics are not primarily those of the world capitalist market but are conceivable only in terms of the internal relations of the feudal mode of production, the transition from an absolute rental regime to a relative rental regime.

The feudal mode of production in Ireland does come to an end in the late nineteenth century. Nevertheless, this demise was not primarily due to the dynamics of the international capitalist market. Rather the feudal rent relationships came to an end because of the developing class struggle between landlord and tenant within the Irish feudal mode of production. With the pursuit of consolidation and rising productivity, the Irish countryside had become more homogenous. This was achieved through the massive elimination of the most disadvantaged sectors of the rural population. While the major class opposition prior to the Famine was the confrontation between landlord and tenant, the tenantry contained within it significant divisions. We have already discussed the position of the cottier as occupying the final subdivision of the land under the absolute rental regime that characterised pre-Famine Irish agriculture. Clark[55] estimates that over half of the agricultural labour force consisted of cottiers and, less numerously, landless labourers. The conflict between landlord and tenant could be reproduced on a smaller scale in antagonism between the tenant and the cottier. Including the small independent farmer, Clark[56] estimates that three-quarters of the population in agricultural districts belonged to the rural poor.

Prior to the Famine, collective action by the rural population consisted of the formation of secret societies or gangs whose members were drawn from the poor. These organisations, collectively referred to as Ribbon societies, attempted to violently prevent eviction and the enclosure of common lands. Frequently, a larger farmer, seeking to rent the land of an evicted tenant, would be the object of this violence. Conacre rents, charged by farmers to cottiers, received special attention. Agrarian outrages were frequently directed at the regulation of wages and employment, reflecting the interests of labourers.[57]

Clark summarises the demographic changes after the famine in the following way:

> ... the percentage of the adult male agricultural labour force comprised of labourers fell from 56 per cent in 1841 to 38 per cent in 1881, while the percentage comprised of farmers and farmer's sons rose from 42 per cent in 1841 to 60 per cent in 1881. The sharpest drop occurred among labourer-landholders; they fell from 30 per cent to 12 per cent while landless labourers remained steady as a percentage of the adult male agricultural labour force.[58]

These figures reflect the clearance of estates and the growing consolidation of farm size under the conditions of relative rental production. The substantial tenants occupying these consolidated farms now formed the largest group in the countryside. This growing class had an interest in peasant proprietorship, an interest that would not have been shared by the inadequately landed majority in the pre-Famine period. In addition, the now more substantial tenants had the resources to pursue their demands.

When the Land War broke out in 1879, Paul Bew has argued that 'the most important forms of struggle were different varieties of highly legalistic strategies'. [59] He contends that the dominant strategy was 'rent at the point of a bayonet'. What this meant was that the tenant refused to pay rent, but only up to the last moment short of eviction, with the Land League covering the legal expenses generated by the delay. Bew observes that this low risk strategy was objectively in the interests of the more substantial tenantry.[60]

Agrarian unrest spread throughout the countryside. In response to this agitation, a series of Land Acts was passed between 1881 to 1909. This legislation brought about a change in the ownership of land in rural Ireland. These Acts included the 1881 Land Act, followed by the Ashbourne Act of 1885, the 1891 Balfour Act, the Wyndham Act of 1903, and finally the Birrell Land Act of 1909. They allowed the Irish tenant farmer to borrow money at increasing attractive rates from the British government in order to buy out the land from the landlords.[61]

With the end of landlordism, peasant proprietorship was established. Once feudalism had been eliminated from the Irish countryside and replaced with a small farming regime, only then was the stage set for the penetration, albeit in a very uneven way, of actual capitalist production in Irish agriculture. If capitalism is identified with modernity, the particular relationship between Britain and Ireland, far from promoting modernisation, was instrumental in keeping modernity at bay in the Irish countryside into the twentieth century.

NOTES

1. It is an open historical question what might have happened under an undisturbed native or Anglo-Norman feudalism. While we can never know the precise character of this kind of development, it is certainly safe to say that it would have been different.
2. R. Dudley Edwards, *An Atlas of Irish History* (London: Methuen, 1973), p. 171.
3. K.T. Hoppen, *Ireland since 1800: Conflict and Conformity* (London: Longman, 1992), p. 33.
4. P. Deane and W.A. Cole, *British Economic Growth, 1688–1959* (Cambridge: Cambridge University Press, 1969), p. 142. For an overview of the reasons for a lack of industrial development, see E. O'Malley, 'The Decline of Irish Industry in the Nineteenth Century', *Economic and Social Review*, 13, 1 (1981).
5. See Dudley Edwards, *An Atlas of Irish History*, p. 160–2.
6. See Hoppen, *Ireland since 1800*, p. 87.
7. W.E. Vaughan, 'Agricultural Output, Rents and Wages in Ireland, 1850–1880', in L.M. Cullen and F. Furet (eds), *Ireland and France, 17th - 20th Centuries* (Ann Arbor, MI:, 1980), p. 187.
8. In Marxian economic theory the income of exploiting classes consists in the products or the value of labour performed by the labouring classes over and above the labour which produces the workers' standard of living. For instance in a capitalist economy profit comes from the surplus labour of the working class.
9. L. Laclau, *Politics and Ideology in Marxist Theory* (London: NLB, 1977).
10. Marx emphasises the role of this extraeconomic domination:

    It is clear, too, that in all forms where the actual worker himself remains the 'possessor' of the means of production and the conditions of labour needed for the production of his own means of subsistence, the property relationship must appear at the same time as a direct relationship of domination and servitude, and the direct producer therefor as an unfree person - an unfreedom which may undergo a progressive attenuation from serfdom with statute labour to a mere tribute obligation. K. Marx, *Capital, Vol. III*. (London: Penguin, 1981), pp. 926–7.

11. They were especially at pains to distinguish the Irish rent situation from the Ricardian concept of rent. See R.D.C. Black, *Economic Thought and the Irish Question, 1817–1870* (Cambridge: Cambridge University Press, 1960), p. 17.
12. J.S. Mill, *Principles of Political Economy* (Toronto: Toronto Press, 1965), p. 193.
13. Cliffe, T.E. Leslie, *Land Systems and Industrial Economy of Ireland, England, and Continental Countries* (London: Longmans, 1870).
14. The Penal Laws were passed at the beginning of the eighteenth century and placed the Catholic population at a severe social and economic disadvantage. Importantly, they made it illegal for Catholics to buy land, obtain a mortgage on it, rent it on a long- term basis, or make a normal profit on such rental. Normal inheritance was also affected.
15. See Leslie, *Land Systems and Industrial Economy of Ireland, England, and Continental Countries*, p. 128.
16. R.W. Horton, *Lectures on Statistics and Political Economy, As Affecting the Condition of the Operative and Labouring Classes* (London, 1832), pp. 8–9.
17. M. Longfield, 'Production - Riches - Enjoyment - Consumption', *Dublin Statistical Society Transactions* Vol. I (1849), pp. 16–17.
18. W.E. Vaughan, 'The Landlord and Tenant Relations in Ireland between the Famine and the Land War, 1850–1878', in L.M. Cullen and T.C. Smout (eds), *Comparative Aspects of Scottish and Irish Economic and Social History, 1660–1900* (Edinburgh: John Donald Publishers, 1977), p. 218.

19. I. Butt, *The Irish People and the Irish Land, A Letter to Lord Lifford* (Dublin: John Falconer, 1867), pp. 56, 58.
20. K. O'Neill, *Family and Farm in Pre-Famine Ireland, The Parish of Killashandra* (London: The University of Wisconsin Press, 1984), pp. 33–5.
21. G. Sigerson, *History of the Land Tenures and Land Classes of Ireland* (London: Longmans, 1871), p. 157.
22. For accounts of these rules, see Lex, *Doings in Party, A Chapter of Irish History in a Letter to the Rt. Hon., The Earl of Derby K.G.* (London: Hatchard, 1860), pp. 15–16; 'Lord Arran's Estate, Diary of the Agent, Co. Donegal 1858–1898' (Public Records Office); 'Report by J.L. Murray on Lord Leitrim's Estate' (National Library, 1864); and 'Diary of Frances Alcorn, Lord Leitrim's Estate, Co. Donegal' (National Library, 1878).
23. F. Seebohm, 'The Land Question, English Tenures in Ireland, Part I', *The Fortnightly Review*, Vol. VI (1869), p. 631.
24. According to Butt, the legal enactments brought into operation in Ireland with regard to the forfeitures of tenants' interests were based on principles diametrically opposed to the Common Law of England:

> Forfeitures were odious in all English courts. Irish legislation has exactly reversed these principles. Commencing in the reign of Queen Anne contemporaneously with the Popery Laws, a number of Acts of Parliament have been passed constituting what is known in Irish jurisprudence as 'the ejectment code', ... The whole object of that code was to expediate and facilitate the eviction of the tenant - to get rid of every formality and difficulty by which the good old wisdom of the common law obstructed the forfeiture of the tenant's estate, and lastly to extend that forfeiture to cases in which, according to the common law, it did not exist. Statute after statute was passed for those purposes ... In Ireland, by statutes passed for the special benefit of landlords, every difficulty which the requisitions of that common law interposed in the way of such an ejectment is swept away. In England it is the duty of the judges to administer the law so as in every doubtful case to protect the tenant. In Ireland it has judicially declared to be their duty in every doubtful case to facilitate his eviction. Butt, *The Irish People and the Irish Land*, p. 188–9.

25. B. Solow, *The Land Question and the Irish Economy, 1870–1903* (Cambridge: Harvard University Press, 1971), p.7.
26. In the most influential recent volumes on the nature of the nineteenth century Irish economy, there was no discussion of the feudal nature of the rent relationship. This suggests implicitly their acceptance of the notion of a capitalist rent relationship. See J. Mokyr, *Why Ireland Starved, A Quantitative and Analytical History of the Irish Economy, 1800–1850* (London: George Allen and Unwin, 1983); and C. O'Grada, *Ireland: A New Economic History 1780–1939* (Oxford: Clarendon Press, 1994).
27. K. Marx, *Capital, Vol. II* (London: Penguin, 1978), p. 283.
28. K. Marx, *Capital, Vol. I* (London: Penguin, 1976), pp. 860–1.
29. K. Marx, *Theories of Surplus Value, Part III* (London: Lawrence and Wishart, 1972), p. 400.
30. *Reports of the Commissioners for Inquiry into the Condition of the Poorer Classes in Ireland, Reports from Commissioners*, Vol. 30–34, Appendix H (1836), p. 673.
31. Ibid., p. 660.
32. T.W. Freeman, *Pre-Famine Ireland: A Study in Historical Geography* (Manchester: Manchester University Press, 1957), p. 21.
33. See *Reports of the Commissioners for Inquiry*, p. 666.
34. M. Cullen, *Life in Ireland* (London: Batsford, 1968), p. 101.
35. G. O'Tuathaigh, *Ireland Before the Famine, 1798–1848* (Dublin: Gill & Macmillan, 1972), p. 135.
36. From the seventeenth century, Ireland developed a form of tenure which was unique to Ireland, which was known as leases for lives renewable for ever. See J. Finlay, *A Treatise on Law of Renewals in Respect to Leases for Lives Renewable for Ever in Ireland* (Dublin: John Cumming, 1829), p. VII. According to Wylie, the standard form of this type of lease consisted of a conveyance to the tenant for the duration of the lives of three specified persons, with a covenant of a fine to be paid on each renewal. See J.C. Wylie, *Irish Land Law* (London: Professional Books, 1975), p. 223.
37. J.S. Donnelly, *The Land and the People of Nineteenth Century Cork, The Rural Economy and the Land Question* (London: Routledge and Kegan Paul, 1975), pp. 51, 53.

38. Ibid., pp.111–12.
39. See Marx, *Capital, Vol. I*, p. 860.
40. See Cullen, *Life in Ireland*, p. 144.
41. See Solow, *The Land Question*, p. 92.
42. See Donnelly, *The Land and the People of Nineteenth Century Cork*, p. 119.
43. Ibid., pp. 113–14.
44. Ibid., pp. 118–19.
45. Landlord-assisted emigration accounted for 22,000 emigrants during the Famine period. This was, however, only about 5% of the total number. See M.E. Daly, *The Famine in Ireland* (Dundalk: Dundalgan Press), p. 106.
46. Absolute rental extraction tended to continue in the post-Famine period in the poorer parts of the West of Ireland with its accompanying labour processes associated with spade husbandry. See P. Bew, *Land and the National Question in Ireland, 1858–82* (Dublin: Gill & Macmillan, 1978).
47. J. Hooper, 'The Yields of Irish Tillage Food Crops Since the Year 1847', *Department of Agriculture and Technical Instruction for Ireland Journal* (1922), p. 226.
48. J. Bell and M. Watson, *Irish Farming, Implements and Techniques, 1750–1900* (Edinburgh: John Donald, 1986), p. 77.
49. See Hooper, 'The Yields of Irish Tillage Food Crops', p. 222.
50. W. Monsell, 'Address at the Opening of the Twenty-Second Session', *Statistical and Social Inquiry Society of Ireland Journal*, Vol. V (1869).
51. J. Lee, *The Modernisation of Irish Society 1848–1918* (Dublin: Gill & Macmillan, 1973), p. 10.
52. R. Pringle, 'A Review of Irish Agriculture, Chiefly with Reference to the Production of Livestock', *Journal of the Royal Agricultural Society of England*, Vol. VIII (1871), p. 45.
53. See Lee, *The Modernisation of Irish Society*, p. 10.
54. D. Jones, 'The Role of the Graziers in Agrarian Conflict, 1870–1910', *ESRI* Seminar Paper, 1978, p. 9.
55. S. Clark, 'The importance of agrarian classes: class structure in nineteenth century Ireland', in P.J. Drudy (ed.), *Ireland: Land, Politics and People* (Cambridge: Cambridge University Press), pp. 14–15.
56. Ibid., p. 16.
57. Ibid., p. 16.
58. Ibid., pp. 21–22.
59. See Bew, *Land and the National Question in Ireland*, p. 221.
60. Ibid., p. 222.
61. See Lee, *The Modernization of Irish Society*, pp. 102–3.

CHAPTER THREE

Was Ireland a Colony? The Evidence of the Great Famine

CHRISTINE KINEALY

The Great Irish Famine was unique in nineteenth-century European history, not only because of the timing, duration and outcome of the crisis, but also because it occurred within the jurisdiction of the United Kingdom, which at the time was the most industrialised state in the world and lay at the centre of a vast empire. The United Kingdom had been created as a consequence of the Act of Union of 1800 when Irish politicians had been persuaded, through a mixture of bribery, bullying, threats and promises, to vote the parliament in Dublin out of existence and instead to send representatives to Westminster.[1] As a consequence, Irish MPs became part of the imperial parliament in London. However, the continuation of an Irish administration at Dublin Castle was an indication that Ireland was not an equal partner within the Union but was to continue to have a quasi-colonial status.

Economic benefit, especially through access to Britain's vast trading network, was to be one of the fruits of the Union for Ireland.[2] Yet, regardless of increased trading links, the Irish economy showed little benefit from being integrated into the British Empire. Moreover, despite the various legislative enactments and high level of intervention by the British government, a real union proved to be ephemeral. Within fifty years of the passage of the Act of Union, Ireland was confronted by a subsistence crisis that was unprecedented in its extent and longevity. The paradox of a medieval famine (in terms of population loss) taking place in the midst of such wealth and resources was commented on at the time. In 1847 Isaac Butt, a leading political economist who was both Protestant and a supporter of the Union, asked how it was possible that:

> ... in a country that is called civilized, under the protection of the mightiest monarchy upon earth, and almost within a day's communication of the capital of the greatest and richest empire in the world, thousands of our fellow creatures are each day dying of starvation.[3]

Nonetheless, the government's response to the Famine (under Robert Peel and John Russell respectively) was shaped by a combination of political, financial, ideological and providentialist views of Ireland and of her place within the United Kingdom and the empire. These attitudes and ambitions had been evident before the first appearance of blight, with Ireland's role within the United Kingdom and the empire being portrayed as one of inferiority to, and dependency on, Britain. As the Famine progressed, successive relief policies provided an opportunity to impose changes on the Irish economy – and Irish character – regardless of the social cost to the people. They also demonstrated that, despite the Act of Union, Ireland was not an equal partner within the United Kingdom. This attitude was not confined to the poor but extended to many Irish landlords, who were also viewed as lazy and unenterprising. If the Irish economy was to modernise and capitalise, therefore, both ends of the economic spectrum needed to be transformed.

This chapter explores how the British government's responses to successive harvest failures after 1845 reflected and reinforced Ireland's inferior status within the United Kingdom. That the poor in Ireland were regarded as being less deserving than the British poor had been evident in the draconian Poor Law Act of 1838. The Irish Poor Law was also viewed as an important tool in the economic transformation of Ireland, which had been a major concern of successive governments prior to the appearance of the potato blight. The various special relief measures introduced after 1845 reinforced the low status of the Irish destitute and were used to expedite the regeneration of the Irish economy. At the same time, British economic interests were protected, even if the outcome was to the detriment of the Irish poor. The repeal of the Corn Laws in 1846 was an early example of a British politician using the crisis as an opportunity to introduce legislation from which Britain, rather than Ireland, would be the main beneficiary. Moreover, throughout the Famine, Ireland was frequently treated as a distinct political entity rather than as an integral part of the United Kingdom. The Poor Law Extension Act of 1847 and the Rate-in-Aid Act of 1849, for example, were attempts to transfer the financial burden of relief to Irish tax-payers thereby denying the principle that the Famine was a British – or imperial – responsibility. Moreover, the refusal of the British government either to close the Irish ports or to restrict food exports, regardless of requests from Irish authorities to do so and despite international condemnation, demonstrated that merchants and British consumers were to be protected. In contrast, the Irish poor were left to the vagaries of an underdeveloped import sector and an unregulated distribution system in which speculators and fore-stallers controlled food supply.[4] Yet, much of the British press continued to portray Ireland as the idle and ungrateful recipient of British tax-payers' – and imperial – generosity. The influential *Times* newspaper, which from 1846 led a campaign against giving additional money to Ireland, warned:

The state of Ireland has become really alarming. A moral has intervened on a physical calamity ... There is a grand national embezzlement in the course of perpetration ... One million souls are depending on the charity of the empire. One million souls are feeding and clothing themselves on the unearned bounty of the British nation.[5]

Two years later, when financial intervention from the British government had virtually ceased, *The Times* opined 'The [Irish] people have always been listless, improvident, and wretched, under whatever rulers ... They have not participated in the great progress of mankind ... We do pity them, because they have yet to be civilized.'[6]

A PROTESTANT STATE?

At the time of the Act of Union the British state was overtly identified with Protestantism. The shared religion of the British population provided them with a common sense of identity and nationality into which Irish (and British) Catholics did not fit. The influence of Protestantism spilled over into other areas, the historian Linda Colley claiming that:

Protestantism coloured the way Britons approached and interpreted their material life. Protestantism determined how most Britons viewed their politics. An uncompromising Protestantism was the foundation on which their state was explicitly and unapologetically based ... what was still the most striking feature in the religious landscape, the gulf between Protestant and Catholic.[7]

The Act of Union demonstrated the privileged place of Protestantism within Catholic Ireland by affirming the minority Church of Ireland as the state church, which was to be partly financed by tithes.[8] Furthermore, the failure to grant Catholic Emancipation meant that the Union was founded on a broken promise and that Catholics remained excluded from the newly-constituted Westminster parliament. Although Catholic Emancipation was granted in 1829, simultaneously a large number of Catholics were disenfranchised simultaneously. Nonetheless, the granting of political rights to Catholics angered some conservative Protestants, particularly members of the Orange Order. The annual 12 July parades were used as a vehicle for demonstrating their opposition, but the resultant violence against Catholics forced the British government to ban political marches. In 1845, however, the ban was lifted and the Orange Order made clear their determination to oppose the movement to repeal the Act of Union.[9]

The food shortages after 1845 were frequently expressed in providentialist terms by leading members of the British government, most notably by an influential evangelical moralist group that included Charles Wood and Charles Trevelyan.[10] As a consequence, the suffering of Irish people was viewed by some politicians in a redemptive way. The Famine also coincided with a renewed Protestant crusade in Ireland that used the hunger of poor Catholics as a vehicle for proselytising. At a meeting of the Presbyterian Synod in Scotland in 1847, it was agreed that:

> The recent awful calamity and famine that has overtaken Ireland, and more especially the fact that this calamity has fallen upon the poorest, appeared to be God's way for preparing their hearts for the reception of the truth. The people are now alive to the selfishness of their priests; and instead of looking upon Protestants as their enemies, they now regard them as their friends.[11]

Evangelical members of the Anglican Church were also active in proselytising. The Temporal Fund, which was established in Belfast following the second appearance of blight, explained its purpose lying in the fact that ' ... an opening had been made for conveying the light of the Gospel into the darkened mind of the Roman Catholic peasantry; they have listened with the deepest attention to the ministers of the church proclaiming the way of salvation while humbly engaged in efforts to rescue their bodies from famine and disease'.[12] The *Banner of Ulster* objected to activities of this group, pointing out that they had introduced a 'spirit of sectarianism' into the provision of relief.[13] Regardless of the condemnation of the work of such bodies in Ireland, even amongst the Protestant press, the government refused to regulate the work of the proselytisers.[14] Instead, private philanthropy became associated with proselytism and Protestantism, despite the fact that most private charity was non-denominational. In the long term also, the work of the evangelical groups increased antagonisms between the main churches in Ireland.[15]

The ideological gulf between Britain and Ireland was also evident in the way in which the poorer classes in Ireland were regarded. At the time of the Union, Ireland represented almost fifty per cent of the population of the United Kingdom. The rapid growth of the Irish population in the decades after 1800 meant that Irish poverty was frequently linked with a belief that Ireland was over-populated. The apparent threat to Britain posed by the Irish poor was explained by Thomas Malthus when he warned a parliamentary committee in 1826 that 'unless some other outlet be opened to them, [they] must shortly fill up every vacuum created in England or Scotland, and to reduce the labouring classes to a uniform state of degradation'.[16]

In 1838 a national system of poor relief, based on the workhouse system, was introduced into Ireland. It was modelled on the 'new' English Poor Law of 1834. The extension of the workhouse system to Ireland had been opposed by a government-appointed Poor Inquiry Commission, which had sat from 1833–36. They had advocated that a programme of public works, land improvement and assisted emigration should be used to alleviate poverty in Ireland. However, the suggestions of the Commission were considered to be too interventionist and expensive.[17] In contrast, the advantage of a poor law was that relief expenditure would be made a charge on local, rather than national, taxation. Although the Irish Poor Law was based on the 'new' English Poor Law, the system of relief introduced into Ireland in 1838 was far more stringent than that provided in either its English counterpart or the Scottish Poor Law.[18] No right to relief was included in the Irish act and no provision was made for outdoor relief, which meant that all aid had to be obtained within the confines of a workhouse.[19] In general, therefore, Irish relief was more punitive and circumscribed than relief available elsewhere in the United Kingdom, reflecting the perception of the Irish poor as undeserving. In addition to providing poor relief, the Irish Poor Law was also regarded by the government as a valuable tool in transforming Ireland from a subsistence to a commercialised economy.[20] By 1845, although 118 of the 130 workhouses were operating, they contained few inmates, suggesting that both as a mechanism for relief and as a tool of transformation, the Poor Law was having little impact. The social dislocation resulting from the Famine, however, was to provide an opportunity to the government to restructure Irish society.

The view of the Irish poor as being different and undeserving did not alter after 1845 when the potato crop failed repeatedly. Throughout the Famine, despite evidence of disease and death, the needs of the Irish poor were regularly subordinated to those of the British working classes. This perception had an impact on relief policies. In 1846, the potato crop also failed in the Highlands of Scotland. Despite more widespread devastation in Ireland, Charles Trevelyan of the Treasury who, *de facto*, had been placed in charge of relief operations in both Ireland and Scotland, decided that the government food depots in Scotland should be first to receive imports of corn. This decision caused considerable consternation amongst relief officials in Ireland.[21] Trevelyan justified his uneven treatment on the grounds that the Irish people (peasant and landlord alike) were lazy and feckless. He came from Cornwall and described himself as a 'reformed Celt', which he contrasted with the 'unreformed Celts' who inhabited Ireland.[22] The Highland landlords were singled out for praise by Trevelyan, who commented that 'It was a source of positive pleasure to turn from the Irish to the Scotch case - in the former every thing both with regard to the people and the proprietors is sickening and disgusting'.[23] Public opinion in Britain was also shaped by stories of abuse of relief systems in Ireland and the laziness of both landlords and tenants, most notably in *The Times* and *The Morning Chronicle*. *The Times* concurrently carried stories of the suffering in Ireland alongside editorial comments suggesting that no more should be done to assist the Irish poor. The ingratitude of the Irish poor, who were being fed at the expense of the English poor, was a persistent theme.[24] At the same time, Irish people were characterised as being culturally inferior. In March 1847, the paper described the Irish population as 'a people born and bred from time immemorial in inveterate indolence, improvidence, disorder and consequent destitution'.[25] A few months later, Irish landlords were referred to as 'a class without social humanity, without legal obligation, without natural shame'.[26] Palpably, Irish people continued to be perceived through a prism of colonial inferiority.

Despite the fact that following the Union Ireland sent 100 MPs to Westminster (which was increased to 105 in 1832), a number of colonial trappings remained. One of the most visible symbols of this ongoing subordinate relationship was the continuation of Dublin Castle, with an Irish administration and a Viceregal court. The Lord-Lieutenant, a Chief Secretary and Under-Secretary remained answerable to the Cabinet in London. The abolition of the Lord-Lieutenancy – which was both unnecessary and expensive if the Union was a reality – was debated in Parliament in 1823, 1831, 1844 and 1849, with even Lord John Russell believing it to be anomalous.[27] Nonetheless, the office survived until 1922.[28] The role of Dublin Castle, however, changed in the 1830s, with attempts made to transform it from being a tool of the Protestant ascendancy. Inevitably, the more liberal and conciliatory approach towards Catholics by the Irish administration incensed a number of Protestants, especially members of the Orange Order. They accused the Dublin Executive of being a 'partisan and anti-Protestant ministry', which rested its power on 'the affection and immunity of these savages'.[29] Throughout the Famine, Dublin Castle was the centre of relief administration in Ireland, although after 1846 they reported directly to Charles Trevelyan of the Treasury. Significantly, each of the Lord-Lieutenants who was in the post during the crisis, that is, Lords Heytesbury, Bessborough and Clarendon, argued for a more liberal approach to relief. Yet, despite the fact they were all political appointments made by the Prime Minister, their advice was repeatedly ignored.

FEEDING BRITAIN

From the first appearance of blight in 1845, the relief policies introduced in Westminster showed a willingness to sacrifice the needs of the Irish poor to the economic interests of Britain. Whilst the response of Peel's government has generally been praised, especially when contrasted with the losses suffered during Russell's administration, he too was operating within certain ideological and economic parameters in which trade – British trade – was paramount. The repeal of the Corn Laws was an early example of how Ireland's distress was used as an opportunity by the government to try to bring about change in Ireland. The trading nexus between Britain and Ireland, both before and after the Union, demonstrated the high level of dependence of Britain on Irish food imports. The fact that so much of the detail of the Act of Union was concerned with imports, exports, duties and bounties was indicative of the high priority that trade had within the political relationship.[30] Moreover, since the 1780s, Britain had become a net importer of corn and after 1800, Ireland played an increasingly vital role in supplying Britain with foodstuffs; between 1815 and 1845 the value of Irish exports almost quadrupled.[31] By 1845 Ireland was recognised as the granary of the United Kingdom, supplying enough corn to feed two million people in Britain. Although corn was a major commodity, vast amounts of livestock, dairy produce, eggs and alcohol were also exported.[32] For example, by 1845, 262,677 cwt. of butter from Ireland was exported to Liverpool annually.[33] Clearly, Ireland was producing an agricultural surplus for trading purposes. Nonetheless, the buoyant commercial sector existed alongside, and was underpinned by, the potato subsistence economy. Britain's dependence on Ireland for so much of her food supply, however, was a cause of concern to some. For *The Times* newspaper, the potato blight and poor corn crop in 1845 was a warning that Britain should stop depending on a 'broke reed' for so much of her annual corn supply.[34]

Whilst Peel had been moving towards a free trade policy since 1841, the potato blight allowed him to bring his timetable for repeal forward. Peel believed that weakening the hold of the symbiotic potato-subsistence and corn-for-export system of production would also be a vital step in bringing about an economic and social regeneration of Ireland. When introducing the Corn Law bill to parliament he argued that 'I do not rest my support of this bill upon the temporary ground of scarcity in Ireland ... the real question at issue is the improvement of the social and moral condition of the masses of the population'.[35] Yet Peel was aware that the repeal would be uneven in its impact, warning that 'If there be a part of the United Kingdom which is to suffer by the withdrawal of protection ... it was Ireland'. He based this opinion on the fact that 'Ireland had not, as England had, the means of finding employment for her agricultural population in her manufacturing districts.'[36] The repeal of the Corn Laws, therefore, although ostensibly tied in with food shortages in Ireland, was ultimately done for the benefit of British manufacturing rather than Irish agricultural interests. At the same time, the combination of potato blight and Corn Law repeal were viewed as the first steps in the agricultural and economic modernisation of Ireland.[37]

The repeal of the Corn Laws also ruptured the Conservative Party and resulted in the fall of Peel's Ministry. Peel was replaced by Lord John Russell in the summer of 1846, just as news of the second, more extensive, appearance of blight was announced. The second potato failure coincided with a poor corn harvest and an industrial recession in east Ulster, which meant that the demand for relief was far higher than in the previous year. Yet, in order not to undermine the position of merchants, the new government promised to import only a small amount of corn to Ireland, leaving the bulk of food imports to the workings of the free market. Consequently, less corn was imported by the Whig government to Ireland in 1846–47 than during Peel's administration.[38] At the same time, the continuation of some corn duties (the Corn Laws were not, in fact, repealed but dismantled over a period of three years) and the existence of the Navigation Laws, which restricted the transport of food, were impediments to a genuine free movement of foodstuffs.

The decision by the government not to interfere in food exports and imports was, at the time, criticised by a wide spectrum of people ranging from nationalists such as John Mitchel and Daniel O'Donnell to senior government ministers such as Lord Bessborough. Following the first appearance of blight in 1845, the Lord-Lieutenant, Heytesbury, requested that ports should be 'opened' to allow an inflow of cheap provisions, and that distillation should be stopped in order to conserve grain supplies for food rather than alcohol.[39] Such actions had been successfully employed in earlier subsistence crises and, in 1846, they also had the support of the corporations of Dublin, Derry, Cork, Limerick and Belfast.[40] Regardless of these requests, the government chose to keep its intervention in regulating food supply to a minimum, with no restrictions placed on exports. The *Belfast Vindicator*, which was the only Catholic newspaper printed in Belfast and had been founded to give a voice to nationalist opinion in Ulster, asserted that 'As long as England is unaffected by the appalling distress that unhappily exists in this country, it will never consent to the proposal of prohibiting the use of grain in distilleries and breweries.'[41]

Whilst exports of corn from Ireland decreased after the harvest of 1846, this was partly due to a poor harvest. In the case of livestock, however, exports increased after 1846; in 1847, for example, 9,992 calves were exported to Britain, which represented a 33 per cent increase over the previous year. In the first nine months of 1847 also, 874,170 gallons of porter and 183,392 gallons of whiskey were exported to Liverpool alone. During the same period, 56,557 firkins of butter were exported to Bristol and 34,852 to Liverpool (a firkin equalling nine gallons), and 3,435 poultry were exported to Liverpool and 2,375 to Bristol.[42] As vast amounts of food left Ireland, relief officials complained that no dependence could be placed on Irish merchants who clearly preferred to export rather than to import food. Henry Labouchere, the Chief Secretary between 1846–47, in a confidential report to Russell, admitted that the consequence of the Whig policies had been 'misery' that was 'impossible to relate', whereas the situation under Peel had been by comparison one of 'comfort and abundance'.[43]

A constant opinion expressed in the nationalist newspaper, the *Nation*, was that Ireland had sufficient wealth, resources and food to make the loss of human life preventable.[44] However, such views were not confined to nationalists. The *Banner of Ulster*, a Belfast-based, Protestant paper, also opposed the policy of allowing food to leave the country and supported the demand for distillation to be banned. It expressed the folly of such policies arguing that:

> The failure in the crop - by politicians in parliament, public writers and speakers out of parliament - is variously attributed to Providence. The remark is true in one sense, for man could not put the rot into potatoes,

but it is false in another, for the harvest was sufficiently abundant to give food for man and beast. The famine - if there be a famine - is man made. We have malted and distilled the famine. That fact must never be forgotten - unless we would lose the lessons that this judgment should teach.[45]

In England also, an editorial in the leading business journal, *The Mark Lane Express and Agricultural Journal*, stated that 'It is in the power of the government to prevent a lamentable crisis in the nation'. They suggested a number of measures that could be taken for this end, including, stopping distillation from corn, removing all duties on corn, allowing spare shipping to be used to bring food into the country, forbidding the giving of corn to horses and other beasts of burden, and allowing sugar to be used in distilleries and breweries. The editorial also posed the question 'What will become of the poor inhabitants of Ireland when England cannot assist? The probability is starvation to death.'[46]

Similar criticisms and reservations were repeated – privately – by two successive Lord-Lieutenants, Lords Bessborough and Clarendon. Bessborough believed that the non-availability of food in Ireland was due to the actions of Irish and British merchants whom, he opined, 'have done their best to keep up prices'.[47] Clarendon took a more cynical view of the role of the merchants, believing that leading members of the government had allowed them to behave badly. He informed Russell that 'No-one could now venture to dispute the fact that Ireland had been sacrificed to the London corn-dealers because you were a member for the City, and that no distress would have occurred if the exportation of Irish grain had been prohibited.'[48] Clearly, market forces worked to the advantage of a small group of merchants and the population of Britain rather than for the benefit of those districts in Ireland which had lost their subsistence crop. This viewpoint was expressed at the time by a wide spectrum of commentators. Isaac Butt condemned the resolution of the British government not to interfere with trade, believing that the decision was made because 'the cabinet were too much influenced by the fear of offending powerful British interests'.[49] This sentiment was echoed privately by Bessborough who observed 'It is difficult to persuade a starving population that one class should be permitted to make a 50 per cent profit by the sale of provisions whilst they are dying in want of these.'[50]

As the Famine progressed Irish poverty was increasingly made the sole responsibility of Irish tax-payers rather than the whole of the United Kingdom. After the harvest of 1847, the Poor Law was designated as the main mechanism for providing both ordinary and famine relief. For the government, the benefit of this change was that the financing of relief would all devolve to Irish tax-payers, effectively landlords. Moreover, on land which was greatly subdivided, landlords were also liable to pay the rates for tenants valued at less than four pounds per annum, which provided an incentive to evict small tenants and thus end subdivision. The increased fiscal responsibility proved to be a heavy burden on some landlords (and in some cases the final financial straw), but the government approved of this outcome and even facilitated the sale of property through the introduction of legislation in 1848 and 1849 known as the Encumbered Estates Acts. The transfer of the tax burden to Irish property exclusively was not only unpopular with Irish landlords but it was also viewed as inappropriate by a number of leading political commentators including the economist, Nassau Senior. Senior argued against throwing the entire responsibility for relief on Irish landlords and pointed out that those in charge of relief operations had treated them 'as if *they* were ignorant of their own country and *we* understood it … as if our superiority of strength implied that of a knowledge of their affairs'.[51] Senior also suggested that the continuation of high levels of exports in the midst of a famine was a sign of real want rather than a buoyant commercial sector.[52]

A number of politicians, including some Irish landlords, were concerned about both the immediate and longer term impact of relief policies. The Marquis of Sligo, who had a reputation as a humane and liberal landlord, informed Clarendon that unless more relief was provided, officials in Dublin and London would be to blame for the resultant thousands of deaths. He accused the government of trying to shift responsibility for the previous year's mortality onto the relief committees in Ireland, when the real culprit had been the policies under which they had been forced to operate.[53] The Whig supporter, the Marquis of Clanricarde, also viewed a dogmatic adherence to the new relief measures as ultimately damaging to the Union between Britain and Ireland. He warned that unless more was done to help the people 'the demand will not just be for repeal, but one more fatal, which will await its solution only until England is involved in a European war'.[54]

Despite viewing the government's policies after 1847 as harsh and misguided, a diverse collection of landlords took advantage of the opportunity available for land clearances. A small number claimed that they were doing so reluctantly. Lord Sligo, who protested that he was being squeezed financially by high taxes and low rent, justified clearing his estate in the autumn of 1848 on the grounds that he felt 'under the necessity of ejecting or being ejected'.[55] The incentive to evict was a further harsh by-product of the transfer to Poor Law relief. In 1847, evictions rose sharply and kept rising until they peaked in 1850, reaching 100,000 persons.[56] Many more were illegally evicted or voluntarily surrendered their holdings in an effort to become eligible for relief, forced to do so by the harsh regulations of the new Quarter Acre Clause, which deemed that anybody occupying more than this acreage of land was not eligible to receive relief. Homelessness and social dislocation, therefore, became a major source of distress and death in the latter years of famine.

The introduction of the Rate-in-Aid in 1849 – a tax on all Irish Poor Law unions, which was then redistributed under the direction of the Treasury to the most distressed unions – was a further instance of Ireland being forced to rely on her own resources. The tax particularly angered tax-payers in Ulster who, despite extensive local suffering, viewed the Famine as being confined to the Catholic west of the country. One local Poor Law Guardian, suggested that the people in the north of the country had not suffered because 'the Northerners are a hardworking industrious people, and the blessing of God is upon their labours. If the people of the South had been as industrious as those in the North, they would not be in the condition they are in.'[57] It was also suggested that the effect of the tax would be to 'keep up an army of beggars, fed out of the industry of Ulster'.[58] More significantly, the Rate-in-Aid demonstrated that despite having undergone four successive years of economic crisis, the Irish Famine was viewed as an exclusively Irish and not a British responsibility. A number of Protestant Ulster newspapers described the tax as being 'anti-Union'. The *Banner of Ulster* warned that the proposed act was 'dangerous to the stability of that Union on which the safety of the Union depends'.[59] The measure was also opposed by Edward Twistleton, an Englishman who was Poor Law Commissioner in Ireland. He argued that if the Union meant anything, then Ireland should be treated the same as any other part of Britain, especially during a crisis. He resigned in protest at the introduction of the tax.[60] Sir Robert Peel also, who since his resignation had given cross-party support to Russell, criticised the measure on the grounds that Irish relief should be kept in line with English practices rather than be treated differently.[61] The MP William Sharman Crawford, who had frequently argued for more liberal relief measures to be introduced, that as all taxes were paid into an Imperial Treasury 'and placed at the disposal of an Imperial Legislature for the general purposes of the United Kingdom', expenditure by the Treasury should similarly be used for all portions of the United Kingdom.[62]

By 1849, policy formulation in London was clearly frustrating Clarendon, the Lord-Lieutenant. He had been appointed in May 1847 and arrived in Ireland believing that less rather than more relief was needed, but that it had to be administered in a resolute manner. Within a few weeks, however, his attitude towards the need for intervention had changed and he found himself in conflict with London, especially the Treasury, over the relief policies. At the beginning of 1849, a small government grant was given to Ireland, which Russell announced would be the final one, despite Clarendon and others arguing that more assistance was necessary. The Lord-Lieutenant also believed government intervention was vital to prevent further wholesale evictions. Whilst Clarendon partly attributed the redemptive policies to the weakness of the Prime Minister, most of his censure was directed against Charles Wood and Charles Trevelyan of the Treasury, and George Grey, the Home Secretary, arguing that relief policy had been hijacked by 'C. Wood, backed by Grey, and relying on arguments (or rather Trevelyanisms) that are no more applicable to Ireland than to Loo Choo'.[63] As the situation in some areas deteriorated further in 1849, Clarendon, in a private communication to Russell, appealed for more intervention, arguing that:

> Surely this is a state of things to justify you asking the House of Commons for an advance, for I don't think there is another legislature in Europe that would disregard such suffering as now exists in the west of Ireland, or coldly persist in a policy of extermination.[64]

A further aspect of the Irish Poor Law which continued to be a source of grievance throughout the nineteenth century was the omission of a Law of Settlement in Ireland. In England, settlement, by which relief could only be obtained in any parish based on residency, had been an integral part of the Poor Law since the seventeenth century. No residence qualifications had been introduced into the Irish legislation in 1838. In 1846, the English legislation was changed to require that a person had to have resided in one parish for five years in order to acquire a settlement. At the time of the Famine, therefore, the English, Welsh and Scottish Poor Laws contained legislation that could be invoked against famine emigrants to Britain who had not acquired a legal settlement. Some British relief officials used the legislation indiscriminately and, at times, illegally. In Liverpool, which was the main port of entry for Irish immigrants, 15,008 were returned back to Ireland in 1847. By 1849, the number of removals had fallen to 9,509 persons and by the 1850s, it had stabilised at about 4,500 people annually.[65] The Removal Laws continued to be a source of grievance with Irish boards of guardians. In 1866, the Irish Poor Law Commissioners again asked for the settlement laws to be removed from British Poor Law legislation, describing them as 'an interference with the personal liberties of the poor, unknown, we believe, in any other part of Europe'.[66] The Removal Laws also demonstrated that Irish immigrants to Britain were there under sufferance rather than by right.

During the Famine, law and order in Ireland continued to be a source of concern to the British government. Even after the Union, the military presence in Ireland remained high, augmented by the establishment of an armed police force in 1814. Robert Peel, who had been responsible for its creation as Chief Secretary, justified this measure on the grounds that 'The Irish needed firm lessons because they could not understand oblique ones'.[67] By March 1846, there were 10,000 armed policemen in Ireland, which made it a proportionately larger force than anywhere else in the United Kingdom.[68] In March 1848, in expectation of a Young Ireland insurrection, 10,000 extra troops were placed in Dublin.[69] The government also relied on the introduction of emergency legislation (including the suspension of Habeas Corpus) to control areas regarded as 'disturbed'. The role played by the military and police presence was admitted by Earl Grey in the House of Lords in March 1846, when he said that he had heard the Home Secretary 'distinctly admit that we had military occupation of Ireland, but that in no other sense could it be said to be governed; that it was occupied by troops, not governed like England'.[70] Leading relief officials were also aware that an increase in crime was likely in view of the parsimony of relief provision. This fear was expressed by the Board of

Works who admitted, 'The government's aim is two-fold - to afford the distressed a subsistence and to preserve the peace of the country.'[71] Within parliament, concern was articulated by George Poulett Scrope, a radical English economist. Scrope opposed the dependence of successive British governments on coercion, arguing that it served only to 'make the people more desperate, encourage the landlords to exterminate them still faster, and aggravate the existing social evils'.[72] His indefatigable attacks on Whig policy throughout the Famine, especially the government's unwillingness to put humanitarian concerns before ideological ones, meant that he was widely respected in Ireland.[73] Scrope's protests, however, had no impact on government policies.

THE POLITICAL CONTEXT

The Famine took place against a backdrop of increasing political polarisation within Ireland represented by a revival of the Orange Order after 1845 and a move to a more radical form of nationalism following the death of Daniel O'Connell in 1847. Within Britain also, there was unrest as the Chartists prepared to present their monster petition to parliament in April 1848. Moreover, the overthrow of King Louis-Philippe in France in February of that year triggered uprisings throughout Europe. The British government in 1848, despite the Chartist unrest, was primarily concerned with political developments in Ireland, even before the French revolution. In December 1847, an Irish Coercion Bill received Royal Assent, making it the thirty-fifth such piece of legislation since the Union. In 1848 also, in response to the threat of a nationalist uprising, Habeas Corpus was suspended.[74] The Young Ireland uprising in July 1848, although easily defeated, contributed to a polarisation within Irish politics. In 1848, as in 1798, the Orange Order offered to act as a counter-insurgency force, describing themselves as a 'native garrison'.[75] In the wake of the nationalist uprising, press opinion in Britain hardened further against relief intervention in Ireland.[76] At the same time, it enabled the Irish poor to be increasingly caricatured as violent and ungrateful.[77]

The belief that Ireland was ungrateful and owed much to Britain had been evident in the British media since the first appearance of blight. In an article in the London *The Times* in February 1847, the writer expressed concern with the ingratitude of Ireland and the fact that no lessons had been learnt during the period of the Union, asking:

> What have we - what has England - done to deserve this perpetual blister of thankless obligations and exacting oblique? ... We have been united to Ireland for 47 years by the ties of legislative association. During that time Ireland has enjoyed all the privileges that England enjoyed ... yet, she claims in alternate tones of supplication and menace that her poor shall be supported by our bounty, her improvidence corrected by

our prudence, and her self-sought necessities alleviated by our mort-
gaged wealth.[78]

The failure of the Irish people to benefit from union with a superior nation was
attributed to the fatal moral failings of the former. Journals and newspapers
which were read by the British middle classes constantly outlined these shortcomings. In 1847, the most devastating of all the Famine years, *Fraser's
Magazine* explained these differences thus:

> The English people are naturally industrious, they prefer a life of honest
> labour to one of idleness. They are a persevering as well as an energetic
> race, who for the most part comprehend their own interests perfectly,
> and sedulously pursue them. Now of all the Celtic tribes, famous every-
> where for their indolence and fickleness as the Celts everywhere are, the
> Irish are admitted to be the most idle and fickle. They will not work if
> they can exist without it.[79]

An alternative point of view was represented concurrently in the *Belfast
Vindicator*, which unequivocally laid the blame for the suffering and starvation
in Ireland on the British government. In an impassioned editorial, the paper
averred:

> The work of death goes on. We are reaping the fruit of English legisla-
> tion. There is scarcely now anyone so foolhardy as to defend the legisla-
> tion by which the country has been reduced to its present deplorable
> condition. All now see the blundering by which this country has been
> ruined ... The blundering absurdity of the famine laws - the neglect, or
> petty insolence of England's hired officials, have brought conviction to
> the minds of all who are not wilfully blind on this side of the channel
> that the real blight of this country has been the blight of foreign legisla-
> tion.[80]

A similar point of view was evident in the findings of a government commission appointed to investigate the continued mortality in County Clare in 1849
and 1850. It concluded that:

> Whether as regards the plain principles of humanity or the literal text
> and admitted principles of the Poor Law of 1847, a neglect of public duty
> has taken place and has occasioned a state of things disgraceful to a civ-
> ilized age and country, for which some authority ought to be held respon-
> sible and would long since have been held responsible had these things
> occurred in any union in England.[81]

In conclusion, throughout the course of the Famine relief policies were controlled by a small ruling clique in Westminster who viewed the distress as a providentialist opportunity to change Ireland for Britain's benefit. The repeal of the Corn Laws was an early example of this aspiration. Ireland was also regarded as a burden and a threat, rather than as an equal partner within the United Kingdom. As a consequence, the opinions of her legal representatives were frequently ignored and the advice of the Dublin Castle administration was marginalised. Instead, policy formulation was designed to protect Britain's economic interests rather than alleviate Irish distress. The refusal to interfere with trade, despite clear evidence that the free market was not operating in many parts of Ireland, the operation of the Law of Removal against famine emigrants to Britain, and the introduction of the Rate-in-Aid, illustrated that British economic interests were paramount. These policies were underpinned by the belief that the population of Ireland was separate, distinct and generally undeserving. Repeatedly, the perceived moral failings of the Irish people were used to justify these forms of intervention.

In 1851, the Great Exhibition was held in London, which was a showpiece for Britain's technical, industrial and financial supremacy. It attracted over one million visitors.[82] Britain's economic performance and self-confidence had not been dented by the catastrophe in one part of the United Kingdom. Instead, her commercial prowess and the rewards of possessing an empire were put on public display. In the same year, the preliminary results of the decennial census were collated in Ireland. The Census Commissioners noted the vast fall in population, yet went on to state:

> ... although the population has been diminished in so remarkable a manner by famine, disease and emigration between 1841 and 1851, and has been since decreasing, the results of the Irish census of 1851 are, on the whole, satisfactory, demonstrating as they do the general advancement of the country.[83]

Although within a six-year period over one million people had died and even more had emigrated the Census Commissioners interpreted the loss of population as having been beneficial to Ireland and, implicitly, to Britain. Apart from the massive population losses, the catastrophe also reinforced existing political and religious divisions within Ireland, and between Ireland and Britain. Within Ireland, Ulster Protestants increasingly interpreted the Famine as a Catholic and southern, rather than a national, disaster.[84] However, discriminatory legislation before, during and after the Famine demonstrated that Irish people (whether Catholic or Protestant, peasant or landlord) were not perceived to be equal to British people, although Catholics had the added disadvantage of following a false God and misguided political leaders. Ironically, northern Protestants, despite feeling abandoned by the British government during the Rate-in-Aid crisis, remained attached to the Union. Instead, the Famine was used to demonstrate their distinctiveness and superiority.[85]

Overall, the responses of the British government during the Famine demonstrated that Ireland had not achieved commensurate status with the population of Britain and that the Act of Union was colonialism under another guise.

NOTES

1. A. Jackson, 'The Irish Act of Union', *History Today*, 51 (Jan. 2001), pp. 19–25.
2. Similar promises had been made to the Scottish parliament in 1707. See C. Kinealy, *A Disunited Kingdom? England, Ireland, Scotland and Wales 1800–1949* (Cambridge University Press, 1999), pp. 6–10.
3. I. Butt, 'The Famine in the Land', *Dublin University Magazine*, xxix (May 1847), p. 501. Butt's politics underwent a radical change and in 1870 he founded the Home Government Association, which laid the foundations for the Home Rule movement.
4. The British government's refusal to close the ports was condemned in the American press, see *Weekly Herald* (New York), 21 November 1846.
5. *The Times*, 10 December 1846.
6. Ibid., 4 October 1848.
7. L. Colley, *Britons. Forging the Nation 1707–1837* (London, The Bath Press, 1992), pp. 18–19.
8. Act of Union, Anno 39 and 40 Georgii III, AD [AU?]1800.
9. *Belfast Protestant Journal*, 21 March 1846, 11 July 1846.
10. P. Gray, *Famine, Land and Politics. British Government and Irish Society 1843–50* (Dublin, Irish Academic Press, 1999), pp. 24–6.
11. *Banner of Ulster*, 26 Oct. 1847.
12. *Belfast News-Letter*, 8 Jan. 1847.
13. *Banner of Ulster*, 8 Jan. 1847.
14. See C. Kinealy and G. MacAtasney, *The Hidden Famine: Hunger, poverty and sectarianism in Belfast* (London, Pluto Press, 2000), pp. 124–39.
15. D. Kerr, *A Nation of Beggars? Priests, People and Politics in Famine Ireland, 1846–1852* (Oxford, Oxford University Press, 1994), pp. 324–5.
16. Thomas Malthus, quoted in B. Inglis, *Poverty and the Industrial Revolution* (London, Hodder and Stoughton, 1971), p. 235.
17. *Letter from N. Senior on the third report of the commissioners of inquiry into the condition of the poor in Ireland*, British Parliamentary Papers, B.P.P. 1837 (90) li.
18. Kinealy, *A Disunited Kingdom*, pp. 68–72.
19. *An Act for the more effectual Relief of the Destitute Poor in Ireland*, 1 & 2 Vic. c.56., 31 July 1838.
20. George Nicholls to Lord John Russell, *Report by George Nicholls to His Majesty's Secretary of State for the Home Department*, B.P.P., 1837, (90) 1, pp. 9–11.
21. Sir Randolph Routh to Trevelyan, 29 October 1846, *Commissariat Series*, p. 207.
22. Charles Trevelyan, *The Irish Crisis* (London, Longman, 1848), which first appeared anonymously in the *Edinburgh Review*.
23. Quoted in T.M. Devine, *The Great Highland Famine. Hunger, Emigration and the Scottish Highlands in the Nineteenth Century* (Edinburgh, John Donald, 1988), p. 91.
24. This attitude was exemplified in a number of *Punch* cartoons, for example, 'Union is Strength' of 17 Oct. 1846, in which England is giving bread and a shovel to Irish peasants and 'The English Labourer's Burden' of 24 Feb. 1849, in which an English labourer is depicted carrying an Irish peasant.
25. *The Times*, 14 March, 26 March 1847.
26. Ibid., 16 April 1847.
27. Lord John Russell, 'Note on the post of Irish Viceroy', PROL, Russell Papers, 30/22/ 6H; no date, 1847.
28. S. J. Connolly (ed.), *The Oxford Companion to Irish History* (Oxford, Oxford University Press, 1998), p. 329.
29. *Ulster Times*, 20 Nov. 1838.
30. Act of Union, Schedule, Number One.
31. C. Ó Gráda, *Ireland: A New Economic History* (Oxford, Oxford University Press, 1994), pp. 162–3.

32. C. Kinealy, 'Food Exports from Ireland 1846–47', in *History Ireland*, 5, 1 (Spring 1997), pp. 32–6; and C. Kinealy, *The Irish Famine. Impact, Ideology and Rebellion* (London, Palgrave, 2002), pp. 90–116.
33. For more on exports, see C. Kinealy, *The Great Irish Famine. Impact, Ideology and Rebellion*, pp. 90–116.
34. *The Times*, 1 Sept. 1845.
35. Robert Peel, *Hansard*, 15 May 1846, pp. 689–91.
36. Debate in House of Commons of Corn Laws, *Hansard*, 5 May 1846, pp. 122–8.
37. See C. Kinealy, 'Peel, Rotten Potatoes and Providence. The repeal of the Corn Laws and the Irish Famine', in A. Marrison (ed.), *Free Trade and its Reception* (London, Routledge, 1998), pp. 50–62.
38. Charles Trevelyan to Sir Randolph Routh, 18 December 1846, *Correspondence Explanatory of the Measures adopted for the Relief of Distress in Ireland from July 1846 to January 1847. Commissariat Series*, P.P. 1847 [761], p. 382.
39. Lord Heytesbury to Robert Peel, 17 October 1845, Lord Mahon and Right Hon. Edward Cardwell (eds) *Memoirs of the Right Honourable Sir Robert Peel* (London, John Murray, 1857) p. 125; ibid., 27 Oct. 1845, p. 138.
40. *Belfast Vindicator*, 1 Nov. 1845.
41. Ibid., 2 Jan. 1847.
42. The composition of individual ship's cargoes to main ports in Britain is contained in the Bills of Entry, Maritime Museum, Liverpool; see also, Kinealy, 'Food Exports', pp. 35–6.
43. Ibid.
44. *Nation*, 30 Oct. 1847.
45. *Banner of Ulster*, 2 April 1846.
46. *Mark Lane Express*, 4 Jan. 1847.
47. Lord Bessborough, Dublin Castle to Russell, Russell Papers, PROL, 30/22/16A, 23 Jan. 1847.
48. Lord Clarendon to Russell, Clarendon Papers, Bodleian Library, 12 July 1847.
49. Butt, 'The Famine in the Land', p. 507.
50. See, for example, Distress Papers in National Archives; also Bessborough to Russell, Russell Papers, PROL, 30/22/16A, 23 Jan. 1847.
51. Nassau Senior, 'Proposals for extending the Irish Poor Law', *Edinburgh Review* (Oct. 1846) pp. 367–414.
52. Ibid.
53. Clarendon to Marquis of Sligo, 14 August 1847. For more on the debates in parliament, including the opposition of Disraeli and Bentinck to Whig policies, see Kinealy, The *Great Irish Famine*, pp. 31–60.
54. Marquis of Clanricarde to Clarendon, 15 Aug. 1847.
55. Quoted in Grey, *Famine, Land and Politics*, p. 180.
56. This figure is generally accepted by historians, including M. Daly and J. Donnolly, but has been challenged by T.P. O'Neill. See T.P. O'Neill, 'Famine evictions', in C. King (ed.), *Famine, Land, Culture in Ireland* (Dublin, University College Dublin, 2000), pp. 29–70
57. *Armagh Guardian*, 12 March 1849.
58. *Hansard's Parliamentary Debates*, col. 62, 1 March 1849.
59. *Northern Whig*, 22 Feb. 1849; *Banner of Ulster*, 22 May 1849.
60. Evidence of Edward Twistleton, *Select Committee on the Irish Poor Law*, 1849, xv, pp. 699–714.
61. Sir Robert Peel to Sir James Graham, 20 Jan. 1849, in Charles Stuart Parker (ed.), *Sir Robert Peel from his Private Letters* (London, John Murray, 1899), p. 501.
62. *Hansard*, 1 March 1849.
63. Clarendon to Duke of Bedford, Clarendon Papers, Bodleian Library, 16 Feb. 1849. For the defence of Trevelyan see Robin Haines, *Charles Trevelyan and the Great Irish Famine* (Dublin, Four Courts Press, 2004).
64. Ibid., 28 April 1849.
65. *Report of the Select Committee on Poor Removal*, 1854 [396] xvii, pp. 570–607.
66. *Nineteenth Annual Report of Poor Law Commissioners*, 1866, p. 14.
67. Quoted in E.J. Evans, *Sir Robert Peel: Statesmanship, Power and Party* (London, Routledge, 1994) p.8.
68. K. T. Hoppen, *Ireland Since 1800: Conflict and Conformity* ((London, Addison-Wesley, 1989), p. 128.
69. L. Curtis, *The Cause of Ireland. From the United Irishmen to Partition* (Belfast, Beyond the Pale, 1994), p. 55.

70. Earl Grey, *Hansard*, House of Lords, 1347, 23 March 1846.
71. Board of Works to Henry Labouchere, 6 Sept. 1846, Distress Papers, quoted in L. Swords, *In Their Own Words. The Famine in North Connaught 1845–49* (Dublin, Columba Press 1999), p. 68.
72. Scope to Russell, Russell Papers, PROL 30 22 5A, 23 June 1846.
73. *The Times*, 14 April 1849.
74. R. Sloan, *William Smith O'Brien and the Young Ireland Rebellion of 1848* (Dublin, Four Courts Press, 2000), pp. 246–7.
75. Petition of Loyal Orange Lodge No.356, Outrage Papers for County Down, National Archives, 29 July 1848.
76. *Illustrated London News*, 29 July 1848; *The Times*, 14 Nov. 1848.
77. L.Curtis, *Nothing but the Same Old Story. The Roots of Anti-Irish Racism* (second ed. Belfast, Beyond the Pale, 1996), pp. 50–54. See also Leslie A. Williams, *Daniel O'Connell, The British Press and the Irish Famine* (Aldershot, Ashgate, 2003).
78. *The Times*, 10 Feb. 1847.
79. Quoted in Curtis, *Nothing but the Same Old Story*, p. 51.
80. *Belfast Vindicator*, 6 Jan. 1847.
81. *Report of Select Committee appointed to enquire into the administration in the Kilrush Union since 19 September 1848*, P.P. 1850, [613] xi, p. xii.
82. E. Royle, *Modern Britain. A Social History 1750–1985* (London, Edward Arnold, 1987), p. 251.
83. *General Report of Census Commissioners for Ireland* (Dublin, 1856), p. lviii.
84. For more on this divide, see C. Kinealy and G. Mac Atasney, *The Hidden Hunger*, Chapter 1.
85. *Armagh Guardian*, 12 March 1849.

CHAPTER FOUR

The Material Implications of Colonialism in Early Nineteeth-Century Ireland

CHARLES E. ORSER JR.

INTRODUCTION

Scholars conducting research from the perspectives of several disciplines over the past few years have repeatedly demonstrated that colonialism is a complex and highly nuanced process that is often ambiguous and difficult to understand with absolute clarity. In numerous empirical studies they have shown the myriad, often unique ways in which the colonialist endeavour has been enacted, and many have stressed both the long- and the short-term impacts of colonialism on both colonialiser and colonialised. This body of research illustrates that at its core colonialism consists of a series of complex interactions between men and women of different cultures and various social classes. Numerous scholars have worked diligently to unravel the many dimensions of colonially-based cultural and social interactions, but many investigators are only now coming to appreciate fully the material side of these associations.

The materiality of colonialism, though inseparable from the process of cultural interaction, is equally complicated and is often quite subtle. Colonialism's material expressions can range from the wholesale construction of planned villages and fortifications (to invent a familiar landscape in an unfamiliar ecological zone) to the flooding of a region with foreign material objects (in an effort to transform a people's traditional culture). As physical things that constitute the tangible embodiment of foreign power and possible long-term domination, the objects of colonialism often work to create new markets and to erode or to destroy an indigenous people's traditionally-constructed material, social, and natural worlds. The full-scale, often overwhelming materiality of the colonialist endeavour often imparts a lasting impression on an indigenous people and their landscape.

Significant issues arise about the adoption and use of foreign objects by indigenous men and women immersed in a colonial setting. What is the meaning of an indigenous culture using the objects created by a colonialist culture? Does the use of these objects mean that the indigenous men and women in effect have accepted the culture of the colonialists?

Questions such as these have significant implication for Irish history, particularly when we consider the early nineteenth century, the years immediately following the passage of the Act of Union. The precise, contextually-rooted nature of social and cultural change and the relationship between material change and social transformation have bedevilled archaeologists and cultural anthropologists for years. Many of the most thoughtful scholars have adopted a multidisciplinary approach in an attempt to bring to bear as much information as possible to the resolution of such questions, and in this sense, archaeology is particularly well-suited to providing unique information about the material expressions of colonialism around the world. Archaeological research by its very nature brings to light fresh information. Much of archaeology's special contribution is embodied in excavated artefacts, tangible objects often handled by both coloniser and colonised as each directly experienced colonialism. Artefacts are the physical expression of the contacts and interactions between members of diverse cultures.

In this chapter I focus on the relationship between colonialism and portable material culture by reference to Ballykilcline, an early nineteenth-century townland in north County Roscommon. Excavations were annually conducted there under my direction from 1998 to 2002.

THE IMPORTANCE OF ARTEFACTS IN THE STUDY OF COLONIALISM

Archaeologists have long been interested in the contacts and interactions of diverse peoples, and the examination of cultural contact situations has become a staple of research for many archaeologists. Archaeologists initially found it relatively easy to recognise the presence of colonising peoples among previously uncontacted peoples by simply examining the artefacts they excavated. Imported objects found at indigenous village sites provided tangible proof that contact, either direct or indirect, had occurred. For archaeologists excavating indigenous sites occupied during the post-Columbian era of European expansion, the identification of colonialism was especially straightforward because of the ease in recognising objects manufactured in European factories.[1] At the same time, however, most archaeologists realised that it was not enough simply to demonstrate that past colonisation, or at least culture contact, had occurred. The historical reality of colonialism could be established in most cases without recourse to archaeological excavation because historians had long chronicled the details of European global expansion. The most interesting questions for anthropologically-trained archaeologists revolved around the meanings of material objects in colonial encounters, and the acceptance or rejection of specific elements of material culture by indigenous men and women.

Many archaeologists initially adopted an acculturation model to explain the transfer of material objects from one cultural setting to another. In this perspective, the higher the percentage of foreign objects at an aboriginal village site, the greater the cultural transformation experienced by the inhabitants of that site.[2] Archaeologists working in places visited by exploring and colonising Europeans found it particularly easy to recognise past acculturation by the indigenous peoples' adoption of European objects.[3]

Some archaeologists eventually came to realise, however, that the use of the acculturation model meant that they would have to assume that all peoples react similarly to the introduction of foreign objects.[4] Archaeologists could use this assumption to devise universal rates of culture change wherever European objects were found at native villages. Archaeologists today are generally unwilling to rely on a concept of cultural universality, and most have abandoned a strict adherence to acculturation as an explanatory mechanism. Culture contact nonetheless remains a viable archaeological research topic around the world.[5] A more sophisticated perspective was reinforced by the growing understanding that even men and women without economic or political power have some measure of control over their destinies.[6] Addressing the weaknesses of acculturation in the archaeological study of African American slavery, for example, one archaeologist observed that it is 'an inaccurate, passive model for a dynamic process' that obscures 'the creation of a community and shared culture among slaves in the context of their struggle against an oppressive system, a system with styles of domination and resistance shaped by specific relations of production'.[7] The same comment could be offered for many other peoples affected by the colonial process.

The archaeologists' turn from acculturation to domination and resistance was part of a growing understanding that the archaeology of modern history is inexorably about capitalism in some fashion.[8] Archaeologists who acknowledged that capitalism creates and maintains social inequalities soon considered the nature of the material relations between 'haves' and 'have-nots'.[9]

Several archaeologists have used excavated information to show that 'have-nots' were not simply dominated by elites. Archaeologists investigating industrial capitalism, for example, have been especially conscious of demonstrating the defiance workers could express both at their jobs and in their homes.[10] In addition to overt work stoppages, industrial workers could show their dissatisfaction by engaging in work slow-downs, product sabotage, equipment damage, frequent absenteeism, and the use of banned substances, like alcohol.

Within recent years a growing number of archaeologists have followed the lead of cultural anthropologists and material culture specialists and have noted that material things are actively engaged in the social world.[11] Archaeologists now recognise that artefacts, in addition to being functionally useful, were also created to carry symbolic meanings, to convey complex messages, and to mediate between diverse individuals and social groups in situationally-defined, complicated ways. Artefacts even play a role in human psychology, affecting 'what a person can do, either by expanding or restricting the scope of that person's actions and thoughts'.[12] Based on these sophisticated understandings, most archaeologists now agree that material objects constitute 'a definitional component of human existence'.[13] In short, humanity simply cannot be conceptualised in the absence of material things.[14]

Given the broad diversity of human cultures around the globe, it is not surprising that certain cultures became associated with distinct kinds of artefacts. Archaeologists are renowned for their ability to relate specific sorts of artefacts with certain past peoples. They regularly link individual artefacts, artefact styles, and unique decorations with past human populations and social groups.

The close connection between specific artefacts and past social and cultural entities is easy to conceptualise for prehistory. For example, archaeologists can easily imagine groups of ancient men and women making clay pots and then decorating them with symbols they conceive to have meaning within their culture. Once archaeologists identify the possible stylistic varieties, they can use them as cultural signposts: every time they unearth a pot with an identifiable decorative style, they can state with some assurance that they have found evidence for a certain past people with whom they associate that kind of pot. Excavators know, for instance, that Neolithic people in County Antrim decorated their bowls both with a whipped cord decoration that extended laterally around the vessel, and with a series of parallel lines running down the vessel from top to bottom.[15] Archaeologists assume that these decorations embodied some social meaning, but their precise message is lost to time.

The above scenario makes perfect sense for many prehistoric contexts because the people who made the pots probably also used them. The pots' makers had embossed them with designs that had specific meaning within the cultural context in which their pots would be used. The rise of market capitalism, however, makes the facile association of artefacts and culturally-relevant symbols considerably more complicated. Beginning around AD 1500 and increasing with time, a growing percentage of people used objects they did not make. As a result, archaeologists studying the modern world are not able to assume that the objects people used were necessarily decorated with symbols and designs that were directly meaningful to them. Consumer choice is thus an especially important matter in colonial situations. The important question is not 'why did the people decorate their pots in a certain style', but rather, 'why did they accept one kind of artefact and not another'?

Archaeologists examining native sites in North and South America have discovered that colonising Europeans flooded indigenous villages with products made in the factories of their home countries. So overwhelming was the influx of new goods that one historian has labelled it the 'First Consumer Revolution'.[16] Archaeologists working at colonial-period sites throughout the

Americas regularly unearth the material remains of the colonialist enterprise. After spending years studying glass beads, brass kettles, iron knives, and other objects, anthropological archaeologists have learned how native peoples used these new things, how they adapted them to their traditional ways of life, and how they were changed by their presence. Some native peoples resisted and even rejected the inflow of foreign objects to their villages.

Issues concerning the introduction of foreign artefacts into a traditional culture are especially pertinent to early nineteenth-century rural Ireland because they directly relate to the wider concerns of cultural identity and cultural maintenance in a colonial setting. Important questions involve the retention of a traditional mode of life in the face of an often overwhelming influx of mass-produced, foreign-made goods, many of which, by their presence alone, may modify traditional patterns of life. For this reason, material culture cannot be ignored when investigating the question 'Was Ireland a Colony?' A brief consideration of one common commodity, tea, offers insights about the significance of material culture.

When the Dutch first imported tea to Europe in 1610, they brought Chinese porcelain teapots along with them. Entrepreneurs in Europe soon built an entire industry around the manufacture of the so-called 'china' required for the proper brewing, serving, and drinking of tea.[17] Tea drinking in Europe was originally restricted to the upper class, but non-elites had also adopted the practice by the late eighteenth century. Accordingly, the explosion in tea imports to Ireland between 1772 and 1811 is staggering, rising 512 per cent for black tea alone.[18]

Drinking tea, however, represented more than just acquiring a new taste. It also demanded a wholly new material culture, composed, in the best circumstances, of a teapot, tea cups, saucers, spoons, a creamer, and a sugar bowl (which also required another non-European commodity). At the same time, drinking tea became a social engagement imbued with a special etiquette and ritual.[19]

In light of the social significance of tea, an archaeologist who finds tea cup fragments at an abandoned village site in the Irish countryside must decide whether the tea drinkers also enacted the social practices and attitudes that could accompany the consumption of this foreign substance. Though it may initially seem quite trivial, answering this question can assume paramount importance in a colonial situation where the archaeologist must decide whether the acceptance of tea equates with the acceptance of new social and cultural customs. We may well ask in an Irish context whether the presence of English tea cup fragments at rural village sites carries any special meaning about the loss of Irish identity or the success of English cultural domination. Put another way, do cultural and social implications accompany the simple drinking of tea?

This simple question, though supremely important to the archaeology of modern Ireland, cannot now be resolved. As I write this, archaeologists have simply not conducted enough detailed research on the nineteenth century to propose an informed answer. Some view of the complexities inherent in the material world of colonialism can be gained, however, by examining a townland in north County Roscommon, called Ballykilcline.

THE VIEW FROM BALLYKILCLINE, COUNTY ROSCOMMON

Ballykilcline was a townland of about 610 acres (247 ha) located in north County Roscommon, on the eastern shore of Lough Kilglass. In 1841 almost 500 people lived at the townland as tenant farmers.

The initial effort to create a foreign colony in Roscommon involved the garrisoning of an English force in Roscommon Castle in 1566, but the colonial history of Ballykilcline began in the 1650s when the Cromwellians leased several plots of land in the area of their faithful soldiers, including Nicholas Mahon, the occupant of Strokestown Park House.[20] The Mahons held a lease on Ballykilcline until May 1834, when negotiations with the Crown disintegrated. The lands of Ballykilcline then came under the administrative control of Her Majesty's Commissioners of Woods, Forests, Land Revenues, Works, and Buildings. Upon taking control of the townland, the Commissioners discovered that the townland was divided into 'seventy-four distinct Tenancies'. The tenants were merely tenants at will, and so they did not hold long-term leases giving them the legal right to live in the townland.

The Crown's agents soon learned that the tenants were not inclined to pay their rents for the year 1836. In the minds of the agents, this action undoubtedly illustrated why the area around the townland was 'proverbial in this part of the county for its wickedness'.[21] To solve the non-payment problem quickly, the Commissioners issued notices to the tenants requiring them to surrender possession of their holdings. Fifty-two of them complied and were reinstated as 'care-takers' with a small monthly allowance. One condition of this arrangement was that the tenants, now mere occupiers of the land, were required to surrender possession immediately upon the Crown's demand. Some tenants, however, 'absolutely refused to give up the Possession or to account with the Crown's Receivers for the Value of the Holdings in their Occupation',[22] and they instituted a rent strike. When the Crown's receivers called on the recalcitrant tenants, several of them who had originally agreed to surrender refused to do so. Faced with the volatile situation, the Under Secretary asked the police to assist the rent collectors in their duties. The police feared for their safety and declined to intervene, stating that any effort to collect the rents would cause 'a certain Breach of the Peace and probable personal Injury to those employed'.

The British government then decided to institute legal proceedings against eight 'ring leaders' of the rent strike, and ordered their arrest. On 6 April 1842, a process server attempted to give notice to the eight tenants, but a mob assembled and he was 'driven off the Lands'. The process server – with apparent police assistance – was able to deliver subpoenas to only four of the 'ring leaders'.

One month later, the Clerk of Quit Rents informed the remainder of the Ballykilcline tenants that they were required to pay their arrears in Strokestown, the nearest market town, on 31 May. The tenants dutifully appeared on the appointed day, but only one of them – the Protestant minister who lived in the Glebe – agreed to pay the required amount. The others refused to pay 'saying they had not the Money, and that the Rent fixed upon their Lands was too much and more than they could pay'. The tenants then made a formal petition to the Commissioners, asking forgiveness, and stating that they had been victimised by 'high, enormous Rents'. As a further show of strength, they appended a bold statement to the end of their petition: If the Commissioners did not agree to forgive their arrears payments, they would be forced to send a petition directly to 'Her most Gracious and Illustrious Majesty, tending to the Fraud and Imposition they are subjected to'.

Instead of accepting the terms of the petition, the Commissioners began to press for a legal solution to the rebellion, and in their official record began to refer to the tenants as 'Intruders on the Crown Lands of Ballykilcline, in the County of Roscommon'. Eviction was the most drastic solution available, but even with this threat hanging over them, the tenants continued their open resistance. In a letter dated 8 April 1843, the Sub-Sheriff of County Roscommon stated that when he had arrested one of the 'ring leaders' in Strokestown, 'the roads on every Side of me were surrounded, and the Prisoner would be certainly rescued from me had I not got him into One of the Police Stations along the Road'. The tenants attacked the police station and the sheriff could only get his prisoner to the Roscommon jail by taking an indirect route.

By 1844 the tenants still refused to pay their rents and the Crown still sought to force payment. In May the bailiffs employed to serve the rent notices found the tenants more intractable than ever. The Crown's agent reported that when the bailiffs attempted to serve notice, 'they were attacked by the Tenants, and not having the Protection of the Police were obliged to retreat, after only effecting the Service of Six or Seven of the Notices, and were it not that by chance they met a few Policemen on Duty they would certainly have been killed, as it was with the greatest Difficulty and fixed Bayonets that the Police could keep the Mob from them'. The tenants were 'armed with Sticks, Stones, and Shovels' and used 'threatening Language' when chasing the bailiffs away from their homes. The obviously exasperated agent then asked the Commissioners' permission either to evict the tenants and to lock their houses, or to 'throw down the Houses of the refractory Tenants … [to] make an Example among them'.

Faced with the reality that the tenants were in a state of overt rebellion, the Commissioners decided that eviction was ultimately the best solution.

The tenants of Ballykilcline must have realised at the same time that they were out of options, because in May 1846 they sent a petition to the Commissioners, describing themselves as: '459 Individuals of moral industrious Habits, exemplary, obedient, and implicit to their Landlady or Landlord, which is the Cause of bringing them into Contempt, but are penitent and regretful for any Misunderstanding which has occurred in the Event of the Case in question'.

The historical record indicates that the tenants succeeded in their rent strike because the so-called 'ring leaders' were never entirely arrested. But the strike can also be considered a failure because it ended with the full eviction of the tenants in 1847–48, at the height of the Great Starvation.[23] In any case, the final years of the townland's history are largely defined by the tenants' refusal to pay their rents. The sequence of historical events reveals much about the residents' reaction to their social roles as the Crown's tenants, but archaeological research provides additional insights into the cultural life of the townland's residents and presents another perspective on the nuances of cultural maintenance in colonial settings.

During five consecutive summers in 1998–2002, excavations were undertaken in the extreme north-west corner of Ballykilcline, on land occupied, from about 1800 to 1848, by Mark Nary and his sons, Luke, James, and Edward. The Narys participated in the rent strike, but the records do not indicate that they were 'ring leaders'. The authorities, however, did identify two of their close relatives as active ring leaders.

Excavation focused on the two Nary house sites indicated both on the 1837 Ordnance Survey map and on a special plat drawn in 1836 by Dublin-based surveyors hired by the Commissioners. One practical advantage offered by the Nary site is that the land has remained virtually undisturbed since the Crown's agents pulled down and destroyed the tenants' houses. The surface of the ground, in pasture since 1848, revealed no evidence of the former dwellings, and the precise house locations were found using sophisticated geophysical imaging methods.[24]

The excavations at Ballykilcline demonstrate without question that the British market extended to the townland and that at least the Narys were eager consumers of English-made goods, even though they were in open rebellion against the Crown. The ceramic sample excavated from the Nary house sites is most informative. Of the 10,341 artefacts collected during those years, 6,686 (or 64.7 per cent) were ceramic shards. The high percentage of ceramic finds is not unusual because of a number of practical factors: glazed ceramics are durable; they tend not to deteriorate in most soils; and when dropped, a ceramic bowl or plate tends to shatter into several pieces. What is somewhat surprising, however, is that almost half (48.8 per cent) of the shards are from white, thin-bodied, 'refined' earthenwares, undoubtedly manufactured in England.[25]

The production of refined earthenware was never a major industry in early nineteenth-century Ireland, though a fine earthenware tradition did exist throughout the eighteenth century.[26] As a result, the vast majority of refined vessels found inside an Irish home during the early decades of the nineteenth century would be English-made.[27] Between 1800 and 1810 alone, Wakefield reported that Ireland imported £643,786 worth of 'earthenware'.[28] In addition to the fine earthenwares, excavators also unearthed over 2,500 shards of red-bodied, thick 'coarse' earthenware from an important but largely unexamined indigenous industry.[29]

The tangible presence of the ceramic artefacts at Ballykilcline raises several important questions about the local economy, including issues of supply and demand, the precise routes of transport, and the number of English dishes that actually came into the townland. Because the residents of Ballykilcline were likely to have purchased the ceramic vessels represented by the excavated shards, the vessels' presence in specific houses even raises questions about household economy and intra-townland social inequality.

Archaeologists find it difficult to provide economic information from ceramics shards alone, even for those produced by nineteenth-century factories. Nevertheless, a relative idea of the exchange value of the ceramics recovered from the excavations at Ballykilcline can be devised. After making a careful examination of early nineteenth-century price lists and potters' records, archaeologist George Miller created four price groups for mass-produced, English ceramics.[30] Undecorated wares were the least expensive. Vessels with minimal decoration – shell-edged, sponge-decorated, and 'factory-made slip-wares' – came next, followed by hand-painted wares. The most expensive vessels were those decorated with intricate transfer-printed designs, most often in shades of blue.

Ceramic salespeople, of course, marketed their wares as whole vessels rather than shards. Analysis of the ceramic sample from the two Nary houses at Ballykilcline revealed a minimum of at least 127 different refined earthenware vessels. This sample includes 31 plates, 1 platter, 35 tea cups, 24 saucers, 8 bowls, 1 teapot, 11 pitchers, 3 pitchers or jugs, 7 mugs, 1 tile, and 5 unknown vessels. Of these vessels, 53 (41.7 per cent) are transfer-printed and 49 (38.6 per cent) are minimally decorated. This distribution means that fully 80.3 per cent of the sample falls into the two highest cost categories for nineteenth-century English refined ceramics.

IMPLICATIONS OF THE CERAMIC EVIDENCE

Such a large relative percentage of English-made ceramic vessels at the house sites of the Narys was unexpected for two reasons. In the first place, neither house was completely excavated. Excavation instead uncovered about three-quarters of one house and less than a quarter of the second. The imported ceramics thus have a large presence in this relatively small area. In the second place, in writing about pre-famine life, historical observers often remarked about the paucity of material culture in the homes of Ireland's rural population. Arthur Young mentioned the presence of 'crocks', and defined them as 'the iron pot of an Irish cabbin [sic]', but added that to the Irish 'a hog is a much more valuable piece of goods [sic] than a set of tea things'. In her diary of life as a landlord's wife in County Wicklow in the 1840s, Elizabeth Grant described the material emptiness of one of her tenants' homes: 'I saw no bedclothes, straw below, some sort of dark cloth above; there was a pot and a plate or two and a basin and a spoon.' She further said that her tenants 'spend their money very foolishly' and regarding meals, that 'They have not fuel indeed to cook one, nor pot nor pan nor griddle nor crock to prepare one in, most of them at least.'[31]

As may be expected, nineteenth-century novelists were more expressive in their descriptions. William Carlton described a cabin in *The Black Prophet* as: the 'tables and chairs were crazy; the dresser, though clean, had a cold, hungry, and unfurnished look'. Anthony Trollope provided an even darker image in *The Kellys and the O'Kellys*: 'It isn't that the chairs and tables look filthy, for there are none. It isn't that the pots, and plates, and pans don't shine, for you see none to shine.'[32]

Verbal images, coupled with comparable pictorial images from the same period, combine to present a picture of the typical Irish tenant farmer as devoid of an extensive material culture, a perception that to some extent persists today. At least two implications stem from this perception: first, that an archaeologist seeking to excavate the site of a rural tenant family's house should expect to find little in the way of material culture, and second, that the rural Irish, being devoid of a material culture, were perfect candidates for colonisation from the east.

The presence of English ceramics in such relative abundance at Ballykilcline raises many consequential questions about internal colonialism and its long-term effects. First, the appearance of the refined earthenwares demonstrates that the residents of Ballykilcline both desired these imports and had the economic capital to purchase them. The artefacts suggest that the people had no qualms about participating in the British marketplace. In fact, the abundance of so many vessels of various decorations suggests that they willingly bought into the economic system being pressed around the world under the auspices of the same colonial power that sought to dominate them. Excavations around the world demonstrate that English ceramics were in the vanguard of English colonial activities.[33]

Linked with this interpretation is the intriguing idea that the residents of Ballykilcline used their withheld rent money to enter the marketplace. They took their economic fate into their own hands by keeping their funds, and thereby raised their own material standard of living. If this interpretation is true, their action constitutes a fascinating and powerful response to colonial domination. Whereas historical records indicate rather clearly that the tenants rejected the idea of paying rent to live on the land, the excavated artefacts reveal that they readily bought into their oppressors' colonial material culture.

Archaeological research at Ballykilcline also allows for a further investigation into the broader relationships between the material culture of resistance and cultural identity. A prominent idea in the archaeology of resistance is that men and women who occupy subordinate social positions may use material objects to express their distinction from the power elite. This conscious usage is perhaps easiest to envision in situations where the resisting men and women craft their own distinctive artefacts. A classic example discovered purely by archaeologists is provided by the low-fired, unglazed 'colonoware' pottery made by African slaves along the eastern seaboard of the United States and in the Caribbean during the seventeenth, eighteenth, and early nineteenth centuries.[34] Archaeological convention makes it relatively easy to imagine the producers of these pots imprinting them with meaningful cultural symbols, and archaeologists have identified many of the decorations on colonoware vessels as decidedly African and Native American in character.

It is more difficult to understand how non-elites used mass-produced objects for group identification and expression. Research in African American archaeology is again instructive. In an important study of late nineteenth- and early twentieth-century consumerism among African Americans living in Annapolis, Maryland, archaeologist Paul Mullins has convincingly demonstrated how African Americans used seemingly insignificant artefacts – like inexpensive porcelain statuettes – to symbolise their entry into the broader consumer culture.[35] Rather than constituting mere knick-knacks, the small statues can be interpreted as embodying powerful social meanings, in effect representing the rightful entry of African American men and women into an economic order from which they had long been excluded.

Mullins discovered, however, that the African American adoption of inexpensive porcelain statuettes represented more than the interaction of economics and social attitudes. The practical effects of racial designation and racism provided key insights into the consumption patterns of African Americans. The effects of racism on both the Irish and throughout Ireland are well documented,[36] and racism must be taken into account when analysing nineteenth-century Irish archaeological contexts both in Ireland and elsewhere.[37] Little doubt exists that the oppression of the Irish had racial overtones. The inclination to equate the physical appearance and culture of the Irish with those of Africans and African Americans is also well known, but material comparisons were also made. For example, many early nineteenth-century writers compared rural Irish cabins to the kraals of the so-called 'Hottentots'. W.M. Thackeray, Asenath Nicholson, and Jonathan Pim all mentioned the kraal by name.[38] It was probably no accident that in the early nineteenth century the Khoi Khoi, pastoralist herders of southern Africa – misnamed 'Hottentots' – 'lived in a condition in some ways more degraded than that of slaves'.[39] The *Oxford English Dictionary* includes one gloss of 'Hottentot' as: 'a person of inferior intellect or culture; one degraded in the scale of civil-isation, or ignorant of the usages of civilised society'. Equating the square Irish cabin with the squat, mat-covered, inverted bowl-shaped Khoi kraal is merely ideological; it bears no resemblance to reality.[40]

Given such statements, we may easily extrapolate that a racialised percep-tion of the Irish may have been widespread in some social circles. If this view permeated society, we may expect that the effects of racial categorisation should have been translated into material terms. The enforced inferiority of rural Irish men and women thus should be apparent in the collections from Irish archaeological sites. The problem is, however, that archaeologists have yet to develop ways to identify the material effects of racialist attitudes. The collection excavated at Ballykilcline exhibits no obvious indications that racist beliefs were pressed on the townland's residents. Our inability to see the material effects of racism in the artefacts may simply signify, as Mullins dis-covered in his study of African American life in coastal Maryland, that oppressed men and women must sometimes hide their material gains from the elites who hold power over them. Tangible expressions of material progress thus may be subtle. They may also only appear inside rural cabins, where such expressions do not have the potential to cause the rent to be raised. The pos-sible distinction between the interior furnishings of a rural cabin and its out-side appearance suggest the oppressive power of colonialist administration.

In the context of early nineteenth-century Ireland, it may be possible that the tenants of Ballykilcline had to devise mechanisms to keep any social or economic advances hidden from view. Tenant secrecy may partly account for some of the outsiders' comments about the debased condition of rural Irish men and women. At Ballykilcline specifically, one of the Crown's agents unsuc-cessfully attempted to convince the Commissioners that the tenants only feigned destitution, stating that they lived 'in a State of comparative Affluence'.[41] The agent's obvious frustration is probably an indication that British bureaucrats were incapable of imagining that Irish tenant farmers could accumulate wealth of any sort. One of the tenants' greatest collective strengths, therefore, may have rested in their landlords' prejudice against the so-called 'Celtic Race'; in perceiving them as forever poor and morally corrupt, they could not envision Irish tenants as using their rent monies to increase their material standard of living. Like Elizabeth Grant, they may only have been able to imagine that Irish tenant farmers would squander their meagre funds, and forever live as 'bog trotters'.

The archaeological material from Ballykilcline raises a further issue con-cerning the correlation between artefacts and resistance history. The histori-cal record is unequivocal in stating that the residents of Ballykilcline were engaged in a protracted and occasionally violent rebellion against their land-lords, the British Crown. The artefacts, however, indicate that at least one family of non-rent-paying tenants fully embraced English commodities. Only one artefact in the sample from the five years of excavation implies any kind of resistance. This tiny artefact is a single fragment of a white clay smoking pipe bowl stamped 'PEAL' for Repeal. Little is currently known about pipes of this sort, except that they were probably part of an industry geared towards marketing O'Connell.[42] Its presence at Ballykilcline suggests that at least one of the townland's residents did not approve of the economic and political status quo. Given the faint appearance of the letters on the pipe, one could make the case that the political views of the pipe's owner were not actually openly expressed. The pipe may represent an extremely muted protest.

In light of the presence of this one tiny pipe fragment, it is possible to imagine that the purchase of English ceramics may have been conceptualised as an act of covert resistance on the part of the Ballykilcline tenants. While believing in repeal of the Act of Union, they may also have been actively, albeit clandestinely, working to improve their standard of living. The presence of the latest and most durable ceramics then available may be an indication of this strategy. Rather than representing cultural capitulation, the English dishes in the rebelling tenants' homes may have been a personal way of resisting debasement.

The presence of the tiny Repeal pipe at Ballykilcline perhaps demonstrates the subtle power that artefacts can exert. Mass-produced artefacts may be used by indigenous peoples to impart messages in colonial settings that were not intended by the original artefact makers. In some cases, the messages may not even be obvious to the artefacts' users. Ceramic colour provides a useful example. A brilliant white body was one of the most important physical characteristics of the English ceramics manufactured during the early nineteenth century. As English potters worked diligently to imitate the hard-paste, opaque, Asian porcelains that accompanied tea to Europe, the colour of their so-called 'chinas' became increasingly whiter as they perfected the productive process. As a result, English 'creamwares' manufactured in the late eighteenth century have a slightly greenish cast, the 'pearlwares' of the early nineteenth century have a bluish cast, and the 'whitewares', first produced in the early nineteenth century and still made today, are stunningly white.[43]

In colonial situations, and particularly in early nineteenth-century Ireland, it would be a mistake to overlook the colours of ceramic dishes. In fact, the brilliance of the imported, English ceramics is extremely significant because it stood in stark contrast to the traditional Irish coarse earthenwares. Excavations reveal that local Irish potters decorated their coarse earthenware vessels with earth-toned glazes in shades of green, brown, tan, pale yellow, and black. At the same time, excavated shards indicate that Irish potters made wares in familiar, utilitarian forms, such as large bowls and wide-mouthed crocks, meant for kitchen and dairy usage.[44]

Isaac Weld, who surveyed County Roscommon in 1830 for the Royal Dublin Society, understood the importance of ceramic colour. Writing about what he called 'the worst cabins' in the county, Weld was startled by the colours he saw around him:

Every thing around these hovels, until the potato shews [sic] its green leaves, appears dark; the house, the soil, and even the garments of the women, consisting commonly of deep brown, accord so nearly in colour with the appearance of the surrounding objects, that on many occasions, the groups of females sitting before the doors, would be undistinguish-able [sic], were it not for the white caps of linen or muslin, which, if they do not preserve their original hue, are nevertheless still conspicuous.[45]

If Weld could have looked inside one of these so-called 'hovels', he undoubt-edly would have been struck by a similar contrast between the traditional, coarse earthenware bowls and the 'modern', white dishes manufactured in England. He, in fact, did argue that the superior quality of the English fine earthenwares would quickly supplant the traditional wares; not only were they better, he said, but also cheaper.

Art historians who have considered the importance of colour have observed that colours and art styles can be used to create 'visual ideologies', or visual attempts to alter a people's understanding or conception of the world around them.[46] The introduction to the Irish countryside of huge amounts of starkly white, brightly decorated, English ceramics – as demonstrated by the findings at Ballykilcline – may be interpreted as but one part of a larger ideological bat-tle for the hearts and minds of Irish men and women. In addition to making the tenant farmers dependent on the British economic system, the goal of a visual ideology that included ceramics would have been to make them think like members of the British Empire. Ceramics were assumed to help promote the colonisation of the Irish mind.

CONCLUSION

It is impossible to know how or indeed even whether the men and women of Ballykilcline were being 'modernised' or 'Anglicised' by their white tea cups and other imported dishes. But by resisting their rent payments and purchas-ing the most modern ceramics on the market, the tenants may have had the best of both worlds, even if only briefly.

Archaeological research conducted all over the world has demonstrated that archaeology provides a path-breaking way to provide new information about the material dimensions of colonialism. One value of archaeological research is that the analyses can simultaneously be both minutely site-specif-ic and broadly comparative. The actions of the Ballykilcline tenants were com-plicated and undoubtedly enacted within several interconnected social net-works. The role of material objects in those networks is only beginning to be closely examined. A more complete picture of tenant life will emerge as more archaeologists begin to conduct research on sites occupied during the early nineteenth century. Research now suggests that the many messages present-ed by the artefacts – which were the personal objects used by the tenants in their homes – may be deciphered by a simple willingness to consider artefacts as social documents deeply engaged on both sides of the colonialist struggle.

NOTES

The archaeological research at Ballykilcline was conducted under excavation licence 98E0297, administered by Dúchas, The Heritage Service, Dublin. I wish to thank their staff, as well as the staff at the National Museum, for all their assistance and guidance. This study results from research funded by grants from the Famine Commemorative Commission, the National Committee for Archaeology, the Heritage Council, and Illinois State University. I especially wish to acknowledge the assistance of archaeologist John Waddell and geophysicist Kevin Barton, as well as that of my field directors, Katherine Hull, Stephen Brighton, and David Ryder, and all the students who conducted the excavations. I am also grateful for the assistance of the landowners, all those people in Strokestown who offered much needed help, and the Roscommon County Council. Special thanks are also due to Janice Orser for all her assistance during the preparation of this essay.

1. J.D. Birmingham, D. Bairstow and A. Wilson (eds), *Archaeology and Colonisation: Australia in the World Context* (Sydney: Australian Society for Historical Archaeology, 1988); S.L. Dyson (ed.), *Comparative Studies in the Archaeology of Colonialism.* (Oxford: British Archaeological Reports, 1985); W.W. Fitzhugh (ed.), *Cultures in Contact: The European Impact on Native Cultural Institutions in Eastern North America, A.D. 1000–1800* (Washington, DC: Smithsonian Institution Press, 1985).
2. P. Farnsworth, 'Missions, Indians, and Cultural Continuity', *Historical Archaeology*, 26, 1 (1992), pp.22–36; G.I. Quimby and A. Spoehr, 'Acculturation and Material Culture: I', *Fieldiana: Anthropology* 36 (1951), pp. 107–47; J.R. White, 'Historic Contact Sites as Laboratories for the Study of Culture Change', *The Conference on Historic Site Archaeology Papers* 9 (1975), pp. 153–63.
3. C.E. Orser, Jr., *A Historical Archaeology of the Modern World* (New York: Plenum, 1996), pp. 60–6.
4. I. Brown, 'Historic Artifacts and Sociocultural Change: Some Warnings from the Lower Mississippi Valley', *The Conference on Historic Sites Archaeology Papers* 13 (1979), p.118.
5. G. Connah, *The Archaeology of Australia's History* (Cambridge: Cambridge University Press, 1993); A.L. Crowell, *Archaeology and the Capitalist World System: A Study from Russian America* (New York: Plenum, 1997); C.R. Ewen, *From Spaniard to Creole: The Archaeology of Cultural Formation at Puerto Real, Haiti* (Tuscaloosa: University of Alabama Press, 1991); L. Falk (ed.), *Historical Archaeology in Global Perspective* (Washington, DC: Smithsonian Institution Press, 1991); C.L. Lyons and J.K. Papadopoulos (eds), *The Archaeology of Colonialism* (Los Angeles: Getty Research Institute, 2002); J.D. Rogers and S.M. Wilson (eds), *Ethnohistory and Archaeology: Approaches to Postcontact Change in the Americas* (New York: Plenum, 1993).
6. N.B. Dirks (ed.), *Colonialism and Culture* (Ann Arbor: University of Michigan Press, 1992); R. Guha, *Dominance Without Hegemony: History and Power in Colonial India* (Cambridge: Harvard University Press, 1997); E.W. Said, *Culture and Imperialism* (New York: Alfred A. Knopf, 1993).
7. J.E. Howson, 'Social Relations and Material Culture: A Critique of the Archaeology of Plantation Slavery', *Historical Archaeology*, 24, 4 (1990), p. 81.
8. M.P. Leone, 'A Historical Archaeology of Capitalism', *American Anthropologist*, 97 (1995), pp. 251–68; M.P. Leone and P.B. Potter, Jr. (eds), *The Recovery of Meaning: Historical Archaeology in the Eastern United States* (Washington, DC: Smithsonian Institution Press, 1988); *idem*, *Historical Archaeology of Capitalism* (New York, NY: Kluwer Academic/Plenum, 1999); B.J. Little, 'People with History: An Update on Historical Archaeology in the United States', *Journal of Archaeological Method and Theory*, 1 (1994), pp. 5–40; C.E. Orser, Jr., 'Plantation Status and Consumer Choice: A Materialist Framework for Historical Archaeology', in S.M. Spencer-Wood (ed.), *Consumer Choice in Historical Archaeology* (New York: Plenum, 1987), pp. 121–37
9. B. Frazer (ed.), 'Archaeologies of Resistance in Britain and Ireland', *International Journal of Historical Archaeology*, 3 (1999), pp.1–129; P.P.A. Funari, M. Hall and S. Jones (eds), *Historical Archaeology: Back from the Edge* (London: Routledge, 1999); R.H. McGuire and R. Paynter, eds,

The Archaeology of Inequality (Oxford: Blackwell, 1991); D. Miller, M. Rowlands and C. Tilley (eds), *Domination and Resistance* (London: Unwin Hyman, 1989).

10. Useful examples are: M. C. Beaudry, L. J. Cook and S. A. Mrozowski, 'Artifacts and Active Voices: Material Culture as Social Discourse', in R.H. McGuire and R. Paynter (ed.), *The Archaeology of Inequality* (Oxford: Blackwell, 1991), pp. 150–91; M.S. Nassaney and M.R. Abel, 'The Political and Social Contexts of Cutlery Production in the Connecticut Valley', *Dialectical Anthropology*, 18 (1993), pp. 247–89; P.A. Shackel, *Culture Change and the New Technology: An Archaeology of the Early American Industrial Era* (New York, NY: Plenum, 1996).

11. M. Shanks and C. Tilley, *Re-Constructing Archaeology* (Cambridge: Cambridge University Press, 1987), p. 117.

12. M. Csikszentmihalyi and E. Rochberg-Halton, *The Meaning of Things: Domestic Symbols and the Self* (Cambridge: Cambridge University Press, 1981), p. 53.

13. S. Jhally, *The Codes of Advertising: Fetishism and the Political Economy of Meaning in the Consumer Society* (London: Francis Pinter, 1987), p. 1.

14. A case for the indispensability of material objects to humans has been made most forcefully by archaeologist M.B. Schiffer, *The Material Life of Human Beings: Artifacts, Behavior, and Communication* (London: Routledge, 1999).

15. J. Waddell, *The Prehistoric Archaeology of Ireland* (Galway: Galway University Press, 1998), p. 43.

16. J. Axtell, *Beyond 1492: Encounters in Colonial North America* (New York: Oxford University Press, 1992), pp. 125–51.

17. J.N. Pratt, *The Tea Lover's Treasury* (San Ramon: CA: 101 Productions, 1982), pp. 104–6.

18. E. Wakefield, *An Account of Ireland, Statistical and Political, Volume II* (London: Longman, Hurst, Orme, and Brown, 1812), p. 40.

19. R. Roth, *Tea Drinking in 18th-Century America: Its Etiquette and Equipage*. United States National Museum Bulletin 225 (Washington, DC: Smithsonian Institution Press, 1961). Further information on the material culture of tea drinking appears in D. diZ. Wall, 'Family Dinners and Social Teas: Ceramics and Domestic Rituals', in C. E. Hutchins (ed.), *Everyday Life in the Early Republic* (Winterthur, DE: Henry Francis du Pont Winterthur Museum, 1994), pp. 249–84.

20. T. Cronin, 'The Elizabethan Colony in Co. Roscommon', in H. Murtagh (ed.), *Irish Midland Studies: Essays in Commemoration of N. W. English*, (Athlone: The Old Athlone Society, 1980), p. 109; G. Hanley, 'Nicholas Mahon and 17th Century Roscommon', *The Irish Genealogist*, 3 (1961), pp. 228–35.

21. J. O'Donovan, *Letters Containing Information Relative to the Antiquities of the County of Roscommon, Collected During the Progress of the Ordnance Survey in 1837* (Bray: Michael O'Flanagan, 1927), p. 57.

22. All quotes in this section are taken from 'Lands of Ballykilcline, County Roscommon, Returns to Orders of the House of Lords, Dated 16th and 19th February 1847'. London: House of Lords, 1847.

23. R.J. Scally, *The End of Hidden Ireland: Rebellion, Famine, and Emigration* (New York: Oxford University Press, 1995), pp. 105–29.

24. C.E. Orser, Jr., *A Report of Investigations for the First Season of Archaeological Research at Ballykilcline Townland, Kilglass Parish, County Roscommon, Ireland*. Submitted to Dúchas, The Heritage Service, Dublin, 1998.

25. I. Weld, *Statistical Survey of the County of Roscommon, Drawn up under the Direction of the Royal Dublin Society* (Dublin: R. Graisberry, 1832), p. 165.

26. M. Archer, *Irish Delftware: An Exhibition of 18th Century Irish Delftware at Castletown House, Celbridge, Co. Kildare*. (Dublin: Irish Printers, 1972); P. Francis, *Irish Delftware: An Illustrated History* (London: Jonathan Horne, 2000); *idem, A Pottery by the Lagan: Irish Creamware from the Downshire Pottery, Belfast, 1787–c. 1806* (Belfast: Institute of Irish Studies, Queen's University, 2001); M. Reynolds, 'Irish Fine-Ceramic Potteries, 1769–96', *Post-Medieval Archaeology*, 18 (1984), pp. 251–61.

27. M. Dunlevy, *Ceramics in Ireland* (Dublin: National Museum of Ireland, 1988), pp. 21–2; G. O'Brien, *The Economic History of Ireland from the Union to the Famine* (Clifton, NJ: Augustus M. Kelley, 1972), pp. 364–5; M.S.D. Westropp, 'Notes on the Pottery Manufacture in Ireland', *Proceedings of the Royal Irish Academy*, 32 (1913), pp. 1–27; *idem, Irish Pottery and Porcelain* (Dublin: The Stationery Office, 1935).

28. Wakefield, *Account of Ireland*, p. 39.

29. C.E. Orser, Jr., 'Of Dishes and Drains: An Archaeological Perspective on Irish Rural Life in the Famine Era', *New Hibernia Review*, 1 (1997), pp. 120–35; *idem*, 'In Praise of Early Nineteenth-

Century Coarse Earthenware', *Archaeology Ireland*, 14, 4 (2000), pp. 8–11; *idem*, 'Vessels of Honor and Dishonor: The Symbolic Character of Irish Earthenware', *New Hibernia Review*, 5 (2001):83–100.

30. G.L. Miller, 'Classification and Economic Scaling of 19th Century Ceramics', *Historical Archaeology*, 14 (1980), pp. 1–40; *idem*, 'A Revised Set of CC Index Values for Classification and Economic Scaling of English Ceramics from 1787 to 1880', *Historical Archaeology*, 25, 1 (1991), pp. 1–25.

31. A. Young, *A Tour of Ireland with General Observations on the Present State of that Kingdom Made in the Years 1776, 1777, and 1778* (London: Cadell and Dodsley, 1780), p. 26; E. Grant, *The Highland Lady in Ireland: Journals, 1840–50*, eds. P. Pelly and A. Tod (Edinburgh: Canongate, 1991), pp. 128, 281.

32. W. Carlton, *The Black Prophet: A Tale of Irish Famine* (London: Simms and M'Intyre, 1847), p. 33; A. Trollope, *The Kellys and the O'Kellys, Or Landlords and Tenants* (London: Penguin, 1993), p. 54. Also see C.E. Orser, Jr., 'Can There Be an Archaeology of the Great Famine?' in C. Morash and R. Hayes (eds), *'Fearful Realities': New Perspectives on the Famine* (Dublin: Irish Academic Press, 1996), pp. 77–89.

33. The case for North America is well known, but for other locales, see R. Auger, 'Sixteenth-Century Ceramics from Kodlunarn Island', in W.W. Fitzhugh and J.S. Olin (eds), *Archaeology of the Frobisher Voyages* (Washington, DC: Smithsonian Institution Press, 1993), pp. 147–51; J. Birmingham, *Wybalenna: The Archaeology of Cultural Accommodation in Nineteenth-Century Tasmania* (Sydney: Australian Society for Historical Archaeology, 1992); A.Y. Ogedengbe, 'An Historical Archaeology of Zungeru Colonial Settlement: A Case Study', in K. W. Wesler (ed.), *Historical Archaeology in Nigeria* (Trenton, NJ: Africa World Press, 1998), pp. 273–310; C. Schrire, *Digging Through Darkness: Chronicles of an Archaeologist* (Charlottesville, VA: University of Virginia Press, 1995); A. Wilson, 'The Failed Colonial Squire: Sir John Jamison at Regentville', in J. Birmingham, D. Bairstow and A. Wilson (eds) *Archaeology and Colonisation: Australia in the World Context* (Sydney: Australian Society for Historical Archaeology, 1988), pp. 123–38.

34. Colonoware pottery has spawned a huge and expanding literature in historical archaeology. For the basics, see the pioneering studies: L. Ferguson, 'Struggling with Pots in South Carolina', in R. H. McGuire and R. Paynter (eds), *The Archaeology of Inequality* (Oxford: Blackwell, 1991), pp. 28–39; *idem*, *Uncommon Ground: Archaeology and Early African America, 1650–1800* (Washington, DC: Smithsonian Institution Press, 1992); *idem*, '"The Cross is a Magic Sign": Marks on Eighteenth-Century Bowls from South Carolina', in T. A. Singleton (ed.), *I, too, Am America: Archaeological Studies of African-American Life* (Charlottesville, VA: University of Virginia Press, 1999), pp. 116–31.

35. P.R. Mullins, *Race and Affluence: An Archaeology of African America and Consumer Culture* (New York: Kluwer Academic/Plenum, 1999); *idem*, 'Racializing the Parlor: Race and Victorian Bric-a-Brac Consumption', in C. E. Orser, Jr. (ed.), *Race and the Archaeology of Identity* (Salt Lake City, UT: University of Utah Press, 2001), pp. 158–76.

36. T.W. Allen, *The Invention of the White Race, Volume I: Racial Oppression and Social Control* (London: Verso, 1994); L. Curtis, *Nothing but the Same Old Story: The Roots of Anti-Irish Racism* (Belfast: Sásta, 1994); L.P. Curtis, Jr., *Apes and Angels: The Irishman in Victorian Caricature* (Washington, DC: Smithsonian Institution Press, 1971); L. Gibbons, 'Race Against Time: Racial Discourse and Irish History', *Oxford Literary Review*, 13 (1991), pp. 95–113; P. Hainsworth (ed.), *Divided Society: Ethnic Minorities and Racism in Northern Ireland* (London: Pluto, 1998); N. Ignatiev, *How the Irish Became White* (New York, NY: Routledge, 1995); R.N. Lebow, *White Britain and Black Ireland: The Influence of Stereotypes on Colonial Policy* (Philadelphia, PA: Institute for the Study of Human Issues, 1976); R. Lentin and R. McVeigh (eds), *Racism and Anti-Racism in Ireland* (Belfast: Beyond the Pale, 2002); D. R. Roediger, *The Wages of Whiteness: Race and the Making of the American Working Class* (London: Verso, 1991); B. Rolston and M. Shannon, *Encounters: How Racism Came to Ireland* (Belfast: Beyond the Pale, 2002); H. Waters, 'The Great Famine and the Rise of Anti-Irish Racism', *Race and Class*, 37 (1995), pp. 95–108.

37. C. E. Orser, Jr., 'The Challenge of Race to American Historical Archaeology', *American Anthropologist*, 100 (1998), pp. 661–8; *idem*, *Race and Practice in Archaeological Interpretation* (Philadelphia, PA: University of Pennsylvania Press, 2003).

38. W.M. Thackeray, *The Irish Sketchbook* (Dublin: Gill & Macmillan, 1990), p. 101; A. Nicholson, *Ireland's Welcome to the Stranger: or, Excursions through Ireland in 1844 and 1845, for the Purposes of Personally Investigating the Condition of the Poor* (London: Charles Gilpin, 1847), p. 260; J. Pim, *The Condition and Prospects of Ireland, and the Evils Arising from the Present Distribution of Landed*

Property: With Suggestions for a Remedy (Dublin: Hodges and Smith, 1848), p. 116.

39. R. Elphick, *Kraal and Castle: Khoikhoi and the Founding of White South Africa* (New Haven: Yale University Press, 1977), p. 180.

40. Contemporary images of the Khoi Khoi kraal can be found in: W.J. Burchell, *Travels in the Interior of Southern Africa, Volume I* (Cape Town: C. Struik, 1967). The only possible correlation between Khoi housing and that of rural Ireland could be the rounded, domed-roofed creat, common in the Late Middle Ages. See Kieran D. O'Conor, *The Archaeology of Medieval Rural Settlement in Ireland* (Dublin: Royal Irish Academy, 1998), pp. 94–6; and D. Dickson, *New Foundations: Ireland, 1660–1800* (2nd edn, rev., Dublin: Irish Academic Press, 2000), p. 22.

41. House of Lords, 'Lands of Ballykilcline', p. 76.

42. G. Owens, 'Constructing the Image of Daniel O'Connell', *History Ireland*, 7, 1 (1999), pp. 32–6; R. uí Ógáin, *Immortal Dan: Daniel O'Connell in Irish Folk Tradition* (Dublin: Geography Publications, 1996).

43. See, for example, I. Noël Hume, *A Guide to Artifacts of Colonial America* (New York, NY: Alfred A. Knopf, 1972), p. 128.

44. D.L. Brown, 'Ceramic Functional Analysis: The Redwares of Late Eighteenth- and Nineteenth-Century Gorttoose Village, County Roscommon, Republic of Ireland'. Unpublished senior research thesis, Illinois State University, Normal, 1998.

45. Weld, *Statistical Survey*, p. 316.

46. N. Hadjinicolaou, *Art History and Class Struggle*, trans. L. Asmal (London: Pluto, 1978).

PART II
POLITICS/HISTORY

CHAPTER FIVE

'Ireland's last fetter struck off': The Lord-Lieutenancy Debate 1800-67

PETER GRAY

For much of the first two-thirds of the nineteenth century the office of the Irish lord-lieutenant was a contested constitutional site. This is evident from the debates surrounding the series of attempts (ultimately abortive) to abolish it and replace the viceregal system of executive governance based at Dublin Castle with direct rule from Westminster. The abolition debates gave articulation to a vigorous, if ultimately unresolved, controversy over Ireland's constitutional status within the United Kingdom and the British Empire, involving significant claims and counter-claims over the incomplete character of the Act of Union, the continuing 'colonial' status of Ireland, and the survival of 'national' political institutions.

This pre-Home Rule controversy reinforced the dualistic ambivalence that characterised British (and many Irish) constructions of Ireland's constitutional condition. Pulled in opposite directions by the contrasting imperatives of British integrationism and the practicalities of governing an intractable society shaped by previous colonial practice, British observers ultimately found themselves incapable of reconciling constitutional theory with governing realities. Although each had their advocates, neither the contrasting models of Scotland or the West Indies colonies were found to offer a satisfactory answer to the problem of legitimising the executive government of Ireland.

The lord-lieutenancy debate was limited largely to the period between the 1820s and the emergence of the Home Rule campaign in the 1870s. Polarisation over the more profound constitutional changes embodied in the Home Rule Bills eclipsed the lesser (if still symbolically charged) question of the lord-lieutenancy. In 1871–2 and again in 1885 Gladstone floated the idea of the Prince of Wales replacing a ministerial appointment as the resident representative of the Crown, but his concern appears to have been as much with the survival of the monarchy as a useful institution as with the underlying constitutional problems of Ireland.

At any rate, his plans for a supra-political Edwardian viceroyalty were scuppered by a combination of Saxe-Coburg-Gotha family politics, Irish nationalist opposition, and parliamentary hostility towards further royal 'extravagance'.[1]

However, the issues raised in the early nineteenth-century debates continue to have resonance more than a century later. The idea that integrated direct rule would promote full political participation within a uniform British nation-state, and thereby marginalise Irish nationalism, attracted British radicals and liberals and their Irish Unionist allies in the nineteenth century. The same constitutional panacea – sweeping away anything that smacked of constitutional or national difference – continues to appeal to a section of Unionism in Northern Ireland, and to elements of the British right, to the present. The ultra-integrationist language voiced by British and Irish advocates of viceregal abolition in the nineteenth century was strangely re-echoed in the integrationist campaigns within Ulster Unionism led by Enoch Powell from the mid-1970s and later taken up by the so-called 'Campaign for Equal Citizenship' in the 1980s and fitfully advocated by Robert McCartney and his accident-prone UKUP in the 1990s.[2]

THE IRISH VICEROYALTY AND THE UNION

Motions or bills to abolish the Irish lord lieutenancy and the viceregal court, either replacing the position with a secretary of state for Ireland or transferring all Irish executive powers to the home secretary, were introduced into the Westminster Parliament in 1823, 1830, 1844, 1850, 1857 and 1858. The first three were brought forward by Joseph Hume, a Scot and a leading 'economical' radical. Those of 1857 and 1858 were proposed by one of Hume's successors in the radical leadership, John Arthur Roebuck. These backbench initiatives were attempts to push government or the main opposition party into action; although they failed, they attracted increasing support in the Commons and from the British press. When the long-serving viceroy Lord Carlisle retired from office in 1864, it was thus hardly surprising that a further press and pamphlet campaign attempted to re-open the question.

The exception to these unofficial campaigns, and by far the most significant initiative, was the 1850 abolition bill, proposed by the Whig-Liberal government itself. Lord John Russell's bill obtained a large Commons majority at its second reading but was lost due to lack of time at the end of the session. Russell's ailing government did not have an opportunity to reintroduce the measure before it fell in 1852, but this official acceptance of the principle of abolition could not but alter the terms of the debate.

Before looking at the language of the debate, a brief summary of the power and political standing of the lord lieutenant may be helpful. The office had its roots in the twelfth-century position of the king's lieutenant governor or 'locum-tenens', an institution of fluctuating importance and nomenclature, held at different times by energetic agents of the monarch, by sinecurists, and by members of the leading Anglo-Irish families. After a period of inactive absenteeism, the lords lieutenant of the later eighteenth century had again become active executive officers, managing with the assistance of the Irish chief secretary and other Dublin Castle officials the often intractable Irish Parliament on behalf of the British government.[3]

The 1800 Act of Union created the new polity of the United Kingdom of Great Britain and Ireland with a unified legislature, but it left the executive apparatus in Dublin virtually unchanged. John Foster, one of the Act's bitterest opponents, warned that the anomaly of abolishing the legislature while leaving the lord lieutenant and Dublin Castle departments intact would make Ireland 'a colony on the worst of terms',[4] but this line of criticism did not become widespread in the Union debates. The absence from the Act of any mention of the executive was later to lead to sharp debate on what had been the intentions of the framers of the Union.[5] Yet, while the abolition of the separate post of chancellor of the Irish exchequer in 1816 indicated that the Dublin executive was not sacrosanct, the offices of lord lieutenant, chief secretary and under secretary were to survive until the establishment of the Irish Free State in 1922.

One of the objections raised after 1800 to the lord lieutenancy was the simultaneous role it played in both the 'efficient' and 'dignified' aspects of the constitution, as Bagehot would later define them. As head of the Irish executive, the holder possessed significant statutory and prerogative powers over security and legal matters (including the power of mercy) and over other developing areas of administration such as the poor law commission and board of works. He also held considerable patronage powers. On the other hand, as viceroy he was also the monarch's representative in Ireland, the apex of the Irish court and the focus of official ceremonies that traced their origins to Anglo-Norman times. Lords lieutenant continued, however, to be government appointments, the incumbent invariably departing with the fall of the governing party at Westminster. They were usually appointed from the British nobility or diplomatic corps (in the first half of the nineteenth century only Wellesley and Bessborough were of Anglo-Irish background). One early twentieth-century historian of the institution, a Catholic liberal-unionist, lamented that the political dimension of the office had continually damaged its symbolic power, yet insisted that it was the mode of government best suited to the Irish character, as 'a country peopled by the descendants of kings could not be expected to have an instinctive respect for any form of Government savouring of Republicanism, or any that left wholly to the imagination the majesty of the Sovereign ruler'.[6] Subsequent events were to reveal this to be wishful thinking, but the conflicts inherent in the institution of the lord lieutenancy had long been a subject of heated controversy.

In the wake of the Union, internal tensions arose as the chief secretary's position grew in status and responsibility vis-à-vis the viceroy. Resident in London for half the year, and sometimes a full member of the Cabinet (which the lord lieutenant usually was not), a strong chief secretary such as Robert

Peel tended to usurp some of the executive powers of his nominal superiors. At the same time, the relatively junior ranking of chief secretaries frequently limited their weight in government. Moreover, the home secretary also had administrative responsibility for Ireland, and as a constant member of the Cabinet almost always outranked both lord lieutenant and chief secretary.[7] Sometimes, as in the later 1830s under lords lieutenant Mulgrave and Ebrington, this confused executive structure could be made to operate smoothly, but too often in this period the internal divisions attracted public attention and fuelled calls for rationalisation. The nadir was probably the period 1841–44 when the liberal Tory chief secretary Lord Eliot frequently found himself at odds with the reactionary under secretary Edward Lucas and Orange-leaning viceroy Earl de Grey.[8]

INTEGRATIONIST INITIATIVES

Oppositional criticisms of the lord lieutenancy touched initially on traditional radical and liberal objections to the costs of maintaining 'the farce of a vice regal court' out of public monies. The Duke of Northumberland (one of the wealthiest peers in England) offered in 1829 to forego half of his £30,000 annual salary, but the government, conscious that career diplomats might not have the private income necessary to finance the (already somewhat diminished) panoply of the Dublin court, declined to accept the proposal. On the other hand, in 1852 the prime minister had to warn Lord Eglinton of the political inexpediency of too lavish a scale of entertainment at the Irish court.[9]

The abolition debate was not, however, primarily about public money. The full-scale assault on the viceroyalty launched by Joseph Hume in 1823 was grounded on a more profound critique. Alongside his objections to the administrative inefficiencies and excessive cost of the office, Hume made it explicit that his chief motivation was ideological: a radical-integrationist understanding of the 'Irish difficulty'. Ireland's essential problem, Hume asserted, lay in the incompleteness of the Union, and the continuation of a colonial form of government in Dublin:

> England, Scotland and Ireland, were called the united kingdom; but, were they united in the spirit or intention of those who promoted the Union? Had Ireland participated of those promised blessings of the British constitution, and been a source of prosperity and of power to the empire? It was expected that, by the Union, the interests of England and Ireland would be so completely amalgamated ... that Ireland should become the same country as England. But, up to the present time, Ireland had been governed as our slave colonies were, by a viceroy and colonial establishment; and Jamaica might be called, with as much propriety, a part of the united kingdom as Ireland.[10]

Hume declared he was sure that Pitt's intention in 1800 had been to introduce just such a 'complete union', but that executive corruption and special pleading had subsequently prevented this, just as they had the promised grant of Catholic emancipation.

Like many other British radicals and liberals in this period, Hume's integrationism did not stop at the amalgamation of political institutions. The abolition of the lord lieutenancy symbolised and would promote a more profound alteration in British-Irish relationships. The aim of the Union had been, he argued in 1830, 'not alone to unite the two countries in name, but to blend them into one complete and perfect whole'. This meant 'assimilating the habits of the people', explicitly by 'raising' the Irish to the level of the British, for 'if Ireland were once set free from the burthen of a separate and a bad government it would speedily rise, both in civilization and prosperity, to a much higher grade than it had ever reached'.[11] Hume's model was his native Scotland – a society which, according to the Whiggish doctrine that exercised hegemony over much of its middle classes in this period, had been raised out of unenlightened backwardness by the 1707 Union with England.[12] Hume preferred total executive integration, but other Scots took a more ambiguous view of the legitimacy of distinct ministerial representation for the component parts of the United Kingdom: in 1836 Henry Cockburn urged the replacement of the anomalous office of lord advocate with a secretary of state for Scotland, a reform not enacted until 1885.[13]

The revival of Irish Repeal agitation in the 1840s merely convinced Hume of the rectitude of his previous statements: 'take away the local Government', he asserted, 'and one great cause of discontent would be removed'.[14] Other radicals echoed Hume on this point. To Bernal Osborne the lord lieutenancy was 'a proof of national serfdom', demoralizing Ireland and weakening England.[15] To J.A. Roebuck, succeeding Hume as the leading radical advocate of abolition in the 1850s, abolition would remove the 'last badge of subjection' and undo the legacy of conquest. Ireland would cease to be a distinct entity and would be merged into the greater England that he understood the United Kingdom to embody:

> I want every county in Ireland to be like a county in England, and every parish in Ireland to be like a parish in England, and that she should not call herself Ireland, but a part of the United Kingdom of Great Britain and Ireland ... What I mean is that Ireland should be part of England - really a part ... I want an equal law for Irishmen and Englishmen. I do not want the distinction of Irishmen to exist. Cork ought to be like York.[16]

While Roebuck failed to persuade a Commons majority that the time was expedient for winding up the Irish executive, his motion did stir the London *Times* into endorsing the principle of assimilation in 1857. The office of viceroy, its editorialist declared, was a badge of provincialism; such proconsular forms might be necessary in far-flung imperial territories, but were retrogressive in Ireland.[17] The paper returned to the theme in 1864, when it criticised Palmerston's failure to take advantage of Carlisle's retirement to act decisively to end the constitutional anomaly. The continuation of the office suggested that 'all Ireland is merely a colony when it is in reality just as much an integral part of the empire as England or Scotland'. The political consequences of this ambiguity were dangerous: 'The feeling of Ireland has always been to speak of herself and her institutions as opposed to England and Scotland. Nothing can be more impolitic or more pernicious than retaining any office which countenances such an idea.'[18]

Such integrationist rhetoric was not restricted to British commentators. One anonymous Irish pamphleteer urged Lord John Russell in 1847 to end the constitutional anomaly of viceregal rule, which he claimed had been poisoning Anglo-Irish relations since the reign of Henry II. The Union of 1800 had been intended by Pitt to be an incorporating one; it followed that the survival of the lord lieutenancy was constitutionally illegal and merely symbolised Ireland's continuing inferiority. In this writer's view the UK government and parliament had 'violated the principle of the Union in casting on Ireland, as if a colony or province, a Deputy or Local Governor, under whom its people were to be subjected, instead of living like their fellow-subjects in Great Britain, free and under the immediate and direct government of the Crown.' Only abolition, the author concluded, would promote the necessary amalgamation of the English, Scottish and Irish into a single people.[19]

'Eblanensis', the Irish author of an *Appeal to Caesar: or Ireland's last fetter struck off* (1864), was equally scathing about both the corruption and partisanship allegedly inseparable from the lord lieutenancy, and the insult this compromised office presented to the most 'dignified' element of the constitution: 'we want equal-handed justice!', the author declared, 'Justice unalloyed! Justice direct from its highest, purest source! We want not Satraps nor Proconsuls, Governors nor Deputies, nor Viceroys. In fact, we want our Sovereign's rule direct!!!' The lord lieutenant and Irish executive not only inhibited self-reliance, corrupted the system of justice, and gave false hopes to 'the ignorant and disaffected to look upon Ireland as still a separate kingdom, not an integral part of the united kingdom', but by interposing between Ireland and the unifying majesty of the crown, it obstructed the full realisation of a common British nationality.[20] Like most integrationists, 'Eblanensis' was convinced that the viceroyalty was responsible for the absence of royal state (as opposed to private) visits to Ireland, and of the establishment of an Irish Balmoral. This was more than a complaint about Ireland's inequitable share of royal favour; it was a lament that Ireland was being denied the integrative magic of a regular royal presence.

Other Irish voices were also raised against the viceregal office. Not surprisingly, many of these were Irish Whig-Liberals engaged in building 'imperial' careers at Westminster and who had committed themselves wholeheartedly to the one-nation principle. Thomas Spring Rice (from 1839 Lord Monteagle) endorsed Hume's 1830 motion on the grounds that 'the present tendency was to assimilate the two countries', and that 'Castle Government' was redundant in an era of rapidly improving communications (a theme continually stressed by integrationists). Accordingly, Spring Rice 'valued a single steam-boat more than a whole wilderness of Lord Lieutenants'.[21] Others, such as the former Catholic Association orator and Whig-Liberal junior minister Richard Lalor Sheil in 1850, and the former chief secretary Sir William Somerville in 1857, echoed these opinions. Sheil urged that this 'badge of colonial inferiority' be removed, and that the moral transition initiated by the Famine be further promoted by abolition; Somerville hoped such a step would not denationalise Ireland, but 'unprovincialize' it, and render it 'more imperial in character'. From this liberal-imperialist perspective, Ireland could never truly fulfil its destiny as part of the imperial mother-country so long as the institutional reminder of its own colonised past remained in place.[22]

In contrast to these liberals, most Irish Conservatives opposed the abolition of the viceroyalty (not least as it was consistently proposed by radicals and liberals), but there were some exceptions. Angered by the Whigs' anti-landlord policy during the Famine, and irritated by Lord Clarendon's energetic and provocative style in the office, the *Dublin Evening Mail,* organ of the Irish landed interest, toyed with the idea of abolition in 1847. The corruption of patronage and the craven competition for viceregal favour had, in the paper's opinion, demeaned the Irish character and inhibited concerted resistance on the part of the abortive 'Irish Party'.[23] Perhaps more significantly, a number of Ulster Conservatives broke ranks in 1857–58 to support abolition, and were promptly accused by their southern colleagues of promoting the jealousy of the brash industrial town of Belfast and its hinterland towards the ancient institutions of Dublin.[24] This north-south split was accentuated by Conway Dobbs, MP for Carrickfergus, who asserted that Ulster (implicitly as a distinct political entity) was in favour of any step that would 'complete the Union'.[25] This assertion of 'Britishness' as a primary and integrating identity was by no means universal in the north, but it was of significance for the future that tensions within Irish Conservatism should have arisen on this constitutional issue.

THE 1850 ABOLITION BILL

The most significant initiative in the abolition campaign was Russell's government bill of 1850. This marked a shift for integrationism from the margins to the centre of British politics and indicates in part the success of radical advocates in persuading the Whig-Liberal elite of the logic of their proposal. Signs of this change could be detected by early 1844, when the economist and political commentator Nassau Senior placed abolition in his programme for Irish amelioration published (with the approval of the party's leadership) in the

Edinburgh Review. Senior's principal objection was less to the colonial character of the office or to the holder's appearance as a '*quasi* King' in Ireland, than to the party-politicization of the viceroyalty, which rendered Dublin 'the nucleus of faction and intrigue, and [brought] the political warfare "home to men's business and bosoms"'.[26] His recommendation of replacement with a fourth secretary of state was to become Whig policy, but had a low priority for several years.

Russell's motivations in proposing the abolition of the viceroyalty in 1850 were multiple. The bill was drawn up at a time of acute fiscal problems, when the administration was reeling from the combined assaults of the radical left and the protectionist right. However, retrenchment was not its primary objective, and Russell disappointed many, Peelites as well as radicals, by insisting on the creation of an Irish secretaryship of state (to be filled by Clarendon) rather than submerging the Irish executive wholly into the Home Office.[27]

Moreover, it is clear that a policy of abolition had been agreed three years earlier. Although one later commentator discerned a personal antipathy towards the office dating from his father's unhappy viceroyalty in 1806–07,[28] it seems more likely that Russell's attitude before his first premiership was more ambivalent. What led him to take a decision in 1847 was a combination of the frustrations produced by the crisis of Irish policy in 1846–47 (when the distant and ailing lord lieutenant and weak chief secretary had offered a limited counterweight to the Treasury and Cabinet majority at Westminster), and the circumstantial deaths of both the popular incumbent Lord Bessborough and Daniel O'Connell. During Bessborough's terminal illness Russell had decided to transfer powers to an Irish secretary of state who would spend half the year in each country.[29] When discussion with colleagues made it clear that immediate abolition was inexpedient, Lord Clarendon was dispatched as lord lieutenant on the explicit understanding that he would serve only three years and prepare the ground for reform.[30]

The continuing crisis of the Famine and the threat of nationalist and agrarian rebellion in 1847–49 prevented any early resolution. The Queen and Prince Albert after initial support grew hesitant about abolition, Clarendon was anxious to retain tight personal control in Ireland, and Russell was disposed to be patient.[31] By September 1849, however, with much of his Irish policy already in tatters, Russell was eager for a success. The very frustration of seeing his (and Clarendon's) policies destroyed at Westminster had taken its toll:

> The evil I have found, and of which you must have had some experience yourself, is that the proposals of a Lord Lieutenant of Ireland, come they from Normanby, Bessborough or yourself are looked upon as exclusively Irish, and against which exclusive spirit English statesmen are bound to guard themselves and their country ... When the Union with Scotland was made, Lord Somers with consummate wisdom insisted upon abol-

ishing the Scotch Privy Council, and then made the two countries really one, though the laws were different and the Church different – Ireland with the same law as England, and the Established Church the same has remained a separate kingdom, owing to the short-sighted plans of Mr Pitt.[32]

Two years in Dublin had led Clarendon to develop some scepticism towards Russell's enthusiasm for 'Englishing' the government of Ireland. Yet, while he felt that Ireland could not be treated like Scotland, and that only a permanent local official could hope to understand Irish conditions and feelings, he became more amenable as the economic and political crisis eased. Furthermore, the unexpectedly successful royal tour of Ireland in August 1849 had opened up the possibility of regular visits, undermining any residual case for the viceregal court.[33] By May 1850 Clarendon was promoting the bill as an essential step in the elimination of Ireland's culture of political dependency.[34] Russell presented his bill to the Commons on 17 May 1850 as the completion of a long-considered plan. His speech touched on all the principal grounds already made for abolition: the suitability to Ireland of the Scottish model of integration, the unnecessary inefficiencies and adverse effects of the dual administration, the preferability of regular royal visits and the completion of the work left unfinished by Pitt in 1800.[35] Russell's insistence on abolition reflected his Whiggish concern for the primacy of constitutional forms in resolving the 'question of Ireland'; the bill paralleled his Irish franchise reform measure of 1850. Clarendon's views were more ambivalent, but he too was prepared to use integrationist arguments in private, insisting that the government of Ireland as a colony was 'humiliating to me *as an Irish man* ... Ireland is entitled to be placed on a footing of perfect equality with England and Scotland, and treated as an inseparable part of the Imperial Unity instead of an outlying dependency'.[36] Both were to be disappointed. Despite a large second-reading majority, the bill was dropped due to lack of time. In a session which saw the ministry severely buffeted on foreign policy and financial issues, Russell ultimately had to admit that he could not also risk the parliamentary guerrilla tactics threatened by Irish and English opponents of the abolition of the lord lieutenancy.[37]

ANTI-ABOLITIONISM: CONSERVATIVE, NATIONALIST AND IMPERIALIST

What objections were raised by those opposed to the abolition of the viceroy? Perhaps surprisingly, there was some overlap between the expressed opinions of Irish Conservatives and constitutional nationalists. There was, firstly, a pronounced Dublin lobby which objected equally to the threatened financial loss which the city's merchants and artisans might suffer from the closure of the court, and the final elimination of its status as a capital city. Dublin MPs and

lord mayors, both Tories and Repealers, were vigorous opponents of the measure throughout the period.[38] Petitions were prepared by the Corporation and
commercial bodies in 1850 and 1864 in defence of the viceroyalty, and rumours
that the Irish legal institutions were also under threat were exploited by the
motions' opponents.[39] Clarendon regarded the overt popular opposition of
1850 with some disdain,[40] but at a time of continuing political insecurity the
dangers of further alienating the capital's artisan and mercantile classes could
not be discounted.

Others warned that abolition smacked of the pernicious principle of 'centralization', further removing the power and status of local elites and transferring these to Westminster. The ignorance of British MPs had, it was claimed,
already led to damaging legislation and 'rule by boards' in Ireland, the loss of
the viceroy would mean the end of all Irish influence over both law and patronage – greater absenteeism would be the inevitable result.[41] The evils of centralization were also vigorously bemoaned by the independent-minded Irish
liberal Torrens McCullagh. No lover of the lord lieutenancy in principle, he
nevertheless opposed any suggestion that the home secretary be made responsible for Ireland. Ireland required equal, not identical, institutions; Parliament
should not, he insisted:

> forget the moral, social, political, and religious differences between the
> two nations. Of these the Channel is but in truth a very inadequate sym-
> bol ... but the thirst of centralization is ... insatiable; for it would not only
> gulp the sea, but it would fain believe that those popular wants and pas-
> sions with which the dark and restless waves have been so often com-
> pared, can be got rid of by simply refusing to see or heed them more.[42]

McCullagh's stance is remarkable given that he held the position of private
secretary to the chief secretary in 1850, and was thus speaking against the very
abolitionist policy of the government he then served.[43]

Irish Tories were yet more defensive of the lord lieutenancy as an emblem
of the sort of loyal Irish nationality with which they felt comfortable: the institution was for them something distinctive, approachable, and unthreatening.
Presenting the Dublin petitions in 1850, Lord Londonderry warned that the
proposed abolition of the Irish court contravened the political contract underlying the Union.[44] Joseph Napier preferred a Burkean defence, arguing that the
viceregal system's 'distinguishing lineaments ... had been stereotyped by the
hand of God', and that the viceroyalty was one of those 'national peculiarities
which nothing could efface; the land of Burke and of Wellington might cling to
her national feelings with pride, and at least without rebuke.'[45] In this organi-
cist ideal, the lord lieutenant and his Dublin court symbolised the distinct
identity of the Anglo-Irish political class within the larger British polity.

Nationalists might be expected to be more hostile towards an institution
that could indeed be seen as symbolising Ireland's colonial subjugation; yet here

again the response was mixed. Revolutionary nationalists were by definition excluded from the parliamentary debate, but did cast a shadow over proceedings (especially in 1850). One Repealer who supported the abolition bill argued that, irrespective of individual intentions, the lord lieutenancy had operated as a divisive force in Ireland, as the office was a 'bauble' that inhibited the creation of national unity.[46] Others, however, anxious to distance themselves from extremism in the aftermath of the 1848 rising, argued that abolition would further promote the separatist agenda by provocatively 'crushing all national feeling in Ireland'. E.B. Roche was sure that 'if the bill passed, the cry of national redemption would go forth to excite a people who were both patriotic and sensitive.'[47]

There was, however, a more considered O'Connellite position on the lord lieutenancy. Daniel O'Connell had demonstrated himself adept at exploiting executive divisions within Tory administrations, and in using his influence over liberal viceroys such as Wellesley, Mulgrave and Bessborough to promote his own political ends. A political pragmatist, he regarded the office as one that created opportunities which might be turned against Westminster. His political lieutenant Dillon Brown made this explicit in 1844, stating that following the repeal of the Union the office of viceroy would survive, but be nationalised under the influence of a restored Irish Parliament.[48] O'Connell's blunt warning in 1830 that any attempt to proceed to abolition would anger the people of the country, was cited by the chief secretary in 1844 as a continuing reason for inaction.[49] Significantly, Russell committed himself to act only after O'Connell's death in May 1847, leading to charges of hypocritical expediency from the bill's Tory opponents.[50] With the Repeal movement fragmenting the timing might have proved right, but constitutional nationalism had not disappeared, and O'Connell's son Maurice continued to argue that the institution was capable of reform, and that abolition would merely strike the first blow for complete separation.[51]

Ultimately neither the Irish Conservatives nor the Repealers were responsible for the survival of the lord lieutenancy. It is evident that the intellectual case for removing the symbol of colonised status was won, so far as Parliament and the British public were concerned, by Hume, Roebuck and their allies. Once Russell declared himself converted to the principle of integration in 1850, most of the political elite openly endorsed the correctness of the 'colonial' interpretation of the Irish executive. Sir Robert Peel, who had previously resisted abolition, announced himself persuaded that the communications revolution had now made it possible to introduce 'a system of unity'.[52] Even the Conservative Lord Naas, later to be chief secretary in 1852 and ultimately viceroy of India, was convinced that 'the present system of governing that country partook very much of that pursued with reference to the colonies, while it possessed nothing whatever of its efficiency'.[53] Subsequent argument focused more on the timing and modalities of abolition than on its principle.

What prevented governments from re-opening the question again after

1850 was quite simply the overwhelming sense that, however embarrassing Ireland's colonial administration might be to an idealised image of the United Kingdom, in practical terms administrative assimilation was too dangerous. The Liberal chief secretary in 1857, Edward Horsman, declared that with the Famine only eight years in the past, Ireland was still too unstable for such an experiment. The prime minister, Lord Palmerston, cited both Carlisle's personal popularity in Ireland and, more ominously, the need for a strong local government to defend the status quo.[54] Russell himself in 1858 backed away from his previous commitments, unable now to see any practical way of proceeding.[55]

Lying behind this failure of nerve was a damning speech made by the kingdom's most revered figure in 1850. In the Lords' debate on abolition, the Duke of Wellington had spelled out explicitly the ultimate rationale for the continuance of the office of lord lieutenant – as the resident civil authority without whom the military could not act in the event of rebellion. Security was the bottom line: with many urban corporations now under nationalist control and the home secretary (or putative Irish secretary) far away in London, only the viceroy could secure the permanence of British rule.[56] This was a defence that Wellington had maintained since at least 1834, when he had feared that the Whigs and O'Connell were conspiring to abolish the office as an impediment to their anti-Protestant political agenda. He had also seen his role in the Repeal crisis of 1843–44 as that of badgering the then lord lieutenant into taking decisive military and judicial measures to put down O'Connellism.[57] Wellington's strictures concerned members of Russell's Cabinet in 1850, and continued to underlie government reluctance to act subsequently.[58]

The 'national security' defence of the office appealed not only to Tories, but also to many centrist Liberals. Attempting to dissuade his friend Clarendon from accepting abolition in 1849, Charles Greville, the clerk of the privy council, voiced an opinion about Irish government and the country's place in the empire that was widely shared (and echoed on occasion by Clarendon himself):

> Ireland is as unfit for 'constitutional' government as the Punjaub, and attempts ... to put Ireland and England on the same level is a mockery and delusion, and practically leads to nothing and confusion and disorder in every shape ... and impunity for every species of outrage. What Ireland requires is such a government as Strafford's or Cromwell's, or the rule of a Nicholas or a Napoleon, who could legislate as well as administer, and who would be under no necessity of deferring to public opinion and what are called popular feelings, which mean pride, bigotry, obstinacy, and the perpetuation of the most momentous abuses.[59]

Such attitudes appeared to many fully justified by the emergence of Fenianism as an active force in the mid-1860s. Even the *Times*, an enthusiastic supporter of Roebuck's motion up to 1864, was by 1866 looking to a new lord lieutenant as 'a model ruler of Ireland - dispassionate, firm and persistent'.[60] For a defender of the institution nearly half a century later, it remained axiomatic that the best viceroy was not the most popular or the most 'improving', but one, like Lord Spencer, who demonstrated greatest firmness in the face of rebellion and agitation.[61]

In conclusion, what does the lord-lieutenancy debate tell us about the 'problem of Ireland' in the early and mid-nineteenth century? Unquestionably I believe it reveals much about the unresolved discrepancy in British thought between the constitutional (and social) theory of the Union as the engine of assimilation, and the pragmatic imperative of retaining control through the maintenance of colonial (or quasi-colonial) instruments of governance. It also says much about the predominant Irish tendency (paradoxically Conservative as well as nationalist) to utilise or subvert the very emblems of conquest to retain a sense of historical nationality. The romantic novelist Charles Lever spoke for both these constituencies when he wrote in 1864 of the symbolic significance of the viceroyalty, 'this one remnant that recalls a time when we used to fancy ourselves a people'. He articulated a feeling that many theorists have identified as one of the distinguishing strategies of resistance to colonisation, the inversion of imposed symbols: 'Why, therefore, might not we Irish like to wear as an honour what was instituted as a penalty, and exhibit from pride what took its rise in repression?'[62]

NOTES

1. Richard Shannon, Gladstone: heroic minister 1865-1898 (London: Allen Lane, 1999), pp. 92-3, 109-11; James H. Murphy, *Abject Loyalty: Nationalism and Monarchy in Ireland during the Reign of Queen Victoria* (Washington, D.C.: Catholic University of America Press, 2001), pp. 188–90, 230–42.
2. For a robust critique of Ulster Unionist integrationism and its insistence on the non-colonial nature of the Union of 1800, see John McGarry and Brendan O'Leary, Explaining Northern Ireland: broken images (Oxford: Blackwell, 1995), pp. 93-5, 100, 126-37.
3. For general histories, see J.T. Gilbert, History of the viceroys of Ireland (Dublin: James Duffy, 1865); and Joseph Robins, Champagne and silver buckles: the viceregal court at Dublin Castle, 1700-1922 (Dublin: Lilliput Press, 2001).
4. John Foster, Speech of the Right Honourable John Foster, Speaker of the House of Commons of Ireland, delivered in committee, on Monday the 17th day of February, 1800 (Cork: James Haly, 1800), p. 26.
5. The silence of the two major monographs on the Act on the future of the executive suggests that the subject was simply not considered by Pitt and his ministers. See G.C. Bolton, The passing of the Irish Act of Union (Oxford: Oxford University Press, 1966); and Patrick M. Geoghegan, The Irish Act of Union: a study in high politics 1798-1801 (Dublin: Gill & Macmillan, 1999).
6. Charles O'Mahony, The viceroys of Ireland: the story of the long line of noblemen and their wives who have ruled Ireland and Irish society for over seven hundred years (London: John Long, 1912), p. 342.
7. For a full discussion of the Irish executive, see R.B. McDowell, The Irish administration 1801-1914 (London: Routledge and Kegan Paul 1964), pp. 52-77
8. See Norman Gash, Sir Robert Peel (Harlow: Longman, 1986 edn), pp. 393-401.

9. Hansard's Parliamentary Debates, first series, XVII, 528 [8 June 1810: Tighe]; ibid., second series, I, 470 [17 May 1820: H. Parnell]; O'Mahony, The viceroys of Ireland, pp. 233-5; Allen Warren, 'Disraeli, the Conservatives and the government of Ireland: Part 1, 1837-1868', Parliamentary History, 18, 1 (1999), p. 53.
10. Hansard, second ser., IX, 1215-16 [25 June 1823].
11. Ibid., XXIV, 555-64 [11 May 1830].
12. See Colin Kidd, Subverting Scotland's past: Scottish Whig historians and the creation of an Anglo-British identity 1689-1830 (Cambridge: Cambridge University Press, 1993).
13. John F. McCaffrey, Scotland in the nineteenth century (Basingstoke: Macmillan, 1998), p. 58.
14. Hansard, third ser., LXXIV, 834-41 [9 May 1844].
15. Ibid., XCI, 202-10 [17 May 1850].
16. Ibid., CXLVI, 1048-55 [7 July 1857].
17. The Times, 11 June 1857.
18. Ibid., 7 Oct. 1864
19. Anon., A letter to the Right Honourable Lord John Russell ... on the misgovernment of Ireland, and the necessity of the immediate abolition of its lord lieutenancy and local government (London: H. Hurst, 1847), pp. 19, 31.
20. Eblanensis, Appeal to Caesar, or, Ireland's last fetter struck off: in which the reasons for continuing the lord lieutenancy are considered (London: T. and W. Boone, 1864). Similar assimilationist arguments continued to be made later in the century, see Henry L. Jephson, 'Irish statute law reform', Journal of the Statistical and Social Inquiry Society of Ireland, 7 (1876-79), pp. 376-7.
21. Hansard, second ser., XXIV, 566-8 [11 May 1830]; but cf. his later more ambivalent (post-Famine) views in Hansard, third ser., XCII, 474-5 [27 June 1850].
22. Ibid., XCI, 1451-4 [17 June 1850], CXLVI, 1070-5 [7 July 1857].
23. Dublin Evening Mail, cited in The Times, 7 June 1847.
24. Hansard, third ser., CXLIX, 757 [25 March 1858: Vance].
25. Ibid., 751-3
26. [Nassau Senior], 'Ireland', Edinburgh Review, LXXIX (Jan. 1844), 257-9.
27. C.C.F. Greville, A journal of the reign of Queen Victoria, from 1837 to 1852 (3 vols., London: Longmans, Green and Co., 1885), III, 314, 338-9 [20 Feb., 6 June 1850].
28. O'Mahony, Viceroys of Ireland, pp. 211-12.
29. Russell, Memo on the post of Irish viceroy, [May 1847], Russell Papers, Public Record Office, Kew, PRO 30/22/6H, fols 372-3; Lord Lansdowne to Russell, 5 May 1847, ibid., 6C, fol. 246.
30. Greville, Journal, III, 80-6 [2, 3 May, 7 June 1847]. For a fuller account of Clarendon's appointment, see Peter Gray, Famine, land and politics: British government and Irish society, 1843-1850 (Dublin: Irish Academic Press, 1999), pp. 168-71.
31. Russell to Clarendon, 28 Sept., 15 Oct. 1847, Clarendon Deposit Irish, Bodleian Library, Oxford, Box 43; Clarendon to Russell, 10 Oct. 1847, ibid., Letterbook I; Murphy, Abject Loyalty, pp. 102-3.
32. Russell to Clarendon, 4 Sept. 1849, Clarendon Deposit Irish., Box 26.
33. Clarendon to Russell, 11 Sept. 1849, 13 Jan. 1850, ibid., Letterbook 4, Letterbook 5. In fact, Victoria visited Ireland again only in 1853, 1861 and 1900.
34. Clarendon to Russell, 4 May 1850, Clarendon Deposit Irish, Letterbook 5.
35. Hansard, third ser., XCI, 171-84 [17 May 1850].
36. Clarendon to C. Villiers, 14 June 1850, Clarendon Deposit Irish, Letterbook 5.
37. Hansard, third ser., XCII, 899-900 [4 July 1850]; Russell to Clarendon, 2 July 1850, Clarendon Deposit Irish, Box 26.
38. See Hansard, third ser., XCI, 192-6 [17 May 1850: Grogan], 211-18 [Reynolds]; CXLVI, 1075-8 [7 July 1857: Vance].
39. Speeches of the marquis of Londonderry and the duke of Wellington on the presentation of the petitions against the bill for the abolition of the lord lieutenant of Ireland (London: John Olliver, 1850), pp. 30-2; [Anon.], 'Removal of the Irish law courts', Irish Quarterly Review, I (March 1851), 1-21; The Times, 1 Nov. 1864.
40. Clarendon to G.C. Lewis, 17 March 1850, Harpton Court Papers, National Library of Wales, Aberystwyth, C/1047.
41. Hansard, third ser., XCI, 1014-6, 1018-20 [10 June 1850: Hamilton, Dunne]; CXLIX, 761-4 [25 March 1858: P. O'Brien]. One legal writer welcomed Russell's Bill as likely to open Irish eyes to the insidious workings of 'centralization' since 1800, [Anon.], 'Imperial centralization',

Irish Quarterly Review, I (March 1851), 134-47.

42. Hansard, third ser., XCI, 1442-51 [17 June 1850]; see also ibid., CXLVI, 1055-62 [7 July 1857].
43. For McCullagh's independent stance on other policy issues, see Gray, Famine, pp. 149, 176-7.
44. Hansard, third ser., XCII, 458-66 [27 June 1850].
45. Ibid., XCI, 1421-7 [17 June 1850].
46. Ibid., 196-202 [17 May 1850: W. Fagan].
47. Ibid., 202, 217 [M. O'Connell, Reynolds], ibid., 1420 [17 June 1850].
48. Ibid., LXXIV, 859-61 [9 May 1844].
49. Ibid., second ser., XXIV, 574 [11 May 1830]; third ser., LXXIV, 846-7, 853 [9 May 1844: Eliot, Bellew].
50. Ibid., third ser., XCII, 461 [27 June 1850: Londonderry].
51. Ibid., XCI, 1016-18 [10 June 1850].
52. Ibid., 1407-16 [17 June 1850]. It had been rumoured as early as 1844 that Peel might give way over abolition, but was 'too timid' to proceed. Nassau Senior to Richard Whately, [March 1844], Nassau Senior Papers, National Library of Wales, Aberystwyth, C634.
53. Hansard, third ser., XCI, 1438-9 [17 June 1850].
54. Ibid., CXLVI, 1086-92, 1093-6 [7 July 1857]. For Carlisle's paternalistic defence of his office, and his personal popularity, see J.J. Gaskin (ed.), The viceregal speeches and addresses, lectures and poems of the late earl of Carlisle (Dublin: McGlashan and Gill, 1866), pp. 80-4, 91-5; [Charles Lever], 'The Irish viceroyalty', Blackwood's Edinburgh Magazine, XCVI (Nov. 1864), p. 606.
55. Hansard, third ser., CXLIX, 766-9 [25 March 1858].
56. Ibid., XCII, 468-71 [27 June 1850]. This was widely distributed in Speeches of the ... duke of Wellington on the presentation of the petitions against the bill for the abolition of the lord lieutenant of Ireland (London, John Oliver, 1850).
57. Wellington to Roden, 1 Sept. 1834, in John Brooke and Julia Gandy (eds), The prime ministers' papers: Wellington. Political correspondence I. 1833-Nov. 1834 (London: HMSO, 1975), pp. 657-60. For Wellington's actions in 1843-44, see P. Gray, 'Wellington and the government of Ireland, 1832-46', in C.M. Woolgar (ed.), Wellington studies III (Southampton: Hartley Institute, 1999), pp. 203-26.
58. Lansdowne to Russell, [May 1850], Russell Papers, PRO 30/22/8D, fols 256-7.
59. Greville to Clarendon, 26 Oct. 1849, Clarendon Deposit, c.522.
60. The Times, 4 July 1866.
61. O'Mahony, Viceroys of Ireland, pp. 267-70, 276-87.
62. Lever, 'Irish viceroyalty', p. 604.

CHAPTER SIX

Local Government in Nineteenth-Century Ireland

VIRGINIA CROSSMAN

The parallels between the administrative structure of the government of Ireland and that of many overseas colonies have frequently been remarked upon.[1] Less commonly noted is the degree to which the administration of the localities also had strong colonial overtones. Irish resident magistrates, for example, performed a role comparable to that of government agents in India and Ceylon, being sent into the Irish countryside to live among the people and bring order and discipline to the local community. Reliance on officials such as RMs (Resident Magistrates) reflected both the relatively disturbed state of Ireland, and the reluctance of the imperial government to permit Irish people to administer their own affairs. Irish people came into more frequent contact with government agents than their counterparts elsewhere in the United Kingdom, the gradual intrusion of the state into the lives of the people having started earlier and becoming more far-reaching in Ireland. One effect of this, a contributor to the *Fortnightly Review* noted in 1885, was 'daily to give emphasis to the fact that the whole country is under the domination of an alien race'.[2] The administration of the localities impacted on and informed Irish responses to British rule.

This study examines the structures of Irish local government in the nineteenth century, and analyses perceptions of its conduct. It does so in order to explore Ireland's relationship to the United Kingdom and the Empire. Were the Irish localities governed as an integral part of the metropolis or as an outpost of empire? And to what extent did local administrators in Ireland share or resist an imperialist mindset? It will be argued that the conduct of local government, often seen as a training ground for national government, became a litmus test of political maturity. It provided a means of assessing the conduct of Irish landlords and the fitness of the Irish people for self-government.

The administrative history of the British empire in the nineteenth century was dominated by two apparently contradictory developments: the moves towards colonial autonomy and imperial unity. Laissez-faire attitudes combined with economic necessity and geography encouraged metropolitan governments to leave local authorities to administer local affairs, funded by local taxes. The result was the development throughout the Empire of a wide variety of constitutional and administrative practices reflective of and influenced by local conditions and circumstances. At the same time, a growing belief in Britain's imperial mission, the spreading of good government, western 'civilisation' and Christianity, reinforced the paternalistic and authoritarian nature of imperial rule in many Crown Colonies. The administrative history of nineteenth-century Ireland is similarly characterised by two divergent tendencies. Successive British governments attempted to integrate Ireland into the United Kingdom, whilst at the same time responding to the particular circumstances of the country by introducing institutions which had no equivalent in Britain. Moreover, even where the administrative structure of Ireland followed that of Britain – under the poor law, for example – the relationship between central and local government was conducted on very different terms.

In the White Dominions, the tradition of colonial autonomy fostered the move to responsible government, leading colonies such as Canada and Australia to become internally self-governing during the nineteenth century. As J.M. Ward has noted, British politicians increasingly came to agree that 'British institutions should be granted as nearly as local circumstances and colonial status permitted to all British possessions overseas that were thought capable of working them smoothly according to British notions of political equity'.[3] This was initially taken to rule out not only non-European populations, who were assumed to be incapable of responsible self-government, but also some European populations such as the white settlers of Trinidad and South Africa, who were not trusted to rule mixed populations without supervision. In order to qualify for self-government, colonial populations needed to demonstrate that they could and would conduct themselves according to British standards of political and administrative behaviour. As we shall see, Ireland failed to meet these criteria. Both the 'settler' and the 'native' populations of Ireland were judged to be incapable of administering the country in an efficient and impartial manner.

The system of local government that developed in Ireland was modelled on that of Britain. The earliest representatives of central authority in the Irish localities, the county sheriff and local magistrates were adjuncts of the legal system imported to Ireland from England, and the division of Ireland into counties and boroughs again followed an English exemplar. The main divergence between English and Irish administrative practice was in the survival in Ireland of the grand jury which became the chief organ of Irish county administration. In England the administrative functions of the grand jury were by the nineteenth century largely performed by parish vestries and by magistrates sitting at quarter sessions. But if the structure of local government appeared to grant Ireland metropolitan status as part of the United Kingdom, its conduct and administration indicated a much more dependent status. Thus while the system of local and superior courts was modelled on that of England, the state played a much more active role in Ireland in overseeing the local administration of justice and regulating the proceedings of local courts.

In England, local magistrates who presided over petty and quarter sessions were believed to operate impartially and with the consent and confidence of the local population. In Ireland there was little public confidence in the local magistracy, the majority of whom were drawn from the Protestant landed gentry. Magistrates who were not inactive or incompetent, were generally believed to be corrupt. One Irish landowner attributed the disordered state of counties Tyrone and Donegal in 1813 to 'the deficiency of proper resident [i.e. local] magistrates, who would take the trouble to act without prejudices and partiality'.[4] Conscious that this situation did little to encourage public respect for, or confidence in, the law amongst the Catholic population, British ministers caused the magisterial lists to be revised on a number of occasions in order to weed out unsuitable people. A determined effort was also made, particularly under Whig and Liberal administrations, to appoint more Catholic magistrates.

Ministers further attempted to improve the image and authority of the law by strengthening the professional element over the amateur. This meant appointing legal officials such as assistant barristers and crown solicitors, and increasing numbers of stipendiary (better known as resident) magistrates. Once again, the idea was to improve the efficiency and efficacy of the legal process and to lessen the degree to which the law was seen to be the instrument of Protestant landlords. Assistant barristers were originally appointed to act as 'a constant assistant to the justices' at quarter sessions, their duties later being extended to the hearing of minor civil suits.[5] Resident magistrates appeared to those responsible for the government of Ireland to offer many advantages over ordinary magistrates. They were active and, in theory at least, they were impartial, being assumed to be more detached than ordinary magistrates and less influenced by local feeling. Moreover, if they proved unsatisfactory, they could simply be removed or dismissed.

Ordinary magistrates were seen as representatives of the Protestant landed elite, more concerned to enforce their own personal dicta than the letter of the law; RMs represented a supposedly neutral justice system. By the end of the nineteenth century, however, a notable shift in emphasis had taken place in the RM's role. Having originally been conceived in part as a check on the excesses of the Protestant Ascendancy, RMs came to be seen as providing a necessary counterbalance to popularity-hunting Catholic magistrates, who, according to one RIC (Royal Irish Constabulary) officer, 'came into court with the object of assisting the defendant if possible'.[6] Popular criticism of the Irish magistracy, like that directed at other local institutions, tended to reflect a sense of exclusion. It was not so much the existence of partiality or corruption that was resented but the fact that others were benefiting.

A relatively high degree of central regulation and control was also evident in the enforcement of the law in Ireland. During the course of the nineteenth century, the administration and enforcement of emergency powers were increasingly taken out of the hands of local magistrates and entrusted to government officials. The Irish constabulary, in contrast to police forces in Britain that were under the control of local authorities, was directed and controlled from the centre. Members of the constabulary were forbidden from serving in their home counties in order to prevent personal or local feeling influencing their performance. Organised along military lines and accommodated in barracks, this was a force serving not the locality, but the state. Its primary role was that of enforcing the law and suppressing disorder, thus maintaining the authority of government, and, as such, it came to be seen as the model for colonial police forces throughout the empire.

The extent to which the RIC provided an exemplar for colonial police forces has come under question in recent years,[7] but it remains the case that Irish experience of policing was closer to that of many colonies, than to that of Britain. The crucial point being that whereas in Britain the emphasis by the later nineteenth century was on policing by consent, in Ireland, as in many colonies, the police were frequently obliged to operate by coercion. Thus they were always in danger of being perceived not as a public service but as a symbol of an alien and illegitimate government. In Britain far more of police time was devoted to the detection of crime than in Ireland, where the main priorities remained the protection of life and property and the maintenance of social order. Similarly, although by the end of the nineteenth century the majority of Irish policemen came from the Catholic community, their officers were still predominantly Protestant. This division mirrored that in many colonial police forces where 'native' constables were officered by white Europeans.

Ireland can be seen as providing an interesting intersection of colonial experience in relation to policing. In white colonies, as colonial government became more established, police forces gradually abandoned a coercive role and moved towards policing by consent. The Canadian North West Mounted Police, for example, had originally been established in 1873 in order to secure the northwest territories in the wake of the Red River uprising. By the early years of the twentieth century the force was increasingly taking on a service role, 'delivering veterinary services, fighting prairie fires and conducting the census'.[8] In black colonies, by contrast, police forces largely remained as an arm of state, a symbol of imperial authority. In Ireland, the move towards policing by consent, and the performance of a service as well as a security role, is evident in the development of the RIC during the second half of the nineteenth century. The imposition of duties such as the distribution and collection of voting papers for the election of poor law guardians, the compilation of statistical returns and the inspection of weights and measures, helped, as Elizabeth Malcolm and William Lowe have argued, 'substantially to transform and domesticate the force's character'.[9]

The process of domestication was, however, a patchy and partial one. It was hampered, and ultimately negated, by the politicisation of the RIC during the Land War and subsequent nationalist campaigns. While police duties in much of Ireland did take on a domestic character, in disturbed districts where the police were used to enforce the payment of rent, and to arrest those suspected of political disaffection, they continued to perform a coercive role. Like their counterparts in Britain and elsewhere in the empire, the RIC enforced the prevailing values of order, respectability and morality. Their response to prostitution, for example, was to remove evidence of this activity from public view, and to try and prevent the women involved from disturbing social or public order.[10] In this regard the RIC could be said to have played a role characteristic of colonial police forces in helping to construct 'the colonial social order'.[11] The most immediate contact point with authority for most colonised people, the police personified stability and order and were duty-bound to identify and neutralise potential threats to the political, social and moral fabric of society.

Central government intervention in and supervision of local authorities was, therefore, a characteristic feature of the development of local administration in Ireland during the nineteenth century. In part this reflected the changing nature of the state, and the growing degree of state regulation evident throughout the United Kingdom. Central regulation of certain aspects of economic and social organisation, was, as Oliver MacDonagh observed, 'based from the start, on the United Kingdom as a single administrative unit. Ireland might have its own inspector or inspectors, but only in the same way as Yorkshire or East Anglia'. Nevertheless, Ireland displayed a high degree of what MacDonagh termed 'administrative idiosyncrasy', noting that 'in the fields of education, economic development, police, prisons, and public health ... the state intervened to a degree and in a fashion scarcely conceivable in contemporary Britain'.[12] He attributed this to the poverty of Ireland as well as to the relatively weak and inchoate nature of local government, but it was also due to the belief that Irish people were not capable of administering the growing range of powers and responsibilities imposed on local bodies effectively and impartially.

Throughout the nineteenth century Irish local administrators were accused of inefficiency, corruption and partiality. At the beginning of the century the grand jury system came under attack on account of its exclusive character and its association with financial malpractice. Grand jurors were nominated by the high sheriff from the leading property owners of the county (excluding peers). County cess, which provided the funds expended by the grand jury on local works, was levied on the occupier rather than the owner of land. Grand jurors, who were overwhelmingly Protestant, were thus responsible for spending money raised from their tenants, who were overwhelmingly Catholic. Grand jurors were also condemned for abusing the system for their own personal gain. William Maxwell attributed the appalling state of the roads in the west of Ireland in the 1820s to the 'atrocious system of peculation'[13] carried on by grand juries. The alleged level of abuse was such as to cause alarm even within the Protestant Ascendancy. The Limerick landowner, and Whig politician, Thomas Spring Rice, maintained that under the grand jury system,

> public burthens have augmented in a most formidable progression: the
> public works have deteriorated in a similar ratio. The landlord is lowered

in general estimation, by his acquiescence in a corrupt system; the peasant is impoverished and the community is plundered.[14]

There was a growing realisation that the behaviour of grand juries reflected badly on the Irish land-owning class as a whole, reinforcing an impression in Britain, and abroad, of widespread irresponsibility and inefficiency amongst the local elite. The French writer, Gustave De Beaumont expressed a common view when he noted that while the English landowner acted as a 'patron of the soil and its inhabitants', the Irish proprietor was simply 'desirous of deriving ... the greatest profit possible'. De Beaumont's solution was for government in Ireland to be centralised. 'What Ireland wants', he maintained, was 'a strong administration ... beneath whose shadow the middle classes might grow up, develop themselves, and acquire instruction, whilst the aristocracy would crumble away'.[15]

Some British politicians were tempted to agree, believing that a more centralised system, with a greater input from the metropolis, was bound to be more efficient. Ireland, Lord Anglesey declared in 1831, 'wants a Bonaparte (*sic*)'.[16] Many others, however, distrusted centralisation as a departure from English traditions and practices. As Robert Peel had warned the Irish chief secretary in 1828, 'to take [local administration] into the hands of Government is to widen the distinction between England and Ireland and postpone the period at which Irish local affairs can be satisfactorily managed by local authorities'.[17] The desire to maintain some kind of administrative parity between Britain and Ireland shaped government policy throughout the century. Thus the response to Irish poverty adopted by the Whigs in the 1830s was to introduce the workhouse system that was already operating in Britain. When introducing legislation to replace Irish grand juries with popularly elected county councils in 1892, Arthur Balfour candidly admitted that 'nobody supposes that any new machinery will work more efficiently than that which already exists. The main object of establishing the new machinery is to remove any sense of unequal treatment between the three portions of the United Kingdom'.[18]

Faced with the problem of how to improve the quality of local administration in Ireland, ministers tended to adopt a piecemeal approach, addressing particular problem areas rather than the administrative structure as a whole. A series of reforms was introduced in the early decades of the nineteenth century, for example, to provide for a more satisfactory scrutiny of, and accounting for, grand jury expenditure. Perhaps more importantly, however, the grand jury was increasingly eclipsed as an organ of local administration by the poor law board. The poor law provided an alternative administrative structure to that of the grand jury system, and one which was more representative of rate-payers' interests while still providing a major role for local landowners.

Poor law boards were composed partly of guardians elected by the ratepayers, and partly of local magistrates sitting ex officio. In the post-Famine period, the boards were given a wide range of responsibilities in addition to their management of the workhouse. Thus the administration of local dispensaries was transferred from grand juries to poor law boards in the 1850s, and the latter also acted as the administering authority under health and safety legislation such as the Sanitary Act of 1866, and the Public Health Acts of 1874 and 1878. The expanding responsibilities and importance of poor law boards were reflected in the level of local expenditure. Whilst the level of county cess, which had risen dramatically in the first half of the nineteenth century from £0.4m in 1803 to £1.3m in 1840, remained fairly static in the second half of the century, poor law expenditure rose from £0.75m in the mid 1850s to £1.4m in 1886.[19]

One of the advantages of the poor law system in the eyes of its advocates was the opportunity it afforded for the promotion of local co-operation and development. It was hoped that the experience of working together on poor law boards would bring the various classes in Ireland together, creating a bond of union between them which would help to reduce sectarian and partisan feeling. In their annual report for 1841, the Poor Law Commissioners explained that they

> had always considered that the organisation of the [poor law] unions and the creation of a local machinery for their government, would afford important facilities for the introduction of other local improvements in Ireland. Hitherto there has been a want of means for the origination and carrying out of such objects, but the union authorities now afford the means and possess the requisite degree of influence and consideration, for setting on foot and supporting undertakings calculated to benefit its inhabitants.[20]

The hope that poor law boards would act as some kind of social and political cement knitting Irish society together into a stable and integrated organism was to be frustrated. Much to the dismay of the Poor Law Commissioners, politics intruded. As early as 1840 the Commissioners had expressed their regret that 'much excitement and party feeling should have been exhibited'[21] in some electoral contests and the following year they rejected recommendations from their own assistant commissioners to change the voting procedure. The Commissioners were worried that,

> if there be an assemblage of the voters, and if speeches be addressed to them by or on behalf of the several candidates, popular excitement will probably be produced, and ill-feeling created, that will agitate men's minds long after the election has passed, and prove an impediment to the calm and cordial working of a Board of Guardians constituted under such circumstances. Guardians might then also be returned pledged to some particular line or conduct, and fettered in the free exercise of their judgement upon the questions which arise in the administration of the law.[22]

Party politics, the Commissioners clearly felt, had no place in local administration. This, however, was to ignore the reality of local affairs. Poor law elections in England were frequently fought along factional or party lines,[23] and in the far more deeply divided society of Ireland, it was inevitable that politics would influence both the choice and the conduct of local administrators. Until the 1880s the number of electoral contests was relatively small with the vast majority of candidates being returned unopposed, but this situation was to change when the exhortations of the Land League prompted far greater numbers of tenant candidates to challenge landlord representatives. The resulting shift in power on many poor law boards was to produce a highly politicised system. Home Rule increasingly dominated the political agenda at both national and local level, and popular representatives were quick to use whatever platforms were available to them to demand self-government. Just as ex officio poor law guardians sought to protect the interests of landlords, guardians elected as tenant representatives sought to protect the interests of tenants.

The institutions of local administration thus reflected the divisions and tensions of Irish society as a whole, causing them to be evaluated in relation to wider political issues and objectives. Grand juries remained an anathema to Irish Nationalists, symbolising the continuing power of the Protestant Ascendancy, whilst Unionists contrasted the quiet efficiency of grand juries with the populist antics of poor law boards. Writing in 1888, the Irish Conservative, Robert Staples, condemned the way in which boards of guardians had used their powers 'with a view rather to the injury of political opponents than to the furtherance of public ends'. Sites for cottages erected under the Labourers Acts were

> invariably selected upon the holdings ... of those conspicuous for their anti-Nationalist sympathy or independent conduct. Outdoor relief has been lavishly distributed to persons evicted on account of their obedience to the no-rent manifesto ... Contracts are given to tradesmen and others remarkable for their Nationalist sympathies, quite regardless of the interests of the ratepayers.[24]

As a consequence and reminder of the growing confidence of the nationalist movement, the politicisation of local government, and of poor law administration in particular, could only be a cause of concern to those determined to keep Ireland within the United Kingdom. Allegations of mismanagement served to deflect attention away from the signs of a widespread rejection of British rule, onto the alleged failings of nationalist guardians. In 1892 a government memorandum catalogued cases of 'oppression' by public bodies, including numerous instances of contracts being taken away or awarded for political reasons. A contract to supply meat to Kanturk workhouse, for example, was taken away from one merchant when he refused to stop supplying the police and given to his cousin, 'an advanced nationalist', at a higher price.[25] What constituted oppressive or partisan behaviour was, of course, a highly subjective judgement. Unionists condemned the activities of nationalist boards, but saw nothing wrong when landlord-dominated boards granted relief to the families of injured policemen, or employed officers with landlord and unionist connections. Moreover, at the same time as lamenting the intrusion of party politics into the poor law boardroom, Conservative ministers such as Arthur Balfour were busy injecting party politics into other areas of the Irish administration, including policing. And when nationalists complained of the partisan character of the administration as a whole they were met with incomprehension.

By the later nineteenth century self-government was as much a local as a national issue. An editorial in *United Ireland* in 1882 declared that 'the most pressing necessity to local, political, and social life' in Ireland was

> to abolish its incubus, the existing system of local government. All the local power is held by the landlords and the nominees of the Castle. From the Castle to the grand juryroom, all the boards and bodies ... are the camps and strongholds of the English garrison. They must be routed before we can breathe freely in Ireland.[26]

Central supervision of the poor law system was a cause of increasing resentment among nationalist guardians. Grand juries operated relatively free from central interference. Poor law boards conducted their business under the watchful eye of the Poor Law Commissioners (replaced in 1872 by the Local Government Board) who were empowered to dissolve any board that failed to administer the poor law according to the statutory regulations. Local government inspectors were far more involved in the day-to-day running of poor law unions than was the case in Britain. Drawn predominantly from the ranks of the Irish gentry, the political sympathies of the majority of local government inspectors lay with the landed classes. Most regarded ex officio guardians as being inherently superior to their elected colleagues, being better-educated and more experienced in management and administration.

Giving evidence to a parliamentary select committee in 1885, inspectors Richard Bourke and George Spaight contrasted the efficient administration of boards dominated by ex officio guardians with those controlled by elected guardians. The latter, Bourke maintained, 'save money upon some things where they should spend it, and spend it lavishly very often where they should save it; it is their ignorance chiefly, I think, of public affairs which leads to that'.[27] Spaight recounted a story of an elected guardian on the Cahirciveen Board who had applied for poor relief for himself claiming that he was as much in need of relief 'as anybody in the union'.[28] Such anecdotes reinforced unionist prejudices regarding the unsuitability of the majority of elected guardians for the demands of local office.

One local government inspector who evinced a more open-minded attitude towards the Irish people found that his views brought him into conflict with colleagues and his superiors. W.L. Micks was moved from the south-west district, after he attempted to settle a dispute between a local landowner and his tenants over rent levels. According to police reports, Micks had entirely taken the tenants' side, so that 'the landlord could not have accepted the terms proposed ... without giving a complete victory to the Plan of Campaign'.[29] The inspector had already been the subject of complaint from local officers when he recommended a man for the post of poor rate collector, who was 'the strongest possible Nationalist and known by the Police to be a leading boycotter and organizer of outrages'. According to the Divisional Magistrate, Colonel Turner, poor law boards under Micks' charge had repeatedly been reported for bad management and corrupt conduct, 'but as far as I know nothing is done to improve or correct things'.[30] The Local Government Board judged that Micks had compromised his position by allowing his 'strong and very advanced liberal opinions on political questions ... to obtain publicity' in the district. Since he would no longer be able 'to inspire confidence, and to cause local parties to regard him as perfectly impartial',[31] his removal was deemed to be essential. This view prevailed despite a plea on the inspector's behalf from the Catholic Bishop of Limerick who argued that his removal would be seen as a punishment for attempting to settle the dispute on the Vandaleur estate. According to the Bishop, Micks commanded 'the respect of people of all shades of opinion', and his attempt at mediation 'had the approval of all classes'.[32] This letter probably did more to confirm than to lessen official disapproval of Micks' behaviour.[33]

Unionists defended central supervision as a necessary safeguard and one that was valued and appreciated by Irish people. Poor law guardians, it was claimed, were 'accustomed to the sway exercised over their proceedings by the Local Government Board, and do not resent it; there is scarcely a meeting at which some matters are not referred to the Local Government Board for their opinion and advice'.[34] But this rosy view was contradicted by nationalist writers who railed against the 'autocrats at the Customs House',[35] whose actions were dictated by political not administrative considerations. 'If it is a Nationalist Board of Guardians that is to be suppressed', an editorial in *United Ireland* observed in 1890,

> or a Nationalist newspaper that is to be boycotted out of Government advertisements, or merely a Nationalist evicted tenant to be dismissed from a humble post under the Poor Law, then the Local Government Board as a branch of the Castle, is ever ready to do its share of the duty in a way worthy of coercion, and to do it with a will.[36]

By the early years of the twentieth century the power of the Local Government Board was a regular subject for attack by nationalist critics of the British rule, who condemned it as being 'at once bureaucratic and autocratic'. It was chaired by 'a Protestant of anti-popular opinions and a pronounced party man', and of the nine general inspectors, it was noted, six were Protestant.[37]

That there were some grounds to nationalist complaints is clear from the memoirs of Sir Henry Robinson, who served as vice-president of the Local Government Board from 1899 until 1922, having previously been a local government inspector and commissioner. Robinson's view of the Irish people was typical of the imperial governing elite. In his memoirs the Irish are depicted as charming, child-like creatures whose attempts to exercise any kind or administrative or governmental responsibility required constant monitoring and frequent intervention. Local relief officers, he recalled, were typically

> recruited from the peasantry with no qualifications required save that they should be able to read and write. Anxious, simple-minded people they were, desperately afraid of responsibility, but with a perfectly childish reverence for the traditions of the service, and a burning desire to follow the law, as they interpreted it, to lengths which outdistanced all considerations of common sense.[38]

As vice-president of the Local Government Board, Robinson endeavoured to ensure that his staff contained a mixture of nationalities, believing that it was unwise to rely on Irishmen alone. As he explained to the Royal Commission on the Civil Service in 1913, he had observed

> the characteristics of the three, English, Irish and Scotch, and, working together, they make a really perfect combination. The Englishmen ... have been stolid, sensible, highly competent persons. The Scotchman is a rock of common-sense, accurate, and cautious. The Irishman is brilliant, resourceful and quick, but he is rather impulsive and wants the steadiness of the English and Scotch. An office with all three nationalities represented is perfectly equipped.[39]

The difficulty facing opponents of Irish self-government at local level was that by the end of the nineteenth century the existing structure of local government in Ireland appeared increasingly anachronistic in relation to the rest of the United Kingdom. And with the introduction of democratic local government in England in 1888, it was generally accepted that it was only a matter of time before a similar system was established in Ireland. Nationalists welcomed this prospect as long overdue, and as a first step on the road to self-government. Unionists, on the other hand, were convinced that unless any reformed system was carefully hedged around with safeguards to protect the interests and influence of the Protestant minority, it would represent a further step on the road to ruin. This was certainly Arthur Balfour's view. He accepted that the grand juries would have to be replaced by county councils. But he was worried that the election of councils on a parliamentary franchise (as in England) would hand power over to people who were 'very poor ... very ignorant [and] in all probability very extravagant'. Such people, he feared, 'directly by their votes, and indirectly through the patronage exercised by their

Representatives ... will serve the interests of their political party regardless of the necessities of sound administration'. Local affairs would thus be entrusted to a class 'not only incompetent to manage them with economy, but bitterly hostile to those who can so manage them, and who have so managed them in the past'.[40]

Balfour's proposals for reform included restrictive franchises and extensive central checks and controls. Not surprisingly, Irish nationalist politicians rejected these proposals out of hand, denouncing them as an insult to Ireland. In John Redmond's words the 1892 local government bill was an illogical and grotesque measure based 'upon the principle of distrust of the people, framed upon the supposed inferiority of the Irish race'. The Irish people were being treated as 'totally unfit for self-government ... a set of tools who would at once proceed, if permitted, to squander their own money'. Redmond went on to reject the argument that the actions of certain poor law boards had demonstrated the need for reserve powers to deal with recalcitrant or irresponsible elected bodies. The incidents of boards being dissolved were, he claimed,

> simply incidents in the political and agrarian war [which formed] no justification for a proposal which is based upon the supposed probability of Irish county councillors being corrupt and oppressive. There is nothing in the Irish character, nothing in the history of Irish representative bodies, to justify the belief that county councils in Ireland will be one whit less honest and capable than those bodies which have been granted, free from oppressive restrictions, to England and Scotland.[41]

When local government reform eventually reached the statute book in 1898 it was closely modelled on the English system. The measure was presented by the Chief Secretary, Gerald Balfour, as the inevitable consequence of reform in Britain and as a prerequisite for economic and social development in Ireland. 'You cannot', he informed the commons, 'put old wine into new bottles and in my judgement the reform of local administration in Ireland has now become almost a condition of the further reforms which I hope ultimately to see accomplished'.[42] Speaking in the House of Lords, however, the former viceroy, Lord Londonderry, reiterated earlier warnings of the dangers of reform. The result, he predicted, would be an enormous amount of extravagance, jobbing and maladministration: 'If gentlemen such as those who sat in [certain poor law] unions are to be elected to the county councils what hope have we for any economical or efficient work to be done in the future?'[43]

With the emergence of a national campaign for self-government, the administration and control of Irish local affairs became political issues in a way that they were not in the rest of the United Kingdom. The dichotomy that lay at the heart of much British policy throughout the nineteenth century was that a great many politicians, Conservative and Liberal, clung to the belief that the Irish were capable of behaving like English people, whilst refusing to allow them the freedom to do so. Ireland would only be permitted to have local self-government, an editorial in *United Ireland* suggested in 1890, if local authorities 'will submit their will in all things to the views of the Coercionists ... The Irish local authorities can have money, if they won't spend it, they can have power, if they won't use it'.[44] As the Belfast MP, Thomas Sexton, observed during the debate on the local government bill of 1892, it was hardly surprising that having made coercion the permanent law of Ireland, Balfour was finding it difficult to devise a satisfactory form of democratic local government. 'Elective government', he declared, 'whether local or general, presupposes a foundation of civil liberty, and you can no more found a satisfactory or permanent scheme of elective Local Government upon the statutory regime which you have created in Ireland, than you can build a fortress on a swamp'.[45]

In structure and administration local government reflected Ireland's anomalous position within the empire. It was part both of the metropolitan centre and of the colonial fringe. Structurally, Ireland followed Britain, but administratively, different practices and criteria applied. This divergence was, as the nineteenth century progressed, increasingly to call into question the actuality and benefits of the Union of 1800, and, in a wider sense, of Ireland's place within the United Kingdom and the empire.

British imperialists assumed that British institutions of government, and particularly representative institutions, were superior to those of other countries. This assumption often came to be shared by the peoples they governed. From its inception in 1885, the Indian National Congress demanded the extension of British parliamentary institutions, arguing that as British citizens the people of India were entitled to the rights and privileges of British people. Daniel O'Connell had advanced similar arguments in 1835 when calling for the reform of Irish municipal corporations, arguing that the only means of preserving the connection between Britain and Ireland was 'by allowing the Irish people to share the advantages of the British institutions'.[46]

Irish nationalists from O'Connell to Redmond sought to convince the British that Ireland deserved to be treated as the other constituent parts of the United Kingdom, and that the Irish people could be trusted to adhere to British administrative practices and standards. There were others, however, who refused to accept the validity of such standards. Speaking in Dublin in 1883 Tim Healy declared that

> he had always refused and would refuse to 'civilise himself'. They were threatened by Mr Gladstone with the forces of civilisation. If he was allowed to put his interpretation on the forces of civilisation he would say that so far as the House of Commons was concerned, the first great force of civilisation was the dinner napkin ... he had no respect for this fetish dignity.[47]

Healy's declaration can be seen as part of the process by which a significant body of Irish nationalists came to reject English values along with English rule. Cultural nationalism aimed to create an Irish identity that owed nothing to England or to English culture. An independent government, it was hoped, would sweep away the administrative detritus of British rule and establish authentically Irish institutions at both national and local level.

The Democratic Programme of the First Dáil declared in 1919 that 'The Irish Republic realises the necessity of abolishing the present odious, degrading and foreign poor-law system, substituting therefore a sympathetic native scheme.'[48] Boards of guardians were formally abolished in 1925 and replaced by county boards of health and public assistance empowered to grant outdoor relief to all needy persons. No longer would the poor be obliged to enter the workhouse in order to receive relief.[49] In other respects the structure of local government in independent Ireland remained largely unchanged, though many of its functions were gradually transferred either directly to central government, or to administrative boards. Indeed, local authorities tended to be regarded with as much suspicion and disfavour by Irish government ministers as they had by their British predecessors. Healy recalled being told by a Free State minister in 1926 that county councils represented 'the Magna Charta of jobbery'.[50] Such comments are further evidence of the extent to which Irish political attitudes, as well as administrative structures, were shaped by the legacy of British rule.

NOTES

1. See, for example, D. Fitzpatrick, 'Ireland and the Empire', in A. Porter (ed.), *The Oxford History of the British Empire: The Nineteenth Century* (Oxford: Oxford University Press, 1999), pp. 495–8.
2. 'Local Government and Ireland', *Fortnightly Review*, 44 (1 July 1885), p. 8.
3. J.M. Ward, *Colonial Self-Government: the British Experience 1759–1856* (London: Macmillan, 1976), pp. 328–9.
4. Abercorn to Whitworth, 2 Oct. 1813, Public Record Office of Northern Ireland (hereafter PRONI), Abercorn Papers, D623/A/85/68.
5. R.B. McDowell, *The Irish Administration 1801–1914* (London: Routledge, 1964), p. 113. Assistant barristers were renamed chairman of quarter sessions in 1858, and county court judges in 1877.
6. J. Regan, 'Memoirs of District Inspector John M. Regan', PRONI, unpublished typescript, c. 1960, p. 49.
7. R. Hawkins, 'The "Irish Model" and the empire: a case for reassessment', in D. M. Anderson and D. Killingray (eds), *Policing the Empire: Government, Authority and Control, 1830–1940* (Manchester: Manchester University Press, 1991), pp. 18–32.
8. G. Marquis, 'The "Irish Model" and Nineteenth-Century Canadian Policing', *The Journal of Imperial and Commonwealth History*, 25, 2 (May 1997), p. 212.
9. W.J. Lowe and E. Malcolm, 'The Domestication of the Royal Irish Constabulary', *Irish Economic and Social History*, xix (1992), pp. 30–2.
10. M. Luddy, '"Abandoned Women and Bad Characters": prostitution in nineteenth-century Ireland', *Women's History Review*, 6, 4 (1997), pp. 485–503.
11. See Anderson and Killingray, *Policing the Empire*, p. 9.
12. O. MacDonagh, 'Ideas and Institutions, 1830–45', in W.E. Vaughan (ed.), *A New History of Ireland. V. Ireland under the Union, I: 1801–70* (Oxford: Clarendon Press, 1989), p. 206.
13. W.H. Maxwell, *Wild Sports of the West* (London, 1832), I. 41–42.

14. T. Rice, *Inquiry into the Effect of Irish Grand Jury Laws* (2nd edn, London, 1815), pp. 19–20.
15. G.A. de la Bonniere de Beaumont, *Ireland, Social, Political and Religious*, ed. W.C. Taylor (London, 1839), I. 288; II. 213–14.
16. Anglesey to Holland, 3 Sept. 1831, PRONI, Anglesey Papers, D619/27B, f. 36.
17. Peel to Gower, 26 Dec. 1828, British Library (hereafter BL), Peel papers, Add. MSS 40336, f. 187.
18. Memorandum on Irish Local Government, 2 Nov. 1891, Public Record Office, London (hereafter PRO), Cabinet papers, CAB 37/30/38.
19. See V. Crossman, *Local Government in Nineteenth-Century Ireland* (Belfast: Institute of Irish Studies, 1994), pp. 40, 52.
20. *Seventh Annual Report of the Poor Law Commissioners*, HC 1841 (327), xi. 360.
21. *Sixth Annual Report of the Poor Law Commissioners*, HC 1840 (245), xvii. 424.
22. *Seventh Annual Report of the Poor Law Commissioners*, HC 1841 (327), xi. 352.
23. D. Fraser, 'The Poor Law as a Political Institution', in D. Fraser (ed.), *The New Poor Law in the Nineteenth Century* (London: Macmillan, 1976), pp. 111–27.
24. R. Staples, 'Local Government in Ireland', *Fortnightly Review*, 27 July 1886, pp. 107–8.
25. Particulars of known cases of oppression on the part of public bodies such as Corporations or Boards of Guardians, 1 March 1892, National Archives of Ireland (hereafter NA), Chief Secretary's Registered Papers (hereafter CSORP), 1892/4813.
26. *United Ireland*, 21 Oct. 1882.
27. *Report from the Select Committee of the House of Lords on the Poor Law Guardians (Ireland) Bill; together with the proceedings of the Committee and minutes of evidence*, HC 1884–85 (297), x. 326.
28. Ibid., 361. The same story was told to the American writer William Hulbert when he was touring Ireland a few years later. See, W.H. Hulbert, *Ireland Under Coercion: the Diary of an American* (Edinburgh, David Douglas,1888), pp. 207–8.
29. Turner to Ridgeway, 9 Aug. 1888, NL, CSORP, 1888/21874.
30. Ibid.
31. Robinson to Ridgeway, 21 Nov. 1888, NL, CSORP, 1888/22789.
32. Bishop of Limerick to Balfour, 7 Nov. 1888, ibid.
33. This episode does not seem to have permanently damaged Micks's career. He was appointed secretary to the Congested Districts Board in 1891 and became a Local Government Board commissioner in 1898.
34. *The Times*, 11 March 1892.
35. *United Ireland*, 12 Feb. 1887. The Local Government Board had its offices in the Customs House in Dublin.
36. *United Ireland*, 16 Aug. 1890.
37. *Light on the Local Government Board*, National Library of Ireland, privately printed pamphlet, n.d. (c. 1900).
38. Sir H. A. Robinson, *Further Memories of Irish Life* (London, Herbert Jenkins, 1924), p. 25.
39. Quoted in L. W. McBride, *The Greening of Dublin Castle: The Transformation of Bureaucratic and Judicial Personnel in Ireland 1892–1922* (Washington DC, Catholic University of America Press, 1991), p. 79.
40. Memorandum on Irish Local Government, 2 Nov. 1891, PRO, Cabinet papers, CAB 37/30/38.
41. J. Redmond, 'The Irish Local Government Bill', *Fortnightly Review*, 1 May 1892, pp. 623, 630–1.
42. *Hansard 4*, liii, 1227 (21 Feb. 1898).
43. *Hansard 4*, lv, 558 (21 July 1898).
44. *United Ireland*, 10 May 1890.
45. *Hansard 4*, iv, 1316 (19 May 1892).
46. *Hansard 3*, xxix, 1315 (31 Jan. 1835).
47. F. Callanan, *T.M. Healy* (Cork: Cork University Press, 1996), p. 81.
48. Quoted in R. Barrington, *Health, Medicine and Politics in Ireland 1900–1970* (Dublin: Institute of Public Administration, 1987), p. 91.
49. Outdoor relief was available under the poor law system in certain circumstances but its provision was discouraged by the Local Government Board on grounds of cost.
50. T.M. Healy, *Letters and Leaders of My Day* (London, Thornton Butterworth, 1928), II. 434.

CHAPTER SEVEN

Hunting and Shooting: Leisure, Social Networking and Social Complications

Microhistorical Perspectives on Colonial Structures and
Individual Practices: The Grehan Family, Clonmeen House,
Ireland, late Nineteenth and Early Twentieth Century

NICOLA DRÜCKER

This exact Account of my Time will make me more sensible of
its value: it will dissipate the illusion which makes us consider
only Years and Months, and disregard Hours and Days.

Mr. Gibbon's Journal[1]

Tue 7/11/1882   Drove "Patience" to Rosnalee. 24 minutes.
Shot there 28 pheasants. 27 rabbits 1 cock.
Guns: P. Fitzgerald. Young Pike. Self &
Leader. Had to stay to dine & sleep. Very
cold & heavy showers.[2]

Stephen Grehan's Diary

INTRODUCTION

In a striking way Stephen Grehan's diary entry mirrors the contemporary
virtues and intentions expressed on the title page of *The Private Diary*.[3] From
1857 onwards, all male Grehan family members kept commercially printed
diaries. The above extract follows a set pattern. The destination is noted,
Rosnalee, the country house and estate of the Leader family. The combination
used of 'time' and 'value' introduces the idea of efficiency, punctuality and
utility. The focus on even smaller sections of time hints at a growing sophisti-
cation. Precision and minuteness were also made possible by appropriate
goods,[4] i.e. a watch, a gun and a diary.

Such small units, be it of time, place or subjects, are the main constituents of microhistorical research. The development of such *Close-ups* creates a different historical context, presenting us with new results. Both these new contexts and new results have to be compared and connected to those of other historical approaches, in particular research in traditional 'macro-oriented' political history.

This essay sets three subjects – Esther Chichester and Stephen Grehan, and their estate, Clonmeen, Co. Cork – into their particular context,[5] and evaluates their points of interaction in a period of British rule and rising Irish nationalism.

A careful study of primary sources was begun in 1996 when I was introduced to the Grehan Papers, a collection of family and estate papers generated by the Grehan family of Clonmeen, Co. Cork over a period of 150 years, held in University College Cork. The documents span the period of 1702 until 1975.

Hunting and Shooting were a common activity within the Grehan family. Considered a form of leisure, these activities also enabled social networking and functioned as a catalyst for social complication and conflict. These pursuits reflect the involvement of the two individuals[6] and one house – their experiences, ideas and decisions as well as emerging events which were part of Anglo-Irish social realities.

Within this microhistorical perspective I will focus especially on the analysis of colonial structures and individual practices. Colonial structures as a form of power and rule pervade public and private spheres. So too do individual practices influence the relevance of public rule and private life. The lifetimes of Esther Chichester (b. 1860) and Stephen Grehan (b. 1858) can be also characterised, on the one hand, as a decisive period for British imperialism, but also as a period where nationalist ideas developed in Ireland, the government of which had been unified with Great Britain since 1800. What did Esther Chichester and Stephen Grehan contribute to the concept and practice of colonialism?

CONTEXTS

The Archive

The introductory quotations – one of them a conviction combined with an implicit advice and the other a record of a day narrated in factual detail – provide insight for the microhistorical researcher but they previously had a clear contemporary function and significance for their authors.

The following study is based on the Grehan Family Papers, donated by Peter A. Grehan to University College Cork. Letters, diaries, photographs, maps, plans, ledgers and legal documents reflected, and formed part of property, possessions, family and individual history and identity.[7] These documents

1. Esther Chichester and Stephen Grehan ([no date or number] BL/EP/G)

2. Clonmeen House, Ireland ([no date or number] BL/EP/G)

represent not only the historical contexts of their origination but also contain their own 'historiography'. When being passed on within the family from generation to generation, they were constantly 'edited': material was added, other material was thrown out, rearranged or redistributed within the family network. Items of daily and personal relevance, ranging over private and public matters, organically created in the course of everyday life, gradually survived their owners and consequently changed their function and meaning.[8]

In this way the Grehan Papers bear the characteristics of a family possession.[9] However, a further change of genre took place when the material was handed over to the Boole Library Archives Service. As a fond, i.e. a set of organically created material, of archival value, access to the material was transformed. Originally private and relevant to one family's history, the Grehan Papers were catalogued and partly re-grouped. This meant that a new structure was introduced and the documents were organised under these four main headings: 'Legal Records', 'Estate Administration', 'Family and Personal Papers' and 'Records of Related Families'.[10] This clear differentiation between a legal, an economic and a personal area, i.e. the distinction between the public and the private realm, is related to the western philosophical tradition. Questions arise: Were the records deliberately created in these categories or are they imposed? Do Stephen Grehan's records mainly represent the so-called public, associated with a male area of rationality and rule, while Esther Chichester's records rather concentrate on private issues linked to a supposedly female world of emotions, family and individual identity?[11]

Public access and storage are now regulated through the Archives Service. During my research, Peter A. Grehan fortunately mediated between archival material, family history, personal experiences and cultural contexts.

Esther Chichester was born in 1860. Due to a scarcity of primary sources only some circumstances of her upbringing can be described. Her father was Lieutenant Colonel Charles Raleigh Chichester, a member of the Catholic English gentry, who, lacking landed property, pursued a military career. He married Esther's mother, Mary Josephine Balfe, who inherited her father's estate at Runnamoat, Co. Roscommon. More than likely this landed property was decisive for the arrangement of the marriage. Charles Raleigh Chichester was concerned with developments in landholding during the 'Land War' in Ireland and he expressed his convictions in a booklet *Irish Landlordism*, which he wrote in response to a publication on rents by a member of the Irish Catholic clergy.[12]

Chichester expected the clergy not to stir up the Irish population but to support the status quo, i.e. recognise the legislative, judicial and executive supremacy of the landed gentry. He identified himself with the privileges of the landed gentry and the changes brought about by the British Empire – the Union had an immediate effect on the estate Runnamoat, which officially became part of Britain. Class awareness rather than solidarity in religion entered into his convictions. Chichester's concept of nationality was very flexible. Despite being English, his marriage to a daughter of an estate in Ireland turned him into an 'Irish landlord' as the title of his booklet shows. However, the patrilinear principle of inheritance and lineage rendered Mary Josephine Balfe's and Charles Raleigh Chichester's offspring members of the English Catholic aristocracy.

Esther was educated at the girls' boarding school 'Convent of the Sacred Heart', Roehampton in, England. Esther's and her siblings' upbringing in the English tradition in Irish circumstances further brought them closer to an English than an Irish nationality. This concept of nationality expresses the identification with one's local tasks as a member of a certain class within the framework of the British Empire.

Esther Chichester, who had suffered from breathing difficulties since at least 1882, died in 1900. Stephen Grehan's ancestors were Catholic merchants in Dublin – members of the Irish Catholic Bourgeoisie. In 1830, his grandfather, Stephen Grehan, became the first Catholic Director of the Bank of Ireland. Around the same time he also inherited the estate Clonmeen. The next generation, i.e. his son George Grehan, graduate of Trinity College Dublin and his wife Mary O'Reilly of Coolamber, Co. Westmeath, spent the first years of their marriage in Dublin. Their son, Stephen Grehan, was born in 1858. After the premature death of Mary O'Reilly in 1859, George Grehan permanently settled in Clonmeen, which he had started to manage in the 1840s.[13] In this way, Stephen Grehan, the only child, was the first Grehan to grow up in a land-owning family on the estate in Clonmeen.

Stephen Grehan was educated at home and sent on a Grand Tour d'Europe in 1877 as symbolic accomplishment and completion of his education. From the middle of the nineteenth century not only the landed classes completed this tour, but a growing number of wealthy newcomers also took on this custom.[14]

Stephen Grehan and his father George Grehan were attracted by the prestige of the landed elite. They aspired to upward mobility within the class structure. In the second half of the nineteenth century, the aristocratic elite were gradually losing their exclusive power, while some members of the middle class improved their status and started imitating the cultural practices of the landed class. Newcomers were often characterised by the desire to be acknowledged as upper class in their aspirations, and by their efforts to distinguish themselves from their former class.[15]

George Grehan promptly became involved with local government, becoming High Sheriff in 1859, magistrate for the County of Cork in 1858 at least until 1877 and Justice of the Peace in 1875–76.[16] The combination of his father's directorship, his own professional status and the influence of a sense of crisis within the landed system, facilitated his quick acceptance by the landed elite. Stephen Grehan continued his father's participation in local government which was considered a landlord's duty. In 1879, he was awarded a Commission of the Peace, became High Sheriff in 1883 and in 1888 was promoted within the county establishment to Deputy Lieutenant.[17]

In 1883 Esther Chichester and Stephen Grehan married. This event, following some romantic correspondence, granted him entry into *Burke's Landed Gentry* – 'Grehan of Clonmeen'[18] – thus promoting him from mere landowning or the 'nouveau riches' status to that of the landed gentry. The planned marriage of Esther and Stephen was also the occasion for George Grehan to transfer his landed property, the Clonmeen and a Tipperary estate, to his son.[19]

Clonmeen lands were located alongside the Blackwater river in Co. Cork – a region which was a major centre of English colonisation and conquest. Luke Gibbons gives an apt definition:

> Conquest was not restricted to military and political subjugation, but involved the classical colonial patterns of confiscation and plantation of land, and systematic attempts to extirpate native law, language, religion, and culture.[20]

At least from 1500 onwards, the area was dominated by the O'Callaghans of Clonmeen, a Gaelic clan. But Elizabeth I held some lands as a grant to the O'Callaghans as early as 1573. The clan ruled the area from their stronghold, Clonmeen Castle, until *c*.1650 when Lord Muskerry and Irish troops were defeated by Cromwell's troops under Lord Broghill in the battle of Knockbrack. Subsequently, Sir Richard Kyrle, a Cromwellian Officer, was rewarded with lands at Clonmeen.

Documents indicate unbroken presence of Church of Ireland vicars in Clonmeen Parish from as early as 1591 onwards. Catholic religion was suppressed after the Cromwellian victory. The Augustine monastery, near Clonmeen Castle and constructed by the O'Callaghans, was replaced by a Protestant church built on the same grounds.[21] In the late seventeenth century the Gaelic chief Donogh and his wife Ellen O'Callaghan were transplanted to Co. Clare. Their lands were granted to various people, the most influential being Sir William Petty, who played a key role in the post-Cromwellian colonial redistribution of Irish land and who wrote the survey, *Hiberniae Delineatio quod hactenus licuit perfectissima* (1683).[22]

Further complications regarding landownership followed in Penal Times until John Roche of Dublin bought the Clonmeen lands in the late eighteenth century. When his nephew Stephen Grehan succeeded to the lands, he and his son George extended the estate, partly facilitated by the Encumbered Estates Commission. Two houses were built: a Georgian style residence in 1841 and in 1893 Esther Chichester and Stephen Grehan added another, even bigger Victorian country house, referred to as Clonmeen House.

Clonmeen House and estate clearly reflected the lifestyle of Stephen Grehan and Esther Chichester. Labourers on the homefarm and servants in the house shared this space, some permanently, others during working hours. But there also was the term 'Clonmeen' – a traditional local place name which existed independently from ownership changes. It was a recognised townland with relevance for tenants and other local residents. So 'Clonmeen House and estate' or also 'Clonmeen' relate to various possible sites of interaction between different groups of people. Given the above outlined colonial context of Clonmeen, this situation can be also described as a 'contact zone':

> [...] the space of colonial encounters, the space in which peoples geographically and historically separated come into contact with each other and establish ongoing relations, usually involving conditions of coercion, radical inequality, and intractable conflict.[23]

Mary Louise Pratt chose the term 'contact' to emphasise the impact of subjects, their co-presence and interaction.[24] In a strange but different way my historical research in the archive, and the encounter with the material resembles a new contact zone, set down in order to reconstruct the past reality of the Clonmeen contact zone partly. The contact between researcher and the Grehan archives is not reciprocal, and the historical context is post-colonial after the establishment of an independent nation state, the Republic of Ireland.[25]

A Microhistorical Approach

Microhistorical studies require a clear framework to deal with small units such as one place or a distinct point of time.[26] The focus point of this paper 'hunting and shooting' needs to be set in a larger context as regards timespan, historical environment and individual lives as has been done briefly in the above section.

In addition, the study of colonial structures is an important issue. Luke Gibbons sees Ireland as 'a colony *within* Europe':

> [...] Ireland's anomalous position at once within and outside Europe gives issues of race, nation, class and gender a new complexity, derived from an intersection of both metropolis and subaltern histories.[27]

Although Ireland ceased with the Act of Union to be a self-governing colony, colonial structures remained a valid issue. First, as Britain's oldest colony[28] conquered from the late sixteenth century onwards, certain long-established ideas, experiences and traditions were ingrained in common practice. This was independent of any legal act. Secondly, the integration of Ireland's government into central government immensely increased the impact of British rule, although certain concessions had been promised, for example, Catholic emancipation. Thirdly, the era of British expansion continued throughout the nineteenth century. British imperialism reached another peak in the 1870s with formal imperialism and increased European competition for colonies in order to defend or obtain hegemony in Europe.

Thus, after the Act of Union, Ireland could be considered as one part of a colonising motherland. Or Ireland could be perceived as a role model for

3. Shooting party ([no date] BL/EP/G, Box 3, 60)

4. Shooting party ([no date] BL/EP/G, Box 2, 53)

achieved colonisation, i.e. finally and utterly conquered with established colonial structures. In either scenario, there was a continuity of resistance against British rule. The question of Irish identities and their formation would be central to all perceptions in this situation of conflict. Individual perceptions of the particular situation around Clonmeen will be examined in the next section.

A key requirement for a microhistorical approach is a high density of primary sources. Analytical methods also come from neighbouring subjects, such as literary analysis, biographical and cultural studies, and aim at a non-ethnocentric and non-teleological evaluation of all kinds of 'texts', i.e. written, oral or visual material.[29] With this approach, influenced by Geertz's method of 'Thick Description',[30] networks, cracks, gaps and wide differences – conflicting and conforming elements – become visible. Primary documents show multiple and heterogeneous realities created by recording individuals. These are only fragments – of realities, of records and of readings – a complete reconstruction of past social realities is impossible.[31]

Continuing re-focusing between smaller and larger contexts, i.e. micro- and macrohistorical perspectives or the history of everyday life and traditional political history, brings about insight on the three subjects treated here.[32]

Thus, the discussion of selected primary sources in the outlined framework shows a historical situation at Clonmeen of 'overlapping territories and intertwined histories'.[33] And to complete, of interrelating lives.

HUNTING AND SHOOTING

Cultural Practice

These two photographs show two different shooting parties. Photograph 3 was taken prior to 1900 and features Esther Chichester sitting on the fence (third woman from the right). Men, women, children, dogs and horses are grouped – the men and boys displaying guns and the women holding umbrellas. One woman is mounted on a horse.

Photograph 4 shows more men than women and a boy at another shooting party which also appears more elaborate due to the tent.

They are group portraits – most of the eyes are focused on the camera and consequently on the observer, conveying a sense of cohesion. But this cohesion applied to the action of 'being photographed' only – any further meaning remains uncertain. Photography is selective and edited in its depiction of reality, both by the photographer and his or her subjects.[34]

Hunting and shooting were considered suitable sports for the landed class, or in other words the leisured class. The gentry perceived leisure as attitude, a concept which goes back to Greek society where strength in arts, sports, discourse, military endeavours and political action was aspired to. Apart from their individual satisfaction, this privileged male class considered leisure to be a public good.[35]

In order to underline leisured status, all sporting and social activities were rated of superior importance on the estate, with the result that even farm labourers were asked to perform duties related to sports.[36] Hunting and shooting were socially representative events carried out within the landed class, but they could be also very individual experiences, for example, lonely rough shooting in the mountains or occasionally a lonely pursuit of a fox. The results and success added to one's social prestige within the gentry. On a personal level sport was the 'only outlet in life'[37] – an emotional activity and a space for emotions – hinting at an extremely restricted and regulated lifestyle.

Shooting was considered a male activity with only a few exceptions. However, gentry women were required as audience and for provisions since they were expected at lunch breaks, or for the occasional walk home.[38] This also explains why women were portrayed on the above photographs.

Esther Chichester recorded shooting events and results in her diary. There is no indication if she wrote these entries because of her genuine interest, identification with the activities of her husband, intended complete record keeping or any other reason. It would be worth investigating whether Stephen recorded likewise Esther's activities as precisely in his diary in order to identify mutual interests and priorities.

24[Dec 1888]	Gentlemen went out shooting. Agnes & I walked over the bogs with them.
[...]	
28	Shot bog. Papa shot a pheasant stayed out till they had finished & was rather tired inconsequence Concy & I walked & she jumped or rather crossed several drains
29	Stephen took a family group. Also picture of Peter Magrath at 2 o'clock about 93 tenants assembled for a feed & dance. I danced 4 jigs
30th	Sunday. I did not go to Church owing to bronchitis. We took a family group in the afternoon.
[...]	
1st Jan [1889]	Went to last Mass. The Irwin boys & Raleigh & Charlie shot 5 pheasants round house & got 26 rabbits we left before 4 & drove into Castlerea. Awfully cold & had not enough wraps on caught train & had a most uncomfortable journey to Mallow which we reached before 2 A.M. slept there.[39]

Her diary entries are very concise. From photographs being taken, one can conclude that this action was considered a special event. Subsequently, the possession of these photographs would have been of considerable value to the Grehan family.

Peter Somerville-Large suggests that shooting parties were perceived by women as mainly boring. He quotes Lady Clodagh Anson, who described them as:

> awful things. ... The men went off after breakfast, and all the wives sat around in the drawing room making unattractive things in wool, generally in very bright colours if they were for "the poor". [...] Afterwards you walked with the guns, getting home gratefully at dusk, changing into a tea gown for tea, then you 'rested', why I don't know, unless the hostess wanted to get rid of you to write letters. You changed again for dinner, of course, a very long affair with six or seven courses. How does one live through such things?[40]

Unfortunately, Somerville-Large does not provide the source, date or context of this quote. It is evident that Lady Clodagh Anson considered this type of female leisure too formal and inactive. From an early age Stephen Grehan recorded his shooting efforts in his diary. When 16 he noted:

> '1/1/1874:   Heard 12 Mass. went down to river before lunch. no duck. rode after lunch with Johnnie O'Brien to père M...
> [...]
> 28/1/1874:   Went to shoot by the river. Sent bird up to Dublin to be stuffed.'[41]

In a diary shooting was recorded as an activity but also as a story of success – sometimes the exact outcome was noted. The stuffed bird referred to above has the significance of a trophy, a luxury good and a material piece of evidence. In this way it also documents that Stephen Grehan expected and aspired to prestige as a sportsman and an accepted member of his social class.[42]

The keeping of a gamebook is a further practice in this context. Apart from reflecting minuteness in record keeping as regards numbers and dates, it shows the shooter's success. Although prestigious items in this way, Stephen Grehan's game lists do not have the expensive design and layout of other game books.[43] They are rather shabby looking notebooks, one of them was reused. However, they cover the period from 1875 until 1912 and list date, district, animal killed, remarks and season's totals.[44] The title page of his second game register is covered with several handwritten versions of Stephen Grehan's name, his signature, various years and a comment on himself: 'Le nom d'un fou se trouve partout!!'[45] It is evident that the aspirations of serious and complete bookkeeping were only marginally met.

Hunt meets were a social and sports event for both men and women of the landed class. The breakthrough for women only occurred in 1879 when the empress Elizabeth of Austria visited Ireland to hunt and thus rendered female participation in the sport respectable and even desirable.[46]

Ambitions, competition and achievements were noted and recognised in a similar way as shoots. Hunting events functioned as accepted meeting points for family members, neighbours, guests, young people and fiancées, like Esther and Stephen. As long as certain social codes were kept, for example, chaperones as company for unmarried women, there seemed to have been the same anticipation and involvement on the side of the women as of the men.

In 1882, a few months before their wedding, Stephen Grehan noted in his diary:

> Tue 26/9/1882   Went to Mallow by 12–30. Hunt-meeting. R & Cis drove in & met me. Old court-people Also played tennis Esther & Christine came back to Clonmeen.[47]

Esther wrote too in a letter to Stephen in November 1882:

> [...] The next two meets I hear are the Frank's place & Dromore – They run I believe in this direction from Carrig Miss Barry is going to ride I should so like to go too – but can't without a chaperone – isn't it a nuisance! when I shall be a qualified chaperone myself in two months! [...][48]

In later years, Esther, was more reluctant to hunt but still enjoyed it. Her diary reads:

> 26/12/1893   I went out to the hunt against my inclination but found I liked it & fell quite at home. - No sport before I came home so had one jump only.[49]

Stephen Grehan was heavily involved in the local Duhallow Hunt Club.[50] Consequently, Esther and Stephen's son and daughters became involved in hunt meets as well. Their daughter May Grehan (b. 1884) wrote a full article on 'Sports & Games' in the Family Journal of February 1903;[51] featuring hunting, racing, billiards and the weather – the prevailing winter preoccupations. It appears that in this aspect of life, women had become fully integrated, at least in the physical enjoyment and strains, and in the social aspects.[52]

> *Hunting*: We have had very bad sport indeed with the Duhallows, I am sorry to say.
> On the 26th inst. Father & I drove 12mls. to a meet at Cahermee, our horses having slept the night with the Whites, only to draw covert after covert blank - we actually had a blank day.
> We had to brave an awful shower of snow at the beginning & my hands got so cold that I could hardly hold my reins. However it cleared up afterwards & people tried to forget the scarcity of foxes by talking to friends exchanging all the latest bits of news. And each fresh detail of

the great success of the Barings's dance which took place on 23rd becomes known to those who had not the luck of being there become more & more envious of those who had. [...] Castle Cor, where we meet on 28inst. ought to give us a run, as a fox was seen there two days ago.

Last week when we met at Newberry Manor on 21st Feb. we had a short but nice little run over some very high fences. One girl who was wearing an old habit got hung up & might have had a very nasty fall but she escaped with a small cut on her forehead.[53]

Obviously, old-fashioned riding-dresses had a negative impact on performance. This incident points to the issue of gendered dress codes: their social meaning and restriction (of movement).

Hunt balls were a major social entertainment in the landed class and strengthened their network and solidarity. Here young people were introduced to society accompanied by their parents. Hunt balls were as much a part of Stephen Grehan's life as his children's.

Stephen Grehan's diary:
23/1/1877:   Wet. Shot with rifle. Drove to Lombardstown & went to Mallow to Hunt Ball. Pap came.[54]

Family Journal (1903):
Mr & Miss Grehan were at a dance given by Mr & Mrs Baring (M.F.H. of the Duhallow's at Avondhu Mallow, the night of 23rd & 24st inst.
The dance was an excellent one & everybody seemed to enjoy it thoroughly. Dancing was kept up vigorously until after 3.[55]

Stephen Grehan's enthusiasm for hunting is obvious in his choice of his hunting clothes as a costume for a fancy dress ball, another aspect of social life. Interestingly the same diary gives evidence of his opinion concerning his involvement in local politics and government. Compared to the diary entries of that year, his comments on this matter are extremely emotional and in contrast with the rational, authority-conscious attitude expected of a man in the nineteenth century.[56]

Mon 15/3/1880   Jury Sworn for Criminal Business
Tue 16/3/1880   *Gd* Jury discharged. Very stupid work. Awfully glad its over.
[...]
Fri 2/4/1880   Went to Cork by 10–32 for Relief Fund Ball. *A Capital Ball* - nearly 400 attended
                Fancy Dress - I went in hunt uniform.
Sat 3/4/1880   Came home by 4–30 train - [57]

Apart from this outburst, most diary and personal records of Esther Chichester and Stephen Grehan show very few emotions. Peter A. Grehan, who grew up as a member of the gentry, learned that no gentleman would show emotion.[58] Interestingly enough both hunting and shooting are sports in which a high amount of aggression is displayed and thus worked as a general source of emotional release. Whether this worked in the same way for women cannot be investigated here. Hunting and shooting also involved another group of people who were thought of as a different class. In Clonmeen three men worked in the stable, three in the garden and twenty-two were noted as 'labourers' in 1907.[59] They took care of the horses, hounds, game, riding gear and guns. A Grehan daughter mentioned her own anticipation and their work in the *Family Journal*, not mentioning names but using the passive voice:

> [...] We have I think played our last game of croquet & tennis for 1903. There seems little chance of the ground ever drying again.
> We can however look forward with pleasure to the *Hunting & Shooting*. The hunters are being exercised daily for 2 hours each & saddles & habits are being looked over & renewed.[60]

For the landlord, these appurtenances had further significance. The attitude of Stephen Grehan, for example, towards his horses, dogs and guns reveals personal attachment. He cares for them, reports on their behaviour or performance and they obviously have an important personal meaning for him.[61] When away on a Tour d'Europe in 1877, Stephen wrote to his father in Clonmeen:

> [...] I have a wretched pen, any prospects of game? I hope no pheasants were killed during the mowing. Will you tell Mr Patsey to give my gun a good oiling, it is more than a month since it was put in the case.
>   Do all the dogs still hunt waterhens? Any fishing? [...]?[62]

Yet at the same time, these items take on a further significance when seen as necessary attributes of the landed class. In this way, they become competitive symbols of status. Not only the quality of a single item or animal was of importance but also the abundance of such resources was an issue.

'Land' was another crucial aspect of hunting and shooting. Inviting shooting parties or hunt meets always involved a display of one's estate: its size, its appearance and its natural resources – be it agricultural produce, forests or fauna. Whereas shooting took place in a designated area on the estate, hunting events could lead in any direction depending on the chase. However, since the starting point would always be near a country house, the direct neighbourhood would witness and be affected by the sport.

Such display of property manifested the landlord's power in this space and structure. The hunt also included lands leased to tenants. Therefore, the landowner did not only show his social and economic status but also his political

5. A meet in front of rural house ([no date] BL/EP/G, Box 1, 139/197)

power over his landed property and its inhabitants. Thus, public and private spheres consisted of individual actions, experiences and ideas. The 'public' and 'private' area are not understood as dichotomies but as integrated and produced. Hunting and shooting have individual as well as social implications; the Grehan family, visitors and labourers contributed to their outcome. Class and leisure concepts outside the Grehan family impacted on their aspirations and actions. Power structures in the Grehan family and at Clonmeen further shaped their social contexts and were dependent on material or political resources. They were as much pervaded by material interests and emotions as by colonial structures and attitudes. Medick and Sabean have developed the point that distinct roles within a family are also a product of continuities in a family history and their social environment.[63]

Conflict on Land and Hunting

The hounds are relaxing on the road adjoining a stone house. A man on a horse, a participant in the meet, stands even closer to the building – on its 'lawn'. Three men are leaning with their back against the house. It might well be their house and they could be tenants of the hunting landlord. There could have been some sort of conversation between the two parties.

The photograph reflects the ample space and movement of the hunting class and a confined and humble representation of the rural people. Anne McClintock's analysis is to the point: 'Photography was both a technology of representation and a technology of power.'[64]

A microhistorical approach to social complications between the landed and the tenant or farmer class is limited through the availability of primary sources. First, the Grehan Papers were filtered and compiled by this family of one side only. The other side can only be seen indirectly, in documents generated by the Grehans, for example, this photograph. The quiet, unspectacular and immobile presence of the rural people in this setting which was further turned into a static photographic document might disguise ongoing conflict in a colonial contact zone.[65]

The indirect documentation of these people at Clonmeen has a further facet – their activities and lives were recorded and then transmitted without their consent. Whereas some texts, for example, diaries and letters, were created in view of some sort of audience, subjects in other archival documents only appear in a passive way, without an intention to be fixed on paper or in an archive.[66] In this case, the Grehan family, representing the upper class, had the material resources and power to write and transmit (now historical) texts from their own perspective. Other inhabitants of Clonmeen were restricted by access to education, free time and consumer goods in the creation of primary sources.

The amount of photographs taken by professionals and amateurs in the Grehan Papers are evidence of the importance they gave to this new medium. The possession of a camera and photographs points at cultural and individual practices developing with this new technology.[67] Who was being photographed in which context? In what way did the subjects present themselves? Which photos were shown around and which were thrown out? What was the interest of the amateur photographer, who in the nineteenth century was necessarily part of the wealthy class? Especially in 1881–82 Stephen and Esther Grehan experienced conflict between the landed class and farmers or tenants in North Cork. Developments in the 'Land War' and the consequent Land Act of Gladstone (1881) left traces in Esther's letter to Stephen:

> [...] Mr. Morrogh heard bad news about the hunting yesterday the curate in Doneraile who is most anxious that the hunting should be allowed told him that all Buttevant farmers have signed a paper saying that they will prevent the hunting Some Doneraile farmers who were asked to sign it also, refused - [...][68]

'Stopping the Hunt' was a major national campaign as part of the Land League (founded in 1879) agitation in the season of 1881–82, but further disturbances and conflicts subsequently continued to occur.[69] In the poor law union of Kanturk the hunt was stopped once, and in Mallow three times. The Duhallow foxhounds were disrupted *c.* 26 November 1881, suspended on 7 December 1881 and resumed in January 1882.[70]

Hunting, which was considered the symbol of a gentleman's pleasures and rule over their estate's land and population, became loathed by tenants and some farmers who claimed co-determination[71] and took to various forms of protest, for example, poisoning hounds, gathering at decisive spots or signing resolutions.

These mass protests were also aimed against coercion, for example, the Protection of Person and Property Act in March 1881. This act had been passed in order to limit the influence of the Land League by enabling the authorities to arrest and detain without trial. Since agitation of the League continued, many members as well as Parnell (October 1881) were arrested. Consequently, protests increased and contributed to a compromise between the British government and Parnell in the Kilmainham Treaty (1882), in which a further Land Act was promised.[72]

The local Duhallow Historical Journal describes another form of protest in 'The Land League Hunt'. In protest of rack rents paid to the landlords Leader, Longfield and La Tuish, who were neighbours of the Grehans' with larger estates, 'a poach-up of all local landlord estates was ordered'.[73] O Nunain described, how tenant farmers associated themselves with the Land League, and complained about the exclusive hunting rights of the landlord. This is how O Nunain recounts the incident:

> In 1885 the spirit of Dromtariffe tenant farmers was still unbroken and having banded themselves together in the Land League were looking forward to the day, when they would again own the lands on which they worked and out of which they had been driven after the great battle of Knockbrack in 1651. [...]
>
> In Dromtariffe outside help was sought. Word was sent to the Maoilinn men who were well known in the Land League circles. With them came men from Castleisland and Coisceim including John Twiss and his greyhound Bran. The parish of Dromtariffe was poached from Ardrahan to Gurteen westwards to Dromagh. They even entered the lawn of Leader's Great House. There when William Leader threatened to shoot John Twiss' hound, Twiss drew a revolver and threatened to shoot Leader if he did so. Leader withdrew but promised that it would not be the end of the matter. Some years later Twiss was arrested and tried for the murder of James O'Donovan at Glenlara, found guilty and hanged. He proclaimed his innocence even from the gallows.
>
> A second poach-in took place on a working day. Leader's gamekeepers and workmen were engaged at farmwork and retreated from field to field before the poachers. Father Con O'Sullivan the Parish Priest saw the poachers as he passed by in his pony trap. He stood up in the trap and cheered the huntsmen who filled the trap with hares, rabbits and pheasants. [...][74]

Narrated in a national tone with strong moral appeals to perceived injustice, this account addresses landownership as the key issue during the conflict. The protest against landlord practice is justified by the colonial past. The battle of Knockbrack brought about the defeat of Irish troops by Cromwellian soldiers and is remembered as a local event with continuing consequences.[75] In addition, the support of their case by the Parish Priest plays an important role.

The re-interpretation and re-invention of hunting by the rural inhabitants is remarkable. They attacked a pre-eminent occupation of the landed class, reversed the practice of demonstrating one's property by trespassing the core lands of the estate, the 'lawn'. They laid claim to the concept of leisure by choosing a working day and keeping the killed animals as profit. The response to the violent protest of the landlord Leader was further menace. In this way, they harshly protested against the contemporary power structures in land and rights distribution, and expressed their own desire to participate in the cultural practice of hunting.

This phenomenon could be also described, as by Pratt, as 'transculturation' –'subordinated or marginal groups select and invent from materials transmitted to them by a dominant or metropolitan culture'.[76] The protesters appropriated hunting, a mode of dominant representation, to express their own claims.

These protests definitely have to be seen in connection with the boycotting of high rents, protesting against evictions, intimidation and ambushes; i.e. other forms of mass protest and resistance against the land tenure system and the demand for Home Rule or the end of British rule in Ireland.

During the Land War, Clonmeen could also be described as a 'conflict zone'.[77] The events described above would have been known at Clonmeen, in particular since the Grehans were acquainted with the Leaders and joined the Leaders' shooting parties. The Land League was also active around Clonmeen.

This is how workmen at Clonmeen, whose fathers or who themselves were employed, recall the events in the late nineteenth century. It is important to note that this typewritten manuscript has characteristics of oral history: the structure of the sentences, the rhetorical construction and the content. It comprises 400 years of Clonmeen history in three pages. Sheehan et al. wrote in 1938:

> [...] The landlord [Stephen Grehan] exercised no special powers over his tenants, save alone the collection of half-yearly rents [...] He reserved all game and fishing sites for himself, and exercised the strictest watch over these, not allowing even a dog to walk on his preserves. At one time, his estate was a noted haunt for hares. A local story is told of a curate in this parish, Father O'Riordan, who had a hobby for hounds. This curate's residence was situated on the estate. One day he took out his hounds to exercise them in the fields nearby. He was seen, and reproached by the game-keeper. The matter was reported to the Landlord, who also forbade the curate to bring his hounds on the land. The curate is supposed to

have remarked to his friends, when telling the story that the day would come, when there wouldn't be a hare in Clonmeen. Strange enough, those words have come true. It became a regular rabbit warren, all over the estate, so much so, that they had to be poisoned at regular intervals, owing to the extensive damage being done by them. [...][78]

The introductory sentence is a plain understatement of the story to come. The story resembles a biblical allegory of egoism, power and greed. With the help of divine intervention – through a curate – the landlord is punished. Obviously the curate and his friends retold this story so many times that Sheehan et al. refer to it in their account as a local story.

Oddly enough, Stephen Grehan's gamebook gives evidence of the curse of the curate. In the season of 1886–87, 31 hares and 160 rabbits were shot, whereas in 1891–92 only 9 hares and 3657 rabbits are registered ...[79]

This particular kind of storytelling and understanding of the past is part of a subaltern culture and resistance to colonial structures. Sheehan et al. judge the past situation at Clonmeen only implicitly as colonial: they remember the transplantation of the O'Callaghans after Cromwell, narrate in 'Catholic'–'Protestant' dichotomies and they refer to the succeeding landlord Stephen Arthur Grehan as the 'occupier'.[80] Both local accounts relate to colonial conquests in the seventeenth century. They attack the exclusive (hunting) rights and power of the landlord and they claim the support of the local Parish Priest for their cause.

Workmen of Clonmeen, a generation after campaigns like 'Stopping the Hunt', interpret their past as colonial. Through their own oral culture they transmit stories of individuals and constitute a local identity.

In 1893 Stephen Grehan recorded:

Thu 2/3/1893   Went to Cork for Unionist Meeting at Assembly Rooms. Good Meeting.[81]

There is no evidence in the Grehan Papers as to whether the political conflict on hunting and land issues shaped, changed or affected his political conviction.

Abroad

Stephen Arthur Grehan recorded in his diary:

Sat 24 December 1932
    Heard tiger had killed near Pattan and we went off after breakfast - [...?] started about 2pm, when beaters within 100yd tiger roared and galloped out to Oxley who missed, then came past me, I got him with left barrel to my great surprise - a big one, 9'[ft] 7 1/2" [inches] between pugs great excitement in camp - skinned by 11pm.[82]

6. Stephen Arthur Grehan in India ([no date or number] BL/EP/G)

Esther and Stephen Grehan's only surviving son is featured with a fallen tiger. Stephen Arthur Grehan holds the gun and is surrounded by natives, who acted as beaters and whose position in the photograph underlines their minor importance for the photographer.

This photograph shows not only the tiger as an exotic good – and the connected issues of transport, leisure time and finances, it also documents the material and cultural power of the Grehan family to hand down their history.[83]

The diary entry, again, provides facts and a sequence of events, but the pride of the hunter can be read between the lines. The numbers, i.e. distances and size of the tiger, underline Stephen Arthur's excitement. He was so impressed that he wrote a short story recalling the experience, entitled 'A Christmas Eve Tiger', in which he elaborated the diary entry but without really adding any new insights on the hunt and the shoot.[84] It is set in a British Army Camp in Gogra, India. What is the relationship between 'Stopping the Hunt' and, a generation later, new hunting and shooting terrain for the Grehans in Britain's 'Crown Colony'? How did Esther, Stephen and Stephen Arthur Grehan judge colonial politics? Various Land Acts (between 1885 and 1909) facilitated a transfer of land from the landowner to the tenants. Stephen Grehan also sold land to his tenants through the Irish Land Commission. Landlords became more dependent on the opinion of the local people. Some gentlemen were forced to restrict hunting and searched for new 'undisturbed' hunting areas abroad.[85]

In the late nineteenth century the landed class mixed socially with the military and police forces which were present in Ireland. Military careers were considered suitable, as regards class and income, for sons of the landowning class. Stephen Grehan, who supported the anti-home rule movement, agreed with this. His son and several husbands of his daughters were members of the British Army. Judging from their enthusiasm for the British Empire, one can assume that imperial values were at least latently present in the previous generation.[86] Keith Jeffery points out that the Empire provided careers in imperial service, in particular for members of the declining Irish gentry, who gradually lost their tasks and a *raison d'être* in Ireland.[87] India was one such destination.[88]

In 1914 Stephen Arthur Grehan (b. 1895) joined the Royal Military Academy in Woolwich and then participated in the First World War, being promoted to acting major. He was the first Grehan to serve in the British Army. From 1920, he did service in Mesopotamia. He was sent to India from 1932 until 1937, first at Meerut, then as commander of the Mountain Battalion.[89]

Judging from letters Stephen Arthur wrote in 1920 to his father at Clonmeen, his imperial attitudes were evident.

> General Headquarters,
> Mesopotamian Expeditionary Force
> May 19th, 1920
>
> Dear Bo,
> [...]
> The country [Ireland] seems to be in an appalling state judging by todays wireless news - I shouldn't be in the least surprised to hear any time that you are all taking a trip out of the country, but then I suppose you cant very well do that & leave everything to chance - It is hard to see how they can get the country settled without martial law & a great deal of bloodshed - I cannot see that the present (or any) home rule bill can be of the slightest use until the country is quiet & outrages are stopped. I hope you have ordered the I Times to come out as, except for Reuters, one is very out of touch here. [...][90]

A second letter:

> General Headquarters,
> Mesopotamian Expeditionary Force
> 2/7/1920
>
> Dear Bo
> [...] It is a pity that he [Joss Ryan, fiancé of his sister Aileen] is Indian Army - the I.A. is rather unsettled now that they are giving commissions to Natives & also the political situations seems by no means secure; Fancy having a nigger subaltern in your mess or, worse still, being commanded by a Nigger! I cant see how they are ever going to get subalterns to join in future, as a fellow joining now is bound to be junior to some native - the whole of our prestige in India has been built up & main-

tained through keeping the native in his place & now they go & put him on absolute equality with the Sahib! They say here that the feeling among the old regular native officers is very much against it. [...][91]

Stephen Arthur seemed very comfortable with the military environment. His thoughts about the use of martial law and physical violence to settle Ireland might have been the same for India or any other country he was serving in. He had a clear concept of his own racial and consequently political superiority. Due to his chosen career, he had declared himself loyal to Britain and thus, identified himself with a British motherland or an 'Irish Empire'[92] by serving in her colonies. However, some of Stephen Arthur's attitudes may have shifted by the 1930s when Photograph 6 was taken. Nevertheless, Stephen Arthur Grehan, as a newcomer, supported not only elitist social and cultural practices but also the British political and cultural elite in the field of international relations. Thus, one could conclude that colonial attitudes were internalised, expressed and then passed on.

Close relatives of Stephen Arthur simply express personal worry about his well-being abroad. In 1932, his father recorded in his diary: 'Stevie and Cecily left. He for India she to see him off - ... I wonder whether I shall ever see dear old Stevie again. His Batts is due home in 1936.'[93] Stephen Arthur's wife, Cecily Gaisford St. Lawrence, wrote to his sister Magda Grehan in the same year: 'How I hate this India business - it seems such a bad time to go out there now with so much unrest.'[94] Prestige and careers were less important when communicating on a personal level.

Ironically, and also as a result of internalised colonial structures on the part of the Irish gentry, new hunting areas were usually other, more recently subjugated parts of the British Empire, for example, Africa and India. Stephen Arthur Grehan transferred his cultural practice of hunting and shooting to India, where he as a member of the British army, again represented a part of the ruling society. In this way, he exported and supported with his service abroad existing power and cultural structures which were loyal to the British Empire. One can go a step further and state that this particular tiger hunt and its circumstances are an example that the general Irish social experience of having been colonised was converted to subsequent colonising efforts of other societies.

Unfortunately, there are no documents in the Grehan Papers referring to the opinions of the Indian natives on the above-described situation. So the question if there are similarities between the reactions of the inhabitants of the hunting and shooting area in Gogra, India and Clonmeen, Ireland has to be left unanswered.

However, at that time the Indian nationalist movement spearheaded by Gandhi was active in protests against British presence and demands for independence were finally granted in 1947.

CONCLUSION

I have undertaken to apply a microhistorical approach to the Grehan Papers and to the question of social interaction at Clonmeen. In particular I have examined hunting and shooting as both individual and colonial practices.

Clonmeen as a place can be understood as a 'contact zone'. Set in one colonial environment, this analysis shows records made by the Grehans differ in their form and contents from those of local non-gentry residents. While the quoted records of the neighbours show close links to oral tradition and narrate historical and contemporary experiences of injustice and protest, the evaluated Grehan documents rather mirror detailed record keeping, often referring to measurements or specific personal events in letters and diaries. Furthermore, there is a certain continuity in the type and style of records that were created and then survived in the Grehan Papers. The activities of hunting and shooting for instance are only described from the perspective of leisure and social networking, with scarce exceptions. Both groups mention and relate to each other in the surviving documents, but it is evident that the 'texts' of the Grehan Papers also convey the family's comparably unlimited access to material resources for documentation, time for their creation and space for their storage.

At Clonmeen there were at least these two different modes of passing on beliefs and understandings. The local accounts based in an oral tradition tend to go back to English colonisation in the seventeenth century, which signified for the locals the beginning of their present situation. The written documents of the Grehans on the other hand have the characteristics of a material possession. Their contents are too specific and are not designed to be remembered through oral transmission.[95] Both groups of sources constitute relations to and understandings of history – of family history and local history – and thus contribute to identity formation. The workmen of Clonmeen and other inhabitants in the area mentioned in the Duhallow Historical Journal clearly view nineteenth century North Cork as colonial, and as dominated by the landowning class. The unrestricted use of this territory for hunting and shooting parties was a tangible sign of this domination. This view is rooted in their own experiences, interpretation and ideas. In contrast, Esther Chichester, Stephen Grehan and their children attribute a different meaning to their hunting and shooting practices. These activities were prominent in their daily lives, were personally enjoyable and any disturbance of this leisure pursuit of the elite and powerful was disapproved of. Judging further from Stephen Grehan's support for the Unionist cause and Stephen Arthur Grehan's membership of the British Army, one can draw the conclusion that they both considered Ireland in the nineteenth century and early twentieth century to be an integral part of Great Britain. They expressed conformity with British values, pursued British careers and moved in British social circles. This sense of belonging to – as in being part of – the motherland and Empire, whether Irish or British, was also conveyed through cultural practices and social networks when hunting and shooting.

It is difficult to assess how directly Esther Chichester or working women at Clonmeen were involved in shaping or expressing this kind of political commitment since there is no explicit evidence in the sources. The marriages of some of Esther and Stephen's daughters with members of the British Army are a hint at female support and agreement with this loyalty.

In any case, the actions of the subjects of this analysis were consistent with and enhanced colonial structures and social relations. On the other hand, these same actions tended to intensify local protest against these established structures.

Additional research could investigate to what extent both groups knew of the other's experiences, ideas and convictions. In what way did communication take place in the 'contact zone'? Were opinions negotiated or did they simply co-exist due to a lack of communication?

While all actions at Clonmeen were related to their particular contexts, they were still based on individual perceptions and consequent individual decisions. This applied to Father O'Riordan exercising his hounds on the Grehan estate as well as to Stephen Arthur Grehan's imperial tiger hunt. As the records of the Grehan family show, individuals actively participated in representing themselves in the public and private spheres, and in emotional and rational matters, sometimes developing their role rather than merely fulfilling their allotted place. Nevertheless, although he largely despised the operation of local politics, Stephen Grehan took up the role assigned. Likewise, Esther Chichester's presence at shooting parties underlined her public role.

A microhistorical approach can reveal the impact of colonial structures on the private and public worlds of individuals as well as the impact of individuals on these structures. Individuals shape their social realities in such a way as to identify with or adhere to a desired social group.[96]

NOTES

1. *The Private Diary: Arranged, Printed, and Ruled, for Receiving an Account of Every day's Employment, for the Space of One Year: with an Index and Appendix* (9th edn, London: John Taylor, Bookseller and Publisher to the University of London, [1830]), title page. It was kept daily in 1830 by an unknown person. Ryan of Inch Family Papers, University College Cork, Boole Library Archives Service, National University of Ireland, Cork.
2. National University of Ireland, Cork, Boole Library Archives Service, Descriptive List of Boole Library/Estate Papers/Grehan – this will be abbreviated: 'BL/EP/G'. '[...]' stands for deliberate omissions whereas '[...?]' means that these parts of the document were not readable and thus caused omissions. *T. J. & J. Smith's Scribbling Diary with Almanack for 1882.* (London), Stephen Grehan, BL/EP/G 737.
3. See *The Private Diary*.
4. 'Appropriate goods' – this notion carries double significance: they reflect expectations and conventions of contemporary society and they are material possessions ('*Appropriate:* 'to make one's own', from the Latin *proprius*, 'proper', 'property', J. Clifford, 'Collecting ourselves', in:

S.M. Pearce (ed.), *Interpreting Objects and Collections* (London: Routledge, 1994), p. 261.
5. Social reality is the '*Produkt aus der triadischen Interaktion Mensch-Mensch-Umwelt*' (G. Rosenthal, 'Geschichte in der Lebensgeschichte', *BIOS- Zeitschrift für Biographieforschung und Oral History*, 2 (1988), p. 7); and '*die Gesamtheit der Perspektiven in ihren Wechselbeziehungen zueinander*' (G.H. Mead, 'Die objektive Realität von Perspektiven', quoted in: G. Rosenthal, 'Geschichte in der Lebensgeschichte', p. 10).
6. I agree with Rosenthal, who understands the individual as a producer and product of collective and individual history. See Rosenthal, 'Geschichte in der Lebensgeschichte', p. 5. Ginzburg aptly speaks of a permeable ego, i.e. of connected inner and outer worlds. See C. Ginzburg, 'Mikro-Historie. Zwei oder drei Dinge, die ich von ihr weiß', *Historische Anthropologie*, 1 (1993), p. 192.
7. This function became redundant when Clonmeen House and estate was sold in the 1970s – the subsequent donation emphasises this crucial rupture and loss.
8. Ideas about material culture are relevant in the case of archival documents. Photographs are immediate consumer goods whereas other archival 'texts' reveal aspects of material culture. The Grehan Papers as an entity are a possession and in this way a 'good'. "Consumer goods" meanings could be shaped over a potentially long life, not merely the moment of purchase, raising questions of motivation and the qualitative aspects of desirability', P. Glennie, 'Consumption within Historical Studies' in D. Miller (ed.), *Acknowledging Consumption. A Review of New Studies* (London and New York: Routledge, 1995), p. 178.
9. Note the difference to the other related genre 'collection': 'One of the distinctions between "possessing" and "collecting" is that the latter implies order, system, perhaps completion,' N. Aristides, 'Calm and uncollected', *American Scholar*, 57, 3 (1988), p. 330, quoted in: S.M. Pearce, 'The urge to collect', in S. M. Pearce (ed.), *Interpreting Objects and Collections* (London and New York: Routledge, 1994), p. 158.
10. C. Quinn, *Descriptive List Grehan Family Papers*, University College Cork, Boole Library Archives Service, National University of Ireland, Cork.
11. Cf. N. Goswani, 'Public and Private', at Postcolonial Studies at Emory (http://www.emory.edu/english/bahri/pub.html), Fall 1996, p. 1.
12. Cf. C.R. Chichester, *Irish Landlordism*, reprinted from the *Dublin University Review* (Dublin: Sealy, Bryers and Walker, 1887), BL/EP/G 505. He refers to a publication of the same year by Father Finlay, *Rent and the Payment of Rent*.
13. See Quinn, 'Introduction', *Descriptive List Grehan Family Papers*, pp. I-II.
14. J. Böröcz, 'Travel-Capitalism: The Structure of Europe and the Advent of the Tourist', *Comparative Studies in Society and History*, 34 (1992), p. 710.
15. F.M.L. Thompson, 'Britain', in D. Spring (ed.), *European Landed Elites in the Nineteenth Century* (Baltimore, MD: John Hopkins University Press, 1977), p. 30.
16. *Purcell's Commercial Cork Almanac* (Cork: Purcell & Company, 1858), p. 67; *Purcell's Commercial Cork Almanac* (Cork: Purcell & Company, 1877), p. 95; *Francis Guy's County & City of Cork Directory 1875–1876 (Cork: Guy and Co., 1879).*
17. Award to Stephen Grehan in 1879, BL/EP/G 800; Commission as Deputy Lieutenant, award for Stephen Grehan, 23 Feb. 1888, BL/EP/G 801.
18. *Burke's Landed Gentry of Ireland* (10th edn, London: Harrison & Sons, 1904), p. 235.
19. '*Nov 82* Grehan with Chichester, Copy Head of Settlement by intended husband. W Roche & Sons, 4 Stephen's Green', BL/EP/G 201(11).
20. L. Gibbons, 'Ireland and the Colonization of Theory', *Interventions*, 1, 1 (1998/89), p. 27.
21. Cf. J. Grove White, *Historiographical and topographical notes, etc. on Buttevant, Castletownroche, Doneraile, Mallow, and places in their vicinity*, Vol. 1 (Cork: Guy & Company, 1905), pp. 278–9; Vol. 2 (Cork: Guy & Company, 1911), pp. 219, 222, 223, 225, 228, 231, 235, 236.
22. W. Petty, *Hiberniæ Delineatio quod hactenus licuit perfectissima (1683)*. (Newcastle on Tyne: Frank Graham, 1968 - first edition reprinted)
23. M.L. Pratt, *Imperial Eyes. Studies in Travel Writing (*London: Routledge, 1992), p. 6. Structures of power and rule are outlined in the essay 'Herrschaft als soziale Praxis' by A. Lüdtke, in A. Lüdtke (ed.), *Herrschaft als soziale Praxis. Historische und sozialanthropologische Studien (*Göttingen: Vandenhoeck & Ruprecht, 1991), pp. 9–66.
24. See Pratt, *Imperial Eyes*, p. 7.
25. J. Clifford described museums as contact zones and to some extent this serves for archives as well. J. Clifford, 'Museums as Contact Zones', in J. Clifford (Ed.), *Routes. Travel and Translation in the late twentieth century (*Cambridge, MA and London: Harvard University Press, 1997), pp.

188–219. It can be argued that Ireland had reached a post-colonial situation with its integration into the United Kingdom in the nineteenth century but the developments in the early twentieth century point to a self-perception of the Irish as colonial in the nineteenth century.

26. Important microhistorical studies are D.W. Sabean, *Property, production, and family in Neckarhausen, 1700–1870* (Cambridge: Cambridge University Press, 1990) and R. Isaac, *The Transformation of Virginia. 1740–1790* (Williamsburg, VA: The University of North Carolina Press, 1982).

27. See Gibbons, 'Ireland and the Colonization of Theory', p. 27.

28. Cf. N.P. Canny, 'The Ideology of English Colonization: From Ireland to America', *William and Mary Quarterly*, 30 (1973), pp. 575–98.

29. See Ginzburg, 'Mikro-Historie', pp. 175, 179, 181, 183. Also H. Medick, 'Mikro-Historie', in W. Schulze (ed.), *Sozialgeschichte, Alltagsgeschichte, Mikro-Historie* (Göttingen: Vandenhoeck & Ruprecht, 1994), p. 43.

30. 'Doing ethnography [i.e. "thick description"] is like trying to read (in the sense of "construct a reading of") a manuscript – foreign, faded, full of ellipses, incoherencies, suspicious emendations, and tendentious commentaries, but written not in conventionalized graphs of sound but in transient examples of shaped behaviour.' C. Geertz, 'Thick Description: toward an interpretative theory of culture', in C. Geertz (Ed.), *The Interpretation of Cultures* (No place: Basic Books, 1973), p. 9–10, 20, 28, 30.

31. 'Social reality' is a 'Produkt aus der triadischen Interaktion Mensch-Mensch-Umwelt'; see Rosenthal, 'Geschichte in der Lebensgeschichte', p. 7; and Ginzburg, 'Mikro-Historie', p. 185.

32. See Ginzburg, 'Mikro-Historie', p. 185.

33. E.W. Said, *Culture and Imperialism* (London: Vintage, 1994), p. 1.

34. P. Bourdieu, 'Die gesellschaftliche Definition der Photographie', in P. Bourdieu et al., *Eine illegitime Kunst. Die sozialen Gebrauchsweisen der Photographie* (Frankfurt: Suhrkamp Verlag, 1983), pp. 85, 93–5.

35. P.A. Stokowski, *Leisure in Society. A Network Structural Perspective* (London and New York: Mansell, 1994), p. 4. She proposes to develop a sociology of leisure by asking 'how are the relations between social actors [...] patterned for leisure, and what do the relational patterns in this social environment mean for the behaviors and feelings of the actors involved?' (p. 8). This question is related to this analysis but too narrow when concentrating on the concept of leisure and social actors.

36. Peter A. Grehan, 'The Code of a Gentleman', not published, 1997, p. 1.

37. Correspondence with Peter A. Grehan, 17 July 1999.

38. Cf. ibid., and P. Somerville-Large, *The Irish Country House. A Social History* (London: Sinclair-Stevenson, 1995), pp. 338–9.

39. 'Notebook containing daily diary entries by Esther Chichester Grehan [...]', 31 July 1888–29 November 1889, BL/EP/G 837.

40. See Somerville-Large, *The Irish Country House*, p. 339.

41. *Small Scribbling Diary with Almanack for 1874* (London), Stephen Grehan, BL/EP/G 729.

42. Cf. also Correspondence with Peter A. Grehan, 17 July 1999.

43. See Somerville-Large, *The Irish Country House*, p. 338.

44. Notebook of Stephen Grehan, then used as game list 1875–79, BL/EP/G 359; 'Notebook recording details of game shot, 1876–1892', BL/EP/G 360 (catches of fish were also recorded); 'Game book, 1894–1912', BL/EP/G 361.

45. See 'Notebook recording details of game shot, 1876–1892'.

46. See Somerville-Large, *The Irish Country House*, p. 329.

47. See *T. J. & J. Smith's Small Scribbling Diary with Almanack for 1882* (London).

48. Esther Chichester at Old Court, Doneraile, to Stephen Grehan, 12 November 1882, BL/EP/G 681.

49. *Lett's Rough Diary or Scribbling Journal for 1893* (London, Paris and Melbourne), Esther Chichester, BL/EP/G 838.

50. The Grehan Papers certify his membership at least from 1887–1921; in 1890 Stephen Grehan was Honorary Secretary.

51. The Family Journal was compiled by the Grehans and families they were related to or friendly with. In particular, the generation of Esther's and Stephen's children collected and wrote articles on social events in this handwritten journal which was then circulated among the families.

52. There is no indication in the Grehan Papers that girls and women had gained at this later point of time access to active shooting participation.

53. Family Journal, Issue No. 5, Feb. 1903, BL/EP/G 1392, pp. 18–19.

54. *T. J. & J. Smith's small scribbling Diary with an Almanack for 1877* (London), Stephen Grehan, BL/EP/G 732.

55. This is one brief notice of recent events among others that were collected on the first pages of the journal. It refers to the same dance as May Grehan described above; Family Journal, Issue No. 8, May 1903, BL/EP/G 1393, p. 2.

56. Cf. N. Goswani, 'Public and Private', at Postcolonial Studies at Emory (http://www.emory.edu/english/bahri/pub.html), Fall 1996, p. 1.

57. *T. J. & J. Smith's small scribbling diary with Almanack for 1880*, Stephen Grehan, BL/EP/G 735.

58. See Grehan, 'The Code of a Gentleman', p. 1.

59. Notebook detailing items given to workmen at Christmas and other occasions, begun by Esther Grehan, 1887–1917, 24 December 1907, BL/EP/G 307 (23).

60. Family Journal, Issue No. 11, Sept.1903, BL/EP/G 1395, p. 17.

61. 'Women, in particular, used consumer goods both to establish their families' abstract attributes (status, lineage), much as men used land, and to recognise and negotiate personal qualities of taste, sociability and worth. Their wills consistently reveal a self-conscious, emotional involvement in household goods, clothing and personal effects. Such intensity of meaning appears only occasionally among men, and is largely restricted to guns and animals.' P. Glennie, 'Consumption within Historical Studies', p. 179.

62. Letter from Stephen Grehan to George Grehan, Zermatt, 4 Aug. 1877, BL/EP/G 598.

63. Cf. quotes from Grehan family members of different generations. H. Medick & D. Sabean, 'Emotionen und materielle Interessen in Familie und Verwandtschaft: Überlegungen zu neuen Wegen und Bereichen einer historischen und sozialanthropologischen Familienforschung', in H. Medick and D. Sabean (eds), *Emotionen und materielle Interessen: sozialanthropologische und historische Beiträge zur Familienforschung* (Göttingen: Vandenhoeck & Ruprecht, 1984), pp. 35–45.

64. A. McClintock, *Imperial Leather. Race, Gender and Sexuality in the Colonial Contest* (New York: Routledge, 1995), p. 126.

65. Cf. ibid.: 'The immobility of the sitter conceals behind the surface of the photograph the violence of the colonial encounter.'

66. A. Farge, *Le Goût de l'archive* (Paris: Éditions du Seuil, 1989), pp. 15–16.

67. 'Material Culture invested with new meanings linked social characterisation to everyday cultural practices, through consumer goods' availability to express wealth (through accumulation of goods); social standing (through differentiation in possessions); and cultural position (where particular possessions 'flagged' certain cultural discourses).' P. Glennie, 'Consumption within Historical Studies', p. 178.

68. Esther Chichester at Old Court, Doneraile, to Stephen Grehan, 18 October 1882, BL/EP/G 664.

69. L.P. Curtis Jr, 'Stopping the Hunt, 1881–1882: an Aspect of the Irish Land War', in C. H.E. Philpin (ed.), *Nationalism and Popular Protest in Ireland* (Cambridge: Cambridge University Press, 1987), p. 391.

70. See Curtis Jr, 'Stopping the Hunt', pp. 349–402.

71. Ibid., p. 402.

72. Ibid., p. 376; and M.J. Winstanley, *Ireland and the Land Question, 1800–1922* (London and New York: Methuen 1984), p. 29.

73. S. O Nunain, 'The Land League Hunt', *Seanchas Duthalla* (1989), p. 55.

74. Ibid.

75. Cf. above: 'I. Contexts – The archive'.

76. Pratt, *Imperial Eyes*, p. 6.

77. This does not imply that conflict does not take place in contact zones. Cf. the notion of 'conflict zone': Clifford, 'Museums as Contact Zones', p. 207.

78. 'The Landlord', typewritten manuscript by: John F. Sheehan, Banteer, from the late Jeremiah Sheehan, Banteer and Michael Sheehan, Inchidaly. Donald Lehane, Banteer, from Joseph Lehane, Banteer, 8 Oct. 1938, p. 24.

79. See 'Notebook recording details of game shot, 1876–1892' BL/EP/G 360.

80. 'The Landlord', typewritten manuscript by: John F. Sheehan, Banteer, from the late Jeremiah Sheehan, Banteer and Michael Sheehan, Inchidaly. Donald Lehane, Banteer, from Joseph

Lehane, Banteer, 8/10/1938, pp. 23–5.

81. *Lett's No 33 Rough Diary 1893* (London, Paris and Melbourne), Stephen Grehan, BL/EP/G 747.

82. *Walker's Year by Year Book. A condensed, comparative record for five years, for recording events most worthy of remembrance* (London), 1932–36, Stephen Arthur Grehan, BL/EP/G 923.

83. The materiality of history as our inherited legacy brings out two of the main branches of material culture studies. The first of which is the study of historical artefacts and the second lies in the wider connotations of the term materialism.' Editorial, *Journal of Material Culture*, 1, 1 (1996), p. 3.

84. 'A Christmas Eve Tiger', *W. 4 Writing efforts*, [no date], Stephen Arthur Grehan, BL/EP/G 548.

85. See Curtis Jr, 'Stopping the Hunt, 1881–1882', p. 402.

86. Medick and Sabean mention the '*Scharnierfunktion der Familie*' for social differentiation: Medick & Sabean, 'Emotionen und materielle Interessen in Familie und Verwandtschaft', p. 48.

87. K. Jeffery, 'Introduction', in K. Jeffery (ed.), *'An Irish Empire'? Aspects of Ireland and the British Empire* (Manchester and New York: Manchester University Press, 1996), p. 17.

88. Cf. the essay by T.G. Fraser, '"Ireland and India"' on their relations within the British Empire, in: K. Jeffery (ed.), *'An Irish Empire'? Aspects of Ireland and the British Empire*, pp. 77–93.

89. Cf. A.J. Cornwell, Hon. Obituarist, 'Major S. A. Grehan', *The Oratory School Magazine*, 132 (1972), p. 119.

90. Letter from Stephen Arthur Grehan, Mesopotamia, to Stephen Grehan, 19 May 1920, BL/EP/G 1166.

91. Letter from Stephen Arthur Grehan, Mesopotamia, to Stephen Grehan, 2 July 1920, BL/EP/G 1166a.

92. 'But the Empire as a vital and viable system was not always irrelevant to Irish people or Irish concerns, nationalist or Unionist. Ireland, as part of the metropolitan core of the Empire, supplied many soldiers, settlers and administrators.' – K. Jeffery, 'Introduction', in K. Jeffery (ed.), *'An Irish Empire'? Aspects of Ireland and the British Empire*, p. 1.

93. *Charles Letts Self Opening Diary, 1932*, Stephen Grehan, BL/EP/G 786.

94. Letter from Cecily Gaisford St. Lawrence to Magda Grehan, 16 Feb. 1932, BL/EP/G 873.

95. It is important to note that there is no positive evidence the Grehans were without oral traditions nor is the non-existence of other written sources in the Clonmeen locality a certainty.

96. Cf. the attraction of closeness to power and 'Eigensinn', which affected solidarity with rule as well as resistance; A. Lüdtke, 'Geschichte und Eigensinn', in: *Alltagskultur, Subjektivität und Geschichte*, edited by Berliner Geschichtswerkstatt (Münster: Westfälisches Dampfboot, 1994), pp. 143, 151.

CHAPTER EIGHT

The Sinews of Empire: Ireland, India and the Construction of British Colonial Knowledge

TONY BALLANTYNE

The question of Ireland's relationship to Britain and Britain's imperial project stands at the heart of recent debates over revisionist approaches to the interpretation of the Irish past. Ireland's exact status within the empire, the role of British dominance in Irish 'underdevelopment', and Britain's place in the definition of Irish identities are not only difficult questions of historical interpretation but also are the heart of competing visions of Ireland's present and future. In the early 1990s, Francis Fukuyama might have proclaimed that the collapse of European communism and the end of the Cold War marked the 'death of history' in an age of globalization, but the Irish public's sustained interest in the past and the heated nature of recent scholarly exchanges over 'revisionism' suggests that in the Irish case history continues to occupy a central place in political and cultural life.[1]

Critics of revisionism have reacted to what they see as a 'cynical' debunking of national heroes and a systematic attempt to discredit the Irish nationalist tradition.[2] For Brendan Bradshaw, revisionism has been characterised by an 'invincible' and 'corrosive scepticism' and an 'inquisitorial approach'.[3] Bradshaw argues that the role of the historian of Ireland is to produce a 'holistic' present-centred public history that traces the development of, and thereby fortifies, the nation.[4] The historian, in Bradshaw's view, becomes the myth-maker for the national community, detailing the catastrophic nature of the Irish past and celebrating the heroic resistance of its rebels and nationalist leadership. This heavily teleological narrative celebrates Ireland's achievement of independence as the culmination of a 'national consciousness' that (we are told) was at least a millennium old and affirms Ireland's supposedly unique status as a European colony which was able to throw off its imperial oppressor.[5]

Bradshaw's privileging of national history not only silences important local traditions and identities, but also profoundly dislocates Irish history from its broader contexts. National and nationalistic histories have the inherent tendency to remove the unit of study from the complex networks and global forces that condition its nature and shape its development. In his important critique of Eurocentric history Eric Wolf argued that: 'Concepts like "nation," "society," and "culture" name bits and threaten to turn names into things. Only by understanding these names as bundles of relationships, and by placing them back into the fields from which they were abstracted, can we hope to avoid misleading inferences and increase our share of understanding.' Most importantly, Wolf warned that nations function like analytical 'billiard-balls': they are seen as self-contained and clearly delineated objects which occasionally collide with other nations (in wars or revolutions) but remain essentially unaltered: national histories reify and homogenise their objects of study.[6]

Moreover, a narrow focus on the development of national consciousness has led to an overemphasis on nationalist resistance and struggle and Irish history is then reduced to a series of English atrocities and Irish rebellions, ultimately leading to independence. Within such an analytical tradition, history is narrated through the lens of the 'national(ist) struggle', an approach that implicitly designates much of everyday life, popular culture and cultural mentalities as irrelevant to the national past. Moreover, this focus on resistance, which is also common in the historiographies of colonial India and Australasia, can obscure as much as it reveals. The full range of responses to British expansion, including accommodation, adaptation, apathy and collaboration as well as resistance and cultural persistence, have to be recovered.[7] A sensitivity to Ireland's role in the British imperial state's sinews of power – its crucial role as a food-supplier, military recruiting ground and 'model colony' – must balance attempts to recover, what David Lloyd terms, the 'occult spaces' of cultural resistance and 'living on'.

Thus simple national or coloniser-colonised models are incapable of charting the multiple positions and shifting significance of Ireland within the global networks created by British imperialism. Although the Act of Union in 1801 marked the formal end of Ireland's status as a dependent kingdom and provided for substantial parliamentary representation in London, Ireland remained under the control of a 'colonial' style administration: the Lord-Lieutenant oversaw an administration which exercised increasingly centralised authority and deployed sophisticated tools of surveillance and coercion, most notably in the form of the Irish Constabulary (founded in 1836). The geopolitical prominence of garrison towns and the continued presence of English- and Scottish-born troops created an atmosphere of 'occupation' and 'colonisation' and this was further reinforced by the imperial mentalities of the administration. As David Fitzpatrick has observed: 'Ireland's rulers [in the nineteenth century], whether grim or benevolent, tended to regard the Irish as a separate and subject native population rather than an integral element of a united people.'[8] The partial and incomplete nature of the Union and the continued emphasis on Ireland's otherness, brought home most forcibly in the popular simian stereotypes of the nineteenth-century press, underpinned Ireland's multiple positions within the British colonial system. At once metropolitan and colonial, Ireland's status was often ambivalent, frequently double-natured: it enjoyed parliamentary representation but was subject to a coercive regime; after 1801 Ireland was part of an parliamentary Union but nevertheless functioned as a testing ground for systems of control and suppression later deployed in distant colonies, and throughout the nineteenth century the Irish, although supposedly a component of a unified 'British' people, were identified as racial 'Others' and were frequently compared to 'lowly' Africans.

But surveying Ireland's status within the empire requires us not only to consider whether Ireland fulfilled the criteria for it to be designated a colony, but we must also locate its place within the broader dynamic of British empire-building. This means, of course, we have to examine not only Ireland's absorption into, and role in sustaining, Britain's imperial 'military-fiscal' state, but also its relationships with the other components of the British imperial system. Of course there is a huge literature focusing on one aspect of these relationships: Irish migration to British settler colonies (or former colonies in the case of the United States) and the construction of diasporic communities. But migration is only the most obvious of these imperial ties. Given the prominent role of Irish Catholic missionaries in the Christianisation of parts of Asia, Africa and the Pacific, especially those areas under British influence, the place of Ireland's Roman Catholic community within an empire that was frequently seen as a bulwark against Popery and irreligion requires careful reconsideration. Equally pressing, however, is the need to recover the intellectual networks and values that linked the empire together: what Andrew Porter has recently termed the 'empires of the mind'.[9]

Transnational and cross-cultural approaches, which locate Irish development in contexts that transcend or cut across the borders of the modern nation, are well developed in the historiography of early modern Ireland. Steven Ellis has stressed that late fifteenth-century and sixteenth-century Ireland must be interpreted within the wider context of Tudor courtly politics and state-building. Ellis has argued that the Tudor period witnessed the construction of a 'second Tudor kingdom which was co-extensive with the island of Ireland and its inhabitants.' This project has led Ellis to rethink the basic terminological and analytical frameworks for Tudor Ireland, a research agenda which has stimulated an ongoing debate.[10] While Ellis's preferred interpretative unit is the 'British Isles', several historians, most notably Nicholas Canny, have placed early modern Ireland in the broader context of the construction of a British Atlantic world. In this approach the colonisation of Ireland is seen as part of Britain's 'westward enterprise', a system of trade, migration and knowledge-circulation where images and ideologies were actively transplanted from Ireland to British North America.[11]

Some isolated studies have made similar arguments for a later period, as they have suggested that Ireland was particularly prominent as a centre of intellectual and governmental innovation in Britain's second empire (*c*.1765–1870). Given its proximity to Britain and its importance in domestic British politics Ireland was a site where important debates over the nature of religion and peasant communities were waged and new forms of governance and control were developed. For several generations historians emphasised that the 'Irish model' of policing that emerged in the post-Union period was fundamental to patterns of discipline and government throughout the empire.[12] Richard Hawkins has demonstrated the shortcomings of such a sweeping view; nevertheless he also establishes the flexibility and popularity of the Royal Irish Constabulary as a reference point in debates over policing throughout the empire, including India.[13] More importantly, S.B. Cook has clearly established the centrality of Ireland as a reference point in land-policy formation in India, as British administrators (but also Indian and British news-paper men, pamphleteers and polemicists) fashioned an explicitly comparative discourse laden with analogies and comparisons between Ireland and India.[14] Cook's work reaffirmed the earlier studies of Clive Dewey that sketched the importance of the British tradition of political economy and the 'rehabilitation of the peasant proprietor' that underpinned the marrying of Ireland and India in British debates over tradition and social structure.[15] More recently still, C.A. Bayly has reconnected Irish and India historiographies in an important lecture that explored the possibility of a 'connective' or 'comparative' imperial histo-ry that examines both the construction and dismantling of British authority in India and Ireland within a common analytical framework.[16]

Although the links between Indian and Irish nationalisms have been thor-oughly explored, Hawkins, Cook, Dewey and Bayly provide numerous exam-ples of the various ideologies and networks which tied Ireland and India together within the British imperial system.[17] From the mid-eighteenth cen-tury until the middle of this century elaborate webs of military recruitment, intellectual exchange and political interdependence joined Ireland and India. These networks were imperial in nature; they were a complex set of relation-ships engendered by British expansion into Asia from the mid-eighteenth cen-tury on, as British imperial ambitions gradually 'swung to the east' after the loss of the American colonies. Although the Irish continued to play a visible and important role in the Atlantic empire, this new eastward drive created fresh opportunities for Irish people of various religious and social backgrounds. The Irish were prominent colonial servants in India, playing a crucial role as soldiers, doctors, and administrators: indeed at least four Irishmen rose to the position of Viceroy or Governor-General. The prominence of these servants of the British empire was such that many nineteenth- century English commen-tators complained that India was subject to an 'Irish Raj'.

But Keith Jeffery has recently warned that simply cataloguing such con-nections may not 'materially advance our understanding. Indeed it may simply be a contribution to the "just fancy that" school of history'.[18] This is an impor-tant point and it is a warning frequently disregarded by a range of historians, amateur and professional, over the last sixty years.[19] Here I hope to venture beyond the 'just fancy that' approach of identifying Irishmen who rose to power or fame in India, or noting some of the connections between Irish and Indian nationalists, to focus on the role of Irish administrators in the production of knowledge regarding Indian society. Recent Indian historiography has stressed the importance of knowledge communities in the construction of British hegemony, and this study attempts to examine the influence of Irish antiquarians, folklorists and linguists in the British imperial system. The remainder of this study has two parts: the first examines the genesis of these Irish-Indian connections from the 1780s through to the mid-nineteenth century, focusing upon the strong connections that linked Celticism and Orientalism as discourses of governance and cultural analysis. The second part of the piece explores the Irish role in the construction of British colonial knowledge about India, sketching the position of Irish universities as training-grounds for imperial service and the role of these Irish-trained scholar-administrators in India during the final decades of the nineteenth century.

Although academic nationalist interpretations and many popular views of the Irish past stress the turbulent and violent nature of the British–Irish relationship, seeing Ireland as a 'restless dominion', it seems that despite the heightening tensions of the late eighteenth century many Irish leaders were intent on political reform rather than bloody revolution. It was the inequities and sectarian nature of the state that was under attack, rather than the state itself.[20] Political and economic ties with Britain were very important for most sectors of Irish society and the British empire assumed greater economic and social significance for many Irish people: R.B. McDowell has suggested that in this period 'Irish men were very conscious of belonging to the empire'.[21] The rapid expansion of British imperial holdings in Asia and the Pacific after the loss of the American colonies generated considerable interest, even amongst sworn enemies of the Dublin administration. Thus, for example, we find Theobald Wolfe Tone excitedly writing to the Duke of Richmond in 1790, suggesting the foundation of a British military colony in the 'Sandwich Islands' [Hawai'i]. Tone argued that such a base would allow the British to harry Spanish galleons sailing from the Peruvian coast to Manila, provide a new staging station for the trans-Pacific fur trade, function as a potential plantation-colony and serve as a base for a British attack on the west coast of South America, which Tone was certain would fall to the 'first bold invader'.[22] C.A. Bayly has observed that Tone's proposal reminds us that 'a desire to participate in British imperial ventures at this time was in no way incompatible with revolutionary nationalist aims'.[23] This plan not only reflected Tone's hopes that England would 'cut the very sinews of Spanish commerce' (echoing a long tradition of anti-Catholic and anti-Spanish feeling dating back to the days of Drake), but also his profound interest in Britain's empire. An avid reader, he digested newly published discussions of the Pacific and South America produced by British explorers such as Anson and Cook in addition to the accounts of 'the Bucaniers' who were his 'heroes'; and he took great delight in visiting East India Company ships at Deptford.[24] His brother and fellow-enthusiast William Henry Tone was a pioneering ethnologist in India, producing two important accounts of the Maratha military and political system that the East India Company was intent on overthrowing.[25]

That William Henry Tone should make an notable contribution to the 'military orientalism' which influenced the military strategy of the East India Company is not really as surprising as it may at first seem, as by the close of the eighteenth century Irish intellectual life increasingly operated within a globalized analytical framework created by British imperial expansion. The drive of the British merchants, navy and army into Asia and the Pacific was dependent on the collection of information regarding the new regions and peoples that fell under British influence. Recent historians have made it clear that British expansion was dependent on intelligence-gathering, the 'turning' of indigenous networks of communication and the construction of new forms of knowledge control and dissemination: the sinews of empire included postal systems, printing presses, learned societies and colleges as well as the army, police and law courts.[26] While the 'discovery' of the indigenous communities of the Americas broadened European horizons, it was only with the new wave of European expansion into the Pacific and the interior of Asia that a truly global information order was born as the last major gaps in the 'great map of mankind' were filled in.[27] From the late seventeenth century European intellectual and cultural life was stimulated by the encounter with the Asia-Pacific region: chinoiserie and an admiration for Confucianism was followed by an 'Oriental [or more particularly an Indian] renaissance', and a 'Pacific craze'.[28] These cosmopolitan discourses focused on the renovating potential of the exotic, stressing that European culture might be revivified through an engagement with 'purer', more 'simple' social forms.

Ireland was woven into these Enlightenment discourses on cultural difference as there was a sufficient cultural and economic disjunction between Ireland and England for it to be seen as 'exotic' and 'other'. English readers, it seems, were as taken with descriptions of Gaelic bards and great Celtic warriors, as they were with descriptions of Hindu holy men, Muslim despots and dusky Pacific maidens. But such exoticism, a striking element of these Enlightenment texts, provided the 'local colour' within a series of discourses which were essentially comparative as they traced shared cultural features and common patterns of historical development. The two most important models that shaped British understandings of world history in the late eighteenth century, 'Mosaic ethnology' and the Scottish philosophical history tradition, both asserted the fundamental unity of humanity and structured nature of history.[29] Under these influences even the most exotic and seemingly unique of practices were in fact familiar: for example, the Hindu gods Brahma, Vishnu and Shiva were, in fact, the Trinity, and the druids of Britain were the representatives of a pan-Oriental form of Buddhism which supposedly stretched from Egypt to Southeast Asia.[30]

The strength of this comparative sensibility is clearly seen in the work of Charles Vallancey, who was one of the first to marry Celticism and Orientalism. The English-born son of Huguenot émigrés and a leading military engineer (and later Chief Surveyor of Ireland), Vallancey attempted to create a rich archive documenting Irish history and culture. Vallancey, whose ethnology was moulded by the continued importance of the monogenism of the Christian framework as well as Enlightenment cosmopolitanism, believed that the analysis of the Irish past was best undertaken in a comparative light. In his *Vindication of the Ancient History of Ireland* (1786), Vallancey argued that Irish culture exhibited profound affinities with a range of 'Eastern' traditions. On the basis of manuscript sources and extensive comparative vocabularies, Vallancey asserted that the Irish were in fact Pheno-Scythians who had migrated from the Caspian Sea to Ireland via Persia, Africa and Spain. As such the Irish could boast a proud cultural heritage that stretched back to the dawn of civilisation. This, of course, had political implications that were made even clearer when Vallancey drew parallels between the Irish experience of English domination and the destruction of Carthaginian culture by the Romans.[31]

Although modern historians have tended to dismiss Vallancey's ethnology as speculative and amateurish, his work operated within well-established norms of European scholarship and reflected the growth of intellectual networks that spanned the empire. By the late eighteenth century, British colonial knowledge was never simply a product of the particular factors operating in a specific colony; rather it was shaped by broader networks of intellectual exchange, against the backdrop of the shifting patterns of metropolitan ideologies and intellectual fashions. While Celticists like Vallancey and Joseph Cooper Walker were dependent on 'native learning' and local informants, their work was also profoundly shaped by their engagement with British Orientalism.[32] Vallancey's early work was influenced by the work of Sir William Jones's studies of Persian and drew heavily upon the work of William Marsden and J.Z. Holwell on Asian history. If anything his engagement with British Orientalism grew over time, as his later *The Ancient History of Ireland, Proved from the Sanscrit Books of the Bramins of India* (1797) was moulded by the notorious work of the Sanskritist Francis Wilford on Indian geographical knowledge.[33] But Vallancey's engagement with Orientalist learning was not unique; it fact other leading figures in Irish intellectual life had close ties with India. Edmund Burke, of course, was prominent in debates over the East India Company and was a frequent correspondent of Sir William Jones, while the leading Irish antiquarian Joseph Cooper Walker also exchanged ideas about Irish and Indian music with Jones, parallels which he examined in his *Historical Memoirs of the Irish Bards*.[34]

As related bodies of knowledge, both Orientalism and Celticism were discourses of governance grounded in the desire to understand a (subject) people who were now under British authority. The East India Company's Bengal administration was reluctant to impose alien systems of law and administration on the 20 million subjects it was responsible for after 1765. Hastings insisted that Indians should be governed by their own laws and argued that 'in all suits regarding inheritance, marriage, caste and other religious usages and institutions' the correct Muslim and Hindu legal traditions should be 'invariably adhered to'. Nathaniel Brassey Halhed, a leading Orientalist in the Company's employ, suggested that 'a well-timed toleration in matters of religion, and an adoption of such original institutes of the country, as do not immediately clash with the laws or interests of the conqueror' would strengthen the Company's authority.[35] These East India Company men believed that Orientalist knowledge would also facilitate a richer appreciation of Indian culture in addition to a deeper attachment to empire. Warren Hastings maintained that Britons 'should not fear to place, in opposition to the best French versions of the most admired passages of the Iliad or Odyssey, or of the 1st and 6th Books of our own Milton, highly as I venerate the latter, the English translation of the Mahabharat'.[36] Moreover, he hoped, the publication of accounts of Indian language, philosophy and religion 'will impress us [the British] with a more generous sense of feeling for their natural rights'.[37]

Celticists were also articulating similar arguments in the late eighteenth century. What is striking about the development of Celticism in this period is the heavy interdependence between a strengthening interest in antiquarianism and philology and the political agenda of the Patriots. This group of leading Protestants were resentful of the restrictions imposed by London on Irish trade (especially within the empire) and the limited opportunities for the Irish-born in British and imperial administrations. The Patriots hoped to win commercial freedom, significant constitutional concessions and cultural respect from London. Sylvester O'Halloran, a leading Patriot antiquarian and physician, stated that his *Introduction to the Study of the History and Antiquities of Ireland* was motivated by a 'natural reverence for the dignity and antiquity of my native country' which he saw as Ireland rather than Britain, and suggested his work was a response to English and Scottish authors who represented the 'Irish nation as the most brutal and savage of mankind, destitute of arts, letters, and legislation'.[38] Vallancey, of course, had elaborated a defence of Irish cultural achievement in his *A Vindication of the Ancient History of Ireland* by claiming a long and glorious lineage for Gaelic culture. The influential Patriot Lawrence Parsons, who defended Vallancey's scholarship, hoped that the project pursued by Vallancey and other antiquarians would 'relieve this country from the unjust charges of ignorance and barbarism'.[39] Thus these Patriot antiquarians, who were arguing for greater constitutional rights and a share in the empire for Ireland, grounded their arguments for administrative reform in an assertion of the quality and value of Ireland's indigenous culture. Moreover, as Leerssen has suggested, the Patriot Celticists of the late eighteenth century produced a 'Gaelicized' vision of the Irish past, which identified the nation with Gaelic culture and articulated a profound identification between this sector of the Anglo-Irish literary elite and Ireland's Gaelic past.[40]

Vallancey's legacy lingered on in the debates over round towers and the origins of Irish culture that raged in the 1830s and still flared in the late nineteenth century. These debates reflected a common European concern with the links between Europe and Asia (which was commonly seen as the cradle of humanity), a desire to reconstruct the peopling of Europe and to establish national origins through the construction of cultural genealogies.[41] Comparative philology and ethnology occupied a central place in European intellectual life in the early nineteenth century and strong philological/ethnological traditions developed in both Scotland and Ireland. Although considerable Scottish attention was directed towards the ongoing Ossian debate, a powerful Scottish tradition of linguistic Orientalism focused on the languages of Southeast Asia and emerged in the works of Edinburgh-trained East India Company men, most notably John Leyden and John Crawfurd.[42]

Irish philology was less fixed on empire as antiquarians continued to clash over the legacy of Vallancey's diffusionism. These debates were primarily conducted within the institutional framework of the Royal Irish Academy. In October 1827, for example, L.C. Beaufort presented a long 119 page paper to the Academy that suggested pre-Norman Irish architecture was shaped by Ireland's cultural origins in the 'unchanging east'.[43] Drawing particularly on the work of Sir William Jones, but also an array of other British and continental Orientalists, Beaufort attempted to substantiate further the oriental origins of the Irish people. Tracing similarities between Irish and Middle Eastern and South Asian material culture, Beaufort identified an endless stream of analogies, affinities and resemblances: the houses of 'India and Caubul' echoed the design of the 'Irish cabin'; Irish round towers were suggestive of the pagodas of Asian temples; Irish spirituality seemed to be an offshoot of Hindu sun-veneration and Zoroastrianism. Thus, for Beaufort, the allied development of Orientalism and Celticism clearly revealed the eastern, but 'chiefly ... Persian origin' of 'many customs' found in Ireland.[44]

Arguments over the origins and development of Irish culture intensified in the early 1830s when the 'Origin and Uses of the Round Towers' was designated as the topic for the Royal Irish Academy's prize essay for 1830. Although George Petrie's winning essay, which was finally published as *The Ecclesiastical Architecture of Ireland* in 1845, presented a detailed critique of the diffusionist tradition and established the medieval ecclesiastical origins of the towers, it was the runner-up Henry O'Brien's essay (along with the Academy's rather inept handling of the competition) that stimulated public debate. O'Brien's *The Round Towers of Ireland (or the Mysteries of Freemasonry, of Sabaism, and of Budhism, Now for the First Time Unveiled)* insisted that the phallic symbolism of the round towers affirmed the oriental influence which had imprinted Ireland's culture, a heritage which could be traced back to an ancient form of fertility worship supposedly practised by Zoroastrians in Persia and by Buddhists.[45] O'Brien's argument, which many reviewers saw as exceedingly indelicate, caused a furore and O'Brien died amidst a flow of harsh reviews and

personal attacks; but his death did not mark the end of the diffusionist tradition.[46] It was resurrected by Ulick Bourke's *Aryan Origin of the Gaelic Race and
Language* (1875), a work that bolstered the diffusionist paradigm through a
heavy engagement with the works of James Cowles Prichard, Max Müller, and
Henry Sumner Maine. Bourke's avowed aim was to popularise the 'Aryan' origins of the Irish and to use it to instil pride in the attainments of the Irish past.
Bourke's argument was closely tied to his advocacy of the Irish language and
his role as a spokesman for a 'revivalist populist nationalism'.[47]

Meanwhile, diffusionist arguments were being developed in a more rigorous manner and used to a very different end in England. The leading British
ethnologist James Cowles Prichard followed Vallancey's lead by insisting on
the eastern origins of the Irish and on the unity of Druidism with Indian religious traditions. While Prichard rejected Vallancey's speculative sensibility,
adopting a more rigorous comparative method shaped by his Scottish training
and Jonesian philology, he realised that his work had political and racial relevance: he hoped that his work would counter the rising wave of British
Teutonomania and polygeneism.[48] By stressing the unity of Celtic language
and religion with the mainstream of Indo-European cultural development,
Prichard challenged the increasingly rigid lines drawn between the liberty-lov-
ing Anglo-Saxon Englishman and backward Celt by Thomas Arnold, John
Kemble and Benjamin Thorpe, the leading apostles of the Anglo-Saxon
revival.[49]

By the peak of Prichard's career new, more concrete, links between India
and Ireland were emerging, as Britain's colonial project in India increasingly
drew on Irish expertise and personnel. Irish involvement in the East India
Company was well established and the reliance of the Company on Ireland as
a recruiting ground was particularly marked, as Irish troops composed 48 per
cent of the European soldiers serving in the Bengal army between 1825 and
1850 (and the majority of these soldiers were Irish Catholics).[50] Although
much attention has been directed at the rebellion of the Connaught Rangers
in 1920, Irish soldiers were generally loyal and consistent servants of the Raj.[51]
The rebellion of the Connaught Rangers attracted a great deal of attention in
both the British and Irish media, but this essentially reflected the crisis in
British–Irish relations. From the perspective of South Asian military culture
the rebellion was less remarkable, as mutinies (of both Indian and European
troops) were fairly regular occurrences and the rebellion of the Connaught
Rangers was relatively small in scale (especially in comparison to the military
rebellions at the heart of the struggle against the British in 1857–8) and quickly contained. A narrow focus on rebellion and resistance must not efface the
deep-seated Irish interest in, and profit from, South Asian military service.

Ireland also provided intellectual capital for the Raj as well as raw man-
power. This was particularly the case with surveying which was, of course,
essential in the construction of imperial authority. In both contexts the colonial administration attempted to construct a dense archive of geographical

information that would facilitate the exploitation of resources and revenue reserves, improve strategic planning and speed up the movement of troops. The diverse material collected in the unpublished reports of the Ordnance Survey and in the settlement reports and district gazetteers of India offered colonial administrators an insight into the topography, socio-economic structure, historical development and customs of local societies.

Moreover, from the early 1830s the Ordnance Survey of Ireland served as a key reference point for the Great Trigonometrical Survey of India.[52] The Ordnance Survey built upon the earlier tradition of Irish military surveys, in particular extending the work that Irish military engineers had pursued under Vallancey's direction in the south of Ireland between 1776 and 1796.[53] Captain Henry Kater, a meteorologist and assistant on the East India Company's early surveys, was influential in the debates in the late 1820s that fixed the eventual scale and organisation of the Ordnance Survey; but generally the flow of ideas was from Ireland to India.[54] George Everest, the Surveyor-General of India, established an important relationship with Thomas Frederick Colby, director general of the Ordnance Survey (1820–47), and visited the Irish survey on Colby's invitation. Everest believed that the Irish model, especially its technologies and institutional structure, should be transplanted to India in order to improve the state of British geographical knowledge and ultimately shore up imperial authority. The other leading figure in colonial surveying in India, Thomas Best Jervis, extended these arguments, stressing that the division of labour employed in Ireland would be even more advantageous in India. The dull repetitive work at the heart of the survey would be delegated to local workers trained in a limited range of simple tasks, while the officers would be able to focus on the computations and scientific issues. This system would expose Indians to the usefulness of science and inculcate disciplined and conscientious work patterns amongst the indigenous population.[55] These links between the Ordnance Survey and the Great Trigonometrical Survey of India were further cemented by the exchange of personnel, as all engineer cadets were sent to the Ordnance Survey for training prior to being sent to India.[56]

The increasing interdependence of Irish and Indian forms of colonial knowledge and government was cemented from the mid-1850s as a result of the reorganisation of the administrational system of British India. Until 1855 the East India Company recruited through elaborate networks of patronage. While Scots were prominent from an early stage, relatively few Irishmen served in the rank and file of the Company administrators in the eighteenth or early nineteenth century. Between 1805 and 1815 Haileybury College, the Company's main training institution, received only twenty-two applications from Irishmen out of a total of 492.[57] But this patronage system was abolished in 1855 under the direction of the Secretary of State for India, Sir Charles Wood. Wood instituted a new regime based on an open competitive examination, a system that was the backbone of officer training until the independence of India in 1947.[58] Effectively this shift passed the responsibility of preparing young men for Indian service from Haileybury to the Universities of Ireland and Britain. The Irish universities quickly seized upon the opportunities this reorganisation presented, as they instituted courses in zoology, oriental languages, and Indian history with the aim of preparing their students for the exam. This reorientation was swift and effective: between 1855 and 1863 24 per cent of all Indian Civil Service (ICS) recruits were educated in Ireland, as opposed to an average of around 4 per cent in the early nineteenth century.[59] Trinity College Dublin (TCD) was particularly prominent as a training institution; this reflected both a persistent interest in imperial careers amongst the Protestant middle-class, but also the strength of the College's programme in oriental languages. In the late nineteenth century TCD produced on average seven ICS men per year and by 1912 a total of 180 had entered the service, an extremely significant contribution to the tiny white elite responsible for the administration of India. In the late 1850s and early 1860s potential ICS men were trained by the prominent Sanskitist Professor Rudolf Thomas Seigfreid, an influential member of the board responsible for reorganisation of the Indian Civil Service, and the German-trained William Wright who ultimately occupied the chair of Arabic at Cambridge. In 1861 Mir Alaud Ali, a native of Oudh who added Persian and Hindustani to the College's offerings, succeeded Wright in the chair of Arabic at Trinity.[60] The breadth of Trinity's linguistic programme was further extended by Robert Atkinson, Professor of Sanskrit and Comparative Philology between 1871–1907, who claimed ability in Hebrew, Coptic, Sanskrit, Arabic, Telugu, Tamil, Persian and Chinese in addition to Celtic, classical and romance languages. Although Atkinson was not renowned for his research, he provided a highly effective and broad grounding in oriental languages that gave TCD graduates a head start over many of their colleagues.[61]

But the Queen's Colleges of Belfast, Cork and Galway also placed a heavy emphasis on their role as training institutions for empire. Galway graduates, for example, were prominent in the Indian medical and engineering services as well as filling various imperial or quasi-imperial positions from Cochin China to Mauritius. In fact the ability to produce more candidates for the ICS and imperial service was a fundamentally important function of the Queen's Colleges and was a key litmus test in assessing their success. In 1901, the Royal Commission on University Education in Ireland questioned Alexander Anderson, Professor of Natural Philosophy and President of Queen's College Galway, over the performance of the college. The Commission's sustained questioning was aimed at discerning whether the College was a 'complete failure', a 'relative failure', or simply a 'failure'. Anderson's defence rested on the number of 'well-known men' educated in the College and their successful post-graduation careers; the list of graduates entered into evidence was thick with men who had served abroad, especially in India.[62]

Although the proportion of Irish recruits levelled out as the late nineteenth century progressed, Irish administrators were extremely prominent in the late nineteenth century. Raj. S.B. Cook's excellent *Imperial affinities: nineteenth century analogies and exchanges between India and Ireland* has documented the profound impact of Irish land policy and Irish administrators in the debates surrounding Indian land legislation in the late nineteenth century. Cook clearly establishes that Irish ICS men were central in ensuring the greater protection afforded to *raiyat*s (substantial peasants) by the *Bengal Tenancy Act* (1885). This Irish influence was resented by both *zamindar*s (large land-holders) and English commentators, one of whom denounced the *Act* as the product of 'Home Rulers and Fenians', adding that bill had the 'Irish marks of the beast upon its face'.[63]

Not only were Irish ICS men at the forefront of legislation that afforded some protection to the peasants of Bengal, but they also exhibited a strong interest in preserving the culture of rural communities. By the late nineteenth century British Orientalism had moved away from a narrow focus on the classical heritage of Sanskrit texts, to focus increasingly on 'little traditions' and local customs which deviated considerably from the teachings of this canonical Sanskritic tradition.[64] Between the mid 1870s and the 1920s two TCD graduates, William Crooke and George Grierson, shaped this new body of knowledge. Their researches into vocabularies and patterns of rural life, artisan traditions and popular religion not only revealed the immense diversity of Indian life, but also defended the validity of these traditions against the incursion of western norms.[65] Both men received training in oriental languages at TCD and their interest in rural and folk traditions reflected the prominence of Irish antiquarian debates during their education and the influence of the English 'Arts and Crafts' movement.[66] Grierson's monumental nineteen volume *Linguistic Survey of India* (1903–) mapped the massive linguistic variation of South Asia, revealing the region's complex patchwork of regional languages, local dialects and sub-cultures. While this work was of great value to anthropologists and historians it was of great utility to colonial administrators, as Shahid Amin has observed: 'In the exercise of power, Englishmen [and Irishmen too!] could not afford to do away with Indian words.'[67]

While Grierson, whose work was characterised by meticulous ethnographic detail and patience, would have harboured deep doubts about Charles Vallancey's early work on Irish and oriental languages, he was nevertheless a culmination of an Irish Orientalist tradition established in the late eighteenth century. Well-prepared in Indian languages by his Trinity training Grierson, like so many other Irishmen, both Protestant and Catholic, made their careers in an imperial world. Although Ireland had won its independence by the end of Grierson's career, powerful links continued to bind Ireland and India up to the decolonisation and partition of India in 1947.

To conclude, modern Irish disinterest or hostility towards the British imperial project should not blind us to the crucial role played by Ireland and the Irish in the maintenance of two centuries of British power in India. This essay has provided further evidence of the limits of models for Irish history that primarily focus on Irish resistance to British imperialism: late nineteenth-century observers, whether Irish educators, British journalists, or Indian politicians stressed the prominent role of the Irish, both Catholic and Protestant, in the Raj.[68] Peasants feeling the pressure of population growth and rural poverty, middle-class Catholics hungry for success and status, and Anglo-Irish keen to assert their value to Britain's imperial venture all found the opportunities offered by service in India lucrative. This essay also suggests that further research is required into the role of the Irish in imperial personnel networks, as the existing historiography on the Irish diaspora largely focuses on North America and the British settler colonies. Although the Europeans of India may represent a 'failed' colonial community, there is no doubt that this Irish involvement in India was an important but largely overlooked component in the Irish historical experience. This 'Irish Raj' also tells us something rather profound about the nature of the empire itself. Although post-colonial critics have often stressed the fractured, fragmentary and brittle nature of the empire, quite the opposite seems true. British imperial authority rested on complex networks of military recruitment, social communication, and intellectual exchange. Like India (which functioned as a crucial centre of ideas, capital and personnel for the Indian Ocean and the Pacific), Ireland functioned as a key sub-imperial centre within these networks: it provided the soldiers, doctors and administrators for the colonies; it functioned as a testing-ground for new legislation and systems of government; and Irish culture provided a surprisingly frequent reference point for understanding the indigenous cultures of Asia and the Pacific. Ireland together with India occupied a central place in the discourses and practice of modern British empire-building: Ireland's colonial status might still be debated, but its central role in the sinews of the British empire can not be doubted.

NOTES

I would like to thank Tadhg Foley, William O'Reilly, Steven Ellis, Terry McDonough and Nicholas Canny of the National University of Ireland, Galway for their responses to earlier versions of this study. Many of the arguments here develop those articulated in T. Ballantyne, *Orientalism and Race: Aryanism in the British Empire* (London: Palgrave, 2001).

1.   F. Fukuyama, *The End of History and the Last Man* (London: H. Hamilton, 1992).
2.   D. Fennell, 'Against Revisionism' in C. Brady (ed.), *Interpreting Irish History. The Debate on Historical Revisionism 1938–1994* (Dublin: Irish Academic Press, 1994), pp. 181–90.
3.   B. Bradshaw, 'Nationalism and Historical Scholarship in Modern Ireland' in C. Brady (ed.), *Interpreting Irish History. The Debate on Historical Revisionism 1938–1994* (Dublin: Irish Academic Press, 1994),pp. 191–216.
4.   Ibid., p. 209.
5.   At a 1998 paper delivered in Galway, Bradshaw prefaced an agenda for Irish history in the next millennium by asserting the uniqueness of the Irish historical experience. He also suggested, in response to a question from Nicholas Canny, that it is difficult for non-Irish historians to 'understand' the Irish past, implying that histories should be produced from within the national community.

6. E.R. Wolf, *Europe and the People Without History* (Berkeley, CA: University of California, 1982).
7. D. Fitzpatrick, 'The Geography of Irish Nationalism', *Past and Present*, 78, pp. 113–44.
8. D. Fitzpatrick, 'Ireland and the Empire', in A. Porter (ed.), *The Oxford History of the British Empire: Volume III - the Nineteenth Century* (Oxford University Press: Oxford, 1999).
9. A. Porter, 'Empires in the Mind' in P.J. Marshall (ed.), *Cambridge Illustrated History of the British Empire* (Cambridge: Cambridge University Press, 1996), pp. 185–223.
10. S.G. Ellis, '"More Irish Than the Irish Themselves"? the "Anglo-Irish" in Tudor Ireland', *History Ireland* 7, 1 (1999), pp. 22–6; S.G. Ellis, *Ireland in the Age of the Tudors, 1447–1603: English Expansion and the End of Gaelic rule* (London: Longman, 1998); S.G. Ellis, *Tudor Ireland: Crown, Community, and the Conflict of Cultures, 1470–1603* (London: Longman, 1985).
11. D.B. Quinn, *The Elizabethans and the Irish* (Ithaca, NY: Cornell University Press, 1966); N. Canny, *Kingdom and Colony: Ireland in the Atlantic World, 1560–1800* (Baltimore, MD: Johns Hopkins University Press, 1988); J.H. Andrews, *A Paper Landscape: the Ordnance Survey in Nineteenth-Century Ireland* (Oxford: Clarendon Press, 1975).
12. C. Jeffries, *The Colonial Police* (London: Max Parrish, 1952).
13. R. Hawkins, 'The "Irish Model" and the Empire: a Case for Reassessment', in D.M. Anderson and D. Killingray (eds), *Policing the Empire: Government, Authority and Control, 1830–1940* (Manchester: Manchester University Press, 1991).
14. S.B. Cook, *Imperial Affinities: Nineteenth-Century Analogies and Exchanges Between India and Ireland* (New Delhi: Sage, 1993).
15. C. Dewey, 'The Rehabilitation of the Peasant Proprietor in Nineteenth Century Economic Thought', *History of Political Economy*, 6 (1974), pp. 321–36; C. Dewey, 'Celtic Agrarian Legislation and the Celtic Revival: Historicist Implications of Gladstone's Irish and Scottish Land Acts, 1870–1886', *Past and Present*, 64 (1974), pp. 30–70.
16. C.A. Bayly, 'Ireland, India and the Empire: 1780–1914', *Transactions of the Royal Historical Society* X (sixth series), 2000, pp. 377–97.
17. See, for example, I.M. Cumpston, 'Some Early Nationalists and Their Allies in the British Parliament, 1851–1906', *English Historical Review*, LXXV, 1976, pp. 279–97; H. Brasted, 'Indian Nationalist Development and the Influence of Irish Home Rule, 1870–1886', *Modern Asian Studies*, 1980, 12, pp. 37–63; R.P. Davis, 'India in Irish Revolutionary Propaganda, 1905–22', *Journal of the Asiatic Society of Bangladesh*, 1977, 22, pp. 66–89.
18. K. Jeffrey, 'Introduction', in K. Jeffrey (ed.), *An Irish Empire?: Aspects of Ireland and the British Empire* (Manchester: Manchester University Press, 1996), p. 17.
19. The best examples of this approach are: N. Kapur, *The Irish Raj: Illustrated Stories about Irish in India and Indians in Ireland* (Antrim: Greystone, 1997); and M. Mansoor, *The Story of Irish Orientalism* (Dublin: Hodges). While T. Fraser, *Partition in Ireland, India and Palestine: Theory and Practice* (London: Macmillan Figgis & Co, 1944) presents a detailed comparative analysis, his essay in Jeffrey's edited collection is a broad overview that simply describes Irish involvement in India rather than offering sustained analysis of its development or significance. See T.G. Fraser, 'Ireland and India', in K. Jeffrey (ed.), *An Irish Empire?: Aspects of Ireland and the British Empire*, pp. 77–93, 1984.
20. N. Canny, 'Irish Resistance to Empire?: 1641, 1690 and 1798', in L. Stone (ed.), *An Imperial State at War: Britain from 1689 to 1815* (London: Routledge, 1994).
21. R.B. McDowell, 'Ireland in the Eighteenth Century British Empire', in J.G. Barry (ed.), *Historical Studies IX* (Belfast: Blackstaff Press, 1974), p. 49.
22. T Bartlett (ed.), *Life of Theobald Wolfe Tone* (Dublin: Lilliput Press, 1998), pp. 414–8.
23. C.A. Bayly, *Imperial Meridian: the British Empire and the World, 1780–1830* (London: Longman, 1993), p. 128; also see T. Dunne, *Theobald Wolfe Tone: Colonial Outsider. An Analysis of his Political Philosophy* (Cork: Tower Books, 1982).
24. See Bartlett (ed.), *Life of Theobald Wolfe Tone*, p. 25.
25. W.H Tone, *A Letter to an Officer of the Madras Establishment: Being an Attempt to Illustrate Some Particular Institutions of the Maratta People* (London: J. Debrett, 1796); W.H Tone, *Illustrations of Some Institutions of the Mahratta People* (Calcutta: Times Press, 1818).
26. C.A. Bayly, *Empire and Information: Intelligence Gathering and Social Communication in India, 1780–1870* (Cambridge: Cambridge University Press, 1996); B. Cohn, *An Anthropologist Among the Historians and Other Essays* (Delhi: Oxford University Press, 1987); B. Cohn, *Colonialism and its Forms of Knowledge: the British in India* (Princeton, NJ: Princeton University Press, 1996).
27. P.J Marshall and G. Williams, *The Great Map of Mankind: British Perceptions of the World in the Age of Enlightenment* (London: Dent, 1982).

28. W.W Davis, 'China, the Confucian Ideal, and the European Age of Enlightenment', *The Journal of the History of Ideas*, 54, 4 (1983), pp. 523–548; O. Impey, *Chinoiserie: the Impact of Oriental Styles on Western Art and Decoration* (London: Oxford University Press, 1977); R. Schwab, *Oriental Renaissance: Europe's Rediscovery of India and the Orient, 1680–1880*, trans. G. Patterson-Black and V. Reinking (New York, NY: Columbia University Press, 1984); Marshall and Williams, *The Great Map of Mankind*, p. 218.

29. T.R. Trautmann, *Aryans and British India* (Berkeley, CA: University of California, 1997); J Rendall, 'Scottish Orientalism: from Robertson to James Mill', *The Historical Journal*, 25, 1 (1982), pp. 43–69.

30. J.Z. Holwell, *Interesting Historical Events, Relative to the Provinces of Bengal, and the empire of Indostan*, 3 vols. (London: T. Becket and P.A. de Hondt, 1765–71); C. Vallancey, *An Essay on the Antiquity of the Irish Language: Being a Collation of the Irish with the Punic language* (Dublin: S. Powell, 1772), pp. 28–9.

31. Valluncey , p. 3.

32. J. Leerssen, *Remembrance and Imagination: Patterns in the Historical and Literary Representation of Ireland in the Nineteenth Century* (Cork: Cork University Press, 1996), p. 70; cf. C.A. Bayly; and R. Rocher, 'British Orientalism in the Eighteenth Century: The Dialectics of Knowledge and Government', in C. Breckenridge and P. van der Veer (eds), *Orientalism and the Postcolonial Predicament. Perspectives on South Asia* (Philadelphia, PA: University of Pennsylvania Press, 1993), pp. 215–49.

33. F. Wilford, 'On Egypt and Other Countries Adjacent to the Cali River, or Nile of Ethiopia, from the Ancient Books of the Hindus', *Asiatic Researches*, 3 (1792), pp. 295–462.

34. Lord [John Shore] Teignmouth (ed.), *The Works of Sir William Jones*, 13 vols. (London: John Stockdale and J. Walker, 1807), vol. II, pp. 123–3; J.C. Walker, *Historical Memoirs of Irish Bards* (London: T. Payne & Son, 1786), pp. 4, 126.

35. P.J Marshall (ed.), *The British Discovery of Hinduism in the Eighteenth Century* (London: Cambridge University Press, 1970), p. 142.

36. Ibid., pp. 187–8.

37. P.J. Marshall, 'Warren Hastings as Scholar and Patron', in A. Whiteman, J.S. Bromley and P.G.M. Dickson (eds), *Statesmen, Scholars and Merchants: Essays in Eighteenth-Century History Presented to Dame Lucy Sutherland* (Oxford: Clarendon, 1973), p. 256.

38. S. O'Halloran, *An Introduction to the Study of the History and Antiquities of Ireland: in Which the Assertions of Mr. Hume and Other Writers are Occasionally Considered* (London: J. Murray, 1772), i.

39. L. Parsons, *Observations on the Bequest of Henry Flood, Esq. to Trinity College, Dublin: With a Defence of the Ancient History of Ireland* (Dublin: Bonham, 1795).

40. J. Leerssen, *Mere Irish and Fior-Ghael: Studies in the Idea of Irish Nationality, its Development and Literary Expression Prior to the Nineteenth Century* (2nd edn, Cork: Cork University Press, 1996), pp. 359, 364.

41. See Schwab, *Oriental Renaissance*.

42. See Rendall, 'Scottish Orientalism', pp. 43–69.

43. L.C. Beaufort, 'An Essay upon the State of Architecture and Antiquities, Previous to the landing of the Anglo-Normans in Ireland', *Transactions of the Royal Irish Academy*, XV (1828), p. 115.

44. Ibid., pp. 110–13,115–16, 195, 199–206

45. H. O'Brien, *The Round Towers of Ireland (or the Mysteries of Freemasonry, of Sabaism, and of Budhism, Now for the First Time Unveiled)*(London: Whittaker, 1834).

46. See Leersen, *Remembrance and Imagination*, pp. 112–20.

47. See Leersen, *Mere Irish and Fior-Ghael*, p. 140; U. Bourke, *The Aryan Origin of the Gaelic Race and Language* (London: Longmans, Green and Co, 1875). [AU?]

48. J.C. Prichard, *The Eastern Origins of the Celtic Nations: Proved by a Comparison of their Dialects with the Sanskrit, Greek, Latin and Teutonic Languages. Forming a Supplement to the Researches into the Physical History of Mankind* (London: S. Collingwood, 1831); R. Young, *Colonial Desire. Hybridity in Theory, Culture and Race* (London: Routledge, 1995).

49. G. Stocking, Jr. (ed.), *Researches into the Physical History of Man*, [J.C. Prichard] (Chicago, IL: Chicago University Press, 1973); Young,'Introduction', *Colonial Desire*.

50. K. Jeffrey, 'The Irish Military Tradition', in K. Jeffrey (ed.), *An Irish Empire?: Aspects of Ireland and the British Empire* (Manchester: Manchester University Press, 1996), p. 94.

51. See A. Babington, *Devil to Pay: the Mutiny of the Connaught Rangers, India, July, 1920* (London: Leo Cooper, 1991).

52. M.H., Edney, *Mapping an Empire: the Geographical Construction of British India, 1765–1843*

(Chicago: University of Chicago Press, 1997), pp. 35, 201.

53. See Andrews, *A Paper Landscape*, p. 3.
54. Ibid., p. 19ff.
55. See Edney, *Mapping an Empire*, pp. 76–7.
56. Ibid., pp. 281–5.
57. See McDowell, 'Ireland in the Eighteenth Century British Empire', p. 55.
58. C. Dewey 'The Education of a Ruling Caste: the Indian Civil Service in the Era of Competitive Examination', *English Historical Review*, 88 (1973), pp. 262–85; R.J. Moore, 'The Abolition of Patronage in the Indian Civil Service and the Closure of Haileybury College', *The Historical Journal*, 7, 2, pp. 26–57.
59. See Dewey, 'The Education of a Ruling Caste'.
60. R.B McDowell and D.A. Webb, *Trinity College, Dublin, 1592–1952: An Academic History* (Cambridge: Cambridge University Press, 1982), pp. 233–4.
61. K.C. Bailey, *A History of Trinity College Dublin* (Dublin: University Press, 1947), pp. 198–9.
62. Royal Commission on University Education in Ireland, *Minutes of Evidence Taken at the First Nine Sittings Held in Dublin* (Dublin, 1901)0
63. C.T. Buckland, *Publications of the London Committee formed to oppose the Bengal Tenancy Bill* (London, 1884), p. 18.
64. See Bayly, *Empire and Information*, pp. 354–7; and S. Amin (ed.), *A Glossary of North Indian Peasant Life* [William Crooke] (Delhi: Oxford University Press, 1989).
65. Amin (ed.), *A Glossary of North Indian Peasant Life*, p. xxii.
66. See Bayly, *Empire and Information*, pp. 354–7; McDowell and Webb, *Trinity College*, pp. 233–4; Bailey, *A History of Trinity College Dublin*, pp. 199–203.
67. Amin (ed.), *A Glossary of North Indian Peasant Life*, p. xxii.
68. For example, *The Hindoo Patriot*, 16 July 1881 and 15 Feb. 1885; *The Englishman*, 16 Sept. 1880.

PART III
IDEOLOGY

CHAPTER NINE

Defining Colony and Empire in Early Nineteenth-Century Irish Nationalism

SEAN RYDER

CHANGING THE QUESTION

It may seem odd that Ireland's relation to Britain was rarely described as 'colonial' in the nineteenth century, even by separatists. Leading nationalists like Daniel O'Connell usually made a clear distinction between Ireland's political status and the status of Britain's colonies in Asia, Africa, Australia, North America and New Zealand. Colonial activity in itself was not necessarily seen in a negative light – an Irish nationalist like William Smith O'Brien could be a whole-hearted advocate of 'colonization' schemes in Australia at the same time as he argued for Irish self-determination.[1] The situation may seem particularly incongruous to a present-day reader, given that since the mid-twentieth century the project of nationalism has been strongly associated with 'anti-colonial' and 'anti-imperial' discourse – an association much influenced by anti-imperial struggles in Africa and Asia. That Irish nationalism in its formative period did not, on the whole, make use of anti-colonial critique says several things about the complicated relationship between Ireland and the British state at the time, and about the internal dynamics of Irish nationalism, as well as offering instructive insight into the historically-determined nature of language itself. It does not necessarily mean that Ireland was not a 'colony' in some important senses of the word, nor does it mean that Irish nationalists were deluded or self-contradictory. As this essay will demonstrate, there are reasons for the relative absence of anti-colonial critique which have a great deal to do with what was possible and strategic in terms of political discourse at that particular historical moment, and cannot be taken as a measure of what Ireland's 'objective' political and cultural status may have been.

The issue of Ireland's 'colonial' or 'non-colonial' condition in the nineteenth century has become a topic of current debate, recently surveyed by Stephen Howe, David Fitzpatrick and others.[2] Works by Howe and Liam

Kennedy have expressed scepticism about the validity of the designation 'colonial' when applied to Ireland, on several grounds: that the term 'colony' was not generally applied to Ireland by eighteenth- and nineteenth-century politicians; that many Irish people were in fact enthusiastic contributors to the imperial project; or that economic statistics show that Ireland is not comparable to 'real' colonies in Africa and Asia. A contrasting argument is made by David Lloyd, who has suggested that Kennedy and others are missing the point. Lloyd proposes that 'the designation colonial' ought to be understood as a 'rational abstraction', which is a

> concept that can only function ... at the point when the phenomenon it designates and unifies have emerged in their full material actuality ... [R]etrospectively, we can see the work of the East India Company as a phase of colonialism, though the word itself may not have been used.[3]

With hindsight, in other words, we can see that nineteenth-century Ireland exhibits characteristics of a colony, whether or not nineteenth-century commentators had the ability or insight to say so. Joe Cleary too, in his immensely perceptive summary of the debate over Ireland's colonial status, draws attention to the limited usefulness of semiotic analysis and political consciousness in attempting to ascertain whether Ireland was or was not a 'colony'. He persuasively redefines Ireland's colonial condition in historical materialist terms. Ireland, he argues, was a colony because of its position in an emergent cpitalist world-system – not just because of its political relation to Britain, or on account of what contemporary commentators believed. Such an interpretive frame is flexible enough to allow for local differences among colonial histories without deying the existence of certain shared experiences produced by operations of the global economy, experiences that are 'colonial' because they are fundamentally shaped by a country's relation to metropolitan, imperial centres of capital.

The purpose of this essay, however, is not to determine in a purely empirical sense whether Ireland was in fact a colony in the nineteenth century. Instead it tries to probe what is meant by asking the question itself, and how inextricably linked to the vagaries of language and discourse any answer to it must be. This is not simply a retreat into a version of the argument that we are condemned to grope forever within a 'prison-house of language', as if language's unstable or creative relation to extra-linguistic reality disqualifies it as a source of historical illumination. Language can be powerfully instrumental as a force for change and liberation regardless of whether it acts as a reliable vehicle for the conveyance of 'objective truth'; in fact it is a resource that is all the more interesting for its multiplicity of functions and complexity of signification.

Some of the relevance of this to the question of judging Ireland's coloniality may be glimpsed through constructing even a partial genealogy of the terms 'colony' and 'empire' within Irish political discourse. The terms 'colony' and 'empire' have never been used solely to denote social, political and economic formations; they have also been used in a utilitarian way to perform rhetorical functions, and to provoke ethical and evaluative responses. To describe a situation as 'colonial' is to put into play, sometimes deliberately, a wide range of possible meanings and connotations which vary according to history and context, and which greatly exceed the role of the merely descriptive. By paying attention to language as a historical phenomenon in its own right, viewing it as more like a performance than a mirror, terms like 'colony' and 'empire' can themselves be seen as contributors to the process of historical change and the evolution of Irish culture. They are never neutral descriptors of such change. From this perspective, the question – was Ireland a colony? – proves interesting not for the affirmative or negative answers it may generate, but for the rich insight it may provide into the dynamics of language and historical agency.

Tracing the usage of 'colony' and 'empire' in nationalist commentaries about Ireland is therefore not a matter of judging the perspicuity of those writers who recognised Ireland's 'true' colonial nature, nor, on the other hand, a matter of judging the accuracy of those who denied it. Instead it is to see that Irish nationalism's evolution was at an important level a linguistic struggle to define its object and function: to find the right language to define Ireland's political and cultural identity, and to mobilise the kinds of arguments that would secure Ireland's uniqueness and independence. What makes this particularly complicated is that this process of political definition and analysis undertaken by nationalist writers is both enabled by the discursive conventions available to it and constrained by these discourses, be they political, economic, educational, religious, racial, or otherwise. Discursive conventionality may sometimes be strategically enabling, as when it allows Irish nationalist arguments to participate in the mainstream political discourse of the day. But it can also be constraining, as when it limits the possibilities for radical political critique, or for a fundamental re-imagining of the terms in which political argument is conducted. It is also possible to find intriguing moments when Irish nationalism appears to have transgressed the conventions of those discourses it inherited, and opened up new possibilities for national self-definition. When, for instance, several tribes from southern Africa formed an alliance to resist British encroachment in 1847, the *Nation* newspaper broke the usual conventions of Victorian racial discourse by expressing political solidarity with the native Africans. Complaining that 'There seems to be more true civilisation in Kaffirland than in Ireland', the article quotes the (presumably translated!) words of a chieftain named Krieli, who had organised a confederacy of tribes to 'bury our past misunderstandings and unite against the common enemy as one Kafir nation'. The *Nation* writer exclaims:

> We wish them success with all our souls. The English have no more business in the country of the Kafirs than in China, or India, or in New Zealand, or in Ireland.[4]

Because of the rhetorical link made here between the victims of colonial settlement and imperial aggression across the globe, Ireland has been effectively
identified as a 'colony', since southern Africa, New Zealand and India were
certainly perceived to be 'colonies' in the press of the day. In a way that was
unconventional for the time, Irish people have been identified with 'colonised'
people of different races. But what is also significant in this case is the ven-
triloquising of the 'subaltern' voice of Krieli, since it allows the colonised
native to be represented as essentially civil and heroic, a departure from the
more usual stereotype of the African as merely barbaric. Such radical analogies
between the Irish and the natives of other colonies were not always welcome,
even in the pages of the *Nation*.

As we shall see shortly, though, this kind of text represents a significant
transitional stage in the discourse on colony and empire. One of the most obvious indices of this transition is the shift from the eighteenth-century use of the
term 'colony' to mean the culture of the *colonisers*, to the twentieth-century use
of the term 'colony' to evoke the culture and figure of the *colonised*. It is striking, as Ania Loomba has pointed out, that for most of its history the word
'colony', which derives from the Latin term for 'farmer-settler', has been
defined in terms only of settlers and their relationship to a parent state – even
the *Oxford English Dictionary* (OED) definition has not historically registered
any recognition of the people displaced or absorbed by such activity.[5] As the
'colonised' became literally more visible within the discourses of colony and
empire, more obvious possibilities arose for developing an anti-colonial critique
based on principles of natural justice and the rights of indigenous peoples.

Given the historicity of language and discourse, it is misleading to try to
answer the question of whether analogies between Ireland and other colonies
– at whatever level – may have been scientifically 'correct'. This appears to be
the question behind Liam Kennedy's critique of Irish colonial analogies, in
which he sets out to statistically prove Ireland's non-colonial status.[6] But neither can the question of analogy be answered by a simplistic readings of what
nineteenth-century writers and analysts themselves had to say (or failed to
say) about the relationship between Britain and Ireland. Vocabularies and
meanings are dynamic: language is not solely a matter of finding the correct
word to describe a static object, it is often a matter of mobilising vocabularies
and meanings in specific circumstances, in order to get certain things done.
The reactive nature of the *Nation* article cited above, written as an immediate
response to news from the Cape, alerts us to the fact that the choice of language within Irish nationalism was often highly pragmatic and strategic.
Rather than devising a foundational set of definitions and principles, which
would fix the essential nature of Irish identity or the constitutional position of
Ireland, the political writings of the period show terms like 'colonial', 'imperial' and 'national' being used in quite flexible ways, varying from text to text,
even from week to week. Depending upon factors such as audience, immediate political events, the conventions of genre, and the changing legal sanctions

of the state itself (such as 'gagging acts'), nationalist writers tended to choose their language expediently rather than for ideological consistency, or scientific accuracy.

The remainder of this essay proposes to examine, firstly, some characteristics of the English-language discourse on 'colony' and 'empire' in the eighteenth and nineteenth centuries, especially as it related to Ireland; and secondly, to examine the various ways Irish nationalists adopted and adapted this discourse in the early nineteenth century. The purpose is not to decide objectively the question of Ireland's coloniality but to show what the concept might have meant in the early nineteenth century, and to suggest the variety of ways in which nationalism mobilised those meanings.

VOCABULARIES OF COLONY AND EMPIRE

There are two distinct senses in which the terms 'colony' and 'empire' were employed in the late eighteenth and early nineteenth centuries: one was as a legal/descriptive term, the other was as a term evoking moral concerns. It was as a legal term that Ireland's 'colonial' (or non-colonial) character was first theorised. In *The Case of Ireland's being Bound by Acts of Parliament in England, Stated* (1698), William Molyneux made a technical distinction between countries which had been settled as a result of conquest, and were therefore to be called colonies, and those which had been settled as a result of mutual agreement, and which retained the status of kingdoms, even if in some respects absorbed into a larger political entity. Molyneux argued that because the native Irish had voluntarily submitted to Henry II, Ireland had not strictly speaking been 'conquered'. Since it had not been conquered, it could not technically be a colony: rather it was a kingdom of its own which had entered into a compact with the English king. Molyneux was very explicit, for example, in his distinction between Ireland's condition and the colonial status of the North American settlements:

> Does it not manifestly appear by the constitution of *Ireland*, that 'tis *a Compleat Kingdom* within itself? Do not the Kings of England bear, the Stile of Ireland, amongst the rest of their kingdoms? Is this agreeable to the nature of a *Colony*? Do they use the title of Kings of *Virginia*, New *England*, or Mary-land?[7]

Molyneux's argument, not surprisingly, privileged the status of the Protestant Ascendancy in Ireland. It provided that class with a rationale for relative independence from Britain, yet also justified its continuing power over the Gaelic and Catholic population. Molyneux, for instance, argued that even if one believed Henry II had indeed employed invasion and conquest as his methods, the fact was irrelevant given that he had only employed them against the natives:

> it was only the *Antient Race* of the *Irish*, that could suffer by this
> Subjugation; ... the *English* and *Britains* ... retain'd all the Freedoms and
> Immunities of *Free born* Subjects.[8]

The 'English and Britains', and their descendants in Ireland – in other words, the
settler culture – are here allowed the status of free citizens, while the Gaelic
'colonised' are excluded from such privileges. One might say that the legislative
independence which Molyneux was attempting to justify was less a form of
'decolonization' than a reconfiguration of the existing colonial rule.[9] Nevertheless,
Molyneux continued to be invoked as an important patriotic authority by various
forms of Irish nationalism well into the 1840s. His respectable political pedigree,
and the fact that his arguments were based upon the discourse and principles
that underpinned the British state itself, made his name tactically useful, even
for a subsequent nationalist who might wish to reconcile those very cultural and
religious divisions that Molyneux had been happy to enforce (between Protestant
and Catholic, and between Anglo-Irish and Gaelic).

In spite of Molyneux's rejection of the term on legal grounds, by the late
eighteenth century 'colony' became a word quite commonly applied by nationalists to describe Ireland's status. While Molyneux's name and authority continued to be invoked by Henry Grattan and the Ascendancy patriots, Grattan
found that deploying the term 'colony' was a strategically useful way of signifying the de facto condition of Ireland prior to 1782. For Grattan, 'colony' had
a strongly emotive function, signifying degradation, insult and subjection
rather than simply describing a constitutional condition. In his declaration of
independence in the newly-established Irish parliament he proclaimed:

> Spirit of Swift! Spirit of Molyneux! Your genius has prevailed! Ireland is
> now a nation! ... She is no longer a wretched colony.[10]

Grattan's use of colony here is enabled by the association of 'colonial' status
with English misrule, an association which had been accentuated by the
American war of independence and its assertion of the rights of colonists to
self-determination. Like Molyneux, Grattan believed that, legally speaking,
Ireland was not a colony: he argued, however, the English government had
treated it like one – and this was the real source of grievance. The term
'nation' in Grattan's discourse performs the same function as 'kingdom' in
Molyneux's – that is, as a sign of the properly elevated and independent status the island ought to enjoy. Of course, this nationality belonged only to the
Protestant Ascendancy; the Gaelic and Catholic 'natives' were excluded from
parliament, and thus denied constitutional political agency.

In the 1790s Wolfe Tone and the United Irishmen adopted a great deal of
the same rhetoric, but with some important and radical modifications.
Referring to the process that led to the establishment of 'Grattan's parliament', an anonymous United Irishmen address in 1792 remarked that

> the part of the [Irish] nation which is truly colonial, reflected that
> though their ancestors had been victorious, they themselves were now
> included in the general subjection; subduing only to be subdued, and
> trampled upon by Britain as a servile dependency ... they resisted British
> dominion, renounced colonial subserviency, and followed the example of
> a Catholic parliament just a century before ... in 1782 Ireland ceased to
> be a province and became a nation.[11]

This writer's analysis of Ireland's relationship to Britain at this point is essentially the same as Grattan's, but the United Irishmen took the analysis further
by drawing attention to the exclusive nature of the Protestant 'nation' which
had been established in 1782. Wolfe Tone radically extended the concept of
Irish nationhood to include those who had been excluded by Molyneux and by
the Irish Protestant 'nation' – the 'natives', the Catholics and 'men of no property'. Tone's work provides a powerful and novel foregrounding of the rights of
the Irish 'colonised' (without actually employing that term) on the basis of
natural law.[12]

In this the republican Tone was an unlikely ally of the conservative
Edmund Burke, whose critique of the Irish Protestant Ascendancy – which he
deemed a plebeian oligarchy – was based upon the fact that it practised a form
of despotism over the Irish Catholics. Burke extended his critique to make
analogies between Irish Catholics and other victims of oppressive rule, including the colonised of Asia. In an important passage from his 1795 letter to Sir
Hercules Langrishe, Burke explicitly links the Irish Catholics to the subjected
people of India, and both to those European peoples subjected to 'Jacobin'
tyranny:

> I think I can hardly over-rate the malignancy of the principles of
> Protestant ascendancy, as they affect Ireland; or of Indianism as they
> affect these countries, and as they affect Asia; or of Jacobinism, as they
> affect all Europe and the state of human society itself ... Whatever tends
> to persuade the people, that the *few*, called by whatever name you
> please, religious or political, are of opinion, that their interest is not com-
> patible with that of the *many*, is a great point gained to Jacobinism.[13]

Colonies, for Burke, are potential sites for tyranny, but not because the establishment of colonies is inherently wrong. Colonies, being essentially commercial in purpose in the late eighteenth century, are simply more vulnerable to a
loss of political virtue, a concern at the heart of Burke's political vision. It is
commerce that can easily become corrupt and greedy, controlled by the interests of an unscrupulous minority, and when this is linked to political control,
the result is despotism.

In the nineteenth century, the term 'colony' took on further connotations
as material and political circumstances changed. After a period when the idea

of colonization had been subject to extensive critique, and during which European wars occupied much of the energy and resources of Britain, the idea of colonial plantation had a significant revival, both in the form of 'colonization schemes' and in the increasing use of penal colonies as a way of siphoning off the 'criminal element' from mainstream British society.[14] The emigration and land improvement schemes proposed by Edward Gibbon Wakefield and his supporters focused especially on the settlement of New Zealand, Australia and Canada, reviving the eighteenth-century ideals of Britain's civilising mission, but adding the argument that the establishment of colonies would resolve population and economic problems within Britain itself. Wakefield's own idea of a colony, unlike Burke's, reinstates the exclusive focus on the settler as the colonial subject, much like Molyneux:

> A colony therefore is a country wholly or partially unoccupied, which receives emigrants from a distance; and it is a colony of the country from which the emigrants proceed, which is therefore called the mother-country ... [T]he national character of the states formed by colonization must greatly depend on the character of the institutions of government which the first settlers obtain.

Wakefield uses this definition to argue in favour of political independence for settler colonies:

> Regarding colonial government, therefore, as an essential part of colonization, the question remains whether the government of the colony by the mother-country is equally so. Is the subordination of the colony to the mother-country, as respects government, an essential condition of colonization? I should say not.[15]

Although Ireland figures in this discourse of colonization as a possible site for 'internal colonization', meaning essentially the agricultural improvement of waste lands, Wakefield excludes Irish people in general from participation in these overseas colonial projects. Although they are British citizens, their slavish behaviour makes them unsuitable for colonial emigration. The causes of this alleged slavishness for Wakefield seem to waver between the historicist view that the Irish people have been degraded by circumstances, and the resolutely anti-historicist view that they are racially different to the industrious Anglo-Saxon:

> ... the hordes of Irish-pauper emigrants who pour into North America, British and American, are, in considerable proportion, virtually slaves by means of their servile, lazy, reckless habit of mind, and their degradation in the midst of the energetic, accumulating, prideful, domineering Anglo-Saxon race.[16]

The Young Ireland nationalist leader Smith O'Brien's enthusiasm for Irish colonization schemes can be understood in the light of these comments. To argue
in favour of Irish participation in colonial plantation, as O'Brien did, was to
argue against racial stereotyping such as Wakefield's, and to assert the fundamental dignity and civility of Irish people. It thus fit strategically with one of
Irish nationalism's fundamental precepts. The Irish deserved to be recognised
as 'freemen' rather than slaves, civilisers rather than barbarians.

The racialisation of the discourse on colonies and colonialism is a more
prominent feature of the later nineteenth century than it is of the early half.
One early and noteworthy example is Robert Knox's work, *The Races of Men*,
first published in 1852, which ironically echoes Molyneux's denial that Ireland
had ever truly been a colony. Unlike Molyneux, Knox sees this as a rationale for
the continued coercive occupation of Ireland rather than its liberation.
Racialising the Irish-British relation, Knox argues that the two races can never
be assimilated; therefore the extermination of the 'Celtic race' would be welcome:

> Ireland is not a colony, but merely a country held by force of arms, like
> India; a country inhabited by another race ... The really momentous
> question for England, as a *nation*, is the presence of three sections of the
> Celtic race on her soil: ... and how to dispose of them.[17]

In spite of Knox's denial of Ireland's 'colonial' status, his racialised figure of
alien native is structurally similar to the figure of the 'colonised' in twentieth-
century discourse. In this case the recognition of this figure becomes a pretext
for its obliteration.

None of the writers cited thus far used the term 'colonialism' to describe
the activity of colonial conquest and settlement. Even the verb 'colonization'
used by Wakefield does not carry quite the same meaning as 'colonialism' –
that is, it lacks the sense of being an ideological or theoretical project.
Colonization is an activity; colonialism is a whole structure or system in which
activity takes place. In fact the earliest use of 'colonialism' in the sense of 'the
colonial system or principle' dates only from 1886, according to the *OED*. It is
instructive to note that this 1886 quotation, taken from an anti-Home Rule
tract, reads 'English Colonialism works well enough', while the most recent
quotation in the *OED* entry is from 1957, and reads 'Colonialism is the com-
monest term of abuse nowadays throughout half the world' – an indication of
the connotative transformation undergone by the word between the nineteenth and twentieth centuries.

The term 'imperialism' has a similarly late history. One of its earliest
appearances in English occurs in 1851, where it is used in a negative way to
describe the oppressive and hubristic French regime under Napoleon III.[18]
The preferred term for British imperial activity was simply 'empire' well into
the later nineteenth century. Edmund Burke's own definition of 'empire' lacks

the acquisitive, expansionist associations we now associate with 'imperialism'; Burke simply defines an empire as 'the aggregate of many states under one common head'.[19] Nearly a century later, George Cornewall Lewis, in a much-cited definition of empire, repeats the same basic formula, focusing on the purely legal denotation of the word:

> The entire territory subject to a supreme government possessing sever-al dependencies (that is to say, a territory formed of a dominant country together with its dependencies) is sometimes styled an *empire*, as when we speak of the British empire. Agreeably with this acceptation of the word empire, the supreme government of a nation, considered with ref-erence to its dependencies, is called the imperial government, and the English parliament is called the imperial parliament as distinguished from the provincial parliament of a dependency.[20]

Lewis's definition, however, comes out of a context in which the British empire had become extremely complex. Technical distinctions between crown colony, charter colony, dependency, dominion, province, territory and settle-ment, for example, were often made for legal purposes. The term 'empire' itself became flexible in order to accommodate this multiplicity. Koebner and Schmidt describe three basic ways of defining the British Empire in the nine-teenth century:

> There were two great complexes of overseas dominion, each adminis-tered by a specific department – the *Colonial Empire* and the *Indian Empire* ('our empire in the East'). For *the British Empire* or *the Empire* there remained two basic interpretations. It was possible and sometimes thought necessary to let those names stand for the whole comprehensive system constituted by the United Kingdom and all its dependencies. One could, on the other hand, without denying the applicability of this broadest interpretation, use the name in a more restricted sense to mean only the United Kingdom, so that the Colonies and the Indian Empire were regarded as dependent on the British Empire rather than being parts of it ... Between the interpretation which stressed the dominion over dependencies and the other which looked to the greatness of the native country there was still room for yet a third. It dwelt on the con-nexion between Great Britain and those dependent countries which had been completely or to a large extent built up by settlers originating from her soil. It focused its attention on the relation between the 'Mother-country' and the 'Colonies'.[21]

In 1841 the Wakefieldian Herman Merivale, like Cornewall Lewis with the term 'empire', attempted to limit the increasingly widely-ranging signification of the term 'colony':

> And I may here mention that throughout these Lectures the term Colony is used in the ancient and proper sense, and not that which has passed from official into general usage, in which it comprehends every species of foreign possession – military stations, such as Gibraltar and Malta; conquered districts, possessed by native inhabitants with a very slight admixture of the conquerors, such as Ceylon; mercantile emporia, such as the factories of European powers on the coast of Africa. By a Colony I understand a territory of which the soil is entirely or principally owned by settlers from the mother country.[22]

Given the multiplicity of meaning for these words in the nineteenth century, it is not surprising that the precise application of the terms colony and empire should also prove difficult and controversial in present-day historiographical and critical discourse.

The possibilities for anti-colonial critique were also bound up with forms of discourse. Of course, in a strictly terminological sense, there could be no anti-imperialism or anti-colonialism before the words imperialism and colonialism existed. Nevertheless, as we have seen with Burke, in the eighteenth century a critique of 'empire' was certainly possible: not from the ideological basis that empire-building was wrong in itself, but from the more general moral perspective that like any other human activity, it became immoral when dissociated from virtue. The ideal vision of empire promulgated in the eighteenth century was one of 'flourishing and commercially viable colonies, populated with free British subjects, that served as bulwarks of trade, prosperity, naval strength and political virtue for the parent state'.[23] Benevolent views like these were challenged late in the eighteenth century by crises such as the American colonial rebellion and criticism of the conduct of the East India Company. Even so, the harmful effects of the Burkean loss of virtue were most often defined in terms of the effects on the parent and settler cultures rather than the culture of the indigenous 'colonised'. The problem with the British empire in Asia, for instance, was not considered to be its effect on the 'native' populations but rather its potential as an unfortunate source of 'luxury, effeminacy, profligacy and debility' which might taint the virtue of the colonist, and ultimately undermine British traditions of liberty and civilisation.[24]

This radical critique of empire which continued into the early nineteenth century in the writings of Richard Cobden and others drew upon a particular vocabulary current in England since the seventeenth century, derived from classical republicanism. This discourse, which in turn shaped the language of the eighteenth-century Irish patriots and nineteenth-century Irish nationalists, articulated political and social critique through a set of binary oppositions. The ideal political state was one based upon a society of 'freemen' who behaved according to a self-generated constitution which encouraged personal liberty and responsibility. Set in opposition to this quasi-democratic, anti-authoritarian model were those regimes based upon centralised rule, which

curtailed freedom for all but the elite. The vocabulary associated with the latter form of government included despotism and tyranny, slavery and serfdom,
priestcraft and popery, luxury and corruption. Often this opposition was translated into historical terms as the conflict between virtuous, democratic Saxon
culture and feudal, despotic Norman culture. (It was not difficult for Irish
nationalists like Thomas Davis to later adapt this model to Irish history – in
his poem 'Celts and Saxons' the Irish ironically occupy the position of the
Saxons in the English radical tradition, with the Norman yoke translated into
a yoke of the 'Anglo-Norman' variety.[25])

Thus it is that early nineteenth-century critics of empire, such as Cobden
and Goldwin Smith do not so much attack the effects of colonial and imperial
rule upon the colonised as they attack the morally corrupting effect on the
imperial culture itself. They argue that the greed, ostentation and wasteful-
ness which seem to accompany empire prevent England from properly enjoy-
ing the fruits of her greatness and industry and civilisation. Cobden and others were also able to utilise the classical and historical associations evoked by
the term empire, bringing an almost scriptural dimension to their critique:

> I believe that the desire and motive for large and mighty empires, for
> gigantic armies and great navies ... will die away ... I don't feel sympathy
> for a great nation, or for those who desire the greatness of a people by the
> vast extension of empire ... we have had great empires at all times – Syria,
> Persia and the rest. What trace have they left of the individual man?[26]

Cobden's target is again the hubris which will destroy the imperialists themselves. In one of the earliest uses of the word 'imperialism', Charles Dilke in 1861
also worried about the effect that imperial despotism had upon English virtue. In
Dilke's argument, imperialism refers not just to overseas expansion, but is something practised by a European country (in this case, France) over its own subjects:

> Virtually, in annexing any Eastern country, we destroy the ruling class,
> and reduce the government to a mere imperialism, where one man rules
> and the rest are slaves. ... not only is our government in India a despot-
> ism, but its tendency is to become an imperialism, or despotism exer-
> cised over a democratic people, such as we see in France.[27]

Goldwin Smith, in his *Irish History and Irish Character* (1861), drew upon
these negative, Napoleonic connotations of the term 'imperialism', and managed to link it to Irish racial characteristics. Smith argued that there was a
'strong tendency to what is called Imperialism' inherent in the 'Keltic race',
which was 'opposed to the Constitutionalism to which the Teutonic races
tend'. It was apparently making 'even the highly civilized Kelt of France, familiar as he is with theories of political liberty, almost incapable of sustaining free
institutions'. Assuming the racial homogeneity of Celt, Irish and French,

Smith argued that it was as characteristic of the Irish as of the French to favour the rule of persons rather than that of institutions. Thus in an extraordinary turn, it is the Irish who are 'imperialists' at heart, not the British.[28]

Of course, the critique of imperialism was much less common than the celebration of it in English political discourse of the nineteenth century. By 1868, a writer in *The Spectator* is able to use 'imperialism' as a positive term when applied to England, speaking of 'imperialism in its best sense'. This means that it is sometimes a binding duty to perform 'highly irksome or offensive tasks', such as the defence of Canada or the government of Ireland.[29] This sense of the moral duty is a continuation of the eighteenth century rationale for empire: the argument being that Britain's enlightened, libertarian civilisation was one which could only benefit those who became associated with it. In this way, a writer in the *Edinburgh Review* was able to rationalise the idea of empire on the basis that it was actually a superior form of organisation than the nation itself. The British empire connected

> scattered dependencies ... with one great whole infinitely more powerful, civilised, free than any separate fragment could be ... The subordination of national or provincial independence ...[bestows] the true citizenship of these realms.[30]

IRISH NATIONALISM AND THE ANTI COLONIAL CRITIQUE

The preceding gives some sense of the context which shaped the early nineteenth-century Irish nationalist discourse on colony and empire. Nationalists like O'Connell, O'Brien, Davis and Mitchel made use of the existing vocabulary and models in a wide variety of ways. Sometimes it was argued that Ireland was by definition an integral part of the empire, and that its problems would be resolved not by separation, but by proper imperial participation (O'Connell and Smith O'Brien). At other times the moral critique of empire found in Burke and Cobden was employed to argue that Ireland would never flourish within the British empire – not because it was an empire, but because it was British, and therefore incorrigibly iniquitous (John Mitchel). Occasionally, as we have seen already with the *Nation*, a critique of British imperial invasion and occupation was based on a sense of solidarity with those who had been victims of such aggression (Thomas Davis). These arguments never resolved into a coherent theorisation of Ireland's colonial or imperial identity, and were always complicated by strategic moves and demands, which could sometimes push O'Connell into a more radical position than usual, or, on the other hand, could pull Davis back from the more radical implications of his cross-cultural analogies. There were, in other words, a range of opinions represented on the question of Ireland's colonial status.

The figure of Daniel O'Connell is a useful starting point, given his powerful effect on Irish political discourse of the early nineteenth century. O'Connell and his followers did not tend to use the term 'colony' to describe Ireland's political or cultural status. He repeatedly defined Ireland's status as 'provincial', not 'colonial': 'I have seen Ireland a Kingdom – I reproach myself with having lived to see her a Province'[31] – the word 'province' for O'Connell carrying the same emotive weight, and sense of degradation, that 'colony' did for Grattan. In the tradition of Molyneux and Grattan, his concern was to gain for Ireland the kind of constitutional justice it deserved, but always within an imperial frame. The problem was that Britain had relegated Ireland to an inferior constitutional position, absorbing it into the United Kingdom as a subordinate appendage, rather than accepting it as an autonomous Kingdom which happened to have the same monarch as England.

Molyneux's argument was strategically useful to O'Connell, in spite of its contradictions, and its exclusion of the very populace – the 'native Irish' and Catholics – that O'Connell spent his political career trying to mobilise. The 1782 parliament which represented the culmination of Molyneux's arguments was a model which O'Connell was keen to utilise in his arguments for the repeal of the Union. For one thing, it provided a counter-example to the violent and destructive events of the 1798 rebellion – a political act from which O'Connell was eager to dissociate his movement.[32] Grattan's parliament was a reformist rather than revolutionary model, a model which could conceivably win liberal support within the existing British parliamentary structure, and which therefore might be thought to have some reasonable chance of success.[33]

In refusing to apply the term 'colony' to Ireland, O'Connell was motivated by other factors. The idea of Ireland being a sister-kingdom did not merely serve as a way of making the Anglo-Irish feel superior: it gave the entire island a political and cultural status equal to other European kingdoms. The settler/native distinction which Molyneux uses could be blurred without much difficulty in order to appeal to a mass popular audience. One could still have the dignity of being the subject of a kingdom without having democratic access to political power. The imperial idea itself did not cause ideological problems for O'Connell's thinking, either: in fact his notion of empire derived very much from the eighteenth-century idea of empire as guarantor of liberty. Tom Steele, reflecting orthodox O'Connellism in a speech in 1846, 'disdained the attainment of a selfish Irish nationality ... [at the sacrifice of the] sublime principle of universal liberty' – a liberty that for some political theorists could best be maintained by participation in the British multinational empire.[34] Much was made in O'Connellite rhetoric of the contributions Irish people had made to the empire economically, culturally and militarily, in order to prove Ireland's loyal commitment to empire, even when treated unjustly by British governments. The Young Irelander Thomas D'Arcy McGee in the *Nation* in 1847 expressed similar pro-imperial sentiments:

I do not see why we should insist on considering ourselves conquered.

There is an ancient, and advantageous, and a natural connection between England and Ireland – that of the crown – which, until this island drifts from its moorings, or England becomes hopelessly criminal, no sane man will seek to separate.[35]

The argument here is little different to *The Times* of the same year:

The condition of Ireland is, directly, the condition of the British empire. No legislative union can tighten - no Utopian separation could dissolve - that intimate and close connexion between the two islands which has been formed by the hand of nature, and consolidated by the operations of time ...[36]

And indeed, the argument utilised by O'Connell about Ireland's integral place in the empire could be turned, with little difficulty, into an entirely opposite argument *against* Repeal, as in James Grant's 1844 book *Impressions of Ireland and the Irish*:

There is one way, and one way only, of crushing repeal. That is by rendering Ireland in reality what it is nominally – an integral part of the British empire ...[as opposed to treating it as] a conquered province.[37]

Insisting on Ireland's status as a kingdom within an empire also discouraged any attempt to compare Ireland's experience to other nineteenth-century colonial situations, like Canada or Australia. For such comparisons to be made, either Ireland had to be understood to be a colony, or else the colonies had to be understood as kingdoms – which meant seeing the indigenous peoples of North America or Australia as having produced an equivalent civilisation to the Gaelic and Norman cultures of Ireland. Given the dominant Eurocentric view which tended to relegate such cultures to noble savagery at best, it was more strategically useful for nationalists to compare Ireland to other European nations, especially ones like Belgium, Hungary or Norway with which certain historical parallels could be drawn, and certain comparative statistics about population, agricultural output and land ownership could be produced.

This is not to say that O'Connell himself did not utilise colonial analogies when occasionally convenient, or make principled links between his arguments for Irish freedom and the freedom of oppressed people elsewhere. O'Connell's long-standing and unwavering views on slavery are well known, and earned him some notoriety even with Irish nationalism in the 1840s, when his strong abolitionist line was seen as potentially damaging to the Repeal movement in the United States. For O'Connell, slavery was by definition repugnant to natural law, for Africans as well as for Irish or any other people.[38] In this, his views were somewhat more in the radical eighteenth-century tradition than were the views of some of his contemporaries, most notably John Mitchel, who while denying that the Irish deserved to be treated as slaves, was not averse to the idea of slavery as such. O'Connell did also make reference to the dispossession and slaughter of the aboriginal people of Australia and New Zealand, attacking the imperial policies which had caused such an evil: 'There are your Anglo-Saxon race! Your British blood! Your civilizers of the world …'[39] Yet this condemnation is not one which directly seeks solidarity or identification between the Irish and the Maori or aborigines: rather it is mobilising the critique of the improper conduct of empire by the British – highlighting the hypocritical chasm between their civilising ideals and their corrupt practices.

The idea of colonial settlement in itself was not a problem for O'Connell any more than it was for William Smith O'Brien. The latter, as noted already, was a strong advocate of Wakefieldian colonization as a remedy for Irish as well as British economic ills. O'Brien, like O'Connell, condemned the genocide of all Tasmania's indigenous people, but also felt that 'a few thousand savages' had no right to control large tracts of fertile territory.[40] From the perspective of missionary activity, too, the colonization of Asia and Africa by Britain opened up positive possibilities for both Catholic and Protestant organisations. In a significant example of the kinds of contradiction which arose in nationalist discourses of the time, the O'Connellite paper *The Pilot* in 1829 foresaw exciting possibilities for Catholic missionary work in the expansion of the empire – without acknowledging the historical irony that it was imperial expansion in Ireland that had been responsible for the persecution of Catholics.[41]

The compatibility of nationalism with an acceptance of the inherent validity of empire was further illustrated by the evocation of the figure of 'King Daithi' in Young Ireland rhetoric. According to legend, the fifth-century Irish king embarked on an imperial foray into France, successfully conquering territory all the way to the foot of the Alps. About to engage the Romans in battle, he committed an act of impiety towards a Christian hermit and was killed by an act of divine retribution. The tale of Daithi was a useful myth in so far as it gave ancient Ireland a legendary imperial past cognate with other major European nations. It also demonstrated that far from being perpetual victims and failures in war, the Irish could on occasion raise themselves to the level of imperial conquerors.[42] The legend also dovetailed with O'Connell's frequent reminders of the heroic contribution that Irish soldiers had made to the expansion and defence of the British empire since the eighteenth century – again proof of Ireland's capacity for loyalty, order and discipline.

One of Daithi's champions in the 1840s was Thomas Davis, who in fact provided Irish nationalism with its most complex and sustained perspective on nineteenth-century colony and empire. Davis's analysis of Irish history, most systematically articulated in the essay 'Udalism and Feudalism' (1841) is founded, contra Molyneux, upon the idea that Ireland had indeed been conquered by Henry II. The result of this conquest was Ireland's subjection to the rule of a feudal aristocracy that remained at the heart of the problem of

Ireland. Davis sets Ireland's experience within a broad European context: admitting that the Celts themselves had been conquerors in their day, and that European history in general was essentially a history of serial conquests. Ireland's special case, however, derived from the fact that its feudal social and economic structure had never progressed to the modified and liberal stage it had in England, and which produced there a large class of 'yeoman', and enabled England's growth as a commercial empire and parliamentary state. For Davis Ireland is less a colony than an anachronistic relic in the history of western European nations. Aristocracy persisted longer here than elsewhere, and was maintained by force:

> The origin of the Irish aristocracy is in confiscation. The nature of that aristocracy results from their alienage – first, of country, then of religion. Their power was founded on conquest; and though penal laws, carrying out what confiscation began, increased their sway during three-fourths of the last century; and though ejectment acts and insurrection have continued their legal sway, yet their real power rests, as it originated, in the force of British regiments, recruited by inconsiderate Irishmen.[43]

Citing Gustave de Beaumont frequently as an authority – especially his comment that 'it is necessary to abolish the principle of aristocracy in Ireland' – Davis identifies the class system as the source of Ireland's social and political evils. The country Davis presents as a model for what Ireland's political economy ought to be is Norway, a country never conquered or feudalised, and based upon the solid economic and political foundation of small farm proprietorship: 'the Norwegians have always been freemen'.[44] This kind of analysis enables Davis to mobilise the language of English radicalism, designating Irish peasants as 'serfs', a term which carries the same emotive force as 'slave', but also signals a precise economic meaning of 'the feudal subject'.

Davis's political rhetoric, which draws heavily on English radicalism, also draws upon the vivid metaphoric language and tone of Thomas Carlyle. One of Davis's essays from the *Nation* describes the British Empire as

> a sort of world-hydra, as Carlyle would call her. From Canada to the Cape, from Ireland to Australia, from India to China to Western Africa, and the distant realms of South America, no nation but has felt the teeth, and claws , and venom, of this incongruous and pitiless monster ... She has rotted away by her avarice and vices, half the population of Australia and Polynesia; and cleared out, with bullet and bayonet, the 'last man' from the great island of Van Dieman – thus accomplishing at the Antipodes that extermination so often and vainly tried in Ireland.[45]

Davis is more willing than many of his contemporaries to pursue the possible analogies between Ireland and other, non-European victims of imperialism. In his 1837 address to the Dublin Historical Society, for instance, Davis compares the experiences of Ireland and India under the British Empire – proclaiming that Ireland has actually fared worse, given that extermination was not a feature of the conquest of India. He also extends his critique of empire to include other examples of imperial brutality, such as the Ottoman Turks, and the Boers in southern Africa.[46] While his critique does not become a fully ideological critique of imperialism itself, Davis is nevertheless laying the ground for such a critique; demonstrating that despotic iniquity is not exclusive to a corrupt British state. It appears to be a feature of empire in many cases.

Yet Davis's analogies are also constrained in interesting ways. Davis wished to transcend the ethnocentric assumptions that prevented comparison between European and non-European people, but to do so had to avoid deploying the powerful binary matrix whereby European and non-European were defined exclusively by their differences to each other. The way he overcame this, especially in his early articles on the British invasion of Afghanistan in the *Citizen*, was to suggest that prior to imperialist invasion, societies like Afghan society were in fact organised much like pre-feudal European society. Adapting the English libertarian vision of a proto-democratic, freeborn Saxon society that supposedly existed before the imposition of the Norman yoke, Davis represents Afghanistan as a nation similarly inhabited by 'freemen' who are supporters of 'the old cause', battling against a foreign tyrant determined to 'enslave' them. By making Afghanis into a kind of rugged eastern version of the English yeoman, Davis succeeds in constructing his analogy, though at a price which involves translating Afghan society into terms derived from English political culture.[47]

One of Davis's early editorials in the *Nation* illustrates this grafting of European political ideals onto non-European struggles. In the process Davis affirms the priority of nation over empire in a direct reversal of the argument of the *Edinburgh Review* contributor cited above:

> Affghans are led by this, their great misfortune to a self-sacrificing union, and firm faith in nationality and freedom, they shall resume their high estate. For great is the strength of a young nation ... Empires go down before its running ...[48]

The article goes on to make comparisons between Ireland, Afghanistan, Tyre and Sidon, Athens, Israel, early Rome, Switzerland, Holland, America, and Circassia. All of these have displayed specific heroic qualities in resisting the aggression of despotic empires. These analogies are, of course, very selective. Certain nations do not qualify – China, for instance:

> The villainy of England may excite our anger, but we cannot *much* pity the Chinese, we despise them *so much*. Had they shown signs of manhood we would honour them and grieve for them.[49]

Among other things, the constraints imposed by Victorian discourse on gender are evident here. The need to distance Irish national character from any association with 'feminine' weakness or cowardice outweighs the advantage of anti-imperial solidarity. Imperialist aggression may not always arouse sympathy for its victims: those who do not appear to fit the model of the heroic, masculine 'freeman' are not worthy of comparison.[50]

Yet in spite of the limitations, produced by the discursive context in which he was working, Davis' contribution to the analysis of empire is a remarkably consistent attempt to give attention to the perspective of the 'subaltern'. He was not quite the first to do this in an Irish context – as we have seen Tone's and even Burke's championing of Catholics in the eighteenth century gave prominence to the rights and sufferings of the 'colonised;' and it may also be argued that Thomas Moore's *Irish Melodies* (1807–18) and *Lalla Rookh* (1817) offered a literary voice to subaltern experience. Moore's songs often take as their central theme cultural dispossession, and the condition of melancholy which defines a significant part of the Irish character for Moore is shown often to derive from the effects of colonization or imperial conquest. But Davis, unlike Tone and Burke, takes up in some detail the theme of the cultural loss and dispossession which results from colonial or imperial rule, and in doing so makes a contribution which foreshadows the twentieth-century work of anti-imperial critics like Frantz Fanon and Ngugi Wa Thiong'o, who have focused upon the traumatic psychological and cultural after-effects produced in the colonised subject. Davis's articles in the *Nation* from 1842 to 1845 argue the need to preserve those relics and reminders of the pre-colonial past before they are entirely lost, be they Celtic and prehistoric antiquities, or old Irish melodies and poems. Most famously, his two articles on the Irish language argue that the language loss produced by conquest and colonial rule produces negative psychological and cultural consequences for colonised or oppressed people. This is a form of critique which goes beyond the moral and legalistic critiques of earlier nationalism, and takes as its central focus the experience of those who have been colonised:

> To impose another language on such a people is to send their history adrift among the accidents of translation – 'tis to tear their identity from all places – 'tis to substitute arbitrary signs for picturesque and suggestive names – 'tis to cut off the entail of feeling, and separate people from their forefathers by a deep gulf – 'tis to corrupt their very organs, and abridge their power of expression.[51]

What we see here, then, is an interestingly transitional phase in the development of anti-colonial and anti-imperial critique. As in many of the writings that emerged from nineteenth-century Irish nationalism, eighteenth-century English-language discourses on empire and colony begin to shift into the vocabulary and strategies we more commonly associate with twentieth-century anti-colonialism. Such texts provide us with evidence of the complicated nature of Irish–British relations, and the widely differing perceptions of those relations among Irish nationalists. These various perceptions are not just a reflection of a simple debate about Ireland's colonial or non-colonial status, however. As we have seen, for Irish nationalists the answer to the question – 'Was Ireland a colony?' – could never be simple. It was inevitably conditioned by factors such as the shape of the discourses of the time, the nature of the writing occasion, and the strategic demands of the moment – as indeed is the case for present-day critics and historians.

NOTES

1. The title of a recent biography of O'Brien plays on this paradox; see R. Davis, *Revolutionary Imperialist: William Smith O'Brien 1803–1864* (Dublin: Lilliput, 1998).
2. S. Howe, *Ireland and Empire: Colonial Legacies in Irish History and Culture* (Oxford: Oxford University Press, 2000), *passim*; D. Fitzpatrick, 'Ireland and the Empire', in A. Porter and A. Lo (eds), *The Oxford History of the British Empire, Vol. 3: The Nineteenth-Century* (Oxford: Oxford University Press, 1999), pp. 499–504; P. Clayton, *Enemies and Passing Friends: Settler Ideologies in Twentieth-Century Ulster* (London: Verso, 1996), pp. 1–12; L. Kennedy, *Colonialism, Religion and Nationalism in Ireland* (Belfast: Institute of Irish Studies, 1996), pp. 35–74.
3. D. Lloyd, *Ireland After History* (Cork: Cork University Press/Field Day, 1999), p. 7.
4. 'Resistance to the English in Africa', the *Nation* 16 Oct. 1847, p. 860.
5. A. Loomba, *Colonialism/Postcolonialism* (London and New York: Routledge, 1998), pp. 1–7.
6. See Kennedy, *Colonialism, Religion and Nationalism in Ireland*, pp. 167–81.
7. Cited in D.G. Boyce, *Nationalism in Ireland* (3rd edn, London: Routledge, 1995), p. 103.
8. Quoted in J. Hill, 'Ireland Without Union: Molyneux and his Legacy', in J. Robertson (ed.), *A Union for Empire* (Cambridge: Cambridge University Press, 1995), p. 280.
9. See Lloyd, *Ireland After History*, p. 7 for a general description of this phenomenon.
10. H. Grattan [Jr], ed., *Speeches of Henry Grattan*, 4 vols (London: Longman, Hurst, Rees Orme and Brown,1822), vol. 1, p. 123.
11. From a 1792 'Address to the Delegates for promoting a reform in Scotland', quoted in L. de Paor, 'The Rebel Mind: Republican and Loyalist', in R. Kearney (ed.), *The Irish Mind* (Dublin: Wolfhound, 1985), pp. 168–9.
12. See for example 'An Argument on Behalf of the Catholics of Ireland', (1791) in S. Cronin and R. Roche (eds), *Freedom the Wolfe Tone Way* (Tralee: Anvil, 1973), pp. 102–24.
13. *Writings and Speeches of Edmund Burke: Volume IX*, ed. R.B. McDowell (Oxford: Clarendon Press, 1991), p. 667. See Luke Gibbons, *Burke and Ireland* (Cambridge: Cambridge University Press, 2003) and T.O. McLoughlin, *Contesting Ireland: Irish Voices Against England in the Eighteenth Century* (Dublin: Four Courts Press, 1999), pp. 161–88 for a lengthier discussion of Burke's anti-imperial arguments applied to Ireland.
14. See A.G.L. Shaw, *Convicts and the Colonies* (London: Faber, 1966), p. 17.
15. E. Gibbon Wakefield, *A View of the Art of Colonization* (London: J. W. Parker,1849), p. 16.
16. Ibid., p. 175.
17. R. Knox, *The Races of Men: A Philosophical Inquiry into the Influence of Race over the Destinies of Nations* (2nd edn, London: Renshaw, 1862), pp. 375, 378.
18. R. Koebner and H.D. Schmidt, *Imperialism: The Story and Significance of a Political Word, 1840–1960* (Cambridge: Cambridge University Press, 1964) p. 10.
19. Cited in the *OED* entry for 'empire'.
20. Cited in Koebner and Schmidt, *Imperialism*, p. 39.
21. Ibid., p. 37.
22. H. Merivale, *Lectures on Colonization and Colonies* [1841] (London: Longman, Brown and Green,1861), p. xii.
23. K. Wilson, 'Empire of Virtue: The Imperial Project and Hanoverian Culture, c.1720–1785', in L. Stone (ed.), *An Imperial State at War: Britain from 1689 to 1815* (London: Routledge, 1994), p. 132.

24. Ibid., p. 153.
25. T. Davis, *Poems of Thomas Davis* (Dublin: Duffy, 1846), p. 27.
26. See Koebner and Schmidt, *Imperialism*, pp. 31–2.
27. From C. Dilke, *Greater Britain* (1868); cited in Koebner and Schmidt, *Imperialism*, p. 24.
28. Cited in Koebner and Schmidt, *Imperialism*, p. 18.
29. *The Spectator*, 11 Jan. 1868, vol. 41, p. 38.
30. Koebner and Schmidt, *Imperialism*, pp. 41–2.
31. Speech quoted in W. Fagan, *The Life and Times of Daniel O'Connell*, 2 vols (Cork: J. O'Brien, 1847–48), vol. 1, p. 116.
32. See further discussion in S. Ryder, 'Young Ireland and the 1798 Rebellion', in L. Geary (ed.), *Rebellion and Remembrance in Modern Ireland* (Dublin: Four Courts Press, 2000), pp. 135–47.
33. Compare Smith O'Brien's argument that criticism of empire was likely to make English less receptive to the idea of Repeal; see R. Davis, *The Young Ireland Movement* (Dublin: Gill & Macmillan, 1987), p. 206.
34. Quoted in the *Nation*, 7 Feb. 1846, p. 261.
35. T.D. McGee, letter to editor, the *Nation*, 16 Oct. 1847, p. 360.
36. *The Times*, 25 Jan.1847; cited in E. Lengel, 'A "Perverse and Ill-Fated People": English Perceptions of the Irish, 1845–52'. *Essays in History*, 38, <http://etext.lib.virginia.edu/journals/EH/EH38/Lengel.htm>, 1996.
37. J. Grant, *Impressions of Ireland and the Irish*, 2 vols (London: H. Cunningham, 1844), vol. 2, pp 189–90.
38. See D.C. Riach, 'O'Connell and Slavery', in D. McCartney (ed.), *The World of Daniel O'Connell* (Dublin: Mercier,1980), pp. 175–85.
39. McDonagh, *O'Connell: The Life of Daniel O'Connell 1775–1847* (London: Weidenfeld and Nicolson, 1991) p. 302.
40. See Davis, *Revolutionary Imperialist*, p. 321.
41. See Davis, *Young Ireland Movement*, p. 207.
42. See, for example, T. Davis, 'The Fate of King Daithi', and J.C. Mangan, 'The Expedition of King Daithi', both in *The Ballads of Ireland*, ed. Edward Hayes, 2 vols (Edinburgh: A. Fullerton, 1855), pp. 64–69.
43. T. Davis, *Essays Literary and Historical*, ed. D.J. O'Donoghue (Dundalk: Pendalgan Press,1914), p. 63.
44. Ibid., p. 64.
45. 'England's Mission', the *Nation*, 18 Feb. 1843, p. 201.
46. See J.N. Molony, *A Soul came into Ireland: Thomas Davis 1814–1845, A Biography* (Dublin: Geography, 1995), p. 28.
47. Ibid., pp. 53–4.
48. 'Afghanistan: The Triumph of Crime', the *Nation* 26 Nov. 1842, p. 105.
49. 'Poor China', the *Nation*, 26 Nov. 1842, p. 104.
50. See S. Ryder, 'Gender and the Discourse of Young Ireland Cultural Nationalism', in T.P. Foley et al. (eds), *Gender and Colonialism* (Galway: Galway University Press, 1995), pp. 210–24.
51. See Davis, *Essays*, p. 97.

CHAPTER TEN

'Becoming a Race Apart': Representing Irish Racial Difference and the British Working Class in Victorian Critiques of Capitalism

AMY E. MARTIN

In a letter to Engels in December 1869, Karl Marx reported on his progress in organising the British proletariat in Victorian London. He wrote of numerous discussions among the members of the General Council of the First International (FI), but in particular of their recent attention to the 'Irish question'. Marx had prepared a presentation for the council in which he set forth his own ideas about the importance of Ireland to the revolutionary politics of the FI. He explained to Engels:

> The way I shall present the matter next Tuesday is this: I shall say that quite apart from all the 'international' and 'humane' phrases about jus-tice-for-Ireland – which are taken for granted in the International Council – it is in *the direct and absolute interests of the English working class* to get rid of their present connection with Ireland ... I long believed it was possible to overthrow the Irish regime by way of the English working-class ascendancy. This is the position I always represented in the *New York Tribune*. A deeper study has now convinced me of the opposite. The English working class will never achieve anything before it has got rid of Ireland. The lever must be applied in Ireland.[1]

This bold statement encapsulates an understanding of relations between England and Ireland that Marx had developed over the course of the late 1860s. By urging the end of the 'present connection with Ireland', Marx argues for the necessity of the end of Ireland's Union with Britain. It is one of the few moments in his monumental corpus on the capitalist mode of production that colonialism and anti-colonial nationalism would play such a prominent, indeed a primary role in both his economic analysis and his theory of proletarian revolution. For in his call for 'get[ting] rid of their present connection with Ireland', Marx asserts that the success of the agenda of radical Irish nationalists – Repeal of the Act of Union and an independent Ireland – was the condition of possibility for the revolution of English workers.[2]

In other letters and articles during the late 1860s and early 1870s, Marx articulates a more elaborate theory of the importance of Ireland to the overthrow of the capitalist mode of production in Britain. He contends that aside from the economic importance of Ireland, continued British rule accomplished three other key things. First, he identified Ireland as:

> ... the bulwark of the *English landed aristocracy*. The exploitation of this country is not only one of the main sources of their material wealth; it is their greatest *moral* strength. They represent in fact *England's dominion over Ireland*. Ireland is, therefore the *grand moyen* by which the English aristocracy maintains *its rule in England* itself.[3]

Here Marx begins to engage with the question of British national identity and nationalism. The exploitation and domination of Ireland provide the British ruling classes with a 'moral strength,' a powerful image of themselves as effective colonisers which in turn secures them not just economic but hegemonic power in Britain. This national identity in turn extends to the working class:

> All English industrial and commercial centers now possess a working class *split* into two *hostile* camps: English proletarians and Irish proletarians. The ordinary English worker hates the Irish worker because he sees in him a competitor who lowers his standard of life. Compared with the Irish worker he feels himself a member of the *ruling nation* and for this very reason he makes himself into a tool of the aristocrats and capitalists *against Ireland* and thus strengthens their domination *over himself*. He cherishes religious, social and national prejudices against the Irish worker. His attitude is much the same as that of the 'poor whites' towards the 'niggers' in the former slave states of the American Union. The Irishman pays him back with interest in his own money. He sees in the English worker both the accomplice and the stupid tool of *English rule in Ireland*. This antagonism is artificially sustained and intensified by the press, the pulpit, the comic papers, in short by all the means at the disposal of the ruling classes. *This antagonism* is the *secret of the impotence of the English working class*, despite its organization.[4]

This passage provides us with a complex and fascinating analysis of the ways in which the power of the British ruling classes was maintained in part by an ideology of anti-Irish prejudice. Rather than engage with the historical accuracy of Marx's analysis, I want to make a more fundamental observation about his remarks concerning the significant place of Ireland in capitalist Britain. Marx is *unable* to diagnose the problems of class politics in Britain without engaging seriously with both British and Irish nationalism and attendant ideas of national identity. He reveals how the revolutionary politics of the British proletariat is defused by a particular construction of Britishness; that construction of national identity is understood through Britain's colonial domination of Ireland. This colonial and racial 'antagonism' dismantles the radical organisation of the working class, producing fractures at the core of its politics. It does so through the production of a nationality that seemingly transcends class relations through recourse to ideas of national difference and, as Marx indicates with his American analogy, the discourse of race.

Marx identifies this problem as bound up with the category of nation. He writes, 'in Ireland, it is not only a simple economic question but at the same time a *national* question, because the landlords there are not, as in England, the traditional dignitaries and representatives of the nation but its morally hated oppressors'.[5] At the same time, the disabling condition of the British proletariat is secured by an ideology in which their identity is constructed as 'member[s] of a ruling *nation*' (Marx's emphasis). In these letters on Ireland, Marx, in an otherwise uncharacteristic move, takes the question of nationalism and the category of the nation quite seriously. In fact, Irish anti-colonial nationalism becomes a necessary catalyst for the revolutionary overthrow of capitalism in Britain. This move rests on the recognition of an ideology of British national identity that takes shape through the justification of colonialism in Ireland and through 'religious, social and national prejudices against the Irish worker'.

Marx's writings on Ireland are just one important example of how, in Victorian Britain, critiques of capitalism were inseparable from the question of Ireland. In this essay, I argue that this moment in Marx's letters in fact emerges from an ideological formation that begins in early Victorian writings on capitalism and class conflict. Thus, this essay contextualises this unusual and resonant moment in Marxist thought through a retrospective approach – by looking back at the writings of two early Victorian critics of the capitalist mode of production, Friedrich Engels and Thomas Carlyle. I want to argue that Marx's turn towards Anglo-Irish relations and questions of race and nation is not anomalous but in fact typical. These letters exemplify an obsession in various studies of capitalism in Britain with the place of Ireland in Britain's most pressing national questions. Therefore, whether towards conservative ends in the case of Carlyle or as part of a burgeoning radical politics in the work of Engels, early Victorian engagements with Britain's capitalist transformation turned to Britain's relations with Ireland as central to their analysis.

In the case of Carlyle's 1839 pamphlet, *Chartism*, a preoccupation with Irish immigrants is central to his elaboration of just the kind of divisive racist and nationalist politics to which Marx alludes. This politics is at the heart of his hugely influential idea of 'the condition of England question', an ideological

formation which transformed Britain's political landscape and literary production during the 1840s. Building on Chris Vanden Bossche's assertion that
'Carlyle [considered] the condition of Ireland a key to understanding the condition of England',[6] I suggest that, for Carlyle, the national crisis facing Britain
is a crisis of Britain's relation to Ireland. Carlyle's formulation of the 'condition
of England question' demonstrates clearly how early Victorian constructions of
the working class become fully imbricated with Irish racial stereotypes and
how ideas about Britain's capitalist condition are also profoundly informed by
fear of the cultural and racial mixing of the 'Saxon' and the 'Celt'.[7]
Conservative panic concerning the possibility of revolution in England is
inseparable from rising anxiety about the integrity of Englishness and
Britishness in the face of the 'counter-colonization' of the imperial nation
through the first large-scale immigration of colonial subjects.[8] In other words,
in a prefiguration of Marx's letters, the crisis that Carlyle identifies in his apocalyptic assertion of national disintegration is, I argue, as much a crisis of immigration and national identity as it is a crisis of class relations. When Carlyle represents England's condition as that of a diseased national body, the disease
with which it is infected is Irish in origin.

In Engels' *The Condition of the Working Class in England*,[9] which draws significantly on Carlyle's pamphlet, attention to British colonialism in Ireland and to
subsequent Irish immigration reveals how the categories of race, colonialism
and nation are at the centre of Marxist politics in its incipient stages. Engels'
revolutionary politics concerning English proletarian radicalism differs greatly
from Carlyle's prophylactic approach to Chartism. But, Engels' chapter, 'Irish
Immigration', shows a surprising point of agreement between the two on the
critical role of Irish immigration in producing discontent among British workers through a flooding of the labour market, a lowered standard of living, and
the introduction of a tendency towards violence against the British state.
Engels shares with Carlyle an analysis of Irish immigrants as a contaminant of
sorts – the source of the economic, cultural, and racial degeneration that has
in turn engendered class consciousness and working-class radical politics. Like
Carlyle, Engels attributes this degeneration to the racial identity of the Irish:
their biological 'uncivilized' temperament and an innate predisposition 'to kill
their oppressors' (CWC 309). However, in order to press this understanding of
Irish immigration into the service of his dialectical analysis of revolution in
England, Engels must reframe this racialism outside the anti-immigrant politics of Carlyle. He encourages miscegenation between the calm, rational
English worker and the violent, insurrectionary Irish worker; Irish racial temperament must be transmitted to the English proletariat not just through
'daily contact' but by means of 'intermarriage' (CWC 139). Engels' project
takes on a eugenic dimension as he imagines a way to transfuse 'Irishness' into
the English nation and thereby to harness Irish violence in the service of revolutionary politics. This observation seeks not to dismiss Engels' work as
racist, but to open up new historical lines of inquiry for the ways that Marxist

analysis and politics from its beginnings was forced to reckon with categories such as race that are often seen as marginalised in classic Marxist thought.

By juxtaposing the work of these two intellectuals, it is also not my intention to ignore or to render insignificant the very important political differences between them. Instead, I want to suggest that their incompatible politics makes their similarities all the more striking. Reading the early writings of Engels and Carlyle comparatively provides an opportunity to see how both hegemonic and counter-hegemonic analyses of class conflict and of revolutionary possibility were inseparable from questions of imperial security, race, immigration, and national integrity. This conjunction is important enough that it persists and takes new forms in the work of Marx and the politics of the First International in the 1860s and 1870s.

It is important to read these texts as emerging out of a particular historical crisis[10] that began with the Act of Union of 1801 and then intensified after Catholic Emancipation in 1829. The Act of Union refashioned the British nation, creating the precarious new entity, 'the United Kingdom of Great Britain and Ireland', through the legal and juridical absorption of a colony into the imperial nation. Even the grammar of this legislative creation reflects the ambivalence with which it was riven from the beginning. The name, 'United Kingdom', reflects a primary insistence that its various parts are solidly unified. However, Ireland remains attached by the conjunction 'and', a grammatical reminder of the limits of incorporation and the spectre of a continued recalcitrance which no union could obscure. Such a close reading makes apparent the ways in which the Act of Union placed the Irish in a liminal and contradictory position. They were national subjects incorporated into the nation-state through parliamentary and economic structures and given the title of citizens, but they remained a colonised and alien population, were denied certain fundamental rights of citizenship, and continued to be constructed as culturally, religiously and racially other. This position rendered Irish masses within the newly created United Kingdom indecipherable in relation to questions of national belonging, internal yet persistently foreign.

The Act of Union also unwittingly created a problem of quarantine with which both Engels and Carlyle grapple. Union was ratified in large part as a legislative response to 'Irish receptivity to French ideas',[11] to anti-colonial insurgency that had long been seen as a dangerous manifestation of the anarchy inherent to the unruly Irish. However, while the creation of the United Kingdom extended the suppressive reach of the British state to Ireland in a more direct manner, Irish violence and revolutionary potential were now in a sense absorbed into the British nation; state domination became easier, but any sort of quarantine of insurrection within the borders of Ireland became difficult if not impossible. From the beginning, the implications of union as a form of colonial domination left British politicians and thinkers grappling with serious questions: how should the Irish be brought into the nation? should they or could they assimilate? how could Irish difference be accommodated within the UK without producing violent and degenerative effects? These questions only intensified after the ratification of the Catholic Emancipation Bill of 1828, legislation which began to dismantle some of the legal disabilities to which Catholics residing in the UK were subject. As state discrimination against the Irish on the basis of religion began to lose some of its force, racial and cultural constructions of difference came to the fore as primary modes of articulating the enduring separateness of Ireland from the United Kingdom.[12]

Hence, in the wake of Union and Catholic Emancipation, the kind of attention to these questions exhibited by Carlyle and Engels is far from anomalous, and during the 1830s, political concerns about Ireland only intensified due to increasing Irish immigration to Britain. Even before a flood of immigrants arrived in Britain during the great famines of the mid-1840s, what Kerby Miller calls 'the prefamine exodus'[13] began when a steady stream of Irish entered Britain as permanent emigrants or seasonal migrants looking for work. By 1841, just two years after the publication of *Chartism*, the British census recorded more than 415,000 Irish in England and Scotland, a figure which did not include seasonal labourers and the children of earlier emigrants.[14] This Irish presence provoked widely disseminated xenophobic discourses on the influence of these immigrants, particularly their effect on the English working class and their politicisation.[15] This backlash was exacerbated by the appearance of a demand for Repeal of the Act of Union on many Chartist platforms, some alliances between Irish nationalists and working-class radicals, and the seemingly prominent role of the Irish in the most radical Chartist politics, which had begun to advocate physical force as a legitimate tactic of political struggle.[16]

When examining the historical context of early Victorian anti-Irish discourse, we must also consider one other aspect of this historical conjuncture. Stuart Hall has defined modern crisis as periods in which the capitalist means of production cannot reproduce itself without significant transformation.[17] Hall's definition allows us to understand Irish immigration to Britain during the 1830s in a more complex frame; the national integrity of Britain was not only threatened by a form of colonial domination that ruptured and reorganised the nation's boundaries, but by the capitalist mode of production's ever increasing demand for surplus labour. The continued expansion of British industrialisation demanded and attracted a reserve army of labour from the feudalized periphery of the newly created United Kingdom.[18] Therefore, post-Union economic decline in Ireland created the material conditions necessary to allow continued capitalist development in Britain.[19] Not only did the newest form of colonial control create a dissolution of national boundaries that threatened the nation's stability and self-conception, but the capitalist mode of production required this same crossing and confounding of boundaries in the form of the immigration and migration of labourers. Stuart Hall has described this process as a 'tension between the tendency of capitalism to develop the nation-state and national cultures and its transnational imperatives [—] a contradiction at the heart of modernity'.[20] Applying Hall's formulation to the Act of Union and subsequent immigration, it becomes clear that Irish immigration during the 1830s and 1840s serves as the lens that brings into focus an extended national crisis precipitated by the conjoined projects of colonialism and capitalist expansion. The English working class became the doubly vulnerable site of permeability and instability; Union dismantled the national boundaries that separated the British proletariat and Irish subjects, while capitalist production demanded that the British working class absorb surplus population, perceived as racially other and inherently insurrectionary, into the nation as necessary labour-power.

   This essay calls attention to the way that, in early nineteenth-century conservative and progressive interventions regarding the working class, the discourse of race is required to identify and analyse the complex crisis I have described and to resolve it accordingly. I am not suggesting that the discourse of Irish racial difference first appears during the early Victorian period.[21] In keeping with the work of Luke Gibbons and Mary Hickman who argue that racial stereotypes about the Irish pre-date the nineteenth century, I am attempting to rethink a transformation of a long-standing discourse of Irish racial difference, a transformation that takes place during the first half of the nineteenth century in Britain. Hazel Waters and Kevin Whelan have presented compelling arguments that anti-Irish racism, while having powerful antecedents for centuries, crystallised in its most explicit form during the Great Famine.[22] However, Carlyle's *Chartism* shows that this crystallisation after 1846 occurs as the culmination of a process begun in the previous decade. In the case of both Carlyle and Engels, pre-Famine racialist discourse provides a way to think through the transformations effected by the development of the capitalist mode of production and the possibility of revolution in Britain. Therefore, this essay investigates this shift in the ideological work that the discourse of race performs in early Victorian Britain. Race provides a way to represent what is perceived as the critical role of Irish subjects in the inextricable diseases of industrialisation and discontent. For Carlyle and Engels, a racialized conception of Irishness enables them to imagine two radically different cures for the chronic affliction of class conflict in Britain.

*   *   *   *

Very little critical attention has been directed to the central place of Irish immigration in Engels' earliest work on the English proletariat, *The Condition of the Working Class in England*. For example, Steven Marcus' comprehensive study, *Engels, Manchester, and the Working Class*, seldom mentions Engels' analysis of Irish immigration to Britain; he describes the chapter titled 'Irish Immigration' as an appendage of sorts 'which acts as a footnote to and additional confirmation of the arguments advanced in the chapter on competition'.[23] In his ground-breaking history, *The Making of the English Working Class*, E.P. Thompson writes a short section on the Irish that ends with an affirmation of Engels' analysis of Irish immigration as 'the precipitate which brought the more disciplined and reserved English workers to the point of political action'. Thompson acknowledges that '[w]e may dispute Engels' language of "nature" and "race"' concerning the Irish, but 'we need only replace these terms to find that his judgement is valid'.[24] Besides for this brief disavowal of 'nature' and 'race' (which leaves unexplained how such terms could possibly be replaced without compromising the content of Engels' study), Thompson does not undertake any substantive engagement with these terms or with their critical place within Engels' understanding of the condition and politicisation of the working class in England.

As Marcus points out, Engels' small chapter on 'Irish Immigration' appears after his explication of competition between workers for employment. In 'Competition', Engels first employs the example of the Irish immigrant to demonstrate how both wages and standards of living are lowered by the introduction of competition. He writes:

> The Englishman, who is not yet wholly uncivilised, needs more than the Irishman, who goes about in rags, eats potatoes and lives in pigsties. This does not prevent the Irishman competing with the Englishman and gradually dragging down his wages and standard of living to his own level. Certain jobs can only be performed by workers who have reached a certain degree of civilisation and practically all industrial employment falls into this category ... The newly-arrived immigrant from Ireland would make a poor factory worker. His level of culture is so low that he camps in the first stables that he comes across and if he got a decent cottage he would be evicted every week because he squanders wages in drink and cannot pay the rent. (CWC 90)

Despite what Engels describes as the 'uncivilized' state of Irish immigrants, they play a key economic role as 'surplus population', a reserve of labour power 'available to produce the great quantities of goods which are needed during the few months when the business boom reaches its climax'. (CWC 97–8) However, Engels is absolutely clear that 'the real reason for the existence of the superfluous population is the competition of the workers among themselves' which allows factory owners to lengthen the work day and to lower wages. (CWC 94) These passages reveal the significance of Irishness within the dialectical materialism that Engels is beginning to theorise in 1845. In fact, he argues that the biological material of the Irish cultural and racial character is the synergist for an intense state of competition which subjugates workers within the English labour market so efficiently. Therefore, the influence of competition would not be nearly so effective without the introduction of a surplus population which is specifically *Irish*. The culturally specific standard of living that Irish immigrants carry with them is represented with a portrait of domestic chaos and drunken disorder.

In the next chapter on 'Irish Immigration', the racialist dimension of Engels' analysis becomes completely clear. The chapter begins with a brief statistical account of Irish immigration to Great Britain which estimates that 'over a million have emigrated to Britain, and fifty thousand more are coming in year by year'. (CWC 104) Engels then continues his detailed description of the Irish national character, asserting that these immigrants are 'uncouth, improvident, and addicted to drink' and 'introduce their brutal behavior' into the English proletariat. However, he interrupts himself with a sudden exclamatory gesture: 'Let Thomas Carlyle speak on this subject.' At this point, the text is overtaken by an extended citation of 'Chartism'. Carlyle's text serves an evidentiary function, supporting Engel's previous assertions concerning Irish national character. Engels follows this citation by stating: 'Carlyle's description is a perfectly true one if we overlook his exaggerated and prejudiced defamation of the Irish national character.' (CWC 105) However, this disclaimer, strangely reminiscent of E.P. Thompson's, proves empty; despite the brief acknowledgement of Carlyle's 'defamation' of Irishness, Engels uses this passage as a springboard for his own racialist characterisation of Irish immigrants and their influence on the British proletariat.

Indeed Engels proceeds to enumerate the same essential Irish attributes that Carlyle describes in *Chartism*. The only difference between the racial discourse in these texts is representational strategy; while Carlyle offers the reader a vivid portrait of the 'wild Milesian' who becomes both a metaphor and a synecdoche for Irishness, Engels' writes in a documentary register of the socio-economic and cultural impact of the Irish on Britain. Engels rehearses a catalogue of traits which characterise Irishness – indolence, intemperance, unsanitary living habits which pollute Britain, and a general lack of 'civilization'. For example, writing of Irish 'filth', Engels provides accounts of the 'abnormal method of rearing livestock in large towns' which includes allowing pigs to share family sleeping quarters and 'the custom of living in one room' which has not 'spread widely among the English'. These anecdotes combine ideas about laziness, domestic disorder, animality, and the pollution of the nation. Thus, while industrialisation sets in motion the degeneration of working class conditions, the infusion of Irish customs into the nation intensifies such degradation. Engels asserts that '[I]t is not surprising that a social class already degraded by industrialisation and its immediate consequences should be still further degraded by having to live alongside and compete with the uncivilised Irish.' (CWC 107) In other words, the capitalist mode of production can only produce the most intense degeneration of the proletariat when coupled with the effects of Union and immigration.

If Engels intends only to recapitulate the stereotypes of Irishness in *Chartism*, then what do we make of his disclaimer in which he seems to reject Carlyle's 'exaggerated and prejudiced defamation of the Irish national character'? I want to argue that we can read this ambivalent textual moment as typical of Engels' desire to have two seemingly contradictory discourses at work in his analysis of Irish immigrants. At times, Engels seems to take an anti-essentialist position, attributing those characteristics that he notes in the Irish population to the living conditions found in Ireland as a result of colonial rule. He writes that, '[s]ociety neglects the Irish and allows them to sink into a state bordering upon savagery. How can society complain when the Irishman does, in fact, become a habitual drunkard?' (CWC 106–7) This analysis allows Engels to incorporate Irish immigrants into his understanding of the capitalist mode of production, making the Irish subject to the same exploitation as the British working class. He also begins to find justification for the Irish discontent which becomes so central to his vision of impending revolution in Britain.

However, this anti-essentialism is often subsumed by an insistence that Irish national character is ultimately racial in origin. If Irishness were produced solely by historical conditions, then reform might remedy the problem, a possibility which Engels rejects wholesale. As we will see, in order for Engels to press Irish immigrants into the service of revolutionary politics, their national character must be innate and immutable. Therefore, Engels posits race as the basis of Irish difference. In 'Irish Immigration,' he writes, 'One may depend upon seeing mainly Celtic faces, if ever one penetrates into a district which is particularly noted for its filth and decay.' Thus the presence of Irish faces serves as an index of squalor, and racial and national character are written onto Irish bodies in the form of visible, detectable physical difference: 'These faces are quite different from those of the Anglo-Saxon population and are easily recognisable.' Language and accent serve as supplementary indices of Irishness, as Engels writes, 'The Irish, of course, can also be identified by their accent, for the true Irishman seldom loses the sing-song, lilting brogue of his native country. I have even heard the native Irish language spoken in the most densely-populated parts of Manchester.' (C 105)

In a later chapter titled 'Proletariat on the Land', Engels extends his racialist analysis, arguing:

> The English are indeed responsible for the fact that poverty strikes the Irish a little sooner than it would otherwise do. But they cannot be held responsible for the poverty itself ... The actual manner in which poverty strikes the Irish may be explained by the history, traditions, and national characteristics of the people. The Irish have a strong affinity with the Latin races such as the French and the Italians. (CWC 308)

In other words, Irish poverty finds its cause in a national disposition which is the direct expression of racial identity. According to Engels, race singularly determines the socio-economic conditions in Ireland which are carried by Irish immigrants to the new locations in which they settle. He also insists on the affinity of the Irish with 'the Latin races such as the French and Italians'; this comparison gestures towards a shared racial genealogy with nations imagined to have a revolutionary disposition expressed in their national history and sets up the Irish as a potential revolutionary force in Britain.

In the chapter that follows 'Irish Immigration,' Engels continues his exploration of the effect of the Irish on the British working class, writing:

> It has been observed that the arrival of the Irish has degraded the English workers, lowering both their standard of living and the level of their behavior. On the other hand the Irish immigrants have helped to widen the gulf that separates the capitalists from the workers, thus inevitably hastening the approaching cataclysm ... we must welcome any circumstances which bring the disease [of capitalism] to its climax. (CWC139)

At this moment, we can see how Engels envisions Irish immigration as a productive force fuelling the dialectic of history towards revolution. He redeploys the discourse of the disease of the social body to represent the capitalist mode of production, but he argues that the disease cannot be cured; rather it must be 'brought to a climax' through the heightening of class conflict into a 'cataclysm.' In order for this to occur, the Irish must affect Britain not only economically and culturally but most importantly, racially:

> The Irish immigration is hastening this process [the inevitable movement towards revolution] because the passionate, excitable sides of the Irish character have had their effects on the English workers. In many ways the English are to the Irish as the Germans are to the French. In the long run this union of the livelier, more mercurial and more fiery temperament of the Irish with the stolid, patient, and sensible character of the English can only be mutually beneficial. The harsh egotism of the English middle classes would have kept its hold much more firmly on the English proletariat, if it had not been for this Irish element. It is in the nature of the Irish to be generous to a fault and to be swayed almost wholly by sentiment. *Through intermarriage and by daily contact in the workaday world these Irish attributes have softened the cold and rational aspects of the English character.* In these circumstances it is not surprising that the working classes have *become a race apart* from the English bourgeoisie. (my emphases, CWC 139)

'The Irish character', which Engels has identified as racial in origin, transforms the fixed temperament of the English proletariat. As an innately 'stolid, patient, and sensible' subject, the English worker does not possess the 'fiery temperament' necessary to incite a dramatic political revolution; Irish immigrants must provide the ignition for revolutionary upheaval. The racial temperament of the Irish is transfused into the British masses, transforming the legislative union of Great Britain and Ireland and the political union between working-class radicals and Irish nationalists into a racial union as well. The suggestion of 'intermarriage' implies that reproduction allows for the materialisation of working-class subjects who embody the double racial character that is ideal for revolutionary action. Therefore, at the crux of Engels' argument, miscegenation becomes a necessary catalyst for revolution in England.

The consequences of this racial fusion are twofold. First, as the above passage demonstrates, the gulf between the working class and the bourgeoisie is transformed from an economic division into an immutable division of race. As a result, '[t]he middle classes have more in common with every other nation in the world than with the proletariat which lives on their own doorsteps'. (CWC 139) Engels rethinks Disraeli's infamous description of class difference as the bifurcation of Britain into 'two nations' and reconstructs that division along the axis of race. This new profound split makes class conflict more intense, and less able to be ameliorated by any prophylactic measures such as Reform legislation or even the extension of suffrage that Chartists demand. For Engels, racialism provides the condition of possibility for the destruction of British national cohesion.

Second, the transfusion of Irish blood into the British national body 'add[s] an explosive force to English society'. (CWC 309) What must be transmitted is not simply racial difference, but a racial character that contains within it the means to trigger revolution. Since Engels constructs the Irish as 'passionate', mercurial and fiery, Irish bodies carry within them a predisposition to violence not possessed by the British proletariat. Engels reminds his readers that '[t]he Irish people have resisted oppression in two ways' – agitation for Repeal of the Union and 'acts of violence'. He states that '[c]rime is endemic in the rural districts [of Ireland] and not a day passes without the perpetration of some serious breach of the law. Nor do the Irish hesitate to kill their oppressors ...' (CWC 309) Therefore, the most important element of Irishness is a predisposition towards violence – a raced tendency to resist oppression through brutal and criminal means. Through contact, intermarriage and miscegenation, the Irish propensity for transgressing the law and for the murder of oppressors will infect the English worker with the temperament necessary to strike out against the bourgeoisie and the British state. The English working class are faced with their own racial lack which translates into the failure of their radical politics; Irish blood is required to hasten the development of class consciousness and then to transform Chartism into active, violent upheaval. For Engels, working-class identity in England cannot be theorised without an account of the racial consequences of immigration; racial discourse works as an indispensable element in the dialectical movement of history toward class conflict and revolution.

*   *   *   *

How can we understand Engels' reliance on racial discourse in his earliest work on the English working class? Does this racism somehow undermine the searing critique of the capitalist mode of production and the early dialectical materialism that is at work in his 1844 study? In order to answer these questions, we must turn to Carlyle's work in *Chartism* four years earlier. This small pamphlet, however conservative, contained a public indictment of capitalism by a major early Victorian intellectual, an indictment that was to have far-reaching consequences in the social realist literature of the 1840s as well as in the arena of parliamentary politics. It was this aspect of Carlyle's intervention that made it so attractive to Engels. In a sense then, Engels' particular understanding of Irish immigrants and revolution can be understood as an engagement with Carlyle's formulation of the 'condition of England question' that appeared in 1839.

In *Chartism*, a strange amalgamation of potentially radical critique of capitalist expansion with conservative panic about working-class radicalism, Carlyle assesses current class conflict and working-class radicalism in Britain and declares a national crisis. He articulates this crisis as an urgent query facing the English nation: the 'condition of England question'.[25] To represent and to explore this national emergency, Carlyle imagines early Victorian England as a diseased national body.[26] For Carlyle, Chartist politics and other manifestations of working-class discontent are outward signs of an illness ravaging England – 'symptoms on the surface [which] you abolish to no purpose, if the disease is left untouched.' (C 3) In his metaphoric pathologization of working-class insurgency, Carlyle insists that his intervention is an attempt to provide an epidemiology, a comprehensive study of the causes, transmission, and potential cure of Chartist agitation.[27]

Literary critics have most often read Carlyle's biomedical trope of national crisis in relation to domestic problems facing early Victorian Britain such as the growth of working-class;[28] ruling-class failure to govern properly; the dominance of a laissez-faire ideology in social and economic policy in Britain; the erosion of religious, moral, and political authority within the nation; and industrialisation's corruption of what Carlyle saw as an effective social order.[29] Yet a careful reading of this recurring image reveals that disordered class relations and related domestic conditions cannot be the *only* cause of England's ailment. While such forms of disorder figure largely in Carlyle's exploration of Chartism, his metaphor presents the unmistakable suggestion of infection by foreign contagion. What alien infectious agent has penetrated England's boundaries and, through pollution of the working class, serves as the catalyst for the disease of proletarian disaffection?

According to Carlyle, the source of this infection is Ireland. He names Irish immigration to Britain, a phenomenon that he connects with colonialism, as 'the sorest evil this country has to strive with' (C 28), the means of transmission of an infection which adulterates the body politic with working-class unrest and revolutionary potential.[30] Carlyle figures the Irish immigrant as 'the ready made nucleus of degradation and disorder' who carries to Britain the misery of Irish poverty and a 'degraded National character'. (C 28) At the close of his chapter on the English working class, he writes boldly, 'Ireland is in chronic atrophy these five centuries; the disease of nobler England, identified now with that of Ireland, becomes acute, has crises, and will be cured or kill'. (C 35) By tracing briefly the discourse of disease in Carlyle's pamphlet, we see immediately the central place of Irish immigrants in his analysis of class conflict and proletarian radicalism in Britain.

These immigrants overwhelm and destabilise the British labour market and introduce a 'pestilence' which takes hold of a national body already weakened by forms of domestic disorder. Carlyle declares:

> [t]here is one fact which Statistical Science has communicated, and a most astonishing one; the inference of which is pregnant as to this matter. Ireland has near seven millions of working people, the third unit of whom, it appears by Statistical Science, has not for thirty weeks each year as many third-rate potatoes as will suffice him. It is a fact perhaps the most eloquent that was ever written down in any language, at anydate of the world's history. (C 25)

This hyperbolic passage insists upon the momentous global importance of the historical phenomenon of Irish economic decline. The enormously significant 'fact' of Ireland's condition is 'pregnant' in relation to the 'condition of England question'; this use of reproductive language throws into relief the Malthusian underpinnings of Carlyle's analysis. The evocation of overpopulation and of millions of starving, indolent bodies across the Irish Sea inaugurates Carlyle's apocalyptic vision of the impending destruction of the English nation. If the expansion and development of the capitalist mode of production causes the demoralisation of British workers, Irish immigrants are the primary catalyst for this process.

This argument culminates in Carlyle's painstaking construction of a vision of 'Irish national character'. (C 26) Carlyle contends that the dominant, essential qualities of Irish national identity are criminality, treachery, anarchy, and dishonesty, a total alienation from 'the truth'. (C 27) These characteristics combine to form a general state of barbarism,31 one which is not only alien to Englishness but a terrifying, irreversible inversion of British civilisation. 'Savagery' has taken a biological hold in each Irish body, encoded and carried in blood, until the disorder 'circulates through every vein, of [the people]'. Once this internalisation and transmutation are complete, the Irish are emptied of all human content and become a 'no-thing', (C 27) a kind of living vacuum devoid of civilisation. In relation to Britain, each Irish subject is a 'Sanspotatoe', (C 28) a lack who looks to consume that which has been denied him or her.

This disturbing portrait of Irish national character becomes an almost hysterical form of racism when Carlyle begins to describe Irish immigrants to

Britain. In what I am calling the 'wild Milesian' passage – which Engels cites at length in his chapter on Irish immigration – Carlyle writes:

> But the thing we had to state here was our inference from that mournful fact of the third Sanspotatoe, — coupled with this other well-known fact that the Irish speak a partially intelligible dialect of English, and their fare across by steam is four- pence sterling! Crowds of miserable Irish darken all our towns. The wild Milesian features, looking false ingenuity, restlessness, unreason, misery and mockery, salute you on all highways and byways. The English coachman, as he whirls past, lashes the Milesian with his whip, curses him with his tongue; the Milesian is holding out his hat to beg. He is the sorest evil this country has to strive with. In his rags and laughing savagery, he is there to undertake all work that can be done by mere strength of hand and back; for wages that will purchase him potatoes. He needs only salt for condiment; he lodges to his mind in any pighutch or doghutch, roosts in outhouses; and wears a suit of tatters, the getting on and off of which is said to be a difficult operation, transacted only in festivals and the hightides of the calendar. The Saxon man if he cannot find work on these terms, finds no work. He too may be ignorant; but he has not sunk from decent manhood to squalid apehood ... (C 28)

In this lengthy narrative, every 'third Sanspotatoe' enters the British nation easily due to the proximity of Ireland and the low cost of transportation. Such immigrants 'darken all our towns'. The metaphor of 'darkening' represents the process of national degeneration in Britain that the Irish presence generates. The descriptive, 'darkening', also literally implies the unsanitary living habits that Carlyle associates with the Irish – the 'filth' of Irish working-class ghettoes that sully English and Scottish cities. This metaphor also offers a figurative representation of the cultural and racial pollution of British civilisation. Carlyle identifies the sites of this contamination as 'our' urban centres, employing the first person plural to consolidate British national belonging in the face of an Irish invasion.

Arrival in Britain transforms the 'Third Sanspotatoe' into the 'wild Milesian', the synecdochal figure of the Irishness transfused into Britain. Carlyle imagines this Milesian as an Irish pauper who, while begging on the roadside, is whipped by an English coachman – a vignette which embodies Carlyle's vision of the relations between Ireland and Britain. The image places the English figure physically above the roadside beggar and also seated upon a coach, a signifier of British technological superiority, of the coachman's stable place within the nation's class structure, and of his skilled labour. The coachman must fend off the Irish pest beneath him with physical violence; thus, Irish immigrants are immediately associated with economic parasitism that demands violent suppression. The Milesian is described as willing to perform unskilled labour for wages below the British national standard; his presence transforms the labour contract. For Carlyle, the first and most striking effect of the presence of the Milesian is the degeneration of the national economy produced by falling wages, increased unemployment, and a growth in the number of the working class who, in order to survive, either enter state-sponsored workhouses or become indigent.

In addition, the Milesian's 'savagery' is composed of other attributes which typify Irishness – irrationality, 'false ingenuity', and mockery of English civilisation; these characteristics of Irish national identity are expressed through Irish culture. Carlyle redeploys stock images of Irish rags and filth, reinforcing a long-standing stereotype that the Irish had a much lower standard of personal and domestic hygiene than the British. Such unsanitary conditions are synonymous with supposed Irish superstition and Catholic idolatry, as the Milesian changes his suit of tatters only 'in festivals and the hightides of the calendar'; while Carlyle writes little of Irish Catholicism in *Chartism*, this image makes clear the way that Roman Catholic religious practices serve as evidence of Irish inferiority.[32] Bodily degradation is mirrored by the 'barbaric' living conditions of Irish domestic space, a standard of living akin to the animality of 'pighutch[es] or doghutch[es]'; even the simplicity of the food eaten in the households of a 'root-devouring' (C 26) people who need 'only salt for condiment' becomes a stigmatising signifier of savagery. These aspects of Carlyle's Milesian reinforce Anne McClintock's argument that 'English racism also drew deeply on the notion of the *domestic* barbarism of the Irish as a marker of racial difference', leading to the formation of an 'iconography of domestic degeneracy'.[33]

Carlyle's imagining of 'the wild Milesian' also associates the Irish with criminality, particularly various forms of the 'drunken violence' (C 28) that he calls to his readers' attention throughout *Chartism*. Carlyle makes use of a tradition that describes the 'natural' Irish temperament as unstable, violent, and unpredictable. In an 1834 travel narrative published several years before *Chartism*, Henry Inglis, a close friend and correspondent of Carlyle's throughout the 1830s, wrote that for the English, '[t]he very name [Ireland] forces to our recollection images of shillelaghs, and broken heads, and turbulence of every kind'.[34] Here Inglis claims that, in British popular memory, Ireland is synonymous with violence in many forms. This statement exemplifies the way in which resistance to colonial domination was depoliticised and translated into 'irrational' violence produced by the essential instability and criminality of the Irish. Through the prism of racialization, anti-colonial violence is abstracted into general 'turbulence'. The stereotype of Irish predisposition to violence was posited as the expression of an inherent insanity: 'emotional instability, mental disequilibrium, or dualistic temperament'.[35] In other words, in this construction of the 'wild Milesian', Carlyle engages in both the racialization of violence and what Michel Foucault calls 'the psychiatrization of criminal danger'.[36] He then suggests that this national predisposition to criminal insanity is exacerbated by uncontrolled consumption of alcohol, the 'liquid Madness' of the Irish (C 35).

The Milesian passage suggests two primary markers of difference that express Irish national character in legible form and that allow for the identification of Irish immigrants despite the absence of what Franz Fanon called an 'epidermal schema' of race. Carlyle first identifies the 'partially intelligible dialect of English' spoken by the Irish as an emblem of their barbarism. Language, accent, and a supposed inability to master the English language inscribe Irish bodies circulating throughout Britain with an audible difference that ensures their detectability and that therefore differentiates them from the British working class.[37] These linguistic markers also signify the inability of the Irish to assimilate into English culture and the failure of a long-standing project of cultural imperialism.

Carlyle supplements this linguistic difference with an insistence on corporeal markers of Irishness. Halfway through the Milesian passage, he shifts his narrative into the second person; readers are exhorted to scrutinise proletarian faces and to discover in them the imagined signs of mass Irish immigration. He informs his reader that *'wild Milesian features,* looking false ingenuity, restlessness, misery, and mockery, *salute you* on all highways and byways' (my emphases, C 28). Irish difference operates in a visual economy; physiognomy 'salutes' those who witness it, making the identification of Irishness possible by reading the inscription of barbaric attributes onto the very features of immigrants. At the same time, Carlyle never describes the distinctive physical features of the Milesian, leaving the reader in the throes of a scopic drive to discern national character in the faces of passers-by. Like the symptoms of the diseased national body that require scrutiny, the faces of the working class must be read constantly for signs of racial difference that they may express.

Carlyle's complex representation of the 'wild Milesian' reveals that his understanding of Irishness in 1839 exists at the crossroads of two discourses. At the start of *Chartism,* Carlyle claims that Irish national character has been created by historical conditions, centuries of poverty and misrule that led to the degradation of the people as a whole. As we have seen, this difference has solidified into a permanent identity that cannot be reversed simply by altering historical circumstances; degeneration has created a kind of sedimentation of barbarism which is contained in and expressed upon the surface of Irish bodies. Therefore, Carlyle's construction of Irishness contains a racialist and racist dimension, but one which constructs race as a mutable biological identity forged by historical conditions. This logic is in keeping with Etienne Balibar's suggestion that while the distinction between cultural racism and biological racism can be a useful tool of analysis, it is important to remember that 'culture can also function like a nature, and it can in particular function as a way of locking individuals and groups a priori into a genealogy, into a determination that is immutable and intangible in origins'.38 Indeed, in the case of Carlyle, cultural racism figures history as an agent which transforms culture into nature.

This racial imaginary then ineluctably slides into and becomes inextricable from a discourse on racial genealogy which implies an immutable ancient basis for the national character of the Irish. For, as Carlyle's descriptive term 'Milesian' suggests, he imagines Irishness as originating from racial descent as well as historical conditions. Throughout the nineteenth century, the term 'Milesian' signified a racial mythology that traced the origins of the Irish people to ancestors in Egypt and Spain who eventually settled in Ireland.39 This genealogy was widely disseminated in the works of the Scottish scholar MacPherson, texts with which Carlyle was certainly familiar. When Carlyle invokes this account of racial origins, he differentiates the genealogy of the Irish people from the English who can claim an Anglo-Saxon heritage which, later in *Chartism*, becomes critical to Carlyle in his myths of empire as Britain's national and racial destiny. Therefore, the Irish difference of which he writes is simultaneously the result of an historically contingent process of degeneration and of essential racial descent; it is expressed in an articulation of cultural racism and biological, naturalised racism.

Hence, the transformation of Britain occasioned by the Act of Union, industrialisation, and subsequent immigration is not only economic, cultural, and political, but ultimately racial. Carlyle imagines that a blood transfusion of sorts has taken place, and the anarchy which is Irishness circulates through the veins of Britain's national body. Following the depiction of the wild Milesian, he describes this process as an invasion:

> American forests lie untilled across the ocean; the uncivilized Irishman, not by his strength but by the opposite of strength, drives out the Saxon native, takes possession in his room. There abides he, in his squalor and unreason, in his falsity and drunken violence, as the ready-made nucleus of degradation and disorder ... This soil of Britain, these Saxon men have cleared it, made it arable, fertile, and a home for them; they and their fathers have done that. Under the sky there exists no force of men who with arms in their hands could drive them out of it; all force of men with arms these Saxons would seize, in their grim way, and fling (Heaven's justice and their own Saxon humour aiding them) swiftly into the sea. But behold, a force of men armed only with rags, ignorance and nakedness; and the Saxon owners, paralysed by invisible magic of paper formula, have to fly far, and hide themselves in Transatlantic forests. (C 28–29)

Here, Carlyle anticipates the 'cure' for the condition of England question which he presents at the close of *Chartism* – the global emigration of the surplus British workers who might serve as the agents of Britain's imperial destiny. Irish immigration to Britain is the unfortunate circumstance which makes

the emigration of the British working classes necessary. In a reworking of colonial discourse, standard iconography of the engulfment of new territories and
their subsequent cultural, social and political regeneration is inverted into a
dystopic narrative of the counter-colonization of Britain. Once the British
state absorbs Ireland into the UK and Irish immigrants begin to enter Britain,
the fantasy of *the civilizing mission*, of the march of progress through the spread
of English government and culture around the globe, is replaced by a reverse
trajectory. Two racially distinct, masculine nations[40] – 'the Saxon men' and 'the
uncivilized Irishman' – struggle to occupy Britain. As the militarised might of
the Saxons fails, they are subsumed by 'a force of men armed only with rags,
ignorance, and nakedness' who stand as the phantasmic antithesis of
Britishness. We see a paranoid fantasy in which colonial violence is turned
against the imperial centre which is then engulfed and its national subjects
expelled. The British nation is now colonised by the savagery it was destined
to civilise, and this colonization of the working classes, their eviction from
Britain,[41] indicates that this unimaginable conquest is almost complete.
Indeed in the fourth chapter of *Chartism*, the reader discovers that the 'finest
peasantry in the world' is not England's working class, but refers ironically to
Irish immigrants who are 'streaming in on us daily.' (C 31) In the end, capitalist expansion allows England to be consumed by her dangerous colony, and
'Ireland, now for the first time, in such strange circuitous way, does find itself
embarked in the same boat with England, to sail together, or to sink together;
the wretchedness of Ireland, slowly but inevitably, has crept over to us and
become our own wretchedness.' (C 30)

Victorian respondents to *Chartism* as well as recent Carlyle scholars have
criticised the pamphlet for its lack of proposed solutions for the disease which
Carlyle so extensively diagnoses.[42] Indeed Carlyle does not offer any suggestions for remedying the crisis produced by capitalist development and post-
Union Irish immigration. He ends his pamphlet with two propositions – education of the working class[43] and emigration of the British proletariat in the
service of imperial expansion. While Carlyle barely mentions the 'wild
Milesian' when suggesting these measures, it is possible that, like other politicians and commentators of the 1830s who imagined schemes of resettling the
Irish in the New World,[44] he had hopes for directing the 'Third Sanspotatoe'
to the colonies rather than Britain. He gestures to this solution when he mentions 'American forests [that] lie untilled' while Irish immigrants flood a nation
which lacks the employment they seek. Still, no more explicit reference is
made to government-subsidised plans for Irish immigration.

Perhaps to look for such concrete propositions in Carlyle's pamphlet is
beside the point though. Instead, what may be most important about *Chartism*
is not a vision of socio-political change or the suggestion of any palliative measure, but the text's transformation of the discourse that articulates British
national crisis and by extension national identity. By disseminating a discourse
of Irish difference in 1839, Carlyle's analysis of Irish immigration itself serves

as a solution for the 'condition of England question' occasioned by industriali-sation and class conflict. In an essay titled 'Class Racism', Etienne Balibar writes suggestively of a transformation in nationalist ideology that begins in early Victorian Britain:

> [Disraeli] indicates the path which might be taken by the dominant classes when confronted with the progressive organization of the class struggle: first divide the mass of the 'poor' (in particular by according the qualities of national authenticity, sound health, morality and racial integrity, which were precisely the opposite of the industrial pathology, to the peasants and the 'traditional' artisans); then progressively dis-place the markers of dangerousness and heredity from the 'labouring classes' as a whole on to foreigners, and in particular immigrants and colonial subjects, at the same time as the introduction of universal suf-frage is moving the boundary line between 'citizens' and 'subjects' to the frontiers of nationality.[45]

Carlyle's influential anti-Irish politics and representations of Irishness partic-ipate in just the displacement that Balibar describes. The phantasmic figure of the 'wild Milesian' and the terrifying image of the imperial nation colonised by 'savage' immigrants – these Carlylean discourses perform the exclusion and expulsion of those who are simultaneously 'foreigners … immigrants and colo-nial subjects'. In other words, Carlyle's racist anti-immigrant politics postu-lates a consolidating vision of British national identity that synthesises the working classes with the rest of Britain through the marginalization of Irish subjects. This nationalist politics renders unnecessary even the extension of suffrage – a Chartist demand – but also a legislative possibility raised by the limited yet significant Reform Act of 1832.[46] This emerging form of British nationalism offers a symbolic share in a coherent, unified national identity as a compensatory substitute for and a displacement of the rights of universal cit-izenship as envisioned by working-class radicals. In the face of the historical crises precipitated by capitalism and colonialism, Carlyle relies on the dis-course of race to redraw the boundary lines of nationality and to subordinate the potentially revolutionary difference of class to the difference between cit-izens and colonial subjects, between British and Irish, between Saxon and Milesian Celt. Therefore, I would argue that anti-Irish racism and the British nationalism with which it is imbricated serve as two of the primary ideological agents through which the British working class is hegemonized and through which the British nation is mobilised as an imagined racial unity with a com-mon imperial destiny.

For Carlyle, this refiguring of the British nation in relation to Irish nation-al character is one of the prophylactics that might prevent a revolution in Britain. He writes:

For that the Saxon British will ever submit to sink along with [the Irish] to such a state, we can assume as impossible ... *there is a 'Berserkir-rage' in the heart of them* [the British], which will prefer all things, including destruction and self-destruction to that. Let no man awaken it, this same Berserkir-rage! *Deep-hidden it lies, far down in the centre, like genial central-fire*, with stratum after stratum of arrangement, traditionary method, composed productiveness, *all built above it, vivified and rendered fertile by it*; justice, clearness, silence, perserverance, unhasting unresting diligence, hatred of disorder, characterise this people; *their inward fire we saw, as all such fire should be, is hidden at the centre. Deep hidden; but awakenable and immeasurable — let no man awaken it! With this strong silent people have the noisy vehement Irish now at length got common cause made.* (my emphases, C 30)

This passage begins with a rejection of the apocalyptic vision of degeneration that Carlyle presented earlier in *Chartism*. Employing the rhetorical strategy of a ominous warning, Carlyle cautions that Irish immigrants might awaken an essential 'Berserkir-rage' hidden at the racial core of the British, one which until now has been sublimated into the work of British civilisation. As the catalysts for the violent disaffection of the British proletariat, the Irish have disturbed the racial temperament of the Saxons now that '[w]ith this strong silent people have the noisy vehement Irish now at length got common cause made'. This statement refers not only to the 'common cause' created by Union and immigration, but to developing political alliances between British proletarian radicals and some Irish anti-colonial nationalists commonly lamented in conservative Victorian politics.[47]

I call attention to this passage because I believe that it explains the ideological function of the nexus of anti-Irish racism and Saxon nationalism that we find at work in *Chartism*. This racist ideology serves to redirect the 'rage' of the masses from the ruling classes and the British state into a xenophobic channel, diverting it towards the Irish immigrants in their midst. Identifying the Irish as the limit of a raced British nationality disrupts real and potential political organisations which might encompass working-class radicals and immigrant colonial subjects; it also resolves the crises of national integrity created by Union. In Balibar's words, the category of immigration functions as 'a solvent of "class consciousness"'.[48] Carlyle's anti-Irish racism and his vision of Britain hegemonize the British working classes by interpellating them as members of a racially homogenous nation of Saxons; class politics is subordinated to the imperative to reconsolidate national identity in the face of immigration. This political project requires an identification of the racial character of the Irish and the exclusion of the 'wild Milesian' who is Britain's racial and immigrant other.

*   *   *   *

My reading of Carlyle's *Chartism* returns us to Engels' eugenic understanding of revolutionary possibility in early Victorian Britain and allows us to read his attention to Irish immigrants in a wider political frame. For it seems that by 1845, the political terrain concerning class conflict and revolution had already been mapped out through ideologies of race and nationalism. In fact, the discourse of Irish racial difference allows Engels to imagine a repair of the schism that is enacted by Carlyle's anti-Irish racism. By reworking Carlyle's racist and nationalist ideology into a narrative of miscegenous possibility, Engels finds a way to contest both the displacement of 'the markers of dangerousness and heredity from the "labouring classes" as a whole on to foreigners, in particular immigrants and colonial subjects'.[49] He imagines a way to challenge the redirection of proletarian discontent from the dominant classes to immigrant populations. In an inversion of Carlyle's project, Engels' racialism does not produce a fantasy of national reconciliation but provides the condition of possibility for the destruction of British national cohesion. Yet, he accomplishes this not by contesting or rejecting this racialism; instead, he works within the discourse of Irish difference, attempting to articulate it with his own revolutionary politics.

By 1869, however, the great costs of racialism and racism left intact had revealed themselves, as Marx would write eloquently of 'a working class *split* into two *hostile* camps' and would try to find a way to negotiate that divide. Victorian critiques of capitalism continued to face the problem of Anglo-Irish relations throughout the nineteenth century. In fact, Engels would justify his own attention to Ireland in the preface to the 1892 edition of *The Condition of the Working Class in England*. He describes the decade of the 1840s as the period during which the development of the British world market began to rapidly expand; he recognises the integral role of Ireland in the transnationalization of capital through imperialism:

> England was to become the 'workshop of the world'; all other coutries were to become for England what Ireland already was – markets for her manufactured goods, supplying her in return with raw materials and food. England the great manufacturing centre of an agricultural world, with an ever-increasing number of corn and cotton growing Irelands around her, the industrial sun! [50]

Engels identifies the importance of Ireland as an economic model for the development of the capitalist world market. In this essay, I hope to have shown that this economic expansion co-existed with a coterminous process of the construction of interrelated British and Irish national identities that began in the 1830s. Capitalist expansion required ideologies in which Britain worked to represent itself as an organic whole conceptualised through the exteriorisation of the Irish nation now harnessed to it. Critiques of capitalism had to come to terms with the way that race served such an ideological function. As Marx wrote, 'This is why the Irish question is so important for the social movement in general.'[51]

NOTES

1. Original emphasis, Marx to Engels, 10 Dec. 1869, in K. Marx, *The First International and After, Political Writings: Volume 3*, ed. D. Fernbach (New York, NY: Penguin Books), pp. 166–7.
2. Marx called directly for the English workers to make Repeal of the Union 'an article of their *pronunziamento*'. Marx to Engels, 30 Nov. 1867, ibid., p. 161. At the same time, he continually expressed his distaste for many Fenian nationalists and their politics, writing 'I don't like being involved with people like [them]', p. 159.
3. Original emphases, Marx to Meyer and Vogt, 9 April 1870, ibid., p. 168.
4. Original emphasis, ibid., p. 169.
5. Original emphasis, Marx to Kugelman, 29 Nov. 1869. ibid, p. 165.
6. C. Vanden Bossche, *Carlyle and the Search for Authority* (Columbus, OH: Ohio State University Pres, 1991), p. 127.
7. Histories of these stereotypes can be found in L.P. Curtis, *Apes and Angels: The Irishman in Victorian Caricature* (rev. edn, Washington DC: Smithsonian Institute Press); and R.N. Lebow, *White Britain and Black Ireland: the Influence of Stereotypes on Colonial Policy* (Philadelphia, PA: Institute for the Study of Human Issues, 1976). More recently, see L. Gibbons, 'Race Against Time: Racial Discourse and Irish History', in *Transformations in Irish Culture* (Notre Dame, IN: University of Notre Dame Press, 1996), pp. 149–63.
8. One of the most compelling articulations of this argument can be found in M. Hickman, *Religion, Class and Identity: The State, the Catholic Church and the Education of the Irish in Britain* (Aldershot: Avebury, 1995).
9. Throughout this essay, I cite F. Engels, *The Condition of the Working Class in England*, trans. W.O. Henderson and W.H. Chaloner (Stanford, CA: Stanford University Press, 1958). Henceforth this text will be cited parenthetically as CWC.
10. Here I am relying on Stuart Hall's definition of crisis. In his generative reading of Gramsci, Hall asserts that it is necessary 'to distinguish between "organic historical movements, which are destined to penetrate deep into society and to be relatively long-lasting", from more "occasional, immediate, almost accidental movements". In this respect, Gramsci reminds us that a crisis, if it is organic, can last for decades. It is not a static phenomenon but rather, one marked by constant movement, polemics, contestation, etc., which represent the attempt by different sides to overcome or resolve the crisis and to do so in terms which favour their long term hegemony.' See S. Hall, 'Gramsci's Relevance for the Study of Race and Ethnicity', in D. Morley and K. Chen (eds), *Stuart Hall: Critical Dialogues in Cultural Studies* (New York, NY: Routledge, 1996) p. 422. Therefore, using this definition, I would argue that the multifaceted crisis that I describe as the context for reading Carlyle and Engels lasts throughout the 1830s and 1840s rather than appearing as an 'immediate', relatively brief crisis.
11. R. Foster, *Modern Ireland 1600–1972* (London: Allen Lane, 1988), p. 282.
12. I'm not suggesting that anti-Catholicism was replaced by national and racial discrimination against the Irish. Rather while these discourses were always articulated, I would argue that the passing of Catholic Emancipation legislation marked a shift in the structure of their artic-ulation. Perhaps one could say that rather than religion also being a raced category, race now became a more primary identifactory structure that was articulated with persistent anti-Catholic discourse. A similiar argument concerning the co-existence and imbrication of anti-Irish racism and anti-Catholicism is made by Hickman in *Religion, Class, and Identity*.
13. K Miller, *Emigrants and Exiles: Ireland and the Exodus to North America* (New York, NY: Oxford University Press, 1985) p. 1.
14. T.W. Freeman, 'Land and People, c. 1841', in W.E. Vaughan (ed.), *A New History of Ireland. Vol. V Ireland Under the Union 1801–1870* (Oxford: Clarendon Press, 1989).
15. Historians of Irish immigration to Britain have engaged in extensive debate about the exis-tence and pervasiveness of anti-Irish xenophobia and racism in Britain. In particular, Sheridan Gilley has argued that most British stereotypes about the Irish during the nineteenth centu-ry were 'national not racial'. However, Gilley's rejection of anti-Irish prejudice as racial is

grounded in large part in his own racism; he writes, 'Unlike Anglo-Saxons and Celts, Caucasian and Negroes are in fact different races, defined by objective physical characteristics, most notably skin color.' See S. Gilley, 'English Attitudes to the Irish, 1780–1900', in C. Holmes (ed.), *Immigrants and Minorities in British Society* (London: George Allen and Unwin, 1978), pp. 85 and 90. This essay rejects such work, calling into question its assumption that race is an objective material difference rather than a socially constructed category of identification that is historically contingent and that may rely on criteria of identification other than skin colour.

16. See D. Thompson, 'Ireland and the Irish in English Radicalism before 1850', *Outsiders: Class, Gender and Nation* (London: Verso, 1993), pp. 103–33.

17. S. Hall, *The Hard Road to Renewal: Thatcherism and the Crisis of the Left* (London, Verso, 1988), p. 98.

18. Eric Hobsbawm describes the role of the Irish as a 'reserve army' of unskilled labour which provided British industry with the capital of a 'mobile vanguard' of labour. E. Hobsbawm, *Industry and Empire: from 1750 to the present* (London: Penguin Books, 1970), pp. 309–12.

19. See Marx's striking description of this process in the chapter titled 'The Working Day' in K. Marx, *Capital Volume I*, trans. Ben Fowkes (New York, NY: Penguin Books, 1976) pp. 340–416.

20. S. Hall, 'Our Mongrel Selves', *New Statesman and Society*, 19 June 1992, p. 6.

21. For more on pre-Victorian racial discourse concerning the Irish, see J. Leesson, *Mere Irish and Fior Ghael* (Notre Dame, IN: University of Notre Dame Press, 1996).

22. H. Waters, 'The Great Famine and anti-Irish Racism', *Race and Class*, 37, 1 (July–Sept. 1995), pp. 95–108. K.Whelan presented this argument in a lecture, 'The Famine and its Aftermath: A Post-Revisionist Perspective', delivered at the Irish Studies Seminar of Columbia University in 1994.

23. S. Marcus, *Engels, Manchester, and the Working Class* (New York, NY: W.W. Norton, 1974), p. 204.

24. E.P. Thompson, *The Making of the English Working Class* (New York, NY: Vintage Books, 1966), p. 443.

25. This phrase appears at the very start of *Chartism* as the title of the first chapter. Throughout this article, I cite the second edition of T. Carlyle, *Chartism* (London: Chapman and Hall, 1842). Henceforth, the pamphlet will be cited parenthetically in the text as C.

26. Throughout this essay, I come up against the problem of employing the terms 'British' and 'English' consistently. Carlyle uses the terms interchangeably, but his frequent references to 'England' and 'the English' function in the way described by Catherine Hall: 'Englishness marginalizes other identities, those from the peripheries, the Welsh, the Scottish, and the Irish. In constructing what it meant to be English, a further claim was constantly being made – that Englishness was British, whereas those on the margins could never claim the right to speak for the whole..' See C. Hall, *White. Male, and Middle Class: Explorations in Feminism and History* (New York, NY: Routledge, 1992), p. 206. Following Hall's analysis, I use the terms 'English' and 'England' when necessary to reflect Carlyle's use of this descriptive, keeping in mind their metonymic function and the power relations that these terms belie. However, in my own analysis, I employ 'British' whenever possible in order to mark the hegemonic inclusion of Scottish and Welsh populations within Carlyle's understanding of Englishness.

27. Carlyle's use of the trope of disease also echoes the rhetoric of middle- and upper-class panic about literal contagion in the 1830s, such as cholera and typhus, epidemics which were seen to emanate from working-class neighbourhoods in urban centres and to contaminate Britain as a whole. See J. Arac, *Commissioned Spirits: the Shaping of Social Motion in Dickens, Carlyle, Melville and Hawthorne* (New York, NY: Columbia University Press, 1979), pp. 29–30. In addition, Carlyle redeploys the figuration of revolutionary politics as a disease, a metaphor common in British conservative reaction to the French Revolution several decades earlier. See D. Pick, *Faces of Degeneration: A European Disorder, c. 1848–1918* (Cambridge: Cambridge University Press, 1989).

28. In particular 1839 saw major acceleration of mass proletarian protest in the form of the General Convention of the Industrious Classes which presented to Parliament a petition demanding the ratification of the Charter; the petition contained approximately 1,280,000 signatures. One of the primary debates at the Convention was the use of 'physical force' as a supplement to or even a replacement for constitutional agitation. For a general history of the Chartist movement, see A. Briggs, *Chartism* (Gloucester: Sutton, 1998).

29. Critics who have stressed the importance of these domestic conditions in Carlyle's *Chartism* include R. Williams, *Culture and Society: 1780–1950* (New York, NY: Columbia University Press,

1958); and J. Rosenberg, *Carlyle and the Burden of History* (Cambridge, MA: Harvard University Press, 1985).

30. Mary Poovey points out that early Victorian reports on the conditions of the poor, such as James Phillip Kay's 1832 pamphlet titled 'The Moral and Physical Condition of the working Classes ... in Manchester', not only identity Irish immigrants as the cause of cholera epidemics, but also use this discourse of epidemic to represent socio-political unrest in Britain. See M. Poovey, *Making a Social Body: British Cultural Formation, 1830–1864* (Chicago, ILL: University of Chicago Press, 1995), pp. 56–64.

31. See S. Deane, 'Civilians and Barbarians', in *Ireland's Field Day* (London: Hutchinson, 1985), pp. 33–42.

32. In my reading, Catholicism is not the cause of Irish barbarity but its signifier. This analysis is in keeping with Mary Hickman's suggestion that in the eighteenth and nineteenth centuries, '[r]arely were the defects of the Irish character portrayed as the consequence of Catholicism itself, rather the Irish refusal to embrace Protestantism was due to the debased character of the Celt ...' See Hickman, *Religion, Class and Identity*, p. 27.

33. A. McClintock, *Imperial Leather: Race, Gender, and Sexuality in the Colonial Contest* (New York, NY: Routledge, 1995), p. 53.

34. Cited in R.N. Lebow, *White Britain and Black Ireland*, p. 53.

35. See Curtis, *Apes and Angels*, p. 51.

36. See M. Foucault, 'The Dangerous Individual', in L.D. Kritzman (ed.), *Politics, Philosophy, Culture: Interviews and Other Writings, 1977–1984*. (New York, NY: Routledge, 1988), pp. 125–51. Foucault identifies this process as beginning during the first three decades of the nineteenth century in Europe. It is worth noting the relevance of Foucault's analysis of the 'dangerous individual', a concept which emerges from 'a knowledge-system capable of characterizing a criminal individual in himself [sic] and in a sense beneath his acts; a knowledge-system able to measure the index of danger present in an individual ... [and] which might establish the protection necessary in the face of such a danger'. Foucault describes this concept as part of a discourse of degeneration and also as emerging from a transition in which '[t]he social 'body' ceased to be a metaphor and became a biological reality and a field for medical intervention'. Building upon this genealogy, Carlyle and Engels seem to rely on the medico-juridical concept of the 'dangerous individual' and to identify Irish immigrants as such.

37. See C. Wills, 'Language Politics, Narrative, Political Violence', *Oxford University Review*, 13, 1–2 (1991), p. 53.

38. See E. Balibar and I. Wallerstein, *Race, Nation, Class: Ambiguous Identities* (London: Verso, 1988), p. 23.

39. See S. MacManus, *The Story of the Irish Race: A Popular History of Ireland* (New York, NY: The Devin-Adair Company, 1944). According to the *OED*, this mythological genealogy was first noted in *Edmund Spenser: A View of Present State of Ireland*, W.L. Renwick (ed.).

40. As is apparent, Carlyle also identifies the Irish immigrant as male and as the bearer of an anarchic inefficient masculinity which stands in opposition to the stolid 'Saxon manfulness' of British subjects. In both instances, the male working-class body becomes the metonym for national identity.

41. It is difficult to miss the irony of Carlyle's narrative in which British citizens are 'evicted' by Irish immigrants. The evictions which typified the settlement of Ireland and other colonies is transplanted and replayed on British soil in yet another inversion of imperial destiny.

42. For example, see Vanden Bossche, *Carlyle and the Search for Authority*, p. 96.

43. While Raymond Williams sees Carlyle's call for education of the working class as an important progressive thread running throughout 'Chartism,' my own understanding of this proposition is in agreement with David Lloyd and Paul Thomas's critique of Williams. They argue that most bourgeois and some proletarian calls for the education of the working classes must be understood as part of the emergence of the ethical state in the Victorian era, serving the ideological function of forming working-class subjects into docile citizens. They write, 'Educating the poor was not just a Victorian philanthropic obsession. It merits reading as an ideology, since it served at once as a means (and often as *the* means) to shelving dangerous political reforms, and at the same time, operated as an important mechanism of social control,' D. Lloyd and P. Thomas, *Culture and the State* (New York: Routledge, 1998).

44. For historical accounts of such schemes of emigration designed to relieve conditions in Ireland believed to be caused by overpopulation, see H.J.M. Johnston, *British Emigration Policy 1815–1830: 'Shovelling out Paupers* (Oxford: Clarendon Press, 1972); and D. Fitzpatrick, *Irish*

Emigration 1801–1921 (Dublin: Economic and Social History of Ireland, 1984).

45. See Balibar and Wallerstein, *Race, Nation, Class*, p. 210.
46. For more on the history of the complex relationship between Chartism and various forms of Irish nationalism, see J. Belchem, 'English Working-Class Radicalism and the Irish, 1815–50', in R. Swift and S. Gilley (eds), *The Irish in the Victorian City* (London: Croom Helm, 1985), pp. 85–97.
47. See Balibar and Wallerstein, *Race, Nation, Class*, p. 20.
48. Ibid., p. 210.
49. F. Engels, 'Preface to the English Edition of 1892', in *The Condition of the Working Class in England*, p. 366.
50. Marx to Engels, 10 Dec. 1869, in Marx, *The First International and After*, p. 167.

CHAPTER ELEVEN

Irish Political Economy Before and After the Famine

TERRENCE McDONOUGH, EAMONN SLATER and THOMAS BOYLAN

INTRODUCTION

This essay will argue that the Famine in nineteenth-century Ireland represented a turning point in the theoretical basis of Irish economic thought.
Prior to the Famine, Irish political economy was inward looking, seeking to constitute political economy as an objective science uniquely suited to the resolution of social divisions. After the Famine, Irish political economy became excep-
tionally outward looking, seeking inspiration in the broader field of the social sciences, specifically in history, sociology and jurisprudence. Even within economic orthodoxy, fresh arguments were sought to justify a change in land policy. We
will argue that while the demonstrative power of the Famine itself surely had an
influence on this transformation, the social changes wrought in the wake of the
Famine were also significant. The problematic character of the Irish agricultural
economy and the proposed solutions to this problem form an essential background to developments within political economy. More than this, the creation
of an emerging class of substantial tenants in the wake of the Famine clearances
created the social basis for the altered perspectives on Irish political economy.

Before the Famine, classical political economy, based in a utilitarian framework and advocating a policy of laissez-faire, was dominant in Ireland both at
the level of the academy and attempts at popular education in economic matters. Indeed, in the work of Longfield and others, Irish political economy in
this period anticipated the development of marginal theory in economic
thought. After the Famine, classical political economy was largely abandoned
and alternative frameworks of thought were sought. This quest led in several
directions. Ameliorist social science was introduced to Ireland by the
Statistical and Social Inquiry Society of Ireland. T.E. Cliffe Leslie and John
Kells Ingram founded an historical school of economics, which inspired modern institutional economics in the tradition of Veblen. Finally, a basis for the

rehabilitation of the customary rights of the Irish peasantry was sought in the translation and analysis of the Celtic Brehon Law tradition. Each of these new intellectual directions were to drive Irish political economy across disciplinary boundaries, boundaries between economics and sociology, economics and history, and economics and jurisprudence.

Both the transformation of Irish agriculture under pressure for consolidation of holdings and the new thinking in the economics profession altered the terrain upon which solutions to Ireland's development problems were sought. The creation of capitalist farming on the English model was abandoned as not taking into account local particularities and progress was sought in the creation of an independent peasantry.

PRE-FAMINE POLITICAL ECONOMY IN IRELAND

In the pre-Famine period, Ireland became a key stomping ground for the development of the conservative political implications of classical political economy. Indeed, Irish political economy managed to produce a kind of radical orthodoxy which was well ahead of its advent in Britain. In the work of Bishop Whately and Mountifort Longfield, Irish political economy became more Catholic than the pope, where papal authority in this case rested with the Ricardian tradition.

Strangely, it was the anachronistic and colonial character of Irish society which made it ripe for the ideological application of the most advanced elements of economic science. A predominantly feudal society, suffering from a late transition to capitalism, proved fertile ground for the latest in bourgeois political economy. A deeply divided society was the legacy of the English colonial imposition of a kind of bastardised feudalism on Ireland, a feudalism not founded in a history of the evolution of mutual rights and obligations between a native peasantry and a native (or at least assimilated) ruling class. Without a system of mutual rights and obligations, agrarian relations within the Irish estate suffered from a more radical schism than existed in landlord/tenant relations in mainland Britain before the advent of capitalist relations in agriculture. To this radical economic inequality were added differences in nationality and religion consequent on the colonial conquest and the transplantation of a ruling class which was English in origin. These latter differences were especially consequential in that they closed off the most powerful of the traditional ideologies establishing a common principle of identification across the class divide. The British ruling elite in Ireland could appeal to neither patriotism nor the Church in commanding a common allegiance from the exploited strata of the population. The Anglo-Irish ascendancy, largely descended from the Cromwellian invaders of the 17th century, had maintained a British cultural identity and a loyal Protestantism which separated them from the Irish Catholic majority. From the beginning, the colonial background had impoverished the moral economy of Ireland. Colonial Ireland generated an ongoing legitimation crisis for the state and the economic elites. A concerted attempt was made to fill this ideological vacuum with political economy. It was hoped that the most advanced elements of metropolitan social science and ideology could provide the crucial legitimation for an Irish economy caught in a kind of colonial time warp.

While it lacked the emotional resonances of nationalism and religion, English political economy was in many ways well suited to the ideological task it was called upon to perform. Political economy claimed a scientific impartiality and ironically an ideological neutrality. It assumed the capability of adjudicating conflicting social claims. In a religiously divided society, political economy was a secular system of thought. Its universal validity superseded religious and moral discourse. Indeed, its elaboration of utilitarianism as the basis for personal and public choice obviated the need for moral principles at all, reducing all questions to a calculation of utility.

While claiming impartiality, political economy was at the same time highly and quite pointedly partisan. It devoted considerable energy to defending existing social and economic relations. It was dedicated to a policy of free trade and most especially laissez-faire, confident of the identity of the pursuit of self-interest and the pursuit of public interest. In promulgating the principle of government non-interference, political economy was especially concerned to defend property rights. Looking to the success of capitalist agriculture in the English countryside, political economists found justification for applying this doctrine of the inviolability of property rights to the Anglo-aristocracy's landed estates.

The pivotal figure in this regard was Richard Whately, the Anglican Archbishop of Dublin from 1831 to 1863. Before his appointment to religious office in Dublin, Whately had been Drummond Professor of Political Economy at the University of Oxford, where he had succeeded Nassau Senior. Whately did not allow his religious duties in Ireland to sap his interest in political economy. While in Dublin, he established the first Professorship of Political Economy at Trinity College. He was the first president of the Dublin Statistical Society and was widely regarded as 'the father of economic science in Ireland'. He also served on the Board of National Education, interesting himself particularly in the spread of economic ideas into the schools. To this end, he wrote the text, *Easy Lessons in Money Matters*, which quickly became the bestselling work on economics in the nineteenth century.

In 1848, in the midst of the Famine, Whately contended political economy was 'the only means which existed of rescuing the country from convulsion', and went on to say:

> It was a mistake to suppose that religion or morals alone would be sufficient to save a people from revolution. No; they would not be sufficient, if a proper idea of Political Economy was not cultivated by that people.

A man, even of the purest mind and most exalted feelings, without a knowledge of Political Economy, could not be secured from being made instrumental in forwarding most destructive and disastrous revolutions.[1]

As a form of irrefutable knowledge, political economy imposed consensus. It presented existing social relations as harmonious and beneficent, between nations, between employers and employees, and, crucially, between landlords and tenants. Through the agency of competition, individual, class and national interests coincide.[2]

Wealth was to be achieved through thrift over the generations. Any redistribution of property would only ultimately strike hardest at the poor. After a redistribution of wealth

the rich would have become poor, but the poor, instead of improving their condition would be much worse off than before. All would soon be as miserably poor as the most destitute beggars are now. Indeed, so far worse, there would be nobody to beg of.[3]

Whately concluded that

the rich man, therefore though he appears to have so much larger a share allotted to him, does not really consume it; but is only the channel through which it flows to others. And it is by this means much better distributed than it could have been otherwise.[4]

Whately's enthusiasm for political economy did not extend to the work of David Ricardo and the vast majority of the occupants of the Whately professorship at Trinity were anti-Ricardian. Ricardo's framework, while laissez-faire in outlook, contained within it elements which could be used to undermine the Whatelian vision of universal social harmony. This was especially true with regard to the labour theory of value, and Ricardo's analysis of landlord consumption as a drag on economic progress.[5] Whately's first appointment to the professorship, Mountifort Longfield, produced a new economic theory, which according to Schumpeter, 'overhauled the whole of economic theory and produced a system that would have stood up well in 1890'.[6]

Longfield, in Black's[7] estimation, constructed an extraordinary complete marginal theory of value and built upon it a new, non-Ricardian theory of distribution. Longfield rejected the Ricardian ideas of the subsistence theory of wages and the view that the productivity of agricultural land plays a decisive role in determining the return on investment. He developed a theory of profit that linked the return on capital to the marginal productivity of machinery employed in production. Profits, rents and wages were all determined by the laws of supply and demand.[8] His theory emphasised price instead of value, and scarcity instead of the cost of production.[9]

This original school of economic thought was continued within the work of the next Whately professor of political economy, Isaac Butt, who took over the chair in 1836. Butt urged his students to pay serious attention to Jean Baptiste Say and Nassau Senior as well as to Longfield's work. According to Moss, Butt was able to combine Say's and Longfield's works to produce an early statement of the marginal productivity theory of imputation:

> Say had argued that the value of factors of production is derived from [use] value of the products they helped to produce. Say did not explain, however, how the total value created by factors in combination could be imputed to each factor individually. Butt found in Longfield's writings the principle that determines the proportions in which value created by factors in combination is divided among them. That principle is none other than Longfield's concept of 'capital efficiency' whereby competition assures that the unit of capital employed with the least efficiency sets the rental price of the rest.[10]

It fell to William Neilson Hancock, who succeeded to the Trinity chair in 1846, and who was to initiate the Dublin Statistical Society in 1847, to draw out the implications of this conservative political economy for Irish economic policy. Hancock first had to confront the apparent contradiction between a theoretical framework which advocated laissez-faire a priori and a Famine-ravaged Irish economy which cried out for reform. Hancock neatly resolved the problem in the following way:

> What is the advantage it is said, of interfering with existing arrangements? We are taught by *laissez-faire* to leave things as they are, and trust that they will come right in time. Now, this reasoning is quite true if we suppose it to be applied to a state of affairs in which there is no legislative or other interference with the enterprise of individuals. But where such interference *does* exist, to leave things as they are is to perpetuate interference.[11]

What Hancock is arguing is that aspects of the legal code appropriate to feudal relations of production have persisted in Ireland. These remnants were interfering with the efficient operation of the market, which could otherwise be expected to resolve Irish agricultural problems. Hancock sets out to investigate these legal interferences and how they impede the development of an Irish economy based upon laissez-faire principles. In a series of six papers read before the Dublin Statistical Society, between 20 November 1848 and 30 April 1849, Hancock looked at how legal impediments affected the agriculture of Ireland. In 1850, these papers were published in book form.[12]

Hancock argued that the poor state of Irish agriculture was in part caused by the legal structure, which prevented the free transfer and sale of land, and thereby hindered the application of capital to Irish agriculture. The vendor of land had to produce sixty years' title to every acre on offer. This was a time-consuming and expensive process as in Ireland at that time there was no general register of land. To find a sixty-year title for land, Hancock reckoned that about 20 per cent of the selling price was needed to cover the cost of the legal searches.

Hancock[13] also criticised legal restraints on the power of the landlord to alienate land. Hancock suggests that fee in tail and life estates[14] should become fee simple estates. This would give the holder of the estate the right to sell it and pay off the estate's debts. In order to achieve this legal position, it would be necessary for the government to provide a parliamentary title to the landed estate by creating a general register. Hancock's policy suggestion in this regard was enacted by the government in the Encumbered Estates Act of 1849.

As regards the tenantry, Hancock favoured establishing the legal right of the tenant to his improvements and fixtures. The tenant should have a right to either compensation or be able to take the improvements away with him. There is an implicit tendency in Hancock's work to see Ireland as made up of harmonious productive agents with common interests. This especially comes to the fore when Hancock emphasises how the same laws effect the insecurity of both landlord and tenant. The structure of the existing legal impediments is not blamed on any existing ruling class but on the folly of past generations. Hancock summarises the core of his argument in the following way:

> The doctrine of *laissez-faire* teaches us, that in all industrial undertakings we may rely on the best results being produced by private enterprise, if it be only emancipated from the restrictions which the ignorance and folly of past generations have allowed to become sanctioned by law.[15]

Papers reaching roughly the same conclusions as Hancock's were presented to the Society by John A. Lawson, Edward Lysaght, William Hearn, and Jonathan Pim.

Notwithstanding Hancock's support for the tenant's right to improvements, the political economists of the Dublin Statistical Society were in the main unsympathetic to the demands of the nascent Tenants Right Movement. Lysaght saw the Movement as prejudicial to all classes of the community on three counts. Firstly, converting the landlord's rent into a fixed rent would deprive him of all interest in the improvement of the land. Secondly, absenteeism by landlords would be encouraged since they would not be able to increase their income by having residence on their respective estates. Thirdly, the quantity of food produced would be decreased because fixed rents would eliminate 'the present system of competition rents', within which

> ... unless a tenant raises from his farm, agricultural produce of as large a market value, at as small a cost of production as others could at the time his rent was fixed, he cannot continue to pay the same rent, and must soon resign the farm to a tenant of more skill and industry.[16]

POLITICAL ECONOMY AFTER THE FAMINE

After the Famine, Irish political economy underwent a sea change. Prior to the Famine years, Irish economic difference was something to be cured through the application of the standard remedies. The lack of confluence between Irish field systems and British structures was thought to merely underline the need for the more vigorous application of metropolitan political economy. The unorthodox character of the Irish economy was regarded as a sufficient reason for the promulgation of orthodox political economy. In the post-Famine period, Irish economic difference was to have different theoretical consequences. Increasingly, the unique features of the Irish economy, and importantly the specific historical development behind these features, was understood as calling for innovations in economic analysis. Some of these innovations would be found within the framework of traditional political economy. More striking, however, was the pursuit of alternative theoretical frameworks.

The year 1855 marks a turning point in the deliberations of the Statistical Society. In this year, the Society merged with the Social Inquiry Society. Black points out the significance of this development:

> The objects of the Statistical Society were correspondingly enlarged and its business became 'the promotion of the study of statistical political economy and jurisprudence ...' The Society could now be said to deal with social science in the widest sense ...[17]

This development also marked the beginning of a fragmentation and diversification of the theoretical outlooks employed by the members of the Society in understanding Irish society. The tenor of the contributions begins to drift from the deductive methodology of classical political economy to a more inductive collection of facts, statistics, and comparative studies. Ameliorist approaches are taken to social problems and questions of morality loom larger in the Society's discussions.

Perhaps the most dramatic indication of these changes can be found in the work of Hancock. Beginning in 1855, Hancock increasingly concerned himself with an advocacy of the preservation of the family as the natural unit of society. Women and men each had a specific role or function within the family. A consistent dedication to this principle led Hancock to begin to challenge the universal applicability of a political economy which would call the special role of women into question:

> ... it is urged that the principles of free trade require that all employments should be thrown open to women; that it is tyranny and oppression to oppose any restriction; that existing misery and distress arise from arrangements and prejudices against the employment of women.[18]

In a paper read in 1859, Hancock begins to reject the consequences of the unfettered practice of capitalism in agriculture. The paper was entitled 'On the Bothy System of Lodging Farm Labourers in Scotland; its violation of the Family Principles; its condemnation by the Free Church of Scotland; the conclusions to be deduced from the facts stated, and their application to Ireland'.[19] The bothy system was a housing scheme for farm labour, employed by the capitalist tenant farmers in Scotland, where both sexes were lodged together in a hut or outhouse.[20] Hancock quotes a report on the social conditions of the Scottish bothies made by a Committee for the General Assembly of the Free Church of Scotland:

> The nearly unanimous testimony of the returns is to the effect that almost every form of moral evil has sprung from the bothy system, and especially that it has been a great foster parent of Sabbath-breaking, drunkenness and illegitimacy in the districts in which it prevails.[21]

Hancock then links the bothy system with the development of capitalism in Scotland, where the concentration of capital has consolidated the small croft holdings. He argues this linkage should call into question our support for a laissez-faire approach to capitalist development in agriculture:

> In many of the returns to the General Assembly the system is said to have been caused by the introduction of improved farming, the throwing of several farms into one, and the demolition of the old cottages, as being no longer necessary under the new system of husbandry ... Now, when we find improved agriculture in Scotland is attended with the development of the Bothy System with such results as we have seen, it is plain that we cannot place unlimited confidence in capitalist farmers, that the well-being of the labouring classes, which after all, form the bulk of our population, will be safe in their hands without some public opinion to control them.[22]

This questioning ultimately results in a call from Hancock for the preservation of the small farm:

> ... I believe that both large and small farms should exist, and neither to be excluded, and that the forced destruction of small farms, which has been so much favoured in Scotland and in Ireland, is as injurious as forced subdivisions in France.[23]

This new view of Hancock's is a complete rejection of his earlier work in the 1840s, in which he argued for the elimination of legal impediments within the Irish land system in order to make way for the unfettered dynamics of the market. He concludes his paper with a clear statement of his new theoretical position:

The care of wealth has now, as ever, a tendency to hardness of heart, which moral discipline is necessary to control. It has, too, a tendency to generate strong selfishness and a want of consideration for others. I have referred to this point of the subject at such lengths to show that social science does not sanction any law of competition as a substitute for the important moral duties that devolve on every owner of wealth and every employer of labour.

No mere material progress, however great or splendid, can release us from the moral discipline which human nature has always and must ever require.[24] (p. 381)

Hancock's aggressive substitution of moral discipline for the discipline of the market marks a turning point in his thought.

A related development is the introduction of Comtist sociology to Ireland and Irish political economy. On the one hand, Comte's system was positivist in that it held that all social phenomena were data from which a comprehensive science of history could inductively be built. On the other hand, in common with Hancock's developing perspective, Comtists believed that the object of a better understanding must be an improvement in the moral basis of society. Comte went so far as to establish an alternative religion of 'humanity'.[25]

Comtist sociology as a system was enthusiastically brought to Ireland by John Kells Ingram. Ingram held that political economy could not be isolated from other branches of social science. Indeed, economics must be considered a subordinate branch of the more inclusive science of sociology and could only be understood with reference to society as a whole. Ingram contended:

> we cannot isolate the study of one organ from that of the rest, or of the whole. We cannot break up the study of the human body into a number of different sciences, dealing respectively with the different organs and functions, and, instead of a human anatomy and physiology, construct a cardiology, a hepatology, an enterology. It is not of course meant that special studies of particular organs and functions may not be undertaken ... but ... it is essential to keep in view their relations and interactions, and that therefore they must be treated as forming part of the subject-matter of one and the same science.[26]

By analogy, Ingram argues,

> There is one great science of Sociology; its several chapters study the several faces of social existence. One of these faces is that of the material well-being of society, its industrial constitution and development. The study of these phenomena is one chapter of Sociology, a chapter which must be kept in close relation with the rest.[27]

Ingram believed that the then current difficulties of economics could be traced partially to the attempt to consider the economy as the object of a separate science. The problems economics faces will not be resolved 'unless it (economics) be linked in close connection with the general science of society - unless it be, in fact, subsumed under and absorbed into Sociology.'[28] This understanding of the economy accorded more importance to the differing political and cultural institutions of various times and places. In common with the other post-Famine intellectual currents, Comte's sociology rested the explanation of social phenomena in their historical development. This preference for historical explanation was underlined by Ingram's active participation in the founding of the 'English' historical school of economics.

Irish economists had a disproportionate influence in the formation of the historical school. Ingram was a prominent proponent and published the only full scale treatment of the history of economic thought from the historical point of view.[29] Even more influential was T.E. Cliffe Leslie. Leslie opened what has been called the English Methodenstreit in a series of articles in the 1870s. Leslie argued against what he considered to be an overly abstract deductivism in classical political economy. He contended instead that economic understanding must advance through the inductive consideration of the specific character of particular economies.[30]

Influenced by the work of Sir Henry Maine, Leslie believed that explanation must rest with the historical development of particular times and places:

> ... every branch of the philosophy of society, morals and political economy not excepted, needs investigation and development by historical induction; and that not only the moral and economic condition of society, but its moral and economic theories and ideas, are the results of the course of national history and the state of national culture. Contemporary social phenomena, such as the statistician explores, though indispensable to the researches and verification of the economist and the moralist, are regarded ... as but the latest links in chains of sequence connecting the past and the future, and as marking steps in a movement in which there is both continuity and change.[31]

The English historical economists in Ireland saw their approach as consistent with social reform. Ingram saw his project as 'describing objectively existing economic relations, not as immutable necessities, but as products of a gradual historical past, and susceptible of gradual modification in the future ...'[32] Leslie's conviction of the inadmissibility of universal principles led him to reject the English land ownership pattern as the solution to Ireland's agricultural ills. Instead, he fervently supported peasant proprietorship.

Leslie's first article on the Irish Land problem in 1866 was entitled 'Political Economy and the Tenure of Land.' Leslie begins by posing the following problem:

The proposal of the Government to give the tenantry of Ireland some legal security for improvements has been encountered by an objection, claiming to possess the authority of an economic maxim and seeking to stifle *in limine* all legislation in favour of tenants, on the ground that it is a settled principle of political economy that the management of private property should be left to private interest; and that the relation of landlord and tenant being one of contract, the sole duty of the state is to enforce the performance of contracts.[33]

Leslie continues:

The question arises whether the interpositions of the law are really violations of the policy of non-interference, except to secure the protection of property and the performance of contracts? I shall endeavour to show that such interferences not only are based on the very principle of economical policy on account of which the state does interfere to protect property and enforce contracts, but fall far short of affording the degree of security which the position of tenants and the interests of the public, especially in Ireland, require.[34]

Leslie advocates that the state should intervene in the landlord and tenant relationship in order to provide security for the tenant ensuring an adequate return for his improvements. This security goes beyond the right of sale of improvements and also includes the right to a long lease.[35] Since the market in land in Ireland has not produced this type of long lease, the state must intervene:

But since tenants cannot obtain under contract the security they require, the state, upon the narrowest view of its province and duties, should interfere to afford them such security.

There is one thing which private enterprise cannot produce, and that is security; and to afford it is universally acknowledged to be the proper business of the state. When, therefore, contracts do not by themselves give such security, or exclude it, the state should interfere for the same reason that in ordinary cases it interferes to secure the performance of contracts. For why does the state interfere to enforce contracts, save to promote confidence, and to encourage industry, invention, thrift, and improvement.[36]

Having established the necessity of state intervention in favour of the tenant on grounds of economic principle, Leslie deepens the analysis by arguing that the present insecurity of Irish tenants is itself the result of the historical intervention of the state:

The landholders of Ireland are not only, in the same sense as those of England, the creatures, the tenants of the state, but they are the creatures of a violent interference with pre-existing rights of property. Moreover, by further violent interference in the shape of penal laws, directed expressly against industry and accumulation on the part of the bulk of the people, and precluding the acquisition of property and capital and the rise of other industries, the state forced the great mass of the population to become competitors for the occupation of land as a means of subsistence. They were thus placed even more at the mercy of the landlord than the Egyptians were at the mercy of the Pharaoh in the famine, for their lands as well as their cattle and money were gone, and nothing remained to exchange for bread but their bodies and their labour.[37]

Leslie has employed an historical framework to understand the particular character of rent in Ireland. According to Leslie, the state cannot really intervene impartially to protect the private contract between the landlord and tenant, because the state has already played an historical role in undermining the position of the tenant, leaving him at the mercy of the landlord. The colonial character of the Irish past lies close to the centre of Leslie's analysis. The consequence of this particular interference by the state is the specific historically determined character of the Irish rental market:

Instead of the conditions to which the maxim of noninterference applies, is a system of interference which has made the landlord independent of all exercise of frugality and improvement, and deprived the tenant of all security for it.[38]

Leslie is arguing that the historical specificity of the Irish situation demands the abandonment of general principles and the application of specific remedies. In Ireland, at least, these remedies include provisions for increasing tenant security.

Despite the role of colonial violence in his analysis, Leslie was not an Irish nationalist. Indeed the prospect of too radical change filled him with unease. In 1868, Leslie takes up the political implications of economic unrest among the dispossessed tenant farmers:

And although it may not be denied that many of the former holdings were too small for even secure subsistence, the sweeping conversion of small farmers into labourers is, whether they go or stay, a revolution full of danger to both England and Ireland, as one may see in their darkening looks.[39]

Not only dispossession but also insecurity breeds dangerous political trends:

> Instead of the conservative rural class of small farmers, with a fair secu-
> rity to improve, mixed with small proprietors, improving their own lands
> (which ought to have been the transformation effected after the
> famine), the real transformation is that a revolutionary and dangerous
> class has been established. Fenianism, in its worst form, is the direct
> result of the suspension of leases, the consolidation of farms, and that
> emigration to which so many proprietors have looked for the regenera-
> tion of Ireland.[40]

The urgency of the political situation pushes Leslie beyond merely advocating
increased security but actually proposing the need for peasant proprietorship,
as the following indicates:

> A combination of measures is necessary to arrest the progress of sedition,
> to encourage improvement in farming, to facilitate the rise of a class of
> yeoman and peasant proprietors, ... but also a complete liberation of the
> transfer of land from legal restrictions and difficulties, so that farmers
> might buy land as well as hold it securely. For this end primogeniture and
> entail must cease and a simple system of the transfer of land by regis-
> tration must be introduced.[41]

In this passage, Leslie is calling for the transformation of class relations in
Irish agriculture, substituting a countryside dominated by sturdy yeoman proprietors for one in which peasants live in thrall to hereditary landlords. In seeking historical insight into the Irish land question, Leslie discovered a framework within which the goals of the substantial peasant could be rationalised
and represented to British policy-makers.

A further current to emerge in Ireland in the post-Famine period was the
application of the historical jurisprudence of Sir Henry Maine to the study of
the Celtic Brehon Law tradition. In common with the historical school of economics which he influenced, Maine argued that social norms were the result
of a long historical and evolutionary process. No programme, however
advanced, could succeed if it found itself at variance with prevailing, historically established custom. In societies less advanced than Victorian Britain, the
customary was to be given more weight than the contractual.

Maine put especial emphasis on the evolution of property, as Dewey indicates in the following:

> At the core of Maine's thought there lay a complex of tightly-knit evolu-
> tionary trends; from status to contract, from patriarchy to liberty, from
> political organisations based on kinship to political organisations based
> on territorial propinquity, from polygamy to monogamy, from animism to
> monotheism, from magic to science - and from collective to individual
> property. Property, like the political and social institutions with which it

was linked, had to fit into an evolutionary framework; and an already hallowed framework was at hand. The notion that the historical movement of property had been from collective to individual forms was not new. It was as old as the 'state of nature'. What Maine and the historical school did was to restore the theory, adducing fresh evidence of a kind acceptable in an age attuned to new methodologies.[42]

Accordingly, the primitive form of property was a form of collective property, centred around the village community in which there was egalitarian redistribution of land among the village members. The historical jurists believed that these primitive communities passed through identical evolutionary phases, though at differing speeds.[43] The Irish application of these principles found expression in the publication of *The Ancient Laws and Institutes of Ireland* in six volumes by the Brehon law commission, the first in 1865. On the insistence of several Irish antiquarians, the English government agreed in 1852 to appoint a commission for publishing the ancient laws and institutions of Ireland.

The commission employed two Irish scholars, Dr O'Donovan and Professor O'Curry, who copied and made rough translations of a large number of manuscripts, but both died before the first volume was published in 1865. Following their deaths, the work was taken up by the ubiquitous W.N. Hancock and A.G. Richey, professors of political economy and jurisprudence at Trinity College.

Inspired by Maine's approach, Hancock and Richey reconstructed the character of Early Irish society, finding it based on kinship and status, and, crucially, joint ownership of property. The Brehon Laws material not only proved the existence of collective property in Ancient Ireland, but also indicated that Irish society was starting from a very early stage of social development. A.G. Richey characterises the early Irish society he and Hancock discovered in the Brehon law tracts in the following way:

> The difficulty in understanding any ancient social organisation, such as that of the Irish Gael arises from the necessity of conceiving a society founded upon principles not only unfamiliar to us, but absolutely contradictory to those which we believe to be of universal application and primary necessity. It requires an effort so completely to cast off modern prejudices as to realise a community without a government or executive; without laws, in the modern sense of the term; in which the individual had no rights save as a member of a family; the trade of which was carried on without currency, and uninfluenced by the laws of political economy; in which private, or rather individual, property was scarcely existent; and yet, in the absence of all that we now imagine to be essential to the establishment of a community, was not a chaos, but firmly knit together, and regulated in the minutest details of everyday life by an undefined and unaccountable concurrence of all its members in certain

inarticulate rules as to their conduct in the ordinary circumstances of life, the sum of which is expressed in the word 'custom'.[44]

Irish primitive society was contrasted with modern industrialised society, where the political state is fully developed and the Law deals with each individual separately, where private property is the rule and the owner of this property has full power to dispose of it as he wills, and where the concept of contract has superseded the concept of status and customary relationships. According to Hancock and Richey's researches, Irish rural society was closer to its Gaelic origins than to contemporary English society. Indeed Richey contends that 'one of the most remarkable facts in the history of the Celtic inhabitants of Ireland is, that they continued, during the entire historic period, to exist without important change in their civilization and social system ...'[45]

Hancock and Richey suggested that English commercial ideas with regard to property relationships were imposed upon a society which had not emerged from its status-phase, and legislation in advance of its condition had only produced dislocation, agitation, and anomie.[46] The historicists attributed agrarian unrest to a conflict of laws – a conflict between Gaelic customs and English contractual laws. They criticised the concept of 'free trade in land' as socially disruptive of the indigenous customs of the Irish peasantry and recommended a policy of comprehensive tenant rights to the Irish farmers. This legal historicism was instrumental in providing theoretical support for Irish land reform.

Hancock was directly influential in formulating proposals for compensation for disturbance and improvements which were adopted by Gladstone in his Land Act of 1870.[47] These recommendations appeared in Hancock's *Report on the Landlord and Tenant Question in Ireland from 1860 till 1866*. The other major inspiration underlying Gladstone's Land Act of 1870, was George Campbell,[48] who published his *The Irish Land* in 1869. By comparing the historical evolution of Indian and Irish Land tenure systems, Campbell was able to propose the Indian solution to the Irish problem, i.e. rehabilitation of the tenant's customary rights.

The historicist framework of analysis was the ideological vehicle used for the passing of Gladstone's two Land Acts of 1870 and 1881, as Dewey suggests in the following:

> ... Irish tenants expected the 'Three Fs': fixity of tenure, a fair rent; and freedom of sale. It was these rights that Gladstone's second Land Act conceded ... Two commissions of inquiry - the Richmond commission appointed by the outgoing Conservative ministry and the Bessborough commission appointed by the incoming Liberals - agreed that the 'Three Fs'should be conceded (both in 1881) ... But the main thrust of the Bessborough Commission's case for full occupancy rights was historicist. The Bessborough report consisted of an extended re-statement of the historicist case put by Campbell twelve years before.[49]

In Campbell's argument, as with Hancock and Richey, it was the inherent conflict between English law and Irish customary laws which was the root of the problem:

> In Ireland there are two sets of laws - the English laws, and the laws or customs of the country, which, enforced in a different way are as active and effective. In the clashing of these two systems lies the whole difficulty.[50]

While the conflict appeared to embody the clash of two legal systems, the indigenous and the English, the clash had its economic basis in the confrontation of two classes within the one feudal landholding system. An enforcement of the customary laws involved meeting the economic demands of the tenantry, while the laws of the political state tended to buttress the economic position of the Irish landlords. The somewhat contradictory attempt to formalise the customary laws of the tenantry into the statute laws of the political state was in effect an attempt to undermine the existence of landlordism in Ireland.

Innovative approaches to the question of land tenure were not confined to the elaboration of alternative theoretical frameworks. Within British political economy the case for peasant proprietorship was the critical agenda of a dissenting strand of thought, of which Richard Jones, W.T. Thornton, and John Stuart Mill were the leading spokesmen. Of these Mill was unquestionably the most effective and influential in supplying the intellectual and analytical momentum to the political movement of the 1870s to rehabilitate the peasant proprietor. Ireland played a very substantive role in Mill's argumentation in defence of peasant proprietorship, and the central figure in Ireland who exerted the most profound influence on Mill was unquestionably John Elliot Cairnes. Born in County Louth, Cairnes was the sixth occupant of the Whately professorship and also held professorships at Queen's College Galway and University College London. Cairnes is widely considered to be the last great practitioner and defender of the Ricardian system.

Cairnes' writings on peasant proprietorship emerged within the mid-1860s and were concentrated within a relatively short span. These writings took place within the context of an ongoing dialogue on Ireland between Mill and Cairnes at this time. Mill for his part was extremely sensitive to the fact that his advocacy of peasant proprietorship represented a major deviation from the norms of classical political economy and felt obligated to produce an elaborate apologia. Cairnes, in contrast, felt no such need. Having engaged the issue, he provided a cogently articulated frontal attack on the absolute rights of private property and a powerful case for peasant proprietorship within a very short period of time.

In 1864, Cairnes published his first article on Ireland in the *Edinburgh Review*. In that same year, Mill set about revising the fifth edition of his celebrated

Principles of Political Economy, and in this context he invited Cairnes in October 1864 to 'make any improvement that you can suggest, and especially to know if there is anything which you think it would be useful to say on the present state of Ireland'.[51] In the fifth edition, Mill had displayed an extraordinary optimism with regard to the post-Famine Irish economy, arguing that the large decrease in the population, along with the work of the Encumbered Estates Act, made the introduction of the English agricultural system possible on a large scale in Ireland. Mill conceded that peasant proprietorship was perhaps desirable, but held it was 'no longer indispensable'. He concluded that Ireland did not now require 'what are called heroic remedies'.[52] In the event Cairnes was in overall agreement with Mill's account of the situation and clearly shared Mill's basic optimism about the future.

Later that year, in response to a query from Mill concerning the state of the cottier class, we get further insight into Cairnes' evolving assessment of the problem. Writing to Mill on 6 December 1864, where he promises Mill a fuller and more detailed account, Cairnes indicated that in his view the class of cottier tenants had been greatly reduced. Nevertheless, he felt that the issue of over-population still represented a major problem, and that if the standard of living was to be raised for the mass of the Irish working population, it would mean 'dissociating them altogether from their present mode of life'.[53] What Cairnes envisaged as the means of dissociation included: the provision of small parcels of land, the development of economic activity outside agriculture, and continued emigration. Of these he felt that were it not for emigration the population would again be reduced to starvation. In fact Cairnes argued that 'even with the emigration I feel very sanguine it will not be avoided'.[54] Even within the short period between October and December 1864, Cairnes had shifted to a considerably more pessimistic position with respect to the future of the cottier and labouring classes.

The more detailed account of conditions in Ireland which Cairnes had promised Mill emerged as *Notes on the State of Ireland* (1864), which were sent by Cairnes in late December 1864. These *Notes* contained a more elaborate articulation of Cairnes' position on Ireland and addressed a number of aspects of the problem, including the arguments in favour of peasant proprietorship. It is on this aspect of his contribution that we will concentrate here.

In the course of examining the position of the small tenant farmer, Cairnes raised the issue of the prospect of a class of peasant proprietors emerging in Ireland. It was in this context also that Cairnes disagreed fundamentally with Mountifort Longfield's position on the question. Cairnes' argument for peasant proprietorship may best be viewed as a systematic rebuttal of Longfield's position. Longfield's arguments rested on three critical assumptions: (i) that in Ireland wherever 'substantial interest exists in land, the owner of such interest almost invariably sublets'; (ii) that the natural disposition of the Irish people was careless and improvident and given to 'dash and show', which represented precisely the opposite of traits that should characterise peasant proprietors; and (iii) that the peasant proprietor regime belonged to an earlier and more primitive state of society and could therefore be expected to disintegrate under the impact of economic and social development.[55]

Cairnes disagreed with Longfield with respect to all three assumptions and in the course of his response he articulated his defence of peasant proprietorship. With respect to Longfield's criticism of subletting, Cairnes argued that the tendency to sublet was the natural and inevitable consequence of former social and political conditions, which Cairnes felt had more affinity with the ethics of 'feudal and medieval' arrangements. He argued these ethics were now rapidly passing away as far as the landlord class was concerned. If this was true for the landlords, would it not, argued Cairnes, trickle down to the classes below them, thereby neutralising the 'landlord passion' in the lower classes? With respect to Longfield's ethnic characterisation of the Irish as 'careless and improvident' and incompatible with peasant proprietorship, Cairnes did accept that 'no doubt the Irish disposition is careless and improvident'. Nevertheless, he refused to accept the inevitability of Longfield's position, and raised the question as to whether we are 'to suppose that these qualities are ineradicable?' Cairnes argued that the presence of these dispositions could be explained historically, and in order to eradicate them it was all the more necessary to provide for peasant proprietorship. Cairnes stated his position directly and unambiguously as follows: 'regarded from this point of view, peasant proprietorship appears to me to be exactly the specific remedy for the prevailing Irish disease'.[56]

Finally, Cairnes rejected Longfield's historicist argument that peasant proprietorship belonged to an earlier and primitive condition of society by citing France and the northern states of America to demonstrate that peasant proprietorship was the prevailing form of land tenure. Cairnes in fact viewed the English system of tenure rather 'as an exception to the prevailing order of democratic progress than as indicating the rule'. This was a theme that was to recur elsewhere in Cairnes' writings. Even if Longfield's argument was conceded, Cairnes still maintained that it would be 'good policy to encourage this system as a transitional expedient to help Ireland forward in its course '.[57] Clearly Cairnes' thinking was shifting in favour of a more radical reassessment of the Irish situation, and that within a very short period of time.

By January 1865, it became clear to Cairnes that merely facilitating land transfers, as represented by the work of the Landed Estates court, a mechanism that was for Cairnes less than satisfactory, would do little to solve Ireland's problems. For Cairnes it became evident that 'more radical remedies are necessary'.[58] Cairnes' articulation of his more 'radical remedies' was contained in a series of articles published in *The Economist* between September and November 1865 and they represent arguably some of his most significant writings on Ireland.

The Economist articles constituted a cogent case for peasant proprietorship, rejecting the view that the only possible or desirable future for Irish agriculture lay in the creation of large farms based on the English model. At the level of policy, the articles argue for a modest scheme of tenant-compensation, compatible with the principles of free trade, as a step to promote peasant proprietorship. But underlying this modest proposal was a stringent critique of the accepted theory of private property in land. This represented a radical shift in Cairnes' thinking, and it rested on a number of basic premises. Land, Cairnes argued, differed from the other agents of production in a number of respects: (i) it was 'absolutely indispensable to the most human needs', and at the same time was absolutely limited in quantity; (ii) unlike the great mass of commodities, it was not 'the creation of any man's industry'; and (iii) in the productive process it could be 'greatly improved or deteriorated according to the treatment it receives'.[59]

For Cairnes, individual property in land was not only different from other forms of property, it was in fact subordinate to them, in that it did not derive from 'that act which forms in the last resort the natural title deed to almost all other wealth – human labour'. For Cairnes, the cultivator's right to the value he added to land was for this reason more fundamental than the landlord's rights to the property in the land. In Ireland, Cairnes argued, this 'conflict of principles' had already occurred, and in this conflict the labourer had the 'paramount claim'. He argued that the situation in Ireland was now demanding a more extensive analysis and 'a larger theory of the facts' of land tenure. Notwithstanding his trenchant commitment to a basically deductive methodology in political economy, Cairnes was displaying, as he did elsewhere in his economic writings, a decidedly empiricist approach to the situation in Ireland emphasising the distinctive character of the Irish situation. The English agricultural model, for Cairnes, was totally inappropriate to Ireland, and as a result what he termed 'English theory' was clearly at variance with 'Irish ideas', certainly with regard to landed property, and did not now explain Irish 'fact'. Developing this theme, Cairnes viewed the 'peculiar Irish notion' in relation to landed property as being in fact a more universal phenomenon than the 'approved doctrine' of the English classical position. He was highly critical of the accepted theory, which took no account of the different concept of landed property which characterised the Irish situation, a concept, he argued, which had 'a solid foundation in fact'. Cairnes rejected the English doctrine of 'open competition and contract as the remedy of all social disorders arising from land tenure', and argued that the relationship between landlord and tenant was not an ordinary contract but one that demanded 'from the State a large supervision and control'. Clearly Cairnes' thinking had moved to an altogether more radical interrogation of the rights of property, of the limitations of the applicability of the English model, and of the need for state intervention in the domain of land tenure.[60]

The most significant impact of these writings was arguably the extent to which they influenced one of Mill's most controversial and radical works, the pamphlet *England and Ireland* in 1868, a document which greatly influenced the radical wing of the Liberal Party. Cairnes himself returned to this topic when he published his celebrated paper 'Political Economy and Land' in 1870. In this paper he examined again the basis of property in land. He reiterated his doctrine of the qualified rights of ownership along with his arguments for state intervention in dealing with land. Through the course of the 1860s, Cairnes emerged as one of the foremost intellectual architects of the subversion of the absolute rights of private property in land, and the need for State intervention to facilitate the case for peasant proprietorship.

All of the post-Famine innovations in political economy took place in the context of the reorganisation of the rental relationship which followed the Great Hunger. This reorganisation had changed the balance of class forces on the ground. The institution of the relative rental regime described in Chapter 2 involved an attempt by Irish landlords to increase the efficiency of the Irish tenantry as food producers and consequently rent producers. The goal was an increase in the rate of rental extraction. Crucial to this particular transition was a necessary decline in population. Along with decreasing the population, it was essential for the landlord to prevent subletting and family subdivision, and encourage the consolidation of estate farms. The Famine period must be seen as a watershed, not because it was in itself the cause of the evolution of this different strategy for the extraction of rent, but because it allowed the landlords to overcome the resistance of the tenants. During and after the Famine, population declined drastically due to starvation, disease and emigration. Significantly, the average size of holdings almost doubled. Grazing increased in economic importance. Subdivision declined.

The Irish countryside had thereafter become more homogenous. This was accomplished through the massive elimination of the most disadvantaged sectors of the rural population. In consequence, the rural class structure was simplified to one of landlords, tenants and wage workers, with the now more substantial tenants forming the largest group. The pursuit of the relative rental regime had created a large and growing class of people who had an interest in the transition to peasant proprietorship, an interest not shared by the inadequately landed majority in the pre-Famine period. In addition to an interest in peasant proprietorship, the growing class of substantial tenants had the resources and the will to push their demands.

It was the growing importance in the Irish countryside of this substantial tenantry which placed the demand for the restriction of the property rights of the landlord on the political agenda. Peasant proprietorship was, in the eyes of these farmers, the ultimate and logical outcome of this development. This new social force provided the political base for the changing policy prescriptions of Irish political economy. It was the potentially revolutionary force behind what would previously have been regarded as a radical proposal. Perhaps ironically, it was also the conservative force which made safe the granting of the demand. This potent mixture of rebellion and restoration provided the climate in which the political economics of land reform could be creatively discussed.

CONCLUSION

We have discussed the development of a number of novel approaches to the study of economic questions which developed in Ireland in the post-Famine period. These included the social ameliorism of the post-Famine Hancock, Comtean sociology as espoused by Ingram, and the British historical school of economics as developed by Ingram and Leslie. Finally, we have discussed the application of Henry Maine's legal historicism to the study of the Irish Brehon law tradition. When each of these new frameworks was applied to the development of Irish agricultural policy, they lent support to the voluntary recognition of tenant right at minimum and at maximum the establishment of peasant proprietorship. Cairnes also sought to defend the peasant proprietor, but through innovations within the frame of Ricardian orthodoxy. All this is in sharp contrast to the prescriptions of pre-Famine political economy which advocated the dismantling of legal impediments to the market in land and freedom of contract between the holders of the respective factors of production. Before the Famine, economists like Whately and the early Hancock generally looked forward to the institution of the English system of capitalist agriculture in Ireland. After the Famine, the peasant proprietor received increasingly favourable notice. Just as the particular character of the Irish colonial economy before the Famine conditioned the adoption of a conservative version of classical political economy and its associated policy prescriptions, so the changing character of the agricultural economy after the Famine lay the social basis for the opening up of the boundaries of political economy and the transformation of social science's recommended remedies.

NOTES

1   T.A. Boylan and T.P. Foley, *Political Economy and Colonial Ireland* (London: Routledge, 1992), p. 130.
2.   Much of the argument in the foregoing five paragraphs can be found in ibid.
3.   Ibid., pp. 89–90.
4.   Ibid., p. 90.
5.   According to Moss (p.15), candidates for the chair sat an open examination, which Whately corrected and from which he made his own selection. The consequence of this was that:

   It is impossible to say exactly how much influence Whately was able to exert on the actual content of the lectures of the early Dublin Professors, but it does seem clear that, had a Ricardian applied for the job in 1832, his chances of being selected would have been almost nil.

   See L. Moss, *Mountifort Longfield, Ireland's First Professor of Political Economy* (Ottawa: Green Hill, 1976).
6.   J. Schumpeter, *History of Economic Analysis* (London: George Allen and Unwin, 1967), p. 465.
7.   R.D.C. Black, 'Trinity College Dublin and the Theory of Value, 1832–1863', *Economica*, 12, 47 (1945), p. 141.
8.   E. Roll, *A History of Economic Thought* (London: Faber and Faber, 1978), pp. 340–1.
9.   R. Vance, 'On the English and Irish Analysis of Wages and Profits', *Dublin Statistical Society Transactions*, I (1847), pp. 3–4.
10. See Moss, *Mountifort Longfield*, p. 110.

11. W.N. Hancock, 'On the Use of the Doctrine of Laissez-Faire, In Investigating the Economic Resources of Ireland', *Dublin Statistical Society Transactions*, 1 (1847), p. 3.
12. W.N. Hancock, *Impediments to the Prosperity of Ireland* (London: Simms and McInture, 1850).
13. W.N. Hancock, 'On the Economic Causes of the Present State of Agriculture in Ireland, Part II - Legal Impediments to the Transfer of Land', *Dublin Statistical Society Transactions*, 1 (1848b).
14. Fee in tail estates dictated that succession should remain in the family while life estates conferred ownership only during the lifetime of the heir.
15. W.N. Hancock, 'On the Economic Causes of the Present State of Agriculture in Ireland, Part I', *Dublin Statistical Society Transactions*, 1 (1848a), p. 6.
16. E. Lysaght, 'A Consideration of the Theory That the Backward State of Agriculture is a Consequence of the Excessive Competition for Land', *Dublin Statistical Society Transactions*, II (1851), p. 7.
17. R.D.C. Black, *The Statistical and Social Inquiry Society of Ireland, Centenary Volume, 1847–1947* (Dublin: Eason, 1947), p. 13.
18. W.N. Hancock, 'The Effects of the Employment of Women in Occupations Atended with Publicity, as Illustrated by the Result of the Factory System at Bradford', *Statistical and Social Inquiry Society of Ireland Journal*, II (1860), p. 439.
19. W.N. Hancock, 'On the Bothy system of Lodging Farm Labourers in Scotland; It's Violation of the Family Principles, Its Condemnation by the Free Church of Scotland, the Conclusions to be Deducted from the Facts Stated, and Their Application to Ireland', *Statistical and Social Inquiry Society of Ireland Journal*, II (1859).
20. I. Carter, *Farmlife in Northeast Scotland, 1840–1914, The Poor Man's Country* (Edinburgh: John Donald, 1979), p. 119.
21. See W.N. Hancock, 'On the Bothy system of Lodging Farm Labourers in Scotland', pp. 376–7.
22. Ibid., p. 380.
23. Ibid., p. 378.
24. Ibid., p. 381.
25. See J.K. Ingram, 'The Present Position and Prospects of Political Economy', in R.L. Smyth (ed.), *Essays in Economic Method* (London: Duckworth, 1962 [1878]); and R.B. Ekelund, 'A British Rejection of Economic Orthodoxy', *Southwestern Social Science Quarterly*, 47, Sept. (1966), pp.172–180.
26. See J.K. Ingram, 'The Present Position and Prospects', pp. 49–50.
27. Ibid., p. 50.
28. Ibid., p. 55.
29. J.K. Ingram, *A History of Political Economy* (Edinburgh: Adam and Charles Black, 1888).
30. See G.M. Koot, 'T.E. Cliffe Leslie, Irish Social Reform and the Origins of the English Historical School of Economics', *History of Political Economy*, 7, 31(1975), pp. 312–36, and G.C.G. Moore, 'T.E. Cliffe Leslie and the English Methodenstreit', *Journal of the History of Economic Thought*, 17, 1 (Spring 1995), pp. 7–77.
31. T.E. Cliffe Leslie, *Essays in Political and Moral Philosophy*, (Dublin: Hodges, Foster, and Figgis, 1879), p. v.
32. Quoted in Coats, A.W. 'The Historicist Reaction in English Political Economy, 1870–90', *Economica*, 21, May (1954), pp 143–53
33. T.E. Cliffe Leslie, 'Political Economy and the Tenure of Land', *Fortnightly Review* (1866), also in *Land Systems and Industrial Economy of Ireland, England and Continental Countries* (London: Longman, 1870), p. 117.
34. Ibid., p. 118.
35. Ibid., p. 126.
36. Ibid., p.127.
37. Ibid., p.128.
38. Ibid., pp.128–9.
39. See Cliffe Leslie, *Land Systems and Industrial Economy*, p. 43.
40. Ibid., p. 44.
41. Ibid., pp. 48, 51.
42. C. Dewey, 'Images of the Village Community, A Study in Anglo-Indian Ideology', *Modern Asian Studies*, 6, 3 (1972), p. 308.
43. C. Dewey, 'Celtic Agrarian Legislation and the Celtic Revival: Historicist Implications of Gladstone's Irish and Scottish Land Acts, 1870–1886', *Past and Present*, 64 (1974), p. 41.

44. A.G. Richey, *A Short History of the Irish People* (Dublin: Hodges, Figgis and Co., 1887), p. 35.
45. Ibid., p. 13.
46. See Dewey, 'Images of the Village Community', p. 318.
47. R.D.C. Black,. *Economic Thought and the Irish Question, 1817–1870* (Cambridge: Cambridge University Press, 1960), p. 63.
48. G. Campbell, *The Irish Land* (London: Trubner, 1869).
49. See Dewey, 'Images of the Village Community,' p. 61.
50. See Campbell, *The Irish Land*, p. 6.
51. T.A. Boylan and T.P. Foley, "John Elliot Cairnes, John Stuart Mill and Ireland: some problems for political economy," in Antoin E. Murphy (ed.), *Economists and the Irish Economy from the Eighteenth Century to the Present Day* (Dublin: Irish Academic Press, 1984) p. 99.
52. Quoted in Ibid.
53. Ibid., p. 100.
54. Ibid.
55. Ibid., p. 102.
56. Ibid., pp. 102–3.
57. Ibid. p. 103.
58. Ibid. p. 104.
59. Ibid. p. 105.
60. Ibid.

CHAPTER TWELVE

Two Kinds of Colony: 'Rebel Ireland' and the 'Imperial Province'

PAMELA M. CLAYTON

INTRODUCTION

This study is based on the conceptualisation of Ireland as a colony, despite its incorporation into the United Kingdom from 1800 until 1921. This argument is made in the face of the relative neglect of Ireland in the academic literature in English on colonialism and imperialism and a lack of agreement on this issue even within Ireland itself. It was, more specifically, a mixed colony in that it contained a large minority of settlers, of whom a large number lived in Ulster. These had a disproportionate amount of influence on the British political establishment and disproportionate economic power. They shared a sense of identity and national allegiance that differed from that of the majority of Irish people.

Ulster's position as a settler colony within the larger island was, for most of the twentieth century, almost completely overlooked in the academic literature.[1] The history of its foundation is often held to be irrelevant today. Its privileged relations with the metropolis and determination to remain part of the United Kingdom of Great Britain and Ireland against the wishes of a growing majority are ignored by the large number of academics for whom the conceptualisation of a late twentieth-century conflict as springing from a settler colonial society is still distasteful. There have, however, been a few academic works arguing that the original settlement of Ulster is still at the root of the divisions in modern Northern Ireland, and that Ireland can be compared in various ways to other settler colonies, such as Rhodesia, Kenya, South Africa, Israel and Algeria.[2]

The Irish colonial experience included two contradictory elements, both shared by other colonised peoples. On the one hand, there was an intensification of the long tradition of subjecting the Catholic Irish to racist stereotyping, whose content and motivation was almost identical to that experienced by indigenous peoples in other parts of the British Empire. On the other hand,

Irish Catholics played a part in the empire not only as subjects but as agents of the imperial power in the maintenance of the empire.

Despite this, towards the end of the nineteenth and the early twentieth centuries, as the struggle for and against Home Rule intensified, one line of division that emerged concerned the part played by Catholics and Protestants in the imperial project. Protestants made much of their loyalty to the empire which, it was alleged, both differentiated them from the rest of Ireland and deserved the reward of continued membership of the United Kingdom. Irish nationalists colluded in this Protestant self-image by painting its tradition as anti-imperial and by downplaying Catholic participation in empire. An examination, however, of the historic participation of the two groups in the British empire casts doubt on this radical distinction.

The first section addresses the issue of Ireland as a mixed colony. The second illustrates the racist stereotyping to which the Irish, in common with other colonised peoples, were subjected, including implications that they were not an 'imperial race' even as they were serving the empire in large numbers. The third examines Protestant claims to imperial loyalty and considers the evidence for and against these claims.

IRELAND AS A MIXED COLONY

Extensive research on the literature on imperialism and settler colonialism up to the 1980s reveals very few even passing references to Ireland. The puzzle of the missing colony was pointed out by Robinson,[3] who noted that it was primarily – but not only – British imperial theorists who paid the least attention to Ireland. There are notable exceptions in the general literature: for example, Wallerstein[4] defines Ireland as a colony whose seizure in the sixteenth century was the prototype for that of North America. Its colonial status was confirmed by the Treaty of Limerick, which asserted that the Crown's authority over Ireland was the same as its authority over the colonies. It was a dependency of the Crown for which Westminster legislated without Irish representation in parliament.

It is true that, in the motley collection of trade colonies, protectorates, dependencies and settlement colonies that constituted the nineteenth-century British Empire, Ireland held a unique position (as indeed every colony did). It was inhabited by white Christians, even if most were Catholics and hence, in the view of some, not really Christians. Many Irish crossed the narrow stretch of water to find work in England, Wales and Scotland. There was a political relationship going back almost a thousand years and, since 1800, Ireland was officially an integral part of the realm of the United Kingdom of Great Britain and Ireland. Indeed, Ireland became an active partner in the British imperial project, for example, in providing soldiers and civil servants for the maintenance of the empire; and the empire was no doubt as dear to the hearts of some Irish men and women as it was to many English, Scots and Welsh.

Ireland's geographical proximity to England is relevant to its colonial history on at last two counts. Firstly, its retention was a strategic necessity, in the light of the dangerous influence of the American and French revolutions and the enmity of Catholic France and Spain. Secondly, when movements and campaigns seeking some degree of self-government re-emerged, they could not so easily be subjected to the punitive measures taken against more distant colonies. News travelled fast and there were still liberals, and later socialists, who subscribed to kindlier doctrines of empire.[5] Rather, at official level, the dual policy of concessions to moderates and repression of 'seditious agitators' was pursued.[6]

On the other hand, the incorporation of Ireland in 1800 should be seen, not as a partnership of equals but rather in the light of the principle, held by the British in the late eighteenth and early nineteenth centuries, that colonies should be under effective metropolitan control.[7] Given that democracy and universal suffrage were far from the thoughts of the British establishment, a legal union rather than British insistence on Ireland's colonial status appeared to circumvent both the moral basis and the danger of any thoughts of Irish self-government or independence. Furthermore, if recalcitrant Irish people could not, by the nineteenth century, be slaughtered with impunity, they could be portrayed as inferior and even sub-human. Ireland had long been subjected to the racist ideology, based on notions of racial and moral superiority, that permeated the nineteenth- century British Empire.[8] The older liberal and humanitarian ethos remained: 'natives' had a right to the law, protection and education, but their immutable inferiority meant that they were permanently unfit for self-determination.[9]

Ireland was not, however, a homogeneous entity but a mixed colony.[10] Parts of it, notably in the northern province of Ulster, had been settled as a matter of official English policy by episcopalian Protestants from Great Britain, and as part of unofficial migratory movements by Scottish Presbyterians. During the nineteenth century, and particularly following the end of official discrimination against Presbyterians and other non-conformists, the different sects put aside the religious differences which had been most manifest in 1798. This was done in favour of their common political interests as Irish but non-Catholic, indeed often anti-Catholic, and economic interests linked to the industrial thrust of Great Britain rather than to rural Ireland. Just as the Union of 1800 did not change the colonial nature of the relationship between Ireland and Great Britain, so the settler mentality, founded at its deepest level on fear of displacement, loss and exile, remained and indeed intensified among Ulster's Protestants as the century progressed. These fears increased with the widening of the franchise and Irish Catholic attempts to win some measure of self-government.

Although there have always been Protestants who identified with a non-

British Ireland and, indeed, Catholics who were content to remain British, by and large there were increasingly two imagined communities, labelled according to sectarian difference, with different perceptions of their interests, their position, their identity, their history, their future and themselves. This divergence, and the parallel differentiated perceptions of the two groups by the metropolis, was an important factor in the failure of British state-building in nineteenth-century Ireland.[11]

It would be inaccurate to say that the metropolis always favoured British settlers over indigenous peoples. Their attitude to their colonial kith and kin was, rather, ambivalent. By the nineteenth century, it was not British policy to create settlements; rather, would-be settlers, such as Cecil John Rhodes, invaded first and demanded British recognition afterwards.[12] Settlers could then be used to demonstrate the British ideological model of empire. Curzon, for example, saw the colonial personality as free, noble, and energetic, forged 'in the furnace of responsibility and on the anvil of self-reliance.'[13]

Less complimentary was the view that settlement colonies were of use in attracting from the metropolis malcontents and surplus labour.[14] Merivale, although enamoured of the notion of British settlers maintaining British supremacy throughout the world, was unimpressed with the reality, accusing settlers of short-term thinking and careless government.[15] Imperial statesmen generally treated them as if 'they constituted a lesser rank in society'.[16] It has even been argued that the nineteenth-century European empires were the result of the attempt by metropolitan governments to 'control the boundless, irresponsible, freebooting and destructive enterprises of pioneers and adventurers'.[17] In the Irish context, the settlers who attracted the most contempt – because they tended to create trouble – were members of the Orange Order which was from time to time banned or forbidden to hold parades.[18]

RACIST STEREOTYPING OF THE IRISH

From 1800, Ireland was no longer legally a colony but part of the United Kingdom, yet the abusive racial stereotyping of the Catholic Irish in general was common in the Victorian era.[19]

One hypothesis advanced is that the effect of these prejudices by the mid-nineteenth century was to 'reduce the Irish Question ... to an apparent conflict between two fundamentally incompatible races', an approach which led to the failure of British policy in Ireland.[20] Furthermore, the stereotypes of 'Paddy the Irishman ... provided ready-made categories for Burmese and Malays to be fitted into'.[21] Another view, however, discerns the abusive stereotype as long predating the modern era: 'widespread and virulent expressions of anti-Irish prejudice predate the industrial revolution. They had been part of the British scene for centuries. The only novelty in Victorian times was the fact that the prejudice was increasingly articulated in the terminology of racial differentiation'.[22]

Fraser's Magazine in March 1847 claimed that 'of all the Celtic tribes, famous everywhere for their indolence and fickleness ... the Irish are admitted to be the most idle and the most fickle'.[23] The nature of the stereotype is of particular interest, in that it was the one applied to 'native' peoples everywhere; the Irish were accused of being lazy, dirty, ignorant, superstitious, content to be poor, uncivilised, violent, irrational, ungrateful, impractical, childlike, easily aroused and easily manipulated by self-serving agitators.[24] They were indeed often compared with 'aboriginal peoples in Africa, the Antipodes and the Orient'[25] and were, according to Lord Salisbury, as unfit for self-government as Hottentots.[26] Dilke saw the Irish among the 'cheaper races' like the Chinese: 'both prolific breeders, hard workers and inveterate migrants'[27]. There was no apparent difficulty in accepting that the Irish could be both indolent and hard workers.

By contrast, the 'Anglo-Saxon race', that is, the modern British, was deemed to be practical, individualistic, business-like, efficient and responsibly mature, an 'imperial race' which was industrious, frugal and adaptable, and essentially masculine.[28] It was, according to Theodore Parker, 'the best specimen of mankind which has ever attained great power in the world'.[29] Attitudes such as 'reason, restraint, self-control, love of freedom and hatred of anarchy, respect for law and distrust of enthusiasm' were inherited and inheritable[30] – but they had not, it seemed, been inherited by the Irish who were inherently incapable of such noble virtues.

These contrasting stereotypes were adopted by Irish Protestants as part of their campaign against Home Rule, including their claims to be the bulwark of the empire.

'ULSTER' VERSUS 'IRELAND': WHICH WAS THE MORE 'IMPERIAL'?

Despite all the racist stereotyping, and the reasons that lay behind it, many of the Catholic Irish were at the same time undoubtedly assisting the British in maintaining their overseas empire, supplying not only soldiers but officers, administrators and settlers from all its provinces. For Ulster Protestants, however, writing in local and provincial newspapers from the third Home Rule crisis onwards, Ulster was 'the imperial province' in contradistinction to 'rebel Ireland', and Ulster Protestants were especially endowed with imperial qualities.[31] This ideological construct, part of the unionist propaganda campaign to remain within the United Kingdom of Great Britain and Ireland, still plays a part in folk memory and ritual. A new branch of the Democratic Unionist Party was named the 'Armagh/North Down Imperial Democratic Unionist Association'.[32] The place of this anachronistic survival of 'the imperialist message' in Ulster Unionism and loyalist ideology has been described thus: 'The Protestant imagined community is not a nation. It remains what it has always been - a beleaguered garrison loyal to the Crown and Empire, defending an Imperial interest in a hostile and rebellious land'.[33]

Pride in 'the generous splashes of red which indicate upon a map of the world the greatest empire ever known'[34] was not confined to the north of Ireland; what is of interest here is the attempt made by Northern Protestants to deny a constructive role in the empire to Irish Catholics, by usurping that role for themselves. It should be noted that many Irish Catholics have bolstered this notion by neglecting or rejecting their own historic part in the empire.

The 'Empire card' was played to the full for British consumption. During the Home Rule crises religion was fused with imperialism in the claim that Ireland separated from Great Britain would be ruled by the Pope,[35] an argument which appealed to Unionists such as Balfour and Milner who claimed that 'loyalty to the empire' rode above elected governments.[36] Ulster Protestants, however, having claimed in the first Home Rule crisis that Ireland's co-partnership in the empire was threatened,[37] came to claim that they played a special and eventually an exclusive role in it. Not only have 'the Empire's best friends'[38] gone out to colonise distant lands,[39] but they are also responsible for 'the great turning-point in the history of the British Empire ... the Battle of the Boyne. Without its Protestantism what would the spirit of England be?'[40] Orangeism is 'the bulwark of Protestantism ... its ramifications are to be found performing their useful functions of welding more firmly the bonds that knit the Empire together in every part of the globe'.[41]

Similar claims for Ulster, as some called Northern Ireland, are found in the 1939–49 period. 'This western outpost of Empire'[42] is a bulwark of imperialism against 'the foes of the Empire, especially in Ireland'.[43] The terms 'the imperial Province', Ulster's 'Imperial birthright and traditions' and the 'Imperial race' which inhabits it abound[44] and the large numbers of Free Staters who volunteered for service are rarely mentioned. Instead Eire's 'sullen neutrality'[45] is frequently contrasted with the Ulster loyalists who are 'proud to stand by Britain and the rest of the Empire'.[46] Even the German air-raids are a 'savage revenge upon Ulster for her loyalty to Britain and the Empire'.[47]

What was the reality behind the rhetoric? Was participation in empire by Ulster Protestants that of 'imperial servitors', that is, the imperialism of second-class citizens, along with Scots and Irish Catholics[48] or did they play such a pre-eminent role in 'empire-building' that it justified their claim that Ulster was 'the imperial province'? Did the Catholic Irish, on the other hand, stand aside from the imperial project?

Irish Contributions to the British Empire in the Nineteenth Century

Before the nineteenth century opened, it can be argued that Irish Protestants had already contributed to the loss of a substantial part of the British Empire in North America in three ways. Firstly, perhaps the majority of the Irish-born personnel in Washington's army in particular, including the generals, were Ulster Presbyterians,[49] although there were also Ulstermen fighting on the British side. Subsequent presidents included a number of 'Ulster-Scots', albeit the extent of their role has been seriously questioned.[50] Secondly and less directly, the Dublin Parliament, which was Protestant, although happy to fund the Irish establishment (a 12,000–man Protestant force within the British army) to maintain English control in Ireland, became reluctant to pay the costs of its other role, that of acting as the empire's strategic reserve outside Ireland. Therefore, London decided to create an American establishment and the taxation they levied in North America to pay for this was the immediate cause of the American revolt.[51] Thirdly, at this time all officers and men in the King's army were supposed to declare themselves Protestants. Although some Catholics supported the British government and wanted to encourage recruitment for the British side, Irish Protestants, afraid of Catholics being armed, did their best to prevent this.[52] Despite Dublin Castle conniving at the enlistment of some Catholics, the war in North America weakened the Irish establishment and this was a contributory factor in the decisive British defeat at Yorktown.[53]

Important numbers of Irish Protestants went to other white settlements. Toronto is proudly proclaimed to be 'virtually an Ulster city'.[54] Eminent émigrés such as John Ballance, the first Liberal Prime Minister of New Zealand, carried with them the Ulster virtues: 'a believer in self-help for the individual and self-reliance for his country (who) epitomised all that is best in the Ulster and New Zealand character'.[55] Ulster Protestants such as Lord Dufferin, Governor-General of Canada 1872–8 and Viceroy of India 1884–8, drew on their Irish background to see in educated Bengalis 'a great deal of Celtic perverseness, vivacity and cunning'.[56]

Significant though the Ulster Protestant contribution was, 'British history' took on a global dimension in important part through the famine-induced Irish Catholic diaspora of the mid-nineteenth century.[57] There were Irish colonial administrators too, usually Anglo-Irish but occasionally Catholics like Anthony Patrick McDonnell. Above all, there were Irish soldiers; and if Irishmen had contributed to the loss of the United States, they were instrumental in the acquisition of the 'jewel in the crown', India. The ratios of recruits for India per 10,000 of population were England and Wales 6, Scotland 10.5 and Ireland 13.4.[58] Two of the British army regiments were entirely raised in Ulster and both took part in the seizure of large parts of India[59].

The East India Company's army had no bar on Catholics and by the time of the Indian 'mutiny' over half of its white soldiers may have been Irish and many of these were Catholic.[60] Nevertheless, the colonial relationship in Ireland was reproduced in India, in that most of the Company's Irish officers were Protestants.[61] Though the proportion of (mainly Catholic) Irish soldiers fell dramatically, that of the mainly Protestant Irish officers fell very little. In 1914 numbers were such that Roberts could warn the government of grave consequences in India if they persisted with Home Rule for Ireland.[62] It appears that their loyalty was considered to be in doubt as far as the empire beyond Ireland was concerned.

Just as Irish Protestants fought both for and against the empire, there were Irish Catholics fighting for enemy forces too, for example, for the French in India.[63] By a curious paradox, the Boer Irish Brigade, formed of Irishmen and Irish-Americans living in South Africa,[64] fought on the side of the Boer settlers, whose descendants in the Hulpdiens South African Defence Force at Voortrekkerhoogte proposed to erect a monument to their memory.[65]

Irish Recruiting 1914–1918 and After

In the First World War Unionists and Redmondite Nationalists competed to prove their loyalty. Redmond was proud to claim that:

> I met Irishmen everywhere ... not merely in the Irish regiments but in every regiment ... almost for the first time in history the Irish Catholic regiments are fighting and dying for England without any shadow of bitterness in their hearts or minds ... Irish soldiers, Catholic and Protestant, have fought and died shoulder to shoulder against a common foe ... Shall not their blood seal a new bond of brotherhood among Irishmen?[66]

Recruiting was brisk in both north and south at first, and 45 per cent of total Irish enlistments were made in the first nine months of the war.[67] Redmond urged his 170,000 National Volunteers to join up both for home defence and foreign service, and many of the UVF did this as well, offering 30,000 for the front, which formed the bulk of the 36th (Ulster) Division. They also claimed to be able to offer 30,000 for Home Defence and, significantly, another 40,000 to defend Ulster.[68] By the end of 1915 it was claimed that Ulster had supplied 49,760 recruits against 45,237 from the other three provinces.[69] These and probably most of the figures supplied by the Northern newspapers were exaggerated in order to prove Ulster's superior loyalty.

In Nationalist Ireland disillusionment began to set in by 1915. Although the country as a whole benefited from higher prices for its foodstuffs, Dublin suffered depression. The scale of casualties was both unexpected and unprecedented, Edward Carson entered the Cabinet, and it was felt that the Irish Catholic contribution was undervalued by the War Office.[70] After the Easter Rising by the Irish Volunteers and its aftermath, recruitment fell in the south. Nationalists refused to countenance conscription, and as the Sinn Fein 'menace' grew recruitment was reported to have fallen in Ulster too: 'recruiting (...) no doubt practically ceased in our Province ... because our people naturally resented depleting the Province of any more of their manhood while the inhabitants of the South and West remained at home in a bellicose mood hostile to what Ulster considers her peculiar interests'.[71]

Undoubtedly, of the 170,000 recruits and reservists supplied in total, Ulster provided about half,[72] proportionately more than in the other three provinces combined (although it received fewer than half the Victoria Crosses awarded to men from Ireland).[73] To prioritise this figure, however, is to discount the thousands of Irish people from the other three provinces who went to work in British munitions factories, and the further thousands of British-based Irish and descendants of Irish immigrants who joined the services.[74] Furthermore, there was a dreadful attrition of lives of men of all creeds and parts of Ireland throughout the war, and at least half of those Irishmen killed were Catholics.[75]

After the establishment of the Irish Free State, it was apparently Northern Ireland which alone carried Ireland's imperial burden. Between 1918 and 1939 regiments raised in Northern Ireland served in Egypt, India, Palestine, Germany, Mesopotamia, Persia and Upper Silesia[76] and they were well represented in post-1945 wars too, such as in Cyprus.[77] However, in the Second World War, when conscription was not applied to Northern Ireland, the rate of volunteering soon fell and industrial productivity in the shipbuilding industry was poor, with high rates of absenteeism.[78] Some ministers even refused to co-operate with the military authorities.[79] It could be argued that 'saving the empire' was no longer so important now that Northern Ireland had de facto independence. Indeed, it was the flow of recruits from the neutral Irish state which went far towards making up the shortfall caused by low levels of volunteering and the absence of conscription. The official figures state that of those Irish people who once again came to the aid of the empire, 43,000 were from the Free State and 38,000 from Northern Ireland.[80] Churchill's famous letter of appreciation to Northern Ireland was inspired by the Stormont government's agreement for United States forces to land there.[81]

CONCLUSION

In the struggle against Home Rule, Ulster Protestants used the rhetoric of imperialism to enable them to claim that, far from fighting for their own interests, they were struggling to maintain a noble ideal, that of 'imperial unity'. In contrast, 'the Irish rebels', as Carson told the Prime Minister, were part of a Bolshevik conspiracy to destroy 'the British Empire ... the greatest element of solidity in the civilised world ... the greatest conservative force for the stability of society'.[82] At the same time, Irish nationalists colluded, for their own reasons, in the Protestant claims that the Catholic Irish had done nothing for the empire.

In reality, however, it was not only Protestant Ireland (that is, Protestants in all four provinces) which made a significant contribution to building and defending the British empire, but Catholic Ireland too. This has no implications for Ireland's status as a de facto if not *de jure* colony. Large numbers of Indians and Africans also fought in British armies or moved to settle other parts of the empire, if no more or less willingly than those Irish forced through poverty to join the army or through famine to emigrate.

What is of interest is that by the early twentieth century a distorted version of the imperial story in Ireland was used by Unionists to bolster their claim to remain within the empire and thus preserve the privileges (however unevenly distributed) over Catholics that their ancestors had won since the time of the Plantation of Ulster. The same distorted version was used by nationalists to deny Catholic participation in the empire in order to show themselves as anti-imperial by tradition. Two peoples who imagined themselves differently, because of their differing structural positions within a mixed colony, were able to feed off the same myth.

NOTES

1. D. Miller, 'Colonialism and Academic Representations of the Troubles', in D. Miller (ed.), *Rethinking Northern Ireland: Culture, ideology and colonialism* (London and New York: Longman, 1998), pp. 3–39.
2. For explorations of Ulster as a settler colony, see *inter alia*, P.M. Clayton, *Enemies and Passing Friends: Settler Ideologies in Twentieth-Century Ulster* (London: Pluto Press, 1996); P. M. Clayton, 'Religion, Ethnicity and Colonialism as Explanations of the Northern Ireland Conflict', in D. Miller (ed.), *Rethinking Northern Ireland: Culture, Ideology and Colonialism* (London and New York: Longman, 1998), pp. 40–54; R. Crotty, *Ireland in Crisis* (Dingle: Brandon, 1986); I. Lustick, *State-Building Failure in British Ireland and French Algeria* (Berkeley, CA: University of California, Institute of International Studies, 1985); M. MacDonald, *The Children of Wrath: Political Violence in Northern Ireland* (Cambridge: Polity Press, 1986); L. O'Dowd, 'New Introduction', in A. Memmi, *The Coloniser and the Colonised* (London: Earthscan Publications, 1990); R. Weitzer, *Transforming Settler States: Communal Conflict and Internal Security in Northern Ireland and Zimbabwe* (Berkeley, CA: University of California Press, 1990).
3 K. Robinson, *The Dilemmas of Trusteeship: Aspects of British Colonial Policy Between the Wars* (Oxford: Oxford University Press, 1965).
4. I. Wallerstein, *The Modern World System I: Capitalist Agriculture and the Origins of the European World-Economy in the Sixteenth Century* (New York, NY: Academic Press, 1974); I. Wallerstein, *The Modern World-System II: Mercantilism and the Consolidation of the European World-Economy, 1600–1750* (New York: Academic Press, 1980).
5. A.P. Thornton, *Imperialism in the Twentieth Century* (London: Macmillan, 1978).
6. B. Porter, *The Lion's Share: A Short History of British Imperialism 1850–1970* (London: Longman, 1975).
7. D.K. Fieldhouse, *The Colonial Empires: A Comparative Survey from the Eighteenth Century* (London: Weidenfeld and Nicolson, 1966).
8. R. Faber, *The Vision and the Need: Late Victorian Imperialist Aims* (London: Faber and Faber, 1966); R.A. Huttenback, *Racism and Empire: White Settlers and Colored Immigrants in the British Self-Governing Colonies 1830–1910* (Ithaca and London: Cornell University Press, 1976).
9. A.P. Thornton, *Doctrines of Imperialism* (New York, NY: John Wiley and Sons, Inc., 1965).
10. See Crotty, *Ireland in Crisis*
11. See Lustick, *State-Building Failure in British Ireland*
12. R.A. Huttenback, *The British Imperial Experience* (Westport, CT: Greenwood Press, 1975); A. Lemon and N. Pollock, *Studies in Overseas Settlement and Population* (London: Longman, 1980).
13. R.F. Betts, *The False Dawn: European imperialism in the nineteenth century* (Minneapolis, MN: University of Minnesota Press, 1976), p. 16.
14. Fieldhouse, *The Colonial Empires: A Comparative Survey.*
15. R.W. Winks, *The Age of Imperialism* (Englewood Cliffs, NJ: Prentice Hall, 1969).
16. Thornton, *Doctrines of Imperialism*, p. 41.
17. H. Lüthy, 'Colonisation and the Making of Mankind', in G.H. Nadel and P. Curtis (eds), *Imperialism and Colonialism* (London: Collier-Macmillan, 1964), pp. 32–3.
18. J. Bardon, *A History of Ulster* (Belfast: The Blackstaff Press, 1992).
19. M. Banton, *The Idea of Race* (London: Tavistock Publications, 1977).
20. L.P. Curtis, *Anglo-Saxons and Celts: A Study of Anti-Irish Prejudice in Victorian England* (Bridgeport, CT: University of Bridgeport, 1968).

21. V.G. Kiernan, *European Empires from Conquest to Collapse 1815–1960* (Leicester: Leicester University Press, 1982).
22. R.N. Lebow, *White Britain and Black Ireland: The Influence of Stereotypes on Colonial Policy* (Philadelphia, PA: Institute for the Study of Human Issues, 1979); see also N. Canny, 'The Ideology of English Colonialism: from Ireland to America', *William and Mary Quarterly*, 3rd series, 30 (1973), pp.575–98; and S. Deane, *Civilians and Barbarians* (Derry: Field Day Theatre Company Limited, 1984).
23. See Lebow, *White Britain and Black Ireland*, p. 40
24. See Curtis, *Anglo-Saxons and Celts*; and Lebow, *White Britain and Black Ireland*.
25. See Curtis, *Anglo-Saxons and Celts*, p. 58
26. Ibid.
27. Ibid., p. 46
28. H.J. Field, *Toward a Programme of Imperial Life: The British Empire at the Turn of the Century* (Oxford: Clio Press, 1982).
29. See Huttenback, *Racism and Empire*, 1976, p. 17.
30. See Curtis, *Anglo-Saxons and Celts*, p. 11.
31. Among numerous references, see editorials in the *Belfast Telegraph*, 4 Jan. 1912, 19 Sept. 1914, 7 Jan. 1916 (published in Belfast, County Antrim); the *Londonderry Sentinel*, 13 July 1912, 13 Aug. 1912, 17 May 1913, 11 June 1914, 6 July 1916, 20 Oct. 1917, 24 Jan. 1918, 5 Feb. 1921, 7 June 1921, 23 June 1921 (published in Derry); the *Impartial Reporter*, 24 Oct. 1912, 14 Aug. 1913, 13 July 1916, 21 Dec. 1916 (published in Enniskillen, County Fermanagh); the *News Letter*, 26 April 1916, 7 July 1916 (published in Belfast, County Antrim); the *Ballymena Observer*, 20 Sept. 1912, 9 March 1917; the *County Down Spectator*, 20 Sept. 1912, 24 Aug. 1917, 2 Aug 1919, 17 July 1920 (published in Bangor, County Down); the *Portadown News*, 8 June 1912, 30 April 1921 (published in Portadown, County Armagh)
32. *Portadown News*, 10 Jan. 1975. Note that this newspaper changed ownership and direction in 1972.
33. D. Bell, 'Acts of Union: Youth Sub-Culture and Ethnic Identity amongst Protestants in Northern Ireland', paper to the Sociological Association of Ireland, Annual Conference, April 1986, p. 12; see also J.R. Archer, 'The Unionist Tradition in Ireland', *Eire-Ireland*, 15, 2 (1980), pp. 47–59.
34. Editorial, *Ballymena Observer*, 29 Oct. 1915.
35. J. McEvoy, 'Catholic Hopes and Protestant Fears', *Crane Bag*, 7, 2 (1983), pp. 90–105.
36. See Porter, *The Lion's Share*.
37. J. Anderson, 'Ideological Variations in Ulster during Ireland's First Home Rule Crisis: An Analysis of Local Newspapers', in C. Williams and E. Kofman (eds), *Community Conflict, Partition and Nationalism* (London: Routledge, 1988), pp. 133–66.
38. Editorial, *Londonderry Sentinel*, 13 Aug. 1912, 20 Oct. 1917.
39. Editorials, *Belfast Telegraph*, 4 Jan. 1912, *Portadown News* 8 June 1912.
40. Editorial, *Belfast Telegraph*, 24 Jan. 1912.
41. Editorial, *County Down Reporter*, 17 July 1920.
42. Editorial, *Portadown News*, 19 April 1947.
43. Editorial, *Londonderry Sentinel*, 13 July 1939.
44. See editorials: *Londonderry Sentinel*, 11 Feb. 1939, 13 Feb. 1939, 13 July 1939, 12 Aug. 1939, 16 Dec. 1939, 23 May 1940, 26 Nov. 1940, 13 Feb. 1943, 15 Jul 1943, 1 March 1949; *Impartial Reporter*, 3 Sept. 1942; *Portadown News* 30 June 1945, 20 July 1946, 11 Jan. 1947, 19 April 1947, 26 June 1948, 29 Jan. 1949.
45. Editorial, *Londonderry Sentinel* 20 June 1940.
46. Editorial, *Londonderry Sentinel* 12 Oct. 1939.
47. Editorial, *Londonderry Sentinel*, 8 May 1941.
48. M. Hechter, *Internal Colonialism: The Celtic Fringe in British National Development 1536–1966* (London: Routledge and Kegan Paul, 1975).
49. Brigadier-General J. Collins, 'Irish Participation at Yorktown', *The Irish Sword: Journal of the Military History Society of Ireland*, 15 (1982), pp. 3–10.
50. H. Morgan, 'Empire-Building: an Uncomfortable Irish Heritage', *Linen Hall Review*, 10, 2 (1993), pp. 8–11.
51. See Collins, 'Irish Participation at Yorktown'.
52. J. Biggs-Davison and G. Chowdharay-Best, *The Cross of St Patrick: The Catholic Unionist Tradition in Ireland* (Bourne End, Bucks: The Kensal Press, 1984).

53. See Collins, 'Irish Participation at Yorktown'.
54. *Ulster Link: a Bi-Monthly Periodical Containing News of the Irish of Today and of the Past in Australia and New Zealand and with Articles on Ireland, and Particularly Ulster*, published in Melbourne, Australia, 212:24 (Jan/Feb 1982).
55. *Ulster Link*, 250:15 (April/May 1988).
56. A.T. Harrison, 'The First Marquess of Dufferin and Ava: Whig, Ulster Landlord and Imperial Statesman', Ph.D. thesis, New University of Ulster, 1983.
57. J.G.A. Pocock, 'British History - Plea for a New Subject', *Journal of Modern History*, 47, 4 (1975), pp. 600–28.
58. P. Cadell, 'Irish Soldiers in India', *The Irish Sword: Journal of the Military History Society of Ireland*, 1 (1950), pp. 75–9.
59. R. Cannon, *Historical Record of the Eighty-Sixth, or The Royal County Down Regiment of Foot: Containing an Account of the Formation of the Regiment in 1793, and of its Subsequent Services to 1842* (London: John W Parker, West Strand, 1842).
60. See Cadell 'Irish Soldiers in India'. See also M.J.P.M. Corbally, *The Royal Ulster Rifles* (Glasgow: Andrew Pearson, 1959); P. Melvin, 'Some Irish Soldiers in India', *The Irish Sword: Journal of the Military History Society of Ireland*, 16 (1986), pp. 225–6; and Revd J.J.W. Murphy, 'Kipling and the Irish Soldier in India', *The Irish Sword: Journal of the Military History Society of Ireland*, 9 (1970), pp. 318–29.
61. See Cadell, 'Irish Soldiers in India'.
62. See Kiernan, *European Empires from Conquest to Collapse*.
63. See Cadell, 'Irish Soldiers in India'.
64. W. McGrath, 'The Boer Irish Brigade', *The Irish Sword: Journal of the Military History Society of Ireland*, 5 (1961), pp. 59–60.
65. *Irish Sword: Journal of the Military History Society of Ireland*, 6 (1964).
66. J. Redmond, 'Foreword', in S.P. Kerr, *What the Irish Regiments Have Done* (London: T. Fisher Unwin Ltd., 1916).
67. D.G. Boyce, *Nineteenth-Century Ireland: The Search for Stability* (Dublin: Gill & Macmillan, 1990).
68. Editorial, *Impartial Reporter*, 20 Aug. 1914.
69. Editorial, *Londonderry Sentinel*, 11 Jan. 1916.
70. See Boyce, *Nineteenth-Century Ireland*.
71. Editorial, *County Down Spectator*, 13 April 1918.
72. See Bardon, *A History of Ulster*.
73. B. Clark, 'The Victoria Cross: a Register of Awards to Irish-born Officers and Men', *The Irish Sword: Journal of the Military History Society of Ireland*, 16 (1986), pp. 184–207.
74. See Boyce, *Nineteenth-Century Ireland*.
75. See Bardon, *A History of Ulster*.
76. See Corbally 1950, I.
77. J.M.C. (Capt.) Lawlor, 'The Unrest in Cyprus from an Infantry Battalion's Point of View', *The Sprig of Shillelagh - Journal of the Royal Inniskilling Fusiliers*, 338, XXX (1956), pp. 473–7; M.J.P.M. Corbally, *Outline History of the Regiments of the North Irish Brigade* (Omagh: Tyrone Constitution Ltd., 1951).
78. B. Barton, *The Blitz: Belfast in the War Years* (Belfast: The Blackstaff Press, 1989), pp. 49–50, 54.
79. For Northern Ireland during the 1939–45 war, see Barton, *The Blitz*; Bardon, *A History of Ulster*; the *County Down Spectator* during the war years is also a good source for complaints about Northern Ireland's role in the war.
80. See Barton, *The Blitz*.
81. See Bardon, *A History of Ulster*.
82. Editorial, *Impartial Reporter*, 5 Aug. 1920.

PART IV
CULTURE

CHAPTER THIRTEEN

Post-Colonial Perspectives on Irish Culture in the Nineteenth Century

TERRENCE McDONOUGH

The founding text of post-colonial theory is Edward Said's *Orientalism* published in 1978.[1] Nevertheless post-colonial criticism only emerged as a distinct category in the late 1980s and 1990s. Influential early volumes included Gayatri Spivak's *In Other Worlds*,[2] *The Empire Writes Back* edited by Ashcroft et al.[3] and *Nation and Narration* by Homi Bhabha.[4] This literature contained a radical rejection of Eurocentrism, an emphasis on the reclamation of their own past by colonised peoples, a critique of the construction of the colonial and exotic 'Other' in Western writing, and an exploration of the doubled, hybrid identity of the colonised. Given the neglect of colonialism in other areas of Irish intellectual life, post-colonial theory found a vacuum and rushed in thunderously to fill it. Marxist literary theory got sucked in on the rush of air and took up a complementary position. The post-colonial perspective quickly became one pole of literary debate and then perhaps the predominant pole in that other positions tended to define themselves against it. In this way Irish cultural studies came to resemble a polarised reflection of the revisionist/anti-revisionist conflict within the history profession. The difference was that in the arena of culture the Ireland-as-former-colony position rapidly occupied the higher ground.

The success of the post-colonial position in Ireland was such that it has had little time to draw its breath and sum up its accomplishments, despite attracting a certain amount of intemperate critique. The purpose of this chapter is to look at what insights post-colonial and allied Marxist studies have brought to the culture of the Irish nineteenth century. The best and most consistent work has opened up two secure areas of study. Both concern attempts to construct Irish identity, one successful, one unsuccessful. The first involves the attempted recovery of a prelapsarian 'authentic' Celtic past and a definition of what is distinctive in Irish identity as coincident with those points at which it is most different from the metropole. The second involves the failure of the

Irish novel to achieve a secure representation of the bourgeois subject in an Irish context. The first romantic effort was historically successful not because it faithfully reflected the reality of Irish society. Indeed the critical consensus is that by its very nature it concealed at least as much as it revealed. It succeeded because it addressed a real need in a colonial and post-colonial society and sought a way through to the other side of the colonial condition. The project of the realist novel on the other hand failed precisely because it elided the particular character of the self and society in the colonised condition of nineteenth-century Ireland.

YEATS

Yeats criticism provides the first solid canonical footing at the beginning of the twentieth century for the post-colonial scholar. Yeats lends himself to colonial interpretation on two somewhat contradictory grounds. The first revolves around Yeats' role in the national movement. Yeats' self-defined role in the construction of an Irish national consciousness through the production of an Irish national literature is of course well documented and hardly controversial. In his Field Day pamphlet Edward Said unequivocally contends that that Yeats' Irish national role is also one of 'decolonization', that Yeats articulated 'the experiences, the aspirations, and the vision of a people suffering under the dominion of an offshore power'.[5] The role of the artist in the colonial situation is magnified because in the presence of the colonising outsider, the land is 'recoverable first only in the imagination'.[6] Said goes on to observe that a great deal of myth-making goes into this kind of 'retrospective decolonization'.[7] One cannot imagine Yeats dissenting. Citing Benedict Anderson, Said concludes that 'like all the poets of decolonization, Yeats struggles to announce the contours of an "imagined" or ideal community ...'[8]

   Yet an analysis of a complex figure like Yeats can hardly end here. If the face Yeats'project turned to Britain was decolonising, the face it turned to Ireland was colonial in another sense. Yeats sought to find a way to maintain the leadership of the Anglo-Irish Ascendancy, the English colony within Ireland, in the face of the rising demand for Irish independence. Yeats' project was one of enfolding the Ascendancy within the emerging nation. To accomplish this Yeats had to strive to overcome three barriers; the barrier of ethnicity, the barrier of class and the barrier of religion.

   Yeats' exploration of Celticism was the vehicle he used to challenge the ethnic barrier. This Celticism had to be parted from any implication of linguistic descent. Cairns and Richards observe that 'if, following Arnold, the true marks of the Celt were to be found in emotion, natural magic, love of colour, quickness of perception and spirituality, rather than the Irish language, such intangible criteria could be deployed to make Celts of Yeats and his Anglo-Irish contemporaries'.[9] Thus the opposition of the Saxon and the Gael could be overcome in the common name of Celt. At the same time, Celticism could also serve as a mark of Irish difference justifying national demands.

Yeats' anti-modernism was deployed in order to address the question of class. Yeats preferred to see an Anglo-Irish aristocracy and a Gaelic peasantry as two complementary aspects of an organic pre-modern community. Both were set beyond 'the filthy modern tide' and the values of the 'greasy till'. Seamas Deane has Yeats observing 'the peasant and the aristocrat, kindred in spirit but not in class, united in the great Romantic battle against the industrial and utilitarian ethic'.[10] This vision of such an anti-modern alliance was integral to Yeats' nationalism. Deane finds Yeats 'eager to discover an aristocratic element within the Protestant tradition and to associate this with the spiritual aristocracy of the Catholic and Celtic peasantry – defining aristocracy in each case as a mark of Irishness and Irishness as a mark of anti-modernism ...'[11] This pre-modern aristocratic Irishness could fuse the Anglo-Irish and the native Irish into a single nation.

While it may seem eccentric to most observers, Yeats' strong interest in mysticism, the occult, and spiritualism was also, in his own view, a healing gesture. It is an attempt to connect with his fellow countrymen and women 'via Celtic "other worldliness", by-passing the influence of Catholicism by reaching what he supposed to be a more fundamental level of their spirituality'.[12] Terry Eagleton applies to Yeats' project a characteristic Gramscian spin and ascerbic judgment:

> Yeats himself ...will swell the ranks of those who sought to convert the Anglo-Irish into a genuinely hegemonic class. Indeed he will be the last great inheritor of that lineage. Viewed subjectively, that tradition was full of sublime good will, generous intentions, dedicated self-sacrifice. Viewed objectively, it represented one of the most devious pieces of political opportunism in modern Irish history.[13]

PAST AND PEASANT

The lineage Eagleton refers to stretches over the nineteenth century, originating in the Celtic Revival of the late 1700s. In his Field Day Anthology essay, Seamus Heaney finds that in Yeats 'the enterprise of several nineteenth century writers found its purpose redefined and its aspiration fulfilled'.[14] The most extensive consideration of the nineteenth century in these terms has been accomplished by Joep Leerssen.[15]

Leerssen argues that the Act of Union marks a rough dividing point in the ideology of Irish opposition to English rule. Prior to the nineteenth century such opposition found its justification in patriotism. Patriotism, an ideal developed in a European context, saw society as a pragmatic association of individuals with common interests. The patriot sought to work for the good of his fellow citizens.

Nationalism on the other hand looked to a people tied together by the natural bond of common descent and a common culture, a national heritage. The outlook of nationalism came to dominate the Irish self-image in the nineteenth century. The particularity of the Irish nation was sought in a glorified pre-conquest past and in the authentic Irish peasantry. In Leerssen's punning summary, it was sought in 'past and peasant'.

Ireland's national identity was first sought in what Leerssen terms auto-exoticism, a 'reflex' which Leerssen finds most characteristically expressed in Lady Morgan's novels. There are two important expressions of this auto-exoticism. The first is the tendency to explain Ireland in terms of its past as if the present is the unfinished business of bygone eras or the Irish present is somehow closer to its past than elsewhere. Such a past is a prelapsarian one before foreign contamination. The second expression is the implicit argument that 'Ireland is most itself in those aspects wherein it is most un-cosmopolitan, most unlike other nations.'[16] The narrators of this type of fiction often adopt the stance of mediating between a mysterious Ireland and the English reading public. Leerssen finds the origin of this divided stance in Ireland's position within the English national system as England's colony.[17]

Leerssen finds these themes replayed throughout the Irish nineteenth century. They were prominent in the work of Irish antiquarians. Leerssen discusses the round tower controversies in some detail.[18] These themes were central to Thomas Moore's *Irish melodies*. After Catholic Emancipation, the register of Anglo-Irish literature changes from one of explaining Ireland to an English audience to a programme of 'uniting settler and native into a common Irish national awareness'.[19] This new programme however draws sustenance from the same resources of past and peasant. Many of these themes emerge in the poetry of Young Ireland and *The Nation*. They are the source of nineteenth-century popular historical narratives like those of Standish O'Grady. Anglo-Irish culture sought to rejuvenate itself in the primitive energies of Irish song and verse, folklore and the Gaelic language. In these efforts, 'the peasantry is not a social group whose lives and actions, sympathies and aspirations take shape in a politically or historically distinct moment, but rather the timeless repository of a primeval, timeless life, primitive in the root sense of that term, aboriginal and untouched by modernising influences from outside'.[20] In these terms the peasantry was ready to be recruited into the Yeatsian aristocratic pre-modern community. In Leerssen's words, rural Ireland could become 'an idyll rather than a problem'.[21]

Leerssen brings his argument to the end of the nineteenth century and ties his twin themes to Yeats and the Irish literary revival:

> The turn of the century initiatives in an imaginative, literary recuperation and celebration of Ireland's nationality were unavoidably constructed on an auto-exoticist self-image. Irish individuality and Irish identity were sought in those aspects in which Ireland was most distinctively un-

> English; as a result, the privileged areas of Irish culture in the literary imagination were the distant, pre-Norman or mythical past and the contemporary native, as yet un-anglicized, peasantry. [22]

Leerssen admits that the attempt to locate and define a national history and identity was characteristic of all European nationalisms but finds the Irish project different in that it was much more fraught and complex than elsewhere: 'many European nationalities in the wake of Romanticism are preoccupied with identity construction; in the case of Ireland, that project is grafted onto a long-standing confrontation with the neighbouring isle, takes its place in a climate of barely contained hostile divisions, carries a burdensome political heritage, and is invested with great, contentious political urgency'.[23] Irish history had to be recovered in the face of a 'particularly violent and disruptive historical development over long centuries of never-resolved conflict'.[24] The distinctive characteristics of the Irish national enterprise are to be found in colonialism, a long history subject to oppressive foreign control and self-estrangement.

JOYCE

Joyce, as could perhaps have been expected, would prove somewhat recalcitrant to conscription in service of the colonial or post-colonial argument. Yet even here a solid footing is achieved after some retreat and equivocation. Joyce is least problematic in Declan Kiberd's reading. Indeed, Joyce is explicitly identified as the first among the great post-colonial writers. Kiberd[25] scratches Joyce's name from the guest list of the rather morose sherry-and-cheese reception in honour of Mann, Proust, Eliot, and Pound and places him at the head of a carnival crew composed of Rushdie, Marquez and Borges. More than this, the progress of Joyce's fiction creates a kind of utopian trajectory both for the ideal colonial intellectual and the ideal anti-colonial revolution.

In Kiberd's view, *Dubliners* unerringly evoked a colonial Ireland as a paralysed 'place of copied and derived gestures, whose denizens were turned outward to serve a distant source of authority in London'. Joyce is likened to 'many another member of an emerging national elite ashamed of his or her colonial setting, and taking bitter consolation in writing it all down'.[26] This reading of *Dubliners* is shared by the other Irish post-colonial critics. Kiberd provocatively sees *A Portrait* as one of the first major accounts in modern English literature of the emergence of a post-colonial elite. Joyce is unrelentingly critical of this new elite and its own self-interested brand of nationalism. In its imitation of English models and advocacy of an exclusionary national ideal, this elite froze the national movement in a stage well short of its full liberatory potential. In *Ulysses*, Kiberd argues, Joyce moves beyond criticism to 'unleash a plurality of voices which would together sound the notes that moved beyond nationalism to liberation'.[27] Kiberd contends

that Joyce's 'spiritual project was to attempt to imagine a meaningful modernity which was more open to the full range of voices in Ireland than any nationalism which founded itself on the restrictive apparatus of the colonial state'.[28]

Many of the writers in the post-colonial tradition would see this utopian
vision of *Ulysses* as a step too far. Joep Leerssen agrees with Kiberd's assessment of the colonial character of the Dublin of *Dubliners* and *A Portrait*.
However, in contradistinction to Kiberd's view of time in Ulysses as a 'world
of cycles and spirals' undermining Enlightenment time and notions of linear
progress, Leerssen sees Joyce revelling in the 'depiction of a Newtonian
Dublin where time and space coexist in a physical dynamic relationship, dominated by movement and crisscrossing trajectories though space and time,
where space divided by time equals speed'.[29] According to Leerssen, 16 June
1904 is 'the day when James Joyce brought the Irish nineteenth century to a
close'.[30] Thus in Leerssen's view Joyce's career contains within it the break
from a colonial to a modernist essentially non-(rather than post-)colonial literature. But to other post-colonial critics this view of *Ulysses* as radically distinct
from the earlier works is bending the stick back too far.

Frederic Jameson, commenting in his Field Day pamphlet on the colonial
conditions of Joyce's writing, found in the polyvocality of Ulysses a refusal of
the crucial modernist category of style. This refusal was in support of Joyce's
avoidance of the self:

> ... style, as a category of some absolute subject, here disappears, and
> Joyce's palpable linguistic games and experiments are rather to be seen
> as impersonal sentence combinations and variations beyond all point of
> view ... whence one's occasional sense that (as with revolutionary modes
> of production) Joyce leaps over the stage of modernism into full post-
> modernism.[31]

David Lloyd agrees with Jameson's denial of the essential modernism of
Ulysses but sees the invocation of postmodernism as a confusion. Colonised cultures such as Ireland's produce 'not a self-sustaining and autonomous organism
capable of appropriating other cultures to itself, as imperial and post-modern
cultures alike conceive themselves to be, but rather at the individual and nation-
al-cultural level, a hybridization ... in which antagonism mixes with dependence
and autonomy is constantly undermined by the perceived influence of alien
powers'.[32] Nevertheless, Lloyd's view of Joyce's 'style' is closer to Jameson's than
to Kiberd's more celebratory view. Ulysses insists 'on a deliberate stylization of
dependence and inauthenticity, a stylization of the hybrid status of the colonized subject as of the colonized culture, their internal adulteration and the
strictly parodic modes that they produce in every sphere'.[33] In the displaced language of the colonised, Lloyd diagnoses 'indices of damage and impetuses to the
dismantling of the appropriative autonomous speaking subject'.[34]

Terry Eagleton develops the themes of Joyce's stylistic innovations and the lack of a centre in the bourgeois moral self. He notes that 'Joyce's literary experiments are inspired, obviously enough by his colonial context: it was the lack of any very serviceable metropolitan traditions which drove him to invent his own outlandish forms'.[35] Eagleton argues that on the colonial edges the easy totalities of classical realist fiction are less attainable because many of the central determinants of the colonial world lie elsewhere in the metropole. He also argues more specifically that 'if the political history of the nation is fissured and disrupted, subject to the authority of another, it is less likely to throw up … realist notions of coherent narrative and self determining characters …'[36]

Kiberd accepts much of this analysis in noting Joyce's 'rejection of the obligation felt by realists to present a coherent, stable, socialized self'.[37] In a more positive vein, Kiberd credits Joyce with the invention of a technique of mythical realism, 'juxtaposing Odyssean marvels against the Irish quotidian'.[38] Realism was the mode suited to a chronicle of the European bourgeoisie, but Ireland was 'split between modernity and undevelopment' and 'no merely realist method could do full justice to that'.[39] Hence Joyce points the way to the more contemporary development of magic realism. In invoking Ireland's blocked development as constitutive of Joyce's literary innovation, Kiberd presents an alternative to his own more celebratory rendering.

The discussions around Joyce's fiction parallel a central insight into the Irish nineteenth century developed by the post-colonial and Marxist schools of literary criticism. This argument concerns the social origins of the failure of Ireland to produce a secure tradition of the realist novel in the nineteenth century. Eagleton links Joyce explicitly to this earlier lineage:

> … in *Ulysses* he also uses his mythological framework to ironize and estrange that more tenacious modern myth which is realism itself. And if he can accomplish this so superbly, it is in part because he is heir to a cultural lineage for which such realism, as the fruit of a developed European civilization, had never been less than profoundly problematic.[40]

David Lloyd[41] observes that accounts of the nineteenth-century Irish novel are troubled by the need to explain its inadequacy in relation to British and continental models. Terry Eagleton broaches such an explanation: 'the realist novel is the form *par excellence* of settlement and stability, gathering individual lives into an integrated whole; and social conditions in Ireland hardly lent themselves to any such sanguine reconciliation'.[42] Following Hegel and Lukacs, Lloyd argues that the most significant aspect of the integrations performed by the novel, that which makes it 'the "epic" of the bourgeois era',

> … lies in its narrations of the socialization of the individual. … it must be emphasized that the individual narrative of self-formation is itself subsumed in the larger narrative of the civilizing process, the passage

from savagery to civility, which is the master narrative of modernity ... it
narrates the passage of an individual or a people-nation from contingent
particularity to universal value ...[43]

Eagleton sees the disrupted course of Irish history as inimical to 'a tale of evolutionary progress, a middle march from a lower to a higher state'.[44] Lloyd[45]
points to the difficulty in locating a common story in a chronicle of conquest
and dispossession. Even if a common story could be located, a divided society,
historically split between the colonial and the colonised, cannot find a neutral
vantage point from which to tell the tale. Leerssen makes this argument bald-
ly and forcefully: '... a tale that is both Irish and a novel is, in a way, a contradiction in terms: a novelistic setting means Anglo-Ireland, means something
cloned from, and indistinguishable from, England itself, means something
imported and without national Irish past; and an Irish setting means Gaeldom,
means straying from novelistic into a romantic register, means something dispossessed, disaffected and without a present and a future'.[46] Leerssen identifies other modes of literary expression as more congenial to the Irish condition.
For instance he sees Lady Morgan's writings less as novels and more as bridges
linking the earlier forms of antiquarian iconography, sentimental comedies,
and traveller's accounts with the later expressions of Irish identity through
poetry, narrative history and drama.

David Lloyd had earlier analysed the minor status of the poetry of James
Clarence Mangan.[47] Mangan's treatment as minor literature was due to his
refusal to ground his portrayal of the Irish colonial subject in major literature's
narrative of the moral bourgeois subject. This argument is parallel with those
presented above. In a later essay Lloyd argues that the failure of the realist
novel in Ireland is due to a much more particular 'conjunction between demographic shifts, rural violence and social movements' which produces a crisis of
representation for the novel rendering it unable to act 'as a hegemonic force in
an unstable society'.[48]

The first part of Lloyd's argument is that the novel generally demands a
middle class that could provide representative or exemplary figures to mediate
political, class and sectarian antagonisms. The second part of the argument is
not that Ireland lacked a middle class in the nineteenth century. It is instead
that the middle class that Ireland did have lacked the necessary stability and
security of achievement. This instability was due to the colonial settlement:
'... lack of proprietorship in land, for reasons directly determined by the nature
and maintenance of colonial occupation, produced the anomalous situation
that social and political, as well as economic, instability was at its greatest precisely in those areas of the country where the largest "middle class" formations
could be held to be emerging'.[49] Lloyd is here identifying the middle class with
the more substantial tenant and grazier. This Irish middle class eludes a representative function in the novel precisely because its middle position makes
it 'the site of maximum instability, whether in terms of its fluctuating eco-

nomic situation or in terms of its political or social affiliations'.[50]

In addition the forms of social conflict, specifically 'agrarian outrages' conducted by secret societies in the pre-Famine period, are only understandable on their own terms within a frame of the moral economy as developed by E.P. Thompson. They are unassimilable to the progressive vision of both the novel and the state-building projects of nationalism and unionism. They had to be represented as irrational, instinctual and spasmodic. It is this very unassimilability which delineates the threat such actions and organisations pose to the established (or establishing) order. In this way Lloyd grounds the problems of the Irish novel, not in a somewhat abstract fracturing of colonial society but in concrete classes, actions and social movements which find their specific ground in the colonial social formation. Lloyd sees the function of the novel as having two sides, both inclusive and exclusive:

> The larger move of the realist novel .... integrat(es) the individual, or the local community, into the larger frame of national society. This entails, however, not only a movement of assimilation but also its necessary logical correlative, the negation or exclusion of what cannot be drawn into identity. One of the problems of the Irish novel, precisely insofar as it conforms to the symbolic mode of realism, is the sheer volume of inassimilable residue that it can neither properly contain nor entirely exclude.[51]

Thus the failure of the Irish nineteenth-century novel is located by these critics in the colonial character of Irish society; in the disrupted character of Ireland's colonial history, in the failure to find a unified narrative viewpoint in a society split between the colonised and the coloniser, and in the colonial dispossession of land which generated an unstable middle class and unassimilable forms of agrarian struggle. This theoretical perspective has been applied to the novels of Lady Morgan, Maturin, Edgeworth, Le Fanu, Lover, Lever, Griffin, the Banims, Stoker, George Moore and finally Joyce.

In the introduction to this volume I argued that the post-colonial and Marxist analysis of nineteenth-century Irish literature constituted one cable of a provisional rope bridge cast over the chasm of neglect of colonialism in the writing of Irish history. I have argued above that this cable consists of two interwoven strands. One strand analyses the construction in the nineteenth century of an Irish identity rooted in a glorified romantic past and the persistence of this past in an idyllic peasantry. This strand is anchored in a canonical consideration of Yeats' career in the early twentieth century. A second strand concerns the failure of bourgeois realism to find secure expression in the Irish nineteenth-century novel. This failure is based in the fractured colonial condition of Irish society. This fragmentation finds its canonical expression in Joyce's work on the banks of the twentieth century.

The foregoing arguments are not intended to establish that the colonial condition of Ireland is the only ground on which to build an understanding of culture in the Irish nineteenth century. Such an argument would, of course, be indefensible. It is only more modestly contended that these arguments establish that a broad field of nineteenth- and early twentieth-century Irish cultural phenomena, from the Celtic Revival to *Ulysses*, cannot be comprehensively understood without reference to a continuing Irish colonial context.

NOTES

1. E. Said, *Orientalism* (London: Routledge and Kegan Paul, 1978).
2. G. Spivak, *In other worlds: essays in cultural politics* (New York and London: Methuen, 1987).
3. Bill Ashcroft, G. Griffiths and H. Tiffen, *The empire writes back: theory and practice in post-colonial literatures* (London: Routledge, 1989).
4. H. Bhabha, *Nation and narration* (London: Routledge, 1990).
5. E. Said, 'Yeats and Decolonization,' in *Field Day, Nationalism, Colonialism, and Literature* (Minneapolis, MN: University of Minnesota Press, 1990), p. 69.
6. Ibid., p. 77.
7. Ibid., p. 78.
8. Ibid., p. 86.
9. D. Cairns and S. Richards, *Writing Ireland: Colonialism, Nationalism and Culture* (Manchester: Manchester University Press, 1988), p. 67.
10. S. Deane, *Celtic Revivals* (London: Faber and Faber, 1985).
11. Ibid.
12. See Cairns and Richards, *Writing Ireland*, p. 68.
13. T. Eagleton, *Heathcliff and the Great Hunger: Studies in Irish Culture* (London and New York: Verso, 1995).
14. S. Deane (ed.), *Field Day Anthology of Irish Writing* (Derry: Field Day Publications, 1991), p. 783.
15. J. Leerssen, *Remembrance and Imagination* (Cork: Cork University Press, 1996).
16. Ibid., p. 38.
17. Ibid., p. 52.
18. A romantic antiquarian position held that the round towers were Eastern in origin and pre-Christian, used in the context of pagan rites. A more positive position contended, consistent with the modern understanding, that they were monastic fortifications of medieval date. Ibid., pp. 108–56.
19. Ibid., p. 101.
20. Ibid., p. 163.
21. Ibid., p. 168.
22. Ibid., p. 221.
23. Ibid., p. 225.
24. Ibid., p. 225.
25. D. Kiberd, *Inventing Ireland: The Literature of the Modern Nation* (London: Vintage, 1995).
26. Ibid., p. 330.
27. Ibid., p. 338.
28. Ibid., p. 345.
29. See J. Leerssen, *Remembrance and Imagination*, p. 228.
30. Ibid., p. 223.
31. F. Jameson, 'Modernism and Imperialism,' in *Field Day, Nationalism, Colonialism, and Literature* (Minneapolis, MN: University of Minnesota Press, 1990), pp. 61–2.
32. D. Lloyd, *Anomalous States: Irish Writing and the Post-Colonial Moment* (Dublin: Lilliput, 1993), pp. 111–12.
33. Ibid., p.110.
34. Ibid., p. 121. The post-colonial critics further observe that this inauthenticity, the exhaustion, or more aptly the absence of the self is intensified in Beckett's fiction and drama.
35. T. Eagleton, *Heathcliff and the Great Hunger*, p. 256.

36. Ibid., p. 298.
37. See D. Kiberd, *Inventing Ireland*, p. 354.
38. Ibid., p. 338.
39. Ibid., p. 339.
40. See Eagleton, *Heathcliff and the Great Hunger*, p. 225
41. See Lloyd, *Anomalous States*, p. 128.
42. See Eagleton, *Heathcliff and the Great Hunger*, p. 147.
43. See Lloyd, *Anomalous States*, pp. 133–4.
44. See Eagleton, *Heathcliff and the Great Hunger*, p. 147.
45. See D. Lloyd, *Anomalous States*, p. 135.
46. See J. Leerssen, *Remembrance and Imagination*, p. 52.
47. See D. Lloyd, *Nationalism and Minor Literature: James Clarence Mangan and the Emergence of Irish Cultural Nationalism* (Berkeley, CA: University of California Press, 1987).
48. See Lloyd, *Anomalous States*, p. 133.
49. Ibid., p. 139.
50. Ibid., p. 140.
51. Ibid., p.152.

CHAPTER FOURTEEN

Ireland in 1812: Colony or Part of the Imperial Main? The 'Imagined Community' in Maria Edgeworth's The Absentee[1]

VALERIE KENNEDY

INTRODUCTION

In *The Absentee*, Edgeworth tries to create Ireland as a nation as an imagined community both in terms of its own internal relationships and in relation to Britain. Her project is ultimately unsuccessful, and the novel is riven with contradictory elements. These may be related to the anomalies and contradictions in Edgeworth's own situation and the historical context of her Irish works. Ultimately, the project of the creation of a fictional imagined community and the fictional resolution of the problem of absentee landlordism founder on the historical contradictions and anomalies that the novel tries to ignore, as well as the tensions between the various generic modes which Edgeworth employs.

As a member of the Protestant Ascendancy, Edgeworth is in an anomalous position in relation to both Ireland and England and their populations. Irish by nationality and by virtue of their historical connection with the country, the members of the Protestant Ascendancy were nonetheless separated from the majority of the Irish population by social class, religion, and, often, language as well. Linked to the English gentry by religion and a shared belief in Enlightenment values, they were not fully accepted as an integral part of the English class system. In addition, the position of an Irish or Anglo-Irish author writing about Irish themes for an English audience made Edgeworth's situation even more problematic. Edgeworth is using Irish subject matter in works published in London by English publishers primarily for an English audience. All her Irish works were published first in London and two of them, *Ennui* and *The Absentee*, were published in her *Tales of Fashionable Life* in 1809 and 1812 respectively. This has the obvious effect of downplaying the Irish contents and themes of the works, perhaps in order to avoid alienating her English audience.[2] Even now, the debate as to whether Edgeworth should be seen as part of the Irish or the Anglo-Irish tradition continues: Jeffares, Moynahan, and Sloan see her as part of the Anglo-Irish tradition, while Calahan and Deane locate her within the Irish one.[3] *The Absentee* mocks Lady Clonbrony's clumsy and ill-fated attempts to 'pass' as English, but her intermediate location between England and Ireland can be seen as a comic reflection of Edgeworth's own situation.

If Edgeworth's position as a member of the Protestant Ascendancy was inherently anomalous, the Act of Union, which came into effect in 1801, made the Ascendancy's situation explicitly contradictory in terms of law and government. After the Act of Union, Ireland was legally part of Great Britain, that is, part of the imperial main, although, in other respects, the country was in a colonial situation vis-à-vis the imperial entity.[4] As Geraldine Friedman says, the position of Ireland after the Act of Union was that of 'an internal colony'.[5] Quoting Oliver MacDonagh, Daniel Hack describes the position of the Protestant Ascendancy after the Act of Union as that of people who were '"domestically ... overlords, but externally ... dependents" in their relation to the English ruling class'.[6] Although Maria Edgeworth, like her father, was in favour of the Union, a character in their *Essay on Irish Bulls*, Phelim O'Mooney, criticises its illogicality. He observes that '"there was something very like a bull, in professing to make a complete identification of the two kingdoms, whilst, at the same time, certain regulations continued in full force to divide the countries by art, even more than the British Channel does by nature"'.[7]

The anomalies and contradictions of post-Union relations between Ireland and Britain and of Edgeworth's position as a member of the Protestant Ascendancy and an Anglo-Irish author writing for an English audience find a parallel in the three types of textual contradiction in *The Absentee*. Firstly, the novel has pretensions to realism, but in fact elides historical realities and differences. Secondly, it attempts to transcend negative stereotypes of Ireland while failing to escape the orientalising attitude that privileges the metropolitan viewpoint and Standard English as its means of expression. Thirdly, it is structured by the incompatible modes of the travelogue and of allegory and romance.

The Absentee claims to offer accurate reporting of conditions in Ireland, and yet at the same time it elides three elements of the real-life Irish situation after the Union. These are the religious, linguistic, and related social and national differences among the Irish as a people, the 1798 rebellion and the British military response to it, and the decline of the city of Dublin after the Union. Secondly, the book shows a self-conscious negotiation with negative images and stereotypes of Ireland and the Irish and with previous well-known textual representations of Ireland. Yet Edgeworth herself is unable to transcend some of these stereotypes. This is probably because the Irish nation as imagined community in the novel is characterised by the contradictions of the orientalising perspective described by Edward Said as typical of the attitude of the coloniser (or the inhabitant of the imperial power) towards the colonised. This perspective privileges Standard English as the metropolitan mode of linguistic expression and the bearer of the moral values of the post-Enlightenment English gentry, thus defining Ireland, its people, and its language as deviations from the accepted norm of civilisation. Finally, in generic terms, the travelogue form of those sections of the novel set in Ireland sits uneasily with the structures of allegory and romance to which Edgeworth resorts to resolve the contradictions of the text.

The source of these contradictions in *The Absentee* lies in Maria Edgeworth's project of trying to create Ireland as a nation as an imagined community and, more specifically, of trying to find a solution to the problem of Irish (and English) absentee landlordism. The nation as imagined community is envisaged as existing both within Ireland and in the relation between Ireland and Britain. If these two versions of the national community are successfully imagined, the anomalies of Edgeworth's own position in relation to both Ireland and Britain can be resolved. Benedict Anderson defines the nation as 'an imagined political community', further specifying that it is 'imagined as both inherently limited and sovereign'.[8] He explains that the nation as a community is imagined since its members will never know, meet, or hear of most of their fellow citizens, and yet the community exists as an image in their minds. He adds that he has used the word, 'imagined', to stress the significance of the style in which nations are imagined as communities, rather than the issue of their falsity or genuineness. In relation to the words, 'community' and 'sovereign', Anderson argues that 'regardless of the actual inequality and exploitation that may prevail in each, the nation is always conceived as a deep horizontal comradeship' embodied in a sovereign state that guarantees religious and other freedoms to its members.[9] All of these definitions are of obvious relevance to what Edgeworth is trying to do in *The Absentee*, and all reveal particular dimensions of the problems she faces. The community she imagines glosses over not only the inequality and exploitation existing in Ireland, but also the facts of religious, linguistic, and class differences. It also completely occludes the most inconvenient historical realities of all, the facts that, in 1812, Ireland did not exist as a separate independent sovereign state, and that religious and other freedoms were not guaranteed.

The imagined community Edgeworth creates involves, in Ireland, the reinsertion of the Irish aristocracy (the Clonbrony family) into the fabric of Irish society, and the creation of a healthy and balanced relationship between landowner, agent, and tenants, as well as between the landowner as husband and his wife. In the context of Ireland and Britain, the imagined community requires of both English and Irish gentry that they reside on their estates. The Irish aristocracy is required to recognise that their major responsibility is to their Irish tenants and consequently that they should return to Ireland. The English gentry too, should return to their country estates rather than bankrupting themselves in London, as the case of Sir John Berryl, which exactly parallels that of Lord Clonbrony, attests. Edgeworth's narrator makes the point explicitly, not to say clumsily, by calling Sir John an absentee, even though, as the narrator says, the width of the Irish Channel does not flow between him and his estate (p. 54). In both cases, moreover, it is the wives' extravagance and frivolity and the husbands' weakness which are seen to be at the root of the problem.

Unfortunately, however, these projects of the creation of Ireland as a nation as an imagined community and the real situation of Ireland as an internal colony of Great Britain are mutually incompatible, in intellectual, cultural, aesthetic, and political terms. The only way in which Edgeworth can create these fictional imagined communities is to rewrite history, occluding or eliding both actual historical events and differences of various kinds between social groups. Consequently, she returns to an orientalising perspective that reinforces rather than displaces the negative stereotyping of Ireland and the Irish that she is attempting to overcome. Similarly, since the creation of the imagined communities is impossible within the realist context of the travel narrative mode, the novel's ending reasserts the structures of allegory and romance through the figures of the marital union of individuals rather than the political Union of countries.

What follows will examine some of the most important historical omissions and transformations of *The Absentee*, before looking briefly at the contradictions and discrepancies of the novel's representation of Irishness, notably its self-conscious examination of issues of stereotyping and representation. These are most clearly seen in the narration of Lord Colambre's journey to Ireland and the interrogation of stereotypes and of previous textual representations of Irishness. Edgeworth attempts to resolve the problems the novel raises through the allegory of the unifying and successful marriage, and through the return of the reformed and reforming landlord to his long-neglected estates. However, Edgeworth's text undermines its own criticism of the absentee landlord phenomenon through its historical omissions and transformations, the reinscription of stereotypes, and the allegorically apt but improbable ending. Since Edgeworth is never able to question the system of landowning as a whole, she is unable to offer any solutions to its inherent injustices.[10]

REWRITING HISTORY: OMISSIONS AND TRANSFORMATIONS

While purporting to be at least partially a realistic account of the contemporary situation in Ireland,[11] *The Absentee* actually omits or transforms certain key historical events or factors. Some examples of omissions are the 1798 and 1803 rebellions and the subsequent presence of a large English military force in Ireland, and the death of 40,000 people in the famine of 1801. Conversely, the work offers a very different account of the effects of the Act of Union on life in Dublin and on absentee landlordism than those offered by most historians and literary critics. Finally, the differences in language and religion between landowners and tenants are glossed over with barely a word, although they are indicated in the subtext of allusions in the narrative.

In *The Absentee*, neither the 1798 nor the 1803 rebellion is mentioned.[12] Neither is the fact that, after 1792, an English military force which was significantly larger than before was present in Ireland, with a mission to maintain law and order. In *The Absentee*, the English military presence in Ireland is both marginalised and allegorised. Negatively, it is represented in the satire of the boorish and ignorant Major Benson and Captain Williamson, and the wealthy but futile Colonel Heathcock. These negative figures are opposed to Lord Colambre, to Sir James Brooke, and to the eccentric but erudite antiquarian, Count O'Halloran. Lord Colambre thinks of joining the army at one point in the text, Sir James is described as 'an officer'on his first appearance in the text, although his military position is barely mentioned thereafter, and Count O'Halloran has served in the Austrian army. All three offer positive images of what a soldier might be or has been compared to the ludicrous Benson and Williamson and the worse than ludicrous Heathcock. But these positive figures are significant in relation to the moral pattern of the novel rather than the political or military situation in Ireland.[13]

Similarly, the novel runs directly counter to the generally accepted interpretation of the effects of the Act of Union on social life in Dublin and on the phenomenon of absentee landlordism. Edgeworth's novel offers a nuanced picture of initial vulgarisation but eventual beneficial change in Dublin, through the commentary of Sir James Brooke, whereas the view of most historians seems to suggest the decline of the city from a colonial capital to a provincial backwater. In the novel, Sir James says that the changes brought about by the Act of Union 'were productive of eventual benefit' in Dublin even though at first they seemed to mean the loss of 'the decorum, elegance, polish, and charm of society' (p. 83). Sir James describes the benefits of the Union at some length. He explains that while at first it led to the dominance of Dublin society by *nouveau riche* 'barbarians', after a relatively short time most of these were compelled to give way to a new society. This was 'composed of a most agreeable and salutary mixture of birth and education, gentility and knowledge, manner and matter' among 'the higher orders'; that is, upper-class Dublin society is imagined in the form of an English-style meritocracy of the gentry. On the other hand, the middle class and tradesmen are described as being divided into two groups, the honest and the dishonest, the latter embodied in the characters of Anastasia Raffarty and her husband (pp. 83–5). This presents the Union in a generally positive light, despite what Lord Colambre sees at Anastasia Raffarty's house at Tusculum and despite the story he remembers his mother telling about the grocer's wife at the reception in Dublin Castle. Moreover, Sir James adds that many former Irish absentees returned home after the Union, improved by 'a new stock of ideas, and some taste for science and literature' which are necessary in polite society in London if not in Ireland. As McCormack notes, Sir James's view of the city contradicts both the critical view of post-Union Dublin expressed in *An Intercepted Letter* and the reader's perception of Mrs Raffarty and her friends in Edgeworth's novel.[14] The imagined community of upper-class manners combined with upwardly mobile good sense, however, is evoked only through Sir James's description.

In contrast to the positive vision of Edgeworth's novel, historical accounts of Dublin in the period after the Act of Union generally talk about the decline of the city. This is usually seen as a result of several factors, one of them being that, once the Irish parliament was removed, many landowners who were part of it removed to London to take up their seats there.[15] Conversely, in *The Absentee*, the ending suggests that not only is Lord Clonbrony's family returning to their estates in Ireland, but that, in the words of Larry Brady, which close the novel: 'it's growing the fashion not to be an Absentee'(p. 266). As more than one critic has noticed, this is clearly wishful thinking on Edgeworth's part as well as Larry's.[16]

Thirdly, both the Catholic religion and the Irish language are marginalised to such a point that they are barely existent in the work at all. There is not the slightest acknowledgement of the fact that these differences of language and religion between landowners and tenantry, in addition to the economic difference, constituted the main elements of the problematic relationship between them. There are only two brief, and idealising, references to religion in the work. When Lord Colambre is visiting those estates of his father's managed by the good agent, Burke, he finds that Protestant and Catholic children attend the same school, and that both the Protestant and the Catholic priests co-operate with Burke in his management of the estate and its people (p. 133). Interestingly enough, in *Ennui*, there is a similar school, also attended by both Protestant and Catholic children. This time, however, McLeod, *Ennui*'s equivalent of Burke, prefaces his description by telling Glenthorn that 'Religion ... is the great difficulty in Ireland'. The topic is not taken up, but the difficulty is at least registered.[17]

As with religion, so with language. In *The Absentee* as in *Castle Rackrent*, Edgeworth is alive to the different types of usage of English by Irish speakers. However, nowhere in *The Absentee* is there any acknowledgement of the fact that many of Lord Clonbrony's tenants, if not the agents or the landlord himself, would probably be bilingual (speaking both Irish and English), if not monolingual speakers of Irish.[18] As regards the different usage of English by Irish speakers, although the narrator is clearly critical of Lady Dashfort's mockery of the Irish brogue she likes to mimic, Standard English is the norm, and divergences from it are seen as deviations to be explained.[19] The fact that Larry Brady is given the task of ending the novel by describing the Clonbronys' triumphant return to their estates can surely be explained more as a matter of narrative tact than as an endorsement of a non-standard form of the language. The moral centres of the work are provided by Lord Colambre and Grace Nugent, both of whom speak impeccable Standard English. Moral rectitude is embodied in correct grammar and pronunciation.[20] By contrast, again, in *Ennui*, the existence of the Irish language is mentioned once, when Glenthorn first meets Ellinor, his old nurse, and declares that he cannot understand her, 'as she spoke in her native language'. Later, Lady Geraldine comments caustically on the failure of the English traveller, Lord Craiglethorpe, to understand his Irish interlocutors, since 'he can't understand their modes of expression, nor they his'.[21] It is true that Lady Geraldine seems to be referring to the divergent use of English by the Irish rather than to the Irish language per se, but the remark is suggestive nonetheless.

The effect of all these occlusions and transformations in *The Absentee* is to downplay the difference between Ireland and England by more or less completely effacing the differences of language and religion between landowners and tenants. In the process, the Catholic, Irish-speaking identity of Lord Clonbrony's tenants and of the majority of the inhabitants of Ireland simply disappears. Moreover, the narrative's endorsement of Sir James Brooke's positive vision of Ireland and Dublin after the Act of Union rewrites some very recent history through decidedly rose-coloured glasses.

NARRATIVE REPRESENTATIONS OF IRELAND: CONTRADICTORY DISCOURSES

If some aspects of Irish history are largely ignored or rewritten in *The Absentee*, there is also a conflict between the demands of the allegorical structure and those of the anthropological or ethnographic pose of observation and documentation that is used in the sections of the work set in Ireland. In subjecting past and present misrepresentations and stereotypes of Ireland and its inhabitants to critical scrutiny, Edgeworth both challenges them and, paradoxically, reinscribes them.

The Irish sections take the form of a travelogue, as Lord Colambre arrives in Dublin and then visits the estates or the houses of the Raffartys, the Killpatricks, Count O'Halloran, and the Oranmores, before finally arriving in his father's domains. The use of the travelogue allows Edgeworth to correct the misrepresentations of Ireland through the process of education which the hero undergoes. Colambre must learn not to over-generalise, and to distinguish between the balanced and fair representations of Ireland of Sir James Brooke and the biased, malicious, and reductive misrepresentations of Lady Dashfort.

Colambre's journey through Ireland offers him a chance to learn and Edgeworth a chance to instruct not only her hero, but also her (English) readers in how to judge both the Irish and the English correctly. Colambre, like Glenthorn in *Ennui*, represents the errors of vision and the belief in misrepresentations that must be corrected. However, despite the explicit critique of misrepresentations in the text, the narrative itself can be seen at times to draw on and reinforce pejorative stereotypes of the Irish of the sort that Edward Said describes as typical of orientalist representations of the colonised Other.

These pejorative stereotypes emerge in the narrative's engagement with the issue of the representation of Ireland and the Irish through its self-conscious negotiation not only with negative stereotypes of Ireland and the Irish, but also with previous textual representations of them. Edgeworth's text shows that aspect of orientalist discourse which Said calls 'the textual attitude'. Said defines this as the preference for 'the schematic authority of a text to the disorientation of direct encounters with the human', especially when such direct encounters contradict the message which the writer wishes to communicate.[22] *The Absentee* may be said to show Edgeworth's endorsement of the textual attitude despite herself. The book criticises previous representations of Ireland and the Irish; yet, even as it does so, it reinscribes them, while some negative stereotypes of both the Irish and the Jews are used in an apparently uncritical way. The narrative discourse is both ambivalent and unstable, both a reflection and a symptom of the anomalies of Edgeworth's position as a member of the Protestant Ascendancy writing about Ireland for an English audience.

Two notable examples of the narrative's engagement with the issues of the textual representation of Ireland are the discussion between Sir James Brooke and Lord Colambre when the latter first arrives in Dublin and the indirect reference to Spenser's description of the Irish as 'barbarous Scythians'.[23] Both are examples of the way Edgeworth incorporates previous representations of Ireland in her text and reinterprets them as she does so.

The first of these occurs at the beginning of the section of the narrative set in Ireland. Shortly after arriving in Dublin, Colambre meets Sir James Brooke, who is to become one of his two trusted guides to the city and the country. When they meet, Sir James, by a happy coincidence, is reading *An Intercepted Letter from China*, an allusion to the anonymous pamphlet attributed to John Wilson Croker. Edgeworth's narrator transforms the account of Dublin in the pamphlet from a satirical critique of the post-Union city to a pleasing description 'in a slight, playful, and ironical style', thus rewriting the original text.[24] As Lord Colambre and Sir James enter into discussion, Sir James speaks explicitly of 'different representations and misrepresentations of Ireland', and goes on to '[touch] on all ancient and modern authors on this subject, from Spenser and Davies to Young and Beaufort' (p. 81). Sir James also points out the dangers of generalising from particular experiences, both to Colambre and the reader. Sir James, says the narrator, saves 'our young observer ... from the common error of travellers – the deducing general conclusions from a few particular cases, or arguing from exceptions, as if they were rules' (pp. 81–2). Later, showing that he has indeed learned the lesson well, Colambre corrects himself when he is tempted to generalise by taking the disastrous state of affairs on his father's estates, which are managed by Nicholas Garraghty, for the image of Ireland as a whole. 'Let me not', he says, 'even to my own mind, commit the injustice of taking a speck for the whole' (p. 162).

   Thus Edgeworth has Colambre reject the over-generalising perspective that has been identified as one of the typical textual strategies of orientalist discourse.[25] Nonetheless, her use of the travelogue necessarily creates Colambre as the authoritative observer, who, like the orientalist, is superior to the people and places he sees. As Deane says, travel literature in the eighteenth century was 'a mode of political critique', which often viewed the foreign elements it described from the normalising and authoritative perspective of the home culture.[26] In the Irish sections of *The Absentee*, as in the rest of the narrative, the narrative perspective is identified with a version of the English point of view. This means that the Irish characters and their language are seen as deviations from a norm which have to be explained before they can be understood.[27]

   The second, and more interesting, example of Edgeworth's negotiation with previous textual representations of Ireland relates to Spenser's *A View of the Present State of Ireland* and specifically to its image of the Irish as 'Scythians'. In *The Absentee*, the phrase, 'barbarous Scythian', is used by Lord Colambre on the occasion of the visit he makes with Lady Dashfort and the English officers to Count O'Halloran. The purpose of the visit reveals Edgeworth's tendentious rewriting of Irish history. For Lady Dashfort's visit to Count O'Halloran is made in order to ask him if the English officers may hunt and fish on his lands during their stay in Ireland. If Count O'Halloran is taken to be a representative of those Gaelic-speaking gentry still in possession of their estates,[28] then the permission that he graciously grants the visiting English officers to use his land may be taken as a reversal of the past and contemporary colonial occupation of Ireland by British troops. Similarly, the significance of the comparison of the Irish to the 'barbarous Scythians' is also reversed.

   In his *View of the Present State of Ireland*, Spenser's Irenius takes the Scythians as the most important analogy to the situation of the inhabitants of Ireland before the arrival of the English. For Spenser and many of his contemporaries, the Scythians, like the Irish, were barbarians.[29] In the scene with Count O'Halloran in *The Absentee*, the Count is in the process of apologising to his visitors for the misbehaviour of the members of his menagerie. He explains: '"a mouse, a bird, and a fish, are, you know, tribute from earth, air, and water, to a conqueror–"', only for Lord Colambre to respond, '"But from no barbarous Scythian!"'(p. 116). Although McCormack and Walker argue that the scene is designed not to deny that the Count is a barbarian but 'to elevate that cultural identification into a higher value' via the allusion to Herodotus,[30] the exchange surely does both. It challenges the view that the Gaelic gentry are barbarians, since the Count and Lord Colambre are the only people present in this scene who have read Herodotus' *History* and who can thus recognise the classical reference. However, the allusion can be taken to refer to Spenser as well, in which case the denial of Scythian barbarity both recalls and reverses Spenser's use of the same race in his work. Far from being a barbarian, Count O'Halloran, like Lord Colambre, is a nobleman and an Enlightenment gentleman, with the classical education that that description implies.

His aristocratic position (and Edgeworth's classbound view of present and past Irish history) is revealed in the narrative comment that follows Colambre's remark. The Count recognises Colambre as 'a person worthy his attention', that is, another educated nobleman, but then turns his attention to his other guests. The narrator says: 'his first care was to keep the peace between his loving subjects and his foreign visitors. It was difficult to dislodge the old settlers, to make room for the new comers; but he adjusted these things with admirable facility; and, with a master's hand and master's eye, compelled each favourite to retreat into the back settlements' (p. 116). Edgeworth offers an image of the accommodation of 'old settlers' and 'new comers' through the 'master's hand and master's eye' which reveals her desire to rewrite past history as well as predict a unified future. The political vocabulary is surely not fortuitous: as McCormack says, it forces us 'to consider who now are subjects and who are foreign visitors'.[31] What it also reveals, though, is Edgeworth's class-consciousness: peace is secured through the action of the master. In this respect the scene anticipates the ending of the work where the return of the Clonbronys is offered as a proleptic image of reform in the management of their estates and the future prosperity of their tenants.

TRANSCENDING OR REINSCRIBING STEREOTYPES: QUESTIONS OF RACE, CLASS, AND LANGUAGE

If *The Absentee* negotiates earlier textual representations of Ireland and the Irish somewhat ambiguously through allusions to them, it also does so through its ambivalent attitude to stereotypes. The narrator explicitly calls Lady Dashfort's stereotyped and reductive views of the Irish exercises in 'the arts of misrepresentation' (p. 107). However, the narrative not only appears to endorse them at certain moments, but also uses other stock images of Irishmen as one of its own techniques of characterisation.

Lady Dashfort's representations of the Irish are discredited firstly because they are malicious and reductive, and secondly because she has an ulterior motive: she wishes to make Colambre disgusted with Ireland so that he will marry her daughter, Isabel. Here the demands of the allegorical structure of the novel coincide with the ethnographic observations of the travelogue genre, and both coalesce around the question of whom Lord Colambre is to marry. Lady Dashfort makes sure that Colambre will meet two types of Irish individual who will impress him most unfavourably. These are the '*squireens*, or little squires' (p. 107, emphasis in the original), and the peasants who cringe and fawn on the gentry. The narrator describes the *squireens* as

> persons who, with good long leases or valuable farms, possess incomes
> from three to eight hundred a year, who keep a pack of hounds; *take out*
> a commission of the peace, sometimes before they can spell (as her lady-

ship said), and almost always before they know any thing of law or justice. Busy and loud about small matters; *jobbers at assizes*; combining with
one another, and trying upon every occasion, public or private, to push
themselves forward, to the annoyance of their superiors, and the terror
of those below them.

They are also described as showing 'the most self-sufficient ignorance, and the
most illiberal spirit' (p. 107, emphasis in the original). The cringing and servile
peasants, for their part, are said by the narrator to show 'their habits of self-
contradiction, their servility and flattery one moment, and their litigious and
encroaching spirit the next' (p. 109).

Edgeworth is at pains to distinguish between Lady Dashfort's misrepresentations of the *squireens* and the peasantry and the narrative view of them,
yet the distinction is not always as clear as it might be. Various words in the
description of the *squireens* are italicised to show that they are the language of
the *squireens* themselves or of Lady Dashfort mimicking them, and one pejorative comment about the *squireens'* ignorance and pretentiousness is explicitly
attributed to Lady Dashfort. However, it is the narrator, not the character, who
describes the *squireens* taking out commissions of the peace 'almost always
before they know any thing of law or justice' (p. 107), and who says that the
peasants described above belong to 'the old uneducated race, whom no one
can help, because they will never help themselves' (p. 109). Moreover, the
ensuing description, not all of which I have quoted here, is arguably also in the
narrative voice. Lady Dashfort mimics the Irish brogue, and the narrator mimics Lady Dashfort mimicking it. Mimicry is a notoriously ambivalent strategy.
As Homi Bhabha has shown, when used by the colonised, it can be subversive,
yet, when used by the coloniser, it can also be a containing gesture and/or a
mechanism of self-defence.[32] The narrator and Edgeworth herself disapprove
strongly of the self-seeking and unscrupulous English aristocrat, and of her
mimicry as mockery. Yet they are also extremely uneasy with the two groups of
people who are being represented here. They are uneasy with the *squireens* who
might be seen as part of a growing middle class and who seem to be encroaching on the territorial, legal, and political monopoly of the Anglo-Irish landowners, 'the society of gentry' (p. 107), as the narrator calls it here. But they are
also very uneasy with those whom the narrator calls 'the lower class of the Irish
people' (p. 109), whose verbal strategies, as Terry Eagleton says, can be seen
as 'at once an effect of colonialism and a form of resistance to it'.[33]

In relation to the question of mimicry, it might be said that Edgeworth's
narrator shows an ambivalent attitude towards both Lady Dashfort *and* the
squireens and the fawning tenants. Lady Dashfort is unambiguously presented
elsewhere in the novel as unscrupulous and amoral, ready to exploit the good-
natured if unsophisticated hospitality of the Killpatricks and of Lady
Clonbrony, and equally ready to indulge in hypocritical character-assassination
at their expense. She also claims to be "mistress of fourteen different

brogues", and to have "brogues for all occasions", and her representations – or misrepresentations – of the Irish are described by the narrator as a 'mixture of mimicry, sarcasm, exaggeration, and truth' (p. 105). Edgeworth's narrator shows Lady Dashfort's aims in using her ability as a mimic to be morally unacceptable, yet the mimicry itself is ambivalently presented. Edgeworth herself is known to have appreciated good mimicry, and had experimented very effectively with it as a narrative technique in her use of the voice of Thady Quirk as the narrator of *Castle Rackrent*.[34] Thady's rhetoric, and that of the peasants whom Lady Dashfort *and* the narrator both deride in *The Absentee*, are indicative of both Edgeworth's relatively sophisticated awareness of the strategic duplicities of the discourse of colonised or subaltern peoples, and her discomfort with them. She never repeated the experiment she made in *Castle Rackrent* with using this type of discourse as the narrative voice, while her ambivalence towards mimicry can be seen in the discursive instabilities of *The Absentee* and some of her other novels.[35]

Thus, even as the text identifies one type of misrepresentation, it seems to create another, motivated by Edgeworth's class and linguistic prejudices. Salvation lies in those members of the gentry who show moral rectitude and who, not at all coincidentally, speak correct English. While non-standard English speakers like Larry Brady and Brian O'Neill are given a more positive role at various other points in the work,[36] the speech of the *squireens* and the cringing peasants is both designated as dialect and shown to be morally reprehensible. It might be argued that if speakers of non-standard English accept the authority of the good (reforming) landlord, they are seen in their turn as morally acceptable, but if they show themselves to be prepared to challenge or exploit the system, they are not. Class and linguistic prejudices reinforce each other and make Edgeworth's critique of misrepresentations of Irishness a very equivocal exercise.

In a similar way, *The Absentee* also draws on stereotypes of both Irishmen and Jews as one of its techniques of characterisation. For example, Sir Terence O'Fay is a version of the stage Irishman, and Larry Brady is a version of the comic postilion. We meet Sir Terence very early in the work when Colambre goes to see the coachmaker, Mordicai. Mordicai himself, as Moynahan has noted, is presented in the terms of 'an ignorant anti-Semitic stereotype',[37] while both Sir Terence O'Fay and the workman, Paddy Brady, are presented as versions of the comic stage Irishman. The whole scene is framed first by the point of view of Lord Colambre, and second by that of the narrator, both of whom speak Standard English, and both of whom judge speakers of non-standard English to be either morally inferior or, at the very least, morally irresponsible.[38]

In the scene at Mordicai's, Sir Terence is described as speaking with 'a strong Irish accent' and as 'telling a good story, which made one of the workmen in the yard – an Irishman – grin with delight' (pp. 8-9). When Sir Terence leaves, the Irish workman, Paddy Brady, challenged to tell his employer something he does not know about Sir Terence, does so. He 'recounted some of sir Terence O'Fay's exploits in evading duns, replevying cattle, fighting sheriffs, bribing *subs*, managing cants, [and] tricking *custodees*'. He does this, says the narrator, 'in language so strange, and with a countenance and gestures so full of enjoyment of the jest, that, whilst Mordicai stood for a moment aghast with astonishment, lord Colambre could not help laughing, partly at, and partly with, his countryman' (p. 9, emphasis in the original).

Once again, the language and the narrative perspective on it are well worth analysis. Paddy Brady uses a variety of legal terms which would in all probability have been unintelligible to Edgeworth's English readers, and which were explained by footnotes to the original text. The use of legal terminology is one of the distinctive uses of English by the Irish that the Edgeworths point out in their *Essay on Irish Bulls*. The fact that Edgeworth uses it in this work as a distinguishing feature of Paddy's language here and of Sir Terence's in a later scene shows her recourse to a familiar Irish stereotype. Once again, italics are used in the text to stress deviant usage[39] which distances the speaker's idiolect from Standard English. Paddy Brady is not necessarily negatively judged in moral terms: he is a member of the labouring class and perhaps cannot be expected to know better, which is itself, of course, a highly patronising point of view. On the other hand, Sir Terence certainly is expected to know better, since he is a friend of Lord Clonbrony and a member of the gentry, although a disreputable one. This is made clear later in the novel when he himself tells tales of helping aristocratic friends to evade their creditors. Grace Nugent, who is, along with Colambre, one of the embodiments of moral rectitude in the work, asks '"Surely this would be ... swindling"' Sir Terence assures her, however, that, '"amongst gentlemen who know the world – it's only jockeying – fine sport – and very honourable to help a friend at a dead lift"' (p. 65). Lord Colambre is silent until the end of the conversation, when he argues that '"family honour"' is much more important than '"the family plate"' (p. 67), a view which the work as a whole endorses.

In the scene at Mordicai's, as elsewhere, Edgeworth's narrator adds considerations of class and language to those of race. As elsewhere in the text, the perspective is that of the educated ruling class, whether English or Irish, here embodied in Lord Colambre, who laughs 'partly at, and partly with, his countryman'. Lord Colambre is explicitly identified as Paddy's (and Sir Terence's) countryman, but his English is carefully differentiated from theirs: he has no Irish brogue, uses no legal jargon, slang, or 'Hiberno-Irish' expressions, and is a model of both Standard English and moral decorum. Moreover, when Colambre sees Sir Terence greet the coachmaker 'with a degree of familiarity which, from a gentleman, appeared ... to be almost impossible' (p. 8), he is outraged and so, clearly, is the narrator. Mordicai is not a gentleman; for Sir Terence to greet him familiarly shows that he is not a gentleman either. Here class and racial stereotypes reinforce each other, although class concerns take precedence over racial ones. This is also true elsewhere in the novel. For example, when Mordicai comes to try to arrest the dying Sir John Berryl for debt, Colambre reveals that the attempted arrest is illegal, and orders Mordicai out of the house, holding the door open for him. 'Seeing [Lord Colambre's] indignant look and proud for[m]', Mordicai hesitates to go through, 'for he had always heard that Irishmen are "quick in the executive part of justice"'. To this hesitation, Colambre responds, '"Pass on, sir", with an air of ineffable contempt: "I am a gentleman – you have nothing to fear!"'(p. 53).

Here class again takes precedence over race, as it does in a slightly different way in the opening scene of the work. Lady Langdale pronounces Colambre to be '"a very gentlemanlike looking young man, indeed"', causing the Duchess of Torcaster to declare that he is '"Not an Irishman, I am sure, by his manner"' (p. 3). In both these cases, Edgeworth is defending the upper-class Irishman from the presumption that he cannot be a gentleman, rather than countering stereotypes related to the nation as a whole.

Indeed, the entire narrative is characterised by the extreme class-consciousness of the characters and the narrator. Recognising a gentleman is a constant theme. In addition to the opening scene, there is the first significant discussion between Colambre and his father, which sets out the moral parameters clearly enough. When Colambre is telling his father of his meeting with Sir Terence, he expresses his regret that '"he does not look and speak a little more like a gentleman"'. Lord Clonbrony defends Sir Terence, retorting that 'he is as much a gentleman as any of your formal prigs – not the exact Cambridge cut, may be', and continuing, '"Curse your English education! 'twas none of my advice – I suppose you mean to take after your mother in the notion, that nothing can be good or genteel but what's English."' This, however, Colambre denies, describing himself as 'as warm a friend to Ireland as your heart could wish', and as someone who hopes that his English education will enable him to become '"all that a British nobleman ought to be"'. At this point Lord Clonbrony concludes, '"You have an Irish heart, that I see, which no education can spoil"' (pp. 21–2).

While Lord Clonbrony thinks in essentialist racial terms, Lord Colambre's (and Edgeworth's) alternative is that of the '"British nobleman"' an entirely imaginary cosmopolitan educated ideal. Colambre's shift from "gentleman" to 'nobleman' is also interesting: he expects an associate of his father's to behave and speak like a gentleman, but for himself he chooses the, apparently, higher term of the nobleman to articulate his sense of his aspirations and responsibilities. The narrator endorses Colambre's view of the issue by saying that, since leaving Ireland, Lord Clonbrony has become 'less of a gentleman', precisely because of his association with those who, like Sir Terence O'Fay, are his moral inferiors.[40] But it is not only the members of the upper class in the novel who are concerned with gentility. Larry Brady, Paddy's brother, who is Lord Colambre's driver in Ireland, sees through his disguise and 'Notwithstanding the shabby great coat ... perceived, by our hero's language, that he was a gentleman', even in the persona of Mr Evans (p. 139). Later in the same scene, the narrator is careful to discredit the 'gauger' or exciseman by identifying him as 'a half kind of gentleman' (p. 144).

Edgeworth's narrator shows Mordicai's and the Duchess's stereotyped views of the Irish to be distorted and prejudiced, but the narrative's perspective on these stereotypes is both unstable and influenced by Edgeworth's class allegiances. Racial stereotypes are challenged, but also at times reinscribed, as with Paddy and Larry Brady and Sir Terence O'Fay, or used uncritically, as with Mordicai, while sometimes Edgeworth's main concern seems to be to offer a positive image of the Irish gentry.

THE PROBLEM OF THE ENDING: ALLEGORY TRIUMPHANT

As several critics have noted, *The Absentee*, like Edgeworth's other Irish works, links private relationships to political issues, mainly through the question of marriage.[41] As McCormack says, marriage is a trope or 'conceit' which is 'employed of Anglo-Irish relations' from Swift to Heaney.[42] Here, as in *Ennui*, the marriage of the hero is bound up with the image and fate of Ireland. The allegorical dimension of the novel works chiefly through several possible marriages, the most important of which is the projected union of Lord Colambre and Grace Nugent.

The anticipated marriage of Grace and Colambre is offered as an essential part of the idealised 'imagined community' created at the end of *The Absentee*. Lord Colambre, as Lubbers has said, 'prodigiously embodies the best traits of the Irish and the English character'.[43] He was born in Ireland but has been educated in England, and specifically, in the narrator's words, at 'one of our great public schools' (p. 6). Edgeworth says 'our', thereby explicitly identifying the narrative perspective with that of the English ruling class. Colambre attempts to be, as he himself says, 'all that a British nobleman ought to be' (p. 21). As the novel progresses it becomes clear that part of the meaning of Edgeworth's idealised concept of the British nobleman is a sense of responsibility for those social inferiors living on his estates.[44] Becoming conscious of this, Colambre travels to Ireland and rediscovers the land of his birth and its people, becoming convinced that he must persuade his parents to return to their estates and become caring and reforming landlords. Colambre, then, represents an idealised version of the landowner belonging to the Protestant Ascendancy, who comes to realise the potential for change and improvement both of his own estates and their tenants. Grace Nugent, conversely, is 'encoded in a network of Catholic and Jacobite traces yet also liberated from hints and rumours of subversive attachments', as McCormack says.[45] That is, her name identifies her not only with a Catholic heritage, but also with an explicitly rebellious one,[46] and with Gaelic popular culture. Despite this, however, when the truth about Grace's parentage is revealed, she is shown to be half-English.

The significance of the projected marriage of Colambre and Grace, then, lies in the fact that they will unify the discrepant religious traditions of the Irish heritage, and provide yet another link between England and Ireland. McCormack notes that Grace is both a Nugent and a St Omar, which 'marks her as a symbol of Catholic resistance', while Colambre 'bears a "union title", a product of the corrupt and exclusively Protestant Irish parliament'.[47] Their marriage, therefore, suggests both religious and political reconciliation. However, neither of these meanings is expressed directly: the issue of religion, as already noted, is never directly approached in the narrative.[48] It is easy to overlook the fact that Grace's father was English, given the wealth of allusions in the narrative which attach Grace herself to Ireland, as noted by McCormack.[49]

Linked to this projected marriage is the return of the Clonbrony family to their Irish estates, which is seen at the end of the narrative through Larry Brady's eyes and described in his words. The ending is controversial, as is the fact that it is Larry Brady rather than the third-person narrator who narrates the Clonbronys' return. Many critics have found the ending unconvincing, from Thomas Davis in 1843 to Seamus Deane in 1997 and Julia Anne Miller in 2000. Deane quotes approvingly Davis's comments that the ending is 'pious Feudalism', since to imagine the landlord's return and reform is 'flat nonsense'. Similarly, Miller notes that despite Colambre's deliberate 'mocking of the apparatuses of state power' in his treatment of Larry Brady's father, 'such machinery is just below the surface of the newly constituted family relations'.[50] McCormack and Hollingworth see the ending in a more nuanced fashion. McCormack argues that the end of the novel 'seeks to suggest a transcending of differences political, aesthetic, and ontological', although he also notes that 'Colambre personally, and residential landlordism generally, will prove wholly inadequate symbols of a restored world'. Hollingworth sees the ending and Larry's narration of it even more positively as 'an effective and impressive marriage of the vernacular medium with the apological message'.[51]

Clearly Larry's narration of the Clonbronys' return to Ireland offers a more positive image of the tenants and their language than Christy's letter does at the end of *Ennui*.[52] Yet it is hard to see it as modifying the endorsement of what Butler calls 'aristocratic cultural hegemony and metropolitan centrism' through the use of Standard English elsewhere in the narrative.[53] Edgeworth needs to make the return of the Clonbronys as acceptable as possible, and to this end the tenantry must be seen to be fully co-operative in the optimistic vision of the positive effects of their return. It is true that the ending is rendered slightly less improbable by Lord Colambre's actions on his visit to the estates earlier in the novel, and by the fact that various Irish characters blame the Garraghty brothers far more than they do the landlord himself. However, Lord Clonbrony does not entirely escape censure. The landlord of the inn at Colambre compares the absentee landlord to 'a West India planter' and the inhabitants to 'negroes' (p. 130). The comparison is given added point by the fact that, as McCormack notes, 'both Ireland and Jamaica were important theatres of conflict in which Britain faced revolutionary violence' in the early nineteenth century.[54] However, Larry's judgement is that 'Lord Clonbrony himself is a very good jantleman, if he was not an absentee, resident in London, leaving us and every thing to the likes of them', that is, the Garraghtys (p. 141), and this is supported by other voices in the novel.

Ultimately, if the ending fails to convince, it is because it shows the novel to be, in Seamus Deane's words, 'an early form of imperial romance', that is, 'not an analysis but a symptom of the colonial problem the country represented'.[55] Edgeworth tries to occupy the middle ground of rationalism, but, in effect, she looks at Ireland from a perspective which is implicated in what it observes both in terms of class and geography. By creating in Lord Colambre an image of '"all that a British nobleman ought to be"'(p. 21), Edgeworth identifies her narrative with a set of class interests masquerading as an external perspective. As Terry Eagleton says, 'this epistemological outside is also a site of power, and thus at the very heart of what it dispassionately inspects'.[56] Despite its overt project of reform and reconciliation, the narrative as a whole shows that the problems in Ireland cannot be satisfactorily encompassed by the imagined community of the novel's ending. This is because the ending reinstates the land-owning class and the system which are two of the major causes of the problem, while still largely ignoring or evading the differences of class, language, and religion which the narrative has nonetheless partially revealed, seemingly despite itself.

NOTES

1. References to the work are included parenthetically in the text. The term, 'imagined community', is taken from B. Anderson, *Imagined Communities: Reflections on the Origin and Spread of Nationalism* (rev. edn, London and New York: Verso, 1996 [1991]), pp. 6–7 and *passim*.
2. For discussion of the effect of the English audience on Edgeworth's writing, see B. Sloan, *The Pioneers of Anglo-Irish Fiction 1800–1850* (Gerrards Cross: Colin Smythe, 1986), p. 26; J.M. Calahan, *The Irish Novel: A Critical History* (Boston; Twayne, 1988), p. 5; D. Hack 'Inter-Nationalism: *Castle Rackrent* and Anglo-Irish Union', *Novel*, 29 (1996), p. 152.
3. See A.N. Jeffares, *Anglo-Irish Literature* (London and Dublin: Gill & Macmillan, 1982); A.N. Jeffares, *Images of Invention: Essays on Irish Writing* (Gerrards Cross: Colin Smythe, 1996); J. Moynahan, *Anglo-Irish: The Literary Imagination in a Hyphenated Culture* (Princeton, NJ: Princeton University Press, 1995); B. Sloan, *The Pioneers of Anglo-Irish Fiction 1800–1850*; J.M. Calahan, *The Irish Novel: A Critical History* (Boston: Twayne, 1988); and S. Deane, *Strange Country: Modernity and Nationhood in Irish Writing since 1790* (Oxford: Clarendon Press, 1997).
4. See Hack, 'Inter-Nationalism', p. 146, n. 3.
5. G. Friedman, 'Rereading 1798: Melancholy and Desire in the Construction of Edgeworth's Anglo-Irish Union', *European Romantic Review*, 10, 2 (Spring 1999), p. 180.
6. See Hack, 'Inter-Nationalism', p. 146, n. 3.
7. R.L. Edgeworth and M. Edgeworth, *Essay on Irish Bulls* (London: J. Johnson, 1802), pp. 111–12.
8. See Anderson, *Imagined Communities*, p. 6.
9. Ibid., p. 7.
10. A point made by T. Eagleton, *Heathcliff and the Great Hunger: Studies in Irish Culture* (London and New York: Verso, 1995), p. 176.
11. In this respect *The Absentee* is like Edgeworth's other Irish works. The preface, notes, and glossary to *Castle Rackrent* explain various Irish customs and traditions as well as the Irish use of

English, and in *Ennui* the characters of McLeod and Lady Geraldine provide guidance both to Lord Glenthorn and the reader about the realities of Irish life.

12. In *Ennui*, on the contrary, the 1798 rebellion is part of the action of the novel; indeed it might be said that Glenthorn's experiences run partly parallel to those of Edgeworth's father. Glenthorn foils a plan by the rebels either to make him their leader or kill him. Since he has previously been suspected of rebel sympathies, he shows his loyalty to the government by enabling them to capture the rebels. Similarly, R.L. Edgeworth was almost lynched by a mob because he was suspected of sympathy with the rebels and the French because of the presence of Catholics in his infantry corps. See B. Hollingworth, *Maria Edgeworth's Irish Writing: Language, History, Politics* (London: Macmillan, 1997), p. 39; W. J. McCormack, *Ascendancy and Tradition in Anglo-Irish History from 1789 to 1939* (Oxford: Clarendon Press, 1985), p. 158. The Edgeworth family home was spared burning and pillage because of R.L. Edgeworth's generally fair and equitable treatment of his tenants.

13. For other comments on the significance of O'Halloran in relation to military relations between England and Ireland, see T. Dunne, *Maria Edgeworth and the Colonial Mind* (Cork: University College, 1984), p. 14; McCormack, *Ascendancy and Tradition*, pp. 152–3. See also the Edgeworths' *Essay on Irish Bulls*, pp. 209–10, where the Irishman in the 'Bath Coach Conversation' is made to present the role of the English military in Ireland in a very favourable light.

14. See McCormack, *Ascendancy and Tradition*, pp. 127–31.

15. For the decline of Dublin after the Union, see E. Curtis, *A History of Ireland* (London: Methuen, 1961), p. 353; R.F. Foster, 'Ascendancy and Union' in *The Oxford Illustrated History of Ireland* (Oxford and New York: Oxford University Press, 1991), p. 183; A.N. Jeffares, *Anglo-Irish Literature* (London and Dublin: Gill & Macmillan, 1982), p. 84; A.N. Jeffares, *Images of Invention: Essays on Irish Writing* (Gerrards Cross: Colin Smythe, 1996), pp. 155, 177; O. MacDonagh, 'Ideas and Institutions, 1830–45', in T.W. Moody and W.E. Vaughan (eds), *A New History of Ireland, Vol. IV, Eighteenth-Century Ireland, 1681–1800* (Oxford: Clarendon Press, 1986), pp. 193–4. MacDonagh explicitly refers to the departure of many Irish landowners for London.

16. See S. Deane, *Strange Country: Modernity and Nationhood in Irish Writing since 1790* (Oxford: Clarendon Press, 1997), p. 73; W.J. McCormack and K. Walker, 'Introduction' to *The Absentee* (Oxford and New York: Oxford University Press, 1988), pp. xxiii–iv and xxix–xxx; Sloan, *The Pioneers of Anglo-Irish Fiction*, pp. 24–5. Surprisingly, Hollingworth in *Maria Edgeworth's Irish Writing*, does not see the ending of *The Absentee* as wishful thinking although he sees the ending of *Ennui* in these terms (p. 132).

17. M. Edgeworth, *Ennui* in *Castle Rackrent and Ennui* (London: Penguin, 1992), p. 216. The school for both Protestant and Catholic children in both novels may draw on Edgeworth's father's school which also catered for both. See J. Moynahan, *Anglo-Irish*, p. 16.

18. In their *Essay on Irish Bulls*, the Edgeworths recognise this fact and state that 'In some counties in Ireland, many of the poorest labourers and cottagers do not understand English, they speak only Irish' (p. 199).

19. Dunne argues that there are two kinds of 'Hiberno-English' in Edgeworth, one seen positively, one negatively. The first is 'a richly varied and eloquent "foreign" language' which she seeks to explain in order to correct anti-Irish prejudice. The other he describes as 'servile, flattering, deceiving; the language of survival as developed by a vulnerable people', about which Edgeworth had more ambivalent feelings. See Dunne, *Maria Edgeworth*, p. 17.

20. See M. Butler, 'Introduction' to *Castle Rackrent and Ennui* (London: Penguin, 1992), pp. 19–20; Deane, *Strange Country*, p. 65; Hollingworth, *Maria Edgeworth's Irish Writing*, pp. 118, 179. Conversely, in their 'Introduction' to *The Absentee*, W.J. McCormack and K. Walker argue that 'While articulating an official code of Enlightenment values, the novel's language proceeds to undermine the normative power of language itself' (p. xxvi). However, they also express reservations about the moral authority to be attributed to the non-standard English of Larry's letter at the end of the work (pp. xxix-xxx).

21. See Edgeworth, *Ennui*, pp. 156, 211.

22. E. Said, *Orientalism* (London: Routledge and Kegan Paul, 1978) p. 93.

23. See also the first note to Edgeworth, *Castle Rackrent*, which also refers to Spenser's *View of the Present State of Ireland*.

24. This information is derived from McCormack and Walker's note to the passage in Edgeworth, *The Absentee*, p. 298.

25. See Said, *Orientalism*, pp. 227–40. Said is talking about orientalist discourse in the twentieth

century, but the features which he distinguishes can be found in such discourse in earlier periods too.

26. See Deane, *Strange Country*, p. 6.

27. See Hollingworth, *Maria Edgeworth's Irish Writing*, p. 29. For a discussion of Edgeworth's ambivalent feelings towards and use of the Irish vernacular form of English, see ibid., pp. 16, 58, 61, 67, 104, 134, 171–9.

28. See Jeffares, *Anglo-Irish Literature*, p. 85; Jeffares, *Images of Invention*, p. 128.

29. See McCormack and Walker, 'Introduction' to *The Absentee*, p. xx; E. Spenser, 'From *A View of the Present State of Ireland (1596)*', in S. Deane et al. (eds), *The Field Day Anthology of Irish Writing*, Vol. I (Derry: Field Day Publications, 1991), p. 182, n. 3.

30. See McCormack and Walker 'Introduction' to *The Absentee*, p. xxi.

31. Ibid., p. xx.

32. See H. Bhabha, 'Of Mimicry and Men', 'Sly Civility', and 'Signs Taken for Wonders', in *The Location of Culture* (London and New York: Routledge, 1994); see Moynahan, *Anglo-Irish*, pp. 20–2, for a discussion of various possible meanings of mimicry in Edgeworth's writings.

33 See Eagleton, *Heathcliff and the Great Hunger*, p. 170. In *Their Fathers'Daughters: Hannah More, Maria Edgeworth, and Patriarchal Complicity* (New York and Oxford: Oxford University Press, 1991), Elizabeth Kowaleski-Wallace quotes a letter by the adolescent Maria Edgeworth which, as she says, criticises both the 'adverse economic practices that exacerbate native "indolence" and that indolence itself', p. 142. The letter thus reveals Edgeworth's ambivalence about the Irish peasantry.

34. See M. Butler, *Maria Edgeworth: A Literary Biography* (Oxford: Clarendon Press, 1972), p. 172.

35. In her *Belinda*, for example, mimicry is again associated with a colonised people, since it is used by the black slave, Juba. See M. Edgeworth, *Belinda* (London: Dent, 1994), p. 207.

36. See Hollingworth, *Maria Edgeworth's Irish Writing*, pp. 174–8. Hollingworth also argues that the critique of Lady Dashfort also constitutes a form of self-criticism on Edgeworth's part, since she, like her character, has a 'tendency to find Irish speech and manners comic and amusing', p. 169.

37. See Moynahan, *Anglo-Irish*, p. 36. See also Thady's extraordinary revelation of his racial prejudices when he describes Sir Kit's Jewish bride as 'little better than a blackamoor' in Edgeworth, *Castle Rackrent*, p. 76.

38. See Butler, 'Introduction'to *Castle Rackrent and Ennui*, pp. 19–20; Deane, *Strange Country*, p. 65; Hollingworth, *Maria Edgeworth's Irish Writing*, pp. 118, 179.

39. See Hollingworth, *Maria Edgeworth's Irish Writing*, pp. 31, 180.

40. M.J. Corbett also draws attention to the issue of class in *The Absentee*. See 'Public Affections and Familial Politics: Burke, Edgeworth, and the "Common Naturalization" of Great Britain', *English Literary History*, 61 (1994), pp. 891–2.

41. See Corbett, 'Public Affections and Familial Politics', pp. 877, 891; Hollingworth, *Maria Edgeworth's Irish Writing*, p. 127; J.A. Miller, 'Acts of Union: Family Violence and National Courtship in Maria Edgeworth's *The Absentee* and Sydney Owenson's *The Wild Irish Girl*', in K. Kirkpatrick (ed.), *Border Crossings: Irish Women Writers and National Identities* (Tuscaloosa and London: The University of Alabama Press, 2000), p. 13. Miller notes the importance of allegory in the novel, pp. 13, 23.

42. W.J. McCormack, *From Burke to Beckett: Ascendancy, Tradition, and Betrayal in Literary History* (Cork: Cork University Press, 1994), p. 11. This use of the marriage trope can be both linked and contrasted to the nationalist rhetoric which sees 'the Anglo-Irish relationship as a forced marriage', R. F. Foster, 'Ascendancy and Union', in *The Oxford Illustrated History of Ireland* (Oxford and New York: Oxford University Press, 1991), p. 209 (facing).

43. K. Lubbers, 'Continuity and Change in Irish Fiction: The Case of the Big-House Novel', in O. Rauchbauer (ed.), *Ancestral Voices: The Big House in Anglo-Irish Literature* (Dublin: The Lilliput Press, 1992), p. 22.

44. Somewhat differently, in *Ennui*, Edgeworth has her first-person narrator, Lord Glenthorn, reflect on the fact that 'a British nobleman' should 'have some notion of the general state of that empire, in the legislation of which he has a share' (p. 254). Here the meaning of the idealised concept is extended from paternalism at home to imperialism abroad, a dimension lacking in *The Absentee*.

45. W.J. McCormack, 'Setting and Ideology with Reference to the Fiction of Maria Edgeworth', O. Rauchbauer (ed.), *Ancestral Voices: The Big House in Anglo-Irish Literature* (Dublin: The Lilliput Press, 1992), p. 54; see also McCormack and Walker, 'Introduction', pp. xxiii–iv;

McCormack, *Ascendancy and Tradition*, pp. 127, 141–9.

46. See Spenser, *A View of the Present State of Ireland*, pp. 191, n. 10. The note refers to the Nugent conspiracy of 1581.

47. See McCormack, *Ascendancy and Tradition*, p. 145.

48. It is also generally neglected in criticism; one exception is the work of McCormack.

49. For example, S. Gilmartin, in *Ancestry and Narrative in Nineteenth-Century British Literature* (Cambridge: Cambridge University Press, 1998) twice calls Grace 'Colambre's Irish cousin', pp. 29, 40. Similarly, J.A. Miller in 'Acts of Union' calls Grace an 'Irish heroine', p. 13. She also notes that Grace's father is 'a respectable English officer', arguing that this is part of Edgeworth's 'narrative alchemy in which the radical elements of Irish gentry are transformed and reclaimed', p. 22.

50. See Deane, *Strange Country*, p. 73; Miller, 'Acts of Union', pp. 29–30.

51. See McCormack and Walker, 'Introduction', pp. xxiv, xxx; Hollingworth, *Maria Edgeworth's Irish Writing*, p. 178. See McCormack, *Ascendancy and Tradition*, pp. 162–4, for further criticism of the ending of the novel.

52. Christy's letter to Glenthorn recounts the disasters which followed Glenthorn's restitution of the Glenthorn estate to the rightful heir, the Catholic Christy. It also returns the property (minus the castle, which has burned down because of the drunken negligence of Christy's son) to Glenthorn, as the man worthy and capable of administering it. Christy's letter shows its author's recognition of his intrinsic inability either to administer the estate or to control his wife or son in a satisfactory way. It thus shows the loyal Catholic tenants as accepting their intrinsic inability to control their own property, and thus legitimates the continued control of Glenthorn. By birth, he is not the rightful heir, but he has shown himself to be both worthy of power and now, after his education in the course of the novel, capable of fulfilling his responsibilities. Christy's letter legitimates both his dispossession and his relinquishment of responsibility. See Edgeworth, *Castle Rackrent and Ennui*, pp. 321–3.

53. Butler is talking about *Castle Rackrent*, but her comment is also applicable to *The Absentee*. See her 'Introduction' to *Castle Rackrent and Ennui*, p. 20.

54. See McCormack, *Ascendancy and Tradition*, p. 155.

55. See Deane, *Strange Country*, pp. 30, 33. Miller also calls the novel a 'national romance'; see Miller, 'Acts of Union', p. 31.

56. See Eagleton, *Heathcliff and the Great Hunger*, p. 176.

CHAPTER FIFTEEN

The Subaltern can Whisper: Secrecy and Solidarity in the Fiction of John and Michael Banim

WILLA MURPHY

When he was a boy, John Banim delighted in escaping the watchful eyes of his schoolmaster to read prohibited romances in secret under hedges and haystacks. A few years later he illicitly courted the daughter of a Protestant gentleman, which involved donning a long grey cloak and sidling up to his forbidden love in church to press cryptic messages into her hand.[1] The hidden places of John Banim's early life in Ireland punctuate the novels and tales he wrote in collaboration with his brother Michael. The boy who liked to read in secret grew up to be the writer who never lost his attraction to the clandestine. Covert distilleries, underground forts, haunted caves, hidden cupboards and cellars, buried treasure and smugglers, illegitimate births, illicit love, secret passwords: the number of secrets in his writing is perhaps outnumbered only by the number of watchful eyes. Glowering, squinting, glaring eyes, lazy eyes, even eyeless sockets stare up from the pages of the Banims' tales. These are perhaps not unconnected details. Ireland during the period in which the Catholic brothers wrote was among the most observed and tabulated societies in Europe, its British rulers perhaps uniquely adept at knowledge production. The British Empire, as Thomas Richards has suggested, was made of paper as well as property.[2] The Banims' fascination with secrecy and surveillance, in tales that play hide-and-seek with their readers, tells us something about the behaviour of the scrutinised. Those societies that are most watched are also most hidden, just as those children who are most supervised learn to be more cunning than candid. When privacy is distrusted and concealment forbidden, secrets multiply.

For liberal reformers like Maria Edgeworth, such secrecy is the dangerous occupation not just of unsupervised children, but more alarmingly of the unruly Irish (which to Edgeworth comes at times to much the same thing).[3] Left to their own devices, both the child and the Irish tenant would seek to escape the jurisdiction of the law and create their own imaginary, superstitious and alternative worlds. In this sense, secrecy characterises not only the world of childhood but the world of the colony as well.[4] Secret societies, with their elaborate allegorical trappings and millenarian prophecies, their costumes and code-words, are places where subject peoples invent a world of their own making, a fictionalised space screened off from the scrutinising eyes of the law, in which they might imagine themselves differently.[5] Edgeworth's progressive ideals tell her that such clandestine activity is a dangerous perversion of the social order, a rejection of community. And when that secrecy takes the form not of children's hideaways but of violent plots among dispossessed tenants, it becomes not just devious but deadly.

D. A. Miller, in *The Novel and the Police*, has shown how the rise of the novel in the nineteenth century coincided with the creation of a professional police force. The story of the novel, he argues, is the story also of a regulating narrative voice, itself implicated in a panoptic mode of vision, exercising a 'supervision' of the world and its readers.[6] The realist novel, with its omniscient narrator, participates in the policing strategies of ruling power – remaining invisible to readers while rendering everything else visible. Reading, then, becomes yet another mode of supervision, part of the cultural wing of state surveillance. The Banims' fiction makes an interesting case study for Miller's theory, not least because Ireland was the laboratory for various British social experiments, including the creation of a professional police force.[7] In one sense, the Banims form part of the attempt to regulate and reform Ireland in preparation for Catholic Emancipation. Their writing strives to supervise and civilise the native Irish, to translate these unrepresentable subjects into words. As David Lloyd has pointed out, the inventors of the Irish novel are involved in a kind of public relations campaign – managing a violent society through fiction, softening scandalous Irish behaviour through narration, lightening a dark and dense landscape through a discourse of reason and openness.[8] But the Banims' fiction complicates Miller's theory, for their narrative voices keep more secrets than they share, drawing the reader into a world not of transparent objects and knowable subjects but one of deep and dazzling darkness.

If secrecy for the likes of Edgeworth is about devious autonomy and the disintegration of the official state, for the Banims it is the gelling agent of unofficial Ireland, fixing the splintered lives of the Irish tenant classes. More than anything else in these tales, it is secrecy that defines the native Irish, gives them a glimmer of a communal identity, allows them to have a sense of themselves. 'The secrets of his inner heart, the Irish peasant keeps concealed to the present hour', explains the narrator of *The Croppy* (1828), 'as well from the oppressors he hates, as from the friends who, if they knew him better, could better serve him'.[9] The *Tales by the O'Hara Family* (1825) might well be taken as an attempt by those who *do* know him better to better serve the Irish tenant. These novels and tales recognise the power of the secret to protect the identity of supervised subjects and demarcate a colonial community. Secrets form the protective shell of the Irish lower classes and, as Foucault has it, darkness affords at least a kind of protection.[10] The Banims' narrative voice speaks the language of a mass-based mystery that allows the subaltern, if not to speak, at least to whisper. *Pace* Homi Bhabha, the colonial subject speaks in a tongue that is secret, but not silent.

Many critics have dismissed the cryptic elements in the Banims' fiction as mere melodrama, pandering to an English audience's appetite for the cryptic and supernatural, exploiting the market value of sensational Irish material.[11] In venturing to forge an Irish national literature or, in David Gilligan's words, to '[break] a literary silence', their project unlocks the secrets of the Irish heart to an English readership.[12] Their writing aims to dispel the 'mists that hang around Irish ground', get to the bottom of the 'muddy well' of Ireland, and portray the Irish peasantry 'as they really [are]'.[13] It seeks to cultivate affection between the politically united cultures, so their inhabitants might 'recognize themselves as belonging to a common country'.[14] Indeed, their writing sometimes has the character of the informer's testimony about it, exposing the Irish to the curious gaze of ruling-class readers in the name of some common good, but ultimately with a view to their own advancement.[15] Like the merchant class its authors belong to, the Banims' fiction faces both ways. It is inside and outside the Irish tenant classes, at once keeper and teller of Ireland's secrets.[16]

Secrecy is central to the Banims' narrative strategy, but not simply in the interests of indulging the melodramatic addictions of a London audience. If their fiction lays some of Ireland's cards on the table, it also plays other cards close to its chest. It at once presents and preserves, shows and screens off the Irish cabin community. Their writing invents a native Irish voice that shares a mouthful of secrets with English readers, but that same voice keeps quiet about a good deal more. The same tongue that breaks a literary silence also creates a deeper one. The Banims' ameliorating ambitions, their attempt to convince readers that English and Irish 'belong to a common country', that they need have no secrets from one other, are belied by the obstructive tales themselves. This double impulse, to expose and to hide, is well articulated by the narrator of *Crohoore of the Billhook* (1825), who addresses the reader in a lengthy aside:

> Indeed, when, as voracious compilers of our history, we are admitted as witnesses where others would be unwelcome, we dislike to reveal all we see and hear .... In this case, it is plain [the reader] must be content with what we choose, or, after due reflection, deem advisable to give him; seeing that we might keep it all to ourselves, were we so inclined, or did it suit our purposes.[17]

Here, secrecy becomes a display of membership, a bulwark between the reader and the Irish people. The first-person plural places the narrator firmly on the side of the crowd, an insider with powerful secret knowledge he may be willing to share. Then again, he may not. The same narrator who beckons us to enter the inner circles of Irish life ends up shutting the door on his readers, giving us the status of unwelcome non-members standing shivering outside a meeting of the secret society known as rural Ireland.

Some anthropologists of secret societies have argued that secrecy has more to do with connection and community than with separation and autonomy.[18] Secrets are for creating solidarity, not just for keeping to yourself. It is part of the mythology surrounding secrets that they are privately owned, silent and hidden from view. The fact is that secrets always get shared; if they didn't they wouldn't be secrets.[19] A secret must be hidden but not completely, otherwise it disappears.[20] As Jacques Derrida has observed, there is no such thing as an 'absolute' secret, for its pleasure and power depend on its being witnessed – or, in being, as the narrator of *The Boyne Water* defines the terror of a road at night, 'almost hidden'.[21] Beryl Bellman has argued that secrecy is founded on the paradox that 'the proscription "don't tell" is at odds with the fact that secrets are constituted precisely by the way they get told'.[22] Secrecy, in other words, is not a form of silence but a form of communication, a way of saying what cannot be said openly.

The Banims' tales make countless references to acts of clandestine communication that reveal the existence of secret knowledge in the act of concealing it – knowing smiles, sardonic looks, nods and winks. Those who know the secret form a community, and the strength of the secret grows in proportion to its being told.[23] A secret shared, we might say, is a secret doubled. It is this doubleness, or double-edged nature of the secret, that the Banims' fiction explores. The same secretiveness that is perceived as the sin of the Irish might also be their salvation; the same secrecy regarded by rulers as an illness threatening to weaken the settled order becomes a source of vitality for those ruled. John Nowlan, the invalid son hidden in a back room of the family cabin at the opening of *The Nowlans* (1826), is described by the narrator as seeming to be at once the 'shame and affliction' but also 'the only hope' of his family.[24] Nowlan, the ruined priest, embodies this paradox of the secret. The Irish are represented in these tales as dark, murky, unknowable. But this darkness becomes a means also of obstruction and revolt, a source of comradeship and interruption of ruling power.[25]

We witness this communal nature of secrecy in the anxieties articulated by ruling-class writers about their tenants. Landowners such as Elizabeth Smith in County Wicklow sense a vast hidden network among the Irish, an invisible community from which they feel excluded. Smith records in her diary that her tenants, an 'extraordinary slippery people' harbour a 'secret enmity' towards her and 'require constant watching'.[26] Here, the terror of secrecy lies less in breaking down community than in binding it fast. Thomas Flanagan has commented that the Banims' domestic tales were shocking and strange to English readers because of their lack of any sense of privacy. Tony Dooling's hearth, for instance, is the scene of endless comings and goings by neighbours, strangers and beggars in the opening scene of *Crohoore of the Billhook*. It is just this invasion of personal space which the Archbishop of Cashel commented on in his testimony to a parliamentary Select Committee in 1825: the 'common people of Ireland ... in travelling ... go into any cabin which they can find, ... though perfect strangers'.[27] It is not insignificant that *The Nowlans* opens with the narrator himself taking refuge from a storm in a stranger's cabin, where he is welcomed with food, conversation, and a makeshift bed for several nights (and it is by this circumstance that the Nowlan family secret is shared). There is too much secrecy in Ireland because there is too much community, too much communication among the lower classes. Francis Blackburne made this connection between population and secret plots in his testimony to a Select Committee, arguing that 'the parts of the country, where insurrections were most prevalent, is extremely dense', and he goes on to describe 'the great increase of people' that sustains such insurgency.[28] That is the real danger Edgeworth, Smith and fellow reforming landowners sense – the existence of a class of people, in Banim's words, too 'snug among themselves'.

Secrecy gives the Irish tenant classes a glimmer of self-awareness, a glimpse of themselves as a group – but this glimmer is perhaps more of a shadow, a knowledge by negation, creating what Ranajit Guha has called in the Indian colonial context a 'negative consciousness'.[29] The preface to *The Boyne Water* bespeaks an identity forged in the shadows:

> I would go far to assist in dispersing the mist that hangs over Irish ground. I would like to see those dwelling on the Irish soil looking about them in the clear sunshine – the murkiness dispelled – recognizing each other as belonging to a common country, and exchanging the password, 'This is my native land'.[30]

Even this future Irish citizen of light and openness speaks the language of the secret society. Irish identity, the Banims seem to suggest, is shaped by secret passwords and handshakes. It cannot escape the obscure places assigned to it by its rulers. As the narrator of *The Croppy* explains,

> Catholics had considered themselves as on all hands they were considered, an unimportant portion, though by far the greater portion, of the Irish people. A century of degradation ... naturally imparted to them this instinct of insignificance ... Even for their rights they had not dared to speak out as a body. Any murmur that escaped them was but the unheard whisper of fear.[31]

Guha argues that colonial rulers made the Indian 'aware of his place in society as a measure of his distance from themselves'.[32] While I am not arguing for a one-to-one correspondence between the political conditions of Ireland and India, nineteenth-century Irish writing articulates a related experience among the Irish tenantry of distance and negation, obscurity and obstruction. In his evidence before a parliamentary Select Committee in 1824, Revd Michael

Collins describes Irish Catholic self-definition: 'They look upon themselves as more or less aliens in their own country'.[33] Similarly, the narrator of *The Croppy* insists, 'Hidden we have called the character [of the Irish peasant], and it is so. ... owing to a long habit of abstraction, banishment even from all inter-change of social thought or feeling with those ranking above him'.[34] The Banims locate the genesis of Irish reticence and secrecy precisely in their dis-tance from official, public society.

The story of Irish Catholics in the post-Union, pre-Emancipation period is an exemplary articulation of Guha's negative consciousness model. The shift of the political centre to London affects Ireland's capacity to imagine itself, to represent itself, to know itself. Irish writers and artists, along with merchants and politicians, regard themselves as a long way indeed from London. Post-Union Ireland formulates its self-image often with a London audience in mind, seeing itself through London lenses, with the result that Irish writing of the period is steeped in what Joep Leerssen has called 'auto-exoticism'.[35] Ireland is a sphinx in a cultural desert – unrepresentable, a riddle, a question mark, a place that always needs explaining and is never understood, inhabited by a people who always needs watching and are never fully seen.[36]

The Banims' novels and tales are replete with optical objects and straining eyes. The overwhelming impression one gets of their characters is that they feel watched. Walls have eyes and ears in their fiction, where servants hang about to eavesdrop and peep through keyholes; where in rural cabins the stranger is welcomed with a strong drink and a roomful of staring eyes. The schoolhouse in *Father Connell* (1842) is like some proto-panopticon, where, 'through the partition separating his bed-chamber from the schoolroom the head of the seminary had bored a good many holes, nearly an inch in diameter, some straight forward, some slantingly, to enable himself to peer into every corner of the study, before entering each morning'.[37] Mrs. Brady in *The Ghosthunter and his Family* (1831) has recurring nightmares about the eyes of the crowd at her son's pending execution: 'you and I are concealin' ourselves in some dark place, from people's eyes,' she recounts to her husband, 'but 'tis no use, Randal'. And their daughter Rose, meanwhile, 'knew her words were lis-tened to; she knew that, even under her father's roof, and with shut doors and windows, she could not be sure of evading the ears which were stretched to catch what she would say'.[38]

The Banims' style itself sounds like that of writers who feel, along with many of their characters, that they are being watched. Within several pages the narrative voice in any given Banim tale switches between 'we' and 'I', and describes the cabin community alternately as 'them' and 'us', giving the impression that the narrator is unsure where he stands. This voice, as many critics have detected, swings from the discourse of the English realist novel to that of the political O'Connellite speech, didactic history lesson, or Gothic narrative. The post-Union Irish voice is insecure, uncertain of its place or role (its place is defined only by its distance from the centre), imbued, that is to say, with a 'negative consciousness'. But a by-product of such distance and darkness is what Thomas Flanagan has called 'the strangely self-sufficient Gaelic world' that is so alive in Banim's fiction.[39] Or, in Banim's words, the Irish peasantry, 'neglected, galled, hard-driven, bitter', believed 'that any appeal to the law of the land was not for them, that laws were enacted invariably not for, but against them, and that if they were not their own legislators, other legislation was for their punishment only'.[40] As a witness to a Select Committee put it in 1824, '[Irish Catholics] feel no respect for the law; they think it meritorious to elude or violate it; they connect no moral obligation with the laws of the land'.[41] The belief of disaffected Irish Catholics that they must become 'their own legislators' is a negative identity transposed. What develops out of this negative image is the form of the Catholic novel, the Catholic politician, the Catholic consciousness movement so characteristic of the years following the Union.

In John Banim's fiction, secrecy possesses transformative power. The secret is where the Irish tenant lives and moves and has his being – the one space where he does so outside the dominion of the colonial ruler.[42] Secrecy in these tales is far from the deviant behaviour of Edgeworth's fiction, where it is figured as a sickness, a contagion spreading invisibly through the Irish peasantry, threatening to worm its way into the big house, into its servants and children. For the Banims, a community built on secrets is a healthy and happy one. Rose Brady in *The Ghosthunter* feels sure that her brother Daniel will keep her secret because 'he possessed, in common with every member of her father's family, an implicit regard for the truth'.[43] The tale's complete title – *The Ghosthunter and his Family* – suggests that secrecy belongs squarely in the company of Irish family values. Rose's father counsels his future son-in-law to be an honourable friend and share his secrets, for only the coward guards his tongue.

Secrets, like rumour, have the status of being what Guha calls 'spoken utterance *par excellence*', anonymous information without a traceable source that serves to link together those who share it.[44] A secret grows in strength as it is told, creates a chain-link effect as it spreads through the community.[45] In his testimony to a parliamentary Select Committee to inquire into the State of Ireland, the Archbishop of Cashel commented that 'a rumour prevailed that a general rising was to take place on Christmas day, a rumour which, although nobody believed, yet every body circulated'.[46] The servant Aileen in *The Ghosthunter* exhibits the uncontrollable, almost physical force created by owning a secret: 'She felt a kind of choking sensation at the root of her tongue, which, we believe, had become really swollen by her incessant efforts to keep down her secret, each time (and that was every two minutes) that her heart sent it up for publication to the world'.[47] Having a secret is a bit like having a mobile phone – the owner feels compelled, by some uncontrollable force, to speak. Secrets create more discourse, not less, as nineteenth-century sexuality for Michel Foucault is the unspeakable which gives rise to a torrent of speech.[48]

In their very form, the Banims' writings attest to this material force of the secret. Their plots often move along by hearsay, gossip, and rumour, bits of information pieced together by the whispering of servants and tenants. The narrator is usually keen to present himself as an insider, a link in the anonymous chain, an alert listener who has become an informed teller. As one of the notes on the Whiteboys in *Crohoore* asserts, 'I obtained my information as to the proceedings of the Whiteboys from actual participators in their misdeeds'.[49] The narrative voice forever asserts the historical basis and flesh-and-blood sources of his secret knowledge, not only to display his credentials, but also to make real the threat of rural unrest to his readers. The secret knowledge he imparts to readers comes with a warning: like the Cave of Dunmore in *Crohoore*, it promises 'something to be discovered, and a threat to the discoverer'.[50] The Banims end up sharing few secrets, but hint at many more, and it is the resultant sense of the existence of a vast community built on secrets that poses a threat to the reader. In his testimony to a Select Committee in 1824, Major George Warburton suggested that the use of secrecy and violence by Rockites served 'to strengthen the system, to cause intimidation ... more to show the power that the party possessed, than anything else'.[51] As the Protestant minister Walker in *The Boyne Water* warns Evelyn, in relation to the Catholic conspiracy, 'to gain you over, [Catholics] must necessarily impart *some* of their secrets'. Telling some secrets, but not all, is the key also to the Banims' narrative strategy. Their writing is at once an invitation to readers to share the secret of Ireland, and a prohibition against such powerful knowledge.

In the Banims' tales it is the 'artless and undisguised' who lose out, who go to pieces in an invisibly cemented society. The straightforward and plain-speaking Patty in *The Ghosthunter* – who is reminiscent of some of Edgeworth's more anodyne heroines – sickens and dies in the face of the endless layers of secrecy surrounding her. It is the cunning Rose, a reservoir of family and community secrets, who survives, indeed thrives, in the shadowy world. Secret societies during the Banims' lifetime depended on the collusion of the community for their survival. Members could disappear back into the community seamlessly, imperceptibly, precisely because of the existence of a network of secrecy. Arthur Young commented on the subject of agrarian secret societies that 'the gentlemen of the country had frequent expeditions to discover them in arms; but their intelligence was so uncommonly good, by their influence over the common people, that not one party that ever went out in quest of them was successful'.[52] It is perhaps no coincidence that *Crohoore of the Billhook* was written, as the narrator tells us 'during the period when Whiteboys began to appear' in the region. The complicity of the community is precisely what Crohoore depends upon when he is on the run, wrongly accused of murdering Tony Dooling. Crohoore baffles his pursuers, and seems by various reports to appear in different places at the same time. All of this is due to 'the prepossessions of the country people [which] continued to obstruct all regular inquiry'. The popular belief that Crohoore communes with the fairies, and is equipped with the power to wither limbs, blight faces and bewitch cows, provides a powerful incentive to the community to keep on his side.

Such a connection between Whiteboys and witches deserves some attention. The Banims' writing is suffused with references to the supernatural and paranormal, and it is no accident that their exploration of the superstitious is never far from their treatment of agrarian unrest. In his *Memoirs of Captain Rock*, Thomas Moore made a causal connection between oppression and the occult – the Irish peasant's belief in miracles, he argued, is 'a natural consequence of his political position. They, whom all means are employed to torment, may be allowed, at least, divine interposition to comfort them'.[53] Because secret societies are formed in part out of the belief that their day will come, it follows that they appropriate apocalyptic and supernatural imagery. But if the secret is to create solidarity, that can only happen if it is one worth telling. Ghosts and goblins, in other words, lend themselves to being talked about more than such quotidian matters as potatoes and pigs.

This paranormal discourse is not unrelated to the epidemic spread of Pastorini's prophecy during the Banims' lifetime, which foretold the extinction of Protestantism on Christmas Day, 1824. The questions put to witnesses in May of that year suggest that government officials made a connection as strong as Captain Rock's between agrarian movements and a belief in miracles: 'Do you not think,' one witness is asked, 'that the natural effect upon the human mind, of believing in a miraculous interposition of Providence, at a particular period of time, would be to affect the people who are disposed to believe, that the accomplishment of prophecy is at hand?'[54] When servants share secrets about their masters in the Banims' tales, it is the fetches and banshees that get them talking. It is the ghosts and fairies that get them eavesdropping, looking through keyholes, waiting with open ears to catch any stray bits of information that might be useful in the future.[55]

Crohoore is a figure of mystery and evasion, a master escape artist who disappears into crowds formed ostensibly to capture him. All of this leads the narrator to comment that he seems 'protected by unearthly friends and agency'.[56] But he is no doubt protected also by some very earthly friends and neighbours. A description of the collaboration of the Irish tenants with known outlaws is found in an extensive note at the tale's end, dealing with 'the last professional Irish robber', who flourished 'a year or so before the first publication of *Crohoore of the Billhook*'. The note tells us that, while 'baffling all pursuit' and 'eagerly sought after in every direction', he

> laid claim to the hospitality of the neighbouring farmers, and his claim was acknowledged. His meals the best each house could furnish, were brought to him in his concealment, and at night he received shelter from his entertainers. He had openly and unconditionally cast himself as a proscribed outlaw on their mercy; and although a large reward was offered for his apprehension, not one was found to enrich himself as his betrayer.[57]

We witness similar obstructive tactics in a magistrate's description of his attempts to bring to justice members of agrarian secret societies: 'it became almost impossible to procure satisfactory evidence against the guilty' since even 'the sufferers from such atrocities ... would steadily refuse to disclose their names or describe their persons'.[58] The United Irish Rebellion of 1798, as Luke Gibbons has noted, created such an oxymoronic culture of open conspiracy, or a mass-based mystery, wherein enlightened republican values were mediated through the conspiratorial network of secret societies.[59] The agrarian movements of the early nineteenth century inherited this populist form of secrecy, so that Whiteboys and Rockites could rely for their safety and anonymity on the implicit support of their neighbours.

This vast network of termite-like peasantry, who seem able like Rory na-chopple, the rapparee of *The Boyne Water*, to 'wind like an eel through an[y] orifice', is a threat to the governing order in Banims' writing. Their narrative spotlight shines more often on the populace than on the alleged protagonist, and is less interested in showing us the interior struggles of the individual than the collective force of the community. The honourable and innocent Pierce Shay, wrongly accused of being a Whiteboy in *Crohoore*, stands alone on the gallows, abandoned by the narrator who is found jostling among the watchful crowd below: 'We were young and giddy on that memorable day, and pushed with childish eagerness to behold so novel a sight'.[60] Secrets shared have the power in these tales to gather mobs, convict men of murder, steal property from the rich, imprison housewives, move Protestant settlers to suicide, burn infants alive. This is the kind of secrecy that promises, as Banim has it, a 'threat to the discoverer', a threat to readers who exist outside the secret. Rory-na-chopple of *The Boyne Water* is the arch-secretkeeper, seemingly capable of 'whispering' his enemies 'to death'. His well-nigh supernatural abilities, taken in the context of a secret's power to solidify a people against their rulers, are not altogether incredible.

Several critics have commented on the jarring experience of reading the Banims because of the movement from horrific violence to domesticity, and from the occult to the commonplace. Such incongruity might be read as an example of the Banims' uneven style, their problems with wedding polite English forms to violent Irish content. But we might also read it as an assertion of an alternative reality, a claim that another version of history exists alongside the official story in a contested country. As Bellman puts it,

> the discovery of a secret leads to a shift in the conception of reality rather than understanding the present reality as coming directly out of the old. The existence of secrets reinforces the idea that there are alternate versions of reality. The concealed information is the key that permits the selection of one over the other.[61]

The discovery of a single secret in these tales can alter our reading of the entire story. Crohoore is discovered at the tale's end to be not a changeling but the true son of the murdered Anthony Dooling. Oonagh in *The Boyne Water*, a figure of mystery and terror living in a cave and believed to have supernatural powers, is finally revealed as no witch but a mother grieving the infant she watched burned alive. As Teresa de Lauretis has written, the secret possesses a disruptive power, a constant potential for opening 'a view from elsewhere'.[62] For the Banims, this 'elsewhere' is Ireland, and the view it offers is an unsettling one for enlightened English readers .

Enlightenment epistemology presumed that realities lie behind appearances, that surfaces conceal depths, that secrets can be rooted out and dragged into the light. The late eighteenth- and early nineteenth-century is a period infamous for its political paranoia, when plots and rumours of plots ricocheted throughout Europe and rippled across the Atlantic, creating ever-widening circles of real and imagined intrigues. As Gordon Wood has argued, conspiracy theory is the logical extension of enlightenment metaphysics, so that reasonable men and women throughout the Anglo-American world – from John Wesley to John Adams – believed that hidden causes were at work determining individual lives and world history. In an increasingly inscrutable condition of shifting classes and subjects, the belief in an underpinning design made scientific sense to those committed to explaining events in terms of human intentions.[63] The realist novel, particularly in its English form, is consequently characterised by the pursuit and disclosure of secrets, and by the assumption that the contents of any secret, like the contents of any self, can be measured and known.

Viewed from the 'elsewhere'of rural Ireland, however, secrecy takes on quite a different aspect. Historians of nineteenth-century agrarian secret societies have suggested that the power and terror of such movements depended precisely on the indeterminacy of their secrets. Michael Beames has noted that Ribbon societies were characterised by 'an aura of mystery' but with objectives which often remained 'vague'.[64] A magistrate giving testimony on disturbances in Ireland in 1816 commented that he 'could not ascertain, that the various combinations which existed in different parts of the country, proposed to themselves any definite object'.[65] Several years later, Matthew Barrington stated in his evidence to a Committee of the House of Lords that Ribbonmen 'seemed not to understand the object for which they were sworn; they were always sworn to be ready when called upon; but they did not seem to know what was the real object'.[66] As the narrator of *Crohoore* insists, the Whiteboys had 'scarcely an object in view.' Such a sense of secrets without substance is echoed by a witness to a Select Committee, who reported, '[The ribbon system's] existence is manifested by its acts, by the oaths of secrecy, and by the use of pass words and signs, but what the precise object of it is I cannot tell'.[67] In all of these cases, the efficacy of the secret is located in its performance or *form*, rather than in its substance. It is this counter-Enlightenment view of secrecy – as custom over content, act over actual – which we find reproduced in the Banims' writing. Their most unsettling characters, like their narrative voice itself, create terror by seeming to have, like Rory na-chopple, 'just a little bit of a sacret'; by 'laughing and chuckling, in a knowing way, together', by, in other words, *practising* secrecy.[68] Bellman's definition, we recall, is that secrecy is practised in the act of telling or not telling, not in the thing told. Rory shows himself to be whispering to the horse, but, significantly, 'no one heard his whisper, if whisper it was'. His power lies in his ability to *appear* to own a secret, at least to those eyes looking to uncover such a mystery. Two definitions of obscurity operate in the Banims' writing: obscurity in the sense of something determinate being veiled, and the inherent obscurity of indeterminacy. Rory-na-Chopple shuttles between these two meanings, making the latter appear the former. The Banims' style itself exists in that ambiguous space, disturbing readers as effectively as Rory disturbs his rulers.

Yet for all of its ability to forge connections between people, secrecy is also symptomatic of a faultline, of some social rupture or conflict.[69] The context out of which Irish secrecy springs is, as the Banims can't stop reminding us, lost property, lost opportunity, lost identity. As they write in *The Ghosthunter*, Irish Catholics are divided subjects: 'compelled to bow before their superiors in public, they indulged against them, in private, a very respectable portion of loathing and abhorrence.'[70] Such subjects are estranged and divided, split between public actions and private beliefs, adept at disguise and equivocation to preserve their true identity. To present the Irish 'as they really were' is what the Banims believed they were up to – and many of their critics believe the same. David Gilligan hears, despite the 'evasiveness and tendentiousness' of their fiction, 'an authentic native voice'.[71] Mark Hawthorne sees the Banims as discarding 'the English veneer' to discover 'an Irish self-image'.[72] Such criticism reproduces the assumption of the existence of some core of native Irish identity waiting to be revealed. But what if that identity is intrinsically indeterminate, not just misunderstood?

The Banims' most successful characters are also their most slippery. Quicksilver creatures, masters of mimicry, they change their voices, dress and opinions as the occasion requires. They are well represented by Rory na-chopple's Rapparees in *The Boyne Water*, who 'wear portions of the uniform of almost every regiment, on both sides, in Ireland', and are well known to be 'not on any particular side'.[73] This mercurial type recurs in their novels and tales: the Bocchochs in *Crohoore*, are described as 'not being a distinct race, or the descendants of one'. These 'Lame Beggars' live by 'counterfeiting', by 'practicing on the charity, the superstitions, the unwariness, or the terrors of their more simple countrymen'; they 'have skill in disguising their local derivation' and 'passed everywhere for strangers'. It is significant that Crohoore, the master of obstruction and evasion, was raised among these shape-shifting Bocchochs.[74] Harry Tresham's self-fashioning servant Larry in *The Fetches* (1825) is another character whose 'cunning, and his watchfullness of himself and others' allows him to mimic 'the words of his betters, grafting everything onto his still predominant brogue'.[75] And Peery Connolly in *The Nowlans* is 'known to possess the power of showing an extraordinary change of character'. This schizophrenic habit, which includes a self-representation as the village idiot in the grip of a dancing disease, allows Peery to eavesdrop on everyone unnoticed and so possess multiple secrets. This 'power' of changing character proves in the novel to be truly that, and the narrator suggests that Peery's 'real fits of aberration were not so frequent as he wished to have inferred; ... there was, occasionally, as much cunning as folly in his extravagance ... if he liked, he might be as wise a man as his neighbors'.[76] The equivocation, obstruction, and mimicry that hides one's true identity is a strategic act of survival, a cunning art of subversion, a refusal to fall into anyone else's categories. Being protean would seem an example of inherent indeterminacy – in the end, there is nothing determinate to be known. The obscurity lies on the side of the object rather than of the subject.

There is a sense that these characters, doubled over with subversive laughter, are double in another way as well. Mixtures of self-assertion and self-cancellation, self-dramatization and self-consumption, they perhaps have no 'inner heart' to protect, no secret identity to preserve. The narrator of *John Doe* describes the peculiar pack of cards used by the Rockites in their subterranean distillery:

> They used cards, which might baffle the discriminating faculties of more accomplished gamesters, as long fingering, and the hue and shape thereby left on each, confounded, to the uninitiated eye, all distinctions of number, colour, and suit. Habit is everything, however; and the present proprietors of these mysterious symbols appeared to recognize their fifty-two subtle sub-divisions, with as much ease, as in a more fashionable hall, gamblers of a higher order distinguish the differences of an untouched pack: though rumour adds that their means for arriving at such conclusions, were not derived from much positive evidence of the marks originally stamped on the pasteboard, but rather from subsidiary hieroglyphics that had gradually succeeded to the original signs, and as gradually become acknowledged ... by the persevering and watchful observers.[77]

Such a detail might be taken as a trope for the loss of an original identity among the shape-shifting card players. Emptied of their original meaning, however, the Banims' native Irish experience also a certain freedom. They become the jokers in the pack, empty of any particular value, but most valuable precisely for their vacuity. A similar concern with identity can be found in Rockite catechisms, which mimic the forms of official catechisms, but with the intention of a very different kind of conversion. 'Q. Who made your coat? A. It never was made, it grew spontaneous, as the wool does on a sheep's back.'[78] Here, hiding or being cloaked is taken to be the Rockite's natural state – so natural, in fact, that the great coat becomes indistinguishable from the body.

Where the Rockite's cloaking ends and his identity begins is no easy question. Secrecy, thus, does not simply shelter a stable inner life distinct from public experience; it figures a radically divided subject. To live a secret for so long is to risk losing one's voice; saying what the ruler wants to hear can cause one to forget what one might have said in the first place. An extensive note in *Crohoore of the Billhook* illuminates this situation of being divided between self-preservation and self-consumption. The note tells the story of a lone woman living in a castle tower, who was 'in connection with a formidable band of free-booters'. As caretaker of their plunder, she 'screened and protected the depredators' from the law, and kept their treasure secret. On discovery of her hideaway by the law, she

> retired into her storeroom with a light in her hand; gathered close around her the easily ignitable flax, then she applied her brand, and was instant-ly enveloped in flame. Her charred remains were found amidst a burnt heap of cinders. With herself she had consumed all direct identification with the freebooters, ... so the object of her self-sacrifice was gained.

Here, protecting one's identity and losing one's identity collapse into the same act. The Banims, like their characters, articulate this wavering Catholic voice, this curious mix of self-assertion and self-cancellation, standing up for Ireland's identity in fictions that defer to English forms. Their narrative voice is split between a public claim that they would go far to bring the two cultures together, and a 'private ire' towards the ruling power that checks such senti-ments; a voice that hints that they do not wish to go far at all. Their loyalties lie at last among the tight-lipped people to whom they want to give a voice. But keeping that voice silent and secret might be the best way of remaining faithful to it.

To ventriloquise might be a way of keeping one's own voice secret, or it might be a way of hiding the loss of it. But what if there is no authentic voice to lose, no hidden heart behind the veils, no rock-bottom Irish self preserved beneath the strata of secrets? Belief on the part of some critics in the existence of an essential Irish self reproduces some of the assumptions of Dublin Castle in its dealings with secret societies. Both presume that secrets hide actual, substantial, knowable objects (and indeed subjects). The Banims' veiling of the Irish heart may mask an anxiety that there is no underlying identity in the first place. At the core of 'the endless etceteras of rustic tattle' and chatter of cabin life in these novels is a painful, powerful silence.[79] The Banims plead Ireland's case to English readers, voice past crimes, give finger-wagging lessons in history and politics, and tutorials in how to rule the country. All of this, how-ever, is done in novels that are mimicries, or forgeries, of English forms and is articulated in a self-conscious, uneven narrative voice.

The psychoanalytic theory of Nicholas Abraham and Maria Torok has much to say about the relationship between secrecy and language. Reality is born out of an experience of traumatic loss, which takes the form of a secret entombed in the psyche. Language is then built around this secret, encasing and protecting it, refusing to articulate this most real of experiences. A secret is sealed off or 'encrypted' in language that covers over, misleads, tries to erase the secret it contains. Significantly, Abraham and Torok argue that such obfuscation can define families and nations as well as individuals. Further, the secrets we carry around are often not our own, but those passed on to us through language. Members of a family or nation carry around other people's secrets.

> Whether it characterizes individuals, families, social groups, or entire nations, silence and its varied forms – the untold or unsayable secret, the feeling unfelt, the pain denied, the unspeakable and concealed shame of families, the cover-up of political crimes, the collective disregard for painful historical realities – may disrupt our lives.[80]

The secret that disrupts the Banims' language, I want to suggest, is that no 'native' Irish voice exists, no Irish heart can be disclosed. Their narrative voice, like the Irish characters they write about, is split and slippery, unable to speak in an 'authentic Irish voice' because there isn't one.[81] There is no heart, no core of identity, no authentic self in a country of supervised subjects driven into secrecy. But the Rorys and the Larrys and the Peerys and the Bocchochs all make a virtue of their non-identity. They are the dissemblers, the destabilisers, shifting identities to meet the situation, and shedding one self to disclose yet another. It is the impression that some true identity, some secret voice, some inner core *might* exist beneath all the layers that keeps the ruler watchful and the reader turning pages; and it is the non-existence of this core that makes the peeling endless. As with the Banims' narrative voice, the power of these characters is in their practice of secrecy, and attests to the fact that the Irish need not have a stable identity, an authentic voice, to disrupt the ruling power. People need not have an actual secret, in the sense of some hidden piece of information, to make outsiders anxious. They only need to *seem* to have one – or to be one.

The narrative voice of the Banims speaks this language of the communal secret, the mass-based mystery, which has the power to solidify a subaltern people against their rulers. Secrecy operates as the friend and weapon of the weak, but it is also a burden which weighs heavily on the very identities it means to defend, warping and splintering them. Secrecy is power and possibility for a colonised people, but also part of their problem. Like the Bocchochs, who are strangers everywhere and so can be equally at home anywhere, or like the corpse in *The Ghosthunter*, whose face is so badly disfigured it can become any face, the Banims mimic voices and forms not their own. Their anxiety, the secret they can't bear to tell, is the impossibility of recovering a lost voice, the futility of doing reconstructive surgery on a disfigured Irish

identity, the hollowness of the search for the 'inner heart' of a colonised people. Like Patty in *The Ghosthunter*, who tries 'not [to] hear [her] own words',
while she whispers her 'withering secret,' the Banims try to ignore the secret
their tales keep telling.[82]

NOTES

1. See Patrick Joseph Murray's *The Life of John Banim* (New York: Sadlier,1885).
2. Thomas Richards, *The Imperial Archive: Knowledge and the Fantasy of Empire* (London: Verso,
   1993). See also C.A. Bayley, *Empire and Information* (Cambridge U P, 1996).
3. For a treatment of Edgeworth's attitude towards secrecy and children, see Willa Murphy, 'A
   Queen of Hearts or an Old Maid? Maria Edgeworth's Fictions of Union' in *Acts of Union*, (eds
   Daire Keogh and Kevin Whelan (Dublin: Four Courts, 2001) pp. 187-201.
4. For discussions of the place of secrecy in children's literature, see Roderick McGillis,
   "'Secrets" and "Sequence" in Children's Stories', *Studies in the Literary Imagination* 18.2 (1985)
   pp. 35-46, and Susan Sherer, 'Secrecy and Autonomy in Lewis Carroll', *Philosophy and Literature*
   20 (1996)pp. 1-19.
5. See Luke Gibbons for a discussion of the uses of allegory among secret societies in
   Transformations in Irish Culture (Cork: Cork U P, 1996) pp. 18-22.
6. D.A. Miller, *The Novel and the Police.* (Berkeley: U California P, 1988) pp. 10. See also Ali
   Behdad,'Visibility, Secrecy and the Novel: Narrative Power in Bronte and Zola,' *Literature,
   Interpretation, Theory* 1:4 (1990) pp. 253-64; and Richard D. E. Burton, 'The Unseen Seer, or
   Proteus in the City: Aspects of a Nineteenth-Century Parisian Myth,' *French Studies* XLII
   (1988) pp. 50-68; and Walter Benjamin, *Charles Baudelaire: A Lyric Poet in the Era of High
   Capitalism* (London: Verso, 1973) on the flaneur as the distant, detached observer who watch-
   es with an alienated gaze.
7. See S. J. Connolly, "Union Government, 1812–23" in W. E. Vaughan, (ed) *A New History of
   Ireland,* vol. 5, 'Ireland Under the Union' (Oxford: Clarendon, 1989) pp. 71.
8. David Lloyd, *Anomalous States, Irish Writing and the Post-Colonial Moment* (Dublin: Lilliput, 1993)
   pp. 125–162, argues that these early Irish novelists were involved in attempts to reorient and
   reform the Irish, in preparation for Emancipation.
9. John and Michael Banim, *The Croppy: A Tale of the Irish Rebellion of 1798* (Dublin: J. Duffy, 1865)
   pp. 280. Though critics have generally denied Michael Banim any important role in the
   authorship of *Tales by the O Hara Family,* the stay-at-home brother provided much local and historical detail to John in London, was the main author of *Crohoore of the Billhook,* and was deeply
   involved in the editing of manuscripts before and after John's death. "My brother and myself",
   he writes in the preface to the New York edition of the Tales, "were joint producers of the
   stories". John and Michael Banim, *The Peep O 'Day; or John Doe* and *Crohoore of the Billhook* (New
   York: D & J Sadlier, 1889). This chapter acknowledges the brothers' literary partnership, and
   names Michael as co-author of the novels and tales. For a different point of view, see especially Flanagan, *The Irish Novelists: 1800-1850* (New York: Columbia U P, 1959), p. 175.
10. Michel Foucault, *Politics, Philosophy, Culture: Interviews and Other Writings, 1977-1984,* trans. Alan
    Sheridan, ed. Lawrence Kritzman (London: Routledge, 1988).
11. Thomas Flanagan, *The Irish Novelists: 1800-1850* (New York: Columbia U P, 1959) reads the
    Banims as attempting to write 'counter-propaganda' during a period of the ubiquity of the
    stage Irishman, but also as aware of the marketability of Irish material. Mark D. Hawthorne,
    John and Michael Banim: A Study in the Early Development of the Anglo-Irish Novel (Salzburg:
    University of Salzburg Press, 1975) reads the Banims as a marriage of the forms of English
    realism with surreal Irish content.
12. David Gilligan, 'Natural Indignation in the Native Voice: The Fiction of the Banim Brothers'
    in Birgit Bramsback and Martin Croghan, (eds) *Anglo-Irish and Irish Literature: Aspects of
    Language and Culture. Proceedings of the Ninth International Congress of the International Association for
    the Study of Anglo-Irish Literature* (Stockholm: Almquist and Wiksell, 1988) p. 78.
13. Murray, *The Life of John Banim* (New York: Sadlier, 1885) p. 104.)

14. John and Michael Banim, *The Boyne Water* (New York: Sadlier, 1881) p. 13.
15. John wrote to his brother that `if either of us could only delineate the peculiarities we daily witness in those we meet, success would be the result' (qtd. in Murray, *The Life of John Banim*, pp. 140–41). This sense of the author-as-government agent is suggested also in Gerald Griffin's introduction to his *Tales of the Munster Festivals*, where he writes that 'The novelist might furnish the statesman and legislator with an index to the dispositions and habits of the people he was to govern, and who were too distant for personal inquiry or observation.' Gerald Griffin, *Tales of the Munster Festivals* (London: Saunders,1827).
16. Several critics have commented on the uneven character of the Banims' writing. Mark D. Hawthorne calls attention to the major difficulties facing the Irish novelist, whose desire to become a spokesman for his people is compromised by a need to sell to a London audience in *John and Michael Banim: A Study in the Early Development of the Anglo-Irish Novel* (Salzburg: University of Salzburg Press, 1975); David Gilligan describes this problem of audience as causing a schizophrenic style, that attempts at once to present and censor the voices of subversive Irish peasants in `Natural Indignation in the Native Voice: The Fiction of the Banim Brothers' in Birgit Bramsback and Martin Croghan, (eds) *Anglo-Irish and Irish Literature: Aspects of Language and Culture. Proceedings of the Ninth International Congress of the International Association for the Study of Anglo-Irish Literature* (Stockholm: Almquist and Wiksell, 1988); Thomas Flanagan sees the Catholic tradesman John Banim as trapped between classes, 'ridiculed by the Ascendancy and deplored by the old Catholic gentry'in *The Irish Novelists: 1800–1850* (New York: Columbia U P, 1959) p. 167.
17. John and Michael Banim, *The Peep O 'Day; or John Doe* and *Crohoore of the Billhook* (Dublin and London: James Duffy, 1865) p. 306.
18. See, for example Beryl L. Bellman, 'The Paradox of Secrecy,' *Human Studies* 4 (1981) pp. 1–24.
19. Nicolas Abraham and Maria Torok argue that secrets, since they point to some original crime, are always shared at the start, and point to an accomplice. See *The Shell and the Kernel*, Trans. Nicholas Rand (U Chicago P, 1994) p. 158.
20. See Jean-Luc Marion, *God Without Being (U* Chicago P, 1991) for a discussion of the theological relationship between secrecy and revelation.
21. Jacques Derrida, *The Post Card: From Socrates to Freud and Beyond.* Trans. Alan Bass (U Chicago P. 1987) p. 53; see also Sean Gaston, "Derrida and the Ruins of Disinterest". *Angelaki* 7:3 (2002) pp. 105–118; Banims, *B W* p. 62.
22. Bellman argues that 'it is the very nature of secrets that they get told' and that secrets are best understood as 'communicative event[s]' (pp. 1, 2). Secrets are 'metacommunicative' because 'it is assumed that there is much more to the message than the content' (p. 8).
23. Bellman suggests that the practice of secrecy involves a 'display of membership', revealing 'the speaker's and the listener's respective participation in the category of persons who share the concealed knowledge' (p. 11). Such a definition of secrecy might help explain the United Irish paradox of a mass-based secret society.
24. John Banim, *The Nowlans* (Belfast: Appletree, 1992) p. 10.
25. See James C. Scott, *Weapons of the Weak* (Yale U P, 1985) for an exploration of everyday forms of peasant resistance, such as foot dragging, dissimulation, desertion, false compliance, feigned ignorance, slander, and obstruction. Scott argues that such forms of class struggle require no coordination or planning, and make use of implicit understandings and informal networks among the peasantry.
26. Elizabeth Smith, *The Irish Journals of Elizabeth Smith 1840-1850*, eds. David Thomson and Moyra McGusty (Oxford U P, 1980), entries for 19, 28 Oct 1845; 13 May 1847.
27. Select Committee on Irish Affairs, Evidence taken before the Select Committee ... to inquire into the State of Ireland, 15 March 1825 (521) ix.278.
28. Select Committee on Irish Affairs. Evidence taken before the Select Committee to inquire into disturbances in Ireland, 13 May 1824 (20) vii.6
29. Ranajit Guha, *Elementary Aspects of Peasant Insurgency* (Oxford U P, 1997) p. 18.
30. John and Michael Banim, *BW 13.* See Terry Eagleton, *Crazy John and the Bishop* (Cork U P, *1998)* pp. 140–157, for a discussion of the way Thomas Moore echoes such sentiments (desiring to dispel the mists of sadness with the sun of freedom, etc.), and yet at the same time enjoys this misty secrecy.
31. John and Michael Banim, *The Croppy: A Tale of the Irish Rebellion of 1798* (Dublin and London: James Duffy, 1865) p. 6.
32. Guha p. 18.

33. Select Committee on Irish Affairs. Evidence taken before the Select Committee to inquire into disturbances in Ireland, 11 June 1824 (20) vii.6.

34. John and Michael Banim, *The Croppy* p. 280.

35. Joep Leerssen, *Remembrance and Imagination* (Cork U P, 1996) p. 38.

36. Literary representations of Dublin in the period after the Union speak of it in images of decay and decline, as a desert, with an eerie emptiness. See, for example, Lady Morgan's *St Clair; or, The Heiress of Desmond* (Philadelphia: S. F. Bradford, *1807)* which calls Dublin a 'dissipated metropolis' (p. 26). Murray p. 17.

38. John and Michael Banim, *The Ghosthunter and his Family* (New York: Sadlier, 1884) pp. 207, 141. Hereafter abbreviated *GH.*

39. Flanagan p. 176.

40. John and Michael Banim, *Crohoore* p. 403.

41. Select Committee on Irish Affairs. Evidence taken before Select Committee to inquire into disturbances in Ireland, 14 June 1824 (20) vii.6.

42. For a discussion of secrecy and the subaltern, see Gayatri Chakravorty Spivak, 'Can the Subaltern Speak?' in Cary Nelson and Lawrence Grossberg, eds., *Marxism and the Interpretation of Culture* (Urbana: U Illinois P, 1988) pp. 271–313.

43. John and Michael Banim, *GH* p. 144.

44. Guha p. 256.

45. Guha argues that solidarity is 'a categorical imprint of peasant consciousness ... a figure of his self-consciousness' (p. 169) and that rumor is 'both a universal and necessary carrier of insurgency in any pre-industrial, pre-literate society' (p. 251).

46. Select Committee on Irish Affairs. Evidence taken before Select Committee to inquire into the State of Ireland, H.L. 1825 (521) ix.275.

47. John and Michael Banim, GH p. 215.

48. Michel Foucault, *The History of Sexuality: An Introduction,* tr. Robert Hurley (Harmondsworth: Penguin, 1990).

49. John and Michael Banim, *Crohoore* p. 407.

50. John and Michael Banim, *Crohoore* p. 253.

51. Select Committee on Irish Affairs. Evidence taken before Select Committee to inquire into disturbances in Ireland, H.L. 26 May 1824 (20) vii.6

52. Quoted in George Cornwall Lewis, *Local Disturbances in Ireland* (Cork U P, 1977) p. 9.

53. [Thomas Moore], *Memoirs of Captain Rock, the Celebrated Irish Chieftain, with some Account of his Ancestors, By Himself* (London: Longman, 1824) p. 248.

54. Evidence taken before the Select Committee to Inquire into Disturbances in Ireland, H.L. 14 May 1824 (20) vii.27.

55. See especially *The Fetches,* where the servant Larry, a master of mimicry, is always on hand to overhear his master's tales of the paranormal, and passes these on to fellow servants. John and Michael Banim, *Peter of the Castle and The Fetches* (New York: Sadlier, 1869).

56. John and Michael Banim, *Crohoore p.* 371.

57. John and Michael Banim, *Crohoore p.* 406.

58. Extract of dispatch from Whitworth to Viscount Sidmouth, Statement of Nature and Extent of Disturbances in Ireland and Measures Adopted by Government. Command Papers 1816 (479) ix.571.

59. Luke Gibbons, "Alternative Enlightenments: The United Irishmen, Cultural Diversity and the Republic of Letters," *1798: Two Hundred Years of Resonance,* ed. Mary Cullen (Dublin: Irish Reporter Publications, 1998) pp. 119–27.

60. John and Michael Banim, *Crohoore,* p. 371.

61. Bellman pp. 14–15.

62. Teresa De Lauretis, *Technologies of Gender: Essays on Theory, Film, and Fiction* (Bloomington: Indiana U P, 1987) p.25.

63. Gordon S. Wood, 'Conspiracy and the Paranoid Style: Causality and Deceit in the Eighteenth Century,' *The William and Mary Quarterly* 39 (1982) pp. 401-44. See also J. M. Roberts, *The Mythology of the Secret Societies* (London: Paladin, 1974) for a discussion of how secret societies were interlocked with 18th century Enlightenment ideology at many points.

64. Michael Beames, *Peasants and Power: The Whiteboy Movement and Their Control in Pre-Famine Ireland* (Brighton: 1983).

65. Command Papers. Statement of Nature and Extent of Disturbances in Ireland and Measures adopted by Government. 1816 (479) ix.572.

66. Evidence taken before Select Committee to inquire into State of Ireland with reference to Disturbances, H.L. 15 April 1825 (521) ix. 302.
67. Evidence taken by Select Committee to inquire into State of Ireland, 14 May 1824 (20) vii.31.
68. John and Michael Banim, BW p. 124.
69. Stanton K. Tefft, *The Dialectics of Secret Society Power in States* (Atlantic Heights, NJ: Humanities Press, 1992) argues that secret societies "constitute loci at which structural conflicts appear", the result of 'structural contradictions within a social formation" pp. 173, 171.
70. John and Michael Banim, GH p. 53.
71. Gilligan p. 78.
72. Hawthorne p. 17.
73. Banim, BW pp. 502, 340.
74. See Niall O Ciosain, "Boccoughs and God's Poor: Deserving and Undeserving Poor in Irish Popular Culture," in *Ideology and Ireland in the Nineteenth Century*, Tadhg Foley and Sean Ryder, eds (Dublin: Four Courts, 1998) pp. 93–99, for a discussion of nineteenth century representations of boccoughs as "tricksters and frauds", p. 96.
75. John and Michael Banim, *Peter of the Castle and The Fetches* (New York: Sadlier, 1869) p. 243.
76. John and Michael Banim, *Nowlans* p. 9.
77. John and Michael Banim, *John Doe* pp. 129–30.
78. Evidence taken before the Select Committee to inquire into disturbances in Ireland, H.L. 24 May 1824 (20) vii.31.
79. John and Michael Banim, *Crohoore* p. 192.
80. Nicholas Rand, "Introduction: Renewals of Psychoanalysis" in Nicolas Abraham and Maria Torok, *The Shell and the Kernel, vol. 1*, trans., ed. Nicholas Rand (Chicago U P, 1994) p. 21.
81. The fact that the Banim brothers collaborated in writing the *Tales by the O Hara Family* is a good emblem of this split voice.
82. John and Michael Banim, GH p. 154.

CHAPTER SIXTEEN

Theatre and Colonialism in Ireland

LIONEL PILKINGTON

INTRODUCTION

Considered within any context, the relationship between theatre and colonialism is a vast and complex subject demanding an extended historical account of the interrelationships between the policies and practices of colonialism within a given society and the practices and institutions of theatrical culture. This essay does not attempt such an overview, but calls attention to a number of critical problems that arise not so much from the general experience of colonialism in Ireland but from the complex specificities of Ireland's transition from British rule to national independence and, in the early 1980s, in the attempted resolution of the conflict in Northern Ireland.[1] Accordingly, the first part of the essay examines the inaugural moment of the Irish Literary Theatre – the joint production of W.B. Yeats's *The Countess Cathleen* and Edward Martyn's *The Heather Field* performed by the Irish Literary Theatre at the Ancient Concert Rooms in Brunswick Street, Dublin on 8 May 1899 – and then goes on to examine Brian Friel's *Translations* performed by the Field Day Theatre Company in the Guildhall in Derry on 23 September 1980.

THE COUNTESS CATHLEEN AND THE HEATHER FIELD (1899)

The opening productions of the Irish Literary Theatre – of W.B. Yeats's *The Countess Cathleen* and Edward Martyn's *The Heather Field* – are sometimes viewed as a watershed moment in Irish theatre history, marking the beginning of Ireland's national theatre movement and of an authentic Irish drama.[2] Even when this is not explicitly stated, Irish drama anthologies and theatre history books tend to view these 8 May 1899 productions of the Irish Literary Theatre as a crucial starting point. This was also, of course, precisely the way in which the founders of the Irish Literary Theatre –W.B. Yeats, Lady Gregory, Edward Martyn and George Moore – wished their project to be considered.

> We hope to find in Ireland an uncorrupted and imaginative audience trained to listen by its passion for oratory, and believe that our desire to bring upon the stage the deeper thoughts and emotions of Ireland will ensure for us a tolerant welcome, and that freedom to experiment which is not found in theatres of England, and without which no new movement in art or literature can succeed. We will show that Ireland is not the home of buffoonery and of easy sentiment, as it has been represented, but the home of an ancient idealism, and we are confident of the support of all Irish people, who are weary of misrepresentation, in carrying out a work that is outside all the political questions that divide us.[3]

In this formulation, the work of the Irish Literary Theatre stands in Arnoldian contrast to caricatures and crude stereotypes of Ireland as portrayed by the colleens and stage Irishmen of nineteenth-century English drama. And yet despite initial nationalist support for the Irish Literary Theatre as a cultural project (the list of names in the opening programme, *Beltaine*, include the Irish Parliamentary Party leader, John Redmond), it is extremely difficult to view this initiative as marking the end of an era – either of colonialism in Ireland or of a particular kind of theatre. Not only did a nationalist theatre already exist in Ireland (Boucicault's Irish plays and a repertoire of popular nationalist melodramas had, for several decades, been regularly performed at the Queen's Royal Theatre, for example), but there had been previous national theatre projects as, for example, in the case of Robert Owenson's 1784 'national' theatre at Fishamble Street or in the 1897 claims of the Theatre Royal.[4] Moreover, the founders of the Irish Literary Theatre either belonged or gave allegiance to the idea of an ascendancy elite. In addition, the plays performed by the Irish Literary Theatre (and, arguably, by much of the early Abbey Theatre repertoire as well) tend to reflect the anxieties, and in some cases the prejudices, of this elite far more than they do the preoccupations of Ireland's Roman Catholic nationalist majority.

Edward Martyn's sympathetic treatment of the leadership tribulations of reforming Irish landlords in *The Heather Field* is a case in point. An Ibsenite study of a landlord in the West of Ireland, the play's protagonist, Carden Tyrrell, is crippled by debt, but clings fervently to his dream of reforming the Irish landscape from its unproductive native state. Although Tyrrell's Sisyphean task – reforming an intractable Irish nature by ridding his estate of heather – is strikingly colonial, this is presented by the play not as an imposition, but as simply quixotic: doomed to failure, that is, not so much because of any intrinsic lack of merit, but because the task is pursued too dogmatically. As Tyrrell's neighbouring landlord, Barry Usher, reminds him, such a scheme must be 'generous and loving', otherwise the land's wild nature will be bound to avenge itself.

> USHER: I do not know whether his treatment was sufficiently kind, as
> farmers say here in West Ireland. .... He was hardly considerate enough,
> perhaps, in the accomplishment of his will.[5]

The play ends with Tyrrell virtually imprisoned in his house ('like Moltke
fighting battles from his study') as a result of the evictions that he has effected as a way of making money. Tyrrell is presented as a landlord myopically
unable to recognise the benefits of the new constructive unionist policy of
'kindness',[6] but he is, nevertheless, meant to come across as a sadly tragic figure for whom the audience has the most sympathy. To this extent, Martyn's
protagonist dramatises a distinction that had recently been clearly articulated
by the Unionist MP, Sir Horace Plunkett in a 1898 lecture, 'The Economic
Movement in Ireland'. Plunkett's argument was that the maladministration of
Ireland lay in its continuance of the seventeenth-century colonial policy of
coercion. Resolving the crisis of government in Ireland meant developing
(British) government for Ireland in a manner that would command consensual support, or, in Plunkett's words, 'modern relations between the government
and the people'. Bluntly put, then, *The Heather Field* is far closer to a unionist
(and British government) viewpoint than it is to nationalist concerns or preoccupations.

And yet, despite the restricted social parameters of the play and its portrayal of the Irish landowning class within a perspective of tragic decline, the
May 1899 production of *The Heather Field* was described in superlatives by
nationalist print media organs such as *The Freeman's Journal, Independent* and the
United Irishman.[7] Nationalist audiences displayed no objection to the play's
unrepresentative characters or Ascendancy preoccupations. Indeed, the only
negative comments about the play emanate from the unionist-oriented *Irish
Times* which disliked Martyn's application of Ibsenite naturalism to Ireland's
landlord class: 'the cold methods of the Norwegian dramatists can never be
applied with any truth to even the Irish landlord ... without parodying the very
essences of Irish life'.[8]

Popular reaction to Yeats's *The Countess Cathleen* was not as sanguine. With its
narrative action set in Ireland in a time of famine and featuring an aristocratic
lady who rescues her superstitious Catholic tenantry from starvation by an act
of magnanimous self-sacrifice, this was, in Majorie Howes's phrase, 'ascendancy nationalism.'[9] As Howes points out, Yeats's play managed to invert an idea
central to nationalist anti-colonial discourse (peasant integrity in the face of
landlord injustice) in order to gather support for Ireland's increasingly discredited tenantry system.[10] In short, *The Countess Cathleen* was a play that seemed to
turn Irish anti-colonialist rhetoric on its head by suggesting that, far from being
foreign or exotic, Ireland's former colonial rulers – the *soi-disant* Ascendancy –
were an indispensable, if not *the* indispensable, part of the Irish nation.

But again popular criticism of the play was relatively muted. Even though
a group of University students protested, most nationalist newspapers and

journals supported the production even if, as in the case of the *United Irishman* and the *New Ireland Review*, this support was rendered with considerable reservation. Interestingly, the one notable objection to Yeats's play arose from a contemporary critic – the polemicist Frank Hugh O'Donnell – who claimed that *The Countess Cathleen* contributed to a colonial stereotyping of Ireland: '[I]f this be a true portrait of Irish Catholic character, every effort of England to stamp out our religion, and incidentally our nationality, is not merely to be justified but to be applauded.'[11] It is this point in particular – the sense that *The Countess Cathleen* endorses a view that Catholic Ireland is, by definition, not fully modern and therefore not ready for political or administrative independence – that may well explain the depth of O'Donnell's irritation. O'Donnell's more florid denunciations, mainly contained in his second letter of objection which *The Freeman's Journal* refused to print, belong to this broader context of offence. Attacking Yeats's Celticism as 'an agreeable diversification' from the stage Irishman and political Irishman of London, O'Donnell claims that *The Countess Cathleen* should be seen *not* as a replacement of anti-Irish stereotypes (the declared aim of the 1897 Irish Literary Theatre prospectus), but as the means for their elaboration and development.

> Instead of Donnybrook and Ballyhooley, or rather by the side of these types, and, as it were, suggesting their development, the genial Anglo-Saxon is asked to regard the fine old Celtic peasant of Ireland's Golden Age, sunk in animal savagery, destitute of animal courage, mixing up in loathsome promiscuity the holiest homes of the Christian Sanctuary with the gibbering ghoul-and-fetish worship of a Congo negro, selling his soul for a bellyful, yelling alternate invocations to the Prince of Darkness and the Virgin Mary. Surely this is a dainty dish to set before our sister England![12]

O'Donnell's juxtaposition of Irish Catholicism with what he regards as the savage primitivism of the African Congo implies a world whose values have been cataclysmically inverted. The extremity of O'Donnell's racist language conveys outrage at his belief that what has taken place in Yeats's play is an inversion of a fundamental distinction: between an Irish civility demanding political independence in the form of equality with other European nation states and the barbarism of an indigenous African culture that justifies Belgian (Catholic) colonialism. If the Irish can be inferred to be anti-modern largely on account of their Catholicism, then the clear implication of such a logic is that they are indeed little more than colonial natives, transparently undeserving of autonomous state institutions. But this, O'Donnell infers, is as absurd as the claim that the Catholic colonial enterprise in Africa is a travesty. O'Donnell's complaints are grossly racist. Nevertheless, they reveal (albeit inadvertently) the degree to which anti-Catholicism was linked to a political discourse that, in its virulent opposition to Irish home rule, nationalists associated with a disgracefully inappropriate colonialism.

The point here is not to claim that the Irish Literary Theatre operated as an attempt to reimpose a colonialist framework on Irish culture. Indeed, if nationalists of the Irish Parliamentary Party and southern Irish unionists were agreed on anything in the 1890s, it was on the uselessness and wildly inappropriate nature of such a perspective. But neither, it must be acknowledged, was the national theatre initiative in any way concerned with establishing the validity of an anti-colonial critique either in the Irish context or elsewhere, or with establishing a form of theatre that would be at odds fundamentally with the forms and conventions of European theatre. To the contrary, the establishment of a national theatre was seen as vitally important because it demonstrated the hegemony of a normative constitutional politics. As one writer put it in 1895 while attempting to explain the contemporary dearth of Irish drama, 'We have been living through real dramas, and have no time for dramas of the imagination.'[13]

BRIAN FRIEL'S *TRANSLATIONS* (1980)

Brian Friel's play *Translations* is one of the few late twentieth-century Irish plays to address aspects of Ireland's colonial history in a manner that evokes parallels with the political conflict in Northern Ireland. Written in post-independence Ireland, and dealing with topics central to Ireland's history of colonisation (mapping, language politics, militant resistance), *Translations*, more than most other Irish plays, seems to warrant the term 'postcolonial.' Friel's play is set in the mid-1830s, a decade before the cataclysmic events of the 1847 Famine and at the start of the Anglicizing project of the national schools system. The particular issue of *Translations*, however, is the Anglicization of Ireland's place names through the re-mapping of local Irish place names by the Ordnance Survey of the British Army.

Politically charged, the action of *Translations* takes place in rural Ireland on the eve of the potato famine and the introduction of English as the emerging dominant vernacular. With its evocation of traditional characters such as the red-coated soldier (Lancey and Yolland), the shawled girl or Cathleen Ni Houlihan figure (Sarah – a potentially dumb woman whom Manus is teaching to speak), the hedgeschoolmaster (Hugh) and traditional motifs such as eviction, potato blight and poteen, Friel's play evokes a nationally distinctive way of life that was about to disappear. Furthermore, in so far as the first act reveals a confrontation between an economically impoverished but educationally superior indigenous Irish-speaking culture and an imperial, but philistine, English military, the play seems to confirm nationalist anti-colonial views of nineteenth-century Irish history much more than it challenges them. Popular nationalist sentiment is appealed to, for example, when, in the middle of Lancey's patronising lecture on the purposes of the Ordnance Survey, the learned Jimmy Jack inquires politely, '*nonne Latine loquitor*', and Lancey replies promptly that he does not speak Irish[14]. The Baile Beag hedge school may be set in a context of a deteriorating economy (the opening stage directions describe the school as littered with 'broken and forgotten implements'[15]) and may face the Anglicizing effects of the Ordnance Survey and the new National School, but, at least in Act 1, these threats are countered by the wit and subversive ingenuity of the locals. The atmosphere at the beginning of the play is one of optimism and exuberance, of an Irish national culture surviving despite severe economic and political disadvantage.

The play's subsequent action alters this perspective considerably. The principal complication occurs when Yolland falls in love, first with the place and the Irish language, and then with Maire, a local woman betrothed to Manus. After their first and only meeting as lovers, Yolland mysteriously disappears, and while the audience does not find out what has happened to him, there are several hints that he has been abducted and probably killed by the invisible Donnelly twins as part of their ongoing guerrilla war against the British. In the final scene Lancey retaliates by threatening to destroy the entire area if Yolland is not found. The play ends therefore with a situation very similar to the conflict in Northern Ireland in the early 1980s: an escalating war between the British Army and the guerrilla tactics of republican paramilitaries dedicated to an anti-colonial war of resistance.

But *Translations* as a whole is suffused with a pervasive irony. Hugh's scorn for English is spoken in English, which the audience understands as Irish. Thus, while Hugh's teaching is based on the view that Gaelic culture and classical culture make 'a happier conjugation', his actual formulation of this view is an etymological pedagogy that demonstrates exactly the opposite: that it is English, not Irish, that has extensive roots in Greek and Latin. Even in terms of its own English-language theatrical medium, this is a play that celebrates, not the possibility of recovering the Irish language as a widely-spoken vernacular, but Ireland's skilful appropriation of English.

As the play proceeds, the audience's awareness of this irony becomes increasingly apparent. Repeatedly, Hugh warns Yolland that part of the attraction of the Irish language and its literature is that Irish has tendencies towards quixotic fantasy and self-deception. Hugh's point is that the attractive richness of Gaelic culture exists in direct correspondence to the material impoverishment from which it arises. Irish is 'a rich language' because it has functioned historically as a compensation for poverty: 'full of mythologies of fantasy and hope and self-deception – a syntax opulent with tomorrows. It is our response to mud cabins and a diet of potatoes; our only method of replying to … inevitabilities…'[16] That Hugh's caveats are delivered with much the same self-indulgent panache as his tossing back of Anna na mBreag's poteen is a further irony that the excited and semi-intoxicated Yolland is unable to detect. At the same time, however, the idea that retaining 'original' names is romantic folly and a form of self-deception is countered by the play's persistent suggestion that names also have an ontological importance that cannot be replaced.

The play's ambivalence towards naming and the Irish language is returned to in the final scene. Here, Hugh abandons completely his earlier exclusive commitment to Irish by lecturing Owen on the importance of accepting the new Anglicized place names and by volunteering to teach Maire English. Hugh draws an analogy between Owen's repudiation of the Name Book ('A mistake, my mistake—nothing to do with us'[17]) and Jimmy Jack's drunken fantasy about marrying Pallas Athene:

> Owen: I know where I live.
> Hugh: James thinks he knows too. I look at James and three thoughts occur to me: A – that it is not the literal past, the 'facts' of history, that shape us, but images of the past embodied in langue. James has ceased to make that discrimination.
> Owen: Don't lecture me, Father.
> Hugh: B – We must never cease renewing those images; because once we do we fossilise...[18]

The implication of Hugh's remarks is that Owen's apostatic commitment to the idea of an autonomous Irish-speaking culture and Jimmy Jack's pathetic fantasies about Athene stem from a similarly flawed perception: a failure to recognise a distinction between history as fact and history as narrative. For Hugh, Jimmy Jack shows this myopia in his belief that the gods and goddesses of classical mythology actually exist, and Owen shows it through his assumption that the Gaelic place names of the area represent a cultural permanence that must not be changed. Both positions, moreover, may be considered as attempts to resolve or to compensate for an impoverished and isolated condition that result, not in an improvement of that condition, but in the sure guarantee that it will continue. So long as Jimmy Jack chooses goddesses rather than real women, then the companionship that he is longing for will never be found. So long as Irish history is thought of in terms of a loss of an almost pre-colonial purity that may be recovered and so long as this purity is regarded as fact, then the present and future will be condemned to a series of violent repetitions. In this way, the conflict between the mysterious Donnelly twins and the British Army in Act 3 is presented by Doalty as an echo of earlier situations and is offered by the play as a whole as a prefigurement of the conflict in Northern Ireland in the early 1980s. The play's concluding emphasis, therefore, is on the dangers of republican militancy and the absolute priority of the (patriarchal) family unit. Crucial to this perspective is Hugh's description of setting out for the 1798 rebellion and then opting out of the uprising because of what he considers to be the more enduring reality of the family.

> Hugh: We were gods that morning, James; and I had recently married *my* goddess, Caitlin Dubh Nic Reactainn, may she rest in peace. And to leave her and my infant son in his cradle – that was hero

ic, too. By God, sir, we were magnificent. We marched as far as –
where was it? – Glenties! All of twenty-three miles in one day.
And it was there, in Phelan's pub, that we got homesick for
Athens, just like Ulysses. The *desiderium nostrorum* – the need for
our own. Our *pietas*, James, was for older, quieter things.[19]

Like Jimmy Jack's commitment to classical mythology, the militant heroics of
the 1798 rebellion, an event central to Irish republican mythology, are presented here as a substitution of abstractions and goddesses for the quotidian
actuality of the domestic.

Hugh's speeches in the final scene offer a radically different perspective,
therefore, on the version of nineteenth-century Irish history presented in Act 1.
That earlier, nationalistically attractive contrast between on the one hand a rich
indigenous culture and a deteriorating economy and, on the other, an imperialist
British military, now appears as a more complicated relation in which the richness
of Gaelic culture may be seen as contributing to economic decline. In the context
of this recognition, Hugh's proposal that the English language should be accepted appears as a sad but compelling alternative. Yet while an acceptance of the
English language is proposed by Hugh as a corrective to the celibate heroics of
Irish republicanism, there is also a definite impression that this change – Irish-
speaking Ireland's surrender to modernity – may also involve an unquantifiable
ontological loss. It is not enough for the English place names to be accepted,
Hugh lectures Owen, they must also be made 'our own ... our new home'. Friel
here defines Irish nationalism not in terms of militant anti-imperialism but, like
Hugh's unfinished syllogisms, as a modernising, and apparently open-ended project of cultural recovery. And in Hugh's final speech – his attempt to recall the
beginning of Virgil's *Aeneid* – whether or not Carthage/Ireland can be restored to
its former plenitude is a problem that is suspended, quite literally, in mid sentence. In short, *Translations* refutes the existence of a single nationalist narrative,
requires a rethinking of the 'facts' of history, and accepts – albeit lugubriously –
an equation between imperialism and modernity.

The suggestion at the end of *Translations* that both the violent resistance of
Doalty and the Donnelly twins and Owen's new-found determination to recover the Irish language are dangerous, mutually-reinforcing illusions may also be
read as an attack on the politics of contemporary Irish republicanism in the
late 1970s. In particular, *Translations* serves as a riposte to a Provisional Sinn
Féin campaign that stressed the separatist potential of the Irish language and
emphasised the colonial origins of the Irish conflict. As a perusal of the Sinn
Féin weekly *An Phoblacht/Republican News* from 1978 to 1980 demonstrates, the
colonial context of the conflict and the fundamental untranslatability of the
Irish language were increasingly important lines of argument. Disparagement
of the Irish language by the British and Irish political establishments is one of
'the more obvious signs that this country is a colony' argues one article,[20] while
a later editorial describes the separatist political potential of the Irish language

as a 'separatism that is built into it, as it is in every language'.[21] Within this context, Friel's suggestion that the differences between languages are a matter of ontological rather than semantic importance bears a distinct political colour. Rejecting the anti-colonial vocabulary of *An Phoblacht*, *Translations* underlines the need for a *via media* of political accommodation based on an acceptance of inherited political and cultural realities. To this extent, *Translations* looks forward to the Anglo-Irish Agreement of 1985 which laid considerable emphasis on nationalists' right to cultural expression in return for their acceptance of the integrity of Northern Ireland as a political unit.

CONCLUSION

This brief consideration of the inaugural productions of the Irish Literary Theatre and of Brian Friel's *Translations* underline the need for a fundamental reconsideration of the ways in which theatre and colonialism in Ireland have, traditionally, been considered. Whereas, for example, the Irish Literary Theatre is sometimes viewed as a watershed moment in so far as it is seen as inaugurating an authentically Irish theatre (in contrast to a previous British-dominated theatre), the narrative content of *The Heather Field* and *The Countess Cathleen* suggests far more of a continuity with Ireland's *ancien régime* than a disruption. Indeed, the political preoccupations of Ireland's ascendancy are represented to such an extent in *The Heather Field* that the play's ascendancy protagonist is presented sympathetically as a quixotic moderniser. But it is in the case of *The Countess Cathleen* that the contradictions of the Irish Literary Theatre as a nationalist anti-colonial force (the equivalent, in theatrical terms, of Douglas Hyde's 1892 essay 'De-Anglicization of Ireland') are best demonstrated. Not only does this play invert popular anti-colonial sentiment in relation to the Famine of the 1840s, but in its depiction of an idolatrous Roman Catholic peasantry, *The Countess Cathleen* was viewed by some as contributing to a contemporary anti-nationalist sentiment. In similar fashion, understanding Brian Friel's *Translations* within the context of contemporary Northern Ireland politics in the early 1980s – and especially in the context of the cultural politics of Irish republicanism – suggests that heralding Friel's play as 'postcolonial' is as 'prematurely celebratory' as it is to describe Northern Ireland itself as post-colonial.[22]

NOTES

1. This essay can be found in a more extended version in chapters 1 and 8 of my *Theatre and the State in 20th Century Ireland: Cultivating the People* (London and New York: Routledge, 2001).
2. See, for example, B. Friel's 'Plays Peasant and Unpeasant', *Times Literary Supplement*, 17 March 1972, pp. 305–6
3. 'To the Guarantors for a "Celtic" Theatre', W. Gould, J. Kelly and D. Toomey (eds), *The Collected Letters of W.B. Yeats: Volume Two 1896–1900* (Oxford: Clarendon Press, 1997), pp. 123–5.

4. See K. Vandevelde, 'Outside the Abbey: The Irish National Theatres, 1897–1913', unpublished Ph.D. dissertation (National University of Ireland, Galway, 2001), p. 34.
5. G. Moore and E. Martyn, *Selected Plays of George Moore and Edward Martyn*, chosen, with an introduction by D.B. Eakin and M. Case (Gerrards Cross, Bucks: Colin Smythe, 1995), p. 221.
6. See A. Gailey, *Ireland and the Death of Kindness: the Experience of Constructive Unionism 1890–1905* (Cork: Cork University Press, 1987).
7. See R. Hogan and J. Kilroy, *The Irish Literary Theatre 1899–1901* (Dublin: Dolmen Press, 1975).
8. See *Irish Times*, 10 May 1899, p.5.
9. See M. Howes, *Yeats's Nations: Gender, Class and Irishness* (Cambridge: Cambridge University Press, 1996), p. 45.
10. Ibid., p. 47.
11. Quoted in *The Freeman's Journal*, 10 May 1899, p. 6.
12. F .H. O'Donnell, *Souls for Gold!: Pseudo-Celtic Drama in Dublin* (London: Nassau Press, 1899), p. 9.
13. W. Barrett, 'Irish Drama?', *New Ireland Review*, 3 (March–Aug. 1895), p. 40.
14. B. Friel, *Translations* (London: Faber and Faber, 1981), p. 30.
15. Ibid., p. 11.
16. Ibid, p. 42.
17. Ibid, p. 66.
18. Ibid.
19. Ibid.
20. See *An Phoblacht/Republican News*, 14 Oct. 1978, p. 7.
21. See *An Phoblacht/Republican News*, 6 Jan. 1979, p. 2.
22. See A. McClintock, 'The Angel of Progress', in P. Williams and L. Chrisman (eds), *Colonial Discourse and Post-Colonial Theory: A Reader* (Harvester: Hemel Hempstead, 1993), p. 294.

CHAPTER SEVENTEEN

The Bog as Colonial Topography in Nineteenth-Century Irish Writing

CATHERINE WYNNE

In John McGahern's *That They May Face the Rising Sun* (2002) a character recalls a childhood memory of a local skirmish from the Irish War of Independence. Jamsie was planting potatoes with his father when an IRA division was ambushed by Black and Tans.[1] The targets fled to the nearby bog but were followed and retrieved by bloodhounds. One was shot dead and the others were arrested. Meanwhile, Jamsie was warned by his father 'not to be looking and to go on dropping the splits as if nothing had happened'.[2] Such activity, Jamsie explains to his audience, operated as a safeguard: 'If we ran or hid they might think we were spies.'[3] Later that evening Jamsie and his brother ventured down to the bog where they heard a tentative cry. One of the IRA men had escaped the bloodhounds by hiding in the river. He was rescued by the boys' father and temporarily hidden in the family loft. However, someone 'had to be made to pay' and shortly afterwards a neighbouring Protestant farmer was shot dead in his byre – shot because he 'was a Protestant and the nearest to hand'.[4] Jamsie's retelling of the story sixty years later demonstrates how the complex socio-political landscape of the Irish War of Independence reverberates in the novel's present moment. The inscribed memory of violence, sectarianism and social unease is a topographical impression: 'I often see myself and my father,' Jamsie concludes, 'planting potatoes on the hill and that line of young men coming up through the bog and think of the changes a short hour can bring.'[5]

What is interesting, in this context, is the manner in which topography and more specifically the bog intersects with socio-political turmoil. In this regard, McGahern's narrative has its counterparts in nineteenth-century Irish fiction and social documentation. In *Realities of Irish Life* (1868), W. Steuart Trench documents a fascinating historical anecdote in which members of the agrarian secret society, the Ribbonmen, raided the house of a Mr Hall in County Tipperary in 1840. After escaping from the house the robbers took refuge in the nearby bog and were only later apprehended when the police investigated suspects' houses and 'in one of them several men with blackened faces and stained with bog-mould were found concealed'[6]. After the prosecution and transportation of these particular Ribbonmen, vengeance was visited on Hall, who was murdered in a field full of people planting their potatoes. Yet when Trench proposed to instigate a search for the assassin in the surrounding area, a colleague cautioned him: 'the murderer never ran; that would at once betray him. He is surely in the field with us at this moment, and is probably one of those now looking at the body and expressing his wonder at who did it.'[7] Trench, as land agent, is divorced from a landscape that he ostensibly manages and is 'compelled to repress [his] feelings and remain an inactive spectator'.[8] The assassin had blended into the surrounding topography and into a body of workers who, like Jamsie's father in the McGahern narrative, reject or conceal knowledge of the event.

Trench's account illustrates the nature of social dis-ease in nineteenth-century Ireland, while McGahern's fictional memory recalls violent political transition. In both narratives, the contest is inscribed in a shifting and ambiguous topography – the bog. Indeed, the bog's initial serving and later undermining of the both the IRA and the Ribbonmen aligns it with this chapter's concerns. The equivocal nature of sodden grounds is a trope which is constantly turned anew in Irish fiction. It is through an examination of the bog motif in literature that the complex, variable and unstable dynamics of colonial Ireland are understood. Here the bog mirrors shifting allegiances and convoluted negotiations. The Irish-born Patrick Brontë conjoins the aesthetic and the topographical in *The Maid of Killarney* (1818) when Captain Loughlean remarks to Albion that the 'generality of Novels are what you Englishmen say of us Irishmen, when you liken us to our own bogs – green, smooth, and tempting, on the surface, but concealing underneath the miry slough, or deadly pool'.[9] Moreover, the Irish novel is replete with bogs, a feature that reflects the complex colonial engagement as superficial relations give way under the strain of repressed political desires and violent social unrest.

The colonial condition of nineteenth-century Ireland is evidenced in the anomalous and unstable depiction of bog and moor. These mutable topographies chart the social, political and agrarian strife of colonial Ireland. A treacherous site of instability, the bog unleashes dark and recidivist forces. As a quagmire of conflicts, it is simultaneously a locus of profit and progress and a point of degeneration and death. In Bram Stoker's *The Snake's Pass* (1890), a text that prefigures the sectarian tensions of McGahern's narrative, the bog is implicated in the politics and psychology surrounding land possession in a colonial context. Here the Catholic gombeenman, Black Murdock, desiring the bogland of his Protestant neighbour, Phelim Joyce, declares: 'I want yer land – I have waited for it, an' I mane to have it.'[10] In *Parnell and His Island* (1887), George Moore narrates his journey through an inhospitable bogland to his County Mayo estate. As an absentee landlord resident in Paris, Moore is both a part of and divorced from the barren landscape that he traverses.[11] Nor does the theme halt there – it re-emerges in the oeuvre of a diasporic writer, Arthur Conan Doyle. In 'The Heiress of Glenmahowley' (1884), the bog is the site of violent agrarian encounter. Given the author's Irish lineage and the narrative's subtle colonial inflections, we can also read *The Hound of the Baskervilles* (1901) in this context, especially given the narrative's preoccupation with land ownership and control.[12] At once mutable and petrifying, shifting landscapes focus and intensify colonial relations. Sodden grounds sustain a primeval past, operate as sites of agrarian and political strife, and seem to promise or, in some cases, threaten a future beyond colonial constraint.

The narrative preoccupation in *The Snake's Pass* centres on the bog. Here the bog's anomaly, its refusal to be fixed in meaning, is evidenced in the diverse accounts of the legends which surround it. These legends provide alternatively pagan and political narratives which are either prehistoric or which record attempts to restore a national history. Fr Peter articulates the legends' antecedents:

> It's a queer thing that men must be always putting abstract ideas into concrete shape. No doubt there have been some strange matters regarding this mountain that they've been talkin about – the Shifting Bog, for instance; and as the people could not account for it in any way that they can understand, they knocked up a legend about it. Indeed, to be just to them, the legend is a very old one, and is mentioned in a manuscript of the twelfth century. But somehow it was lost sight of till about a hundred years ago, when the loss of the treasure-chest from the French invasion at Killala set all the imaginations of the people at work, from Donegal to Cork, and they fixed the Hill of the Lost Gold as the spot where the money was to be found.[13]

The priest further rationalises that the superstitions arose due to the different names given to the hill:

> That most commonly given is Knockcalltecrore, which is a corruption of the Irish phrase Knock-na-callte-cróin-óir, meaning, 'The Hill of the Lost Golden Crown;' but it has been sometimes called Knockcalltore – short for the Irish words Knock-na-callte-óir, or 'The Hill of the Lost Gold.' It is said that in some old past time it was called Knocknanaher, or The Hill of the Snake;' and, indeed, there's one place on it they call Shleenanaher, meaning the 'Snake's Pass.'[14]

This multiplicity of narratives due to the nature of translation only adds to the mystique of the hill. If naming denotes control, then multiplicitous naming signifies not only an absence of control but mirrors the persistent instability of the hill which has, due to the nature of its peaty soil, visibly grown and visibly shifted its location and meaning through time.

According to one local legend, the King of the Snakes once resided on the hill. Of supernatural proportions and brandishing a golden crown, the snake demanded the human sacrifice of a baby once a year. In a gothic fate reminiscent of that of the peasant mother in *Dracula* (1897), who comes to the castle to plead with the vampire to return her baby, the snake legend similarly recounts the tale of a mother whose search for her missing infant results in madness when she encounters the King of the Snakes: 'but what she seen, none could tell, for, whin they found her she was a ravin' lunatic, wid white hair an' eyes like a corpse – an' the mornin' afther they found her dead in her bed wid a black mark round her neck as if she had been choked, an' the mark was in the shape iv a shnake'.[15] The narrative discloses colonial exploitation and aggression while the woman's muting and subsequent strangulation testify to the dangers of seeing in a landscape that often impresses a perilous or fatal knowledge.

However, the legends propagated by the shifting bog deny fixity: there is no single definitive legend. Although the tale may conclude with the King of the Snakes banished by St Patrick into the sea, the snake departs with a threat: 'An' till ye git me crown I'm king here still, though ye banish me. An' mayhap, I'll come in some forrum what ye don't suspect, for I must watch me crown. An' now I go away – iv me own accorrd.'[16] The storyteller further relates that 'they do say that the shiftin' bog wor the forrum he tuk'.[17] But the glint of amusement in the storyteller's eye betrays his ambiguity in relation to the legend he relates. The nature of belief is debated on theological grounds. When one of the company states his disbelief in the snake legend, another retorts: 'Musha! how could Misther McGlown believe anythin', an' him a Protestan'.'[18] McGlown refuses to believe this legend concerning the bog but he adheres to a different one. This legend entails the French landing at Killala in 1798.[19] According to popular lore, two French soldiers burdened with a trunk of treasure were sucked into the bog. One of the old men present gives credence to this legend by stating that his father watched the French soldiers crossing the bog before losing sight of them in the darkness. The story is sufficient to convince the gombeenman, Black Murdock, who is listening at the window. He subsequently employs an Irish, but English-educated, engineer, Dick Sutherland, to help him find the bog's buried treasure.

Stoker's topographical knowledge of Ireland from the mid-1870s was extensive. As Inspector of Petty Sessions, he travelled with the magistrate's court to country areas and legal processes impressed on him the social dynamics of colonial Ireland. 'He experienced rural Ireland', Barbara Belford notes, 'and witnessed how farmers in the countryside suffered under the English landlord system. He watched hearings that ranged from stealing, unpaid rents, and the avoidance of taxes to dog attacks on cattle.'[20] For Stoker, social experience converged with the cultural knowledge that he attained from the folkloric narratives collected by the Wildes. In particular, Lady Wilde records an account of St Patrick and the snake in *Ancient Legends, Mystic Charms, and Superstitions of Ireland* (1887):

> There is a lake in one of the Galtee mountains where there is a great ser-
> pent chained to a rock, and he may be heard constantly crying out, "O
> Patrick, is the *Luan*, or Monday, long from us?" For when St. Patrick cast
> this serpent in the lake he bade him be chained to the rock till *La-an-
> Luan* (The Day of Judgement). But the serpent mistook the word, and
> thought the saint meant *Luan*, Monday.
>
>   So he still expects to be freed from one Monday to another, and the
> clanking of his chains on the day is awful to hear as he strives to break
> them and get free.[21]

The bleak and threatening socio-political landscape of nineteenth-century
Ireland is fuelled by a rich folkloric tradition. This is transposed into a precarious fictional topography in *The Snake's Pass* in which the bog is implicated in
complex social, economic and sexual negotiations.

   Not surprisingly then, the duplicitous nature of the bog's surface deceives
anything which crosses its path into a false sense of security. It absorbs secrets
and propagates legends but it also threatens to regurgitate all it absorbs. The
fertile surface of the mire often hides its fatal power. Sutherland describes to
Art Severn, the English narrator of *The Snake's Pass*, the grim and treacherous
nature of the bog:

> 'Is it a quagmire, then? or like a quicksand?'
>   'Like either, or both. Nay! it is more treacherous than either. You may
> call it, if you are poetically inclined, a "carpet of death!" What you see is
> simply a film or skin of vegetation of a very low kind, mixed with the
> mould of decayed vegetable fibre and grit and rubbish of all kinds which
> have somehow got mixed into it, floating on a sea of ooze and slime – of
> something half liquid half solid, and of an unknown depth. It will bear
> up a certain weight, for there is a degree of cohesion in it; but it is not
> all of equal cohesive power, and if one were to step on the wrong spot' –
> He was silent.
>   'What then?'
>   'Only a matter of specific gravity! A body suddenly immersed would,
> when the air of the lungs had escaped and the *rigor mortis* had set in,
> probably sink a considerable distance; then it would rise after nine days,
> when decomposition began to generate gases, and make an effort to
> reach the top. Not succeeding in this, it would ultimately waste away,
> and the bones would become incorporated with the existing vegetation
> somewhere about the roots, or would lie among the slime at the bot-
> tom.'[22]

Equally, bog and moor evince a dangerously mesmeric attraction. The fictional peasants of *The Snake's Pass* believe that the hill has a hold over Black
Murdock. Despite his wealth, he refuses to leave the desolate area: 'It can

hould tight enough! There may be raysons that a man gives – sometimes wan thing, an' sometimes another; but the Hill houlds – an' houlds tight all the same!'[23] Even outsiders are sucked into its power. Art speaks of the 'invisible charm with which Shleenanaher had latterly seemed to hold' on him.[24] He is plagued by nightmares in which the gombeenman features as the personifica-tion of the snake. Murdock conceives the power of such synonymity while inadvertently articulating the shifting paradigms of colonial dynamics: 'If I am the shnake on the hill – thin beware the shnake.'[25]

A sense of unease and entrapment in sodden ground haunts the characters. Sutherland is plagued by the memory of seeing Murdock attempt to silence Bat Moynahan – who helped him pinpoint the location of the French treasure – by guiding him towards the bog-hole: 'it's a terrible thing to remember! That attempt to murder in the dark and the storm comes between me and sleep!'[26] Art's dream of Murdock incarcerated in a boggy grave is equally prophetic. Indeed, he comes close to sharing Murdock's fate when he slips into the bog. The experience is terrifying: 'No language could describe the awful sensation of that melting away of the solid earth – the most dreadful nightmare would be almost a pleasant memory compared with it.'[27] In similarly vivid terms, Watson describes the 'tenacious grip' of the Grimpen Mire in *The Hound of the Baskervilles*: '[It] plucked at our heels as we walked, and when we sank into it it was as if some malignant hand was tugging us down into those obscene depths, so grim and purposeful was the clutch in which it held us.'[28]

The threat of what lies under the surface of the hill in Stoker's novel invades the unconscious. Such dreams so affect Art's psychological welfare that his inability to sleep causes him to take walks at night. But these strolls are mistaken for 'moonlighting' and consequently he is interrogated by a policeman, who was, we are pointedly told, born in Ulster.[29] Interestingly, this is the novel's only direct allusion to contemporary political violence. The policeman questions Art's activities at night as the novel broaches agrarian unrest, not explicitly but through allegory and legend. Agrarian agitation co-exists in a nebulous manner on this uncontrolled landscape, a point that recalls the historical Ribbon/Hall engagement.

Agrarian conflict, coupled with social unease, is earlier tackled in Anthony Trollope's *The Macdermots of Ballycloran* (1847). Thady Macdermot, a young Leitrim squire, attacks and inadvertently kills his sister's lover. Fleeing the law, he seeks help from a tenant whose cabin stands 'on the edge of a bog'.[30] Corney Dolan, who is a member of a local secret society, agrees to assist Thady's escape to the mountain over Lough Allen if he swears to 'join their society in every respect, whatever might be its laws, and that if they would assist him in his present condition by affording him whatever security might be in their power, he would faithfully conform to all their rules and regula-tions'.[31] In this cabin on the bog, Thady transgresses societal laws and religious dictates. Aughacashel, the mountain over Lough Allen, is infested with the agrarian secret society, the Whiteboys. The place is defined as existing outside the law; rents are rarely paid, potheen stills are in operation, and the boggish landscape is inimical to the forces of order. The area belongs to the society – it is 'their own country'.[32] Isolated by and at odds with this 'horrid mountain', Thady returns to Ballycloran to be tried and executed for murder.[33] Trapped between a decaying landlordism and violent agrarian dispute, he seeks recourse in oblivion. Trollope's Leitrim squire is lost in a landscape where an unstable bog simultaneously mirrors the social and political strife of nineteenth-century Ireland.

Just as Feemy Macdermot is the primary agent of her brother's demise, a potent female sexuality also emerges in later fictions. In *The Hound of the Baskervilles*, Sir Henry is drawn to the moor in pursuit of Beryl Stapleton and ultimately encounters the demon hound. When Art first meets Norah he cannot see her through the darkness of the night. She remains a disembodied voice, and one which compels his return to the area. Later, he meets her on Knocknacar, a site of immense natural beauty and unstable bog. Art's first guiltily voyeuristic glimpse of her is prefaced by the sound of her voice singing the *Ave Maria*. This hymn is significant in a landscape that harbours a pagan residuum as the contest of competing beliefs is inscribed in a topography that is also synonymous with the female. 'As Christians spread through Western Europe', notes Peter Cherici, 'they had difficulty eradicating secret devotion to the female fertility principle personified as a goddess with various names. The quasi-deification of Mary provided a partial solution to the problem, allowing pagans to transfer their veneration of a local goddess to a Christian demi-goddess.'[34] Mary is a contained and constructed female symbol. Indeed, Cherici continues:

> [M]any of the later medieval statues of Mary showed her crushing a snake beneath her foot. In Christian and Hebrew myth, the serpent was a representation of the male devil who tempted Eve in the Garden of Eden. But the pagan meaning of the snake symbol was neither male nor evil. It was an aspect of the Mother Goddess, a beast who exemplified rebirth when it shed its old skin during the growth process. By stepping on the snake, Mary demonstrated her victory over the competing female principles found in pagan beliefs.[35]

Equally, St Patrick's introduction of a Christian patriarchy is symbolised in his banishment of snakes. Befitting the context of nineteenth-century Ireland, the snake's pagan associations with land and fertility, are transmuted to operate as an allegory of voracious landlordism. At the same time, the snake legend in *The Snake's Pass* resists the Christianising process and contemporaneous sectarian division – a point that is rendered explicit when the bog-slide reveals a cave with a Celtic crown.

Norah Joyce, then, is an ambiguous figure. Despite the seeming piety of her hymn, the prudishly repressed Art is shocked by her posture which belies the hymn's sanctity and flouts the dictates of social convention: 'Her knees were raised to the level of her shoulders, and her outstretched arms confined her legs below the knees – she was, in fact, in much the same attitude as boys are at games of cock-fighting ... no self-respecting woman ever sits in such a manner when a man is by.'[36] At the novel's end, Norah's possession of the Celtic crown symbolises her convergence with the goddess of the land. Art must gain control of both female and bog. However, Norah's peasant attributes must first undergo transformation at Continental and English finishing schools before she is fit to become Art's wife. Her containment ensures that she becomes an (Art)ifact. Contrary to this, Sir Henry is not fated to marry Beryl Stapleton. In fact, the closing scenes of the adventure witness him being chased by Stapleton's hound in an eerie re-enactment of the fate of his ancestor, Sir Hugo. The hound's destruction by Holmes marks a new era for this Baskerville as the sexual danger of the landscape is contained. At the same time Sir Henry's unwed state at the novel's close may also indicate a future without an heir.

The Snake's Pass is preoccupied with incarceration, and land, soil and hidden monstrosities equally permeate Stoker's ensuing fiction from the vaults of Dracula's castle, the burial crypts of *The Lady of the Shroud* (1909), to the womb-like orifice of *The Lair of the White Worm* (1911).[37] In *The Lair of the White Worm*, written when Stoker was close to dying, many of the motifs and interests of his various fictions converge in a lurid study of the supernatural in a primitive landscape. Lady Arabella March is a depleted landowner who, in her metamorphic serpentine state, incarcerates herself in mud-holes beneath the surface of the earth. Ultimately, this creature of the mud must be destroyed. Like Dracula, she is trapped in her lair and eradicated. Contrary to the Count though, Arabella is not vampiric, her gynarchic power resides in her vaginal well-hole. The novel returns to the ambivalent nature of marshy grounds and, similar to *The Snake's Pass* and Doyle's *The Hound of the Baskervilles*, the necessity to investigate legend and to instigate progress in order to come to terms with the past and to negotiate a liberated future.

The thrust of these fictions, then, is to destroy creatures preserved or indeed incarcerated, in actuality or in legend, in these landscapes: Holmes eradicates the supposed Baskerville hound and disarms the legend's threat for future generations. The absentee Baskervilles can return with impunity to their hereditary domains and instigate technological reforms. Sutherland unmasks the bog to reveal its pecuniary and geologic treasures. It is not surprising then, that it is Adam Salton – his name an obvious play on the first man and salt of the earth – who reinstates order and control of the landscape in *The Lair of the White Worm*. These three novels articulate a form of post-colonial narrative as degenerate and absentee landlordism and its gombeen offspring are eradicated just as the incarceratory potential of these sites is defused.

Moore's *Parnell and His Island* is equally taken with the thematics of topography, leaving this text, for all its naturalist intentions, infused with gothic imagery of incarceration and constraint. This is rendered explicit when locals escort Moore to the grave of his ancestor: 'After two hundred years the grave has been violated by the peasants for the leaden coffin, and the bones of him who created all that has been wasted – by one generation in terraces, by another in race-horses, and by another in dissipation in Paris, lie scattered about the ground trodden by chance of the passing feet of the peasant.'[38] He condemns the dissolution of his own class that 'allows the peasant to keep [it] in ease and luxury.'[39] At the same time, Moore envisages the inhabitants of Connaught entrapped in cyclical decline: 'The Western Celt is a creature quick to dream, and powerless to execute; in external aspects and in moral history the same tale is told – great things attempted, nothing done; and the physiology and psychology of his country is read in the unfinished pile.'[40] Moore equates the Mayo peasantry with this particular landscape: 'The Irish race is one that has been forgotten and left behind in a bog hole; it smells of the wet earth, its face seems as if made of it, and its ideas are moist and dull, and as sterile as peat.'[41]

Indeed, the centrality of topography in character formation emerged as a quasi-science in the late nineteenth century – a by-product of an imperial ideology that distinguished the Irish at their best as incapable of self-rule and at their worst as simian and rebellious.[42] Yet, contrary to Moore's interpretation, Joseph Simms propounds: 'The hilly counties and highlands of Connemara produce tall, handsome, keen, active, persevering, intelligent men and beautiful women; while the ungainly baboon-faced, pot-bellied rapparees are the natural offspring of the great central plain and interminable bog-land that occupies such a vast proportion of the country.'[43] Not to be outdone in the topographical analysis of genius, Doyle's equally dubious study, 'The Geographical Distribution of British Intellect' (1888), identifies that the 'mental nadir is to be found in the western province of Ireland'.[44] Ostensibly a study of intelligence, this article is primarily a vindication of empire as Doyle establishes that '[m]any races have helped in the making of Great Britain' and that some of the greatest men of intellect emerged from Edinburgh and Dublin.[45] Not surprisingly, Doyle's lineage comes from both locations and the article is testimony to his attempt to harmonise an Irish familial inheritance into a heterogeneous imperial identity.[46]

At the same time, the bog is implicated in economic and political progress. Its significance in Ireland's political future is articulated in *The Snake's Pass*. Jerry Scanlan, in the midst of relating how the King of the Snakes stole a human baby from the neighbourhood every year, is interrupted by one of his listeners:

> 'But did none of the min do nothin'?' said a powerful-looking young fellow in the orange and green jersey of the Gaelic Athletic Club, with his eyes flashing; and he clenched his teeth.
> 'Musha! how could they? Sure, no man ever seen the King iv the Shnakes!'
> 'Thin how did they know about him?' he queried doubtfully.

'Sure, wasn't one of their childher tuk away iv'ry year? But, anyhow, it's all over now! an' so it was that none iv the min iver wint.'[47]

The passage is interesting in several respects. The young man seeks to move away from the confinement and limitation of superstition to pursue an alternative and more liberating ideology. The colours of the jersey (orange and green) are clearly emblematic of the youth's separatist ideals. The piece demonstrates the burgeoning political consciousness among the younger peasant class, a consciousness fuelled in this instance by the nationalistic Gaelic Athletic Association, which was set up in 1884.[48] Significantly, it marks the polarity between a younger, politically aware generation, who are less tolerant of abuse, and an older generation, typified by the storyteller, who fail to question such violation of their class. The snake, on a political level, symbolises an outmoded and frequently corrupt landlord class, with the gombeenman representing another outgrowth of this system. Art, as an Englishman unfamiliar with the complexities of Irish society, seeks an explanation of the term 'gombeen'. Worse than a landgrabber, the gombeen is defined as:

'[A] man that linds you a few shillin's or a few pounds whin ye want it bad, and then niver laves ye till he has tuk all ye've got – yer land an' yer shanty an' yer holdin' an' yer money an' yer craps; an he would take the blood out of yer body if he could sell it or use it anyhow!'
'Oh, I see, a sort of usurer.'
'Ushurer? aye that's it; but a ushurer lives in the city an' has laws to hould him in. But the gombeen has nayther law nor the fear iv law. He's like wan that the Scriptures says 'grinds the faces iv the poor.' Begor! It's him that'd do little for God's sake if the divil was dead!'[49]

Equally, in the dark and violent *Naboth's Vineyard* (1891) set in Ireland's southwestern bog-lands, E. Œ. Somerville and Martin Ross portray a corrupt gombeenman, John Donovan. Donovan abuses his position as local President of the Land League by falsely boycotting and instigating agrarian crimes against the Widow Leonard whose land he covets. The peasants in *The Snake's Pass* see Murdock as operating beyond the jurisdiction of the law; in *Naboth's Vineyard* Donovan is, in effect, the law.

The battle for the control of land in *The Snake's Pass* is reflected in the snake legend but at the same time the anomalous bog defies ownership or processes of law-making and thus mirrors the mythic King of the Snake's defiance of St Patrick. He declares his sovereignty in the region and subverts the power of the saint. In a legalistic debate over land possession the snake ultimately undermines the saint's decrees:

'I didn't obey,' sez he, because I thraverse the jurisdiction.'
'How do ye mane?' asks St. Pathrick.

'Because,' sez he, 'this is my own houldin',' sez he, 'be perscriptive right,' sez he. 'I'm the whole governmint here, and I put a nexeat on meself not to lave widout me own permission,' and he ducks down agin into the pond.[50]

It is hardly surprising that the novel is preoccupied with land ownership at a time when the land acts were negotiating the transfer of possession from landlord to tenant.[51] In fact, Art buys the gombeen's land prior to the latter's decease with the intention of transferring the deeds to Sutherland. The engineer has a strong nationalistic consciousness – one that he shares with Phelim Joyce. He is simultaneously aware of the implications of land possession. When the bog renders forth the French treasure, the skeleton hands of the French soldiers are still clinging to their charge. Sutherland poignantly comments on the revelation while shrewdly observing its significance:

> 'See how the bog can preserve! ... France should be proud of such sons! It would make a noble coat of arms, this treasure chest sent by freemen to aid other – sand with two such supporters!'
> We looked at the chest and the skeletons for a while, and then Dick said: –
> 'Joyce, this is on your land – for it is yours till to-morrow – and you may as well keep it – possession is nine points of the law – and if we take the gold out, the government can only try to claim it. But if they take it, we may ask in vain!' Joyce answered:
> 'Take it I will, an' gladly; but not for meself. The money was sent for Ireland's good to help them that wanted help, an' plase God! I'll see it does'nt go asthray now!'[52]

But the bog unveils other treasures: the Celtic crown of the mythic King of the Snakes and limestone. Hence, the sodden ground preserves a pre-colonial past, reveres a liberationist enterprise and hails an autonomous future. Sutherland initiates improvements which will greatly benefit the prosperity of the area: 'With limestone we could reclaim the bogs cheaply all over the neighbourhood – in fact a limekiln there would be worth a small fortune. We could build walls in the right places; I can see how a lovely little harbour could be made there at a small expense.'[53]

Indeed, the reclamation of Irish bogs was not a new idea. Stoker may have been inspired by the specific commissions which had been established and various schemes which had been set in place from the early nineteenth century which were designed to reclaim these grounds in order to facilitate the alleviation of poverty and to improve agriculture.[54] However, Sutherland's schemes evince a distinctly political thrust. He sees the Irish bogs as sources of potential affluence which could pave the way for economic and, subsequently, political freedom. In a discussion with Art he notes:

> You will hardly believe that although the subject is one of vital interest
> to thousands of persons in our own country – one in which national pros-
> perity is mixed up to a large extent – one which touches deeply the hap-
> piness and material prosperity of a large section of Irish people, and so
> helps to mould their political action, there are hardly any works on the
> subject in existence.[55]

David Glover argues that Sutherland's belief in the Irish bog as a material
resource and as a political motivator is an allusion 'to an influential tradition of
economic analysis best exemplified by Sir Robert Kane's *The Industrial Resources
of Ireland* (1844) "in which the utilisation of peat-bogs, the harnessing of the
rivers and the tides and the exploitation of mineral resources was advocated"
as the basis for national autarky'.[56] This is further affirmed by an article Stoker
published in *The World's Work* in 1907, where he postulates: 'Ireland has certain natural advantages which have largely yet to be exploited. In agriculture,
all growths can flourish which depend on soft air, moisture, and deep soil. The
surrounding seas abound with fish of every kind. The mineral possibilities are
as yet but little known; but there are vast areas of fuel-bog, sufficient alone for
national wealth.'[57] Hence, seventeen years after the publication of *The Snake's
Pass*, Stoker returns to propound his belief in Ireland's natural resources.

   Mindful of these details in the novel, it is worth noting Stoker's discussions
with Gladstone on Irish affairs. The author, in his biography of the actor Henry
Irving, describes one particular visit by the Prime Minister to the Lyceum theatre on 2 December 1890, shortly after Parnell's famous attack on Gladstone
in his manifesto.[58] Stoker had sent Gladstone a copy of *The Snake's Pass* and on
18 November had received a postcard thanking him for the book: 'I hope',
Gladstone wrote, 'to have perused all your pages before we meet again.'[59]
Stoker reveals that they discussed it at length before the performance on 2
December: 'Possibly it was that as Mr. Gladstone was then full of Irish matters
my book, being of Ireland and dealing with Irish ways and specially of a case of
oppression by a "gombeen" man under a loan secured on land, interested him
for he had evidently read it carefully. As we walked across the stage he spoke
to me of it very kindly and very searchingly.'[60] The bog-slide in *The Snake's Pass*
unveils possibilities for a prosperous future, but the historical environment
into which the novel emerged charts an adverse slippage, the sliding away of
Home Rule:

> Now it must be remembered that, in the interval between his getting
> the book and when we met, had occurred one of the greatest troubles
> and trials of [Gladstone's] whole political life. The hopes which he had
> built up through the slow progress of years for the happy settlement of
> centuries-old Irish troubles had been suddenly almost shattered by a
> bolt from the blue, and his great intellect and enormous powers of work
> and concentration had been for many days strained to the utmost to

keep the road of the future clear from the possibility of permanent destruction following on temporary embarrassment. And yet in the midst of all he found time to read – and remember, even to details and names – the work of an unimportant friend.[61]

When Dan McGlown asserts his disbelief in the snake legend and adheres to the alternative legend of the French soldiers, he is opting for an allegory hailing political freedom as opposed to one reifying oppression. In this sense, he mirrors Stoker himself, who supported Home Rule for Ireland. *The Snake's Pass*, then, represents the Parnellian dream of Home Rule at its apex, just as Stoker's dream of harmony between Ireland and England is represented in the marital union of Norah and Art. The celebration of a nationalist ethos is coupled with a desire to return to a pre-sectarian past, free of the nightmare of present politics. This novel, Stoker's first and only novel with an Irish setting, is advocating a change in land ownership, a development of natural resources and, ultimately, political freedom. Ireland disappeared as a literary topos for Stoker's future fictions, but the ambiguous and mutable nature of the bog would certainly resurface in the shifting and potent form of the vampire.

Stoker's contemporary, Doyle, defined himself in a letter to *The Irish Times* in October 1903 as 'a man of Irish blood living outside Ireland'.[62] As a descendent of dispossessed Irish Catholic landlords, Doyle's inheritance is both synonymous with and separate from the fictional topography of 'The Heiress of Glenmahowley'. The story is set in Connaught in 'an enormous area of peat cuttings and bogland'.[63] It charts the adventures of two middle-class English tourists, John Vereker and Bob Elliott, who have reluctantly inherited property in the west of Ireland during the Land War. As the attractions of their possessions pall, Vereker and Elliot embark on a new escapade. Tricked by O'Keefe, the landlord of the local hostelry, 'The Shamrock Arms', they traverse the fortified Clairmont estate, as each tries to win the hand of its reputed heiress. Miss Clairmont is, however, neither single nor rich – the estate is in debt and is soon to be deserted by the family. Similar to Moore's depiction of his Mayo estate, the story represents landlordism in decline as this 'worn-out system, no longer possible in the nineteenth century' gives way under the pressures of social change.[64]

What is more interesting, however, is the manner in which the bog is central to the violent political dynamics that are played out in this region. Early in the narrative, O'Keefe establishes a nearby bog-hole as a local attraction:

> 'There's a hole in the bog,' he suggested with diffidence. 'The same where the boys threw Mr. Lyons of Glenmorris – bad scran to him – afther they shot him. May be you'd loike to see where they found him wid his head in the mud, an' his feet stickin'up. Ah, it was a glad soight, sorrs, for the pisantry that had worked and slaved – the craturs – and then for him to step in wid a dirty foive and twinty per cint reduction in

the rint, and serve notices on them as wouldn't pay. Sure you could take
your food – or a gossoon could carry it – and picnic by the hole.'[65]

His recital on the bog simultaneously fixes it as a place of agrarian conflict and
as a tourist site. Hence, social struggle is immediately localised while its meaning remains equivocal. Their topographical possessions leave the Englishmen
culturally excluded and O'Keefe slyly reminds them of their dangerous inheritance: 'Ah sure you can't judge of the country now while its quoiet,' said our
host. 'Wait till the throubles come round agin – next year maybe, or the year
afther. It's a loively land when the bhoys is out sorra a taste of scenery would
you think about; and bein' landlords yourselves by that toime, you'd see the
cream of the divarsion.'[66] Tourism is a dangerous activity in such an unstable
locale. The dangers of seeing permeate fictional accounts and social documents. In the Hall episode, Trench is exposed as an impotent spectator and in
both this narrative and in McGahern's fictional episode the potato workers
cannot or will not reveal what they see. Agrarian crime is carried out by 'moon-
light' and by individuals in disguise. Similarly, the phosphorus painted hound
of the Baskervilles attacks at night in a barren landscape suffused in superstition.

As a repository of shifting meanings and positions, it is hardly surprising
that the the bog becomes an unstable political signifier. The May 1882 edition
of *Judy, Or the London Serio-Comic* depicts a cartoon entitled 'Helping him out
of the Bog', in which Gladstone bearing a sack of 'Irish Difficulty' traverses the
colonial mire with the aid of his parliamentarian colleagues.[67] Maud Gonne
invokes a similar, but politically divergent, image in her autobiography which
opens with a fanciful account of a train journey from Mayo in 1897:

> Tired but glowing I looked out of the window of the train at the dark bog
> land where now only the tiny lakes gleamed in the fading light. Then I
> saw a tall, beautiful woman with dark hair blown on the wind and I knew
> it was Cathleen ni Houlihan. She was crossing the bog towards the hills,
> springing from stone to stone over the treacherous surface, and the lit-
> tle white stones shone, making a path behind her, then faded into the
> darkness. I heard a voice say: 'You are one of the little stones on which
> the feet of the Queen have rested on her way to Freedom.'[68]

The Gladstone image depicts the complex negotiation of Irish land difficulties
within the imperial matrix, while for Gonne the vision portrays the commitment or sacrifice that is required for the attainment of Irish nationalism. The
figure of the bog operates as an agent of disruption, with shifting and ambiguous social and political allegiances that simultaneously mirror and mask the
instability of the colonised topos. Eruptive and resurgent, sodden ground
intervenes throughout nineteenth-century Irish fiction and documentation
and, as we see in the exemplary case of McGahern's fiction, is an important

trope in contemporary narratives that explore colonial memory. The bog is viscous and unstable by nature, and is untrustworthy, defiant and fickle. It threatens incarceration and death while at the same time it harbours the remains and traditions of an antique past and seems to promise to deliver a liberated future. Indeed, the bog's anomalous nature mirrors the complexities of the precarious and mutable Irish colonial milieu. In *The Snake's Pass*, Sutherland notes that 'even the last edition of the "Encyclopaedia Britannica" does not contain the heading "bog".'[69] For Stoker, the mysterious bog is unrecorded, unwritten, undefined and invariably uncontrollable. Mapping the ur-consciousness of the island, the bog is established as the emblem of colonial politics.

NOTES

1. The Black and Tans were enlisted in 1920 to serve as reinforcement to the Royal Irish Constabulary (RIC). Their name was bestowed on them for their uniform, which comprised a mixture of khaki, black-green caps and police belts. Their presence engendered much fear in an increasingly hostile population just as the Tans' ruthlessness was exacerbated by IRA guerrilla attacks. For an examination of the Black and Tans, see F.S.L. Lyons, *Ireland Since the Famine* ([1963] London: Fontana, 1985), pp. 415–16.
2. J. McGahern, *That They May Face the Rising Sun* (London: Faber and Faber, 2002), p. 240.
3. Ibid., p. 241.
4. Ibid., pp. 242–3.
5. Ibid., p. 243.
6. W. Steuart Trench, *Realities of Irish Life* (London: Longmans, Green, 1868), p. 51.
7. Ibid., p. 53.
8. Ibid.
9. P. Brontë, *The Maid of Killarney or Albion and Flora* (London: Baldwin, Craddock, and Joy, 1818), p. 33.
10. B. Stoker, *The Snake's Pass* (London: Sampson Low, Marston, Searle & Rivington, 1891), p. 41.
11. Moore took little interest in his land until he became troubled by the Land League's campaign for rent reductions. The Land Acts of the 1880s convinced him that disaster was inevitable, and deservedly so, for his class. See A.N. Jeffares, 'A Drama in Muslin', in G. Owens (ed.), *George Moore's Mind and Art* (Edinburgh: Oliver and Boyd, 1968), pp. 3–5.
12. For a detailed study of the colonial associations of the text, see C. Wynne, *The Colonial Conan Doyle: British Imperialism, Irish Nationalism, and the Gothic* (Westport, CT and London: Greenwood Press, 2002), pp. 65–84.
13. See Stoker, *The Snake's Pass*, p. 30.
14. Ibid., p. 31.
15. Ibid., p. 17.
16. Ibid., p. 22.
17. Ibid., pp. 22–3.
18. Ibid., p. 23.
19. John Moore, George's grandfather, joined General Humbert's army that landed at Killala in 1798. After an early successful skirmish at Castlebar Moore was made president of the Republic of Connaught. However, after only one week Humbert and his troops were forced to surrender at Ballinamuck. John Moore died shortly afterwards in jail. See T. Gray, *A Peculiar Man: A Life of George Moore* (London: Sinclair-Stevenson, 1996), pp. 19–20.
20. B. Belford, *Bram Stoker: A Biography of the Author of 'Dracula'* (London: Weidenfeld and Nicholson, 1996), p. 77.
21. Lady Wilde, *Ancient Legends, Mystic Charms, and Supersitions of Ireland*, vol. 2 (London: Ward and Downey, 1887), pp. 123–4. Stoker refers to William Wilde in his text when the cab-driver, Andy compares the scientific research of Dick Sutherland with that of 'Dochter' Wilde. See Stoker, *The Snake's Pass*, p. 72.

22. See Stoker, *The Snake's Pass*, pp. 76–7.
23. Ibid., p. 29.
24. Ibid., p. 102.
25. Ibid., p. 43.
26. Ibid., p. 286.
27. Ibid., p. 331.
28. A. Conan Doyle, *The Hound of the Baskervilles: Another Adventure of Sherlock Holmes* (London: George Newnes, 1902), p. 331.
29. *Parnell and His Island* is explicit in its definition of moonlighting: 'bands of dreamy youths wander about the country at night, breaking into the different cottages, pulling the occupants out of their beds, and shooting in the legs all whom they suspect of wishing to pay their rents, shooting through the head all who might betray them'. See G. Moore, *Parnell and His Island* (London: Swan Sonnenschein, Lowrey, 1887), p. 236. For an historical account, see J. Lee, *The Modernisation of Irish Society, 1848–1918* (Dublin: Gill & Macmillan, 1973), p. 86.
30. A. Trollope, *The Macdermots of Ballycloran*, intro. Algar Thorold ([1847] London: John Lane, The Bodley Head, 1906), p. 399.
31. Ibid., p. 407.
32. Ibid., p. 423.
33. Ibid., p. 428.
34. P. Cherici, *Celtic Sexuality: Power, Paradigms and Passion* ([1994] London: Gerald Duckworth, 1995), p. 104.
35. Ibid.
36. See Stoker, *The Snake's Pass*, p. 98.
37. Seamus Deane reads the soil crisis of *Dracula* as indicative of the similar land crisis facing Irish landlordism. See S. Deane, *Strange Country: Modernity and Nationhood in Irish Writing since 1790* (Oxford: Clarendon Press, 1997), p. 90.
38. See Moore, *Parnell and His Island*, pp. 75–6.
39. Ibid., p. 7.
40. Ibid., p. 55.
41. Ibid., p.99.
42. For representations of the Irish in the nineteenth century, see L. Curtis, *Apes and Angels: The Irishman in Victorian Caricature* (rev. edn, Washington and London: Smithsonian Institution Press, 1997).
43. J. Simms, *Nature's Revelations of Character; or, the Mental, Moral and Volitive Dispositions of Mankind, as Manifested in the Human Form and Countenance* ([London]: privately printed, 1873), p. 331.
44. A. Conan Doyle, 'The Geographical Distribution of British Intellect', *The Nineteenth Century: A Monthly Review*, 24, 138 (Aug. 1888), p. 195.
45. Ibid., 184.
46. For a detailed study of this, see Wynne, *The Colonial Conan Doyle*.
47. See Stoker, *The Snake's Pass*, p. 16.
48. John Hutchinson argues that the GAA 'nationalized the Irish countryside, giving it a defiantly separatist democratic culture'. See J. Hutchinson, *The Dynamics of Cultural Nationalism: The Gaelic Revival and the Creation of the Nation State* (London: Allen & Unwin, 1987), p. 161.
49. See Stoker, *The Snake's Pass*, pp. 27–8.
50. Ibid., p. 20.
51. For a recent study of the various land acts, see P. Bull, *Land, Politics and Nationalism, A Study of the Irish Question* (Dublin: Gill & Macmillan, 1996).
52. See Stoker, *The Snake's Pass*, p. 349.
53. Ibid., p. 84.
54. See Wyse Papers (1830–39), National Library of Ireland, Dublin, for manuscripts of reports of the Commission on Bogs in Ireland.
55. See Stoker, *The Snake's Pass*, p. 70.
56. D. Glover, *Vampires, Mummies, and Liberals: Bram Stoker and the Politics of Popular Fiction* (Durham and London: Duke University Press, 1996), p. 51.
57. B. Stoker, 'The Great White Fair in Dublin: How There Has Arisen on the Site of the Old Donnybrook Fair a Great Exhibition as Typical of the New Ireland as the Former Festival was of the Ireland of the Past', *The World's Work*, IX, 54 (May 1907), p. 573. See also Glover, *Vampires, Mummies and Liberals*, p. 13.
58. For an interpretation of this event, see Lee, *The Modernisation of Irish Society*, p. 115.

59. B. Stoker, *Personal Reminiscences of Henry Irving*, vol. II (London: William Heinemann, 1906), p. 28.
60. Ibid., p. 29.
61. Ibid.
62. A. Conan Doyle, *Letters to the Press: The Unknown Conan Doyle*, comp. with intro. J.M.Gibson and R. Lancelyn Green (London: Secker & Warburg, 1986), p. 66.
63. A. Conan Doyle, 'The Heiress of Glenmahowley', *Uncollected Stories: The Unknown Conan Doyle*, comp. with intro. J.M. Gibson and R. Lancelyn Green (London: Secker & Warburg, 1982), p. 144.
64. See Moore, *Parnell and His Island*, p. 7.
65. See Doyle, 'The Heiress of Glenmahowley', p. 146.
66. Ibid.
67. *Judy, Or the London Serio-Comic*, 30 (3 May 1882), pp. 210–11.
68. M. Gonne MacBride, *A Servant of the Queen* ([1938] London: Victor Gollancz, 1974), p. vii.
69. See Stoker, *The Snake's Pass*, p. 71.

Afterword:
Ireland and Colonialism

TERRY EAGLETON

In the Flann O'Brien novel *The Third Policeman*, policeman MacCruiskeen fashions a series of chests one inside the other, rather like a babushka doll, the last five chests so microscopic that they are invisible even to the most powerful magnifying glass, as indeed are the tools he uses to make them. 'The one I am making now', MacCruiskeen remarks proudly to the narrator, 'is nearly as small as nothing. Number One (of the chests) would hold a million of them at the same time and there would be room left for a pair of woman's horse-breeches if they were rolled up. The dear knows where it will stop and terminate'. 'It is unmentionable', responds the narrator courteously, to which MacCruiskeen replies with becoming modesty: 'Very nearly'.[1]

'Nothing' is a substantial theme in Irish literature. It was Bishop Berkeley who commented in his notebooks that 'we Irish are apt to think something and nothing to be near neighbours',[2] while the Tipperary novelist Laurence Sterne put in a good word for nothingness, 'considering', as he said, 'what worse things there are in the world'.[3] The greatest Irish medieval philosopher, John Scottus Eriugena, believed that God was sheer nothingness;[4] Samuel Beckett seemed to think much the same about humanity; and Edmund Burke thought that very small objects, like very big ones, were sublime.[5] But it is the idea of invisibility, not exactly of nothingness, which is my route from Flann O'Brien to colonialism. There are, one might claim, two kinds of invisibility: one which arises from absence, and the other from over-obtrusive presence. We don't notice what's not there, or what's so grossly, palpably there that we overlook it, like dangerous driving in New Delhi or insincerity in Hollywood. 'As invisible as the nose on your face', one might say.

It is possible to rank different forms of colonialism according to their degrees of visibility. Most palpable of all is what is sometimes known as administrative colonialism, or which we might rather less blandly call coercive colonialism, where one nation forcibly occupies the territory of another, usually of a different ethnic type, generally by armed conquest, annexes it to its political sovereignty, appropriates its land and resources, reduces its natives to second-class status, systematically undermines its culture and maintains a permanent military government there. Nobody could fail to recognise *this* kind of colonialism, except perhaps a few hundred Irish revisionist historians; though there is perhaps rather more reason for people failing to identify the second form of colonialism, which is settler colonialism. This is when they do not only suppress your language and plunder your resources, but actually have the impudence to come and live with you. Why is it plausible *not* to see Northern Ireland as a colony? Several reasons, to be sure; but one is because the colonial settlers there form the majority, and have been there long enough to feel quite as much at home as Celts in Kerry. Indeed they *are* as much at home as Celts in Kerry, a fact which any enlightened opposition to British rule in the province is quite willing to acknowledge.

Even within settler colonialism, however, there are different shades of visibility. Plantation colonialism, for example, means fairly few colonialists buying up huge tracts of land and importing non-native, sometimes slave labour to work it. This is not easy to disguise as radical egalitarianism. Or you can have mixed settlement colonies, made up of both natives and planters, or pure settlement colonies, where the incomers become a demographic majority – perhaps, as in North America and Australia – by dint of exterminating most of the natives. This is a highly recommendable way of rendering your colonial rule invisible, since who exactly are you then oppressing? Once domination is carried to an extreme, annihilating its victim altogether, then in a kind of Pyrrhic victory it would appear to cancel itself out, as Hegel recognised in his great parable of Master and Slave.

Colonialism, in brief, needs resistance in order to figure as colonialism; and if the original natives are exterminated or die off, so that in time nobody even remembers that they were ever there, then you cease over time to be a colonial power. This was the case with the Firbolgs or pre-Celtic inhabitants of Ireland. One reason why the Irish Republic is not a colonialist society today is because the Firbolgs and their ilk aren't around to tell the tale.

But let us also imagine a settler situation in which the occupiers are ethnically, culturally and religiously akin to the colonised; in which their rule is largely benevolent, so that most of the native group do not especially desire independence and take part quite fully in government; in which over long periods the two groups become culturally fused; and in which both groups are politically hostile to the original metropolitan nation, so as to team up in this way too. Let us imagine too that the place is economically speaking a millstone around the neck of the settlers, and that far from profiting from it they would be economically better off shot of it altogether. Would this still count as colonialism? It would in my view, as long as the natives cannot be said to govern themselves as fully as they would in the absence of the settlers; but someone who considers that it wouldn't certainly has a case. Here we have invisibility by assimilation, as a pork pie may be invisible only because I have eaten it.

A further form of invisibility is political integration – when, as in the Act of Union, the colonised nation is incorporated into the metropolitan nation and ceases, legally and politically, to be a separate, subordinate nation. This need not go hand in hand with settler colonialism, though it did so in the case of Ireland. For some observers, this was when Ireland stopped being colonial and started being post-colonial. On this view, Ireland, or part of it, did not become post-colonial in 1921, because it had already been a post-colonial nation for over a century. For other commentators, it did not become a post-colonial society in 1800 because it was not a colonial nation before that date. For some, Ireland is not a post-colonial nation today because post-colonial nations must by definition be poor, backward, dependent, possibly black and probably a long way from Europe. Less emotive observers believe that a society can be at once affluent and post-colonial, since 'post-colonial' is not necessarily shorthand for 'in a wretched condition'. Colonialist or previously colonialist nations can sometimes be more economically devastated than colonised or previously colonised ones.

There is, in other words, a question about different levels or dimensions of colonialisation. A country may be politically equal to another while being socially, economically and culturally subaltern, which one might call a difference between political form and social content. Not only this, but political integration may actually *reinforce* colonial power – partly by masking it ideologically, partly in more practical ways. It may drag you, for example, damagingly in the wake of a much more economically powerful neighbour with whom your political fortunes are supposedly equally shared, as happened in the case of Ireland and Britain. Conversely, in the post-colonial world, political *independence* may actually intensify economic subordination. The fact that you are no longer exploited by a particular imperial nation may mean that you are up for sale to a range of potential buyers, which is why the United States has played such a resolutely 'anti-colonial' role, seeking the dismantling of traditional empires in order to install its own. In the colonial world, integration may actually intensify your oppression – though it may also, we should bear in mind, help to develop the means for freeing yourself from it. The moral of this tale is surely plain: there is no more effective way of dominating a partner than by that formal, legal equality known as marriage, except that, once you break up in a divorce or post-colonial kind of way, the subordinate partner is now free to be dominated by anyone at all. That is what we know as liberation.

Finally, there is that ultimate form of colonial invisibility known as post- or neo-colonialism. Here, what the old lady from Kerry is reputed to have said about the fairies –that she didn't believe in them, but that they were there anyway – forcibly applies. You may not always see the British, Americans, Germans and French in Ireland, but they are there anyway, and by no means just gawking at the Book of Kells. Like the Almighty, capital is now so universal as to be completely invisible, which is why many of the Irish are now devout political atheists, having ceased to believe in colonialism at all. It is important for some of the Irish in the Republic not to believe that the Republic is post-colonial, since this would imply that it was previously colonised, which might in turn suggest that Northern Ireland was still a colony, which might in turn have unpalatable political consequences. Some of the Irish, in short, do not just reject the appellation of 'post-colonial' for the sorts of reasons that conservative academics do, though quite a few of them who reject it for politically quite pressing reasons also do it for conservative-academic sorts of reasons.

Now the problem with Ireland is that at different times and in different places, various of those forms of colonialism have complexly co-existed. If brutal military usurpation well enough describes the Elizabethan or Cromwellian invasions, the situation of the so-called 'Old English' was much nearer to the cultural-assimilationist model. After 1800, you had the political integration model, but also long-term majority settlement in Ulster and – as far as many of the native Gaels were concerned – a continuing minority-coercion model of colonialism too. All of these forms dialectically interacted: the more, for example, integrationism – the Union – was sustained, the more this lent power to the elbow of a disaffected Gaelic nationalism, and so ironically, intensified the more coercive forms of colonial power. Not only this, but the Union also drove a lot of erstwhile nationally-minded Protestants back into their imperial fortress, polarising the situation rather than integrating it. Because of the Union, the political stakes were drastically raised: it was now not just a question of putting down some piddling national liberation movement, but of preventing the much graver catastrophe of the breakup of Britain itself. The more coercive colonialism had created settlement-colonialism in Ulster, i.e. installed a majority colonialist population there, the more the integrationist philosophy of the Union could justify itself by pointing to this anglicisation of the island. But at the same time, the more such settlement took place, the more this aroused native dissidence, and thus spurred on a more militarily repressive brand of colonial power.

Since partition, a mixed settler colonialism has continued to exist north of the border, along with political integration, while post- or neo-colonialism has taken root south of it. It is therefore not at all hard to see why for many people, colonialism is scarcely relevant to Ireland at all. Most of those north of the border want to be British, while those south of it are as politically independent as most liberal capitalist societies now are. Moreover, what we have in the North is a fairly classic situation in which a portion of the settler colonialists refused to decolonise along with the rest of the nation. This then weakens the case of those in that region who *do* wish to decolonise in two ways: first, because formally speaking (if not in the least in fact) they enjoy full civil rights by virtue of political integration with the metropolitan country, and secondly because, since the anti-colonial struggle in the rest of the island was successful, that impetus has long since died away as it has in most of the rest of the globe; many of its memories have become for some merely embarrassing; and Northern republicans thus look more isolated and archaic than ever. Though they are fortunate in this respect to have the Unionists around, since anyone would be hard put to appear archaic in contrast with them. As far as the embarrassment of republican memories goes, there is a parallel with eighteenth-century England, for which Cromwell suddenly became an unspeakable bounder, and English republicanism a perverse and godless creed, for many of those who wouldn't have been what they were without them. Ironically, then, it is the success of the anti-colonial revolution in Ireland which has helped among other things to stymie its completion.

There were two enormous problems for classical British colonialism in Ireland. The first was the cultural chasm between rulers and ruled; the second, deeply related to this, was the fact that over several centuries of government, British sovereignty in Ireland never succeeded in establishing hegemony, as opposed to that blunter, less intricate instrument known as power. It never managed to persuade enough of the unruly Irish to internalise the law and thus lay the conditions for consensual government, which in the long run, as Edmund Burke recognised, is the only sort of government which has any chance at all of holding people down for lengthy periods. Britain was therefore forced to sustain coercive colonialism even throughout the integrationist era, and could not entirely succeed with settler colonialism simply because the Gaelic natives outnumbered the settler natives.

This meant among other things that American-style anti-colonialist patriotism could not really work in Ireland, since this depends on the settlers being the majority. If the British had treated their Irish colonials as genocidally as the American colonisers had treated the native Americans, then, ironically, a 'patriot' Anglo-Irish anti-colonialist movement later on might have had more chance of success. But the Irish Protestant patriots had to mind their backs against the treacherous Catholic rebels, never really trusted them (not even Wolfe Tone did that), and in the end preferred wimpishly to surrender what scant parliamentary independence they had rather than run the risks of political independence of a separatist sort sinking them without trace within the clamorous Catholic nation.

One answer to the question 'Was Ireland a colony?' is 'Why not ask the punters?' Why not consult the Irish themselves? This may seem an eccentric sort of proposal, since if we were to ask whether Communist Poland was a deformed workers state, a degenerated workers state, a species of bureaucratic collectivism, or an instance of state capitalism, we would not necessarily be inclined to ask the first Polish taxi driver we ran into. Equally, it is doubtful that medieval Persians would have been entirely clear on whether medieval Persia belonged to the Asiatic mode of production, or whether the best way of establishing whether Jacobean England was an instance of moderate late-feudal absolutism was to consult Ben Jonson or James I.

With colonialism, however, things are rather different. If a people represents itself as colonised, then this means that they resist that form of rule; one would not neutrally represent oneself as colonised, as one might neutrally represent oneself as asthmatic. And though this is not enough to establish that the form of power in question is in fact colonialist, there is a sense in which it would not be colonialist without it. A people who do not consider themselves to be colonised may simply have acquiesced in colonial rule and identified it with their well-being; but they may also not consider themselves colonised because a colonial occupation no longer has any significant political effects. England is not a colony because the Normans once marched in, since nobody in England, except perhaps for a few Anglo-Saxon revanchists huddled conspiratorially in Home Counties pubs, now thinks this occupation worth resisting, or even mentioning. It is the Firbolg Problem once more: too much settlement has happened since. But if the English had waged a long struggle against the Norman conquest which had survived into our own time, then we might well conclude that we were still dealing with a colonial situation. The world, in short, is not divided between colonial and non-colonial situations, but between live colonial situations and dead ones. Indeed it was an Irishman – in fact the greatest of all Irish political theorists, Edmund Burke – who acknowledged this point by reminding us that all acts of government are acts of usurpation, simply that some of these aboriginal injustices have been eroded by the merciful, oblivion-inducing passage of time. More or less the whole of the globe is colonised territory.

Not to see this is to object to colonization for all the wrong reasons – by which I mean, roughly speaking, for vulgar-nationalist ones.[6] What are the wrong reasons, for example, for demanding a united Ireland? First, the belief that the territory of Ireland is inherently Irish, and that the non-Irish present upon it are therefore alien interlopers. This is a reasonable enough view as long as you accept that all Gaels in Ireland, including Gerry Adams and Martin McGuinness, are therefore going to have to leave the country en masse, perhaps for Philadelphia, since historically speaking they are alien interlopers too. Is it wrong for Ireland to be carved up into different political sovereignties? Not in principle. In principle, there would be nothing wrong with having twenty rather than two different political states on the island, just as there is nothing wrong in principle with Europe being politically divided. Europe is not 'disunited' just because it is composed of different sovereignties, a view entertained only by those who make a fetish of unity as a good in itself. But geopolitical unity is no more a good in itself than is geopolitical division.

Should one demand an end to partition because the Northern Catholics have been so shamefully treated? Again, I think, not in principle. Partition would have been wrong even if the Catholics had been treated a great deal better than they have been – an improbable but not impossible situation. Is partition wrong because it reduces Catholics in the North to a minority? Not quite: there is nothing inherently undemocratic about being a minority, in fact democracy requires minorities, since there will never be unanimous agreement. Some people treat the phrase 'oppressed minority' as though it were a tautology – minorities just are oppressed by virtue of being minorities – which is sentimental nonsense. Millionaires are also a minority, but not a notably oppressed one. People who believe that crop circles are messages from the gods are a minority, but we do not therefore believe that they are automatically entitled to their own state, though it might be a crafty way of getting rid of them. Is what is wrong with Northern Ireland the fact that Catholics are artificially cut off by a border from their ethnic kinsfolk in the Republic? Certainly not: there is no inherent virtue in being cheek by jowl with your ethnic kinsfolk, and sometimes some point in not being.

Should the British not rule over part of Ireland because it means the dominion of one ethnic group over another? Not at all: colonialism is just as bad if the colonialists are of the same ethnicity as oneself. Ethnicity isn't the point. The British were of much the same ethnic stock as their American colonials, but this did not make the situation any more tolerable than, say, British rule in India or Malaysia. All these are bad arguments against colonialism, either fetishistic, nostalgic, sentimental or latently racist. And one of the most wrong-headed arguments of all, though one which has impelled almost every anti-colonial movement of modern history, including much of the Irish one, is the recently invented Romantic dogma that a distinctive ethnic people have a right to their own political state simply because of their distinct ethnicity. This doctrine has wreaked untold havoc in modern politics, and is doing so in the Balkans as I write. The Irish are not entitled to democratic self-determination because they are Irish, or the Tibetans because they are Tibetan; they are entitled to it because to be Irish or Tibetan is to be a human being, and thus to be entitled to self-determination on that ground alone. We are talking, in short, about the radical Enlightenment, nowadays distinctly unfashionable, rather than its Romantic-to-post-modern aftermath. It is people, not peoples, who have the right to self-government - though admittedly there are times when people can only get it as peoples, because that is the way they have been constituted.

Lenin, who was in general rather sound on the national question, even if he is not exactly a post-modern hero, argued that though the self-determination of a minority was a good in principle, it could not take precedence over a majority's right to liberate themselves from such situations as colonial rule. It is a doctrine accepted in somewhat different form by the United Nations today. Of course in Ireland part of the problem is defining who forms a minority and who a majority, and being good at arithmetic will not help here. The point, however, is that culture cannot be allowed to take precedence over politics, which is not at all a doctrine to the taste of post-modernists. It would be a good thing in principle for the Chinese population of Birmingham to have fuller rights to cultural self-expression; but if this involved the non-Chinese of Birmingham waking up one morning to find themselves fully paid-up citizens of the People's Republic of China, it might leave a little to be desired. Cultural self-expression, whatever the post-modernists may dogmatically consider, is by no means an absolute – not, for example, if it jeopardises the collective political framework which guarantees such self-expression for all cultural groups. And cultural self-expression for Nazis is a demand only of Nazis and spineless liberals. Some Northern Unionists have now begun to speak the language of cultural diversity and post-modern pluralism, having no doubt been to school with Sinn Féin; but it is political, not cultural rights which are fundamental, not least because the political is the only way we have of securing cultural rights all round. There is much in my view that is valuable about cultural nationalism; but objections to colonialism, in Ireland or elsewhere, must finally be radical-Enlightenment rather than Romantic ones.

NOTES

1. Flann O'Brien, *The Third Policeman* (London: MacGibbon and Kee, 1967, reprinted London: Picador, 1974).
2. Bishop Berkeley, *Philosophical Commentaries* (London: Dent, 1944), p.124.
3. Laurence Sterne, *The Life and Opinions of Tristram Shandy, Gentleman* (London: Penguin, 1997), p.530.
4. Dermot Moran, 'Nature, Man and God in the Philosophy of John Scottus Eriugena', in Richard Kearney (ed), *The Irish Mind* (Dublin: Wolfhound Press, 1985), p.91–106.
5. Edmund Burke, *A Philosophical Enquiry into the Origin of our Ideas of the Sublime and Beautiful* (London, 1757, reprinted in F. W. Rafferty (ed), *Works of the Right Honorable Edmund Burke* (London: Macmillan, 1925), vol. 1, p.159.
6. I have developed this argument more fully in Terry Eagleton, 'Nationalism and the Case of Ireland', *New left Review*, No. 234 (March/April, 1999).

Notes on Contributors

Tony Ballantyne taught at National University of Ireland, Galway and the University of Illinois, Urbana-Champaign prior to returning home to New Zealand, where he is a Senior Lecturer in History at the University of Otago. He works broadly on the cultural and intellectual history of the British empire and his publications include *Orientalism and Race: Aryanism in the British Empire* and a volume co-edited with Antoinette Burton, *Bodies in Contact: rethinking colonial encounters in world history*.

Thomas A. Boylan holds a Personal Professorship in Economics at NUI, Galway. His research interests include Economic Methodology, History of Economic Thought, Growth and Development Economics. He has published widely in all three areas. He has recently co-edited (with T.P. Foley) a four volume *Anthology of Irish Political Economy*, and the six volume *Collected Works of John Elliot Cairnes*.

Dr Pamela Clayton spent several years teaching in Sierra Leone and Egypt after taking a degree in Government at the University of Manchester. She moved to Northern Ireland in 1980 and lived in Belfast until 1991, during which time she obtained her doctorate from the Department of Sociology, Queen's University Belfast. She has since been employed by the University of Glasgow, where she is Research Fellow in the Department of Adult and Continuing Education.

Virginia Crossman is Lecturer in History at Oxford Brookes University. She has published extensively on local government and administration in nineteenth-century Ireland. Her latest work on the administration of the Irish poor law will be published by Manchester University Press in 2006.

Nicola Drucker worked as Research Officer in the International Famine Centre, National University of Ireland, Cork. She also taught part-time in the Dept. of History, UCC. She holds an MA in History and English from the University of Hannover. Main research interests are 19th and 20th century Irish history within a European and overseas / (post-)colonial framework. Recently she published 'Irish and Alpine Encounters: Tours and travels in 1877' in: *Beziehungen und Identitaeten: Oesterreich, Irland und die Schweiz*, Gisela Holfter et al. (eds.).

Terry Eagleton is Professor of cultural theory and John Rylands Fellow at the

University of Manchester, Britain. His most recent book, *The English Novel: An Introduction*, has been published by Blackwell.

Peter Gray is Professor of Irish History at Queen's University Belfast. He is the author of *Famine, Land and Politics* and editor of *Victoria's Ireland* and *The Memory of Catastrophe*.

Valerie Kennedy is currently Assistant Professor in the Department of English Language and Literature at Bilkent University, in Ankara, Turkey, where she has been since 1997. Before that she taught in universities in Morocco and Kenya. She has published on Dickens, Austen, Eliot, and Hardy, as well as on Said, feminism, and postmodernism. Her book, *Edward Said: A Critical Introduction* was published by Polity Press in 2000, with a Chinese translation published by Rye Publications in 2003. She is currently editing a collection of short stories translated from the Arabic by Ali Azeriah.

Professor Christine Kinealy is a graduate of Trinity College, Dublin, where she completed a Ph.D. on the introduction of the Poor Law to Ireland. She has published extensively on the impact of the Great Famine in Ireland. In 2003, she was the Arlo Browne Visiting Professor at Drew University in the United States. While there, she undertook research on Irish-American nationalism in the 1840s. Her recent publications include, *A New History of Ireland* and *The Great Famine in Ireland, Impact, Ideology and Rebellion*. She is currently researching the history of the 1848 uprising in Ireland.

Amy E. Martin is Assistant Professor of English at Mount Holyoke College where she teaches Victorian literature, Irish studies and postcolonial theory. She is currently completing a book manuscript titled *Alter-nations: Nationalisms and the State in Nineteenth Century British and Irish Culture*. She has published essays in journals such as *The Field Day Review* and *Victorian Literature and Culture*.

Terrence McDonough is Senior Lecturer in Economics at the National University of Ireland in Galway. He has published in Political Economy, American and Irish Economic History, the History of Economic Thought and in Economic Policy. He is co-editor of *Social Structures of Accumulation: The Political Economy of Growth and Crisis* and co-author of *Minding Your Own Business: Economics at Work*. He is currently working on a project in *Globalization from the Perspective of Long Wave Theory* funded by the Irish Research Council for the Humanities and Social Sciences.

Willa Murphy is Lecturer in Irish Writing in English, Academy for Irish Cultural Heritages, University of Ulster. Her research interests include Nineteenth-Century Irish writing, the intersection of theology and literature, and Irish women's writing. She is co-editor of *The Encyclopedia of Contemporary Irish Culture*, forthcoming from Routledge.

Denis O'Hearn is jointly Professor of Sociology at Binghamton University and Professor of Social and Economic Change at Queens University Belfast. The arguments in his chapter in this book appear in greater length in *The Atlantic Economy: Britain, the US and Ireland*, which won a Distinguished Scholarship Award from the American Sociological Association.

Charles E. Orser, Jr. is University Distinguished Professor of Anthropology at Illinois State University. A historical archaeologist, he uses anthropologically informed archaeology to investigate the lives of men and women ignored by official, written history and their interactions with people of power. His books include *The Material Basis of the Postbellum Tenant Plantation*, *A Historical Archaeology of the Modern World*, *Historical Archaeology*, and *Race and Practice in Archaeological Interpretation*. He is also the founding editor of the *International Journal of Historical Archaeology* and the editor of the *Encyclopedia of Historical Archaeology*.

Sean Ryder lectures in the Department of English at the National University of Ireland, Galway. He is editor of *James Clarence Mangan: Selected Writings*, co-editor of *Gender and Colonialism*, and co-editor of *Ideology and Ireland in the Nineteenth Century*. He has published a number of articles on aspects of nineteenth-century Irish nationalist culture.

Eamonn Slater is a Lecturer in the Department of Sociology at the National University of Ireland, Maynooth. He has edited two books with his colleague, Dr. Michel Peillon, *Encounters with Modern Ireland*, and *Memories of the Present*. He is currently doing research on Marx's ideas on ecology and the Irish Famine.

Catherine Wynne is lecturer in nineteenth-century literature at the University of Hull. She has published *The Colonial Conan Doyle: British Imperialism, Irish Nationalism, and the Gothic* and is author of a number of articles and essays on late nineteenth-century fiction, photography, and film. She is currently co-editing, *Victorian Literary Mesmerism*, a collection of essays on literary engagements with mesmerism in the nineteenth century and is working ona monograph on Bram Stoker.

Bibliography

Amin, S. (ed.), *A Glossary of North Indian Peasant Life* [William Crooke] (Delhi: Oxford University Press, 1989).

Anderson, B., *Imagined Communities: Reflections on the Origin and Spread Of Nationalism*, (rev. edn, London and New York: Verso, 1996 [1991]).

Andrews, J.H. *A Paper Landscape: the Ordnance Survey in Nineteenth-Century Ireland* (Oxford: Clarendon Press, 1975).

Andrews, K., N.P. Canny and P.E.H. Hair (eds), *The Westward Enterprise: English Activities in Ireland, the Atlantic, and America, 1480–1650* (Liverpool: Liverpool University Press, 1978).

Arac, J., *Commissioned Spirits: the Shaping of Social Motion in Dickens, Carlyle, Melville and Hawthorne* (New York, NY: Columbia University Press, 1979).

Arthur, W.B., 'Self-reinforcing mechanisms in economics', in P.W. Anderson, K. Arrow and D. Pines (eds), *The Economy as an Evolving Complex System* (Reading, MA: Addison-Wesley, 1988).

Ashcroft, B., G. Griffiths and H. Tiffen, *The empire writes back: theory and practice in post-colonial literatures* (London: Routledge, 1989).

Babington, A., *Devil to Pay: the Mutiny of the Connaught Rangers, India, July, 1920* (London: Leo Cooper, 1991).

Bailey, K.C., *A History of Trinity College Dublin* (Dublin: University Press, 1947).

Baines, E., *History of the Cotton Manufacture in Great Britain* (London: Fisher, Fisher and Jackson, 1835).

Balandier, G., *Sociologie Actuelle de l'Afrique Noir* (Paris, 1963).

Balibar, E. and I. Wallerstein, *Race, Nation, Class: Ambiguous Identities* (London: Verso, 1988).

Ballantyne, T., *Orientalism and Race: Aryanism in the British Empire* (London: Palgrave, 2001).

Barnard, T.C., *Cromwellian Ireland: English Government and Reform in Ireland 1649–60* (Oxford: Oxford University Press, 1979).

Barrett, W., 'Irish Drama?', *New Ireland Review*, 3 (March–Aug. 1895).

Bartlett, T. (ed.), *Life of Theobald Wolfe Tone* (Dublin: Lilliput Press, 1998).

Bayly, C.A., *Imperial Meridian: the British Empire and the World, 1780–1830* (London: Longman, 1993).

Bayly, C.A., *Empire and Information: Intelligence Gathering and Social Communication in India, 1780–1870* (Cambridge: Cambridge University Press, 1996).

Bayly, C.A., 'Ireland, India and the Empire: 1780–1914', *Transactions of the Royal Historical Society X* (sixth series), 2000, pp. 377–97.

Beaufort, L.C., 'An Essay upon the State of Architecture and Antiquities, Previous to the Landing of the Anglo-Normans in Ireland', *Transactions of the Royal Irish Academy*, XV (1828), pp. 101–241.

Belchem J., 'English Working-Class Radicalism and the Irish, 1815–50', in R. Swift and S. Gilley (eds), *The Irish in the Victorian City* (London: Croon Helm, 1985), pp. 85–97.

Belford, B., *Bram Stoker: A Biography of the Author of 'Dracula'* (London: Weidenfeld and Nicolson, 1996).

Bell, J. and M. Watson, *Irish Farming, Implements and Techniques, 1750–1900* (Edinburgh: John Donald, 1986).

Bew, P., *Land and the National Question in Ireland, 1858–82* (Dublin: Gill & Macmillan, 1978).

Bhabha, H., *Nation and narration* (London: Routledge, 1990).

Bhabha, H., *The Location of Culture* (London and New York: Routledge, 1994).

Black, R.D.C., 'Trinity College Dublin and the Theory of Value, 1832–1863', *Economica* 12, 47 (1945).

Black, R.D.C., *The Statistical and Social Inquiry Society of Ireland, Centenary Volume, 1847–1947.* (Dublin: Eason, 1947).

Black, R.D.C., *Economic Thought and the Irish Question, 1817–1870* (Cambridge: Cambridge University Press, 1960).

Blaug, M., 'The productivity of capital in the Lancashire cotton industry during the nineteenth century', *Economic History Review*, 13, 3 (1961), pp. 358–81.

Böröcz, J., 'Travel-Capitalism: The Structure of Europe and the Advent of the Tourist', *Comparative Studies in Society and History*, 34 (1992), pp. 708–41.

Bottigheimer, K., *English Money and Irish Land: the 'Adventurers' in the Cromwellian Settlement of Ireland* (Oxford: Oxford University Press, 1971).

Bottomore, T., *Dictionary of Marxist Thought* (Oxford: Blackwell, 1991).

Bourdieu, P., 'Die gesellschaftliche Definition der Photographie', in P. Bourdieu et al., *Eine illegitime Kunst. Die sozialen Gebrauchsweisen der Photographie* (Frankfurt: Suhrkamp Verlag, 1983), pp. 85–109.

Boyce, D.G., *Nationalism in Ireland* (3rd edn, London: Routledge, 1995).

Boylan, T. and T. McDonough, 'Dependency and Modernization: Perspectives from the Irish Nineteenth Century', in Foley, Tadhg and S. Ryder (eds), *Ideology and Ireland in the Nineteenth Century* (Dublin: Four Courts Press, 1998)

Boylan, T.A. and T.P Foley, 'John Elliot Cairnes, John Stuart Mill and Ireland: some problems for political economy,' in Antoin E. Murphy (ed.), *Economists and the Irish Economy from the Eighteenth Century to the Present Day* (Dublin: Irish Academic Press, 1984).

Boyle, E., 'The Economic Development of the Irish Linen Industry,

1825–1913', unpublished Ph.D. dissertation (Belfast: Queens University, 1979).

Bradshaw, B., 'Nationalism and Historical Scholarship in Modern Ireland', in C. Brady (ed.), *Interpreting Irish History: The Debate on Historical Revisionism 1938–1994* (Dublin: Irish Academic Press, 1994).

Brenner, R., *Merchants and Revolution: Commercial change, political conflict, and London's overseas traders, 1550–1653* (Cambridge: Cambridge University Press, 1993).

Briggs A., *Chartism* (Gloucester: Sutton, 1998).

Brontë, P., *The Maid of Killarney, or Albion and Flora* (London: Baldwin, Craddock, and Joy, 1818).

Buckland, C.T., *Publications of the London Committee Formed to Oppose the Bengal Tenancy Bill* (London).

Bull, P., *Land, Politics and Nationalism: A Study of the Irish Land Question* (Dublin: Gill & Macmillan, 1996).

Burke, E., *Writings and Speeches of Edmund Burke: Volume IX*, ed. R.B. McDowell (Oxford: Clarendon Press, 1991).

Burke's Landed Gentry of Ireland (10th edn, London: Harrison & Sons, 1904).

Butler, M., *Maria Edgeworth: A Literary Biography* (Oxford: Clarendon Press, 1972).

Butler, M., 'Introduction' to *Castle Rackrent and Ennui* (London: Penguin, 1992), pp. 1–54.

Butt, I., *The Irish People and the Irish Land, A Letter to Lord Lifford* (Dublin: John Falconer, 1867).

Cairns, D. and S. Richards, *Writing Ireland: Colonialism, Nationalism and Culture* (Manchester: Manchester University Press, 1988).

Calahan, J.M., *The Irish Novel: A Critical History* (Boston: Twayne, 1988).

Campbell, G., *The Irish Land* (London: Trubner, 1869).

Canny, N., 'Irish Resistance to Empire?: 1641, 1690 and 1798', in L. Stone (ed.), *An Imperial State at War: Britain from 1689 to 1815* (London: Routledge, 1994).

Canny, N., 'The Ideology of English Colonization: From Ireland to America', *William and Mary Quarterly, 30* (1973), pp. 575–98.

Canny, N., *Kingdom and Colony: Ireland in the Atlantic World, 1560–1800* (Baltimore, MD: Johns Hopkins University Press, 1988).

Carlyle, T., *Chartism* (2nd edn, London: Chapman and Hall, 1842).

Carter I., *Farmlife in Northeast Scotland, 1840–1914, The Poor Man's Country* (Edinburgh: John Donald, 1979).

Cherici, P., *Celtic Sexuality: Power, Paradigms and Passion* ([1994] London: Gerald Duckworth, 1995).

Chichester, C.R., *Irish Landlordism*, reprinted from the *Dublin University Review* (Dublin: Sealy, Bryers and Walker, 1887), BL/EP/G 505.

Clark, S. and J. Donnelly (eds), *Irish Peasants: Violence and Political Unrest 1780–1914* (Dublin: Gill & Macmillan, 1983).

Clark, S., 'The importance of agrarian classes: class structure in nineteenth century Ireland', in P.J. Drudy (ed.), *Ireland: Land, Politics and People* (Cambridge: Cambridge University Press, 1982).

Clayton, P., *Enemies and Passing Friends: Settler Ideologies in Twentieth-Century Ulster* (London: Verso, 1996).

Cliffe Leslie, T.E., 1866. 'Political Economy and the Tenure of Land', *Fortnightly Review* (1866), also in *Land Systems and Industrial Economy of Ireland, England and Continental Countries* (London: Longman, 1870).

Cliffe Leslie, T.E., *Land Systems and Industrial Economy of Ireland, England and Continental Countries* (London: Longman, 1870).

Cliffe Leslie, T.E., *Essays in Political and Moral Philosophy* (Dublin: Hodges, Foster, and Figgis, 1879).

Clifford, J., 'Collecting ourselves', in S.M. Pearce (ed.), *Interpreting Objects and Collections* (London: Routledge, 1994), pp. 258–68.

Clifford, J., 'Museums as Contact Zones', in J. Clifford, *Routes. Travel and Translation in the late twentieth century* (Cambridge, MA and London: Harvard University Press, 1997), pp. 188–219.

Coats, A.W., 'The Historicist Reaction in English Political Economy, 1870–90', *Economica*, 21 May (1954) pp. 143–153.

Coe, W.E., *The Engineering Industry of the North of Ireland* (Belfast: Institute of Irish Studies, 1969).

Cohen, M., 'Peasant differentiation and proto-industrialization in the Ulster countryside: Tullylish, 1690–1825', *The Journal of Peasant Studies* 17, 3 (April 1990), pp. 413–32.

Cohn, B., *An Anthropologist Among the Historians and Other Essays* (Delhi: Oxford University Press, 1987).

Cohn, B., *Colonialism and its Forms of Knowledge: the British in India* (Princeton, NJ: Princeton University Press, 1996).

Cook, S.B., *Imperial Affinities: Nineteenth Century Analogies and Exchanges Between India and Ireland* (New Delhi: Sage, 1993).

Corbett, M.J., 'Public Affections and Familial Politics: Burke, Edgeworth, and the "Common Naturalization" of Great Britain', *ELH*, 61 (1994), pp. 877–97.

Cornwell, A.J., Hon. Obituarist, 'Major S. A. Grehan', *The Oratory School Magazine*, 132 (1972), pp. 118–19.

Correspondence with Peter A. Grehan, 17 July 1999.

Crawford, W.H., *Domestic Industry in Ireland: the Experience of the Linen Industry* (Dublin: Gill & Macmillan, 1972).

Cronin, S. and R. Roche (eds), *Freedom the Wolfe Tone Way* (Tralee: Anvil, 1973).

Cullen, L., *Life in Ireland* (London: Batsford, 1968).

Cullen, L.M., (ed.) *Formation of the Irish Economy* (Cork: Mercier, 1969)

Cullen, L.M., *An Economic History of Ireland since 1660* (London: Batsford, 1972).

Cumings, B., 'The origins and development of the Northeast Asian political economy: industrial sectors, product cycles, and political consequences,' in

F.C. Deyo (ed.), *The Political Economy of the New Asian Industrialism* (Ithaca, NY: Cornell University Press, 1987), pp. 44–83.

Curtis, E., *A History of Ireland* (London: Methuen, 1961).

Curtis Jr, L.P., 'Stopping the Hunt, 1881–1882: an Aspect of the Irish Land War', in C.H.E. Philpin (ed.), *Nationalism and Popular Protest in Ireland* (Cambridge: Cambridge University Press, 1987), pp. 349–402.

Curtis, L. Perry Jr, *Apes and Angels: The Irishman in Victorian Caricature* (rev. edn, Washington and London: Smithsonian Institution Press, 1997).

Daly, M.E., *The Famine in Ireland* (Dundalk: Dundalgan Press, 1986).

Davis, R., *Rise of the English Shipping Industry in the Seventeenth and Eighteenth Centuries* (Newton Abbot: David & Charles, 1962).

Davis, R., *The Young Ireland Movement* (Dublin: Gill & Macmillan, 1987).

Davis, R., *Revolutionary Imperialist: William Smith O'Brien 1803–1864* (Dublin: Lilliput, 1998).

Davis, T., *Poems of Thomas Davis* (Dublin, 1846).

Davis, T., *Essays Literary and Historical*, ed. D.J. O'Donoghue (Dundalk, 1914).

Davis, W.W., 'China, the Confucian Ideal, and the European Age of Enlightenment', *The Journal of the History of Ideas*, 54, 4 (1983), pp. 523–48.

de Paor, L., 'The Rebel Mind: Republican and Loyalist', in R. Kearney (ed.), *The Irish Mind* (Dublin: Wolfhound, 1985), pp. 157–87.

de Paor, M. and L. de Paor, *Early Christian Ireland* (London: Thames and Hudson, 1958).

Deane, P. and W.A. Cole, *British Economic Growth, 1688–1959* (Cambridge: Cambridge University Press, 1969).

Deane, S., *Celtic Revivals* (London: Faber and Faber, 1985).

Deane, S., 'Civilians and Barbarians', in *Ireland's Field Day* (London: Hutchinson, 1985), pp. 33–42.

Deane, S. (ed.), *Field Day Anthology of Irish Writing* (Derry: Field Day Publications, 1991).

Deane, S., *Strange Country: Modernity and Nationhood in Irish Writing since 1790* (Oxford: Clarendon Press, 1997).

Dewey, C., 'Images of the Village Community, A Study in Anglo-Indian Ideology', *Modern Asian Studies*, 63 (1972).

Dewey, C., 'The Education of a Ruling Caste: the Indian Civil Service in the Era of Competitive Examination', *English Historical Review*, 88 (1973), pp. 262–85.

Dewey, C., 'Celtic Agrarian Land Legislation and the Celtic Revival: Historicist Implications of Gladstone's Irish and Scottish Land Acts, 1870–1886', *Past and Present*, 64 (1974), pp. 30–70.

Dewey, C., 'The Rehabilitation of the Peasant Proprietor in Nineteenth Century Economic Thought', *History of Political Economy*, 6 (1974), pp. 321–36.

'Diary of Frances Alcorn, Lord Leitrim's Estate, Co. Donegal' (1878), National Library, mss.

Dickson, D. 'Aspects of the Irish cotton industry', in L.M. Cullen and T.C. Smout (eds), *Comparative Aspects of Scottish and Irish Economic and Social History* (Edinburgh: J. Donald, 1976), pp. 100–15.

Dobb, M., *Studies in the Development of Capitalism* (London: Routledge and Kegan Paul, 1963).

Donnelly, J.S., *The Land and the People of Nineteenth Century Cork, The Rural Economy and the Land Question* (London: Routledge and Kegan, Paul, 1975).

Doyle, A. Conan., 'The Geographical Distribution of British Intellect', *The Nineteenth Century: A Monthly Review*, 24, 138 (Aug. 1888), pp. 184–95.

Doyle, A. Conan., *The Hound of the Baskervilles: Another Adventure of Sherlock Holmes* (London: George Newnes, 1902).

Doyle, A. Conan., *Uncollected Stories: The Unknown Conan Doyle*, comp. and intro. J. M. Gibson and R. Lancelyn Green (London: Secker & Warburg, 1982).

Doyle, A. Conan., *Letters to the Press: The Unknown Conan Doyle*, comp. and intro. J.M. Gibson and R. Lancelyn Green (London: Secker & Warburg, 1986).

Dudley Edwards, R., *An Atlas of Irish History* (London: Methuen, 1973).

Dunne, T., *Theobald Wolfe Tone: Colonial Outsider. An Analysis of his Political Philosophy* (Cork: Tower Books, 1982).

Dunne, T., *Maria Edgeworth and the Colonial Mind* (Cork: University College, 1984).

Durie, A., 'The Scottish linen industry in the eighteenth century: some aspects of expansion,' in L.M. Cullen and T.C. Smout (eds), *Comparative Aspects of Scottish and Irish Economic and Social History* (Edinburgh: J. Donald, 1976).

Eagleton, T., *Heathcliff and the Great Hunger: Studies in Irish Culture* (London and New York: Verso, 1995).

Eagleton T., 'Nationalism and the Case of Ireland', *New Left Review*, No. 234 (March/April, 1999).

Edgeworth, M., *The Absentee* (Oxford and New York: Oxford University Press, 1988).

Edgeworth, M., *Castle Rackrent and Ennui* (London: Penguin, 1992).

Edgeworth, M., *Belinda* (London: Dent, 1994).

Edgeworth, R. L. and M. Edgeworth, *Essay on Irish Bulls* (London: J. Johnson, 1802).

Edie, C.A., 'The Irish Cattle Bills', *Transactions of the American Philosophical Society*, 60, 2 (1970).

Editorial, *Journal of Material Culture*, 1, 1 (1996).

Edney, M.H., *Mapping an Empire: the Geographical Construction of British India, 1765–1843* (Chicago: University of Chicago Press, 1997).

Edwards, M.M., *The Growth of the British Cotton Trade* (Manchester: Manchester University Press, 1967).

Ekelund, R.B., 'A British Rejection of Economic Orthodoxy', *Southwestern Social Science Quarterly*, 47, Sept. (1966) pp172–180.

Ellis, S.G., *Tudor Ireland: Crown, Community, and the Conflict of Cultures, 1470–1603* (London: Longman, 1985).

Ellis, S.G., *Ireland in the Age of the Tudors, 1447–1603: English Expansion and the End of Gaelic Rule* (London: Longman, 1998).

Ellis, S.G., '"More Irish Than the Irish Themselves"? the "Anglo-Irish" in Tudor Ireland', *History Ireland*, 7, 1 (1999), pp. 22–6.

Ellison, T., *The Cotton Trade of Great Britain* (London: Wilson, 1886).

Engels, F., *The Condition of the Working Class in England*, trans. W.O. Henderson and W.H. Chaloner (Stanford, CA: Stanford University Press, 1958).

Fagan, W., *The Life and Times of Daniel O'Connell*, 2 vols (Cork, 847–48).

Fanon, F., *The Wretched of the Earth* (New York: Grove Press, 1968).

Farge, A., *Le Goût de l'archive* (Paris: Éditions du Seuil, 1989).

Fennell, D., 'Against Revisionism', in C. Brady (ed.), *Interpreting Irish History. The Debate on Historical Revisionism 1938–1994* (Dublin: Irish Academic Press, 1994), pp. 181–90.

Finlay, J., *A Treatise on Law of Renewals in Respect to Leases for Lives Renewable for Ever in Ireland* (Dublin: John Cumming, 1829).

Fitzpatrick, D., 'The Geography of Irish Nationalism', *Past and Present*, 78 (1978), pp. 113–44.

Fitzpatrick, D., *Irish Emigration 1801–1921* (W. Tempest: Dundalgan Press: 1984).

Fitzpatrick, D., 'Ireland and the Empire', in A. Porter and A. Lo (eds), *The Oxford History of the British Empire, Vol. 3: The Nineteenth-Century* (Oxford: Oxford University Press, 1999), pp. 499–504.

Foley, T.P. and T.A. Boylan, *Political Economy and Colonial Ireland* (London: Routledge, 1992).

Foster, R., *Modern Ireland 1600–1972* (London: Allen Lane and Penguin Books, 1988).

Foster, R.F., 'Ascendancy and Union', in *The Oxford Illustrated History of Ireland* (Oxford and New York: Oxford University Press, 1991), pp. 161–211.

Foucault, M., 'The Dangerous Individual', in L.D. Kritzman (ed.), *Politics, Philosophy, Culture: Interviews and Other Writings, 1977–1984* (New York, NY: Routledge, 1988), pp.125–51.

Francis Guy's County & City of Cork Directory 1875–1876.

Fraser, T.G., '"Ireland and India"' on their relations within the British Empire', in K. Jeffery (ed.), *'An Irish Empire'? Aspects of Ireland and the British Empire*, pp. 77–93.

Freeman, T.W., *Pre-Famine Ireland: A Study in Historical Geography* (Manchester: Manchester University Press, 1957).

Freeman, T.W., 'Land and People, c. 1841', in W.E. Vaughan (ed.), *A New History of Ireland. Vol. V Ireland Under the Union 1801–1870* (Oxford: Clarendon Press, 1989).

Friedman, G., 'Rereading 1798: Melancholy and Desire in the Construction of Edgeworth's Anglo-Irish Union', *European Romantic Review*, 10, 2 (Spring 1999), pp. 175–92.

Friel, B., 'Plays Peasant and Unpeasant', *Times Literary Supplement*, 17 March 1972, pp. 305–6.

Friel, B., *Translations* (London: Faber and Faber, 1981).

Fukuyama, F., *The End of History and the Last Man* (London: H. Hamilton, 1992).

Gailey, A., *Ireland and the Death of Kindness: the Experience of Constructive Unionism 1890–1905* (Cork: Cork University Press, 1987).

Geary, F., 'The rise and fall of the Belfast cotton industry: some problems', *Irish Historical Studies*, 8 (1981), pp. 30–49.

Geary, F. 'The Belfast cotton industry revisited', *Irish Historical Studies* 26 (1989), pp. 250–67.

Geertz, C., 'Thick Description: toward an interpretative theory of culture', in C. Geertz, *The Interpretation of Cultures* (Basic Books, 1973), pp. 3–32.

Gibbons, L., 'Race Against Time: Racial Discourse and Irish History', in *Transformations in Irish Culture* (Notre Dame, IN: University of Notre Dame Press, 1996), pp.149–63.

Gibbons, L., 'Ireland and the Colonization of Theory', *Interventions*, 1, 1 (1998/99), p. 27.

Gibson, D., 'Chiefdoms, confederacies, and statehood in early Ireland', in B. Arnold and D. Gibson (eds), *Celtic Chiefdom, Celtic State* (Cambridge: Cambridge University Press, 1995), pp. 116–28.

Gill, C., *The Rise of the Irish Linen Industry* (Oxford: Clarendon, 1925).

Gilley, S., 'English Attitudes to the Irish, 1780–1900', in C. Holmes (ed.), *Immigrants and Minorities in British Society* (London: George Allen and Unwin, 1978), pp. 81–110.

Ginzburg, C., 'Mikro-Historie. Zwei oder drei Dinge, die ich von ihr weiß', *Historische Anthropologie*, 1 (1993), pp. 169–92.

Glennie, P., 'Consumption within Historical Studies' in D. Miller (ed.), *Acknowledging Consumption. A Review of New Studies* (London and New York: Routledge, 1995), pp. 164–203.

Glover, D., *Vampires, Mummies, and Liberals: Bram Stoker and the Politics of Popular Fiction* (Durham and London: Duke University Press, 1996).

Goswani, N., 'Public and Private', at Postcolonial Studies at Emory (http://www.emory.edu/english/bahri/pub.html), Fall 1996.

Grant, J., *Impressions of Ireland and the Irish*, 2 vols (London, 1844).

Grattan [Jr], H. (ed.), *Speeches of Henry Grattan*, 4 vols (London, 1822).

Gray, J., 'The Irish and Scottish linen industries in the eighteenth century: an incorporated comparison', in M. Cohen (ed.), *The Warp of Ulster's Past: Interdisciplinary Perspectives on the Irish Linen Industry 1700–1920* (New York: St. Martin's Press, 1997), pp. 37–70.

Gray, P., *Famine, Land and Politics: British Government and Irish Society 1843–50* (Dublin: Irish Academic Press, 1999).

Gray, T., *A Peculiar Man: A Life of George Moore* (London: Sinclair-Stevenson, 1996).

Great Britain Parliamentary Papers 'Annual Report of Her Majesty's Civil Service Commissioners' (1890) XXVI.

Green, E.R.R., *The Lagan Valley* (London: Faber and Faber, 1944).

Grehan Family Papers, Boole Library Archives Service, National University of Ireland, Cork.

Grehan, Peter A., 'The Code of a Gentleman', not published, 1997, pp. 1–3.

Grove White, J., *Historiographical and topographical notes, etc. on Buttevant, Castletownroche, Doneraile, Mallow, and places in their vicinity*, Vol. 1 (Cork: Guy & Company, 1905); Vol. 2 (Cork: Guy & Company, 1911).

Habakkuk, H.J., 'Public finance and the sale of forfeited property during the interregnum', *Economic History Review* 14 (1962), pp. 70–88

Hack, D., 'Inter-Nationalism: *Castle Rackrent* and Anglo-Irish Union', *Novel*, 29, (1996), pp. 145–64.

Hall, C., *White. Male, and Middle Class: Explorations in Feminism and History* (New York, NY: Routledge, 1992).

Hall, S., *The Hard Road to Renewal: Thatcherism and the Crisis of the Left* (London, Verso, 1988).

Hall, S., 'Our Mongrel Selves', *New Statesman and Society*, 19 June 1992, p. 6.

Hall, S., 'Gramsci's Relevance for the Study of Race and Ethnicity', in D. Morley and K. Chen (eds), *Stuart Hall: Critical Dialogues in Cultural Studies* (New York, NY: Routledge, 1996), pp. 411–40.

Hall, T., 'Incorporation in the world-system: toward a critique', *American Sociological Review*, 51, 3 (1986), pp. 390–402.

Hancock, W.N., 'On the Economic Causes of the Present State of Agriculture in Ireland, Part I', *Dublin Statistical Society Transactions*, 1 (1848a).

Hancock, W.N., 'On the Economic Causes of the Present State of Agriculture in Ireland, Part II - Legal Impediments to the Transfer of Land', *Dublin Statistical Society Transactions*, 1 (1848b).

Hancock, W.N., 'On the Use of the Doctrine of Laissez-Faire, In Investigating the Economic Resources of Ireland', *Dublin Statistical Society Transactions*, 1 (1847).

Hancock, W.N., *Impediments to the Prosperity of Ireland* (London: Simms and McInture, 1850).

Hancock, W.N., 'On the Bothy system of Lodging Farm Labourers in Scotland; It's Violation of the Family Principles, Its Condemnation by the Free Church of Scotland, the Conclusions to be Deducted from the Facts Stated, and Their Application to Ireland', *Statistical and Social Inquiry Society of Ireland Journal*, II (1859).

Hancock, W.N., 'The Effects of the Employment of Women in Occupations Atended with Publicity, as Illustrated by the Result of the Factory System at Bradford', *Statistical and Social Inquiry Society of Ireland Journal*, II (1860).

Harper, L.A., *The English Navigation Laws: A Seventeenth-Century Experiment in Social Engineering* (New York: Columbia University, 1939).

Harris R.M., *The Nearest Place That Wasn't Ireland: Early Nineteenth Century Irish Labor Migration* (Ames, IA: Iowa State University Press, 1994).

Hawkins, R., 'The "Irish Model" and the Empire: a Case for Reassessment', in D.M. Anderson and D. Killingray (eds), *Policing the Empire: Government,*

Authority and Control, 1830–1940 (Manchester: Manchester University Press, 1991).

Haydu, J., 'Making use of the past: time periods as cases to compare and as sequences of problem solving', *American Journal of Sociology* (1998), pp. 339–69.

Hechter, M., *Internal Colonialism: The Celtic Fringe in British National Development, 1536–1966* (Berkeley: University of California Press, 1975).

Hickman, M., *Religion, Class and Identity: The State, the Catholic Church and the Education of the Irish in Britain* (Aldershot: Avebury, 1995).

Hill, J., 'Ireland Without Union: Molyneux and his Legacy', in J. Robertson (ed.), *A Union for Empire* (Cambridge: Cambridge University Press, 1995), pp. 271–96.

Hobsbawm, E., *Industry and Empire: from 1750 to the present* (London: Penguin Books, 1970).

Hogan, R. and J. Kilroy, *The Irish Literary Theatre 1899–1901* (Dublin: Dolmen Press, 1975).

Hollingworth, B., *Maria Edgeworth's Irish Writing: Language, History, Politics* (London: Macmillan, 1997).

Holwell, J.Z., *Interesting Historical Events, Relative to the Provinces of Bengal, and the Empire of Indostan*, 3 vols. (London: T. Becket and P.A. de Hondt, 1765–71).

Hooper, J., 'The Yields of Irish Tillage Food Crops Since the Year 1847', *Department of Agriculture and Technical Instruction for Ireland Journal* (1922).

Hoppen, K.T., *Ireland since 1800: Conflict and Conformity* (London: Longman, 1992).

Horton, R.W., *Lectures on Statistics and Political Economy, As Affecting the Condition of the Operative and Labouring Classes* (London, 1832).

Howe, S., *Ireland and Empire: Colonial Legacies in Irish History and Culture* (Oxford: Oxford University Press, 2000).

Howes, M., *Yeats's Nations: Gender, Class and Irishness* (Cambridge: Cambridge University Press, 1996).

Hunter, R.J., 'Towns in the Ulster Plantation', *Studia Hibernica*, 11 (1971), pp. 40–79.

Hutchinson, J., *The Dynamics of Cultural Nationalism: The Gaelic Revival and the Creation of the Nation State* (London: Allen & Unwin, 1987).

Impey, O., *Chinoiserie: the Impact of Oriental Styles on Western Art and Decoration* (London: Oxford University Press, 1977).

Ingram, J.K., 'The Present Position and Prospects of Political Economy', in R.L. Smyth (ed.), *Essays in Economic Method* (London: Duckworth, 1962 [1878]).

Ingram, J.K., *A History of Political Economy* (Edinburgh: Adam and Charles Black, 1888).

Irish Customs, *Exports and Imports of Ireland, 1763–1824* (original volumes in National Library of Ireland).

Irish Railway Commissioners, *Second Report of the Commissioners Appointed to*

Consider and Recommend a General System of Railways for Ireland (1837) (original volume in National Library of Ireland).

Jameson, F., 'Modernism and Imperialism', in *Field Day, Nationalism, Colonialism, and Literature* (Minneapolis, MN: University of Minnesota Press, 1990).

Jeffares, A.N., 'A Drama in Muslin', in G. Owens (ed.), *George Moore's Mind and Art* (Edinburgh: Oliver and Boyd, 1968), pp. 1–20.

Jeffares, A.N., *Anglo-Irish Literature* (London and Dublin: Gill & Macmillan, 1982).

Jeffares, A.N., *Images of Invention: Essays on Irish Writing* (Gerrards Cross: Colin Smythe, 1996).

Jeffery, K., 'Introduction', in K. Jeffery (ed.), *'An Irish Empire'? Aspects of Ireland and the British Empire* (Manchester and New York: Manchester University Press, 1996), pp. 1–24.

Jeffrey, K., 'The Irish Military Tradition', in K. Jeffrey (ed.), *An Irish Empire?: Aspects of Ireland and the British Empire* (Manchester: Manchester University Press, 1996).

Jeffries, C., *The Colonial Police* (London: Max Parrish, 1952).

Johnston, H.J.M., *British Emigration Policy 1815–1830: 'Shovelling out Paupers'* (Oxford: Clarendon Press, 1972).

Jones, D., 'The Role of the Graziers in Agrarian Conflict, 1870–1910', *ESRI* Seminar Paper, 1978.

Judy, Or the London Serio-Comic, 30 (3 May 1882), pp. 210–11.

Kane, R., *The Industrial Resources of Ireland* (Dublin: Hodges and Smith, 1844).

Kearney, H.F., 'The political background to English mercantilism, 1695–1700', *The Economic History Review*, 11 (1959), pp.484–96.

Kelly, P., 'The Irish Woollen Export Prohibition Act of 1699: Kearney Revisited', *Irish Economic and Social History*, 7 (1980), pp. 22–44.

Kennedy, L., *Colonialism, Religion and Nationalism in Ireland* (Belfast: Institute of Irish Studies, 1996).

Kiberd, D., *Inventing Ireland: The Literature of the Modern Nation* (London: Vintage, 1995).

Kinealy, C., *This Great Calamity: The Irish Famine 1845–52* (Dublin: Gill & Macmillan, 1994).

Knox, R., *The Races of Men: A Philosophical Inquiry into the Influence of Race over the Destinies of Nations* (2nd edn, London, 1862).

Koebner, R. and H.D. Schmidt, *Imperialism: The Story and Significance of a Political Word, 1840–1960* (Cambridge: Cambridge University Press, 1964).

Koot, G.M., 'T.E. Cliffe Leslie, Irish Social Reform and the Origins of the English Historical School of Economics', *History of Political Economy*, 7, 31 (1975) pp. 312–36.

Kriedte, P., H. Medick and J. Schlumbohm, *Industrialization before Industrialization* (Cambridge: Cambridge University Press, 1981).

Laclau. L., *Politics and Ideology in Marxist Theory* (London: NLB, 1977).

Landes, D., *The Unbound Promethius: Technological Change and Industrial*

Development in Western Europe from 1750 to the Present (Cambridge: Cambridge University Press, 1969).

Lebow, R.N., *White Britain and Black Ireland: the Influence of Stereotypes on Colonial Policy* (Philadelphia, PA: Institute for the Study of Human Issues, 1976).

Lee, J., *The Modernisation of Irish Society, 1848–1918* (Dublin: Gill & Macmillan, 1973).

Leslie, T.E.C., *Land Systems and Industrial Economy of Ireland, England, and Continental Countries* (London: Longmans, 1870).

Leerssen, J., *Mere Irish and Fior-Ghael: Studies in the Idea of Irish Nationality, its Development and Literary Expression Prior to the Nineteenth Century* (2nd edn, Cork: Cork University Press, 1996).

Leerssen, J., *Remembrance and Imagination: Patterns in the Historical and Literary Representation of Ireland in the Nineteenth Century* (Cork: Cork University Press, 1996).

Lengel, E. 'A "Perverse and Ill-Fated People": English Perceptions of the Irish, 1845–52', *Essays in History*, 38, (http://etext.lib.virginia.edu/journals/EH/EH38/Lengel.htm>, 1996.

Lever, C., *Lord Kilgobbin, A Tale of Ireland in Our Own Time* (London: Smith, Elder, 1872).

Lewis, W.A., *The Theory of Economic Growth* (Homewood, IL: Richard D. Irwin, 1955).

Lex., *Doings in Party, A Chapter of Irish History in a Letter to the Rt. Hon., The Earl of Derby K.G.* (London: Hatchard, 1860).

Lloyd, D., *Nationalism and Minor Literature: James Clarence Mangan and the Emergence of Irish Cultural Nationalism* (Berkeley, CA: University of California Press, 1987).

Lloyd, D., 'Race Under Representation', *Oxford Literary Review*, 13, 1–2 (1991).

Lloyd, D., *Anomalous States: Irish Writing and the Post-Colonial Moment* (Dublin: Lilliput, 1993).

Lloyd, D., *Ireland After History* (Cork: Cork University Press/Field Day, 1999).

Longfield, M., 'Production - Riches - Enjoyment - Consumption', *Dublin Statistical Society Transactions* Vol. I (1849).

Loomba, A., *Colonialism/Postcolonialism* (London and New York: Routledge, 1998).

'Lord Arran's Estate, Diary of the Agent, Co. Donegal 1858–1898'. Public Records Office, Don. 11/1, mss.

Lubbers, K., 'Continuity and Change in Irish Fiction: The Case of the Big-House

Lüdtke, A., 'Herrschaft als soziale Praxis', in A. Lüdtke (ed.), *Herrschaft als soziale Praxis. Historische und sozialanthropologische Studien* (Göttingen: Vandenhoeck & Ruprecht, 1991).

Lüdtke, A., 'Geschichte und Eigensinn', in *Alltagskultur, Subjektivität und Geschichte*, edited by Berliner Geschichtswerkstatt (Münster: Westfälisches Dampfboot, 1994), pp. 139–56.

Lyons, F.S.L., *Ireland Since the Famine* ([1963] London: Fontana, 1985).

Lysaght, E., 'A Consideration of the Theory That the Backward State of Agriculture is a Consequence of the Excessive Competition for Land', *Dublin Statistical Society Transactions*, II (1851).

Macbride, M. Gonne, *A Servant of the Queen* ([1938] London: Victor Gollancz, 1974).

MacDonagh, O., *States of Mind: A Study of Anglo-Irish Conflict 1780–1980* (London, Boston and Sydney: George Allen and Unwin, 1983).

MacDonagh, O., 'Ideas and Institutions, 1830–45', in T.W. Moody and W.E Vaughan (eds), *A New History of Ireland*, Vol. IV, *Eighteenth-Century Ireland, 1681–1800* (Oxford: Clarendon Press, 1986), pp. 193–217.

MacManus, S., *The Story of the Irish Race: A Popular History of Ireland* (New York: The Devin-Adair Company, 1944).

Mallory, J.P. and T.E. McNeill, *The Archaeology of Ulster from Colonization to Plantation* (Belfast: Institute of Irish Studies, 1991).

Marcus, S., *Engels, Manchester, and the Working Class* (New York, NY: W.W. Norton, 1974).

Marshall, P.J. (ed.), *The British Discovery of Hinduism in the Eighteenth Century* (London: Cambridge University Press, 1970).

Marshall, P.J., 'Warren Hastings as Scholar and Patron', in Anne Whiteman, J.S. Bromley and P.G.M. Dickson (eds), *Statesmen, Scholars and Merchants: Essays in Eighteenth-Century History Presented to Dame Lucy Sutherland* (Oxford: Clarendon, 1973).

Marshall, P.J. (ed.), *Cambridge Illustrated History of the British Empire* (Cambridge: Cambridge University Press, 1996).

Marx, K., *Theories of Surplus Value, Part III* (London: Lawrence and Wishart, 1972).

Marx, K., *The First International and After, Political Writings: Volume 3*, ed. D. Fernbach (New York, NY: Penguin Books, 1974).

Marx, K., *Capital Volume I*, trans. B. Fowkes (New York, NY: Penguin Books, 1976).

Marx, K., *Capital, Vol. I* (London: Penguin, 1976).

Marx, K., *Capital, Vol. II* (London: Penguin, 1978).

Marx, K., *Capital, Vol. III* (London: Penguin, 1981).

McClintock, A., 'The Angel of Progress', in P. Williams and L. Chrisman (eds), *Colonial Discourse and Post-Colonial Theory: A Reader* (Harvester: Hemel Hempstead, 1993).

McClintock, A., *Imperial Leather: Race, Gender, and Sexuality in the Colonial Contest* (New York, NY: Routledge, 1995).

McCormack, W.J., *Ascendancy and Tradition in Anglo-Irish Literary History from 1789 to 1939* (Oxford: Clarendon Press, 1985).

McCormack, W.J., 'Setting and Ideology with Reference to the Fiction of Maria Edgeworth', in O. Rauchbauer (ed.), *Ancestral Voices: The Big House in Anglo-Irish Literature* (Dublin: The Lilliput Press, 1992), pp. 33–60.

McCormack, W.J., *From Burke to Beckett: Ascendancy, Tradition, and Betrayal in Literary History* (Cork: Cork University Press, 1994).

McCormack, W.J. and K. Walker, 'Introduction' to *The Absentee* (Oxford and New York: Oxford University Press, 1988), pp. ix-xlii.

McDowell, R.B., 'Ireland in the Eighteenth Century British Empire', in J.G. Barry (ed.), *Historical Studies IX* (1974).

McGahern, J., *That They May Face the Rising Sun* (London: Faber and Faber, 2002).

McLoughlin, T.O., *Contesting Ireland: Irish Voices Against England in the Eighteenth Century* (Dublin: Four Courts Press, 1999).

Medick, H., 'Mikro-Historie', in W. Schulze (ed.), *Sozialgeschichte, Alltagsgeschichte, Mikro-Historie* (Göttingen: Vandenhoeck & Ruprecht, 1994), pp. 40–53.

Merivale, H., *Lectures on Colonization and Colonies* [1841] (London, 1861).

Mill, J.S., *Principles of Political Economy* (Toronto: Toronto Press, 1965).

Miller, K., *Emigrants and Exiles: Ireland and the Exodus to North America* (New York, NY: Oxford University Press, 1985).

Mjoset, L., *The Irish Economy in a Comparative Institutional Perspective* (Dublin: National Economic and Social Council, 1992).

Modelski, G. and W.R. Thompson, *Sea Power in Global Politics, 1494–1943* (Seattle, WA: University of Washington Press, 1988).

Mokyr, J., *Why Ireland Starved: a Quantitative and Analytical History of the Irish Economy, 1800–1850* (Boston: Allen & Unwin, 1983).

Molony, J. N., *A Soul came into Ireland: Thomas Davis 1814–1845, A Biography* (Dublin: Geography, 1995).

Monaghan, J.J., 'The rise and fall of the Belfast cotton industry', *Irish Historical Studies*, 3, 9 (March 1942), pp.1–17.

Monsell, W., 'Address at the Opening of the Twenty-Second Session', *Statistical and Social Inquiry Society of Ireland Journal*, Vol. V (1869).

Moore, G., *Parnell and His Island* (London: Swan Sonnenschein, Lowrey, 1887).

Moore, G. and E. Martyn, *Selected Plays of George Moore and Edward Martyn*, chosen, with an introduction by D.B. Eakin and M. Case (Gerrards Cross, Bucks: Colin Smythe, 1995), p. 221.

Moore, G.C.G., 'T.E. Cliffe Leslie and the English Methodenstreit', *Journal of the History of Economic Thought*, 17 1(Spring 1995) pp. 57–77.

Moore, R.J., 'The Abolition of Patronage in the Indian Civil Service and the Closure of Haileybury College', *The Historical Journal*, 7, 2 (1964), pp. 26–57.

Moss, L., *Mountifort Longfield, Ireland's First Professor of Political Economy* (Ottawa: Green Hill, 1976).

Moynahan, J., *Anglo-Irish: The Literary Imagination in a Hyphenated Culture* (Princeton, NJ: Princeton University Press, 1995).

Munck, R., *The Irish Economy: Results and Prospects* (London: Pluto Press, 1993).

Murray, A.E., *History of the Commercial and Financial Relations between England and*

Ireland from the Period of the Restoration (New York: Burt Franklin, 1903).

Murray, J., *Handbook for Shropshire, Lancashire and Cheshire* (London: Murray, 1870).

Musson, A.E. and E. Robinson, *Science and Technology in the Industrial Revolution* (Manchester: Manchester University Press, 1969).

Nordon, P. , *Conan Doyle*, trans. F. Partridge ([1964] London: John Murray, 1966).

Novel', in O. Rauchbauer (ed.), *Ancestral Voices: The Big House in Anglo-Irish Literature* (Dublin: The Lilliput Press, 1992), pp. 17–29.

O'Donnell, F.H., *Souls for Gold!: Pseudo-Celtic Drama in Dublin* (London: Nassau Press, 1899).

O'Donovan, J., *The Economic History of Live Stock in Ireland* (Cork: Cork University Press, 1940).

O'Grada, C., *Ireland: A New Economic History 1780–1939* (Oxford: Clarendon Press, 1994).

O'Halloran, S., *An Introduction to the Study of the History and Antiquities of Ireland: in Which the Assertions of Mr. Hume and Other Writers Are Occasionally Considered* (London: J. Murray, 1772).

O'Hearn, D., 'Innovation and the World-System Hierarchy: British Subjugation of the Irish Cotton Industry, 1780–1830', *American Journal of Sociology*, 100 (1994), pp. 587–621.

O'Hearn, D., 'Irish Linen: A Peripheral Industry', in M. Cohen (ed.), *The Warp of Ulster's Past: Interdisciplinary Perspectives on the Irish Linen Industry, 1700–1920* (New York: St. Martin's, 1997), pp. 161–90.

O'Malley, E., 'The Decline of Irish Industry in the Nineteenth Century', *Economic and Social Review*, 13, 1 (1981).

O'Neill, K., *Family and Farm in Pre-Famine Ireland, The Parish of Killashandra* (London: The University of Wisconsin Press, 1984).

O Nunain, S., 'The Land League Hunt', *Seanchas Duthalla* (1989).

O'Tuathaigh, G., *Ireland Before the Famine, 1798–1848* (Dublin: Gill & Macmillan, 1972).

Owens, G. (ed.), *George Moore's Mind and Art* (Edinburgh: Oliver and Boyd, 1968).

Parsons, L., *Observations on the Bequest of Henry Flood, Esq. to Trinity College, Dublin: With a Defence of the Ancient History of Ireland* (Dublin: Bonham, 1795).

Pearce, S. M., 'The urge to collect', in S. M. Pearce (ed.), *Interpreting Objects and Collections* (London and New York: Routledge, 1994), pp. 157–9.

Petty, W., *Hiberniæ Delineatio quod hactenus licuit perfectissima* (1683).

Pick, D., *Faces of Degeneration: A European Disorder, c. 1848–1918* (Cambridge: Cambridge University Press, 1989).

Pilkington, L., *Theatre and the State in 20th Century Ireland: Cultivating the People* (London and New York: Routledge, 2001).

Poovey, M., *Making a Social Body: British Cultural Formation, 1830–1864* (Chicago, IL: University of Chicago Press, 1995).

Porter, A., 'Empires in the Mind', in P.J. Marshall (ed.), *Cambridge Illustrated History of the British Empire* (Cambridge: Cambridge University Press, 1996), pp. 185–223.

Pratt, M. L., *Imperial Eyes. Studies in Travel Writing* (London: Routledge, 1992).

Prichard, J.C., *The Eastern Origins of the Celtic Nations: Proved by a Comparison of their Dialects with the Sanskrit, Greek, Latin and Teutonic Languages. Forming a Supplement to the Researches into the Physical History of Mankind* (London: S. Collingwood, 1831).

Pringle, R., 'A Review of Irish Agriculture, Chiefly with Reference to the Production of Livestock', *Journal of the Royal Agricultural Society of England*, Vol. VIII (1871).

Purcell's Commercial Cork Almanac (Cork: Purcell & Company, 1858).

Purcell's Commercial Cork Almanac (Cork: Purcell & Company, 1877).

Quinn, C., Descriptive List Grehan Family Papers, Boole Library Archives Service, National University of Ireland, Cork.

Quinn, D.B., 'Sir Thomas Smith (1513–1577) and the beginnings of English colonial theory,' *Proceedings of the American Philosophical Society*, 89 (1945), pp. 543–60.

Quinn, D.B., *The Elizabethans and the Irish* (Ithaca, NY: Cornell University Press, 1966).

Redford, A., *Manchester Merchants and Foreign Trade* (Manchester: Manchester University Press, 1934).

Rendall, J., 'Scottish Orientalism: from Robertson to James Mill', *The Historical Journal*, 25, 1 (1982), pp. 43–69.

'Report by J.L. Murray on Lord Leitrim's Estate, Co. Donegal' (1864), National Library, mss.

Reports of the Commissioners for Inquiry into the Condition of the Poorer Classes in Ireland, Reports from Commissioners, Vol. 30–34, Appendix H (1836).

Riach, D.C., 'O'Connell and Slavery', in D. McCartney (ed.), *The World of Daniel O'Connell* (Dublin: Mercier, 1980), pp. 175–85.

Richey, A.G., *A Short History of the Irish People* (Dublin: Hodges, Figgis and Co., 1887).

Robinson, R., 'Non-European Foundations of European Imperialism: Sketch for a Theory of Collaboration', in Roger Owen and Bob Sutcliffe (eds), *Studies in the Theory of Imperialism* (New York: Longman, 1983), pp. 117–40.

Rocher, R and Bayly, C.A., 'British Orientalism in the Eighteenth Century: The Dialectics of Knowledge and Government', in C. Breckenridge and P. van der Veer (eds), *Orientalism and the Postcolonial Predicament. Perspectives on South Asia* (Philadelphia, PA: University of Pennsylvania Press, 1993), pp. 215–49.

Roll, E., *A History of Economic Thought* (London: Faber and Faber, 1978).

Rosenberg J., *Carlyle and the Burden of History* (Cambridge, MA: Harvard University Press, 1985).

Rosenstein-Rodin, P.N., 'Problems of industrialization of Eastern and South-

Eastern Europe', *Economic Journal*, 55 (1943), pp. 202–11.

Rosenthal, G., 'Geschichte in der Lebensgeschichte', *BIOS- Zeitschrift für Biographieforschung und Oral History*, 2 (1988), pp. 3–15.

Royal Commission on University Education in Ireland, *Minutes of Evidence Taken at the First Nine Sittings Held in Dublin* (Dublin, 1901).

Ruane, J., 'Colonialism and the Interpretation of Irish Historical Development', in M. Silverman and P.H.Gulliver (eds), *Approaching the Past: Historical Anthropology through Irish Case Studies* (New York, NY: Columbia University Press, 1992).

Ryan of Inch Family Papers, Boole Library Archives Service, National University of Ireland, Cork.

Ryder, S., 'Gender and the Discourse of Young Ireland Cultural Nationalism', in T.P. Foley et al. (eds), *Gender and Colonialism* (Galway: Galway University Press, 1995), pp. 210–24.

Ryder, S., 'Young Ireland and the 1798 Rebellion', in L. Geary (ed.), *Rebellion and Remembrance in Modern Ireland* (Dublin: Four Courts Press, 2000), pp. 135–47.

Sabean, D. and H. Medick, 'Emotionen und materielle Interessen in Familie und Verwandtschaft: Überlegungen zu neuen Wegen und Bereichen einer historischen und sozialanthropologischen Familienforschung', in H. Medick and D. Sabean (eds), *Emotionen und materielle Interessen: sozialanthropologische und historische Beiträge zur Familienforschung* (Göttingen: Vandenhoeck & Ruprecht, 1984), pp. 35–45.

Said, E., *Orientalism* (London: Routledge and Kegan Paul, 1978).

Said, E., 'Yeats and Decolonization,' in *Field Day, Nationalism, Colonialism, and Literature* (Minneapolis, MN: University of Minnesota Press, 1990).

Said, E.W., *Culture and Imperialism* (London: Vintage, 1994).

Schumpeter, J., *History of Economic Analysis* (London: George Allen and Unwin, 1967).

Schwab, R., *Oriental Renaissance: Europe's Rediscovery of India and the Orient, 1680–1880*, trans. G. Patterson-Black and V. Reinking (New York, NY: Columbia University Press, 1984).

Seebohm, F., 'The Land Question, English Tenures in Ireland, Part I', *The Fortnightly Review*, Vol. VI (1869).

Senghaas, D., *The European Experience: A Historical Critique of Development Theory* (Leamington Spa: Berg, 1985).

Sigerson, G., *History of the Land Tenures and Land Classes of Ireland* (London: Longmans, 1871).

Simms, J., *Nature's Revelations of Character; or, the Mental, Moral and Volitive Dispositons of Mankind, as Manifested in the Human Form and Countenance* ([London]: privately printed, 1873).

Simms, J.G., *The Williamite Confiscation in Ireland 1690–1703* (Westport, CT: Greenwood, 1956).

Slater, E. and T. McDonough, 'Bulwark of Landlordism and Capitalism: The

Dynamics of Feudalism in Nineteenth Century Ireland', *Research in Political Economy*, 14 (1994).

Sloan, B., *The Pioneers of Anglo-Irish Fiction 1800–1850* (Gerrards Cross: Colin Smythe, 1986).

Solow, B., *The Land Question and the Irish Economy, 1870–1903* (Cambridge: Harvard University Press, 1971).

Somerville, E. Œ. and Martin Ross, *Naboth's Vineyard* (London: Spencer Blackett, 1891).

Somerville-Large, P., *The Irish Country House. A Social History* (London: Sinclair-Stevenson, 1995).

Spenser, E., 'From *A View of the Present State of Ireland (1596)*', in S. Deane et. al. (eds.), *The Field Day Anthology of Irish Writing*, Vol. I (Derry: Field Day Publications, 1991), pp. 175–202.

Spivak, G., *In other worlds: essays in cultural politics* (New York and London: Methuen, 1987).

Stocking, G. Jr. (ed.), *Researches into the Physical History of Man*, [J.C. Prichard] (Chicago, IL: Chicago University Press, 1973).

Stoker, B., *The Snake's Pass* (London: Sampson Low, Marston, Searle & Rivington, 1891).

Stoker, B., *Dracula* (London: Archibald Constable, 1897).

Stoker, B., *Personal Reminiscences of Henry Irving*, 2 vols (London: William Heinemann, 1906).

Stoker, B., 'The Great White Fair in Dublin: How there has Arisen on the Site of the Old Donnybrook Fair a Great Exhibition as Typical of the New Ireland as the Former Festival was of the Ireland of the Past', *The World's Work*, IX, 54 (May 1907), pp. 570–6.

Stoker, B., *The Lady of the Shroud* (London: William Heinemann, 1909).

Stoker, B., *The Lair of the White Worm* (William Rider & Son, 1911).

Stokowski, P.A., *Leisure in Society. A Network Structural Perspective* (London and New York: Mansell, 1994).

Takei, A., 'The first Irish linen mills, 1800–1824', *Irish Economic and Social History*, 21 (1994), pp. 28–38.

Teignmouth, Lord [John Shore] (ed.), *The Works of Sir William Jones*, 13 vols. (London: John Stockdale and J. Walker, 1807).

The Ballads of Ireland, ed. E. Hayes, 2 vols (Edinburgh, 1855).

'The Landlord', typewritten manuscript by John F. Sheehan, Banteer, from the late Jeremiah Sheehan, Banteer and Michael Sheehan, Inchidaly. Donald Lehane, Banteer, from Joseph Lehane, Banteer, 8 Oct. 1938.

The Private Diary: Arranged, Printed, and Ruled, for Receiving an Account of Every day's Employment, for the Space of One Year: with an Index and Appendix (9th edn, London: John Taylor, Bookseller and Publisher to the University of London, [1830]).

Thomas, P. and D. Lloyd, *Culture and the State* (New York, NY: Routledge, 1998).

Thompson, D., *Outsiders: Class, Gender, Nation* (London: Verso, 1993).

Thompson, E.P., *The Making of the English Working Class* (New York, NY: Vintage Books, 1966).

Thompson, F.M.L., 'Britain', in D. Spring (ed.), *European Landed Elites in the Nineteenth Century* (Baltimore, MD: John Hopkins University Press, 1977), pp. 22–44.

Tone, W.H., *A Letter to an Officer on the Madras Establishment: Being an Attempt to Illustrate Some Particular Institutions of the Maratta People* (London: J. Debrett, 1796).

Tone, W.H., *Illustrations of Some Institutions of the Mahratta People* (Calcutta: Times Press, 1818).

Trautmann, T.R., *Aryans and British India* (Berkeley, CA: University of California, 1997).

Trench, W. Steurt., *Realities of Irish Life* (London: Longmans, Green, 1868).

Trollope, A., *The Macdermots of Ballycloran*, intro. Algar Thorold ([1847] London: John Lane, The Bodley Head, 1906).

Vallancey, C., *An Essay on the Antiquity of the Irish Language: Being a Collation of the Irish with the Punic language* (Dublin: S. Powell, 1772).

Vallancey, C., *The Ancient History of Ireland, Proved from the Sanscrit Books of the Bramins of India* (1797).

Vance, R. 'On the English and Irish Analysis of Wages and Profits', *Dublin Statistical Society Transactions*, I (1847).

Vanden Bossche, C., *Carlyle and the Search for Authority* (Columbus, OH: Ohio State University Press, 1991).

Vandevelde, K., 'Outside the Abbey: The Irish National Theatres, 1897–1913', unpublished Ph.D. dissertation (National University of Ireland, Galway, 2001), p. 34.

Vaughan, W.E., 'The Landlord and Tenant Relations in Ireland between the Famine and the Land War, 1850–1878', in L.M. Cullen and T.C. Smout (eds), *Comparative Aspects of Scottish and Irish Economic and Social History, 1660–1900* (Edinburgh: John Donald Publishers, 1977).

Vaughan, W.E., 'Agricultural Output, Rents and Wages in Ireland, 1850–1880', in L.M. Cullen and F. Furet (eds), *Ireland and France, 17th - 20th Centuries* (Ann Arbor: MI, 1980).

Wakefield, E. Gibbon, *A View of the Art of Colonization* (London, 1849).

Walker, J.C., *Historical Memoirs of Irish Bards* (London: T. Payne & Son, 1786).

Wallerstein, I., *The Modern World-System III: The Second Era of Great Expansion of the Capitalist World-Economy* (New York: Academic Press, 1988).

Waters, H., 'The Great Famine and anti-Irish Racism', *Race and Class*, 37, 1 (July-Sept. 1995), pp. 95–108.

Webb, D.A. and McDowell, R.B., *Trinity College, Dublin, 1592–1952: An Academic History* (Cambridge: Cambridge University Press, 1982).

Wilde, Lady, *Ancient Legends, Mystic Charms, and Supersitions of Ireland*, 2 vols (London: Ward and Downey, 1887).

Wilford, F., 'On Egypt and other countries adjacent to the Cali River, or Nile of Ethiopia, from the Ancient Books of the Hindus', *Asiatic Researches*, 3 (1792), pp. 295–462.

Williams R., *Culture and Society: 1780–1950* (New York, NY: Columbia University Press, 1958).

Williams, G. and Marshall, P.J., *The Great Map of Mankind: British Perceptions of the World in the Age of Enlightenment* (London: Dent, 1982).

Wills, C., 'Language Politics, Narrative, Political Violence', *Oxford University Review*, 13, 1–2 (1991).

Wilson, K., 'Empire of Virtue: The Imperial Project and Hanoverian Culture, c.1720–1785', in L. Stone (ed.), *An Imperial State at War: Britain from 1689 to 1815* (London: Routledge, 1994), pp. 128–164.

Winstanley, M.J., *Ireland and the Land Question, 1800–1922* (London and New York: Methuen & Co., 1984).

Wolf, E.R., *Europe and the People Without History* (Berkeley, CA: University of California, 1982).

Wylie, J.C., *Irish Land Law* (London: Professional Books, 1975).

Wynne, C., *The Colonial Conan Doyle: British Imperialism, Irish Nationalism, and the Gothic* (Westport, CT and London: Greenwood Press, 2002).

Wyse Papers (1830–39), National Library of Ireland, Dublin. .

Yeats, W.B., 'To the Guarantors for a "Celtic" Theatre', in W. Gould, J. Kelly and D. Toomey (eds), *The Collected Letters of W.B. Yeats: Volume Two 1896–1900* (Oxford: Clarendon Press, 1997), pp.123–5.

Young, A., *A Tour in Ireland* (London: George Bell, 1882).

Young, R., *Colonial Desire. Hybridity in Theory, Culture and Race* (London: Routledge, 1995).